Market Liquidity

Market Liquidity

Theory, Evidence, and Policy

Second Edition

THIERRY FOUCAULT
MARCO PAGANO
AILSA RÖELL

OXFORD
UNIVERSITY PRESS

OXFORD
UNIVERSITY PRESS

Oxford University Press is a department of the University of Oxford.
It furthers the University's objective of excellence in research, scholarship,
and education by publishing worldwide. Oxford is a registered trade mark of
Oxford University Press in the UK and in certain other countries.

Published in the United States of America by Oxford University Press
198 Madison Avenue, New York, NY 10016, United States of America.

Library of Congress Cataloging-in-Publication Data
Names: Foucault, Thierry, author. | Pagano, Marco, author. | Röell, Ailsa, 1955- author.
Title: Market liquidity : theory, evidence, and policy / Thierry Foucault,
Marco Pagano, Ailsa Röell.
Description: Second edition. | New York : Oxford University Press, [2023] |
Revised edition of the authors' Market liquidity, c2013.
Identifiers: LCCN 2023019461 (print) | LCCN 2023019462 (ebook) |
ISBN 9780197542064 (hardback) | ISBN 9780197542088 (epub)
Subjects: LCSH: Liquidity (Economics) | Securities. | Capital market.
Classification: LCC HG178 .F64 2023 (print) | LCC HG178 (ebook) |
DDC 332/.041—dc23/eng/20230421
LC record available at https://lccn.loc.gov/2023019461
LC ebook record available at https://lccn.loc.gov/2023019462

Sheridan, United States of America

To our families

Contents

I. INSTITUTIONS

Preface

Liquid markets enable people to fund investments that require a long-term commitment of wealth, while retaining the opportunity to access that wealth when needed. Hence liquidity facilitates real investment and enhances economic growth. But market liquidity can be elusive at times, as investors discovered to their cost in the global financial crisis of 2008—a forcible reminder of John Maynard Keynes's 1936 warning that "there is no such thing as liquidity of investment for the community as a whole" (p. 155): markets freeze when everyone is seeking liquidity and no one is willing to provide it.

Aim and Structure of the Book

The central topic of this book is the liquidity of security markets: its measurement, its determinants and its effects. The first part of the book (Chapters 1 through 5) provides the reader with basic modeling and econometric tools needed to understand market microstructure, the area of financial economics that focuses on security market liquidity. This part of the book starts by describing how security markets are organized and how their liquidity can be measured. Then we explain how various market imperfections affect price formation, liquidity, and the speed at which prices reflect news ("price discovery"). Finally, we show how the interaction of order flow and price movements can be used to assess empirically the relative importance of various determinants of liquidity.

The second part of the book investigates how key features of market design affect the level of liquidity, the speed of price discovery, and gains and losses to market participants: we examine limit order book markets with continuous trading (Chapter 6), market fragmentation (Chapter 7), market transparency (Chapter 8), and algorithmic and high-frequency trading (Chapter 9).

The third part of the book is devoted to interactions between market microstructure, asset pricing, and corporate finance. We first explain how liquidity affects the returns required by investors, and therefore asset prices (Chapter 10). Next, we examine how fluctuations in liquidity can be a source of market instability, and contribute to market freezes and financial crises (Chapter 11). The book concludes by explaining how liquidity affects real investment decisions and corporate policies (Chapter 12).

The book provides an introduction to the field of market microstructure, covering theory, empirical work, and policy issues. It is designed as a textbook for intermediate and graduate-level students in economics and finance, as well as for practitioners with some economics training. The level of technical complexity is kept to a minimum, so that only a very basic knowledge of calculus, statistics, and game theory is necessary to tackle the material. The book does not aim to be a comprehensive survey of the field, but a unified and self-contained treatment of the core concepts and techniques in an area that has greatly developed since its inception in the 1980s. As the book is intended to be a teaching and learning tool, each chapter starts with a list of learning objectives—major points that the student can expect to master by working through the chapter. Most chapters also include boxes that describe business stories or quotes from the financial press that illustrate the real-world relevance of the concepts and results presented. The book also comes with a generous supply of exercises, which vary in complexity and focus: some of them require analytical derivations; others ask for empirical work on small data sets provided on the book's companion web site (which also contains supplemental teaching material for registered educators); see http://www.oup.com/us/marketliquidity/. Our experience is that hands-on practice with the end-of-chapter exercises is the best way to master the material in the book. The book is also complemented by a short online course called "Market Microstructure" that covers the material included in Chapters 1 to 4 and in Chapter 9, available for free at Federica.eu: http://bit.ly/3VO5kqC.

What is New in the Second Edition

This second edition has been thoroughly revised to incorporate recent developments in security markets, namely the rise in algorithmic and high-frequency trading (new Chapter 9) and financial market instability (new Chapter 11). In addition, the description of the design and regulation of security markets has been brought up to date throughout the book, with new illustrative examples taken from striking episodes of market malfunction occurring since the last edition. Finally, the insights from research developed in the last decade have been incorporated, and the presentation of some topics has been revised to take into account feedback from users of the book, as well as our own experience teaching from it.

How to use the Book

We can say with some confidence that this is a useful book, having taught from the first edition over the years, and having received positive feedback from many colleagues who adopted it in their courses. Indeed, we have greatly benefited from the feedback received over more than a decade from undergraduate and graduate students at CEMFI, EIEF, EUI, HEC Paris, Imperial College, NBB, Studienzentrum Gerzensee, Summer School of Market Microstructure, Tinbergen Institute, and at the universities of Bologna, Mannheim, Naples, Princeton, St. Gallen, Sydney, and Tilburg. The book can be used as the main source of material for a course in market microstructure or as a complement to other material in asset pricing or corporate finance.

A course that covers most of the book would require thirty to forty lecture hours, depending on the background of the students (plus about ten one-hour exercise sessions). However, importantly, the book is designed to allow a "modular" use of its material: by a careful selection of chapters, it can be adapted to either an introductory course in market microstructure pitched at the level of an advanced undergraduate or master class, or a more specialized and advanced course, possibly at the doctoral level. More specifically, here are some examples of typical courses that can be designed by "slicing and dicing" the material in the book:

(i) For a basic course in market microstructure we would recommend including all of Part I (fifteen to twenty lecture hours depending on students' background). The chapters on the institutional setting (Chapter 1) and the determination of security prices and market liquidity (Chapter 3) are essential. A basic empirical training is provided by the chapters on the measurement of liquidity and on estimating its determinants (Chapters 2 and 5). The theory of market depth (Chapter 4) is highly recommended, although a short course might leave out the sections on imperfect competition. If more time is available, any of the subsequent chapters (from Parts II and III) may be covered: each of them is self-contained, so that they can be chosen in any combination that caters to the interests of the course participants. Each additional chapter would require no less than three lecture hours.

(ii) A master-level course on the architecture of securities markets would start with the basic institutions and theory (Chapters 1, 2, 3, and 4) and then focus on the market design and regulatory issues addressed in Part II (Chapters 6, 7, 8, and 9). Such a course would require twenty to twenty-five lecture hours.

(iii) A master-level or Ph.D. course stressing the relevance of market microstructure for asset pricing and corporate finance should include Chapters 3, 4, 10, 11, and 12 (fifteen to twenty hours).

(iv) A suitable complement for a Ph.D. course in asset pricing would include Chapters 3, 10, and 11.

(v) Similarly, to complement a Ph.D. course in corporate finance or corporate governance, we suggest Chapters 3 and 12.

Acknowledgments

This book has been many years in the writing, as our students, colleagues, and family members know only too well. We have accumulated a large debt of gratitude. We would like to thank the colleagues, coauthors, and mentors who inspired and encouraged our work in the area. A partial list includes Viral Acharya, Anat Admati, Alessandro Beber, Bruno Biais, Patrick Bolton, Jean-Philippe Bouchaud, Margaret Bray, Giovanni Cespa, Jean-Edouard Colliard, Hans Degryse, Olivier Dessaint, Peter Diamond, Jérôme Dugast, Andrew Ellul, Laurent Fresard, Alessandro Frino, Thomas Gehrig, Larry Glosten, Charles Goodhart, Oliver Hart, Joel Hasbrouck, Martin Hellwig, Terrence Hendershott, Johan Hombert, Charles Jones, Frank de Jong, Ohad Kadan, Eugene Kandel, Mervyn King, Pete Kyle, Jean-Charles Lehalle, Stefano Lovo, Albert Menkveld, Sophie Moinas, Theo Nijman, Maureen O'Hara, Christine Parlour, Lin Peng, Ioanid Rosu, Patrik Sandas, Duane Seppi, Chester Spatt, Ernst-Ludwig von Thadden, Erik Theissen, David Thesmar, Dimitri Vayanos, Clara Vega, Paolo Volpin, and Josef Zechner.

We are particularly grateful to Alessandro Beber for providing data, to Andrew Ellul for both data and extensive feedback on the manuscript, and to Lorenzo Pandolfi for his invaluable advice and his painstaking work on the exercises of the first edition and Markus Bak-Hansen for his help in revising the second edition (and suggesting a few exercises). We also thank people who provided us feedback on the first edition (including Keichi Kubota, Dominik Rösch, and René Wells). We also thank the graduate students who at various stages provided valuable feedback and assistance: Gennaro Catapano, Chin-Han Chiang, Dincbas Neslihan, Francesco Paolo Conteduca, Sarah Draus, Maurizio Montone, Roberto Pinto, Jean-David Sigaux, Yuehua Tang, Antoine Thabault, and especially Paul Whelan.

Special mention goes to Roger Meservey for his outstanding copyediting of the first edition. The striking cover was designed by Paola Pagano. We also thank Terry Vaughn and Joe Jackson at Oxford University Press for their encouragement and guidance during the preparation of the first edition.

Over the years, our research for this book was supported by our respective employers: HEC Paris, Università di Napoli Federico II, Imperial College London, and Columbia University's School of International and Public Affairs.

Last but not least, we thank Anne, Carla, and Patrick for their support and their patience in putting up with the countless hours we stole from family time to work on this enterprise.

List of Acronyms

AMEX:	American Stock Exchange
AMF:	Autorié des Marchés Financiers
BBO:	Best Bid and Offer
CDS:	Credit Default Swap
CFTC:	Commodity Futures Trading Commission
CME:	Chicago Mercantile Exchange
DMM:	Designated Market Maker
ECN:	Electronic Communication Network
ESMA:	European Securities and Markets Authority
ETF:	Exchanged Traded Funds
HFT:	High-Frequency Trading
HFTs:	High-Frequency Traders
ICE:	Intercontinental Exchange
IPO:	Initial Price Offering
LOB:	Limit Order Book
LSE:	London Stock Exchange
OTC:	Over the Counter
MiFID:	Markets in Financial Instruments Directive
MiFIR:	Markets in Financial Instruments Regulation
MTF:	Multilateral Trading Facilities
Nasdaq:	National Association of Securities Dealers Automated Quotations
NYSE:	New York Stock Exchange
PFOF:	Payment for Order Flow
PTF:	Principal Trading Firm
RM:	Regulated Market
SEC:	U.S. Securities and Exchange Commission
SI:	Systematic Internalizer
TRACE:	Trade Reporting and Compliance Engine
TSX:	Toronto Stock EXchange

Introduction

Learning Objectives:

- What is this book about?
- Two key concepts in market microstructure: market liquidity and price discovery
- Why do people care about market liquidity and price discovery?
- Which puzzles can market microstructure address?
- The three dimensions of liquidity

0.1 What Is This Book About?

The way securities are actually traded is far removed from the idealized picture of a frictionless and self-equilibrating market offered by the typical finance textbook. In that idealized version of the trading process, all potential participants are present on the market; these participants convey to the market orders that reflect their demand or supply of securities, and they are not affected by actions of other market participants; and an auctioneer balances the quantities demanded and supplied at a single equilibrium price that reflects a consensus view of the security's "fundamental value." Real-world markets do not work like this, for two main reasons.

First, market players are not all simultaneously present on the market. Such continuous presence would be too costly in time, attention, and access costs. At any given point in time, price formation is delegated to the limited number of market participants who happen to be present. Any temporary imbalance between buy and sell orders for a security will have to be absorbed by whoever is present, especially by professional intermediaries who specialize in "making the market." Typically, market makers and other investors will absorb order imbalances only if the price is sufficiently attractive. For instance, to absorb a spate of sell orders investors will require the inducement of a sufficiently low price. As a result, the equilibrium price actually struck at any given instant may deviate from the one that would emerge if all investors participated. These price deviations generate profit opportunities, which in turn will draw in more traders. Over time the deviations are ironed out.

Market Liquidity: Theory, Evidence, and Policy. Second Edition. Thierry Foucault, Marco Pagano, and Ailsa Röell, Oxford University Press. © Oxford University Press 2023. DOI: 10.1093/oso/9780197542064.003.0001

Second, even the limited number of participants who are present at any instant in a real-world security market have quite diverse information about the security's fundamentals: some participants are shrewd market professionals with all the latest news and state-of-the-art pricing models at their fingertips; others do not have such up-to-date information but may try to infer it from the behavior of other participants; still others may trade for reasons that are unrelated to information, for instance a need to liquidate their holdings in order to pay their bills. As a result, the order flow is a complex mix of information and noise, and a consensus price only emerges over time, as the trading process evolves and participants interpret the actions of other traders. This is another reason why a security's actual transaction price might deviate from its fundamental value, which would be assessed by a fully informed set of investors.

This book takes these deviations of prices from fundamental values seriously. We explain why and how they emerge in the trading process, and how and why they are eventually eliminated. Fortunately we can draw on a vast body of theoretical insights and empirical findings on security price formation that has been built up in the last thirty years, forming a well-defined field of financial economics known as "market microstructure." As we shall see, the study of market microstructure illuminates two key aspects of real-world markets that are neglected by textbook asset pricing models: liquidity and price discovery.

Liquidity is the degree to which an order can be executed within a short time frame at a price close to the security's consensus value. Conversely, a price that deviates substantially from this consensus value indicates illiquidity: in an illiquid market, buy orders tend to push transaction prices up, while sell orders tend to do the opposite; in extreme cases, the deviation is so great that it is not worthwhile or feasible to trade at all, and the market freezes. In other words, in an illiquid market, the best price at which a security can be bought (ask price) is considerably above the best price at which it can be sold (bid price). And in fact the difference between these two prices—the bid-ask spread—is a common measure of illiquidity. Liquidity differs greatly among securities and over time, one of the aims of this book is to explain why this is so. For instance, Table 1 shows the bid and ask prices at which U.S. stocks issued by companies of different sizes (measured by market capitalization, that is, the market value of all their outstanding shares) could be sold or bought on January 12, 2021. Clearly, the stock of large companies such as Amazon and Boeing is extremely liquid, with bid-ask spreads in the range of a few basis points: 2 for Amazon and 4 for Boeing (a basis point is a hundredth of 0.01%). In contrast, for smaller companies, the spread is an order of magnitude larger: for instance, almost 4% for Borr Drilling—a substantial illiquidity cost for potential investors.

Liquidity also fluctuates significantly over time. During the financial crisis of 2008, the average bid-ask spreads for stocks listed on the major exchanges

Table 1 Bid and Ask Prices Quoted for Selected U.S. Stocks on January 12, 2021

Stock	Amazon	Boeing	Campbell Soup	Borr Drilling
Market capitalization (bn $)	1566.88	117.65	13.78	0.23
Best bid price	3124.00	207.71	45.48	0.99
Best ask price	3124.75	207.79	45.36	1.03
$ bid-ask spread	0.75	0.08	0.38	0.04
% bid-ask spread	0.02%	0.04%	0.83%	3.96%

worldwide increased dramatically, from about 3% in the first half of 2008 to 6% in the six months following the failure of Lehman Brothers in September. The average spread peaked at over 6.5% in the period of great uncertainty preceding the announcement of the Citibank rescue on November 23.[1] The connection between uncertainty and illiquidity is underscored by the fact that it was financial stocks whose spreads increased the most sharply by far during those months. The spikes in bid-ask spreads on the stock market coincided with even greater disruptions in the interbank market and the markets for credit default swaps (CDS) and many asset-backed securities. The lack of liquidity was so intense that at some points markets simply seized up. This book examines and explicates the causes of such dramatic changes in market liquidity.

Price discovery is the speed and accuracy with which transaction prices incorporate information available to market participants. Markets sometimes display an astonishing ability to locate information about recent events and extract its implications for underlying stock values. For example, in the wake of the space shuttle Challenger explosion at 11:39 a.m. EST on January 28, 1986, the stock market very quickly determined which of the four potential contracting manufacturers was at fault for the defective parts of the shuttle: within fifteen minutes, there was a sell-induced New-York Stock Exchange (NYSE) trading halt in the shares of only one company, Morton-Thiokol. By the end of the day its shares had fallen by 11.86%, while Lockheed, Martin-Marietta, and Rockwell fell by much less (Maloney and Mulherin 2003). By contrast, the general public did not learn of the cause of the crash until two weeks later, on February 11, when Nobel-winning physicist Richard Feynman demonstrated that there were problems with Morton-Thiokol's booster rockets. This episode illustrates the market's ability to create knowledge out of a multitude of individual trades, each of which manages to contribute a small piece of

[1] These numbers are drawn from Beber and Pagano (2013), who analyze daily closing bid and ask prices for 16,491 stocks listed on the exchanges of from 30 countries and present in the Datastream data base.

information to the overall picture. In this sense, "securities markets are a vehicle for amalgamating unorganized knowledge" (Maloney and Mulherin 2003, p. 474).

This episode also illustrates a general but unintuitive point that will receive considerable attention here, namely, that there is a tension between price discovery and liquidity. When price-relevant information gets to the market by means of trading pressure rather than a public announcement, liquidity suffers. In fact, just as it became apparent that the sell orders of some market participants might be based on superior information about Morton-Thiokol's responsibility for the disaster, the market for its shares became most illiquid: the NYSE specialist (market maker) dealing in Morton-Thiokol's stock decided to halt trading, to avoid making a market in a situation where he might very easily lose money to informed traders.

0.2 Why Should We Care?

Why is market liquidity important? Asset managers and ordinary investors care about liquidity insofar as it affects the return on their investments, simply because illiquid securities cost more to buy, and sell for less. Therefore, illiquidity eats into the return. When markets are less than perfectly liquid, investors cannot buy and sell at the same price, and the bid-ask spread is typically wider for large trades. Thus, analysis of the way liquidity arises, builds, or vanishes may be very important in evaluating the portfolio choices of an asset manager or an ordinary investor.

For the same reasons, liquidity is a key concern of all the professionals who specialize in providing securities trading services, such as the trading desks of institutional investors (mutual funds, pension funds, and hedge funds) and retail stock brokers: locating the most liquid trading venue or timing trades so as to minimize trading costs is the key to providing good-quality service.

Beside being a source of costs, the trading process can also be a source of risks for investors. Insofar as liquidity can vary over time in ways that are not perfectly predictable, it can heighten the risk engendered by the unpredictability of assets' fundamentals. So investors will require compensation not only for the expected trading costs associated with illiquidity but also for the additional risks. For both of these reasons, illiquidity affects equilibrium prices, which must discount not only risky future cash flows generated by the asset, but also the future trading costs that its holders may incur and the associated risks. The need to compensate investors for illiquidity creates a link between the field of market microstructure and that of asset pricing, which we will explore in Chapter 10.

But if illiquidity lowers securities prices, affecting the cost of capital for the issuers, then it will also affect these companies' day-to-day decisions on capital expenditure. The global financial crisis of 2008 is a telling example of the linkage between market liquidity, asset prices and economic activity: the drying up of liquidity in several securities markets in 2008 was associated with plunging asset prices and drastic reductions in security issuance and real investment by firms. And although these drops largely represented a correction of previous overpricing and over-investment, the illiquidity of securities markets undoubtedly amplified the effects of the revision in fundamentals. This episode illustrates why policy makers take such a strong interest in the liquidity of securities markets and in how policies and regulations affect it.

Investors, issuers, and policy makers naturally care not just about liquidity but also about the speed of price discovery. This determines the amount of information that at any instant is embodied in the price of a security, and hence how reliable that price is as a reference point for managers' real investment decisions. An informationally efficient price is also useful as a benchmark for evaluating the performance of the firm's management, and for devising equity- and option-based compensation schemes that provide the proper incentives. In short, market microstructure issues prove to be relevant to corporate finance choices, on such matters as capital budgeting and management compensation, as we shall see in Chapter 12.

0.3 Some Puzzles

This book explains a number of puzzling phenomena in securities markets. Let us consider a few specific examples of issues that can be attacked and understood using the analytical tools and empirical methods of market microstructure.

1. **Why does liquidity change over time, and why does it drop at times of crisis?** As we have seen, securities markets became much more illiquid during the financial crisis of 2008, especially in the second half of the year. This also happened at the start of the COVID-19 pandemic of 2020, when the average bid-ask spread on U.S. stocks in the CRSP US Stock database roughly doubled relative to the end of 2019 (Figure 0.1).

   Stock market liquidity also exhibits long-run trends over time: in the U.S. it has been basically improving since World War II, with average bid-ask spreads gradually declining from about 0.6% in the 1950s to about 0.2% around 2000, with an especially large drop in the 1990s (Jones 2002). Moreover, liquidity varies systematically over a much more limited time frame as well: within a single trading day, bid-ask spreads tend to feature

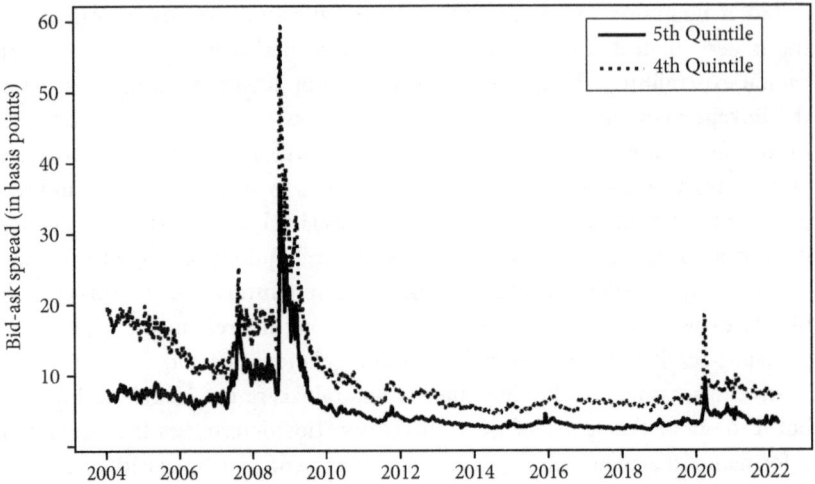

Figure 0.1 10-day rolling average closing bid-ask spread (in basis points) for AMEX, NYSE, and Nasdaq stocks by market capitalization (two first quintiles) in the CRSP data set.
Source: WRDS.

a U-shaped pattern, higher at the open and at the close than during the rest of the trading day. In addition, for individual stocks liquidity tends to drop in connection with special events, such as takeover battles, or in the wake of other dramatic price-relevant events, as exemplified by the Challenger explosion episode discussed above. The models of security price determination presented in Chapters 3 and 4 offer insight into the reasons for these low- and high-frequency empirical regularities, and Chapter 11 will focus more specifically on how market liquidity changes at times of financial instability.

2. **Why do large trades move prices up or down, and why are these price changes subsequently reversed?** One of the most widely observed patterns in securities markets is that a large and sustained flow of buy or sell orders puts temporary pressure on prices: buy orders tend to drive them up, and sell orders tend to push them down, but these price movements are partly or wholly reversed after some time. This is apparent, for instance, in the wake of redemptions of shares of equity mutual funds: to repay the investors who redeem their shares, mutual funds must in turn liquidate part of their stock holdings, and thus generate a wave of sell orders for the corresponding stocks. The average price impact associated with large mutual fund redemptions is shown in Figure 0.2, counting in months from

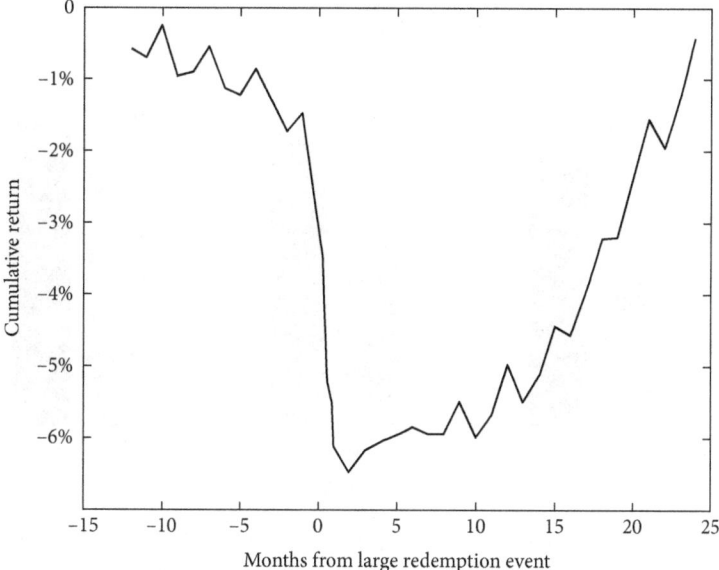

Figure 0.2 Average cumulative return of equities held by mutual funds experiencing large redemptions, counting months from the date of the large-redemption event.

Source: fig. 12 in Duffie (2010).

the date of the large-redemption event.[2] The figure shows that, while the prices of the stocks most affected by mutual funds' sales drop steeply in the month of the redemption, on average they completely recover in the subsequent two years. Chapter 3 will present evidence that such price patterns are not limited to mutual fund redemptions, as they are generally observed for any large security transaction, although often security prices fail to revert fully to the initial level afterwards. The chapter will provide a framework to explain these price responses to large orders.

3. **Why has securities trading become more fragmented?** Practitioners like to say, "Liquidity begets liquidity," meaning that people like to trade at the same time of day and in the same venue as many other market participants. This suggests that security trading should tend to gravitate towards a single trading platform, which would therefore offer greater liquidity to investors than a market fragmented across several platforms. In light of this, it may

---

[2] This figure is from Duffie (2010). Based on data for the net outflows from each mutual fund, Duffie (2010) computes total outflows across mutual funds for each stock, normalized by trading volume, so as to determine price pressure indices for each equity, and then plots the cumulative returns of equities in the top decile according to price pressure, starting from the redemption date.

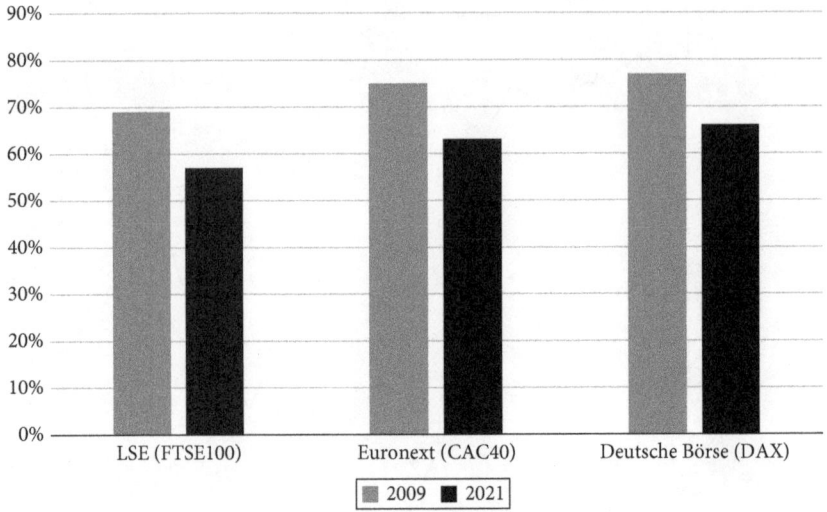

Figure 0.3 Share of trading volume in primary exchange for European stocks.
Source: Cboe Global Markets website (https://www.cboe.com/europe/equities/) and authors' calculations.

appear puzzling that trading in equity markets has become increasingly fragmented over time over the last two decades.

This is illustrated by Figure 0.3, which shows that between 2009 and 2021 the share of trades executed in the primary exchange for a stock (that is, the exchange on which the stock is listed) dropped substantially for stocks belonging to the main European stock indices. This is due to the entry of new trading platforms, which have eroded the share of the main regulated exchanges in the respective stock markets, namely, the share of the London Stock Exchange (LSE) for stocks belonging to the FTSE100 index, Euronext for French stocks included in the CAC40 index, and Deutsche Börse for German stocks included in the Dax index. An even more dramatic drop occurred in the United States, where the NYSE share of total trading volume in NYSE-listed shares dropped from 79.1% in January 2005 to 25.1% in October 2009 (SEC 2010). This drop in the share of trades executed in primary exchanges is part of a long-run trend: at the beginning of the new millennium, most of stock trading volume was concentrated in the respective domestic primary markets. Chapter 7 inquires into the reasons for this increase in the fragmentation of security markets, and its implications for market liquidity and for price discovery.

4. **Why do some traders seek to hide their intended trades, and others to disclose them?** Some traders really keep their cards close to the chest, submitting their orders in a way that does not reveal their true

size. For example, as Chapter 2 demonstrates, they may submit "hidden orders." Alternatively, they may go off-exchange altogether and trade on "dark pools," where orders are not displayed. Indeed, in the E.U. 45% of equity trading occurs outside regulated markets, hence on platforms that are typically less transparent (ESMA 2021a), while in the U.S. 35% of equity trading occurs off-exchange 2021 (SEC 2020). Conversely, some traders appear to seek transparency: for, instance, some of them opt for "sunshine trading," that is, preannounce their trading intentions. For instance, some exchange-traded funds (ETFs) follow trading rules that make their intended trades predictable, as they periodically rebalance their portfolios in order to track public indices. Bessembinder et al. (2016), who study the trades undertaken by a large exchange-traded crude oil ETF, find that both market liquidity and resilience increase significantly around this fund's large and predictable "roll" trade dates. Chapter 8 analyzes market transparency, explaining why it harms some traders and benefits others.

5. **Why are there temporary deviations from arbitrage prices?** The absence of arbitrage opportunities is a central tenet of asset-pricing theory: assets that generate identical cash flows must command the same market price, so that there is no opportunity for profitable arbitrage trading. Nevertheless, there are instances in which the no-arbitrage condition breaks down for non-negligible periods of time. For instance, Deville and Riva (2007) use intraday transaction data to study why it takes time for the French index options market to return to no-arbitrage values after deviating from put-call parity. Similarly, de Jong, Rosenthal, and Van Dijk (2009) document deviations from theoretical price parity in a sample of twelve dual-listed companies, sometimes known as "Siamese twins." These are pairs of companies incorporated in different countries that contractually agree to operate their businesses as a single enterprise, while retaining their separate legal identities and existing stock exchange listings, as in the case of Royal Dutch/Shell. These companies should trade at the same price, yet from 1980–2002 their prices actually differed so much that simple trading rules could produce abnormal returns of nearly 10% per annum in some cases, after adjusting for transaction costs and margin requirements. In Chapter 11 we explore why these deviations can persist, and how they relate to market liquidity.

6. **Why has high-frequency trading become prevalent in stock markets?** In the past two decades, trading has become increasingly automated: orders are more and more frequently generated by computer algorithms, automatically routed to electronic trading platforms to be executed, and often immediately cancelled after being placed on the platform. Such "high-frequency trading," which requires huge investments in technology,

HFT as a share of US equities daily volume
%

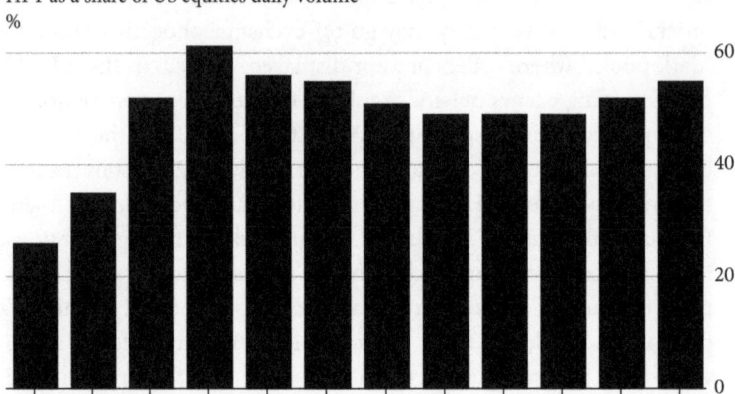

Figure 0.4 Market share of U.S. stock trading volume performed by high-frequency traders.
Source: "How High-Frequency Trading Hit a Speed Bump," *Financial Times*, January 1, 2018.

telecommunication networks, and human capital by market participants, has become prevalent in stock markets. This is illustrated by Figure 0.4: the fraction of high-frequency trading in U.S. stocks rose from less than 30% in 2006 to over 60% in 2009, and then leveled off around 50% in subsequent years. ESMA (2021b) estimates high-frequency trading in E.U. shares to be about 60% of the total, and algorithmic non-high-frequency trading to account for another 15%. Chapter 9 of this book explores what can account for this drastic change in trading technology, and which effects it can be expected to produce on market liquidity, price discovery, and volatility.

0.4 Three Concepts of Liquidity

0.4.1 Market Liquidity

In this book we use the word *liquidity* to indicate the ability to trade a security quickly at a price close to its consensus value, that is, in the sense of "market liquidity." But readers need to be aware that this is only one of three commonly used definitions of liquidity. As they are closely related, these three distinct concepts are often referred to interchangeably in the context of the same discourse in financial press articles and policy discussions. This can be confusing, so it is useful to clarify what liquidity means outside the context of security trading.

0.4.2 Funding Liquidity

When referring to banks or companies, liquidity is generally taken to mean having sufficient cash or the ability to obtain credit at acceptable terms, to meet obligations without incurring large losses. We can refer to this notion as "funding liquidity." Maintaining adequate funding liquidity is particularly important for banks, which typically engage in maturity transformation. That is, they use short-term liabilities (bank deposits or repurchase agreements) to fund long-term assets (loans to companies and households). Hence, to be able to satisfy the claims of their depositors or creditors, they must maintain an adequate buffer of cash and short-term assets that can be readily liquidated. Banks have other options for generating liquidity, such as selling loans, borrowing from other banks, or borrowing from a central bank such as the U.S. Federal Reserve or the European Central Bank. However, it could still happen that, say due to a loss of confidence in the bank, depositors may wish to withdraw funds in excess of the bank's cash reserves plus the amount it can raise by selling short-term assets (such as treasury bills or commercial paper) or obtaining overnight credit on the interbank market. Such a "bank run" is described, in fact, as a liquidity crisis, and in the absence of sufficient liquidity provision by the central bank, the distressed bank will be driven into bankruptcy and forced to liquidate its loan portfolio.

Funding liquidity is related to market liquidity in several ways. First, both have value for the same reason: people want to hold assets that can be immediately transformed into consumption, as for instance when the owner suffers a shock (e.g., a health problem or loss of job) or discovers an unforeseen opportunity (e.g., a very cheaply priced house or a very attractive business project). Since it is hard to insure against such individual-specific liquidity shocks, people try to self-insure by holding demand deposits, which they can withdraw without notice in case of need. That is, they prize funding liquidity. By the same token, investors value market liquidity, that is, they prefer assets that can be sold quickly in case of need at prices not far from their fundamental value.

Second, funding liquidity is itself a prerequisite for market liquidity. For instance, market makers often need access to credit to maintain a large enough inventory of the securities in which they are dealing, because they do not have enough equity. Hence, the more abundant and cheaper is the market makers' funding liquidity, the greater is the liquidity of security markets, in the sense that investors will be able to trade securities in larger amounts at better prices. By the same token, a credit crunch—a drop in funding liquidity—may impair the liquidity of security markets, by forcing market makers to widen their bid-ask spreads and reduce their order size maximum. Chapter 11 analyzes the effect of funding liquidity on price formation in security markets.

Third, the causal relations can also be reversed. That is, market liquidity can be a prerequisite for funding liquidity, because security traders often must post margins (i.e., collateral in the form of cash or securities) to cover the risk that they may not be able to pay for the securities they are buying or deliver those they are selling. This "counterparty risk" can arise if the trader borrows in order to buy the security, or sells short (i.e., without owning it yet). However, margin requirements depend in part on the securities' expected market liquidity: they are typically lower for securities that are expected to be more liquid and less volatile. Hence more liquid markets enable traders to fund their leveraged purchases or short sales more cheaply. This creates a feedback from market liquidity to funding liquidity.

This reciprocal feedback between market and funding liquidity becomes particularly important in times of crisis, when it can lead to liquidity spirals, with market liquidity suddenly drying up for many securities at once, as shown by Brunnermeier and Pedersen (2009). It is important to realize that, however deep and strong the relationship between them, market liquidity and funding liquidity are different concepts, and are accordingly affected by different policy actions: market liquidity by security market regulation and funding liquidity by banking regulation, specifically by the role of the central bank as "lender of last resort." This brings us to a third possible meaning of liquidity, that is, the monetary dimension.

0.4.3 Monetary Liquidity

If we rank assets by market liquidity, the most liquid is obviously cash, which by definition is universally accepted in exchange for goods at very stable terms (except in times of hyperinflation). At intermediate levels of liquidity are financial securities such as bonds and stocks, while at the opposite extreme is real estate, which is so heterogeneous that sale typically requires considerable time and effort, or else a large price concession in exchange for quick sale.

This explains why in practice liquidity is often identified with money itself, whether defined as the cash held by households and firms and bank reserves ("monetary base"), or as broader monetary aggregates that also include bank deposits of various types (M1, M2, or M3). Especially in macroeconomics, this notion of "monetary liquidity" is prevalent. This notion of liquidity also bears some relationship to the previous two: expansion of the money supply by the central bank (say, via open market purchases of bonds or "quantitative easing") increases the supply of funds to banks and thus tends to increase funding liquidity, and with it market liquidity, as we have seen. By the same token, a monetary contraction can be expected to reduce both funding and market liquidity. There is a vast literature that analyzes and documents the link between monetary policy and funding liquidity (see Bernanke and Gertler 1995). Expansionary monetary policy may increase banks' loan supply either directly (bank lending channel) or indirectly by improving borrowers' net worth and thereby their borrowing capacity (balance-sheet channel). Monetary policy has also been shown to affect the liquidity of securities markets: at times of crisis, monetary expansion is associated with greater liquidity in both stock and bond markets, and bond market liquidity is forecast by money flows to government bond funds (Chordia, Sarkar, and Subrahmanyam 2005).

Of course, these relationships are neither mechanical nor stable over time, because banks and other financial intermediaries can generate different amounts of funding liquidity in the presence of the same level of money supply. And conversely, they may respond to an expansion of the monetary base by increasing their reserves with the central bank rather than by increasing their lending.

PART I
INSTITUTIONS

1

Trading Mechanics and Market Structure

Learning objectives:

- How securities markets are organized
- Who sets the rules
- How the organization of securities markets has changed recently

1.1 Introduction

Securities markets are mechanisms for bringing buyers and sellers together and enabling them to trade. Trading may be prompted by various factors: the need to mitigate risks (hedging), the desire to exploit superior information (speculation), or the urge to rebalance one's portfolio (liquidity shocks). In standard treatments of asset pricing, such as the capital asset pricing model (CAPM), the trading mechanism is not laid out explicitly, on the assumption that it does not matter for securities prices. Yet in reality there is a wide variety of trading mechanisms, and market participants pay close attention to their design. Changes in trading rules are often hotly debated, and market organizers carefully fine-tune these rules to improve the competitiveness of their trading platform. This is because the trading rules affect the efficiency of markets as mechanisms to realize trading gains and discover asset values. They also affect the apportioning of gains among market participants, determining, for instance, the fraction of the gain that is captured by specialized intermediaries.

A trading mechanism defines the "rules of the game" that market participants must follow: it determines the actions they can take (e.g., the kinds of orders they can place), their information about other market participants' actions (e.g., whether they observe quotes or orders), and the protocol for matching buy and sell orders (e.g., whether orders are executed at a common price or not). As the possible rules can be put together in a virtually boundless number of combinations, real-world market structures feature great diversity and are constantly

Market Liquidity: Theory, Evidence, and Policy. Second Edition. Thierry Foucault, Marco Pagano, and Ailsa Röell,
Oxford University Press. © Oxford University Press 2023. DOI: 10.1093/oso/9780197542064.003.0002

evolving, so attempting a complete classification is hopeless. It is more fruitful to focus on two prototype trading mechanisms, namely the limit order market (or auction market) and the dealer market.[1] In fact, all securities markets rely, in various ways, on combinations of these two basic mechanisms. Section 1.2 describes how each operates, illustrates market structures that combine elements of both, and shows that each prototypical mechanism itself can vary in important ways, such as the degree of transparency and the frequency of trades.

In limit order markets, all participants (final investors and intermediaries) can interact directly and multilaterally on one trading platform; their bids and offers are consolidated in a limit order book (LOB) according to price priority, so that higher bids and cheaper offers are more likely to be executed. As all participants can trade with each other, trading platforms using this mechanism are sometimes referred to as "all-to-all" trading systems. As explained below, such trading platforms are used in equity and derivatives markets (e.g., options and futures).

By contrast, in dealer markets final investors can only trade at the bid and ask quotes posted by specialized intermediaries, called "dealers" or "market makers," and these quotes are not consolidated to enforce price priority. As prices are often set via bilateral negotiations between dealers and investors (or their brokers), these markets are often referred to as "Over the Counter" (OTC), an old expression referring to decentralized sales, generally occurring over the counter of a shop. Fixed income securities (e.g., Treasuries, corporate bonds, or interest rate swaps), currencies, and interbank loans are often traded in this way. As explained in Section 1.2.2, OTC markets have experienced important changes in recent years (due to automation and regulation) with the emergence of electronic trading systems enabling investors to trade directly with each other ("all-to-all" trading systems) or to request quotes from multiple dealers at the same time ("Request for Quotes" systems or RFQs). Moreover, dealers now use electronic limit order books to trade among each other, in so-called interdealer markets.

Market design matters. Indeed, much of this book distills the results of the large body of research on how market design affects trading costs and price discovery. To provide an idea of the impact that the design of security markets can have on their performance, Section 1.3 briefly previews some empirical studies that compare limit order and dealer markets or investigate markets with different degrees of transparency, i.e., where markets provide different amounts of information about the trading process.

---

[1] These two basic market structures are also known, respectively, as "order-driven" and "quote-driven" markets.

An obvious question is why in practice markets feature different trading mechanisms. As Section 1.4 explains, trading rules are determined by the interplay between regulators, intermediaries, issuers, investors, and the managers of trading platforms. The balance between these stakeholders—and hence the actual trading rules—largely depends on the governance and ownership of the platform. For instance, the platform may be managed for profit or not, and the ownership shares of the various stakeholders (intermediaries, issuers, investors) may vary considerably between platforms and over time. The design of a trading platform must also take into account the possible threat from competing platforms—a concern that in recent decades has become more pressing due to a combination of capital market liberalization, changes in security regulation, and technological advances. In particular, digital and communication technology has radically transformed the trading process, sparking an increasingly lively debate on the impact of new trading technologies on market liquidity, price volatility, and economic efficiency.

1.2 Limit Order Markets and Dealer Markets

1.2.1 Limit Order Markets

A defining feature of the limit order market is that buy and sell orders from all market participants are matched directly in a single marketplace, which can be either the floor of an exchange or a "trading platform" run by a computer (see Figure 1.1).[2] Orders go into a Limit Order Book (LOB), which determines the

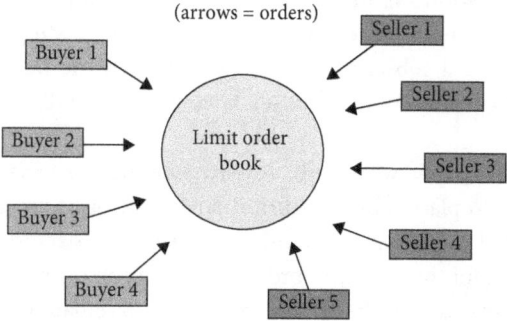

Figure 1.1 Limit order market.

---

[2] However, even when trading occurs on such trading platforms, it may not be completely centralized, as multiple limit order books for the same asset may coexist. As explained in Section 1.4.2 and Chapter 7, such market fragmentation occurs for instance in equity markets in North America and Europe.

priority with which they will be matched with offsetting orders, according to the rules of the market and the characteristics of the orders themselves. In call (or batch) markets, incoming orders are stored in the LOB and then matched at discrete intervals, such as once per day. In continuous markets, they are matched immediately with orders already present on the LOB, if possible; otherwise they are stored in the LOB to await future execution.

Continuous Limit Order Markets

When submitting orders to a continuous limit order market, investors can design them differently depending on their trading needs. The most basic choice, which determines both speed and price of execution, is between limit and market orders. A buy limit order specifies the maximum price at which the trader is prepared to buy a stated amount of the security; similarly, a sell limit order specifies the minimum price the seller will accept for a given amount. A market order only specifies an amount to buy or sell, not the price: it will therefore be executed at whatever price it can fetch on the market.

Limit orders may not find a counterpart with which they can be matched at the specified price. Market orders, by contrast, are filled immediately if there is any outstanding limit order on the other side of the market. Thus, one difference between limit and market orders is that limit orders do not guarantee immediate execution—indeed, they may never be executed at all—whereas market orders are executed immediately upon submission.

The LOB shown in Figure 1.2 illustrates the mechanics of trading in a continuous limit order market. The LOB is a snapshot at a given point in time of all the limit orders awaiting execution. In the LOB, buy limit orders (bids) are arranged in decreasing order of price and sell limit orders (asks) in increasing order. The LOB also shows size and time, that is, the number of shares specified and the time the order was entered in the book. Depending on the market's trading rules, only a subset of the orders present in the LOB may be visible to market participants. As we shall see later, this is one dimension of market transparency.

Consider an investor who wants to buy nine hundred shares. He has two options. One is to place a buy market order for this amount. In this case, the order is executed immediately against the best limit orders to sell (on the ask side): it will first fill the two limit orders placed at the offer price of $74.48 for eight hundred shares, and then be executed for the remaining hundred shares against the limit order at $75.74, so that its average execution price is $74.62. The order of priority in which limit orders on the book are executed depends on their price: aggressively priced orders are filled before less competitive ones. In other words, execution obeys a price priority rule. If two limit orders have the same price, they are filled according to secondary priority rules such as time

Market sell order of 200 (or
limit sell with price < 74.42)

Market buy order of 900 (or
limit buy with price > 75.74)

	Bid			Ask		
Price	Size	Time	Price	Size	Time
74.42	300 100	11:49:39	74.48	300	11:49:35
74.41	100	11:46:55	74.48	500	11:49:40
74.36	400	11:48:30	75.74	100	08:25:17
74.36	400	11:48:32	76.00	150	08:02:02
74.00	13	10:56:00	76.77	20	07:01:01
73.75	5100	11:28:02	77.00	100	09:15:00
72.98	5100	10:56:99	77.06	200	10:14:11
72.15	120	08:01:39	77.35	1000	08:01:39
72.11	20	07:01:01	77.82	20	07:01:01
72.03	20	07:01:01	78.00	300	08:02:00
72.00					9:30:04
71.59		Because of the buy market order, the bid-ask spread				8:01:32
71.11					9:30:04
71.00		widens from 74.48 − 74.42 = **0.06** to 76.00 – 74.42 = **1.58**.				7:01:01
70.35		The market order has "consumed" liquidity.				8:01:35
70.11	20	07:01:01	80.00	350	09:15:00

Figure 1.2 Example of limit order book (LOB).

of submission or pro-rata allocation (fractional execution proportional to limit order size).

The second option for the investor is to place a buy limit order for nine hundred shares. If he specifies a limit price lower than $74.48, the order is entered in the LOB on the bid side and stored for future execution. The level of the chosen bid price determines the likelihood and speed of execution, as more aggressively priced buy orders are executed first according to price priority.

If the investor instead specifies a limit price equal to or higher than $74.48— that is, if he matches or crosses the best price on the ask side of the limit book— then the order is *marketable*: it can be executed at once, at least partially, against stored sell limit orders, in this example those at $74.48. If the order specifies a limit price of $74.50, the remaining hundred shares will appear on the bid side of the LOB as a buy limit order at $74.50. Significantly, the transaction price ($74.48) is determined by existing prices on the LOB, not by the price of the incoming marketable limit order.

The treatment of sellers is analogous. For instance, an investor who wants to sell two hundred shares immediately can either place a market sell order for two hundred shares or a marketable limit order with a price of $74.42 or less. If he is more patient, he can improve his execution by placing a sell limit order for two hundred shares at a price above $74.42, on the ask side of the market. But in this case he runs the risk of non-execution.

Hence, the choice between a market and a limit order involves a trade-off between immediate execution at current market prices and a more favorable transaction price at the cost of delayed and uncertain execution. This trade-off is studied in detail in Chapter 6.

Figure 1.2 can also be used to illustrate the concept of illiquidity, which is discussed in Chapter 2. As a thought experiment, consider a "round-trip transaction," that is, a buy market order followed by an equal-size sell market order. If the market were perfectly liquid, the cost of this round-trip transaction would be zero. Instead, the figure shows that it has a positive cost that increases with its size. If the order size is smaller than three hundred, one buys at $74.48 and resells at $74.42, so that the round-trip cost is $0.06 (i.e., six cents). This cost—the difference between the best bid and the best ask price on the market—is called the "quoted bid-ask spread" and is often used as a measure of illiquidity.

For larger orders, one can compute a similar measure of illiquidity by comparing the average price paid by a buyer placing a large market order and the average price received by a seller for an equally large order. The buy price rises with order size, because the buyer has to "walk up" the schedule of sell limit orders to fill his own buy order. Symmetrically, the sell price is decreasing with the size of the order, as the seller has to "walk down" the schedule of buy limit orders. Thus larger orders are associated with a greater difference between the average execution price for buy and sell market orders—the "weighted average bid-ask spread."[3] A market in which investors can trade large quantities without substantially moving the price—that is, where the weighted average bid-ask spread does not increase much with trade size—is said to be "deep." Therefore, *market depth* is inversely related to the weighted average spread for large trade size. The concept of depth will be made more precise in Chapter 4.

The LOB evolves in real time as market and limit orders are submitted and earlier limit orders are cancelled. For instance, in our example, the submission of a buy market order for nine hundred shares depletes the LOB on the ask side and so widens the bid-ask spread from 0.06 to 1.58. By contrast, if the buyer submits a limit order at $74.45, the bid-ask spread narrows to 0.03. Since market orders widen the spread, they are viewed as consuming liquidity, and traders

---

[3] For instance, in the LOB depicted in Figure 1.2, only eight hundred shares can be bought at $74.48: a buyer looking for one thousand shares would also have to buy one hundred shares at $75.74 and one hundred more at $76.00. As a result, the average price paid per share would be $(74.48 \times 0.8) + (75.74 \times 0.1) + (76.00 \times 0.1) = 74.76$. Conversely, one thousand shares can be sold at an average price of $(74.42 \times 0.3) + (74.41 \times 0.1) + (74.36 \times 0.6) = 74.38$. Therefore, the weighted average bid-ask spread for one thousand shares is $74.76 - 74.38 = 0.38$, rather than 0.06. As a percentage of the mid-quote, the bid-ask spread rises from 0.08% to 0.5%.

submitting these orders are called "liquidity demanders" (or liquidity takers). In contrast, those submitting limit orders are called "liquidity suppliers" (or liquidity makers), since limit orders replenish the LOB.

Box 1.1 Other Types of Order

Limit and market orders are by far the most common kinds of order. But trading platforms often also allow for more complex orders. A *stop order* is an instruction to buy (or sell) only once the price has risen to (fallen to, respectively) a certain level. A stop sell order can be used to limit one's losses on holding a stock if its price nosedives. Moreover, traders can set conditions on cancellation with their orders: *good-until-cancel* orders are valid until they are cancelled, while *good-until* orders are valid until a specified date and *immediate-or-cancel* (or *fill-or-kill*) orders are valid only at the moment they reach the market. Finally, *hidden orders* are limit orders that are stored in the LOB but not displayed to market participants. These orders will be executed in the same way as regular limit orders, but they usually lose time priority against limit orders that are displayed at the same price. A variant of the hidden limit order is the so-called iceberg order, for which a fraction of the actual size is shown to other market participants along with the price. As the order is executed, the hidden size becomes gradually evident to market participants.

Call Limit Order Markets

So far we have considered limit order markets with continuous matching. Another arrangement matches orders at discrete points in time. In this case the limit order market is known as a call (or batch) auction. Before the call auction is held, market participants can submit market and limit orders over a pre-specified time window. During this window, orders gradually accumulate in the LOB without being filled and can in general be cancelled at any time. This pre-auction period stops at some time (which can be deterministic or random), when the price at which eligible orders are executed is set. Unlike in the continuous limit order market, in the call auction all executable orders are cleared at the same price. For this reason, the call auction is sometimes called a single or uniform price auction.

More precisely, at the time of the call auction, all the buy orders in hand are sorted in decreasing order of limit price, with buy market orders treated as at the highest possible price. This determines the cumulative quantity that traders

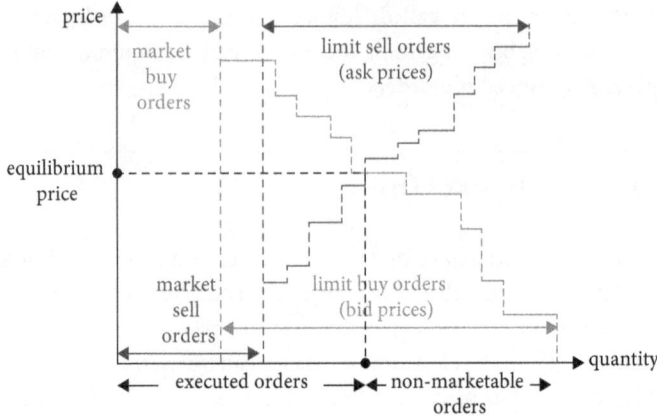

Figure 1.3 Call auction.

are prepared to buy at each possible price. Symmetrically, the sell orders are sorted by increasing limit price, with sell market orders treated as at the lowest possible price. This determines the cumulative quantity that would be sold at each possible price. The resulting demand and supply functions are the two stepwise schedules shown in Figure 1.3.

The price set in the auction—the market-clearing or equilibrium price—is determined by the point where these two stepwise schedules intersect. At this price, orders from all buyers with a bid higher than the clearing price and all sellers with a price below that clearing price are fully executed. Limit orders with a price just equal to the clearing price (the marginal traders) may be partially executed. For instance, in Figure 1.3, the total demand at the clearing price exceeds the total supply, so the marginal buyer will get only partial execution. Buy limit orders below the clearing price or sell orders above it are not filled. It is easy to see that the clearing price maximizes the (voluntary) trading volume, as it leaves no trading opportunity unexploited.

In the past, many exchanges in continental Europe were call markets. In fact, the economist Léon Walras was inspired by the mechanism of the Paris Bourse call auction when he formalized the process by which supply and demand are balanced in competitive markets. Thus, the notion of Walrasian market routinely presented in introductory economics courses is very close to the way trading is organized in call markets. Today, in equity markets, the call auction is often used to determine the opening price (before the start of continuous limit order trading) and the closing price. For instance, the NYSE, the Nasdaq, the Toronto Stock Exchange, Euronext, the London Stock Exchange (LSE), and the Italian Stock Exchange all use call auctions to set opening and closing prices.

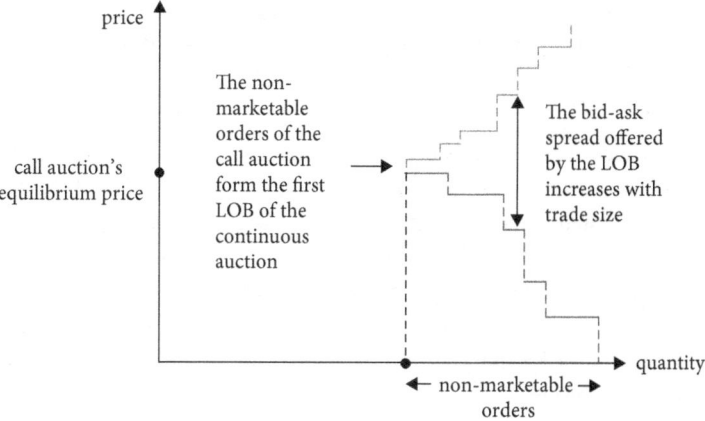

Figure 1.4 Forming the initial limit order book of the trading day.

At the opening, the limit orders that are unfilled in the opening call auction form the initial LOB for the continuous session. Figure 1.4 shows this initial LOB in the case of the call auction displayed in Figure 1.3 and illustrates that the bid-ask spread on the LOB increases with trade size, as noted.

Opening and closing auctions are important for different reasons. At the opening, call auctions play an important role in price discovery: the call auction helps to aggregate information received by different market participants while the market is closed overnight. Meanwhile, closing auctions are becoming increasingly important, as the closing price serves as a benchmark to value institutional investors' portfolios; moreover, as the closing auction attracts a lot of trading interest, it enables asset managers to rebalance their portfolios without the risk of large adverse impact on prices. For instance, for U.S. stocks, closing auctions accounted for about 8% of the daily trading volume in 2018 (Bogousslavsky and Muravyev 2021).

Call auctions are also sometimes used as the only trading mechanism for stocks that are traded infrequently. In this way, market organizers make sure that there is sufficient interest on both sides of the market. They increase the likelihood of finding a counterpart for each side while reducing the risk that the clearing price will be distorted by a temporary imbalance between supply and demand. For instance, on the LSE, SETSqx is a trading platform that runs four electronic auctions a day (alongside a dealer market) for securities that are less liquid than those traded on SETS. Some trading platforms (e.g., Cboe Europe) also run periodic call auctions during the trading, in parallel to the continuous limit order book.

As the trading rules are different in continuous limit order markets and call auctions, traders will not behave in the same way in each case. A formal analysis of price formation and traders' behavior in call and continuous limit order markets is provided in Chapter 4 and Chapter 6, respectively.

Dark Pools

Dark pools are trading platforms that are accessible only to institutional investors (and sometimes financial intermediaries). These are electronic trading platforms operated by stock exchanges (e.g., Turquoise by the LSE, Smartpool by Euronext, or Xetra by the Deutsche Börse), brokers (e.g., BlockCross by ICAP or Blockmatch by Instinet) or banks (e.g., SigmaX by Goldman Sachs or SG CIB AlphaY by Société Générale). These platforms operate in parallel with continuous limit order markets and therefore offer investors an alternative way to execute their orders.

Generally, dark pools do not contribute to price discovery, to the extent that they simply operate as "crossing networks," where traders submit buy and sell market orders and these are periodically crossed at reference prices drawn from other markets, such as the mid-point between the best bid and ask price on the main market for the stock. If there is excess demand (supply) at the reference price, some buyers (sellers) are rationed according to some rule (e.g., time priority or pro rata). Other types of dark pools (e.g., MatchNow, operated by Cboe for Canadian stocks) are not pure crossing networks, allowing traders to submit limit orders, insofar as these offer price improvements relative to the best quotes in the main market.

These trading mechanisms are "dark" in the sense that orders submitted to them are not displayed to the rest of market participants. Moreover, dark pools only disseminate aggregate information on trading volume after executing trades (without revealing information on unfilled orders, for instance). Institutional investors are attracted to dark pools precisely because their opacity reduces the risk of information leakage about their trading intentions (see Chapter 8). The attractiveness of dark pools has increased further in response to the rise of algorithmic trading (see Chapter 9).

Thus, it is no surprise that dark pools have attracted an increasing share of trading volume in recent years: for example, their share of European equity trading rose from less than 1% to about 8% between 2009 and 2016 (Petrescu and Wedow 2017); in U.S. equities markets, trading volume in dark pools rose to about 10% of total trading volume by 2019 (SEC 2020). The growth of dark pool trading—and more generally, off-exchange trading—has attracted regulatory attention: for instance, in Europe the recent MiFID 2 directive capped trading volume in dark pools at 8% of the total in each stock. More broadly, the growth of dark pool trading raises questions about market fragmentation (see Chapter 7) and the optimal level of transparency (see Section 1.2.5 and Chapter 8).

1.2.2 Dealer Markets

In dealer markets, the final investors (or their brokers) do not trade directly with each other, but must contact a dealer, find out his price, and trade at this price, or else try another dealer. So in a dealer market there is a sharp distinction between liquidity suppliers (the dealers) and liquidity demanders (final investors), whereas in a limit order market each participant chooses whether to provide or to demand liquidity.

Figures 1.5 and 1.6 illustrate the trading process in a dealer market. As an example, suppose that Seller 4 wants to sell sixty shares and that he first contacts

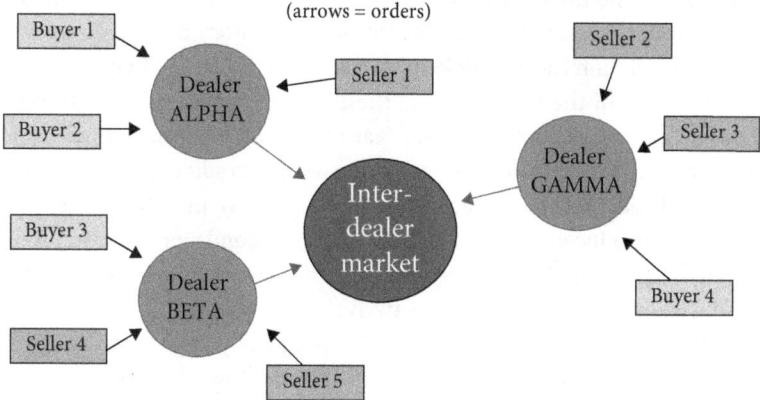

Figure 1.5 Dealer market.

2	ALPHA ZETA	326–329	GAMMA EPSILON IOTA	3
Market Maker Identity Code	Bid Price	Offer Price	Quote Size	Time of Latest Quote Update
ALPHA	326	330	75 × 75	08:53
BETA	324	330	75 × 75	09:14
GAMMA	325	329	75 × 75	09:16
DELTA	323	332	75 × 75	08:53
EPSILON	325	329	25 × 25	09:36
ZETA	326	330	75 × 75	11:30
ETA	325	330	75 × 75	09:45
THETA	325	330	75 × 75	09:23
IOTA	324	329	75 × 75	10:27
KAPPA	323	330	75 × 75	09:45
LAMBDA	325	330	75 × 75	08:53

Figure 1.6 Dealers bid and ask quotes.

dealer Beta. As shown in Figure 1.6, Beta is willing to buy at $324 and sell at $330. Seller 4 can then decide either to sell at $324 or to seek another dealer. In the first case, Beta fills Seller 4's order by buying the security and adding it to his inventory. This exposes Beta to the risk of a sudden fall in the price of the security, and hence a loss on the value of his inventory. To avoid this "inventory risk," Beta can either rebalance his position by trading with a customer who wants to buy the security (for instance, Buyer 3 in the figure) or he can contact other dealers to sell them part or all of his position. As we will see in Chapter 3, the management of inventory risk is a major determinant of bid and ask prices.

Thus, we can distinguish two different segments in dealer markets (as shown in Figure 1.5): the Dealer-to-Customer (D2C) segment, in which dealers serve final investors, and the Dealer-to-Dealer (D2D) segment ("interdealer market"), in which dealers trade with each other to share inventory risk. To do so, dealers use specialized "interdealer brokers" (IDBs) such as ICAP, BGC Partners or BrokerTec (part of the CME group). These brokers have gradually introduced electronic limit order books enabling dealers to trade anonymously and quickly among themselves. Examples of such interdealer trading platforms include eSpeed or BrokerTec (introduced in the late 1990s) in U.S. Treasury markets, MTS (introduced in 1999) in E.U. sovereign bonds, or Thomson Reuters (now Refinitiv) and EBS (Electronic Broker Service) in currencies markets (introduced in 1992 and 1993, respectively).

The volume of trade on the D2D market is typically larger than on the D2C market, as each trade with a given client trickles down to other dealers (via "intermediation chains") until it is passed on to final investors on the opposite side of the market.[4] Eisfeldt et al. (2023) document that in the market for single-name credit default swaps trading among fourteen core dealers accounts for 83% of the total market volume. However, for corporate bonds and currencies, the share of interdealer trading has declined over time, due to the electronification of trading in the D2C market and to regulation (see Section 1.4). For instance, in foreign exchange markets the share of interdealer trading has declined from about two-thirds of total trading volume in the early 1990s to less than one-half (see Chaboud et al. 2023).

In a dealer market, unlike a limit order market, there is no enforcement of price priority: in the example of Figure 1.5, Seller 4 trades with Beta even though he could obtain a better price from Alpha. This can happen because quotes are not necessarily displayed to final investors, who must therefore find the best price

---

[4] For example, in the U.S. municipal bond markets, 23% of transactions initiated by customers generate intermediation chains that involve at least two dealers (see table III in Li and Schürhoff 2018).

by contacting dealers. This search is costly: it takes time and effort and, for this reason, it increases dealers' market power and illiquidity (see Section 10.4).

In contrast, when information on quotes is publicly available, market participants can easily identify the dealers who post the best bid and ask prices. Some dealer markets feature "Multi Dealer Platforms" (MDPs) that consolidate information on the quotes posted by dealers and disseminate it via screens that provide real-time information similar to that in Figure 1.6.[5] Such consolidated information is important, as shown by the example presented in the figure: no single dealer quotes a bid-ask spread of less than 4, but the spread resulting from the consolidation of the quotes (sometimes called the "inside spread" or "market touch" in the United Kingdom) is $329 - 326 = 3$, as is shown at the top of the panel (which also tells us which, and how many, market makers quote the best price on each side of the market). Thus, the market as a whole offers more liquidity than any individual dealer.

Many dealer markets, however, offer far less detail on dealers' quotes. For instance, no real-time information is available in OTC markets such as the U.S. or the European corporate bond market. In currency markets, Reuters and Bloomberg screens do give information on quotes, but this is only indicative: the quotes do not commit dealers to actually trade at those prices.

Dealers' quotes are typically valid only for a limited number of shares. So a large order may be executed by splitting it among several dealers. Suppose that a seller wishes to sell three hundred shares given the dealers' quotes in Figure 1.6. He can execute this order by selling seventy-five shares each to dealers Alpha and Zeta, who post the best bid price, and then another seventy-five each to Gamma and Lambda at the next best bid price. Effectively, the investor is walking down the demand curve resulting from the aggregation of dealers' bid quotes. Similarly, a buyer with a large order will walk up the aggregate supply curve resulting from the dealers' ask quotes. These aggregate demand and supply curves are shown in Figure 1.7. Therefore, as in a limit order market, in a dealer market one can also define a weighted-average bid-ask spread that is also increasing in trade size.

Unlike limit order markets, dealer markets often enable traders to bargain over price and quantity. For instance, instead of searching for a better price, Seller 4 in our example could ask Beta for a better price than 324. If Beta agrees, then Seller 4 gets what is called a *price improvement*. These are common in some dealer markets and result in trades at prices within the quoted bid-ask spread. Moreover, by design, dealer markets allow dealers to establish long-term relationships with their clients and other dealers. They can therefore reward

---

[5] MDPs (such as 360T and SWAPS) have been developed first in foreign exchange markets but are now also used for other asset classes that trade over the counter.

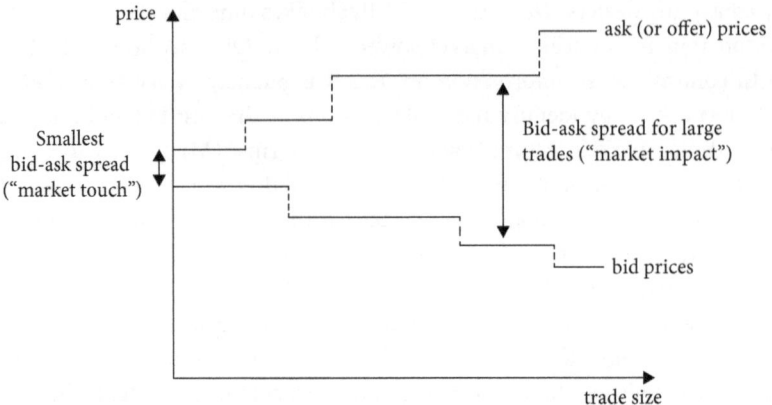

Figure 1.7 Dealer market quotes for various trade sizes.

good or important clients with better prices than other clients. For instance, in the U.S. market for municipal bonds ("munis"), dealers offer better prices to institutional than to retail investors, because institutions trade larger amounts, trade more frequently, and have greater bargaining power. Thus, the network of relationships of dealers and clients is an important determinant of the prices at which they trade in dealer markets (see Di Maggio et al. 2017 for evidence).

Moreover, bargaining may also speed up execution. For instance, an investor with a large order can ask the dealer to quote the price at which he is willing to take the entire order. Typically, this may be worse than the price the trader would obtain by splitting the order among several dealers over time, but it guarantees immediate execution of the full order. This is important to some traders, such as arbitrageurs who must take long and short positions simultaneously in different markets. Thus speed of execution constitutes an additional dimension of market liquidity, sometimes no less important than the cost of trading itself (i.e., the bid-ask spread).[6]

In the past, negotiations between dealers and their clients happened via voice (e.g., telephone) or messaging systems. In today's OTC markets, they have been partially automated with the emergence of Single Dealer Platforms (SDPs), such as "Autobahn" (Deutsche Bank) or "Barx" (Barclays), which are internet portals enabling traders to access prices from one dealer bank for a variety of assets.

---

[6] The importance of speed of execution for investors partly explains why the introduction of the continuous dealer market SEAQ International in London following the 1986 "Big Bang" reforms attracted so much trading in continental European shares. The desire to offer comparably rapid execution also induced continental European exchanges to replace their batch auction system with continuous electronic LOBs (Pagano and Röell 1990).

Moreover, in recent years, due to regulatory pressures following the global financial crisis, new trading systems, called Request for Quotes (RFQs) or click-to-trade, have been introduced in the D2C segments of fixed income and currency markets. For instance, for certain derivatives contracts (liquid standardized Interest Rate Swaps and Credit Default Swaps) in the U.S. the Dodd-Frank Act mandates trade execution on Swap Execution Facilities (SEFs), i.e., electronic limit order books, or RFQ systems, and also requires centralized clearing of trades; a similar regulation was introduced in 2018 in the E.U. as part of the MiFIR directive. RFQ systems enable investors to request quotes from multiple dealers simultaneously, rather than doing so sequentially, to discover the best price. Not surprisingly, such systems increase competition between dealers and have lowered trading costs for their clients. For instance, the mandated introduction of SEFs for dollar-denominated interest rate swaps triggered a reduction in total execution costs of about U.S. $7–11 million per day (Benos et al. 2021), a sizable improvement in liquidity.

1.2.3 Hybrid Markets

Many actual securities markets are hybrids comprising both a limit order platform and a dealer segment, or having a design that mixes features of the two types of market.

For instance, the NYSE has a mix of three different trading mechanisms that operate simultaneously for each stock:

1. An open-outcry market where floor brokers trading on behalf of other investors or on their own account bargain bilaterally.[7]
2. A dealer market with designated market makers (DMM; formerly known as "specialists") for each stock. DMMs have some obligations (e.g., they must post quotes at the best prices for a minimum fraction of the time during the day and their bid-ask spreads cannot exceed a certain threshold). Examples of firms acting as DMMs are Citadel Securities LLC or Virtu Americas LLC.
3. An electronic LOB ("NYSE Arca") for each stock, which allows investors to bypass the DMMs and floor traders.

---

[7] In an open-outcry market, brokers physically meet on a floor to trade. For instance, a broker announces that he is willing to buy 100 shares (a market order) and other brokers respond by shouting ask prices (limit orders) at which they are willing to execute the order. These markets mainly trade derivatives such as futures and options; with the development of electronic trading platforms they are tending to vanish.

Likewise, European exchanges (such as Euronext, Deutsche Börse, and OMX Nasdaq) also rely on DMMs.[8] In this case, DMMs are hired by issuers and commit to maintain their bid-ask spread within a contractually specified limit. In compensation, they receive periodic payments from issuers. Such contracts (unauthorized in the U.S.) can be viewed as a way for issuers to "buy" liquidity and thereby reduce their cost of capital (see Section 11.5.2).

Furthermore, in both the E.U. and U.S. equity markets, investors can trade bilaterally with dealers off-exchange rather than on the respective exchanges' limit order markets. This practice is called "internalization" as it entails dealers executing the orders for their own account. In E.U. equity markets, the banks, broker dealers and high-frequency market makers that operate under the status of "Systematic Internalizers" (SIs) are required to publicly display bid and ask quotes for the most liquid stocks. For other stocks, they have no such obligations. Their market share of total trading volume in E.U. equity markets has risen to 19% in 2020 (ESMA 2021a).

In U.S. equity markets, internalizers (such as Citadel securities, Virtu Securities, G1 Execution Services, sometimes referred to as "wholesalers") accounted for about 27% of total trading volume in 2018 (SEC 2020). A large fraction of internalized trades stems from "payment for order flow" (PFOF) plans. According to these plans, brokers privately route orders with certain characteristics (e.g., orders from retail investors) to dealers, rather than public markets, in exchange for a small fee per share.[9] The dealers that pay for order flow commit to execute market orders at prices that match the best quotes or improve upon them. The large fraction of retail order flow in U.S. equity and options markets that is internalized has raised various concerns about retail investor protection, such as whether internalized orders receive the best prices, and whether migration of orders away from exchanges could harm liquidity. These concerns are analyzed in Sections 7.2.2 and 7.2.3.

The evolution of trading in corporate bond markets is another interesting case in point. The share of electronic trading (via RFQs or all-to-all trading platforms operated by brokers such as TradeWeb or MarketAxess) has been steadily increasing,[10] a trend that has accelerated during Covid-19.[11] Thus, even though the corporate bond market remains a dealer market, it now features

[8] Exchanges use different terminologies to refer to DMMs, even though functions are similar. For instance, DMMs are called "designated sponsors" by Deutsche Börse and "Animateurs" by Euronext.
[9] PFOF was introduced in the 1990s in the U.S. and has always been controversial. The advent of zero commission brokers (like Robinhood) gave a new vigor to this controversy because these brokers earn the bulk of their revenues from payments for order flow.
[10] For instance, O'Hara and Zhou (2021) document that MarketAxess Inc. (the dominant electronic trading platform in U.S. corporate bonds) increased its share of investment-grade corporate bond trading from 10% in 2010 to 17% in 2016.
[11] See "Bond trading finally dragged into the digital age," *Financial Times*, February 21, 2021.

both a standard dealer segment based on bilateral trading and a new electronic segment where customers can simultaneously access the quotes of many dealers.

1.2.4 Brokers vs. Dealers

Dealers differ from brokers, such as Charles Schwab or Robinhood for U.S. retail investors or ICAP for interdealer trades on OTC markets. Brokers only channel the buy and sell orders of their clients to the market, irrespective of whether it is a limit order market or a dealer market, without acting as counterparties for these orders. Dealers, instead, are the counterparties of final investors, and so take inventory risk. Some securities firms (such as Goldman Sachs or J.P. Morgan) offer both services, and are accordingly known as broker-dealers.

A feature that brokers and dealers have in common is that both help final investors to carry out their trades. For this reason, brokers and dealers are often collectively referred to as the "sell side" of the securities industry, whereas final investors (households, institutional investors, firms, and government) are called the "buy side" (since they buy trading services from the sell side).[12] This distinction is important since the two sides often have opposing views on how trading should be organized: as we shall see, a change in trading organization often affects the distribution of trading gains between investors (the buy side) and intermediaries (the sell side).

1.2.5 Market Transparency and Market Data

A market's degree of transparency is determined by the amount of trading information available to participants, both about posted quotes—pre-trade transparency—and realized transactions (transaction prices and traded quantities)—post-trade transparency. This information ("market data") matters to traders, because it enables them to sharpen their estimates of securities' values (as order flows and prices contain information; see Chapter 3) and devise better trading strategies. For instance, as explained in Section 1.2.2, in a dealer market an investor can generally get better terms if he observes all dealers' quotes, and can thus save on the cost of searching for the best price. Here we briefly discuss this important dimension of market structure, leaving a more in-depth analysis to Chapter 8.

---

[12] It is worth emphasizing that these terms do not denote buyers or sellers of securities but of trading services, so that the buy side includes both buyers and sellers of securities.

Transparency varies considerably from market to market. The level of transparency can be very controversial, as it affects how trading gains are distributed between the sell side and the buy side. Intuitively, the demand for brokerage services and dealers' market power are both greater in opaque markets, since it is harder for final investors to identify all trading opportunities. Thus, the sell side is usually less keen on improvements in transparency than the buy side. Moreover, when information on quotes and trades ("market data") is available, it is generally costly, as trading platforms charge significant fees for accessing real-time data. Thus, transparency depends on not only the availability but also the cost of market data. In recent years, this cost has increased, triggering heated debates about the pricing and availability of market data between the trading platforms that provide the data and their users.[13]

In general, electronic limit order markets tend to be very transparent. In these markets, trading platforms provide real-time data feed and charge fees that increase with the granularity of the content.[14] At the least granular level, they only provide the best bid and ask quotes and realized transactions (prices and quantities); at the most granular level, they disclose the entire limit order book, with the exception of hidden limit orders (see Section 1.2.1). In some cases, they even disclose the identities of the brokers submitting limit orders or executed market orders.[15]

Transparency can also vary across dealer markets, depending on whether quotes are displayed centrally through a single screen and whether they are firm or merely indicative. In the latter case, customers still have to contact each dealer directly to verify the actual prices at which a trade will be executed. Since dealer markets are fragmented (deals being struck with individual dealers), it is not easy to ensure that the best quotes are centrally displayed in real time. For example, some dealers may quote prices only on their own proprietary systems. It is even harder to ensure that completed trades and their prices are published promptly, as this requires dealers to report their trades equally promptly to a central market authority. In practice, dealers often oppose prompt publication of trades or try to circumvent rules requiring such publication.

---

[13] See, for instance, "Higher data fees prompt backlash against U.S. equity exchanges," *Financial Times*, November 17, 2017; "European investors complain about soaring costs of data," *Financial Times*, April 4, 2019; or "U.K. regulator to review charges for financial data," *Financial Times*, January 11, 2022.

[14] See Oxera (2019) for estimates of these fees for European exchanges.

[15] The transparency of LOB markets may also change over time. For instance, until 2002 only the best bid and ask prices in the LOB for the stocks listed on the NYSE were disseminated to market participants. Since then, all limit orders have been displayed through the exchange's "OpenBook" system. Another example is Euronext, which terminated disclosure of the identities of the brokers submitting limit orders in 2001.

Computerized trading facilitates data storage and dissemination, but it does not necessarily entail greater transparency in the trading process, for at least two reasons. First, the physical interactions of traders in open-outcry or "floor" markets permit the transmission of a host of informal cues that escape even state-of-the-art electronic systems. If traders are physically present in the same room, their every word and gesture are visible, yielding insights into their trading strategies and the urgency of their trading intentions.[16] Moreover, the electronification of securities trading has facilitated the dispersal of trading across multiple venues (see Section 1.4.3 and Chapter 7), resulting in a fragmentation of market data across these venues. This fragmentation makes it hard to piece together an accurate view of overall market conditions.

To address this issue, the U.S. Securities and Exchange Commission (SEC) required the creation of a consolidated system for quotes and transactions reporting in equity markets in 1975. Pursuant to this mandate, U.S. exchanges report trade and quote data to "Securities Information Processors" (SIPs), which disseminate consolidated data (the best bid and offer prices for a stock across all exchanges and last trade reports) to the public with a very small delay (of a few milliseconds) relative to exchanges' proprietary data feed. In fixed income markets, mandatory reporting of trade prices and sizes (after a delay of fifteen minutes) began in 2002 for corporate bonds via the Trade Reporting and Compliance Engine (TRACE) operated by FINRA (Financial Industry Regulatory Authority) and in 2005 for municipal bonds (via the EMMA system of the MSRB), with a 15-minute delay. In contrast, at the time of this writing, there is still no consolidated tape in U.S. Treasury markets or in E.U. equity and bond markets (but E.U. regulators are considering various options to introduce such a tape).

1.3 Does Market Structure Matter?

The two main functions of a security market are to provide trading services for investors who wish to alter their portfolios, and to determine prices that can guide the allocation of capital by investors and firms. A market is efficient in performing these functions if it enables investors to trade quickly and cheaply (i.e., if it is liquid) and if it incorporates new information quickly and accurately into prices (informational efficiency). Trading rules affect market efficiency on

---

[16] Coval and Shumway (2001) show that changes in the sound level on the floor of the Chicago Board of Trade's 30-year Treasury bond futures forecast subsequent changes in the cost of transacting and volatility. Their interpretation is that the sound level reflects how anxious market participants are to trade at current prices.

both accounts and this book is in part devoted to explaining why this is so. As a preview, we illustrate this point with a few examples below.

Some studies compare trading costs (bid-ask spreads) in limit order markets and dealer markets for matched samples of stocks (i.e., stocks with similar characteristics). Typically they find that trading costs are higher in dealer markets, especially for small orders. For instance, Huang and Stoll (1996) report that, by several measures, trading costs for a sample of Nasdaq stocks, when Nasdaq was still a dealer market, were twice as high as for a matched sample of NYSE stocks, when the NYSE was still primarily a floor market. One possible explanation is that concentrating trading in a single marketplace (in this case the floor of the NYSE) improves liquidity. Chapter 7 explores why and when the consolidation of trading can increase market liquidity.

Changes in trading rules that foster competition among liquidity providers also result in a more liquid market. In early 1997, the SEC introduced new rules (the "Order Handling Rules") that exposed Nasdaq market makers to competition from the general public. The Limit Order Display Rule forced dealers to execute or display any customers' limit orders that offered better prices than their own quotes. This regulatory change (together with the "quote rule" that required dealers trading in multiple venues to make their best quotes available to the public) increased competitive pressures on Nasdaq and led to an immediate and substantial reduction in Nasdaq trading costs (Barclay, Christie, Harris, Kandel, and Schultz 1999).

Changes in market transparency also affect liquidity. For instance, Boehmer, Saar, and Liu (2005) analyze how measures of market liquidity changed when the NYSE started releasing information on limit orders in 2002. They document that this increase in transparency was followed by a drop in the price impact of market orders—a measure of illiquidity alternative to the weighted average bid-ask spread. Similarly, Goldstein, Hotchkiss, and Sirri (2007) and Edwards, Harris, and Piwowar (2007) show that the implementation of TRACE (discussed in Section 1.2.5) significantly reduced bid-ask spreads in U.S. corporate bond markets by increasing post-trade transparency.

Another example of the importance of trading rules is provided by the emergence of electronic trading in fixed income markets: O'Hara and Zhou (2021) document that trading costs are smaller for electronic trades than for voice trades in U.S. corporate bonds, even after controlling for trade size, especially for small trades (for which electronic trading is more prevalent). Electronic trading also had a beneficial spillover effect on the traditional segment of the market, its growth being associated with a decline in trading costs for both electronic and voice trading between 2010 and 2017. This spillover is party due to the fact that electronic trading reduces search costs for dealers' clients and thereby increases competition between dealers.

Market structure also affects the quality of price discovery. Green, Li, and Schürhoff (2010) find that in the United States the prices of Treasury issues react to macroeconomic news much faster than the prices of munis. As the market for Treasuries is more liquid and active, the authors suggest that this is responsible for the different speed of price discovery. In turn, munis' lack of liquidity largely stems from the lack of transparency for their market, as documented by Green, Hollifield, and Schürhoff (2007). Many other studies have explored the impact of market transparency on liquidity and price discovery, as the detailed analysis in Chapter 8 shows.

By affecting liquidity and price discovery, market structure also affects the cost of capital. In Chapter 10, we will see that changes that increase liquidity raise stock prices, as investors require a lower rate of return to invest in more liquid stocks. Similarly, Chapter 12 shows how more efficient price discovery is conducive to better investment decisions by companies.

1.4 Evolution of Market Structure

We have seen that trading platforms are organized in a wide variety of ways. Why do actual trading mechanisms differ so much? This depends largely on who decides the trading rules, which is to say that it depends on the governance of trading platforms. In the past, such governance was partly the result of historical accident, which created different "initial conditions" in the various countries, as Section 1.4.1 explains. In recent decades, however, the governance and organization of trading platforms, especially in equity markets, have tended to converge on one basic model. Section 1.4.2 argues that this convergence reflects the heightened competition in the securities industry, itself the product of the combined pressure of three forces: liberalization of international capital markets, securities regulation overhaul, and advances in information and communication technologies. But technological innovation has transformed security trading over and above its tendency to reinforce competition between trading platforms. Section 1.4.3 describes the enormous impact of technological progress on the automation of order generation, routing, and execution, and the lively debate on the pros and cons of this evolution.

1.4.1 Who Makes the Rules?

The design of trading rules is the outcome of the interplay between government regulation and self-regulation by the trading platforms, such as stock exchanges or trading networks. For instance, in the U.S. much of securities regulation is designed in broad outline by the SEC for equity and bond markets, and by the Commodity Futures Trading Commission (CFTC) for derivatives markets, while it is implemented and specified in greater detail by the self-regulating organizations that govern the markets, such as the NYSE, the Nasdaq and the Financial Industry Regulatory Authority (FINRA). In the E.U., the securities market regulator is the European Securities Markets Authority (ESMA), in coordination with E.U. members' national regulatory agencies (e.g., the AMF for France or Consob for Italy).

The scope of self-regulation and the way it has been used have varied widely over time and across countries. From their inception, stock exchanges have differed very significantly in governance and organization. Many emerged from informal trading. For example, what is widely regarded as the first modern exchange, the Amsterdam Stock Exchange, emerged at the start of the seventeenth century, when trading in the transferable shares of the Dutch East India Company started immediately upon issue in 1602. Trading was at first concentrated outdoors around the Nieuwe Brug in central Amsterdam (in foul weather, the nearby St. Olof's chapel was used), moving in 1611 to a purpose-built centralized merchants' exchange, created to facilitate public trading not just in shares but also in other financial instruments, goods, and insurance (see Petram 2011, for a detailed description of seventeenth-century Dutch share trading). Similarly, the London Stock Exchange (LSE) developed from informal trading that took place around coffee shops in the city, where in 1698 John Casting first published lists of stock prices, entitled "The course of the exchange and other things." Not until 1801 did the exchange turn into an official, regulated stock exchange. The precursor to the NYSE was created in 1792 by a group of stock brokers who signed the Buttonwood Agreement under a buttonwood tree on Wall Street.

Many continental European exchanges, however, were created at the initiative of government authorities and were generally regulated and managed by public agencies, such as local chambers of commerce. The Paris Stock Exchange was established by an order of the Royal Council of State in 1724. By the middle of the nineteenth century, trading was conducted by government-appointed *agents de change* who shouted out prices on the floor and could not trade for their own account: they were strictly brokers, not dealers. In several cases, the exchanges were founded for the express purpose of forming a market specifically for state-issued bonds, not shares or even corporate bonds. This was the case of the Vienna Stock Exchange, founded in 1771 under Empress Maria Theresa, and the Milan Stock Exchange, established in 1808 by a Napoleonic decree and used to trade only government bonds for its first half-century.

Thus, the constituencies that created stock exchanges were quite different, and the differences in governance were persistent. As late as the 1980s, most exchanges were still governed much as they had been at the turn of the twentieth century. These differences in governance shaped the rules of the exchanges, in an illustration of the more general principle that the structure of securities markets is affected by the interests of their controlling constituencies. Depending on the relative power and importance of domestic and foreign intermediaries, institutional investors, and issuers in the share ownership structure, different exchanges pursue different policies. For instance, an exchange that is strictly controlled by a cartel of domestic intermediaries will be more inclined to impede remote access for foreign investors, and more generally will be reluctant to revise the trading system to the detriment of local intermediaries, as in the case of the LSE's protracted resistance to the introduction of an LOB and the NYSE members' opposition to ending floor trading.

More generally, the interests of intermediaries often conflict with those of issuers and investors: the former tend to favor trading rules that protect their rents at the expense of the latter. Chapters 7 and 8 show that such conflicts are a common feature in policy debates about market fragmentation and transparency.

By the same token, changes in the institutional form and governance of exchanges can impact the structure of their markets. Such changes have been frequent in recent years, as most exchanges have been transformed from essentially private clubs (such as the LSE) or semi-public entities (such as the Paris Bourse) into for-profit firms, in which the largest stakes are usually held by major financial intermediaries such as banks, hedge funds, and brokerage houses. The LSE, Deutsche Börse, Euronext, Nasdaq, Hong Kong Stock Exchange, and Toronto Stock Exchange all went public in 2000, while several other exchanges in continental Europe had done so in the late 1990s. The NYSE followed suit in 2006.

1.4.2 Competition between Exchanges

As just noted, from sharply divergent initial conditions, stock exchanges have converged on a similar status as publicly listed companies, through either the privatization of the government-controlled exchanges or the demutualization of those owned and controlled by groups of intermediaries. As for-profit firms, their choices regarding market structure are naturally more and more geared to maximizing shareholders' profits.[17]

---

[17] This organizational form does not prevent deviations from the sole pursuit of profit maximization, where there are private benefits of control. In particular, if the stock exchange is controlled by sell-side firms, these may distort choices regarding market organization so as to serve their own

Table 1.1 Breakdown of Stock Exchange Revenues in 2014 (percent)

Source of Revenue	
Cash and capital markets trading	26
Derivatives and OTC markets trading	22
IT and market data services	19
Post-trade services	16
Financial income and other revenues	9
Listing and issuer services	8

Source: "Changing Business Models of Stock Exchanges and Stock Market Fragmentation," OECD report, 2016.

To understand how this profit orientation altered their choices, note that trading revenues account only for a fraction of the total profits of an exchange (see Table 1.1). Other important sources of revenue are listing fees (paid by issuing firms who list their shares on the exchange), post-trade trading services (payments by traders to clear and settle their trades), and the sale of market data (to investors and other interested parties). For instance, in 2019 Nasdaq reported revenues from the sale of market data and technologies to use and access these data (e.g., co-location) totaling $779 million (versus only $414 million in 2014; see Ernst, Sokobin, and Spatt 2020). The sale of market data is important for European exchanges as well: in 2019 the sale of market data accounted for 11% of the LSE's annual revenue and 19% of Euronext's.[18]

The various services sold by exchanges are complements. Hence, decisions on market structure are made not only considering the impact on trading volume but also with an eye to their effect on listing and data sale revenues. For instance, an exchange may be willing to charge low listing fees in order to attract many issuers and so earn large trading revenues. Or one that operates its own clearing and settlement system may charge low trading fees in order to capture trading flows and charge large clearing and settlement fees.

In recent years, competition has been increasing in all of these business lines. The change in governance has been driven largely by this evolution: the exchanges became publicly listed companies so as to gain the flexibility needed to compete with alternative venues, both at home and abroad. The intensification of competition between trading platforms is the result of three forces:

interests. For instance, if their in-house systems are competing with the exchange's platform in the provision of trading services, they may oppose changes in trading organization that increase the market share of the platform.

[18] Exchange operators do not necessarily sell all these services. For instance, the Cboe does not provide listing services.

1. The removal of barriers to international capital flows has increased firms' propensity for initial public offerings (IPOs) on foreign markets or cross-listing of their shares, and prompted increased cross-border trading by investors. For instance, investors can currently trade many French blue-chip stocks not only on Euronext Paris but also on foreign markets: multilateral trading facilities (MTFs), such as Cboe, or exchanges where the stocks are cross-listed (such as Deutsche Börse and the LSE).

2. Changes in the securities market regulations have also played a role. In the United States, the increased fragmentation resulting from the proliferation of electronic communication networks (ECNs) provided major impetus for creating a new regulatory framework, Regulation National Market System (Reg NMS), in 2005. A major goal of Reg NMS is to organize and facilitate competition between trading platforms. For instance, its order protection rules oblige trading platforms to re-route incoming market orders to the platform that posts the best price at the moment the order is received. Clearly, this rule intensifies the competition for order flow among platforms, and among the liquidity suppliers that operate on each platform (see Chapter 7). In Europe, the Markets in Financial Instruments Directive (MiFID), which went into effect in 2007, also increased competition for order flow between trading platforms. In particular, it abolished the "concentration rule" by which member states could oblige investors to route their orders to the national market. As a consequence, it spurred the creation of many new platforms, operating Europe-wide limit-order books, such as Chi-X (launched in 2007), Turquoise, NASDAQ OMX Europe, Bats Europe (all launched in 2008), and NYSE Arca Europe (launched in 2009).[19]

3. Technological advances in information and communication technologies for securities trading have greatly facilitated entry into the market for the provision of trading services. The cost of setting up an electronic platform such as a LOB is now extremely low, which facilitated the creation of new electronic platforms challenging incumbent markets in the early '90s. For instance, one of the very first electronic limit order market, Island (subsequently renamed INET), emerged at the end of the '80s and challenged Nasdaq (which eventually acquired it). Other such platforms include Archipelago (now part of NYSE), Instinet and BATS (now part of Cboe). Moreover, with smart order-routing technologies (SORs) brokers can easily split orders across markets to get the best prices. Such technologies have lowered the cost of searching for the best price across trading

---

[19] Chi-X and Bats no longer exist and have been acquired by the Cboe.

platforms and so made it easier for exchanges to attract trading business by offering narrow bid-ask spreads and low fees.

Intensified competition for order flow has forced trading platforms to reduce their trading fees. For instance, in 2003, the LSE announced that it would introduce a trading platform for Dutch stocks, EuroSETS. This was spurred by the Dutch brokerage community as a way to lower Euronext trading fees, and in fact Euronext slashed its fees by 50% in early 2004 (Foucault and Menkveld 2008). As a result, trading fees per share are now very small in equity markets (see Chapter 7 for more details).

Another benefit of competition is that it prompted the incumbents to overhaul trading systems and innovate. For instance, for long the NYSE relied heavily on a seriously outdated floor-based system, totally unable to match the execution speed of electronic trading. That trading system gave an informational advantage to members with a seat on the floor; they thus had a vested interest in retaining floor trading. But as competition from new electronic limit order book markets (e.g., BATS) eroded the NYSE's market share, this position became untenable. As a defensive move, in 2006, the NYSE acquired a rival electronic order market, Archipelago, renamed it NYSE Arca, and made it the core of its trading system. By 2009, Arca was processing four-fifths of the NYSE's total trading volume. As of 2017, there were still 205 floor brokers on the NYSE, but they mainly operated at the opening and closing sessions, according to the NYSE website.

Faced with such competition (whether actual or merely potential), the incumbent markets have also reacted by merging to achieve economies of scale and capitalize on liquidity externalities (see Chapter 7). For instance, in 2000 the Paris Bourse merged with the Amsterdam Stock Exchange and the Brussels Stock Exchange (subsequently joined by the Lisbon Stock Exchange), to form Euronext. Then, in 2007, Euronext in turn merged with the NYSE (giving rise to NYSE Euronext), enabling these exchanges to cut overhead costs and build up volume and liquidity. In 2014 the Intercontinental Exchange (ICE) acquired NYSE Euronext, and spun it off as an independent publicly listed company. Since then, Euronext has also acquired the Dublin, Oslo, and Italian Stock Exchanges, in 2017, 2019, and 2021, respectively.

At the time of writing, consolidation has given rise to five mega exchange operators, namely the Intercontinental Exchange, the Chicago Mercantile Exchange, the LSE, Deutsche Börse, and Nasdaq.[20] They have a wide scope of activities, such as the provision of trading and post-trading services in various

---

[20] These exchange operators account for about 50% of the total revenues ($35 billions in 2019) in their industry. See "How exchange operators have grown bigger and bigger," *Financial Times*, December 12, 2020.

asset classes and the design and provision of financial indexes. Their business model is increasingly similar to that of big tech companies, in the sense that they use algorithms to match buyers and sellers of securities and monetize the data generated by this process. To boost revenues from market data (which are proportional to trading volume), they have incentives to reduce their trading fees, and in fact trading fees in electronic limit order markets have declined considerably over time. Moreover, they have acquired providers of data and analytics. For instance, the ICE acquired Interactive Data in 2015 for $15 billion, and the LSE acquired Refinitiv (formerly Thomson-Reuters) in 2020 for $27 billion.

1.4.3 Automation

As we have seen, technology has intensified competition between trading platforms. But the effects of information processing and communication technology on securities trading go well beyond this: over the last half-century technology has completely reshaped the trading process. In the past, securities were bought and sold on trading floors where brokers were in charge of matching the buy and sell orders they received from their clients. But securities exchanges progressively replaced or complemented their trading floors with computerized trading systems. By the turn of the century, 101 out of 120 countries already had electronic trading, and 85 of them no longer had floor trading (Jain 2005). Today, most exchanges use electronic LOBs, and orders are routed via high-speed fiber optic lines.

For the NYSE, this evolution began with the DOT system in 1976, which allowed electronic submission of market orders of up to one hundred shares. Upon reaching the trading floor, the electronic DOT orders for a stock were manually executed by the designated market maker (so called specialist) for this stock. But the NYSE did not become a fully electronic exchange until 2006 with the introduction of the NYSE Hybrid system. By contrast, such exchanges as the Toronto Stock Exchange and the Paris Bourse went over to fully electronic LOB markets quite early (1977 and 1986, respectively). Their trading systems were the blueprint for others.

This technological innovation has allowed traders (brokers, institutional investors' trading desks, proprietary trading firms, etc.) to automate the order submission process, giving rise to so-called *algorithmic trading* (see Chapter 9 for a detailed analysis). Algorithmic trading refers to the use of computers for submitting market and limit orders, and order cancellations according to codified rules ("algorithms"). These algorithms have often been developed by brokers to optimize the placement of large buy or sell orders by institutional investors (e.g., to minimize their trading costs, as discussed in Chapter 2).

Some firms specialize in a particular form of algorithmic trading, called *high-frequency trading* (HFT), which is characterized by the very high speed at which computers submit new orders in reaction to relevant events such as business news reports or changes in the state of limit order books. For instance, the SEC defines *high-frequency traders* (HFTs) as proprietary traders who use "extraordinary high speed and sophisticated computer programs for generating, routing, and executing orders."

Trading speed is often measured by *trading latency*: the time lapse between the moment an electronic message is sent to a trading platform by a trader (for example, a market order to buy shares or a cancellation of a limit order) and the moment feedback is received from the trading platform (for example, on the status of the order). Latencies have become extremely short in electronic securities markets, close to physical limits. For instance, the average exchange-to-trader latency (the average time elapsed between the moment a message is sent by an exchange and the moment it is received by the firm) is 31 microseconds on average for messages about the SPDR S&P 500 Exchange Traded Fund (ETF), whose NYSE ticker code is SPY (Baldauf and Mollner 2020).

High-frequency trading firms (such as Citadel, Virtu Financial, Flow Traders, and Jump Trading) have made large investments to minimize trading latency. For instance, in 2013 alone, the Tabb Group estimated the investment in fast trading technologies at $1.5 billion, twice the amount invested in 2012. Typically, these investments went into establishing fast communication lines between markets, either using fiber optics or microwave transmission, which is 30% faster than fiber optic lines. The first microwave network linking Chicago and New York became operational in 2010. It is used by arbitrageurs to obtain fast information on quotes for index futures traded on the Chicago Mercantile Exchange (CME) and for corresponding ETFs traded on platforms located in the New York area (e.g., NYSE, Cboe, or DirectEdge). Microwave transmission has reduced latency between Chicago and New York to 8.02 milliseconds, close to the theoretical lower bound (about 7.9 milliseconds). Investment by the proprietary trading desks of HFTs is often compared to an arms race, as the purpose is not speed per se but outrunning competitors (see Section 9.4).

Trading platforms have catered to the specific trading needs of high-frequency traders, by increasing the amount of market data made available to them and decreasing their own operating latencies. In fact, they are competing in the speed of disclosure of information on trades and quote updates so as to attract HFT volume and to sell quote information to them. One way they do so is by offering *co-location* services, that is, by renting rack space in their data centers. Co-location enables HFTs to run their algorithms in very close proximity to exchanges' matching engines, so as to race ahead of their competitors in accessing information on trading opportunities and exploiting them.

As a result of these developments, by now HFT represents a significant fraction of the trading activity in electronic markets. For instance, according to ESMA (2021b), in 2018–19 HFT amounted to roughly 60% of total trading volume in European equity markets, and non-HFT algorithmic trading represented an additional 20%. Moreover, HFT has contributed to a very significant increase in the ratio of orders to trades in electronic markets, forcing electronic platforms to increase their processing capacity in the face of a surfeit of limit order cancellations and resubmissions. The dominance of algorithmic and high-frequency trading in today's securities markets is attracting intense public scrutiny: its impact on liquidity, price discovery, volatility, and risk is widely debated, as we shall see in Chapter 9.

1.5 Further Reading

Harris (2003) provides a detailed description of the trading mechanisms and the organization of the securities industry in the United States, and Lyons (2001) describes the structure and functioning of currency markets and offers a theoretical and empirical analysis of their operation. Pagano and Röell (1990, 1993) describe how European trading systems started changing in the 1980s under the pressure of deregulation, competition, and technological innovation. Lee (2000) analyzes in depth the governance of exchanges and their sources of revenue.

Oxera (2019) and SEC (2020) provide accounts of the more recent evolution of the market structure of European and U.S. equity markets, respectively. Description of the evolution of trading mechanisms in currency markets are provided by Chaboud, Rime, and Sushko (2022), Schrimpf and Sushko (2021), BIS (2016), BIS (2020). For fixed income markets, see Bech, Illes, Lewrick, and Schrimpf (2016), and Bessembinder, Spatt, and Venkataraman (2020). Mizrach and Neely (2007) and U.S. Treasury Department (2017) describe the structure of the U.S. Treasury bond market. Duffie et al. (2022) (Chapter 4) provide an overview of trading automation on various markets and its effects.

Pagano and von Thadden (2004) and Dunne, Moore, and Portes (2006) describe and analyze the European government bond market. Biais, Declerck, Dow, Portes, and von Thadden (2006) analyze the European corporate bond market, with special attention to its transparency. European Commission (2017) provides an overview of the evolution of European corporate bond markets.

1.6 Exercises

1. **Call auction.** Graph total market demand and supply curves in {price, quantity} space for a call auction market where the following orders are submitted to a central auctioneer:

    Limit orders to buy: 100 shares at $3.00, 200 shares at $4.00, 200 shares at $3.50, and 500 shares at $2.50.

    Limit orders to sell: 500 shares at $5.00, 600 shares at $3.00, and 500 shares at $4.00.

    Market orders to buy: a total of 500 shares.

    Market orders to sell: a total of 200 shares.

    What is the market clearing price? What quantity of stock is traded? Are all orders that are executable at the market clearing price fully filled?

2. **Continuous order-driven market.** Now suppose that the above orders arrive on the market over time, in the order of arrival that is listed above (that is, at time $t = 1$ the limit order to buy 100 at $3.00 is submitted, at time $t = 2$ the limit order for 200 at $4.00, and so on, continuing until time $t = 9$, when the market order to sell 200 arrives). Track the state of the LOB (show it after each new order has arrived and any transactions are triggered, for $t = 0, \ldots, 9$, in the trading screen format of Figure 1.2) and the time, price and quantity of any transactions that take place. Record the dollar bid-ask spread, that is, the difference between the lowest ask and the highest bid, in the continuous market as it evolves from $t = 5$ onwards.

3. **Comparison: efficiency and market presence.** Consider again the two markets described in questions 1 and 2. Assume that the limit order prices are equal to the order placer's valuation for the block of shares submitted in the order, and think of market orders as placed by agents whose valuation is well outside (above for buyers, below for sellers) the relevant range of trading prices. Which market is Pareto efficient, in the sense that at the end of the trading day there is no pair of agents who could both benefit by trading with each other (i.e., after $t = 9$ in the continuous order-driven market)? Intuitively, why?

4. **Effect of limit order execution on the LOB.** Consider a limit order book (LOB) market. Suppose that the best limit orders on the LOB are:

Bid		Ask	
Shares	Price	Shares	Price
100	90.10	300	91.40
200	89.80	200	92.00
300	89.20	500	92.10
500	89.00	300	93.40

   a. Suppose a sell order of 800 with a limit price of 89.10 reaches the market and is executed. What are the new ask and bid prices after the execution of the order?

   b. How do the bid-ask spread defined by the BBO (best bid and offer) and the market depth available at the BBO change relative to the initial LOB? Explain briefly why.

5. **Effect of limit and market orders execution on the LOB.** Suppose that the best limit orders in the limit order book are:

Bid		Ask	
Shares	Price	Shares	Price
100	59.60	300	61.40
200	59.50	200	61.70
1,000	59.20	500	62.00
500	59.00	300	62.40

Suppose a sell order of 800 with a limit price of 59.30 reaches the market and is executed. Immediately afterwards, a market buy order of 600 reaches the market and is executed.

   a. Explain how these two orders modify the state of the LOB and show what is the final state of the LOB.

   b. Is the final quoted bid-ask spread larger or smaller than the initial one? What is the intuitive reason?

   c. Suppose the sequence of the two orders were the opposite: first the market buy order of 600 and then the limit sell order of 800. Would the final state of the LOB be the same, and would the final bid-ask spread be larger or smaller than the initial one in this case? What is the intuitive reason?

   d. Does this illustrate any general principles? Which ones?

6. **Call auctions and price impacts.** Consider a stock that trades in a call auction market. Just before the call auction clears, the following orders are submitted to the market:

   1. **Sell limit orders:** 5 shares at prices $50, $52, $53, $54, $55, $56, $57, and $58.

   2. **Buy limit orders:** 20 shares at $55, 20 shares at $54, 5 shares at $53, 20 shares at $52, 20 shares at $51, and 20 shares at $50.

      a. If no additional order is submitted, what is the clearing price for the stock? How many shares are traded at this price? What is the bid-ask spread after the call auction?

      b. Suppose that you receive negative information about the stock, which leads you to expect the value of the stock to be $50 in 1 hour.

To profit from this information, you consider posting a sell limit order at $50. You ponder how many shares, x, you should offer, considering increments of 10 shares (10 shares, 20 shares, etc.). Your objective is to maximize your total expected profit, which is equal to the number of shares you sell in the call auction times the difference between the clearing price (accounting for your order) and your estimate ($50) of the value of the asset in 1 hour. You know that other traders have placed limit orders as specified above. If your limit order is tied with other limit orders at the clearing price, the orders placed by other traders will be executed first, because time priority is enforced. What is the optimal size x of your limit order, and what is your expected profit from this order? Justify your answer.

c. You learn that another seller is about to place a sell limit order at $50. Without redoing any calculations, should you consider (i) increasing the size of your sell limit order, (ii) leaving it unchanged, or (iii) reducing it? Explain whether and how your answer depends on the time priority and the size of this limit sell relative to yours.

7. **Continuous auctions.** The table below shows the limit order book of Nestlé at 9:30 a.m. on October 23, 2018, on Cboe (a trading platform for European stocks):

Bid		Ask	
Shares	Price	Shares	Price
1,050	83	1229	83.1
450	82.98	1,183	83.08
470	82.96	1,255	83.6
718	82.94	1,474	83.04
669	82.92	383	83.02

a. What is the quoted bid-ask spread for Nestlé at 9:30 a.m.?

b. If you place a buy market order for 3,000 shares of Nestlé at 9:30 a.m., how much will you pay overall to acquire these shares? What is the effective bid-ask spread on this trade?

c. If you place a sell market order for 2,000 shares, what will be the quoted bid-ask spread and the number of shares offered at the best quotes after this transaction?

d. If you place a buy limit order for 2,000 shares at a price equal to €82.99, what will be the new state of the limit order book after the arrival of this order?

e. The trader who has placed a sell limit order for 383 shares at €83.02 is a dealer. Suppose that Nestlé unexpectedly releases earnings forecasts that are higher than expected at 9:31 a.m. and that, given this news, the new estimate of Nestlé stock price (per share) is €84. If the dealer does not update his quotes, explain what you would expect other market participants to do, and what would be the resulting impact on the dealer.

2

Measuring Liquidity

Learning Objectives:

- The components of trading costs
- How implicit trading costs can be measured from quote data
- What to do when only transaction data are available
- How to take the time dimension in order execution into account

2.1 Introduction

If the structure of a securities market is compared to a car design, measuring market liquidity can be likened to assessing the car's driving performance. Several different aspects of performance need to be considered (for cars, fuel efficiency, speed, safety, etc.), and liquidity has several dimensions as well: trading costs, depth available to customers placing large orders, speed of execution, protection against execution risk, and so on. Liquidity measurement is of paramount importance to practitioners, since illiquidity affects portfolio returns, as Chapter 10 explains. Investors and intermediaries accordingly want to design trading strategies that minimize the effects of illiquidity on their investment performance. Liquidity measurement is also important for researchers and regulators who need to understand the relationship between market structure and performance, just as engineers are keen to understand the relationships between various aspects of a car's design and its road performance.

Illiquidity is often gauged by the cost of trading, which has both an explicit and an implicit component. Explicit costs include broker commissions, transaction taxes, platforms' trading fees, and clearing and settlement fees. As they are charged explicitly to final investors, these are easy to measure. Implicit trading costs are those that arise from the illiquidity of the market; they are measured by the gap between execution price and some benchmark used to proxy for the price that would be obtained in a perfectly liquid market. Commonly, where the data are available, this benchmark is the midquote (the average of the best bid and ask prices) at the time the order is placed or executed.

Market Liquidity: Theory, Evidence, and Policy. Second Edition. Thierry Foucault, Marco Pagano, and Ailsa Röell, Oxford University Press. © Oxford University Press 2023. DOI: 10.1093/oso/9780197542064.003.0003

In practice, professional traders pay close attention to trading costs, and some brokers periodically report summary measures of both components based on the orders executed. For instance, Virtu Financial releases these measures by country for each quarter, as shown in Table 2.1.

The last column in Table 2.1 reports the total trading costs for orders executed by Virtu's brokerage arm in Europe (excluding the United Kingdom) for each quarter (expressed in basis points, i.e., as hundredths of a percent of the value traded).[1] The first three columns break this total down into its components. Implicit trading costs consist of delay costs (second column) and impact costs

Table 2.1 Trading costs (in bps) in European Equity Markets (Ex. U.K.)

Quarter	Delay Costs	Impact Costs	Comm. Costs	Total
2016				
Q1	26	15	8	49
Q2	17	16	8	40
Q3	20	13	8	41
Q4	19	13	7	40
2017				
Q1	17	11	7	35
Q2	12	12	7	31
Q3	15	12	7	34
Q4	16	13	7	36
2018				
Q1	16	12	5	34
Q2	20	11	5	36
Q3	24	12	5	41
Q4	27	15	5	46
2019				
Q1	18	14	5	37
Q2	16	14	5	35
Q3	19	13	5	37
Q4	18	13	5	36
2020				
Q1	24	22	5	51
Q2	22	28	4	54
Q3	24	15	4	43

Source: Virtu Global Cost Review, 2020, available at https://www.virtu.com/ thinking/thought-leadership/.

[1] One basis point (bp) is 0.01%. Thus, a total trading cost of 50 bps means that for a trade of $100, the investor pays a total trading cost of 50 cents. This may seem a small amount but it is not if one considers that the trading volume in securities markets is often large. For instance, in August 2020 the total value traded on the LSE's U.K. order book was £66 billion (source: LSE website). In this case a 50 bps trading cost implies a total illiquidity cost of about £330 million.

(third column). For a buy order, the delay cost is the difference between the midquotes at order execution and submission times; the impact cost is the difference between execution price and midquote at execution time. Explicit trading costs (commissions and fees) are shown in the fourth column as "Comm Costs."

Several interesting facts emerge. First, explicit trading costs are much smaller than implicit trading costs. Indeed, commission costs have declined steadily, continuing a long-term pattern: relative to the mid-2000s, they have dropped by two-thirds. Second, within the implicit costs, delay costs are relatively high, because on average prices move adversely while execution is delayed. Finally, implicit trading costs were largely stable, but rose during periods of market volatility, such as the first and second quarter of 2020, when markets were roiled by the coronavirus pandemic.

Just as someone choosing a car seeks comparative indicators of its performance, traders are interested in measures of implicit trading costs. For instance, a broker who needs to buy five thousand shares of Microsoft will compare its price on Nasdaq (where the stock is listed) to its price on several other platforms where it is traded (Cboe BZX, NYSE, etc.). He must then decide how many shares to buy in each market; whether to split the order over time; and whether to use market orders, limit orders, or a combination of the two.

In this situation, information on implicit trading costs is useful: for instance, the broker may want to trade more on the platform with lower implicit trading costs. Estimating this cost requires detailed data on quotes (e.g., the full LOB in each trading venue) and on past orders (such as the time of their submission, to measure delay cost). When such data are available, traders can assess market liquidity via simple measures of implicit trading costs, such as the quoted bid-ask spread, the effective bid-ask spread, and the realized bid-ask spread, which are presented in Section 2.2. In some cases, regulators oblige trading platforms to publish periodic data on some of these implicit cost measures.[2]

These measures of trading costs require data on bid and ask quotes, but these are sometimes simply unavailable. Even so, implicit trading costs can be measured using time series of recent transaction prices and possibly trading volume. In Section 2.3 we present these additional measures of implicit trading costs: the gap between transaction prices and the volume-weighted average price (VWAP); the estimated price impact of orders; measures of illiquidity based on non-trading; and Roll's measure of illiquidity, which is based on the serial covariance of transaction price changes.

---

[2] Since 2000, the SEC has required platforms that trade stocks listed on Nasdaq or the NYSE to report monthly statistics (known as Dash-5 reports) on their execution quality. These statistics include the average effective bid-ask spread, the average realized spread, and the speed of execution for orders of various sizes and types.

All these measures, however, neglect the time dimension of implicit trading costs: if traders are willing to trickle their orders into the market gradually, they may get a better average price, because with time new counterparties may emerge and post new orders to replace those that have been exhausted—a dynamic dimension of liquidity known as market resiliency. But a gradual execution strategy exposes traders to the risk of incomplete execution. Section 2.4 discusses the notion of implementation shortfall, a measure of execution quality that considers not only the price impact of orders but also the opportunity cost of delayed or partial execution. Traders frequently use this measure to assess their total implicit trading costs on large orders (ex post, after the execution of these orders) and devise trading strategies for minimizing these costs.

2.2 Measures of the Spread

As explained in Section 1.2.1, the most direct way to measure implicit trading costs is to look at market quotes and do a "what if" experiment: what would it cost to make a round-trip transaction, that is, to buy and instantly resell a given amount of securities? Different spread measures give different answers.

2.2.1 The Quoted Spread

The obvious, intuitive measure of the cost of a *small* round-trip transaction is the difference between the best ask quote a and the best bid quote b, that is, the *quoted bid-ask spread* $S = a - b$. If this spread is normalized by the midprice $m = (a + b)/2$, one obtains the relative quoted spread:

$$s \equiv \frac{S}{m} = \frac{a - b}{m}. \tag{2.1}$$

The quoted spread is a good measure of trading costs for orders that are so small that they can be entirely filled at the best quotes, which in the United States are known as the Best Bid and Offer (BBO). The quoted spread for small trades is the most widely reported measure of illiquidity; this is what people mean when they refer to "the" bid-ask spread.

As we saw in Chapter 1, the spread on larger orders can be gauged in a similar way, computing a weighted average bid-ask spread from the quotes posted. For instance, for the buy and sell limit orders posted at a given point in time, suppose that the average execution price for a buy market order of size is $\bar{a}(q)$, and the average execution price for a sell market order of size is $\bar{b}(q)$. The average bid-ask spread for an order of size q is thus $S(q) = \bar{a}(q) - \bar{b}(q)$ and the relative weighted average bid-ask spread is:

$$s(q) = \frac{\bar{a}(q) - \bar{b}(q)}{m}. \tag{2.2}$$

Clearly, when q is so small that the entire offer can be filled at the BBO, this reduces to the spread s in equation (2.1). As the quantity offered at each price is limited, $s(q)$ increases with the trade size q. The deeper the market, the milder the increase in the spread $s(q)$ associated with larger trade sizes q.

The drawback to this method is that it requires data on limit orders or quotes posted in the market at various points in time. Moreover, for trade sizes large enough to exhaust the liquidity offered at the BBO, the LOB at price points beyond the BBO is required. As this information is not always readily available, practitioners and researchers often measure implicit trading costs based on transaction prices alone, or on transaction prices together with the average of the BBO. In the rest of this section, we describe two such measures: the effective spread and the realized spread.

2.2.2 The Effective Spread

The quoted spread reflects the liquidity available at a given point in time for a hypothetical transaction. Instead, one could measure trading costs using the prices actually obtained by investors. This gauge is the *effective half-spread*, defined as the difference between the price at which a market order executes and the midquote on the market the instant before. Suppose that a market buy order for one thousand shares arrives and executes at an average price of 75.50, while the prevailing midquote is 75.45. The effective half-spread on to this order is thus $75.50 - 75.45 = 0.05$ or, as a percentage of the midquote, $0.05/75.45 = 0.066\%$. Formally, the absolute effective half-spread is defined as:

$$S_e \equiv d(p - m), \tag{2.3}$$

where d is the order direction indicator (1 for buyer-initiated and -1 for seller-initiated trades) and m is the midquote on the market prior to a transaction executed at price p. In relative terms, the effective spread is:

$$s_e \equiv d \cdot \frac{p - m}{m}. \tag{2.4}$$

The effective spread can be seen as a measure of a transaction's impact on the price, since it measures the deviation of the actual execution price from the midprice prevailing just before the transaction.[3] This impact (sometimes called "slippage") is positive precisely because the liquidity of the market is limited. Thus, the effective spread averaged across a large number of transactions is a way to gauge market liquidity. The effective spread is likely to increase with the size of the transaction in that (as Chapter 1 explains) larger market orders execute at less favorable prices. So it is useful to sort transactions into size classes before averaging, and get a series of estimates of the effective spread, for various sizes.

As it is based on actual transactions, the effective spread captures any price improvement that market orders may receive when they execute against hidden orders or when they receive a price improvement in dealer markets, as explained in Chapter 1. However, being based on past prices, the effective spread is a retrospective measure of liquidity, in contrast with the quoted spread that relies on prices at which traders can actually trade at a given point in time.

As shown by equation (2.3), to calculate the effective spread one needs transaction prices, the midprice prior to each transaction, and an order direction indicator (buy or sell initiation).

In practice, performing this calculation can be difficult for at least two reasons. First, in theory the effective spread for an order that is split over time should be measured by comparing the average price over the entire order with the market midquote at the time of the first part of the transaction. For an investor assessing the quality of execution of a completed trade, it is a simple matter; one can readily determine the average price—even if the order is executed at multiple price points and/or involves some use of limit orders—and compare it to the initial market midprice. And analyzing such data can help evaluate the effectiveness of trading strategies: whether splitting orders and trickling them into the market improves the average price, and how slowly large orders should be worked. For an econometrician or a regulator analyzing liquidity, however, the splitting of transactions can make it nearly impossible to reconstruct total orders from transaction records. Thus the analysis of market liquidity by such a non-participant may be restricted to the effective spread for smaller transactions placed by an identifiable subset of traders, such as market order placers.

Second, some data sets do not tell whether transactions stem from buy or sell market orders. When this information is not available, one must devise a way to "sign" transactions, that is, to decide for each trade whether $d = 1$ or $d = -1$. One of the most commonly used and accurate methods is the algorithm proposed by Lee and Ready (1991), which is described in Box 2.1.

---

[3] Ideally, one would like to measure trading costs by the difference between the price at which liquidity demanders trade and the fair value of the asset when they trade—the "true" effective bid-ask spread. However, this true effective bid-ask spread cannot be measured directly because the fair value is not observed. Hagströmer (2021) shows that the effective bid-ask spread measured relative to the midquote overestimates the true effective bid-ask spread because liquidity demanders are more likely to submit buy (sell) market orders when the fair value is above (below) the midquote.

Box 2.1 Classification of Trades

The Lee-Ready algorithm is commonly used to classify transactions as buys or sells when this information is not available in the data set. The algorithm works as follows. A transaction is classified as "buyer-initiated" if its price is closer to the prevailing ask quote than to the bid, and as "seller-initiated" if the converse. Any transaction priced exactly at the midquote is classified as a buy if the price is higher than the previous transaction price (that is, on an "uptick"), a sell if lower. The Lee-Ready algorithm and any of its subsequent refinements cannot classify trade initiation with perfect accuracy and so may bias measured transaction costs. Using data sets in which trade directions are observed, Chakrabarty, Pascual, and Shkilko (2015) and Panayides, Shohfi, and Smith (2019) find that the Lee-Ready algorithm is accurate in around 85% and 79% of cases, respectively (that is, about 20% of the trades are misclassified). Jurkatis (2022) proposes a new classification algorithm that outperforms the Lee and Ready algorithm in fast markets (see also Holden and Jacobsen 2014).

2.2.3 The Realized Spread

The quoted spread and the effective spread implicitly adopt the viewpoint of liquidity demanders. That is, they gauge the extra cost sustained by a trader submitting a market order relative to an ideal environment in which trades are made at the midprice. It is tempting to conclude that this extra cost is a gain for liquidity suppliers, the counterparties to all trades by liquidity demanders, but this is not actually the case, because buy and sell orders may exert lasting pressure on prices, to the detriment of liquidity suppliers (e.g., dealers) who absorbed such orders into their inventories.

To illustrate, suppose that a dealer buys 75 shares at $326 when the best bid and ask prices are $326 and $327, respectively. If the dealer unwinds his position immediately at the ask price, he earns a profit of $1 on each share. But if the best bid and ask prices decline to, say, $325.5 and $326.5, respectively, he earns a zero average profit (assuming that he is equally likely to unwind his inventory at the best ask or the best bid price). This example shows that quoted or effective bid-ask spreads are likely to overestimate liquidity providers' gains (and therefore liquidity demanders' trading costs) if after a trade prices move in the direction of the trade.[4]

---

[4] One reason for this is that some market orders may be placed by investors with advance information (see Chapters 3 and 4).

One way to cope with this problem is to compute the *realized half-spread*, that is, the difference between the transaction price and the midprice at some time, Δ, after the transaction (say, a few seconds later), where the interval Δ should be long enough to ensure that market quotes have adjusted to reflect the price impact of the transaction. Let p_t be the price of the transaction at time t, d_t the direction of the market order triggering it, and m_t the midprice at time t. The realized half-spread for this transaction is then given by:

$$S_r = d_t\left(p_t - m_{t+\Delta}\right) = d_t\left(p_t - m_t\right) - d_t(m_{t+\Delta} - m_t), \qquad (2.5)$$

where the first term, $d_t\left(p_t - m_t\right)$, is the effective spread, and the second one, $d_t(m_{t+\Delta} - m_t)$, is the price impact of the transaction, defined as the (absolute) change in the midprice that occurs after it. The overall expression can thus be seen as a measure of the profit earned by the liquidity supplier on the transaction at time t if he unwinds his position at the midprice at $t + \Delta$. Using the definition of the effective spread in equation (2.3) in expression (2.5), one can rewrite the average realized bid-ask spread as:

$$E(S_r) = E(S_e) - E(d_t(m_{t+\Delta} - m_t)). \qquad (2.6)$$

This expression shows that the average realized spread is smaller than the average effective spread if $E(d_t(m_{t+\Delta} - m_t)) > 0$, that is, if on average transactions have a positive price impact. Interestingly, if the effective spread is on average smaller than the price impact, liquidity providers would lose money on average, as $E(S_e) < E(d_t(m_{t+\Delta} - m_t))$. Since in the long run this would drive them out of the market, the effective spread cannot be too low: it must at least compensate them for the adverse price movement following a trade.

The value of the realized spread is sensitive to the choice of the reference post-trade market price (i.e., to $m_{t+\Delta}$). In practice, market participants need time to respond to the information content of transactions with fresh quotes and limit orders. Thus, the choice of Δ depends on how quickly market participants adjust their quotes after a transaction. In transparent and active markets (such as most equity markets), adjustment is generally fast, so a very small value of Δ is appropriate (Conrad and Wahal 2020): too high a value introduces unnecessary noise. In more opaque markets, such as the corporate bond market, information on trades takes more time to be disseminated, and higher values of Δ should be chosen.

Quoted, effective, and realized spreads are used routinely by market participants to evaluate market liquidity. Table 2.2 shows the average quoted, realized, and effective spread and price impact (in basis points) on shares of four large American companies over two trading days in 2020. Three points emerge from

Table 2.2 Average spread measures (in bps) from two trading days in 2020

| Stock | March 16, 2020 (High volatility) | | | |
	Quoted spread	Effective spread	Realized spread	Price impact
Apple	3.2	1.8	0.6	1.2
J.P. Morgan Chase	5.1	2.8	0.9	1.8
Pfizer	3.7	2.4	0.6	1.8
Tesla	18.0	6.5	2.3	4.1
Stock	August 5, 2020 (Low volatility)			
	Quoted spread	Effective spread	Realized spread	Price impact
Apple	1.0	0.5	0.1	0.4
J.P. Morgan Chase	1.3	0.9	0.3	0.6
Pfizer	2.6	1.2	0.6	0.5
Tesla	7.2	2.0	1.1	0.9

Note: The realized spread and price impact measures are computed over a time interval of 5 seconds.
Source: https://research.wpcarey.asu.edu/investment-engineering/.

the table. First, effective spreads are systematically smaller than quoted spreads, which reflects the fact that market participants place orders strategically at times when the quoted spread is particularly small: quotes are averaged over clock time, while effective spreads are averaged over transactions. Second, as expected, realized spreads are smaller than the corresponding effective spreads, which shows that on average market orders had a positive price impact. Thirdly, the spreads varied greatly between the two days. On March 16, 2020, when the broad U.S. stock index S&P 500 dropped by 12%, spreads were much wider compared to a less volatile trading day, such as August 5, 2020.

To see what the numbers in the table imply in terms of wealth transfers between market participants, consider a mutual fund buying $1,000,000 worth of the Tesla stock on March 16, 2020, with a market order: given the effective spread, the fund would pay $650 on the transaction, but only $230 would be earned by the sellers of the stock if they turn around their position after 5 seconds, as following the transaction the Tesla stock will appreciate by 0.041%, so that $410 would be lost due to price impact.

2.3 Other Measures of Implicit Trading Costs

The measures of trading costs considered so far require knowledge of bid and ask quotes at the time of execution (for the quoted spread), immediately before (for the effective spread) or shortly after (for the realized spread). Even when quote data are unavailable, however—as is often the case—implicit trading costs can be measured using transaction data only, as shown below.

2.3.1 Volume-Weighted Average Price

When quote data are not available, the midquote cannot be used as the benchmark for the execution price. One can then use easily observable alternative benchmarks, such as the day's opening or closing price. But often averages of transaction prices over the day are used: a popular benchmark in trading cost analysis is the volume-weighted average price (VWAP) for all transactions in the stock over some relevant interval, normally the entire trading day (though one may also take a shorter interval around the time at which an order was placed). Whatever the benchmark time interval T chosen, we have:

$$VWAP = \frac{\$ \text{ volume of trading}}{\# \text{ of share traded}} = \sum_{t \in T} w_t p_t, \text{ where } w_t = \frac{|q_t|}{\sum_{t \in T} |q_t|}, \qquad (2.7)$$

and q_t and p_t are the size and price of the tth trade.

Investors evaluate their broker's performance in getting a good price for their order by comparing their own price with the day's VWAP. The difference is a mixture of the effective and the realized spreads, as it involves comparison with both pre- and post-transaction prices.

In practice, several problems arise with the use of VWAP as a benchmark for trading costs. First, the average may depend on the order one is interested in itself, if it accounts for a significant proportion of trading volume. In the extreme case, in which execution of a single order (in multiple fills) generates all the day's trades, then a measure of trading cost based on VWAP is automatically zero.

Second, VWAP-based measures of trading costs can be gamed by brokers. Consider, for instance, a broker in charge of executing a large buy market order. Typically, he splits the order and executes it in multiple fills, to avoid having too large an impact on prices. If his performance is judged by the VWAP, the broker has an incentive to trickle the order into the market extremely slowly to ensure that his average execution price is as close as possible to the VWAP. This could lead him to delay trade execution excessively, unduly increasing the risk of non-execution and the client's opportunity cost of not trading. As we will see in Section 2.4, clients can assess the opportunity cost of delay by applying the broader notion of implementation shortfall.

2.3.2 Measures Based on Price Impact

Other measures of transaction costs are based on the extent to which an order generates a reaction in the market price. As we saw in Section 2.2.3, the midprice tends to rise when buy orders arrive, to an extent that is positively correlated with their size. Symmetrically, it tends to fall in the wake of sell orders. Hence the change in the midprice in the wake of a transaction, Δm_t, can be seen as a measure of the price impact generated by that transaction. If this midprice change is proportional to the buying or selling pressure, the relationship can be expressed as follows:

$$\Delta m_t = \lambda q_t + \varepsilon_t, \tag{2.8}$$

where Δm_t is the change in the midprice over a fixed time interval (a half-hour, say, or a day) and q_t is the order (or "order flow"), that is, the total value of buy less sell market orders executed in the same interval. For instance, suppose that in a one-hour interval, the dollar value of all executed buy market orders is $10,000, and that of sell orders $8,000. The order imbalance is +2,000. This differs from trading volume, which in this case is eighteen thousand. Computation of the order imbalance again requires signing market orders. If data on the direction of buy and sell market orders is not available, one can use the Lee-Ready algorithm (Box 2.1).

The intuitive meaning of equation (2.8) is that the net demand during the chosen interval from traders placing market orders puts pressure on the price that is gauged by the coefficient λ. Chapter 4 provides the theoretical underpinning for this equation. The reciprocal of λ can be seen as a measure of market depth (see Chapter 1), in that a lower value of λ means prices are less sensitive to order imbalance. In practice, people often estimate this price impact measure λ by running a regression of the change in the midquote (Δm_t) on the order imbalance (q_t).[5] A closely related approach is the price impact regression presented in Chapter 5.

Stoll (2000) applies a modified version of this approach to daily observations for stocks listed on the NYSE/AMEX and Nasdaq, including a lagged term (q_{t-1}) as an additional explanatory variable to capture a possible reversal of the price impact the following day. He finds that the value of λ is positive for 98% of the stocks and significantly different from zero for 63%. The measure varies considerably across stocks: a one-percentage-point increase in order imbalance has a price impact of 0.75% for lowest-capitalization NYSE/AMEX

---

[5] Another approach is to regress the percentage change in the midquote on the order imbalance scaled by trading volume (i.e., the sum of buy and sell orders).

stocks and 0.52% for the highest-capitalization ones. So, as one would expect, larger stocks seem to have deeper markets, where the price better withstands order imbalances. For U.S. public debt markets, Adrian, Fleming, and Vogt (2017) estimate a price impact coefficient of 0.25 basis points for a $100 million order imbalance in 2-year treasury notes, and of 2.02 basis points for 10-year notes over the 1991–2017 period.

Measuring order imbalances is sometimes difficult, as it requires data on the signed flow of buy and sell market orders. An alternative is to gauge the sensitivity of returns to trading volume (see Hasbrouck 2007, p. 93). While trading volume and order imbalance are certainly distinct concepts, they are likely to be correlated (days with larger order imbalances may well be the days with high trading volume). Therefore, one can estimate a regression of $|\Delta m_t|$ (the absolute value of price changes) on the trading volume Vol_t (the monetary value of the total amount traded) over the same interval (e.g., a day or a month). In this modified version, the slope can be interpreted as a measure of the price change associated with one additional unit of trading volume.

Conceptually this measure is related to the "illiquidity ratio" proposed by Amihud (2002), that is the ratio I_t of the absolute return for a stock ($|r_t|$) to trading volume over a given period (e.g., a day):

$$I_t = \frac{|r_t|}{Vol_t}. \tag{2.9}$$

This is also known as the Amihud ratio.[6] The inverse of this measure,

$$L_t = \frac{Vol_t}{|r_t|}, \tag{2.10}$$

also frequently used, is known as the Amivest liquidity ratio. A low value of this ratio is a sign of market illiquidity.

2.3.3 Non-Trading Measures

Often the level of trading volume in a security or its turnover rate (volume divided by the market capitalization of the security) is used as an indicator of its liquidity—the idea being that a market where many buyers and many sellers congregate will offer better trading opportunities. But there is reason

---

[6] Goyenko et al. (2009) show empirically that the Amihud ratio is a good proxy for price impact, as it is highly correlated with high-frequency measures of price impact.

to doubt that these are good measures of liquidity, because volume tends to increase when new information reaches the market, which is also a time of high volatility and concomitantly wide bid-ask spreads (as we shall see in Chapter 3). So, turnover may increase at a time when trading costs are high. For instance, Fleming (2003) finds that in the market for U.S. Treasury notes trading volume is a weak proxy for liquidity as measured by bid-ask spreads. He also finds that a trading frequency measure (namely, the number of trades executed in a specified interval) is a similarly poor proxy.

However, the frequency with which no trading at all occurs can be a useful proxy for illiquidity in some very thin markets, including many emerging markets. In such markets there are days or even weeks without transactions, in which the exchange simply reports the "stale price" of the last actual trade. Moreover, in these markets real-time quote data are generally unavailable. In a limit order market, this can happen because of the lack of counterparties; in a dealer market, because dealers' bid-ask spreads are perceived as prohibitively costly or unrepresentative of actual trading opportunities.

As no trading is associated with no change in price, Lesmond, Ogden, and Trzcinka (1999) and Bekaert, Harvey, and Lundblad (2007) propose to measure illiquidity as the fraction of no-trade days, defined as days with zero daily returns. The advantage of this measure is that it requires only a time series of daily returns, and no transaction volume data. Bekaert, Harvey, and Lundblad (2007) and Lesmond (2005) reinforce the measure's credibility, showing that it is positively correlated with bid-ask spreads for the limited periods when overlapping data are available, and negatively correlated with trading volume. They confirm this finding by comparing this illiquidity measure with more standard liquidity measures using U.S. data.[7]

Nevertheless, this measure also has a drawback: the maintained assumption that there is no trading whenever prices do not move is not always valid. For instance, on any given day the price of a security may stay level because there is no news about that security, even though trading does take place. Indeed it is precisely in a very liquid market that trades can take place without moving the price! To the extent that such cases occur, identifying non-trading with zero returns leads to an overestimate of the illiquidity of the corresponding market.

[7] In their study, Bekaert, Harvey, and Lundblad (2007) also propose and construct another measure of illiquidity based on no-trade days. Their measure gives greater weight to no-trade days on which there are larger changes in the index of the market on which the stock is listed. The idea is that the change in the index should lead to a change in the price of individual stocks. When no such change is observed for a given stock, this is more likely to be due to absence of trading in this stock, possibly because of prohibitive trading costs.

2.3.4 Measures Based on Return Covariance

Roll (1984) sets out an ingenious method for measuring the bid-ask spread based on transaction prices alone. The idea is that orders will sometimes, at random, hit the ask and the bid price, so that transaction prices bounce back and forth between them, straddling the midquote m_t. The transitory deviations around the midprice are called bid-ask bounce. Intuitively, this bounce engenders negative serial correlation in transaction-to-transaction returns.

This is easiest seen by considering a security whose quotes stay unchanged over the relevant period. Suppose that a buy market order arrives at time t, followed by a sell market order at date $t+1$. The first trade is at the ask price, the second at the bid price, so that the return between t and $t+1$ is negative. Then, one can expect a positive return between $t+1$ and $t+2$, the time of the subsequent transaction: either the next market order is again a sell order executed at the bid price (in which case the return from $t+1$ to $t+2$ is zero) or it is a buy market order executed at the ask price (in which case the return from $t+1$ to $t+2$ is positive). A similar argument shows that after a positive return, one would expect a negative return.

Roll (1984) exploits this intuition to construct an estimator of the bid-ask spread, S, based entirely on the serial covariance of returns. This estimator is called Roll's measure and is derived below. The estimator depends on specific assumptions regarding the order arrival process. After presenting Roll's measure, we shall discuss how it should be adjusted when these assumptions do not hold.

Roll's Measure

To derive Roll's measure, suppose that the security's fundamental value, as captured by the midquote, follows a random walk:

$$m_t = m_{t-1} + \varepsilon_t, \tag{2.11}$$

where ε_t is mean-zero white noise ($E(\varepsilon_t) = 0$ for all t, and $E(\varepsilon_t \varepsilon_s) = 0$ for all $t \neq s$). This variable represents the change in the value of the stock due to new information emerging between time $t-1$ and t. As $E(\varepsilon_t) = 0$, the expected fundamental return is zero ($E(m_t - m_{t-1}) = 0$), which is reasonable for small time intervals (a day or less). In any case this assumption can easily be relaxed (see below).

Now suppose that the bid-ask spread S is constant over time. The ask and bid prices in the market are:

$$a_t = m_t + \frac{S}{2} \text{ and} \tag{2.12}$$

$$b_t = m_t - \frac{S}{2}. \tag{2.13}$$

Transactions are at either the bid or the ask price depending on whether a buy or a sell market order arrives. Thus, the price of the tth transaction can be written:

$$p_t = m_t + \frac{S}{2}d_t, \tag{2.14}$$

where d_t $(= 1$ or $-1)$ indicates whether a transaction is buyer or seller initiated (see Section 2.2.1). Therefore, using equations (2.11) and (2.14), the dollar transaction-to-transaction return is:

$$p_t - p_{t-1} = m_t + \frac{S}{2}d_t - \left(m_{t-1} + \frac{S}{2}d_{t-1}\right) = \frac{S}{2}d_t - \frac{S}{2}d_{t-1} + \varepsilon_t. \tag{2.15}$$

To compute Roll's estimator for the bid-ask spread, we need several additional assumptions on the order arrival process, namely:

a. **Balanced order flow.** Market orders are equally likely to be buy or sell orders: $\Pr(d_t = 1) = \Pr(d_t = -1) = 1/2$ (so that $E(d_t) = 0$ for all t).
b. **No autocorrelation in orders.** Buy and sell market orders are serially uncorrelated, i.e., $E(d_t d_s) = 0$ for $t \neq s$.
c. **No effect on the midquote.** Market orders are assumed to carry no news, meaning that they are uncorrelated with current and future innovations in fundamentals: $E(d_t \varepsilon_t) = E(d_t \varepsilon_{t+1}) = 0$ for all t.
d. **Constant (zero) expected return.** The fundamental value follows a random walk, so that $E(m_t - m_{t-1}) = E(\varepsilon_t)$ is constant and equal to zero for all t.

This set of assumptions regarding the order arrival process and the dynamics of price and quotes constitutes Roll's model. As shown in subsequent chapters, this model is an important element in many market microstructure models.

Under the assumptions of Roll's model:

$$E(p_t - p_{t-1}) = 0.$$

Therefore, using equation (2.15):

$$\begin{aligned}
\mathrm{cov}(p_{t+1} - p_t, p_t - p_{t-1}) &= E\left[\left(\frac{S}{2}d_{t+1} - \frac{S}{2}d_t + \varepsilon_{t+1}\right)\left(\frac{S}{2}d_t - \frac{S}{2}d_{t-1} + \varepsilon_t\right)\right] \\
&= \frac{S^2}{4}E\left[d_{t+1}d_t - d_t^2 - d_{t+1}d_{t-1} + d_t d_{t-1}\right] \tag{2.16}
\end{aligned}$$

$$= -\frac{S^2}{4} \tag{2.17}$$

where we have used the assumptions on the order arrival process and the fact that $E(d_t^2) = 1$: as d_t can be only $+1$ or -1, its square is always 1. As expected, equation (2.17) implies that the bid-ask spread induces a negative correlation in price changes ($\mathrm{cov}(p_{t+1} - p_t, p_t - p_{t-1}) < 0$ if $S > 0$). Moreover, it yields Roll's estimate of the absolute value of the bid-ask spread:

$$S_R = 2\sqrt{-\mathrm{cov}(\Delta p_{t+1}, \Delta p_t)}, \tag{2.18}$$

also known as Roll's measure.

Stoll (2000) reports estimates of the (half) Roll's measure for all stocks listed on the NYSE and Nasdaq (see Stoll 2000, p. 1493, table III). For each stock, he calculates the average daily serial covariance in trade-to-trade price changes over sixty-one trading days. He then reports an estimate of $\sqrt{-\mathrm{cov}(\Delta p_{t+1}, \Delta p_t)}$ by decile of capitalization. Overall, for the NYSE, the half-Roll's measure is 3.81 cents and 11.5 cents for Nasdaq. Obviously this difference is due to differences in the characteristics of the stocks listed on the two exchanges, but even after controlling for market capitalization, for instance, it persists. Stoll (2000), p. 1491, table II also reports the average values of the quoted and the effective spreads for his sample of stocks. On average, the half-quoted spread on the NYSE is 7.9 cents against 12.6 cents on Nasdaq; the half-effective spread, 5.6 against 10.7 cents. The effective spread is smaller than the quoted spread in both markets, since dealers in each sometimes offer price improvement to their clients, which results in trades inside the bid-ask spread. Roll's measure underestimates the quoted spread, and for the NYSE it also underestimates the effective spread.

Extensions
As noted, Roll's measure depends on a series of assumptions concerning the process of order arrival and on stock returns, without which it will not yield an unbiased estimate of the bid-ask spread. We now examine why and in which direction the failure of these assumptions biases Roll's measure. Let us relax them one at a time.

Assumption (a): *balanced order flow.* In reality, market buy and sell orders are not necessarily of equal probability. For instance, at the end of the trading day agents may be more anxious to close out short positions, in which case buyer-initiated transactions would be more prevalent. To account for this, suppose that $\Pr(d_t = 1) = \eta$. When η is different from $\frac{1}{2}$, the order flow is unbalanced: there are more buy orders than sell orders if $\eta > \frac{1}{2}$, conversely if $\eta < \frac{1}{2}$. In the appendix to this chapter we show that in this case the autocovariance of price changes is:

$$\text{cov}\left(\Delta p_{t+1}, \Delta p_t\right) = \frac{S^2}{4} E\left[(d_{t+1} - d_t)(d_t - d_{t-1})\right] = -\eta(1-\eta)S^2. \quad (2.19)$$

Therefore, an unbiased estimator of the bid-ask spread is:

$$S_a = \sqrt{-\frac{\text{cov}\left(\Delta p_{t+1}, \Delta p_t\right)}{\eta(1-\eta)}}, \quad (2.20)$$

which implies:

$$S_R = \left(2\sqrt{\eta(1-\eta)}\right) S_a.$$

Thus, unless the order flow is perfectly balanced $\left(\eta = \frac{1}{2}\right)$, Roll's spread estimator is biased: It underestimates the true spread by a factor of $2\sqrt{\eta(1-\eta)}$. To see intuitively why, note that if almost all transactions are buyer initiated (say, $\eta = 0.99$), the bid-ask bounce is almost nil, as almost all trades are at the ask price. Thus, the covariance of the change in prices is close to zero and Roll's estimate is also close to zero, even though the actual bid-ask spread may be large. Thus, one must adjust the estimate of the covariance (here multiplying it by a factor $[2\eta(1-\eta)]^{-1} \approx 50.5$ to obtain a correct spread estimate.

Assumption (b): *non-autocorrelated orders.* Roll's method is also biased if there is serial correlation in the trade direction d_t. Such correlation may occur in practice because traders slice their orders and execute them piecemeal over time (see Chapters 3 and 9). For example, suppose the direction of market orders is first-order autocorrelated:

$$\Pr\left(d_{t+1} = d_t\right) = \delta.$$

We can then show (see appendix) that:

$$\text{cov}\left(\Delta p_{t+1}, \Delta p_t\right) = \frac{S^2}{4} E\left[(d_{t+1} - d_t)(d_t - d_{t-1})\right] = -(1-\delta)^2 S^2. \quad (2.21)$$

Hence, an unbiased estimate of the bid-ask spread is given by:

$$S_b = \frac{1}{1-\delta} \sqrt{-\text{cov}\left(\Delta p_{t+1}, \Delta p_t\right)} = \frac{S_R}{2(1-\delta)}. \quad (2.22)$$

Thus, unless $\delta = \frac{1}{2}$ (the order flow is serially uncorrelated), Roll's estimator of the bid-ask spread underestimates the bid-ask spread by a factor of $2(1-\delta)$. Choi, Salandro, and Shastri (1988), using the Lee-Ready algorithm to classify transactions, estimate δ to be about 0.7, which implies positive serial correlation in the direction of trade. Then Roll's original measure would again underestimate the true spread by a factor of $2 \times 0.3 = 0.6$.

Assumption (c): *no effect of orders on the midquote.* Roll assumes that changes in the value of the security (ε_t) and the direction of market orders (d_t) are independent. This assumption is problematic if some traders submitting market orders have information on the stock's future payoff. In this case, as will be seen in Chapter 3, the direction of market orders does carry information, and market participants' estimate of the value the security moves in the direction of the order. Specifically, liquidity suppliers permanently revise their value estimate upward after buy orders and downward after sell orders, which implies that ε_t and d_t are positively correlated. This attenuates the bid-ask bounce, which means that Roll's estimator again underestimates the true spread. In this case, obtaining a more accurate estimator requires deeper understanding of the trading process in the presence of asymmetric information. The method will be presented in Section 5.2.

Assumption (d): *non-varying fundamental expected return.* One of the assumptions used to derive Roll's measure is that the expected return is constant and indeed equal to zero: $E(m_t - m_{t-1}) = 0$. However, this assumption may fail: expected returns for a security can vary over time, and if the variations are serially correlated this may be yet another source of bias in Roll's measure. To see this, suppose that:

$$m_t = m_{t-1} + \bar{r}_t + \varepsilon_t. \tag{2.23}$$

where the term $\bar{r}_t$ is the expected component of the return from time t to $t+1$ (that is, $\bar{r}_t \equiv E(m_t - m_{t-1})$) and ε_t is the unexpected component. We index $\bar{r}_t$ by t because it can be time-varying. Then, using equations (2.14) and (2.23), we obtain:

$$\Delta p_t = \bar{r}_t + \frac{S}{2}(d_t - d_{t-1}) + \varepsilon_t. \tag{2.24}$$

Hence,

$$\mathrm{cov}(\Delta p_{t+1}, \Delta p_t) = \mathrm{cov}(\bar{r}_{t+1}, \bar{r}_t) - \frac{S^2}{4}. \tag{2.25}$$

Thus, the covariance of change in prices now depend on two factors: (1) the bid-ask bounce $\left(-\dfrac{S^2}{4}\right)$ whose effect is to make change in prices negatively correlated, and (2) the covariance in expected returns $(\text{cov}\,(\bar{r}_{t+1},\bar{r}_t))$. If the latter is non-zero, then Roll's estimate is biased again. By equation (2.25), an unbiased estimator of the bid-ask spread is:

$$S_d = 2\sqrt{-\text{cov}\,(\Delta p_{t+1},\Delta p_t) + \text{cov}\,(\bar{r}_{t+1},\bar{r}_t)}. \qquad (2.26)$$

If expected returns are positively autocorrelated $(\text{cov}(\bar{r}_{t+1},\bar{r}_t) > 0), S_d$ is larger than the Roll's estimator, which therefore again underestimates the true spread. George, Kaul, and Nimalendran (1991) discuss various ways of correcting for this problem through suitable time-varying estimators of $\bar{r}_t$.

The serial correlation in expected returns may explain why in some samples we find a positive covariance of price changes: in equation (2.25) this happens if $\text{cov}\,(\bar{r}_{t+1},\bar{r}_t)$ is positive and large enough to swamp the bid-ask bounce effect. This was reported even in Roll's original 1984 study, which implements his estimator using daily returns (based on closing prices) and finds that roughly half of the cases show positive serial correlation.[8] Then according to equation (2.18), the spread estimate would be the square root of a negative number— a nonsensical outcome! Harris (1990) shows that positive autocovariances are more likely for low values of the spread. Therefore, in such cases a rough remedy would be to impute a value of zero to the estimated spread. In general, Roll's estimator works better the shorter the time interval over which the returns are measured, so that bid-ask bounce is larger than other determinants of returns.

To sum up, the bid-ask spread induces negative serial correlation in returns, that is, it is a source of price reversals. The idea that illiquidity is a source of reversals is quite general, as Chapter 3 demonstrates. So, estimators for the bid-ask spread can be obtained by measuring the covariance of subsequent returns. These returns can be measured at high frequency (e.g., from trade to trade) or at lower frequency (e.g., from daily close to close).[9] But the accuracy of these estimators depends on the properties of the order arrival and price processes, and they must be fine-tuned accordingly. For instance, exercise 4 asks the reader to derive an estimator of the bid-ask spread in Roll's model when some trades occur at the midprice, as sometimes happens in reality.[10]

---

[8] In contrast, Stoll (2000) finds that for more than 99% of the stocks listed on Nasdaq and the NYSE, the covariance of trade-to-trade returns is negative, as Roll's model implies.

[9] Nowhere do we impose that date t and date $t + 1$ correspond to successive transactions.

[10] Another bias in Roll's estimator arises when there is no trade on a given day, in which case some data bases (such as CRSP) report the midquote instead of a transaction price. If these days are retained in the sample, the estimated cost will generally be biased downwards, because the midquote has no bid-ask bounce.

2.4 Implementation Shortfall

All the measures of trading costs presented so far are static, in that they do not take the time dimension of execution quality into account. In practice, however, large orders from institutions are very often split among several brokers over time (to maintain secrecy about the real size of the desired trade), and the brokers themselves may trickle the orders slowly into the market to get better prices. Thus, there can be a delay between the moment in which a portfolio manager makes his investment decision and the time he starts implementing it. This delay is costly if it is systematically associated with an adverse price movement (see the second column of Table 2.1 for an estimate of delay costs). Moreover, the portfolio manager also faces the risk of a large adverse price movement before the order is entirely filled, perhaps obliging him to cancel part of his order, which results in an opportunity cost.

For these reasons, portfolio managers often use a more encompassing measure of execution quality, namely the "implementation shortfall," first proposed by Perold (1988). This gauge factors in not only the price impact of trades but also the opportunity cost of delayed or unexecuted orders. The basic idea is to benchmark the actual performance of a portfolio against a hypothetical "paper portfolio" in which all rebalancing trades are made instantaneously and fully at midprices. In these conditions, the difference between actual performance and that of the portfolio's paper benchmark is precisely due to all the trading frictions (delays, price impact, and partial execution) encountered by the portfolio manager in rebalancing his portfolio. Thus, the concept of implementation shortfall enables us to disentangle, in the overall return of a portfolio, the portion deriving from the investment strategy of the manager and that depending on the implementation of these ideas, which is the responsibility of the trading desks hired for this purpose.

To understand how the measure of implementation shortfall is constructed and used, suppose that a portfolio manager decides to buy q shares of a stock on day 0 and passes the order to a broker. He plans to evaluate his position at some point in the future, say at date t (his "investment horizon"). In the absence of trading costs (i.e., in a perfectly liquid market), the portfolio manager would buy the shares at price m_0 and evaluate them at time t at price m_t. On paper, his dollar return is therefore:

$$R_p = q(m_t - m_0). \tag{2.27}$$

In reality, however, the portfolio manager will typically buy the stock at a higher price than m_0 because the market is illiquid. And as we have seen, part of the order may go unexecuted. For instance, the manager may decide to stop buying if the price goes too high. If $m_t > m_0$, this results in an opportunity cost. To account for these costs, suppose that only a fraction κ of the manager's buy order is eventually filled, at average execution price $\bar{p}$. Thus, the actual return is:

$$R_a = \kappa q \left(m_t - \bar{p} \right). \tag{2.28}$$

The implementation shortfall, *IS*, is the difference between the portfolio's theoretical, paper return and the actual return:[11]

$$IS \equiv q(m_t - m_0) - \kappa q(m_t - \bar{p}) = \underbrace{\kappa q(\bar{p} - m_0)}_{\text{execution cost}} + \underbrace{(1 - \kappa)q(m_t - m_0)}_{\text{opportunity cost}}. \tag{2.29}$$

Expression (2.29) shows that the implementation shortfall consists of two components: execution cost and opportunity cost. The first term should be familiar by now: it captures the cost of the actual execution at the average price $\bar{p}$ rather than the benchmark price m_0 (i.e., the effective spread). The second component represents the opportunity cost of the forgone returns on the unexecuted portion of the order, $(1 - \kappa)q$. For example, imagine that a client submits a buy order for ten thousand shares when the midquote is \$100, and evaluates the performance of his broker two days later, when the broker has only bought three thousand shares at an average price of \$101.[12] If the current price is 103, then the implementation shortfall is:

$$3{,}000 \times (101 - 100) + 7{,}000 \times (103 - 100) = 3{,}000 + 7{,}000 \times 3 = 24{,}000.$$

To put this figure in perspective, consider that the initial value of the "paper" portfolio in this example is $qm_0 = 1{,}000{,}000$, so that the implementation shortfall is 2.4% of its value.

As observed earlier, there may be a delay between the moment when the portfolio manager makes the investment decision and the moment of implementation. The execution cost component of the implementation shortfall can itself be divided in two components to reflect the cost of this delay. To see this let τ be the date at which the buy order begins to be executed. Then, the execution cost component can be written:

---

[11] The implementation shortfall is computed symmetrically for a sell order, but in that case q is negative (q being the signed order size).

[12] Frazzini, Israel, and Moskowitz (2018) use a sample of large orders submitted by a large asset manager. The average order size of this manager (q) varies between 0.1% to 13% of the average daily volume and it takes about 2.7 days to execute an order.

$$\kappa q\left(\bar{p}-m_0\right) = \kappa q\left(\bar{p}-m_\tau\right) + \kappa q(m_\tau - m_0), \tag{2.30}$$

where the second element $\kappa q(m_\tau - m_0)$ is the delay portion of the execution component of the implementation shortfall. Table 2.1 shows that in practice the delay portion accounts for a significant fraction of total execution cost.

For any given order, one or all components of the implementation shortfall may be negative, as when the broker manages to fill the order at a better average price than the initial price of the paper portfolio. This may happen when the price of the stock goes down after a buy order is issued, or alternatively if the broker is able to use limit rather than market orders. The opportunity cost is negative if the value of the stock declines over the investment horizon ($m_t < m_0$). In hindsight, failing to buy the security turns out to be the better choice and the opportunity cost is negative.

As with the other measures of trading costs, the average implementation shortfall over a large number of orders is a more meaningful gauge than its value for any given order, in that the average filters out the impact of random price variations. The average implementation shortfall is:

$$\mathrm{E}(IS) \equiv \kappa \mathrm{E}\left(q\left(\bar{p}-m_0\right)\right) + (1-\kappa)\mathrm{E}\left(q(m_t - m_0)\right).$$

The opportunity cost component will be positive on average if the direction and size of the orders placed (q) is positively correlated with price changes over the portfolio manager's investment horizon ($m_t - m_0$) so that $\mathrm{E}(q(m_t - m_0)) > 0$. In practice, this positive correlation may exist for several reasons: one's manager may trade based on the same signal as other market participants, the order may exert pressure on prices, or some traders may "front-run" the order (i.e., buy the security to resell it to the buyer at a higher price). Further, brokers often face a trade-off between the execution and the opportunity cost components. By trading patiently (as with limit orders), a broker can generally get a better price and so reduce the execution cost component. But as this strategy increases the risk of non-execution $(1 - \kappa)$, it results in a larger opportunity cost component on average.

The optimal strategy given this trade-off depends on the broker's forecast of the dynamics of the midprice and market liquidity. Again consider a broker with a large buy order. Obviously, if he expects the price to increase, he should increase the execution speed. But, as Chapter 1 shows, buy market orders deplete liquidity on the sell side. In general, after a while, liquidity suppliers will post new quotes and the market will become more liquid. Resiliency, the speed at which liquidity returns to normal after a trade (e.g., how soon a limit order is replenished after the arrival of a large market order), is another dimension of market liquidity. If the resiliency of the market is high, the broker can accelerate the execution of his large order; if resiliency is low, he should trade more slowly. In highly resilient markets, therefore, brokers will be able to achieve both lower execution costs and lower opportunity costs.

In practice, the amount of the implementation shortfall is not negligible in relation to portfolio returns.[13] For this reason, institutional investors increasingly focus on trading cost management in the effort to reduce this cost, often with the help of consulting services from brokerage houses, which now commonly provide so-called trading cost analysis (TCA) services to portfolio managers. Typically, TCA inquires into the sources of the implementation shortfall on a portfolio manager's orders.

2.5 Hands-On Estimation of Transaction Costs

We have presented many measures of transaction costs. The best way to appreciate similarities and differences is for the reader to estimate a few of them and see how their values depend on the characteristics of the stock and how they change in the course of the trading day. For this, we provide data from real-world securities markets, as training grounds for hands-on estimation. In the exercises of this chapter, the reader is prompted to use these data, some of which are available in the companion web site for the book.

2.6 Further Reading

Holden, Jacobsen, and Subrahmanyam (2013) offer an in-depth review of liquidity meaures and empirical evidence on liquidity. The literature has proposed several other measures of illiquidity, in addition to those presented here. The "effective tick" proposed by Holden (2006) is based on the idea that price observations tend to cluster at certain ticks, specifically at rounder increments (price clustering), only due to the bid-ask spread. The measure of the spread is obtained in two steps: first, one estimates the probability of each bid-ask spread from the observed frequencies of prices at the various ticks; second, these probabilities are used to compute the probability-weighted average of each effective spread size.

Another proposed estimator of the effective spread, the LOT measure Lesmond, Ogden, and Trzcinka (1999), is based on the idea that if no trading

---

[13] For instance, Leinweber (1995) reports that the paper return of the Value Line Portfolio (based on the recommendations of the Value Line newsletter) was 26.2% over the period 1971–91 while the actual return was 16.1%, implying an implementation shortfall of 10.1%. Frazzini, Israel, and Moskowitz (2018) estimate the implementation shortfall for actual trades of a large asset manager at 11.8 bps (per order) on average over the 1998–2016 period.

occurs on zero-return days, informed traders must have faced transaction costs exceeding the price change that their information implies. Therefore, the authors propose a maximum likelihood estimator for the transaction cost corresponding to the observed no-trading price interval.

Hasbrouck (2002) sets out two alternative methods for estimating Roll's measure. He notes that in Roll's model both the spread, S, and the variance of the change in the value of the security, $var(\varepsilon_t)$, are unknown parameters. They can be estimated either with the classical method-of-moments or with Bayesian techniques, which involve the specification of a prior. An argument for the Bayesian approach in this context is its ability to accommodate latent (unobserved) data, which in Roll's model include bids, asks, and trade direction indicators, and which are suppressed in the GMM estimation. Since Hasbrouck implements this Bayesian estimation via an iterative procedure known as the Gibbs sampler, the resulting estimate of the spread is known as "Gibbs estimate."

Hasbrouck (2009) compares the Gibbs estimate based on daily closing prices from CRSP with the effective cost of trading based on single-transaction trade and quote data from the TAQ database over the period 1993–2005, and finds that they are highly correlated. This suggests that less data-intensive estimates obtained at the daily frequency are a good approximation of the more precise estimates that can be obtained from intra-daily-frequency data.

Goyenko, Holden, and Trzcinka (2009) effect a similar comparison for a larger set of measures of effective spread and price impact, investigating how closely the measures computed at monthly and annual frequencies and based on daily data are correlated with the corresponding estimates based on intra-daily data from TAQ and rule 605 data. Again, their exercise is designed to identify the measures that, when computed on daily data, best approximate the behavior of their more data-intensive counterparts.

Abdi and Ranaldo (2017) propose another method to estimate the bid-ask spread that improves on Roll's measure by exploiting closing, high, and low prices (as opposed to closing prices only). The advantage of their method is that it is independent of trade direction dynamics, and thus does not require the assumption of serially independent and equally likely trade directions. Instead of the autocovariance of consecutive close-to-close price returns as in Roll (1984), their estimator relies on the autocovariance of close to mid-range returns around the same close price, where mid-range prices are defined as the mean of the daily high and low log-prices.

Determining what trading strategies are optimal to minimize implementation shortfall has become an important issue for practitioners: Bertsimas and Lo (1998) lay out the foundations for this type of analysis; a systematic treatment can be found in Kissell and Gantz (2003). Frazzini, Israel, and Moskowitz (2018) provide examples of execution strategies for orders of a large asset manager (e.g., how these strategies optimally combine limit and market orders) and report estimates the implementation shortfall for on these orders.

2.7 Appendix. Extensions of Roll's Measure

We derive the expressions for the various estimators of the bid-ask spread in Section 2.3.4. Let $\Delta d_{t+1} \equiv d_{t+1} - d_t$. Recall that:

$$
\begin{aligned}
\text{cov}(\Delta p_{t+1}, \Delta p_t) &= \text{cov}\left[\left(\frac{S}{2}d_{t+1} - \frac{S}{2}d_t + \varepsilon_{t+1}\right), \left(\frac{S}{2}d_t - \frac{S}{2}d_{t-1} + \varepsilon_t\right)\right] \\
&= \text{cov}\left(\frac{S}{2}\Delta d_{t+1} + \varepsilon_{t+1}, \frac{S}{2}\Delta d_t + \varepsilon_t\right) \\
&= \left(\frac{S}{2}\right)^2 \text{cov}(\Delta d_{t+1}, \Delta d_t) + \left(\frac{S}{2}\right)\text{cov}(\Delta d_{t+1}, \varepsilon_t) \\
&\quad + \left(\frac{S}{2}\right)\text{cov}(\varepsilon_{t+1}, \Delta d_t) + \text{cov}(\varepsilon_{t+1}, \varepsilon_t).
\end{aligned}
\tag{2.31}
$$

a) Relaxing the assumption of balanced order flow

Consider the case in which the order flow is unbalanced, that is, $\Pr(d_t = 1) = \eta$. Other assumptions are as in Roll's baseline model. In this case, using equation (2.31), we have:

$$
\text{cov}(\Delta p_{t+1}, \Delta p_t) = \left(\frac{S}{2}\right)^2 \text{cov}(\Delta d_{t+1}, \Delta d_t).
$$

By definition:

$$
\text{cov}(\Delta d_{t+1}, \Delta d_t) = E(\Delta d_{t+1} \Delta d_t) - E(\Delta d_{t+1})E(\Delta d_t).
\tag{2.32}
$$

To calculate $\text{cov}(\Delta d_{t+1}, \Delta d_t)$, consider Table 2.3, which shows the various possible realizations for (d_{t-1}, d_t, d_{t+1}) and their probabilities. The table thus allows us to calculate $E(\Delta d_{t+1} \Delta d_t)$ and $E(\Delta d_{t+1})E(\Delta d_t)$. Hence:

$$
\begin{aligned}
E(\Delta d_{t+1} \Delta d_t) &= \eta^2(1-\eta)(-2)(+2) + \eta(1-\eta)^2(+2)(-2) \\
&= \eta(1-\eta)(\eta + 1 - \eta)(-4) = -4\eta(1-\eta),
\end{aligned}
$$

and:

$$
E(\Delta d_t) = \eta(1-\eta)(-2) + \eta(1-\eta)(+2) = 0,
$$

Table 2.3 Probability, Value, and Change of Trade Direction, if $\Pr(d_t = 1) = \eta$

$\Pr(d_{t-1})$		η				$(1-\eta)$		
d_{t-1}		+1				−1		
$\Pr(d_t)$		η		$(1-\eta)$		η		$(1-\eta)$
d_t		+1		−1		+1		−1
Δd_t		0		−2		+2		0
$\Pr(d_{t+1})$	η	$(1-\eta)$	η	$(1-\eta)$	η	$(1-\eta)$	η	$(1-\eta)$
d_{t+1}	+1	−1	+1	−1	+1	−1	+1	−1
Δd_{t+1}	0	−2	+2	0	0	−2	+2	0

so that:

$$\operatorname{cov}(\Delta d_{t+1}, \Delta d_t) = E(\Delta d_{t+1}\Delta d_t) = -4\eta(1-\eta).$$

Substituting this expression into (2.31) and using the assumptions that the order flow and change in asset values are uncorrelated, we obtain:

$$\operatorname{cov}(\Delta p_{t+1}, \Delta p_t) = -4\eta(1-\eta)\frac{S^2}{4} = -\eta(1-\eta)S^2,$$

which is equation (2.19).

b) Relaxing the assumption of uncorrelated order flow
Now consider the case in which the direction of orders is first-order auto-correlated, with constant transition probability, $\Pr(d_{t+1} = d_t) = \delta$, while other assumptions are as in the baseline Roll model. To analyze this case, we have to modify the previous table as follows:
From Table 2.4, we obtain:

$$E(\Delta d_{t+1}\Delta d_t) = \frac{1}{2}(1-\delta)^2(-2)(+2) + \frac{1}{2}(1-\delta)^2(+2)(-2)$$
$$= (1-\delta)^2(-4) = -4(1-\delta)^2$$

and:

$$E(\Delta d_t) = \frac{1}{2}(1-\delta)(-2) + \frac{1}{2}(1-\delta)(+2) = 0.$$

Hence, using equation (2.32),

$$\operatorname{cov}(\Delta d_{t+1}, \Delta d_t) = E(\Delta d_{t+1}\Delta d_t) = -4(1-\delta)^2.$$

Table 2.4 Probability, Value, and Change of Trade Direction, if $\Pr(d_{t+1} = d_t) = \delta$

$\Pr(d_{t-1})$		$\frac{1}{2}$				$\frac{1}{2}$		
d_{t-1}		+1				−1		
$\Pr(d_t)$		δ	(1-δ)			(1-δ)		δ
d_t		+1	−1			+1		−1
Δd_t		0	−2			+2		0
$\Pr(d_{t+1})$	δ	(1−δ)	(1−δ)		δ	(1−δ)	(1−δ)	δ
d_{t+1}	+1	−1	+1	−1	+1	−1	+1	−1
Δd_{t+1}	0	−2	+2	0	0	−2	+2	0

Substituting this expression into (2.31) yields:

$$\mathrm{cov}\left(\Delta p_{t+1}, \Delta p_t\right) = -4(1-\delta)^2 \frac{S^2}{4} = -(1-\delta)^2 S^2,$$

which is equation (2.21).

2.8 Exercises

1. **Quoted spread for different trade sizes.** Consider the LOB of stock XYZ in Table 2.5, which displays the prices, sizes (i.e., number of shares) and times of entry of limit orders present in the LOB, as in Figure 1.2 of Chapter 1. From these data, compute the weighted average quoted spread (in absolute and relative terms) for 100, 500, 1,000, and 2,000 shares. Which side of the LOB is deeper for transactions of 2,000 shares or more?

2. **Measures of the bid-ask spread.** Your fund is considering trading 10-year bonds issued by the Austrian government, and you see that at 9:30 a.m. their lowest ask price is 102.31 and their highest bid price is 99.50. Five seconds later a buy order for a block of €10 million is executed at 102.76. At 10:30 a.m. you check the market again and see that the lowest ask price is 102.55 and the highest bid price is 100.02.

   a. Compute the absolute and the relative quoted spread at 9:30 and 10:30.

   b. Compute the absolute and the relative effective ask-side half-spread at 9:30.

   c. Compare the quoted half-spread with the effective ask-side half-spread (both in absolute and in relative terms) at 9:30. What explains the difference between them?

   d. Compute the absolute realized spread in the 9:30–10:30 interval.

Table 2.5 LOB of Stock XYZ

Bid			Ask		
Price	Size	Time	Price	Size	Time
74.42	300	11:49:39	74.48	300	11:49:35
74.41	100	11:46:55	74.48	500	11:49:40
74.36	400	11:48:30	75.74	100	08:25:17
74.36	400	11:48:32	76.00	150	08:02:02
74.00	13	10:56:00	76.77	20	07:01:01
73.75	5,100	11:28:02	77.00	100	09:15:00
72.98	5,100	10:57:39	77.06	200	10:14:11
72.15	120	08:01:39	77.35	1,000	08:01:39
72.00	20	07:01:01	77.82	20	07:01:01
72.03	20	07:01:01	78.00	300	08:02:00
72.00	100	07:46:19	78.38	1,000	09:30:04
71.59	50	08:02:02	78.60	375	08:01:32
71.11	20	07:01:01	78.64	500	09:30:04
71.00	10	09:30:36	78.87	20	07:01:01
70.35	200	08:00:54	78.95	200	08:01:35
70.11	20	07:01:01	80.00	350	09:15:00

  e. Compare the realized spread computed under point **d** with the absolute effective spread at 9:30 computed under point **b**. What explains the difference between them?
3. **Implicit bid-ask spread in call auction.** In a call auction there is no bid-ask spread, as all trades clear at a single price. However, there is an implicit spread, insofar as the order flow exerts price pressure: the difference between the hypothetical prices that would clear the market if one tried to buy and sell more shares. Specifically, the implicit bid-ask spread for a transaction of size q can be defined as the difference in market clearing price arising from an extra market order of size q to buy and an extra order of size q to sell. Using the data in exercise 1 of Chapter 1, compute the bid-ask spread for transaction sizes $q = 50, 150, 250$, and 350.
4. **Roll's estimator and price improvements.** Consider Roll's model presented in Section 2.3.4. All the assumptions are unchanged, but we do assume that the transaction occurring at time t occurs either at the ask or bid price with probability λ, or at the midprice with probability $1 - \lambda$. Thus, $1 - \lambda$ can be seen as the fraction of trades that receive a price improvement or are crossed by brokers at the midprice. Propose an estimator of the quoted bid-ask spread S for this case.
5. **Empirical measurement of quoted spreads.** The data for this exercise are contained in an Excel file, Ch2_AGF_data.xls available in the companion

website for the book: a record of one day's transactions in the shares of a French company, AGF, on the Paris Bourse. The data comprise:

- time of the transaction
- size of the transaction
- (average) transaction price
- best bid price immediately before the transaction
- best ask price immediately before the transaction
- direction of trade initiation (−1 for transactions below the midprice, +1 above the midprice)

a. For each transaction, compute the absolute spread S in euro (€); compute the relative spread, s and the log spread: $\ln(\text{ask}) - \ln(\text{bid})$; and compare the average of these three measures. Then compute the average absolute spread for each of the 17 half-hour time periods of the trading day and plot a graph of your results showing the intraday evolution of the spread. What kind of pattern over the day would you expect, a priori?

b. Compute and compare the average effective trading cost or "half-spread" in absolute terms, relative terms, and logs.

c. Compute the VWAP for the day. Then calculate the VWAP for buyer- and seller-initiated transactions for the whole day and compare your results with the VWAP benchmark. Repeat, again separately for buyer- and seller-initiated transactions, for transactions divided into three time periods: 9:00–12:00 a.m., 12:00–3:00 p.m., and 3:00–5:30 p.m.

d. Compute Roll's estimate of the bid-ask spread both in euro (€) and in relative terms (using the logarithm of the prices). Then repeat the computations in clock time rather than in transaction time: take the last transaction in every 15-minute time interval. Compare your results with those previously obtained: what explains the difference in Roll's measure?

e. Split the trading day into 15-minute intervals: 9:00–9:15 a.m., 9:15–9:30 a.m., ..., 5:15–5:30 p.m. For each interval, compute the midprice change (from the last transaction of the previous interval to the last one of the current interval; for the first interval take the midprice at 9:06:04 as the initial midprice) and the cumulative signed order flow over the interval expressed as a fraction of the day's total (unsigned) order flow. Perform a regression analysis on the thirty-four data points you obtain in this way, to estimate the price impact parameter λ. Is the estimated parameter significantly different from zero? What is the impact on the midprice of a 1% relative order flow increase?

6. Inferring trade direction. A data set containing a 1-day time series of quote and trade data for Krispy Kreme, listed on the NYSE, is provided in the Excel file Ch2_KrispyKreme_raw_data.xls available on the companion website for the book. This data set contains both transaction data and quote revisions, but no trade direction indicator. (The variable "type" is equal to 1 for transaction data and 0 for quote data.)

    a. For each quote revision, compute the absolute spread S in dollars ($), the relative spread s, and the log spread. Then compute the average absolute spread for each of the 14 half-hour time periods of the trading day and plot a graph of your results showing the intraday evolution of the spread.

    b. Use the Lee-Ready trade classification algorithm to establish trade direction. Then generate a data set containing only transaction data (for each transaction consider the last bid price and the last ask price before the transaction takes place) of the same form as the AGF data set.

7. **Further empirical transaction cost measurement.** Using the data set generated at point **b** of exercise 6 (or alternatively the data in the Excel file Ch2_KrispyKreme_data.xls, which also contains the trade direction indicator):

    a. Compute and compare the average effective trading cost or "half-spread" in absolute terms, relative terms, and logs.

    b. Compute the VWAP for the day. Then calculate VWAPs for buyer- and seller-initiated transactions for the whole day and compare your results with the VWAP benchmark. Repeat, again separately for buyer- and seller-initiated transactions, for transactions divided into three time periods: 9:30–12:00 a.m., 12:00–2:00 p.m., and 2:00–4:00 p.m.

    c. Compute Roll's estimate of the bid-ask spread both in dollar ($) and in relative terms (using the logarithm of the prices); then repeat the computations using not transaction time but clock time: take the last transaction in every 15-minute time interval.

    d. Split the trading day into 15-minute intervals: 9:30–9:45 a.m., 10:00–10:15 a.m., ..., 3:45–4:00 p.m. For each interval, compute the midprice change (from the last transaction of the previous interval to the last one of the current interval; for the first interval take the midprice at 9:30:02 as the initial midprice) and the cumulative signed order flow over the interval expressed as a fraction of the day's total (unsigned) order flow. Perform a regression analysis on the 26 data points you obtain in this way, to estimate the price impact parameter λ. Is the estimated parameter significantly different from zero? What is the impact on the midprice of a 1% relative order flow change?

8. **Implementation shortfall.** Suppose that at time 0 your brokerage firm receives an order from a client who would like to buy a number q of

shares in company XYZ, planning to hold them until some future time t. The midprice of XYZ is m_0 when you receive the order, and the client expects its midprice to be m_t at time t. Although in a perfectly liquid market the client would like the entire purchase to go through at time 0, he realizes that this may not be in his best interest in the rather illiquid market for XYZ shares. So the client's mandate to your firm is "choose the fraction k of the total purchase q that is to be bought between time 0 and time t so as minimize the implementation shortfall." You know that the average price $\bar{p}$ at which you can buy shares for this client between time 0 and t is affected by how much you buy in that interval, according to the function:

$$\bar{p} = m_0 + \lambda kq,$$

where λ is a price pressure parameter.

a. Write the expression for the implementation shortfall in this specific case (using the above expression for $\bar{p}$).

b. Determine the value of k that minimizes the implementation shortfall.

c. How does the optimal k found under point **b** respond to changes in $m_t - m_0$, in q and in λ? What are the intuitive explanations for these comparative statics?

9. **Choice between limit and market orders.** Suppose you wish to buy 100 shares of a stock whose current price is €25 per share, and you are uncertain whether you should place a market order for 100 shares or a buy order with limit price at €26 for 100 shares. You turn for advice to your broker, telling him that you wish to minimize execution risk. He tells you: "it is not clear whether you are better off with either strategy." Is he right, in principle?

10. **Order placement strategy and execution risk.** Consider a security with a final payoff v, which can be traded at time $t = 1$ and/or $t = 2$ at prices:

$$p_t = v + \lambda_t q_t + \epsilon_t, \tag{2.33}$$

where p_t is the price obtained by a customer who places an order of size q_t and λ_t is the price impact parameter, and an innovation ϵ_t that captures the arrival of "news" on the market at time t. The innovation ϵ_t has $E(\epsilon_t) = 0$ and $\text{var}(\epsilon_t) = \sigma_\epsilon^2 > 0$, and is serially uncorrelated.

Consider a risk-averse buyer with mean-variance utility function:

$$U(\Pi) = E(\Pi) - \gamma \text{var}(\Pi), \tag{2.34}$$

where Π is the investor's payoff. The investor assigns value v to each unit of the security, and wishes to place a total order of size Q, so that his payoff is:

$$\Pi = vQ - (q_1 p_1 + q_2 p_2). \qquad (2.35)$$

At $t = 1$ he knows the current price of the security p_1: so both $E(\Pi)$ and var(Π) in (2.34) are conditional on the actual value of p_1, while p_2 is uncertain for the investor.

The investor must decide how to split the total order Q between time 1 and time 2, namely determine q_1 and $q_2 = Q - q_1$ so as to maximize (2.34), where Π is given by (2.35) and prices p_1 and p_2 are given by (2.33).

a. Compute the optimal order sizes q_1^* and q_2^*.

b. Consider the "average split" of the total order Q over time, i.e.:

$$\frac{E(q_1^*)}{Q} \quad \text{and} \quad \frac{E(q_2^*)}{Q},$$

recalling that, from an ex ante perspective, $E(\epsilon_1) = 0$. (i) What would this average split be if the investor were risk neutral ($\gamma = 0$)? Explain the intuition for this "risk-neutral average split." Benchmark your analysis against the case $\lambda_1 = \lambda_2 = \lambda$, where the price pressure is the same in the two periods. (ii) Now consider a risk averse investor ($\gamma > 0$): how does risk aversion affect the average split of the total order Q? Does it accelerate or delay order execution? Explain the intuition for this result, again using the case $\lambda_1 = \lambda_2 = \lambda$ as benchmark.

c. Now consider the "actual split" of the total order Q over time, i.e.:

$$\frac{q_1^*}{Q} \quad \text{and} \quad \frac{q_2^*}{Q},$$

and suppose for concreteness that the price shock at $t = 1$ is positive ($\epsilon_1 > 0$), so that the security is more expensive than usual in the first period. Explain intuitively how this affects the actual split of the total order Q over time, and why.

3

Order Flow, Liquidity, and Security Price Dynamics

Learning Objectives:

- Why and how orders move prices
- Why there is a bid-ask spread
- How prices are formed when orders convey information
- The determinants of market illiquidity
- What inventory risk is and how it affects prices

3.1 Introduction

In principle, asset prices change in response to news about fundamentals, namely, future cash flows and discount factors. But security prices fluctuate continuously, even within extremely short time spans and in the absence of price-relevant news. These movements are responses to incoming orders to buy or sell stocks. Market microstructure theory explains how these intraday price movements are related to the order flow. It identifies illiquidity as one cause of these short-run fluctuations, which can be either transient or longer lasting depending on the motives underlying orders and the way market participants interpret them. If orders are seen as reflecting news about fundamentals, the price movements tend to be long lasting; otherwise, they tend to be reversed quickly.

The prevalence of very short-term price movements and their responsiveness to orders is illustrated in Table 3.1, which reports trade and quote data for the first transactions of a typical trading day (March 26, 2001) for the stock of a large French insurance company, AGF.[1] This stock was traded on Euronext's electronic limit order market until it was acquired by Allianz in 2007. The type of data

---

[1] The companion website for this book reports the same data for the entire day (519 trades).

Market Liquidity: Theory, Evidence, and Policy. Second Edition. Thierry Foucault, Marco Pagano, and Ailsa Röell, Oxford University Press. © Oxford University Press 2023. DOI: 10.1093/oso/9780197542064.003.0004

Table 3.1 Sample Trading Session for AGF on Euronext,
March 26, 2001

Time	Trade size	Price	Direction	Bid	Ask
t	$(|q_t|)$	(p_t)	(d_t)	(b_t)	(a_t)
9:06:04	20	66.70	−1	66.90	67.00
9:06:11	25	66.64	−1	66.65	66.70
9:06:26	18	66.60	−1	66.60	66.65
9:07:18	273	66.42	−1	66.50	66.55
9:07:36	27	66.55	+1	66.15	66.55
9:18:03	100	66.25	−1	66.25	66.35
9:19:37	267	66.20	−1	66.20	66.30
9:23:08	12	66.15	−1	66.15	66.25
9:23:31	157	66.15	−1	66.15	66.20
9:23:38	30	66.10	−1	66.10	66.15
9:26:26	1,000	66.20	+1	66.00	66.20
9:30:10	1	66.20	+1	66.05	66.20
9:30:54	24	66.16	+1	66.05	66.20
9:34:40	90	66.05	−1	66.05	66.20
9:35:39	6	66.05	−1	66.05	66.20
9:36:10	1,000	66.00	−1	66.00	66.20
9:36:14	15	66.20	+1	66.00	66.20
9:39:56	75	66.05	−1	66.05	66.10

given in Table 3.1 illustrates well the type of high-frequency data available on transactions in many markets (see exercise 11 for instance).

For each transaction between 9:05 a.m. and 9:40 a.m., the table displays: (i) the time of the trade, t; (ii) its absolute size, $|q_t|$; (iii) the price, p_t, at which it is executed; (iv) the highest bid quote, b_t, and the lowest ask quote a_t on the limit order book immediately before the trade; and (v) the direction, d_t, of the trade, defined as +1 or −1 depending on whether the party initiating the trade (i.e., demanding liquidity) is buyer or seller. The (signed) *order flow* is thus the absolute trade size multiplied by its direction: $q_t = |q_t| \cdot d_t$.

Clearly, the price varies from one transaction to the next.[2] There is considerable movement even though the time interval is just thirty-four minutes, and this pattern is in no way specific to this particular stock or period. This chapter serves precisely to provide a framework for understanding such intraday stock

---

[2] The transaction price is not necessarily equal to the bid or the ask price just before the transaction. In a limit order market, the depth at the best quotes may be too little to fully execute a marketable order. In this case, the order walks up or down the book (depending on its direction). So the average transaction price can be higher than the current ask or lower than the current bid price. The price can also be strictly inside the quotes if it is a matched trade pre-negotiated outside the main market and entered into the system by a special procedure. For a description of the trading operations in a limit order market, see Chapter 1; for a formal analysis of this trading mechanism, see Chapter 6.

price variations. This framework also helps to explain the factors that determine the other variables appearing in Table 3.1, in particular the order flow and the bid-ask spread. It will also clarify how price volatility, spreads, and order flow are interrelated. Lastly, it will lay the ground work for a more detailed, subsequent analysis of market design issues.

We start with the Efficient Market Hypothesis (EMH), a pillar of modern finance theory, according to which security price changes are induced by the arrival of new information and should follow a random walk. In Section 3.2 we briefly review the EMH to observe that, while useful as a starting point, it does not exactly address the way information gets embodied in asset prices; in particular, it does not assign any explicit role to the variables reported in Table 3.1, such as the bid and ask quotes and the order flow. This is problematic, as price changes do appear to relate to these variables. Specifically, when markets are not perfectly liquid (that is, when the spread is not zero), buy market orders push prices upward, and sell market orders push them downward. The larger the order, the sharper is the price movement, and price volatility is related to the order flow.

These empirical patterns can be reconciled with the EMH by recognizing that the order flow itself provides new information. A series of buy orders is a signal that informed traders may be buying because the stock is undervalued, just as a series of sell orders suggests it may be overvalued. Accordingly, liquidity suppliers should revise their expectations concerning the stock's value based on the observed order flow, and price changes should be partly determined by the order flow.

Section 3.3 sets out a trading model that formalizes this intuition. The model yields several insights. For instance, it explains the existence of the bid-ask spread and relates price changes to the order flow. In this model, the bid-ask spread is a compensation required by liquidity suppliers to offset their potential losses on trades with better informed investors. Thus, the asymmetry of information between the suppliers and the demanders of liquidity determines the market's degree of liquidity.

But in reality, liquidity is also determined by other factors. In particular, liquidity suppliers need to cover the cost of executing orders and maintaining a presence in the market (so-called order-processing costs). Moreover, imperfect competition among them generates rents, which take the form of bid-ask spreads greater than order-processing costs. In Section 3.4, we enrich the model to include both order-processing costs and the rents due to imperfect competition among liquidity suppliers.

Another reason for the existence of a bid-ask spread is the fact that dealers are risk averse. As prices fluctuate during the trading day, liquidity suppliers are exposed to variations in the value of their positions ("inventory risk"), because these positions cannot necessarily be unwound immediately. As a dealer accumulates a long position in the stock, he is exposed to the risk of a price drop; conversely, a short position entails the danger of a rise in the price. If the dealer is risk averse, his quotes should depend directly on his exposure to inventory risk. Section 3.5 analyzes the impact of inventory risk and dealers' risk aversion on bid and ask quotes.

Overall, the models presented in this chapter describe three kinds of cost for liquidity suppliers: (i) the cost of trading with better informed investors (adverse selection costs), (ii) the real cost of processing orders (order-processing costs), and (iii) the cost of holding risky assets (inventory holding costs). Since liquidity suppliers need a larger bid-ask spread to compensate for these costs, each cost category will contribute to market illiquidity. In addition, oligopolistic liquidity suppliers may charge a markup that also fosters illiquidity. Understanding the relative importance of these determinants of liquidity is important for policy-making and market design. For instance, if order-processing costs predominate, then a change in the trading system might be called for. But if adverse selection costs are the main factor, improvements in disclosure and greater parity between traders should be considered.

Thus, it is important to distinguish between the various costs borne by liquidity suppliers. The models presented in this chapter suggest a way to assess their relative importance, because they show that different costs carry different implications for short-term price movements after the execution of a market order. Even though the immediate impact of a market order is the same in all cases (a buy pushes the price up; a sell, down), the subsequent price dynamics differ with the source of market illiquidity, as explained here (summarized in Section 3.6). Specifically, if the bid-ask spread is compensation for adverse selection costs, then the price impact of a market order is permanent, as it leads liquidity suppliers to revise their estimate of the security's value. But if the spread is compensation for order-processing costs or inventory risk, then the price impact of a market order is transient and should dissipate over time; that is, these kinds of cost induce reversals in returns. Moreover, the speed of the reversal differs depending on the relative importance of inventory holding vis-à-vis order-processing costs.

Casual observation of price movements during the day suggests that the immediate price impact of market orders actually has both a permanent and a transient component: in the real world, all kinds of costs matter. Chapter 5 describes various empirical techniques to exploit the implications of the models presented here for assessing the relative importance of adverse-selection costs, order-processing costs, and inventory holding costs.

The analysis in much of this chapter is based on the simplifying assumption that all orders are for a fixed number of shares, which we normalize to 1 so that $q_t = d_t \in \{-1, +1\}$.[3] Trades occur when investors ("liquidity demanders") submit orders to buy or sell; the trades are registered in the sequence in which they occur, just as in Table 3.1. Thus, p_t is the price at which the tth trade takes place, and d_t indicates whether the investor initiating the tth trade is a buyer or a seller. Liquidity is supplied by a pool of traders, whom we call "dealers" or "market makers," but who could also be limit order traders: in this framework, the precise nature of those providing liquidity is irrelevant. Dealers post their bid and ask quotes, at which they are willing to execute sell or buy orders. We denote by b_t^i the bid price posted by dealer i at time t (i.e., what dealer i bids for the stock). Similarly, we denote by a_t^i the ask (or offer) price posted by dealer i at time t (i.e., the price that he asks for the security or at which he offers it for sale). We denote the best ask price by a_t and the best bid price by b_t:

$$a_t = \min_i\{a_t^i\} \text{ and } b_t = \max_i\{b_t^i\}.$$

Investors trade with the dealer that posts the best price: they buy at the lowest ask price a_t and sell at the highest bid price b_t. So the transaction price at time t is either a_t or b_t, depending on the direction of the order that triggers it.

3.2 Price Dynamics and the Efficient Market Hypothesis

Some football clubs are listed on stock exchanges. Not surprisingly, their stock price is very sensitive to their on-field performance: a good showing brings more fans and television coverage, swelling expected revenues. So the outcome of matches affects the club's stock market value. Most matches take place on weekends. On Monday, the stocks of winners rise typically and those of losers fall (Palomino et al. 2009). This illustrates a general principle: new information is a source of price changes. For any security, new information leads investors to revise their estimates of future cash flows. The price adjusts to reflect investors' updated valuation.

The speed of this adjustment is an important issue. For instance, imagine that Ajax Amsterdam meets Juventus in the UEFA Champions League, and Ajax wins in an upset. Assume the closing price for Ajax on the last trading day before the match was €7. In view of Ajax's victory, investors revise their estimate of its stock value (i.e., the discounted value of its expected future dividends) to €7.20. How does its stock price evolve on the trading day after the match? One scenario

---

[3] In Section 3.5, and more extensively in Chapter 4, we will allow investors to place orders of varying size.

could be that it will gradually approach its new fundamental level of €7.20. For instance, a first trade takes place at $p_1 = €7.10$, a second at $p_2 = €7.15$, and so on.

The EMH, however, holds that the adjustment should be instantaneous.[4] According to the EMH, at any point in time, trades are made at a price that is equal to the best possible estimate of the value of the asset, incorporating all available information. We shall refer to this as the "fundamental value" v of the security, which can be thought of as the value once trading is over. Formally, the EMH states that:

$$p_t = \mu_t \equiv \mathrm{E}(v|\Omega_t), \tag{3.1}$$

where μ_t is the market makers' estimate of the security's value v as of time t, and Ω_t denotes the information available to them at that time. The notation $\mathrm{E}(v|\Omega_t)$ indicates the expected value of v conditional on information Ω_t. The absence of a discount factor is justified by the shortness of the interval (intraday).

The conditional expectation μ_t can change only if new information reaches the market. Let the random variable $\varepsilon_{t+1} = \mu_{t+1} - \mu_t$ represent the revision in investors' value estimates induced by the news arriving between time t and $t + 1$, also known as the "innovation" in value. As the innovation at any time captures the effect of news, it cannot be forecast using past information: otherwise, news would not really be news! This means that $\mathrm{E}(\varepsilon_t\varepsilon_s) = 0$, for $s \neq t$ (otherwise past innovations could be used to forecast future ones), and that $\mathrm{E}[\varepsilon_{t+1} | \Omega_t] = 0$, which implies that the expectation of μ_{t+1} as of time t is simply μ_t:

$$\mathrm{E}[\mu_{t+1} | \Omega_t] = \mu_t. \tag{3.2}$$

As $p_t = \mu_t$ at each date, it follows immediately that:

$$p_t = \mathrm{E}(p_{t+1} | \Omega_t). \tag{3.3}$$

Equation (3.3) carries an important implication for the dynamics of stock prices: namely, that the best predictor of future prices, given currently available information, is the current price. In other words, under the EMH transaction prices follow a *martingale*: price changes over a given interval are serially uncorrelated. This can be seen by computing the change of p_t from equation (3.1):

---

[4] Palomino et al. (2009) actually find some evidence that contradicts the EMH: the stock price does not seem to adjust immediately to bad news, or to incorporate all relevant public information.

$$\Delta p_{t+1} = p_{t+1} - p_t = \mu_{t+1} - \mu_t = \varepsilon_{t+1}, \qquad (3.4)$$

so that $\mathrm{cov}(\Delta p_t, \Delta p_s) = \mathrm{cov}(\varepsilon_t, \varepsilon_s) = 0$, since $E(\varepsilon_t \varepsilon_s) = 0$, for $s \neq t$.

Under the EMH, what drives intraday price changes is new information, and assets' prices adjust immediately to the fundamental values given the available information. Hence, any change in price must be due to completely unanticipated information, so that changes cannot be predicted from past information, and particularly from previous price changes.

Let us return to the football club example. On the trading day after the match with Juventus, Ajax opens at €7.20. According to the EMH all subsequent trades should be at this price as long as no new information about Ajax arrives. But suppose that later Ajax announces that its goalkeeper was injured during the match and will be unable to play in future matches. If this worsens Ajax's prospects for the rest of the season, traders mark down their expectations regarding the value of Ajax ($\varepsilon_{t+1} < 0$), and the price immediately drops by $|\varepsilon_{t+1}|$.

The question, however, is how markets become informationally efficient. In other words, what is the *process* whereby equation (3.1) comes to hold? To answer, we need to be more specific about the details of the trading process and the nature of the information that market participants have. Suppose, for instance, that (i) dealers are risk neutral and competitive, (ii) investors do not have more information than dealers, and (iii) trading is cost free. Assumption (ii) implies that the order flow does not contain information; that is, that innovations ε_t and the direction-of-trade indicator, d_t, are independent. If so, dealers have no reason to update their value estimate when they receive buy or sell orders.

Under these circumstances, there is a zero bid-ask spread, and prices do not change in response to orders. To see this, consider how a dealer i sets his ask price at time t, a_t^i. If he sells the stock at price a_t^i, he obtains an expected profit equal to:

$$E\left[(a_t^i - v)\,|\,\Omega_t\right] = a_t^i - \mu_t.$$

Thus, the lowest price at which the dealer is willing to sell is his estimate of the stock's value, μ_t. Since this is the case for all market makers, competition drives their ask price to μ_t. A similar argument shows that the bid price is also μ_t. Thus, dealers offer to execute all orders at price μ_t, the bid-ask spread is nil, and any price movement is entirely attributable to the arrival of public information, not to the order flow.

This is a useful benchmark model, but it fails to capture some important aspects of the intraday trading process. First, empirical studies have shown that intraday price volatility is too great to be explained solely by news (French and Roll 1986 and Roll 1988). This suggests that the trading process itself is a source of volatility. Second, the model fails to capture the simple fact that positive bid-ask spreads are the norm ($a_t - b_t > 0$). Lastly, in practice, intraday changes in prices are often negatively correlated. For instance, for the data reported in Table 3.1, the correlation between successive price changes is negative (–0.45), in line with the empirical evidence summarized by Stoll (2000).[5]

In the rest of this chapter, we show that these different features of the intraday trading process can be captured by relaxing assumptions (i), (ii), and (iii), which is to say, by introducing *frictions*. As we shall see, then, it is no longer the case that the transaction price p_t is equal to the dealers' estimate of the asset value, μ_t. What does determine the price changes between one transaction and the next, Δp_t, and their volatility, $\text{var}(\Delta p_t)$? What are the determinants of the bid and ask quotes, a_t and b_t? What is the relationship between price changes and order flow, q_t? Are changes in prices still serially uncorrelated? We now turn to these questions.

3.3 Price Dynamics with Informative Order Flow

We have seen that under the EMH the price of securities reflects investors' beliefs about these securities' fundamental values, which are continuously updated on the basis of new information, as captured by the term ε_t in equation (3.4). Where does this information come from? It could be generated by public announcements about company performance and macroeconomic news (say, interest rate changes). For instance, prices react to companies' announcements of dividends, insofar as the announcement is really a surprise. But not all information is broadcast simultaneously to all market participants: some investors may be privy to price-relevant information before other market participants, possibly thanks to tips from the company's management or because they have superior analytical skills.[6]

When these investors trade on their private knowledge, their orders convey information to the rest of the market, over and above what is already publicly available. In this environment, market participants will revise their estimate of securities' values in light of the order flow: unusual buying pressure will induce price increases; unusual selling pressure, price declines.

---

[5] There is also considerable debate among scholars on whether the EMH is a good description of price formation at lower frequencies, for instance, monthly or even yearly: see the overview by Shleifer (2000).

[6] Insiders (i.e., employees of a firm, board members, or people with close connections to them) are very well placed to obtain private information. Insider trading is strictly regulated (e.g., insiders cannot trade in the run-up to major company announcements) precisely in order to mitigate the risk of informed trading in the marketplace. Nevertheless, cases of illegal insider trading are frequent and constitute a good example of informed trading.

This feature can explain the existence of a bid-ask spread. To understand this point intuitively, consider the following argument, first presented by Jack Treynor in 1971 under his pseudonym "Bagehot." In principle, dealers are not always as well informed as each and every customer. Traders with superior information will exploit any mispricing by dealers, buying when the ask price is lower than the fundamental value and selling when the bid price is higher. Dealers lose money when they trade with such investors. This is known as "adverse selection": due to the informational asymmetry, market makers tend to attract customers who expect to make a profit at the dealer's expense.[7] To recoup their losses on informed orders, dealers must gain on their business with other traders. They achieve this by means of the bid-ask spread vis-à-vis all customers.

We develop these ideas in the context of a simplified version of the model proposed by Glosten and Milgrom (1985), a cornerstone of empirical and theoretical developments in this field.[8] In this model the ask price exceeds the bid because the former is set in anticipation of receiving a buy order, the latter a sell order:

$$a_t = E(v \mid \Omega_{t-1}, d_t = +1),$$ (3.5)
$$b_t = E(v \mid \Omega_{t-1}, d_t = -1),$$

where Ω_{t-1} is the information known right up to the last trade d_t (recall that in most of this chapter $q_t = d_t$, since order sizes are normalized to 1). A positive bid-ask spread arises because of the informational content of the order flow d_t, which leads dealers to see orders as a source of information additional to that previously available, Ω_{t-1}.

3.3.1 The Glosten-Milgrom Model

Suppose that some traders have better information than dealers: assume that the order at time t is placed by a risk neutral *informed* trader with probability π. An informed trader is defined as one with advance knowledge of v. With the complementary probability, $1 - \pi$, the order comes from a *liquidity* trader, who places a market buy or sell order with probability $\frac{1}{2}$ each. A liquidity trader is an investor who trades for reasons unrelated to information about the value of the security: he may be an individual who needs cash for an unanticipated

[7] For instance, in the extreme case where *all* investors are better informed than the market maker, he will be singled out for a trade *only* when his quotes generate a loss for him. Clearly no one would want to make a market under these circumstances.

[8] Like Glosten and Milgrom (1985), we suppose that all market participants are risk neutral, market makers are perfectly competitive, and traders place orders of a fixed size. But we simplify their setting by assuming that the value of the security has a binary distribution and that the orders placed by liquidity traders are price inelastic.

contingency, or a fund manager, who has to invest a recent cash inflow or rebalance the portfolio.

For simplicity, the terminal value v has binary distribution, that is, it can take two values: v^H or v^L, with $v^H > v^L$. Let θ_t and $1 - \theta_t$ be the probabilities that dealers assign to the occurrence of a high value, v^H, and a low value, v^L. These probabilities reflect the market makers' views *before* observing the $(t + 1)^{th}$ order. The dealers' estimate of the value *after* the tth order is therefore:

$$\mu_t = \theta_t v^H + (1 - \theta_t) v^L. \tag{3.6}$$

As is explained below, dealers' beliefs about the value of the security evolve because the order flow brings new information. In reality, dealers also get information from other channels (economics news, corporate announcements, etc.). But in order to focus on the informational role of the order flow, here we assume that orders are the sole source of new information for dealers. Formally, this means that $\Omega_t = \{d_1, d_2, \ldots, d_t\}$.

Notice that we include the order submitted at date t in the information set used by dealers to determine their quotes at this date.[9] How can that be, if dealers set their quotes *before* observing the order flow at date t? Here, it is important to recall that bid and ask quotes are *contingent* offers: a bid price is the price the dealer offers contingent on receiving a sell order $(d_t < 0)$, and the ask price is an offer contingent on receiving a buy order $(d_t > 0)$. Thus, the answer to the question, "What is the price at which I should execute an order?" must be identical before and after the order is actually received (in this sense, quotes are "with no regrets").

The setting is very similar to the framework developed in Section 3.2, with the difference that now we are more specific about the source of dealers' information. Thus, using the findings of Section 3.2, the ask and bid quotes set by competitive dealers will be:

$$a_t = \mu_t^+ = \mathrm{E}(v \mid \Omega_{t-1}, d_t = +1), \tag{3.7}$$
$$b_t = \mu_t^- = \mathrm{E}(v \mid \Omega_{t-1}, d_t = -1),$$

where μ_t^+ is the dealers' estimate of the security's final value if they receive a buy order at time t, and μ_t^- if they receive a sell order. If the order flow contains information, then it affects dealers' beliefs and we necessarily have $\mu_t^+ \neq \mu_t^-$; hence; $a_t \neq b_t$.

---

[9] We also assume that all dealers have identical information, which means in this case that they all observe the order flow realized at each date. This is a reasonable assumption in a market where trade characteristics (price and size) are reported immediately to all market participants, as in many equity markets. But it is unrealistic in more opaque markets, such as the FX market or the bond market. We discuss these points in greater detail in Chapter 8.

How does the order flow affect dealers' value estimate? For instance, on receiving a buy order should they revise it upward or downward? The answer depends on the *correlation* between the order flow and the value, which is ultimately determined by the way informed traders behave. In this model, they are assumed to be risk neutral and to have only a single trading opportunity. They therefore simply maximize their expected gain from trading, $(v - p_t) d_t$, where d_t is their order and p_t is the transaction price (a_t for a buy and b_t for a sell order). As long as bid and ask quotes lie between v^L and v^H (which will be seen to hold in equilibrium), informed investors will always buy ($d_t = +1$) if they observe $v = v^H$ and sell ($d_t = -1$) if they observe $v = v^L$.

This observation has an immediate implication: the likelihood of a buy order is greater when $v = v^H$ than when $v = v^L$. Conversely, the likelihood of a sell order is lower when $v = v^H$ than when $v = v^L$. This is easily checked. A buy order arises in either of two ways: with probability $1 - \pi$ a liquidity trader arrives and buys with probability $1/2$; with probability π, an informed trader arrives and buys (with probability 1) only if $v = v^H$. Hence, if $v = v^H$, the probability of a buy order is $(1 - \pi)/2 + \pi = (1 + \pi)/2$; but if $v = v^L$, the probability is just $(1 - \pi)/2$ because the informed traders do not buy. Thus, whenever $\pi > 0$, the market maker is more likely to receive a buy order when the security has high rather than low value. For sell orders, the converse is true.

This observation captures the intuitive idea that a sequence of buy (sell) orders is more likely when informed traders are privy to good (bad) news about the actual value of the security. Thus, informed trading induces a positive correlation between order flow and value. Buy orders are in fact good news: a *signal* that the true value of the security is high. Conversely, sell orders are bad news, signalling low true value. Accordingly, dealers must mark their value estimate up when they receive a buy order, and down when they get a sell order:

$$E(v \mid \Omega_{t-1}, d_t = +1) > E(v \mid \Omega_{t-1}, d_t = -1),$$

which implies, $a_t > b_t$. The bid-ask spread is therefore a natural consequence of the fact that buy and sell orders convey different messages: a dealer is willing to execute buy orders at a premium and sell orders at a discount relative to his own estimate μ_{t-1} of the security's value before the tth transaction.

3.3.2 The Determinants of the Bid-Ask Spread

We now compute the ask and bid prices in this model. First consider the determination of the ask price at time t. In a perfectly competitive market with risk neutral dealers, it will be driven down to the point where dealers make zero expected profits, that is, the point at which, on average, the losses they make on trading with informed investors are offset by their profits on business with liquidity traders. The market maker must consider that he may be in one of two possible situations:

1. He may sell to an informed investor and so lose $a_t - v^H$, as informed investors buy only when $v = v^H$. At time $t - 1$, when he sets the ask price a_t, the market maker assigns a probability $\pi\theta_{t-1}$ to an informed buy (i.e., the probability π of an informed investor being active on the market multiplied by the probability θ_{t-1} that the asset has value v^H).
2. He may sell to a liquidity trader and so book a profit of $a_t - \mu_{t-1}$: *conditional on trading with a liquidity trader*, the dealer's estimate of the final value of the security remains unchanged at μ_{t-1} since no new information has emerged since time $t - 1$. The probability of receiving a buy order from a liquidity trader is $(1 - \pi)/2$ (i.e., the probability $1 - \pi$ of a liquidity trader being active on the market multiplied by the probability $\frac{1}{2}$ that he buys).

The possible trading events that can occur on the buy and sell sides at time t are summarized in Table 3.2.

Using these probabilities, we can write the dealer's expected net profit from transactions at the ask price a_t:

$$\underbrace{\theta_{t-1}\pi\cdot(a_t - v^H) + 0\cdot(a_t - v^L) +}_{\substack{\text{expected profit} \\ \text{from trading with} \\ \text{informed customer}}} \quad \underbrace{\tfrac{1}{2}(1 - \pi)\cdot(a_t - \mu_{t-1})}_{\substack{\text{expected profit} \\ \text{from trading with} \\ \text{uninformed customer}}} \quad + \underbrace{\left\{(1 - \theta_{t-1})\pi + \tfrac{1}{2}(1 - \pi)\right\}\cdot 0.}_{\substack{\text{probability} \\ \text{of no ask-side} \\ \text{customer}}}$$

$$(3.8)$$

To give intuition some help, we focus first on the special case of a market maker who is choosing, at time 0, the first ask and bid quotes of the trading day,

Table 3.2 Transaction Probabilities and Underlying Values by Direction of Trade and Trader Identity

Transaction	Identity of trader	Joint probability	Conditional value
	Informed: $v = v^H$	$\theta_{t-1}\pi$	v^H
Buyer ($d_t = +1$) at a_t	Informed: $v = v^L$	0	v^L
	Uninformed	$(1 - \pi)/2$	μ_{t-1}
	Informed: $v = v^H$	0	v^H
Seller ($d_t = -1$) at b_t	Informed: $v = v^L$	$(1 - \theta_{t-1})\pi$	v^L
	Uninformed	$(1 - \pi)/2$	μ_{t-1}

a_1 and b_1. Assume that this market maker estimates the security's value at its unconditional mean $\mu_0 = (v^H + v^L)/2$ (i.e., assigns probability $\theta_0 = 1/2$ to the value being high). Then the expression for the expected net profit (3.8) becomes:

$$\underbrace{\frac{1}{2}\pi \cdot (a_1 - v^H)}_{\substack{\text{expected profit} \\ \text{from trading with} \\ \text{informed customer}}} + \underbrace{\frac{1}{2}(1 - \pi)(a_1 - \mu_0).}_{\substack{\text{expected profit} \\ \text{from trading with} \\ \text{uninformed customer}}} \tag{3.9}$$

If dealers are competitive, a_1 will be such that this expected profit is zero, so that:

$$a_1 = \mu_0 + \pi\left(v^H - \mu_0\right) = \mu_0 + \underbrace{\frac{\pi}{2}\left(v^H - v^L\right)}_{s_1^a}. \tag{3.10}$$

Hence the ask price at time 1 includes a markup $s_1^a = \frac{\pi}{2}\left(v^H - v^L\right)$ over the initial best estimate of the security's value. Naturally, this markup occurs only if there are informed traders ($\pi > 0$) and if they have price-relevant information (that is, $v^H > v^L$). Symmetrically, the bid price b_1 will be:

$$b_1 = \mu_0 + \pi(v^L - \mu_0) = \mu_0 - \underbrace{\frac{\pi}{2}(v^H - v^L)}_{s_1^b}, \tag{3.11}$$

so that the bid price is at a discount $s_1^b = \frac{\pi}{2}(v^H - v^L)$ on the initial estimate. Hence, the bid-ask spread for the first transaction of the day will be:

$$S_1 \equiv a_1 - b_1 = \pi\left(v^H - v^L\right). \tag{3.12}$$

This makes it clear that the bid-ask spread is a compensation required by dealers to cover the loss they incur when trading with better informed investors. This loss is often referred to as the cost of adverse selection, and accordingly known as the adverse-selection cost component of the spread. And while it refers only to the first spread of the day, equation (3.12) reveals that the adverse selection cost is an increasing function of two variables:

1. *The proportion of informed traders, π:* The more prevalent are the orders placed by informed traders, the greater the risk of loss for dealers, who accordingly require more compensation for supplying liquidity. This shows how asymmetric information generates illiquidity, motivating

policies, such as bans on insider trading and disclosure requirements, that are intended to reduce informational asymmetries.

2. *The volatility of the security's value, as proxied by its range of variation,* $v^H - v^L$: The broader the range of possible values, $v^H - v^L$, the larger the losses incurred by dealers in trading with informed investors. Accordingly, dealers require more compensation (i.e., a wider bid-ask spread) as volatility increases. And in practice, other things being equal, spreads tend to be wider for more volatile securities (see Stoll 2000, table I).

The same reasoning allows us to derive the quotes the dealer will set later during the day, after revising his value estimate on the basis of the orders received: the probability θ_{t-1} that he places on the security being of high value, at some later time $t-1$, will presumably no longer be 1/2. Let us turn back to expression (3.8) for the profit the market maker expects from time t transactions at the ask. Setting this equal to zero, we get the competitive ask price at time t:

$$a_t = \mu_{t-1} + \frac{\pi\theta_{t-1}}{\pi\theta_{t-1} + (1-\pi)\frac{1}{2}}\left(v^H - \mu_{t-1}\right)$$

$$= \mu_{t-1} + \underbrace{\frac{\pi\theta_{t-1}(1-\theta_{t-1})}{\pi\theta_{t-1} + (1-\pi)\frac{1}{2}}\left(v^H - v^L\right)}_{s_t^a}. \tag{3.13}$$

Thus, at any time during the trading day, dealers set their ask price a_t above the fundamental value μ_{t-1}. From the first expression, one sees that the difference $a_t - \mu_{t-1}$ is proportional to the probability of receiving an order from an informed trader, conditional on it being a buy:[10]

$$b_t = \mu_{t-1} - \underbrace{\frac{\pi\theta_{t-1}(1-\theta_{t-1})}{\pi(1-\theta_{t-1}) + (1-\pi)\frac{1}{2}}\left(v^H - v^L\right)}_{s_t^b}, \tag{3.14}$$

---

[10] Denoting by I the arrival of a buy order from an informed trader, U the arrival of a buy order from an uninformed trader, and B the arrival of a buy order, the dealer's probability of trading with an informed investor on the buy side is:

$$Pr(I|B) = \frac{Pr(I\cap B)}{Pr(B)} = \frac{Pr(I\cap B)}{Pr(I\cap B) + Pr(U\cap B)} = \frac{\pi\theta_{t-1}}{\pi\theta_{t-1} + (1-\pi)\frac{1}{2}}.$$

The second expression is obtained by replacing the term μ_{t-1} in brackets with the lagged value of expression (3.6), that is, rewriting it in terms of the probabilities of the high and low outcomes. The same reasoning yields the bid price b_t (left to the reader as an exercise).

implying that dealers bid to buy the security at a discount s_t^b relative to μ_{t-1}. Using equations (3.13) and (3.14), we obtain the bid-ask spread S_t at time t:

$$S_t \equiv a_t - b_t = s_t^a + s_t^b \qquad (3.15)$$

$$= \pi \theta_{t-1}(1 - \theta_{t-1})\left(\frac{1}{\pi \theta_{t-1} + (1-\pi)\frac{1}{2}} + \frac{1}{\pi(1 - \theta_{t-1}) + (1-\pi)\frac{1}{2}}\right)(v^H - v^L).$$

This expression for the spread is more general than (3.12), which is the special case of $\theta_{t-1} = \frac{1}{2}$. It remains true that the spread increases with the proportion of informed traders (π) and the volatility of the security's value ($v^H - v^L$). In addition, expression (3.15) shows that the adverse selection trading cost S_t has a third determinant, namely, dealers' beliefs about the value of the security, θ_{t-1}. Unlike the first two, this determinant varies over time, as the market maker changes his value estimate. The spread is greatest when $\theta_{t-1} = 0.5$, as posited in expression (3.12), and falls to zero as θ_{t-1} goes to 1 or 0. To understand this result, suppose that θ_{t-1} is close to 1. This means that dealers are quite confident that the fair value of the security is v^H, so a new buy order is not a surprise—no news—and does not move their value estimate: a_t is very close to μ_{t-1}. But when $\theta_{t-1} = 0.5$, dealers are highly uncertain about the direction of the market, so their beliefs are highly sensitive to the new orders they receive. Accordingly, the revision of their value estimates is substantial. Therefore the spread is greater when dealers are more uncertain about the value of the security. This is why bid-ask spreads often increase in advance of the release of important information, such as macroeconomic data or earnings announcements. This may also explain why the spreads tend to be larger at market openings.

Let us highlight two features of this model. First, it is a highly stylized model of market making, with adverse selection costs the sole component of the bid-ask spread. As we shall see in Sections 3.4 and 3.5, there may be additional determinants as well. Second, since in this model dealers' expected profit is zero, the adverse selection cost eventually bears on the liquidity traders, who—by "paying" the bid-ask spread—lose exactly what informed traders gain. In our setting, liquidity traders' demand is inelastic: it is independent of the price. Intuitively, in reality, one would expect them to be less likely to place orders when the bid-ask spread is greater. As exercise 6 shows, this situation can lead to a market breakdown, where the spread is so wide that no trade occurs at all. This suggests that asymmetric information may also lead to a complete market freeze, as in the interbank market during the crisis of 2007–8.[11]

---

[11] The insight that adverse selection can shut a market down dates back to Akerlof's celebrated piece in 1970 on the market for "lemons."

3.3.3 How Do Dealers Revise their Quotes?

Up to now, in deriving the zero-profit bid and ask prices that competitive dealers will set, we have taken their beliefs about the underlying value of the security as *given*, that is, μ_{t-1} and θ_{t-1} are given. As bid-ask quotes depend on these beliefs (see equation (3.15)), in order to understand how quotes evolve over time, we must explain how dealers form their beliefs in the light of new orders. For instance, on receiving a flurry of buy orders, a dealer should attach more and more weight to the possibility that the security has a high value.

To see how this is done, consider how dealers receiving a buy or sell order at time t, revise the probability that they attach to the value being high, starting from an initial probability θ_{t-1}. Define θ_t^+ as the probability that dealers assign to high value, $v = v^H$, after they receive a buy order at date t, and let θ_t^- be the corresponding probability in the wake of a sell order. Formally,

$$\theta_t^+ \equiv \Pr\left(v = v^H \mid \Omega_{t-1}, d_t = +1\right),$$
$$\theta_t^- \equiv \Pr\left(v = v^H \mid \Omega_{t-1}, d_t = -1\right).$$

To compute θ_t^+ using Bayes' Rule,[12] let A be the event $v = v^H$ and B the arrival of a buy order at time t. Then $\Pr(A) = \theta_{t-1}$; $\Pr(B) = \pi\theta_{t-1} + (1 - \pi)\frac{1}{2}$ (from Table 3.2); and the probability of a buy order when $v = v^H$ is $\Pr(B|A) = \pi \cdot 1 + (1 - \pi)\frac{1}{2} = (1 + \pi)\frac{1}{2}$, since in this case any informed trader will be a buyer. So the probability that $v = v^H$, conditional on a buy order at time t, is given by:

$$\theta_t^+ = \Pr(A|B) = \frac{\Pr(B|A) \cdot \Pr(A)}{\Pr(B)} = \frac{(1 + \pi)\frac{1}{2} \cdot \theta_{t-1}}{\pi\theta_{t-1} + (1 - \pi)\frac{1}{2}}.$$

The derivation of θ_t^- is analogous:

$$\theta_t^+ = \frac{(1 + \pi)\frac{1}{2}}{\pi\theta_{t-1} + (1 - \pi)\frac{1}{2}}\theta_{t-1}, \tag{3.16}$$

$$\theta_t^- = \frac{(1 - \pi)\frac{1}{2}}{\pi(1 - \theta_{t-1}) + (1 - \pi)\frac{1}{2}}\theta_{t-1}. \tag{3.17}$$

---

[12] Bayes's rule states that the conditional probability of an event A given an event B is:

$$Pr(A|B) = \frac{Pr(A \cap B)}{Pr(B)} = \frac{Pr(B|A) \cdot Pr(A)}{Pr(B)}.$$

It is easy to see that $\theta_t^+ > \theta_{t-1}$. Dealers become more bullish about the security when they get a buy order, insofar as buy orders signal that informed traders may have good news. In a symmetrical way, $\theta_t^- < \theta_{t-1}$: dealers become more bearish when they get a sell order, as this indicates that informed traders may have bad news.

Upon receiving a buy order at time t, the dealers' updated expectation of the security's value is the weighted average of v^H and v^L, where θ_t^+ and $1 - \theta_t^+$ are the updated probability weights:

$$\mu_t^+ = \theta_t^+ v^H + \left(1 - \theta_t^+\right) v^L. \tag{3.18}$$

Recalling that the dealers' estimate before receiving the buy order was μ_{t-1}, their revision of the value in the wake of a buy order is:

$$\mu_t^+ - \mu_{t-1} = \theta_t^+ v^H + \left(1 - \theta_t^+\right) v^L - \left[\theta_{t-1} v^H + (1 - \theta_{t-1}) v^L\right] \tag{3.19}$$

$$= \frac{\pi \theta_{t-1} (1 - \theta_{t-1})}{\pi \theta_{t-1} + (1 - \pi) \frac{1}{2}} \left(v^H - v^L\right) = s_t^a.$$

Analogously, in the wake of a sell order:

$$\mu_t^- - \mu_{t-1} = \theta_t^- v^H + \left(1 - \theta_t^-\right) v^L - \left[\theta_{t-1} v^H + (1 - \theta_{t-1}) v^L\right] \tag{3.20}$$

$$= \frac{\pi \theta_{t-1} (1 - \theta_{t-1})}{\pi (1 - \theta_{t-1}) + (1 - \pi) \frac{1}{2}} \left(v^H - v^L\right) = s_t^b.$$

So s_t^a and s_t^b can be interpreted as the changes to dealers' estimates of the asset value: they correspond to ε_{t+1} in the model described in Section 3.2. The model here simply recognizes that the order flow itself is a source of information when orders can come from informed traders. Now that we know the dynamics of dealers' beliefs, we also know how they will set their quotes. As equation (3.7) shows, they will set their ask price in anticipation of a buy and therefore will set $a_t = \mu_t^+$. Conversely, they will bid $b_t = \mu_t^-$.[13]

---

[13] Note that the ask price at time t can be expressed in terms of the belief θ_{t-1} only (without reference to μ_{t-1}) by using (3.16) in (3.18), and similarly for the bid price:

$$a_t = \mu_t^+ = \frac{(1 + \pi)\theta_{t-1}}{2\pi\theta_{t-1} + 1 - \pi} v^H + \frac{(1 - \pi)(1 - \theta_{t-1})}{2\pi\theta_{t-1} + 1 - \pi} v^L$$

$$b_t = \mu_t^- = \frac{(1 - \pi)\theta_{t-1}}{2\pi(1 - \theta_{t-1}) + 1 - \pi} v^H + \frac{(1 + \pi)(1 - \theta_{t-1})}{2\pi(1 - \theta_{t-1}) + 1 - \pi} v^L.$$

Note that we have used two different but equivalent ways to interpret and derive bid and ask prices. In Section 3.3.2, we obtained them by positing that dealers set price markups s_t^a and s_t^b so as to offset the potential losses on trades with better informed agents with the profits on business with uninformed traders. Here, instead, as illustrated by equations (3.19) and (3.20), we derived the markups s_t^a and s_t^b as the revisions to the dealers' estimate of the value of the security following buy and sell orders. That this change is equal to the markup required by dealers to execute a buy order reflects the fact that the order flow itself contains information.

To sum up, the wedge between the dealers' ask price and their prior estimate of fundamentals is both a compensation for the risk of trading with better informed investors *and* an adjustment to the information contained in order flow. Of course, the two approaches produce the same result: equations (3.19) and (3.20) yield the same ask and bid prices as equations (3.13) and (3.14). The advantage of looking at the revision in beliefs is that it enables us to characterize how dealers change their quotes over time in response to the order flow. Therefore, if we specify a time series for the order flow, we can now map out the corresponding time path of quotes, as we do in the next section.

3.3.4 Price Discovery

Buy orders execute at the ask price, sell orders at the bid, so the transaction price at date t is:

$$P_t = \begin{cases} a_t = \mu_t^+ & \text{if } d_t = +1, \\ b_t = \mu_t^- & \text{if } d_t = -1. \end{cases} \tag{3.21}$$

Hence:

$$p_t = \mu_t = \theta_t v^H + (1 - \theta_t) v^L, \tag{3.22}$$

where $\theta_t = \theta_t^+$ if $d_t = +1$, and $\theta_t = \theta_t^-$ if $d_t = -1$. Thus, transaction prices reflect all the information available to market makers at time t, which is to say the information Ω_{t-1} they had at time $t - 1$ plus the direction of the order flow that they receive at time t.

Can we therefore conclude that transaction prices always reflect all available information, as claimed by the EMH? The notion of "all available information" is problematic in an environment in which traders have asymmetric information. Does it mean both public and private information, or only public information?

In other words, in this context does the EMH apply in strong, semi-strong, or weak form?

The semi-strong form states that transactions take place at fair values given all *public* information. In our model, public information at date t is the order flow observed up to this date, $\Omega_t = \{d_1, d_2, \ldots, d_t\}$. As $p_t = \mu_t = E(v \mid \Omega_t)$, the semi-strong EMH holds true in this model. This might seem surprising, insofar as the bid-ask spread is usually construed as a friction that causes temporary deviations of transaction prices from fundamental asset values. But in this model the difference between the execution prices for buy orders and sell orders is due entirely to the fact that they convey different information. Thus, far from being a symptom of inefficiency, the bid-ask spread is part of the mechanism by which dealers incorporate the information contained in the order flow into the price process.

The strong version of the EMH states that transactions always take place at fair values given all public *and* private information. For instance, suppose that informed traders learn that $v = v^H$. If the EMH holds in strong form, then all trades take place at prices equal to v^H (insofar as market participants get no further information). At first glance, it seems impossible for markets to be informationally efficient in this sense. How could prices ever reflect information that is not yet available to all market participants? Yet in this model this is a possibility. To see this, suppose that $\pi = 1$. In this case, the quotes posted by dealers at time 1 (setting $\pi = 1$ in equations (3.13) and (3.14)) will be:

$$a_1 = v^H,$$
$$b_1 = v^L.$$

If $v = v^H$, then informed traders buy and the first transaction of the day is crossed at $p_1 = a_1 = v^H$.[14] Upon observing this transaction, dealers infer that the value of the security is high since all traders are informed and they are buying. Thus, $\theta_1 = 1$, and all subsequent transactions are at v^H (only insofar as no further information arrives, of course). Similar reasoning applies when $v = v^L$. Thus, the strong form version of the EMH holds, despite the fact that dealers initially have less information than some market participants. This is because dealers draw rational inferences from the order flow; that is, they *learn* about private information from the order flow and adjust their quotes accordingly.

Of course, this example is extreme (positing that $\pi = 1$), but it does suggest that prices can adjust gradually to the fair value of the security as dealers learn it

---

[14] In this case, informed investors are just indifferent between buying or not trading. We assume that they buy.

from the order flow. The process by which private information is incorporated into prices and the market becomes informationally efficient is called *price discovery*. Thus, one advantage of the model presented here is that it allows us to study whether and how fast price discovery occurs.

Ultimately these questions bear on the dynamics of dealers' beliefs about the asset's fair value. For instance, suppose as before that $v = v^H$. Equation (3.22) shows that transaction prices will converge to v^H if θ_t goes to 1, in other words, if dealers are increasingly confident that the value of the security is high. Thus, the speed of price discovery is the speed at which θ_t goes to 1. In this model, it can be shown formally that price discovery always obtains in the long run if there are some informed traders in the market ($\pi > 0$) and that its speed increases with the fraction π of informed investors.

A formal derivation of these claims is tedious, but the intuition is simple. In the absence of informed trading, the order flow is balanced, with 50% buy and 50% sell orders. However, with informed trading, the flow is unbalanced and its tendency provides information on value. For instance, if $v = v^H$, the proportion of buy orders will be more than 50%; if $v = v^L$, sell orders will exceed 50%. The speed of the learning process is then determined by how fast dealers become confident that buy orders make up more or less than 50%, which in turn is determined by the proportion of informed traders: buy orders will dominate very quickly if π is close to 1 and $v = v^H$; sell orders will predominate if $v = v^L$.

A good way to illustrate these intuitions is to simulate the model. Assume that $v^H = 102$, $v^L = 98$, and $\theta_0 = 0.5$. Thus, at the start of the trading day, dealers estimate the asset value at $\mu_0 = 100$. Initially, suppose that $\pi = 0.3$ and that the true value of the security is $v = v^H$. On this basis, we draw a sequence of one hundred orders (each of which is a buy with probability $\pi + (1 - \pi)/2 = 0.65$), and record the evolution of dealers' beliefs θ_t associated with this specific sequence of order arrivals, as well as the evolution of transaction prices p_t. For instance, suppose that the two first orders are buys and the third is a sell. Equation (3.16) yields the corresponding dealers' beliefs: $\theta_1 = 0.65$, $\theta_2 = 0.77$, and $\theta_3 = 0.65$.[15] Equation (3.22) gives the corresponding sequence of transaction prices: $p_1 = 100.6$, $p_2 = 101.10$, $p_3 = 100.6$.

---

[15] A convenient way to express the updating of dealers' beliefs θ_t is to recast equations (3.16) and (3.17) in terms of the odds ratio, which yields a linear first-order difference equation:

$$\frac{\theta_t^+}{1 - \theta_t^+} = \frac{1 + \pi}{1 - \pi} \cdot \frac{\theta_{t-1}}{1 - \theta_{t-1}} \quad \text{and} \quad \frac{\theta_t^-}{1 - \theta_t^-} = \frac{1 - \pi}{1 + \pi} \cdot \frac{\theta_{t-1}}{1 - \theta_{t-1}}.$$

Therefore the odds ratio at time t is simply a function of the order imbalance x_t, defined as the cumulative difference between buy and sell orders up to time t:

$$\frac{\theta_t}{1 - \theta_t} = \frac{\theta_0}{1 - \theta_0} \left(\frac{1 + \pi}{1 - \pi}\right)^{x_t}, \text{where } x_t \equiv \sum_{\tau=1}^{t} d_\tau.$$

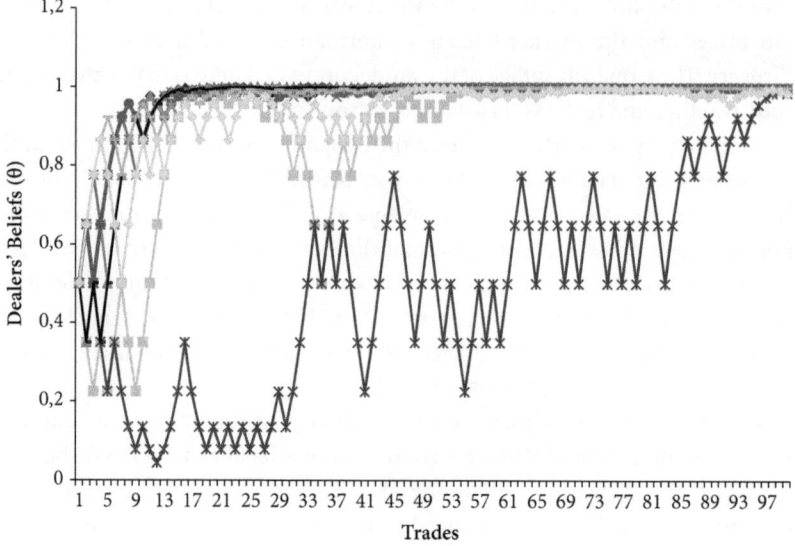

Figure 3.1 Evolution of dealers' beliefs.

We repeat this experiment ten times, drawing ten different random sequences of one hundred orders with the same value of π. Figure 3.1 shows the pattern of dealers' beliefs in each experiment. Clearly, the probability assigned to the high value by the dealers converges to 1 (they eventually discover the correct value), and relatively quickly in most cases.

Next, we measure price discovery by computing the squared difference between the transaction price p_t at date t and v^H ("the pricing error"):

$$PD_t = \left(p_t - v^H\right)^2. \tag{3.23}$$

As dealers learn about the value of the security, PD_t goes to zero; that is, it is an inverse measure of price discovery. Figure 3.2 shows the corresponding evolution for the pricing error in each experiment. Again, in most cases it declines quickly as dealers discover the true value.

To see how the proportion of informed traders π affects price discovery, we run the experiment again with three different values of π: 0.1, 0.5, and 0.9. Figure 3.3 shows the evolution of the squared pricing errors, PD_t (for each value of π) averaged across the ten simulations: $\sum_{i=1}^{i=10} PD_{it}/10$. The middle line summarizes the results for $\pi = 0.5$: on average, full price discovery is achieved after fifteen trades. The bottom line shows that when informed trading is predominant, to the point that nine in ten orders are placed by informed traders, price discovery speeds up considerably: on average, full price discovery

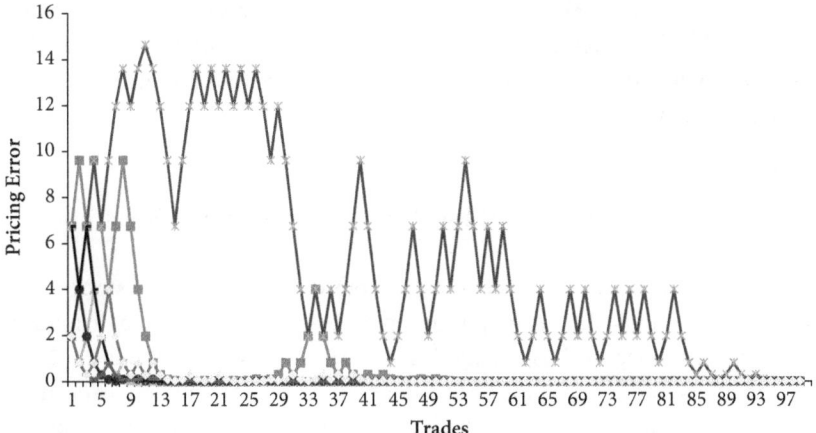

Figure 3.2 Evolution of pricing errors.

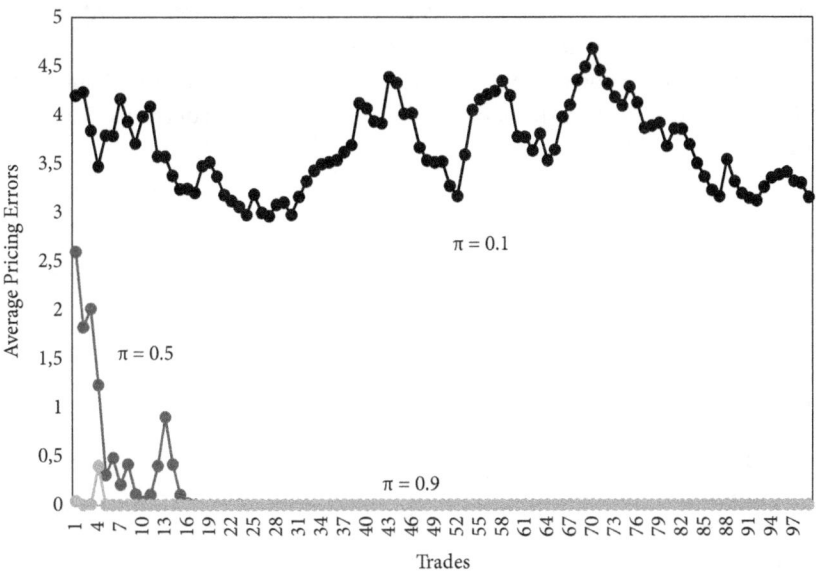

Figure 3.3 Speed of price discovery and the level of informed trading.

occurs after just five trades. In contrast, when informed trading is rare (only one in ten orders placed by informed traders), convergence is much slower—almost imperceptible even after one hundred transactions—because the signal-to-noise ratio in the order flow is much smaller.

These observations on price discovery pose a conundrum for market organizers: more frequent informed trading widens bid-ask spreads and tends to make the market illiquid, as shown in equation (3.15), but it also speeds price discovery. Intuitively, the presence of informed traders is necessary for information to be incorporated in prices. At least in the short run, therefore, there is a trade off between liquidity and informational efficiency.

3.3.5 The Implications for Price Movements and Volatility

Now let us go back to the trade and quote data for the AGF stock in the introduction (Table 3.1). A graphical representation of the price dynamics for AGF is given in Figure 3.4 (considering the first fifty trades on March 26, 2001).

The upper and lower curves chart the best ask and bid quotes, respectively. The dots indicate the prices at which trades take place. It is apparent from the figure that prices adjust in the direction of the order flow. For instance, most of the first ten trades are initiated by sellers placing market orders, and the midprice declines. Conversely, trades twenty-five to forty are mostly triggered by buy market orders, and the midprice rises.

The model developed in this section provides a framework for explaining this effect of order flow on price movements. Recall that (see equations (3.19) and (3.20)):

$$\mu_t^+ = \mu_{t-1} + s_t^a,$$
$$\mu_t^- = \mu_{t-1} - s_t^b,$$

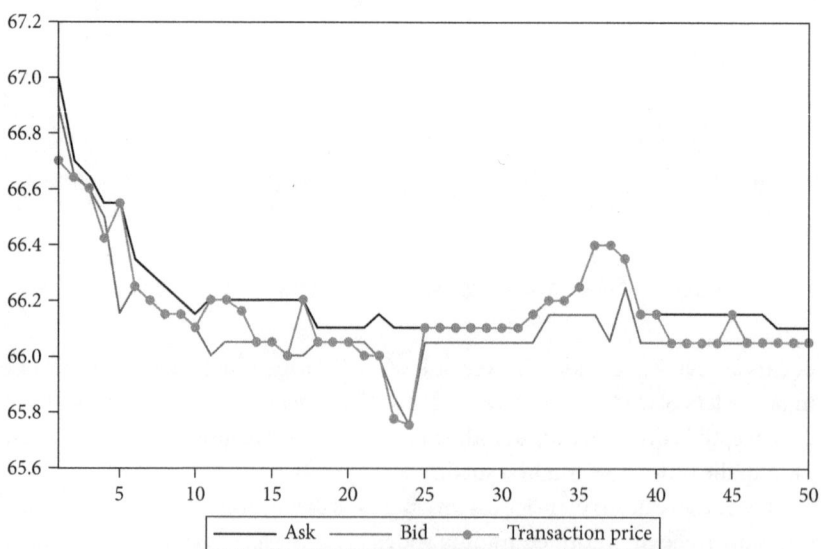

Figure 3.4 Quotes and transaction prices for AGF (fifty first trades of the day).

where the expressions for s_t^a and s_t^b are given by equations (3.13) and (3.14). These equations can be written more compactly as:

$$\mu_t = \mu_{t-1} + s(d_t)d_t, \tag{3.24}$$

where:

$$s(d_t) = \begin{cases} s_t^a & \text{if } d_t = +1 \\ s_t^b & \text{if } d_t = -1. \end{cases}$$

The dealers' estimate of the value of the security after the tth transaction, μ_t, depends on the direction of the order flow; market orders are informative.

Now recall that dealers set their quotes at time t so as to bracket their prior estimate of the security's value, μ_{t-1}, since:

$$a_t = \mu_t^+ = \mu_{t-1} + s_t^a, \tag{3.25}$$
$$b_t = \mu_t^- = \mu_{t-1} - s_t^b. \tag{3.26}$$

Thus they will revise their quotes upward after buy orders and downward after sell orders, exactly as observed in Figure 3.4 for AGF. As an illustration, consider the numerical example analyzed in the previous section ($v^H = 102$, $v^L = 98$, $\theta_0 = \frac{1}{2}$, and $\pi = \frac{1}{2}$). On these assumptions we readily find, from equations (3.13) and (3.14), that $a_1 = 101$ and $b_1 = 99$. Now, assume that the first order is a buy ($d_1 = +1$). This leads dealers to revise the probability of $v = v^H$ upward to $\theta_1 = \frac{3}{4}$ and correspondingly mark up their value estimate to $\mu_1 = 101$. Again using equations (3.13) and (3.14), dealers will raise their bid and ask quotes to $a_2 = 101.6$ and $b_2 = 100$ respectively. If the first order is a sell order, then $\mu_1 = 99$ instead, and $\theta_1 = \frac{1}{4}$. After this trade, dealers lower their bid and ask quotes to $a_2 = 100$ and $b_2 = 98.4$.

As a result, trade-to-trade changes in transaction prices are correlated with the order flow. All transactions take place either at the ask price or the bid price, so that $p_t = \mu_t$. Therefore, equation (3.24) also implies:

$$p_t - p_{t-1} = \mu_t - \mu_{t-1} = s(d_t)d_t. \tag{3.27}$$

Hence, in this framework the difference between the price of the $(t-1)^{th}$ transaction and the tth transaction is entirely determined by the direction of the tth order.[16] The last equation is similar to equation (3.4), except that it explicitly

---

[16] Equation (3.27) implies that the price change in any given time period is proportional to the order imbalance during the period. Thus, it lays the foundation for the price impact regression discussed in Section 2.3.2. Here, the order size is fixed, so only the direction of orders is informative. Chapter 4 considers a more complex environment in which both order direction and size are informative.

relates the change in price ε_t to the order flow d_t: here the price innovation ε_t is equal to $s(d_t)d_t$. This makes sense because, under asymmetric information, the order flow is informative.

Finally, from equation (3.27) we can compute the variance of price changes:

$$\mathrm{var}(\Delta p_t) = \mathrm{var}(s(d_t)d_t). \tag{3.28}$$

Return volatility at time t is thus determined both by the size of the bid-ask spread $s(d_t)$ and by the uncertainty of the direction of the order flow d_t. This shows that trading is also necessarily a source of volatility, being a source of information. Moreover, equation (3.28) suggests that return volatility might not be constant during the trading day, and that it should be correlated with the bid-ask spread. As dealers' value estimate becomes more accurate, their quotes should become less sensitive to order flow, the spread should narrow, and return volatility should decrease. Interestingly, this pattern is observed in equity markets: from the opening to the mid-session, both volatility and bid-ask spreads decline on average, before picking up again as the market close approaches. Of course, our interpretation presupposes that private information is obtained mostly at the start of the trading day or before: if during the day dealers come to suspect that some new price-relevant information—say, a rumor of a takeover bid—is guiding the order flow, they will widen their spreads again, to protect themselves against traders who may have a better sense of the likely outcome.

Expression (3.28) for return volatility is based on the idea that new information affects stock prices only via the orders placed by informed traders. In reality, much new information takes the form of public news, which leads all market participants to revise their quotes and therefore leads to price changes without triggering any trades. Hence, the volatility of stock returns also reflects the variance of price changes induced by such public news. Models with informed trading can easily be adapted to include public news, as will be seen in Section 5.2.1.

3.4 Price Dynamics with Order-Processing Costs

The risk of losing money in trading with better informed investors is the only cost borne by liquidity suppliers that we have considered so far. In reality, however, processing a transaction costs time and money: trading fees, clearing and settlement fees, paperwork and back office work, telephone time, and so on.[17] Naturally, liquidity suppliers also require a compensation for these so-called "order-processing costs." To explore how they affect the bid-ask spread and the resulting dynamics of transaction prices, we extend the framework developed in the previous section by assuming an order-processing cost equal to γ per share. In reality, some of these costs are per transaction, others per dollar traded or per share traded. Most of our results here would also hold if order-processing costs were γ per dollar traded or per transaction (see exercise 1).

3.4.1 Bid-Ask Spread with Order-Processing Costs

Consider again the determination of the bid-ask spread for, say, the tth transaction. Suppose that a buy order is received. To break even, a dealer's ask price must now cover not only the expected loss from trading with potentially informed buyers s_t^a but also the order-processing cost γ. So equation (3.25) must be modified as follows:

$$a_t = \mu_{t-1} + \gamma + s_t^a. \tag{3.29}$$

Dealers simply pass the processing cost on to liquidity demanders. By a similar reasoning, the bid price posted by dealers at time t is:

$$b_t = \mu_{t-1} - \gamma - s_t^b. \tag{3.30}$$

Hence, the bid-ask spread:

$$S_t \equiv a_t - b_t = 2\gamma + s_t^a + s_t^b \tag{3.31}$$

now has two different components: order-processing cost (2γ) and adverse-selection cost $\left(s_t^a + s_t^b\right)$. For practical purposes, it is important to gauge their relative importance in determining the spread. For instance, the policy measures needed to alleviate illiquidity are not the same in the two cases: technological upgrades and rules encouraging competition among trading platforms can reduce processing costs, while action against insider trading may mitigate adverse selection.

How the two components of the bid-ask spread can be measured separately is not obvious, since at first glance they have the same effect. In the next section,

---

[17] Automation reduced some of these costs considerably, but they are still not negligible.

however, we will see that the two components carry very different implications for the dynamics of transaction prices, which gives us a way to estimate the components of the spread using data on order flow and transaction prices.

3.4.2 Price Dynamics with Order-Processing and Adverse-Selection Costs

As trades take place at bid and ask prices, the transaction price at time t can be written as:

$$p_t = \mu_{t-1} + (s(d_t) + \gamma) d_t, \tag{3.32}$$

where $s(d_t) = s_t^a$ if $d_t = 1$, and $s(d_t) = s_t^b$ if $d_t = -1$. As $\mu_t = \mu_{t-1} + s(d_t) d_t$, we obtain:

$$p_t = \mu_t + \gamma d_t. \tag{3.33}$$

Thus, in the presence of order-processing costs, transaction prices deviate from fair value given all public information, including the direction of trade initiation.

The deviation is equal to the processing cost (as $|p_t - \mu_t| = \gamma$). Intuitively, dealers cover this cost by executing buy (sell) orders at a markup (discount) relative to their value estimate based on all public information.

Thus, order-processing costs induce *transient* deviations of transaction prices from fundamental values, so called because these deviations do not correspond to a revision in dealers' value expectations. Accordingly, they are subsequently corrected, at least in part by opposite price movements ("reversals").

To see this, consider the arrival of a buy order at time t and define its short-term (ST) price impact as the deviation of the transaction price from the immediately preceding fundamental value, μ_{t-1}:

$$\text{ST impact} \equiv p_t - \mu_{t-1} = a_t - \mu_{t-1}.$$

Using equation (3.29), one can see that the immediate effect of a buy market order is to push the price up by:

$$\text{ST impact} = s_t^a + \gamma > 0. \tag{3.34}$$

Now consider the long-term (LT) price impact, that is, its effect on the average price at a distant time $t + T$, p_{t+T}. At that time, by equation (3.33), the price will be given by $p_{t+T} = \mu_{t+T} + \gamma d_{t+T}$. Its expected value as of time t is then:

$$E(p_{t+T} \mid \Omega_{t-1}, d_t = 1) = E(\mu_{t+T}|\Omega_{t-1}, d_t = 1) + \gamma E(d_{t+T}|\Omega_{t-1}, d_t = 1) \quad (3.35)$$
$$= \mu_t + \gamma E(d_{t+T}|\Omega_{t-1}, d_t = 1)$$
$$= \mu_{t-1} + s_t^a + \gamma E(d_{t+T}|\Omega_{t-1}, d_t = 1),$$

where the first step follows by the law of iterated expectations and the second by (3.32).

Suppose that $t + T$ is so far ahead that by then the currently pending uncertainty about true value of the asset (v^H or v^L) will have already been resolved–the fundamental publicly revealed (say, $t + T$ is beyond the end of the trading day). Then, the direction of trade at time t (d_t) has no predictive power for its direction at $t + T$ (d_{t+T}). Hence $E(d_{t+T}|\Omega_{t-1}, d_t = 1) = 0$, so that:

$$E\left(p_{t+T}|\Omega_{t-1}, d_t = 1\right) = \mu_{t-1} + s_t^a.$$

Thus the long run impact of the buy order at time t includes only the informational component of the bid-ask spread, and not the order-processing cost γ:[18]

$$LT\,impact = s_t^a. \quad (3.36)$$

Hence, in the long term, only the informational effect persists:

$$ST\,impact - LT\,impact = \gamma. \quad (3.37)$$

In the absence of order-processing costs ($\gamma = 0$), the short-term impact of the buy order is equal to the long-term impact, because the impact is due entirely to the informational content of the buy order. In contrast, in presence of order-processing costs, the short run impact exceeds the long run impact by an amount equal to the processing cost, creating a further temporary price blip at time t.

---

[18] Working out the medium-term effect of the buy order on price is somewhat trickier. Suppose that time $t + T$ is not so distant, and that by then the true value of the security is not yet publicly revealed. In this case d_t has some predictive value for the future order flow d_{t+T}. To see this, consider that a buy order at t leads to an upward revision from θ_{t-1} to θ_t^+ in the probability that the stock has a high value, as described in equation (3.16), and so it increases the probability of further buy orders from informed investors at $t + T$, that is:

$$E(d_{t+T}|\Omega_{t-1}, d_t = 1) > E(d_{t+T}|\Omega_{t-1}).$$

This increased probability is associated with an additional medium-term price impact beyond s_t^a. To see this, compare the expected price at $t + T$ before and after the buy order at time t:

$$E(p_{t+T} \mid \Omega_{t-1}, d_t = 1) - E(p_{t+T}|\Omega_{t-1})$$
$$= s_t^a + \gamma[E(d_{t+T}|\Omega_{t-1}, d_t = 1) - E(d_{t+T}|\Omega_{t-1})] > s_t^a,$$

where we have used equation (3.35). In exercise 10 the reader is asked the precise value of the revision in the expectation of d_{t+T} in this expression.

Thus, after the initial price increase, the price level tends to revert. A similar decomposition can be obtained if the order at time t is a sell order: its immediate effect is to reduce the price, but in the long run the price bounces back and partly reverts to its initial level. Thus, with order-processing costs, trade-to-trade changes in prices will show a negative serial correlation. As Chapter 2 explains, Roll's model exploits this feature to derive an estimator of the bid-ask spread and corresponds to a special version of the current model where the bid-ask spread is due only to order-processing costs. These effects can also be observed in Figure 3.4. For instance, the sequence of buy orders from the twenty-fifth to the fortieth transaction trigger a price increase, but part of it is transient so that after the fortieth transaction the price partly reverts.

To summarize, buy orders and sell orders create upward and downward price pressures, which are permanent only to the extent that illiquidity is due to asymmetric information. The transient component is instead a compensation for the costs borne by liquidity suppliers to accommodate temporary order imbalances.

As order-processing costs and asymmetric information typically coexist, market orders have both permanent and temporary effects. This observation can be used to measure order-processing and adverse selection costs, as Chapter 5 explains.

Box 3.1 Dealers' Rents as an Additional Component of the Bid-Ask Spread

In this section, we interpret γ as a cost per share borne by dealers to execute market orders. But γ may equally well be viewed as a measure of dealers' rents from market power. To see this, suppose that order-processing costs are equal to γ^c and that dealers require an expected profit per share *at least* equal to γ^r on each transaction. It follows immediately that to achieve an expected profit of γ^r for executing a buy market order, dealers must charge an ask price equal to:

$$a_t = \mu_{t-1} + \gamma^c + \gamma^r + s_t^a,$$

so that the term $2\gamma = 2(\gamma^c + \gamma^r)$ in expression (3.31) for the bid-ask spread S_t will reflect not only the dealers' operating costs γ^c but also their non-competitive rents γ^r.

By the same token, we can repeat the reasoning of Section 3.4.2 above to conclude that after the execution of a buy market order the price level will revert by an amount averaging $\gamma^c + \gamma^r$. Similar remarks apply to sell orders. Thus, considering only the dynamics of prices after a trade, one cannot measure separately the order-processing component and the rent component of the bid-ask spread. This implies that what is termed the "order-processing cost" component must be interpreted with care, since it may in fact capture both processing costs proper and the rents captured by dealers in supplying liquidity.

In reality, dealers often earn rents. Indeed, some markets charge a fee on market participants to become dealers. The level of this fee is an indicator of the economic value of being a dealer and is a determinant of the number of dealers. Competition among dealers may be imperfect also due to collusion. In the 1990s, Nasdaq dealers were accused of implicitly colluding on excessive spreads (see Christie, Harris, and Schultz 1994; Christie and Schultz 1994). Chapter 4 offers a more systematic analysis of the way trading rules can affect liquidity suppliers' ability to earn rents at the expense of liquidity demanders.

3.5 Price Dynamics with Inventory Risk

In continuous markets, buy and sell orders from traders seeking liquidity do not arrive at the same time. This creates temporary order imbalances, and one important function of liquidity suppliers is to serve as counterparty when the order flow is unbalanced. For instance, a dealer may execute a sell order for five thousand shares of a stock, which increases his position in it. Next, ten minutes later, he receives a buy order for one thousand shares, which allows him to pare his extra inventory down. Finally, he receives another buy order for four thousand shares, and so reverts to his initial position. Over time, the net position taken by the dealer is zero. His role was simply to balance demand and supply over time.

However, this role exposes the dealer to inventory risk, that is, the possibility of a change in the value of his holdings because of, say, news about the underlying fundamentals. Assuming that dealers are risk averse, they will require a compensating risk premium, known as inventory holding cost—even if they are not at risk of being picked off by traders with superior information. Thus, inventory risk is another important determinant of the bid-ask spread, as was first shown formally by Stoll (1978). Here we analyze the effect of inventory risk on dealers' pricing policy and discuss its implications for the spread and for price dynamics.

In order to isolate the impact of inventory holding costs, we make two simplifying assumptions throughout this section. First, the order flow is not correlated with news about fundamentals; that is, it is not driven by traders with an informational advantage over market makers ($\pi = 0$). Second, dealers have no order-processing costs ($\gamma = 0$).

Before trading at any time t, the representative dealer has cash c_t and a starting inventory of the risky security z_t, where $z_t > 0$ indicates a long and $z_t < 0$ a short position.[19] Marked to market, his initial wealth w_t is the value of his cash and security position before trading at time t, evaluated at time t market price p_t:

$$w_t = p_t z_t + c_t. \tag{3.38}$$

The dealer's concern is how his trade at time t will affect his next-period wealth $w_{t+1} = p_{t+1} z_{t+1} + c_{t+1}$, where z_{t+1} and c_{t+1} are his stock inventory and cash position after trading at time t.

The market is organized as a call auction where the representative dealer is assumed to behave competitively, that is, to take the price p_t as given in choosing the number of shares y_t that he is willing to supply:[20] $y_t > 0$ indicates the dealer's offer to sell y_t shares, and $y_t < 0$ means that he is willing to bid to buy $|y_t|$ shares. Thus the dealer's inventory after selling y_t shares is:

$$z_{t+1} = z_t - y_t, \tag{3.39}$$

and his corresponding cash position after receiving payment for those shares of $p_t y_t$ is:

$$c_{t+1} = c_t + p_t y_t. \tag{3.40}$$

Thus, the dealer's end-of-period wealth, as a function of the amount y_t he sells at time t, is:

$$w_{t+1} = p_{t+1} z_{t+1} + c_{t+1} = p_{t+1}(z_t - y_t) + c_t + p_t y_t, \tag{3.41}$$

using (3.39) and (3.40) in the definition of w_{t+1}.

For ease of exposition, in Section 3.5.1 we start with a static setting with a single trading period, where dealers trading at time 0 expect to liquidate their holdings at a price equal to the fundamental value at time 1, that is, $p_1 = v = \mu_0 + \varepsilon_1$. Then, in Section 3.5.2, we turn to a simple setting with two trading periods, where initially each dealer anticipates that the subsequent value of his inventory will be determined by the future order flow. In this dynamic setting,

---

[19] Since we are considering a representative dealer, z_t must be interpreted as the dealers' aggregate inventory.

[20] In Section 4.3.2, we analyze the imperfectly competitive case in which dealers take account of the impact of their orders on the clearing price (i.e., exert market power). But as we explain there, the effects of inventory risk on price dynamics, our topic in this section, do not qualitatively depend on whether dealers are competitive or not.

prices respond not only to the current order flow but also to the anticipated order flow, so that in equilibrium the pattern of orders, prices, and dealers' inventories over time is jointly determined.

3.5.1 A Static Model: Inventory Risk and Liquidity

Let us first consider a static setting, where trading takes place at time $t = 0$ and the asset pays out its fundamental value v at time $t = 1$. Thus dealers value their final inventory position z_1 at $v \cdot z_1$. Using expression (3.41), their final wealth is:

$$w_1 = v(z_0 - y_0) + c_0 + p_0 y_0. \tag{3.42}$$

Since dealers are risk averse, their objective function is increasing in the expected value of their end-of-period wealth $E_0(w_1)$ and decreasing in its riskiness, which we measure by its variance $var_0(w_1)$.

The most commonly used formulation of the objective function of risk-averse investors (and one that will be used again in Chapter 4) is the linear mean-variance function:

$$U = E_t(w_{t+1}) - \frac{\rho}{2} var_t(w_{t+1}), \tag{3.43}$$

where ρ is a measure of risk aversion. Computing the objective (3.43) for the dealer's end-of-period wealth in expression (3.42) and denoting the variance of ε_1 by σ_ε^2, we get:

$$
\begin{aligned}
U &= E_0(v)(z_0 - y_0) + c_0 + p_0 y_0 - \frac{\rho}{2}(z_0 - y_0)^2 \sigma_\varepsilon^2 \\
&= \mu_0(z_0 - y_0) + c_0 + p_0 y_0 - \frac{\rho}{2}(z_0 - y_0)^2 \sigma_\varepsilon^2,
\end{aligned}
$$

recalling that $E_0(v) \equiv \mu_0$. The dealer chooses his supply of shares y_0 so as to maximize this objective function. The dealer's first-order condition with respect to y_0 is:

$$\frac{\partial U}{\partial y_0} = -\mu_0 + p_0 + \rho(z_0 - y_0)\sigma_\varepsilon^2 = 0,$$

which yields his inverse supply function (i.e., the price at which he is willing to supply a given amount of shares):

$$p_0 = \mu_0 + \rho\sigma_\varepsilon^2(y_0 - z_0). \tag{3.44}$$

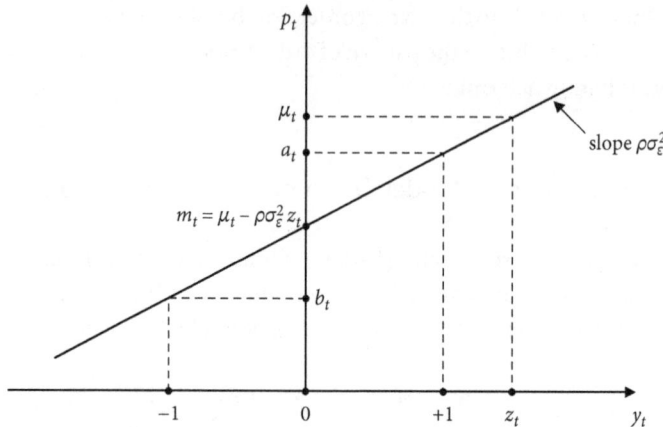

Figure 3.5 Dealers' supply and quotes in the static model with risk-averse dealers.

Thus, as shown in Figure 3.5, if the price equals the fundamental value $E_0(v) = \mu_0$, so that the market offers no compensation for inventory holding costs, the dealer supplies his entire initial inventory z_0, so as to reduce his end-of-period inventory ($z_1 = z_0 - y_0$) to zero. But if the market offers a higher price and therefore a risk premium, the dealer is willing to supply more shares, thus taking a risky short position. The size of the short position depends on the dealer's degree of risk aversion ρ and on the stock's fundamental volatility σ_ε^2: the more risk averse the dealer and the riskier the stock, the fewer shares the dealer will supply. Conversely, if the price is below the fundamental value, the dealer will supply less than his initial inventory: if shares trade at a discount relative to their fundamental value, he is willing to hold a long position until time 1.

In equilibrium, the representative dealer must supply exactly the amount of shares needed to satisfy the incoming order flow, that is, $y_0 = q_0$, where q_0 is the number of shares demanded by investors. Replacing this condition in the dealer's supply function (3.44) yields the equilibrium price:

$$p_0 = \underbrace{\mu_0 - \rho\sigma_\varepsilon^2 z_0}_{\text{midquote } m_0} + \rho\sigma_\varepsilon^2 q_0 = m_0 + \rho\sigma_\varepsilon^2 q_0. \qquad (3.45)$$

Hence the equilibrium midquote m_0 reflects not only the stock's expected fundamental value, but also an inventory risk adjustment: it is the price at which the dealer is willing to hold precisely his initial inventory. As shown in Figure 3.5, the equilibrium price, p_0, depends on whether the dealer receives a buy or a sell order. The ask price for a buy order of size $|q_0|$ exceeds the midquote, reflecting the need to reward the dealer for supplying shares out of his inventory, while the bid price for a sell order of the same size incorporates a discount to reward him for adding one extra unit to it:

$$p_0 \equiv \begin{cases} a_0 = m_0 + \rho\sigma_\varepsilon^2|q_0| & \text{if } q_0 > 0, \\ b_0 = m_0 - \rho\sigma_\varepsilon^2|q_0| & \text{if } q_0 < 0. \end{cases} \qquad (3.46)$$

Figure 3.5 illustrates the ask and bid prices for an order of unit size ($q = 1$). Hence the bid-ask spread is determined by the dealers' risk aversion ρ, the stock's fundamental volatility σ_ε^2 and the size of the trade q, in other words, by inventory holding costs:

$$S = 2\rho\sigma_\varepsilon^2 q. \qquad (3.47)$$

Chapter 4 will further examine the determination of the bid-ask spread in the presence of inventory risk and specifically how market liquidity is affected by the number of dealers competing in the market.

3.5.2 A Dynamic Model: Anticipated Inventory and Prices

A limitation of the static model in the previous section is that it does not take into account that dealers can manage the inventory risk arising from filling orders by unwinding the resulting change in inventory over time. To capture this point, in this section we present a multi-period setting where prices reflect both current inventories and the time path of future inventories, that is, prices react both to the current and the expected order flow. Then, both the immediate price impact of an order and its subsequent persistence depend on how long the resulting change in inventories will last before being unwound by offsetting orders.

These holding-period effects can be simply captured by extending the static model of the previous section to a setting with two trading periods, 0 and 1, where dealers receive orders in both periods and engage in dynamic inventory management. Hence, at $t = 0$ they set their quotes in anticipation of future order flow at $t = 1$. For tractability, the future order flow is assumed to be fully anticipated, that is, dealers already know q_1 when they trade at time 0. At time $t = 2$, the representative dealer liquidates his position in the risky asset at the fundamental value $v = \mu_0 + \varepsilon_1 + \varepsilon_2$, where ε_1 and ε_2 are the two innovations in the fundamental value of the security that become known immediately after trading at $t = 0$ and $t = 1$, respectively.

The dealer's final wealth at $t = 2$ is the sum of his cash and inventory position:

$$w_2 = vz_2 + c_2 = v(z_1 - y_1) + c_1 + p_1 y_1, \qquad (3.48)$$

where in the second step the final inventory z_2 is re-expressed using (3.39) and the final cash balance c_2 using (3.40). Repeating the process again for z_1 and c_1, the dealer's final wealth can be rewritten as:

$$w_2 = v(z_0 - y_0 - y_1) + c_0 + p_0 y_0 + p_1 y_1, \qquad (3.49)$$

which can be rearranged to re-express the dealer's final wealth as the sum of the liquidation value of his initial position and his trading profits at $t = 0$ and $t = 1$:

$$w_2 = (v z_0 + c_0) + (p_0 - v) y_0 + (p_1 - v) y_1. \qquad (3.50)$$

The dealer is facing a dynamic optimization problem, where in choosing supply at time 0, y_0, he needs to anticipate his trading strategy at time 1, y_1. The way to solve problems of this type is by backward induction: first, solve for the optimal trading strategy at time 1 for any given positions inherited from time 0; then, work back in time to find the optimal strategy at time 0, correctly anticipating subsequent optimal choices at time 1 and their impact on trading profits at time 1.

In the first step, i.e., the choice of optimal supply at $t = 1$, y_1, the dealer faces the same static problem analyzed in Section 3.5.1. Thus the equilibrium price at $t = 1$ is given by applying expression (3.45) to time 1 (rather than time 0):

$$p_1 = \mu_1 - \rho \sigma_\varepsilon^2 z_1 + \rho \sigma_\varepsilon^2 q_1. \qquad (3.51)$$

Hence, the dealers' trading profits at $t = 1$ are:

$$(p_1 - v) y_1 = (\mu_1 - \rho \sigma_\varepsilon^2 z_1 + \rho \sigma_\varepsilon^2 q_1 - v) y_1. \qquad (3.52)$$

The market clears in both periods: $y_1 = q_1$ and $z_1 = z_0 - q_0$. Hence, recalling that $v = \mu_1 + \varepsilon_2$, the equilibrium value of trading profits at $t = 1$ is:

$$(p_1 - v) q_1 = [\rho \sigma_\varepsilon^2 \underbrace{(z_0 - q_0 - q_1)}_{z_2} + \varepsilon_2](-q_1). \qquad (3.53)$$

This expression shows that the dealer's profits on his trading at $t = 1$ equal the number of shares purchased at $t = 1$ (that is, $-q_1$) multiplied by their return, which in turn consists of a risk premium compensating the dealer for holding the final inventory z_2 plus the final shock to the fundamental value ε_2.

Inserting this expression for the profits earned at $t = 1$ into equation (3.50) yields the dealer's final wealth, given equilibrium at $t = 1$:

$$w_2 = vz_0 + c_0 - \rho\sigma_\varepsilon^2(z_0 - q_0 - q_1)q_1 + (p_0 - v)y_0 - \varepsilon_2 q_1. \qquad (3.54)$$

Hence, the dealer's objective function at $t = 0$ is:

$$U = E_0(w_2) - \frac{\rho}{2}\text{var}_0(w_2), \qquad (3.55)$$

where the expected wealth is:

$$E_0(w_2) = \mu_0 z_0 + c_0 - \rho\sigma_\varepsilon^2(z_0 - q_0 - q_1)q_1 + (p_0 - \mu_0)y_0, \qquad (3.56)$$

and its variance is:

$$\text{var}_0(w_2) = [2(z_0 - y_0)^2 + q_1^2 - 2(z_0 - y_0)q_1]\sigma_\varepsilon^2, \qquad (3.57)$$

recalling that $\text{var}_0(v) = \text{var}_0(\varepsilon_1 + \varepsilon_2) = 2\sigma_\varepsilon^2$.

The first-order condition of the dealer's objective function with respect to y_0 yields his optimal supply of the security at $t = 0$:

$$y_0(p_0) = \frac{p_0 - \mu_0}{2\rho\sigma_\varepsilon^2} + z_0 - \frac{q_1}{2}. \qquad (3.58)$$

The first two terms of this expression are the supply that the dealer would choose at $t = 0$ if he did not expect to trade again at $t = 1$. The third term is new, and captures the dealer's pre-positioning in anticipation of future order flow: if the dealer expects clients to demand an amount $q_1 > 0$ in the future, he anticipates that his inventory is going to be depleted in the future, and therefore replenishes it at $t = 0$ by half of that amount.

In equilibrium, $y_0 = q_0$, and therefore the price is:

$$p_0 = \mu_0 + \rho\sigma_\varepsilon^2[2(q_0 - z_0) + q_1]. \qquad (3.59)$$

Hence, the initial price reacts not only to current demand for the security but also to future demand, because the inventory management by dealers in anticipation of future demand transfers some of its pressure on the initial price. Otherwise stated, the market price reflects the fact that a position of $z_0 - q_0$ will have to be held for two periods and a position of $-q_1$ will have to be held for one period.

In reality, orders are serially correlated, and thus at $t = 0$ market makers anticipate that the current order q_0 will trigger a subsequent order q_1. To capture this idea in a simple way, assume that $q_1 = \delta q_0$, where positive autocorrelation ($\delta > 0$) may result from the gradual trickling of large orders, while negative autocorrelation ($\delta < 0$) can result from market participants' reaction to attractive prices quoted by market makers ($p_0 \neq \mu_0$).

The resulting bid and ask prices are:

$$p_0 \equiv \begin{cases} a_0 = m_0 + \rho\sigma_\varepsilon^2(2+\delta)|q_0| & \text{if } q_0 > 0, \\ b_0 = m_0 - \rho\sigma_\varepsilon^2(2+\delta)|q_0| & \text{if } q_0 < 0, \end{cases} \tag{3.60}$$

where $m_0 = \mu_0 - 2\rho\sigma_\varepsilon^2 z_0$. So, in the baseline case where the order flow is not serially correlated ($\delta = 0$), the bid-ask spread is doubled compared to the static model (see equation (3.46)), because the inventory risk generated by the absorption of the order flow lasts for two periods. The prospect that the dealer will receive offsetting orders in the future ($\delta < 0$) mitigates his inventory holding costs, and therefore the bid-ask spread. In contrast, if the order flow is positively autocorrelated ($\delta > 0$), the actual holding costs stemming from a given order is larger than in the baseline case. Hence, the size of the bid-ask spread depends on the autocorrelation of the order flow, δ.

In terms of price dynamics, a key implication of this model is that the future order flow, not just the current one, contributes to determine price movements via its effect on dealers' inventories. To see this, use equations (3.59) and (3.51) to write the expected change in the equilibrium price between $t = 0$ and $t = 1$:

$$E_0(p_1) - p_0 = \rho\sigma_\varepsilon^2 \underbrace{(z_0 - q_0)}_{z_1}, \tag{3.61}$$

that is, the expected return on the dealer's position between time 0 and time 1 is per-period risk premium on his inventory position held over this period. Similarly, the expected price change between $t = 1$ and $t = 2$, from equation (3.51), is:

$$E_0(p_2 - p_1) = E_0(v - p_1) = \rho\sigma_\varepsilon^2(z_1 - q_1) = \rho\sigma_\varepsilon^2(z_0 - (1+\delta)q_0). \tag{3.62}$$

Figure 3.6 illustrates the expected price dynamics in the wake of a sell order, i.e., for $q_0 < 0$. For simplicity, in the figure it is assumed that the inventory of dealers is zero before the arrival of the order, both at $t=0$ ($z_0=0$) and before, as no order arrives in the previous period $t = -1$. Hence before the arrival of the order at $t = 0$, the price is simply the asset's risk-neutral valuation: $p_{-1} = \mu$. The price dynamics after the sell order depends on the autocorrelation δ in the order flow. In line with equation (3.60), the price drop and its subsequent reversal are largest if the order flow is positively correlated over time ($\delta > 0$), intermediate if it is uncorrelated ($\delta = 0$) and mildest if it is negatively autocorrelated ($\delta < 0$). Intuitively, if orders are positively correlated over time, then the impact of

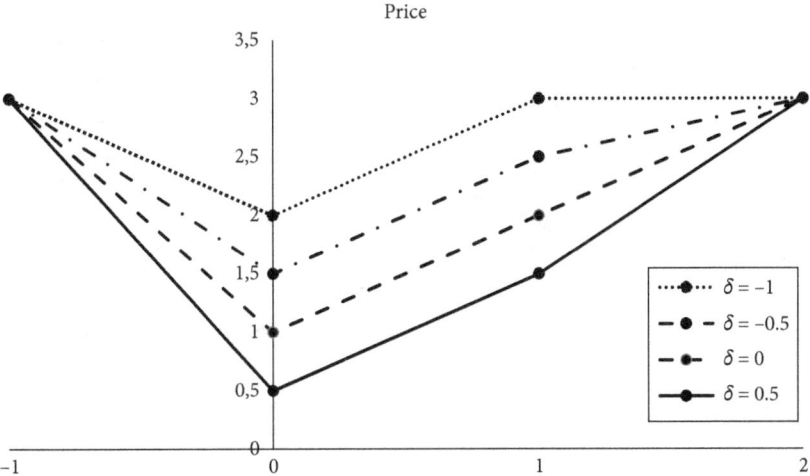

Figure 3.6 Expected prices in the dynamic model with risk-averse dealers.

current orders will be exacerbated by inventory accumulation. Conversely, if orders tend to reverse over time, the price impact of any initial order will be mitigated, because dealers are exposed to inventory risk for a shorter time. Accordingly the stronger is the reversal in the order flow, the milder is the initial price impact, as well as the subsequent reversal, as can be seen by comparing the cases where $\delta = -0.5$ and $\delta = -1$. Figure 3.7 plots the dynamics of inventories in the immediate aftermath of trades (that is, the inventory shown in the figure at any time t is z_{t+1}). Comparing Figure 3.6 and Figure 3.7 one sees that price changes anticipate subsequent fluctuations in inventories: when inventories are expected to rise more in the future, the current price drops more, and therefore both price and inventory display larger subsequent reversals.

As done in Section 3.4, one can measure the expected short-term and long-term impact of a buy order, benchmarked against the midprice at $t = 0$. For simplicity, consider a situation in which market makers start with zero inventory ($z_0 = 0$), and suppose that a buy order $q_0 > 0$ reaches the market at $t = 1$. From equation (3.60) the short-term impact of the order is:

$$\text{ST impact} = \rho\sigma_\varepsilon^2(2+\delta)q_0, \tag{3.63}$$

which is increasing in δ, i.e., in the persistence of the order flow.

Interestingly, in the medium term the order impacts the price by less than in the short term: adding the expected price change between $t = 0$ and $t = 1$ from equation (3.61) to the short-term impact from equation (3.63), the medium-term impact of the buy order on the expected price at $t = 1$ is:

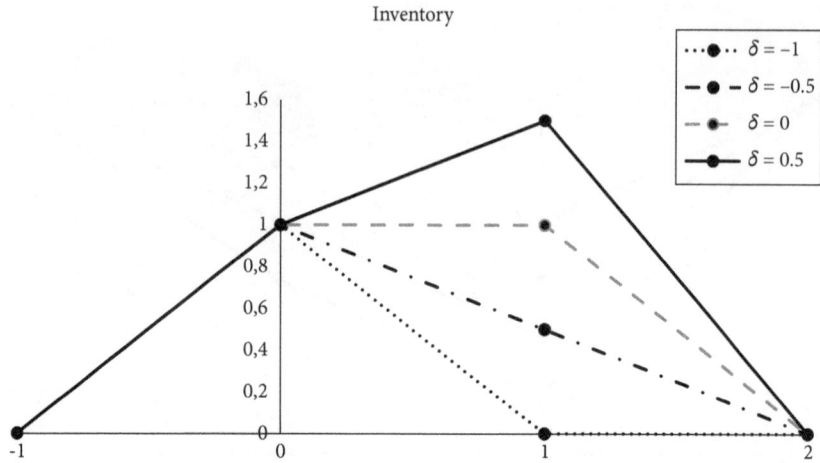

Figure 3.7 Dealers' inventories in the dynamic model with risk-averse dealers.

$$\text{MT impact} = E_0(p_1) - m_0 = \rho\sigma_\varepsilon^2(1+\delta)q_0, \qquad (3.64)$$

which is smaller in absolute size than the short-term impact, highlighting that there is mean-reversion in the expected price.

Of course, the long-term impact of the order is zero, because it is natural to assume that eventually the market makers' inventory goes back to the initial level, so that the price will go back to the initial midquote: in our model, this is implicitly assumed to happen at $t = 2$. As shown in Figure 3.6, the speed of mean reversion depends on the autocorrelation in the order flow: the expected price reverts faster to the initial level the lower is the value of δ. The reason is that, as shown in Figure 3.7, when there is offsetting order flow the market makers can unwind their inventories faster, and therefore their inventory holding cost is smaller.

An important general principle that emerges from this analysis is that the risk premium component of the market price at any moment in time is proportional to the holding time for which a given position will be held, and not only on the expected size of this position over this holding period. Specifically, if market makers anticipate a future time path of inventories $(z_{t+1}, \ldots, z_T)$, then the price at any time t is equal to:

$$p_t = \mu_t - \rho\sigma_\varepsilon^2 \sum_{\tau=t+1}^{t=T} z_\tau, \qquad (3.65)$$

T being the last time at which the dealer expects his inventory to differ from zero. This can easily be checked for $t = 0$ and $t = 1$ for the case with two trading dates considered in this section.[21]

3.5.3 Joint Dynamics of Prices and Inventories: Evidence

The inventory holding cost model analyzed so far yields three main empirical predictions. First, the pressure that orders exert on prices is inversely proportional to the inventory imbalance that they induce and to the persistence of such imbalance. Second, offsetting orders will gradually allow market makers to unwind these inventory imbalances, so that we should observe mean reversion in their inventories. Third, as a consequence, prices should also revert towards the initial level as inventories are unwound: indeed, the path of prices should be the mirror image of that of market makers' inventories.

Consider the first of these three predictions. When a dealer has a long position before trading at date t ($z_t > 0$), buying additional shares is not attractive, as it increases his risk exposure. This will put downward pressure on the price. Conversely, a dealer with a short position is willing to trade at a relatively high price. Hence, the mid-price at date t will deviate from the fair value of the security, and the size of this deviation ($m_t - \mu_t$) is inversely related to dealers' aggregate inventory. This deviation can be called the "price pressure" arising from inventory holding costs.

For stocks listed on the NYSE, Hendershott and Menkveld (2014) find evidence consistent with this prediction. They estimate the relationship between the midquote and dealers' inventories, and obtain a negative coefficient for the price pressure per unit of inventory. Moreover, they find that this price pressure coefficient is much greater (in absolute value) for small-capitalization than for large-capitalization stocks. Specifically, a \$100,000 inventory results in price pressure of 1.01% for small stocks and 0.02% for large stocks. This makes sense, in that fewer people are interested in trading smaller stocks, so it takes longer to unwind the inventories and dealers remain exposed to risk for a longer time. In other words, for small stocks the inventory holding period is likely to be longer than for large stocks. We have shown that price pressure is the product of three terms: the expected inventory holding period, the risk aversion coefficient and the variance of the fundamental. This can be seen by comparing the expression for the midquote in the static model ($m_0 = \mu_0 - \rho\sigma_\varepsilon^2 z_0$) with that in the dynamic model ($m_0 = \mu_0 - 2\rho\sigma_\varepsilon^2 z_0$): in the latter, the price pressure coefficient is twice as

---

[21] To check it, use equations (3.59) for p_0 and (3.51) for p_1, recalling that $q_0 = z_0 - z_1$ and $q_1 = z_1 - z_2$.

large as in the former, because inventories are held for two periods rather than than one.

The second main empirical prediction of the inventory holding cost model is that inventories are mean-reverting. Comerton-Forde et al. (2010) show that the aggregate inventories of NYSE specialists over 1994–2004 fluctuate around an average value of about $200 million. Such fluctuations are also found for individual stocks and corporate bonds, as illustrated by Figure 3.8. The top panel of the figure plots the daily inventory of Apple stock held by a broker-dealer over one year: it is clear that inventory reverts to zero in a matter of days. The bottom panel of the figure instead refers to the corporate bond market, and plots the position of a broker-dealer in a single corporate bond. This illustrates that the speed of inventory mean reversion depends on the activity level of the corresponding market: as the corporate bond market is typically less active, it features slower mean reversion in inventories.

The speed of response of the order flow and mean reversion of inventories not only depends on the market's general level of activity, as illustrated by the comparison between the time pattern of inventories in the Apple stock and in the corporate bond market shown in Figure 3.8. It also depends on other market characteristics, such as the extent of investors' monitoring of the security, and on the salience of price discrepancies, which in turn reflect dealers' risk aversion and the stock's riskiness. Moreover, in practice, dealers actively seek to control their inventory not just by pricing but also by advertising opportunities and soliciting customer orders: they can reduce the holding time of their inventory, and thus accelerate its mean reversion, by eliciting inventory-reducing orders. In line with this prediction, researchers—such as Reiss and Werner (1998) and Hansch, Naik, and Viswanathan (1998)—have found empirically that dealers with long positions are more likely to execute buy market orders; those with short positions, sell market orders. Finally, the speed of adjustment will reflect regulatory limits on the size of dealers' positions, such as short-sales constraints or margin constraints on leverage. Intuitively, the more stringent these constraints, the more apparent the footprints of inventory holding costs on price dynamics.

The third prediction of the model is that, as inventories revert, so do prices, as illustrated in Figures 3.6 and 3.7. This is illustrated by Figure 3.9, which shows the price response to large stock orders placed by clients of a major broker-dealer and executed over three days. The graph is best interpreted as representing the effect of a large sell order, and as such is the empirical counterpart of the price pattern predicted by our dynamic model and illustrated by Figure 3.6.

The mean reversion in prices is faster in more active markets, where inventories revert faster to their desired level (as shown by Figure 3.8). This is documented by Hendershott and Menkveld (2014), who estimate the duration

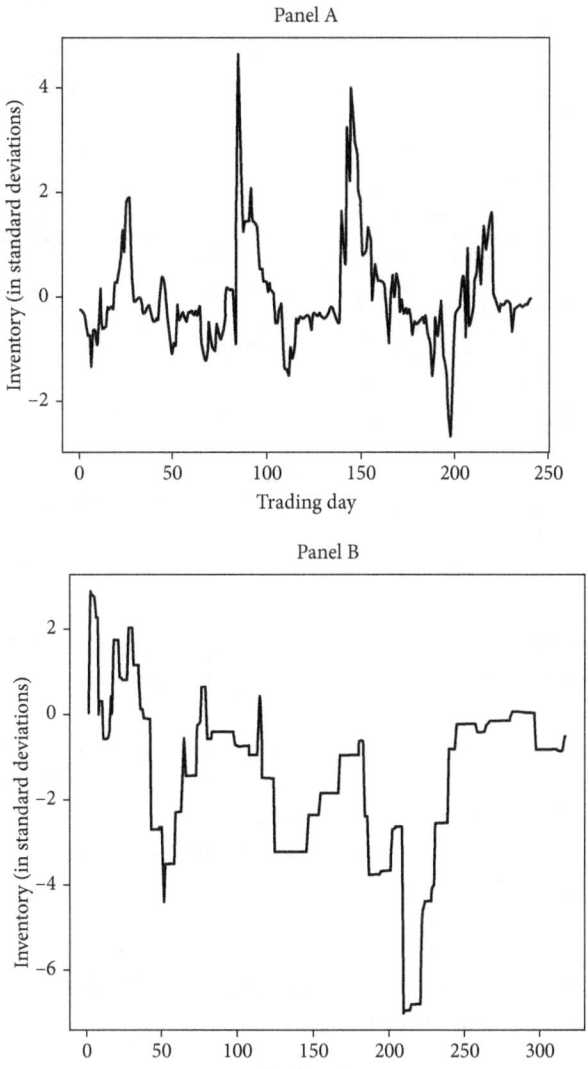

Figure 3.8 Panel A: daily inventory of the U.S.-dollar position of a block market making desk of a major broker-dealer for Apple Inc. stock, after scaling by the sample standard deviation of inventory for the sample period (2010–11).
Panel B: daily inventory of the U.S.-dollar position of a market making desk of a major broker-dealer for a single investment-grade corporate bond, after scaling by the sample standard deviation of inventory levels for the sample period (2010–11).
Sources: fig. 1 and fig. 3 from Duffie (2012).

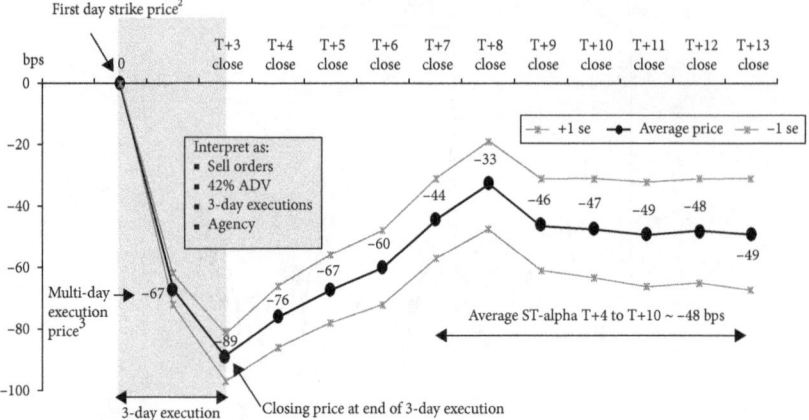

Figure 3.9 Value-weighted average closing prices from when a multi-day execution completes through ten days later. Prices are measured relative to the first-day order arrival price. The sample includes both buys and sells, but the sign of buys is flipped. *Source*: Exhibit 6 from Cai and Sofianos (2006).

of price pressure for NYSE stocks, and find that price pressure lasts longer for small-capitalization stocks (besides being stronger), presumably because trading is less frequent.[22]

Mean reversion in security prices is often observed not only as a result of large orders, as in Figure 3.9, but also when security markets are hit by major shocks, such as the deletion from a widely traded stock market index or a regulatory intervention that forces some intermediaries into fire sales of certain securities, such as low-grade bonds (see Chapter 11).

Box 3.2 Dealers' Inventories, Liquidity, and Volatility Before and After The 2008–9 Crisis

The inventory holding cost model shows that dealers' willingness to accumulate and decumulate inventories in order to serve investors' orders is a key to the market's ability to provide liquidity, and that this willingness depends on the volatility of the fundamentals. So it is no surprise that, with the increase in risk during the financial crisis of 2008–9, dealers' willingness to hold inventories diminished. Their ability to hold large inventories was further impaired by regulatory restrictions on their proprietary trading. Nicole Bullock's article

---

[22] They also measure the contribution of price pressure induced by inventory holding costs to daily volatility, finding that it ranges from 0.17% for large stocks to 1.20% for small stocks.

"Wall Street: inventory reductions 'the death of trading'" (*Financial Times*, March 12, 2012) argues that this has reduced liquidity and increased the volatility of prices in the corporate bond market, as the model analyzed above predicts:

Before the global financial crisis, large Wall Street dealers used to hold big inventories of corporate bonds to facilitate trading for their clients.

When a bond manager such as Jesse Fogarty, of Cutwater Asset Management, wanted to sell a large number of bonds, the dealer would sell some of them to other clients for him and buy some itself to sell down over time, hopefully for a profit.

Since the financial crisis, however, large Wall Street dealers have sharply cut the number of corporate bonds they hold to facilitate this kind of trading for clients or for proprietary positions.

Mr. Fogarty calls this move "the death of trading."

Known in the financial markets as "dealer inventories," these bond holdings reached highs of more than $200bn in 2007, but dropped to less than half that by the end of 2008, as dealers reduced their risk because of the banking crisis.

In the second half of last year, dealers cut their bond holdings again, as they dropped from about $90bn at the start of June to $40bn by the end of February 2012, the lowest level in a decade.

These lower inventories, analysts and investors say, reflect an environment of lower risk-taking by Wall Street banks in the aftermath of the financial crisis and ahead of tighter regulations.

The result is likely to be higher volatility in bond prices, as the buffer is far smaller now.

In addition, the so-called Volcker Rule, a part of the 2010 Dodd Frank Act, could make it impossible for dealers to take these kinds of positions, because it prohibits proprietary trading by banks. At the same time, higher capital costs under Basel III also loom as an impediment to holding bonds on a bank's balance sheet. Many in the market believe the rules, which still need to be finalised, are a big driver of the reduction in inventory that was seen last year.

[...] market participants generally expect lower inventories will increase volatility, as they say happened during last year's sell-off.

As Europe's debt crisis escalated, risk premiums on investment grade and high-yield bonds widened sharply.

"The takeaway is that market liquidity has been reduced," says Chris Taggert, analyst at CreditSights, a research group. "You end up with higher volatility for the simple fact that, without the dealers taking positions, trading volumes will move prices faster."

3.6 The Full Picture

In this chapter, we have seen that an order's short run and long run effects on transaction prices differ depending on what determines the bid-ask spread, that is, whether the source of market illiquidity is adverse selection costs, order-processing costs or rents, or inventory holding costs. In this section we bring these factors together, illustrating qualitatively the type of price response to the order flow that we should observe depending on which of the three underlying forces determines it. Figure 3.10 plots the expected path of the transaction price over time, conditional on a buy order coming to the market at time t. The reason why we plot the expected rather than the actual price path is that, at any time, transaction prices are affected by news on fundamentals as well as by new orders, so that the actual price path is subject to continuous shocks that may conceal the effect of the buy order at time t. By taking expectations of the price at time

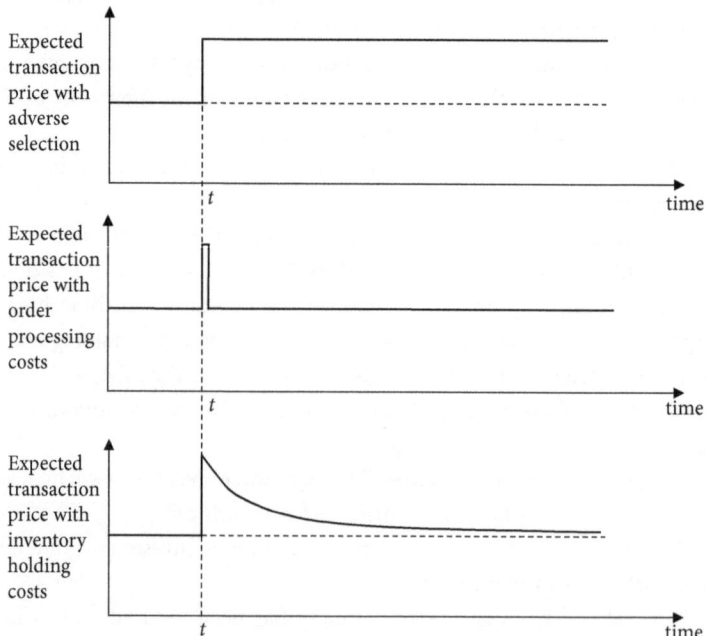

Figure 3.10 Price reaction to a market buy order in different settings.

t, we filter out this noise and highlight the "impulse response" to the buy order submitted at that time.

The top panel of the figure shows that in a setting with adverse selection the price impact of an order is permanent: the buy order induces traders to revise their beliefs about fundamentals upwards and embed this change in beliefs fully and permanently in their quotes. By the same token, in this setting there is no difference between the short run and the long run effect of the order. The middle panel shows that with order-processing costs (but no adverse selection) the buy order induces a temporary upward blip in the transaction price: the effect is present only in the very short run and disappears in the longer term, generating short-term negative autocorrelation in transaction price changes. Merging the time impacts illustrated in the top and middle panels, we have the short-term and long-term price reactions described by equations (3.34) and (3.36), which merge the adverse selection and order-processing cost models.

The bottom panel displays the price path when a buy order is submitted to risk averse dealers: the price reaction is positive in the short term but trails off in the medium term, as shown by equations (3.63) and (3.64). So there is a price reversal as in the middle panel, but the price impact dissipates slowly over time, as the inventories are gradually brought back to target. So again in this case returns should exhibit negative autocorrelation, but at lower frequencies and for longer lags than in the case of order-processing costs.

In the real world, of course, all three effects may be present at once. This is illustrated in Figure 3.11, which shows how all three may contribute to some extent to the positive short-term impact of a buy order, with some reversal occurring quickly as a result of order-processing costs, some further reversal occurring more gradually due to inventory holding costs, and in the long run only the informational effect associated with adverse selection persisting.

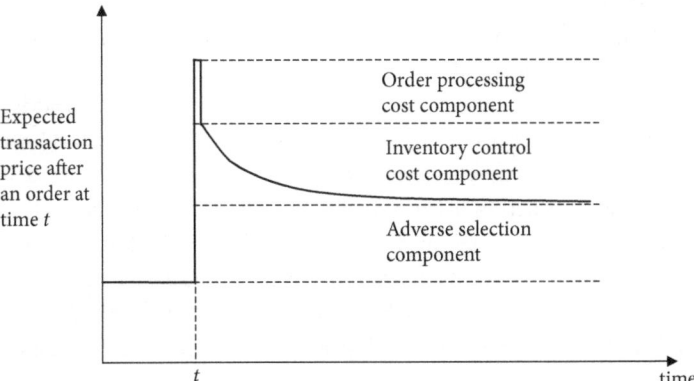

Figure 3.11 Short-term and long-term price responses to a market buy order.

Market microstructure researchers have repeatedly sought to decompose the bid-ask spread into the three components of adverse selection, order-processing costs (plus rents), and inventory holding costs. To identify these components of market illiquidity, researchers exploit the fact that each one has a different effect on the time-series properties of prices and orders, as is shown in the previous figure. Chapter 5 will explain in detail the econometric techniques that are applied to identify these effects and measure the contribution of each source of market illiquidity to the bid-ask spread.

3.7 Further Reading

The model of trading with asymmetric information developed in Section 3.3 is based on Glosten and Milgrom (1985). This model has been extended in many directions. For instance, Easley and O'Hara (1987) consider the possibility of multiple trade sizes for the informed investor; Easley and O'Hara (1992) introduce the possibility of information event uncertainty (that is, the possibility of there being no change in the asset value). In this case, dealers learn not only from the order flow but also from trading volume (the total number of trades over a given period).

One important feature of this model is that liquidity suppliers have less information than some liquidity demanders. In a model related to Glosten and Milgrom (1985), Calcagno and Lovo (2006) provide a theoretical analysis of price competition among dealers when some dealers are better informed than others. In this case, dealers' quotes are informative; the order flow not. Bloomfield, O'Hara, and Saar (2005) show experimentally that informed investors optimally use both market and limit orders when they have the requisite flexibility to do so. Overall, Calcagno and Lovo (2006), the experimental evidence in Bloomfield, O'Hara, and Saar (2005) and empirical evidence in Brogaard, Hendershott, and Riordan (2019) suggest that in securities markets quotes also contain information, in addition to order flow.

The model by Glosten and Milgrom (1985) has also been used to address various policy issues, as we do in Chapter 8. For instance, Diamond and Verrecchia (1987) use it to study the effects of short-sales constraints on price discovery. They show that transaction prices remain efficient in the semi-strong form with short-sales constraints, as in Glosten and Milgrom (1985), but that short-sales constraints slow the process of price discovery. Intuitively, such constraints prevent informed investors from selling a stock when they have bad news, which eventually reduces the speed at which prices reflect informed investors' private information.

Stoll (1978) was the first to relate the bid-ask spread to inventory holding costs. Ho and Stoll (1981) analyze the optimal dynamic pricing policy for a monopolist dealer in presence of inventory risk (see also Madhavan and Smidt, 1993; Hendershott and Menkveld 2014). Amihud and Mendelson (1980) also consider a dynamic model in which dealers are risk neutral but face position limits (i.e., a constraint on the maximum size of their inventory). They show that position limits also generate mean reversion in inventories. Ho and Stoll (1983), Biais (1993), and Yin (2005) study competition between dealers when they have different inventories in various market structures. The empirical literature exploits the idea that inventory effects dissipate in the long run to separate adverse selection from inventory holding costs (see Chapter 5). Given inventory risk, information on the aggregate inventories is informative on the short-term path of prices. Such information may also be a source of adverse selection; its effect is analyzed by Vayanos (1999).

The speed of dealers' inventories' reversion to the mean is sometimes used by researchers as a gauge of the importance of inventory risk in securities markets (see, for instance, Hasbrouck and Sofianos 1993; Madhavan and Smidt 1993; Lyons 1995; Comerton et al. 2010; and Hendershott and Menkveld 2014). Interestingly, the rate of reversion to the mean varies across assets. For instance, Madhavan and Smidt (1993) and Hasbrouck and Sofianos (1993) empirically find a slow rate of mean reversion for the inventories of the specialists in NYSE stocks, whereas Lyons (1995) finds a very high rate of reversion for a dealer in the Deutsche Mark/Dollar market. These differences may reflect differences between assets in price volatility, risk aversion of dealers, or responsiveness of order flow. Recent years have seen the emergence of high-frequency market-makers. These market-makers automate the posting of their quotes and use their speed of access to various trading platforms and information to manage inventory risk very efficiently. As a result, they hold their inventories for a very short period of time (see, for instance, evidence in Menkveld 2013). This suggests that the speed of reversion to mean in dealers' inventories and prices may have increased considerably in recent years.

3.8 Exercises

1. **Bid-ask spread with order-processing costs.** In Section 3.4.1 order-processing costs are assumed to be γ per share traded. Consider the following alternative assumptions:
   a. Assume that order-processing costs are k per transaction. Compute the bid-ask spread in this case and show that it is decreasing with the size

of the transaction. Which features of the technology of trading would lead you to think that this is a realistic model of order-processing costs?

b. Assume that order-processing costs are k per euro traded. Show that the absolute bid-ask spread is increasing in the security's underlying value and the relative bid-ask spread is constant, in contrast with the expressions found in the text where order-processing costs are a constant γ per euro traded, irrespective of the share value.

c. Stoll (2000) reports that Roll's measure ranges from 6.45 cents for small-company NASDAQ stocks to 13.17 cents for large-company NASDAQ stocks (p. 1494). Note that, on average, small-company stocks have a lower price. Which of the following hypotheses is more consistent with this empirical evidence?

(i) Order-processing costs are constant per share traded.

(ii) Order-processing costs are constant per dollar of value traded.

2. **Bid-ask spread and insider trading.** A small risky company's stock is worth either $10 ($v^L$) or $20 ($v^H$) with probability $\frac{1}{2}$ each ($\theta = 1 - \theta = 0.5$).

a. Compute the bid and ask prices set by risk neutral competitive market makers in the absence of informed trading.

b. Compute the bid and ask prices set by risk neutral competitive market makers when they expect one in ten of trade initiators to be informed (to know the stock's true value) and to trade as profit maximizers, while the other nine out of ten are uninformed and buy or sell with equal probability. Assume that all transactions are of the same size.

c. Compute the average trading cost to an uninformed trader and the average gain to an informed one, assuming a unit trade size in both cases.

d. Do you agree with the following statement? "Insider trading does not harm most market participants: it harms only those who are unlucky enough to trade with an insider." Why? Refer to the example in this exercise to illustrate your argument.

3. **Insiders' expected profits in the Glosten-Milgrom model.** Consider the static version of the Glosten-Milgrom model, where market makers set the first ask and bid equilibrium quotes of the trading day. Compute the expression for the expected profits of the insider (only as function of the parameters π, v^H, and v^L. In computing this expression, take into account that the informed trader can trade both in the state in which the security is worth v^H and in that in which it is v^L, and that each of these two states has probability $\frac{1}{2}$). How does this expression vary as a function of the probability of informed trading, π? What is the intuitive rationale for this result?

4. **Imperfectly informed investors in the Glosten-Milgrom model.** Consider the one-period Glosten-Milgrom model, where the security's true value v can be high (v^H) or low (v^L) with probability $\frac{1}{2}$ each. Market makers are competitive and risk neutral, and do not know v. In each period, a single trader comes to the market: with probability $1 - \pi$, he is a noise trader, who buys or sells one unit with probability $\frac{1}{2}$ each; with probability π he is an informed trader, who observes a signal about security's true value. With probability $\rho \in \left(\frac{1}{2}, 1\right]$ the signal is accurate, that is, it coincides with the true value of the security. With probability $1 - \rho$, instead, the signal is mistaken, so that the insider assigns the wrong value to the security. Hence, ρ measures the accuracy of the signal observed informed trader: for ρ close to $\frac{1}{2}$, the informed would be similar to a noise trader; for $\rho = 1$, the insider trader would be perfectly informed.

   a. Write down dealers' expected profits when they receive (i) a buy and (ii) a sell order. [Hint: assume that the informed trader buys the security when his signal equals v^H and sells when it is v^L, so that in each instance with probability ρ he makes profits and with probability $1 - \rho$ he makes losses.]

   b. Compute the bid and ask prices set by risk neutral competitive market markers.

   c. Derive the bid-ask spread as a function of signal's informativeness. How does this result compare with the case of perfectly informed insider trading? Is the market more or less illiquid? Intuitively, why?

   d. Verify whether, given the bid and ask prices derived at point **b**, the insider is actually willing to buy when his signal equals v^H and sells when it is v^L, that is, whether this strategy yields positive expected profits in equilibrium.

5. **Endogenous information acquisition by insiders in the Glosten-Milgrom model.** Consider the one-period Glosten-Milgrom model, where the security's true value v can be high (v^H) or low (v^L) with probability $\frac{1}{2}$ each. Market makers are competitive and risk neutral, and do not know v. In each period, a single trader comes to the market: with probability $1 - \pi$, he is a "noise trader," who buys or sells one unit with probability each; with probability π he is a "potential insider," who learns the security's true value v if he pays a cost c, in which case he will trade on his information to make a profit. (If he does not elect to acquire information, he does not trade.)

   a. Compute the bid and ask prices and the bid-ask spread that market makers set, assuming that they believe the insider will acquire information with some given probability $\varphi \in [0, 1]$?

b. Given these prices, determine the trading profit of an insider who has decided to acquire information.

c. Determine the condition on the cost parameter c in terms of π and $v^H - v^L$ under which the potential insider will never choose to acquire information, even in the most auspicious situation in which market makers do not expect to face any insider trading (i.e., $\varphi = 0$).

d. Determine the condition on the cost parameter c in terms of π and $v^H - v^L$ under which the potential insider will always choose to acquire information, even in the least auspicious situation in which market makers expect to face insider trading with probability π (i.e., $\varphi = 1$).

e. Now consider intermediate values of c for which neither of the conditions determined under points **c** and **d** is satisfied. Determine the value of φ that will make the potential insider indifferent between acquiring and not acquiring information. This endogenous value of φ describes a "mixed-strategy equilibrium" in which the insider randomizes between the two options. How does this value of φ depend on the parameters of the model? Explain your results intuitively.

f. Characterize the equilibrium in the three ranges of the values of c considered in points **c**, **d**, and **e**. Plot the bid-ask spread and the potential insider's net expected profit as a function of the cost c of acquiring information. Explain your graph intuitively.

6. **Equilibrium with price-sensitive uninformed trading.** Consider the one-period version of the model developed in Section 3.3, assuming $v^H = 1$ and $v^L = 0$ with equal probabilities, and the fractions of both informed and uninformed investors are π and $1 - \pi$, respectively. Uninformed investors refuse to trade at a price that is more than δ away from the public estimate μ of the security's value.

a. Compute the zero-expected-profit bid and ask quotes posted by the dealers.

b. Plot how bid and ask prices and the probability of trading vary with π.

7. **Market breakdown in the face of excessive informed trading.** Risk-neutral competitive market makers set bid and ask prices for a security whose final liquidation value v is distributed on $(0, \infty)$ with density:

$$f(v) = \frac{2}{(v + 1)^3}.$$

The liquidation value of the security becomes publicly known after trading; but during trading, it is known only to informed traders who come into the market with probability π and trade a unit to maximize their profit. Noise traders come with probability $1 - \pi$; they buy a unit of the security if their personal valuation is higher than the ask price set by market makers and sell a unit if their personal valuation is lower than the bid price. Noise traders' personal valuations for the security are also distributed with the same density $f(\cdot)$, though independently of the true value v.

Compute equilibrium bid and ask prices, and show that there is a critical value of π beyond which the market breaks down, in the sense that the market makers are unable to set a profitable ask price.

In solving this exercise, you can use the fact that the cumulative distribution function corresponding to density function $f(\cdot)$ is:

$$F(v) = 1 - \frac{1}{(v+1)^2},$$

and also that for this distribution, for any given ask price a and bid price b,

$$E(v) = 1,$$
$$E(v \mid v \geq a) = 2a + 1,$$
$$E(v \mid v \leq b) = \frac{b}{b+2}.$$

8. **Differences in price pressure across stocks.** Can you explain the empirical finding by Hendershott and Menkveld (2014) that the price pressure per unit of inventory is much greater for small-capitalization than for large-capitalization stocks, based on the inventory holding cost model presented in this chapter? How?

9. **Short-sale constraints, liquidity, and market efficiency (inspired by Diamond and Verrechia 1987).** Consider the market for a risky security with uncertain final value v, which can be 1 or 0 with equal probability. As in this chapter, quotes for unit trade size are posted by risk neutral market-makers, and market orders are submitted either by informed traders, who arrive with probability π and know the true value of the stock, or by liquidity traders, who arrive with probability $1 - \pi$ and wish to buy or sell with equal probability.

Traders may be subject to constraints on short selling: an informed trader is short-sale constrained with probability κ_i, and a liquidity trader is short-sale constrained with probability κ_l. If a trader is constrained, he cannot sell when he would like to do so and in this case does not trade. Let d be the direction of the market order: $d = 0$ (*no trade if the trader wants to sell and is short-sale constrained*), $d = +1$ (buy market order) and $d = -1$ (sell market order).

a. Draw the tree for the order arrival process in this model.

b. Calculate the bid and ask quotes, and show that the bid-ask spread does not depend on κ if short-sale constraints are identical for liquidity traders and informed traders, that is, if $\kappa_i = \kappa_l = \kappa$. What happens to the bid-ask spread if $\kappa_i > \kappa_l$ or if $\kappa_i < \kappa_l$? What is the economic intuition for these results?

c. Compute dealers' expectations of the value of the security *if there is no trade*. Show that it is strictly lower than the unconditional expected value of the security if and only if $\kappa_i > 0$. What is the intuition for this finding?

d. Assume that $\kappa_i = \kappa_l = \kappa > 0$. Let $p(d) = E(v \,|\, d)$ be the "price" of the security at time 1 for $d \in \{1, 0, -1\}$. (Note that $p(0)$ is not observable in the form of a quote, because it is the market maker's valuation of the security on receiving no order.) Show that:

$$E(p(d)) = E(v)$$

and that:

$$E(p(d) \,|\, d \neq 0) > E(v) \text{ if } \kappa > 0.$$

e. Suppose that you have data for the transaction prices for stocks traded in a market before the removal of short-sale constraints (time $t - 1$) and after its removal (time t). According to the model presented above, would you expect, on average, to find a negative, zero, or positive return around the date in which the constraint is removed? Can we use this result to evaluate the merits of short-sale constraints?

10. **Predicting future order flow.** In Section 3.4.2, we discuss how the direction of the order flow at future dates t and beyond can be predicted given the current belief θ_{t-1} about the probability of a high value of the stock:

a. Use Table 3.2 to determine $E(d_{t+T} \,|\, \Omega_{t-1})$ for any $T \geq 0$, given the current belief θ_{t-1}.

b. Use equation (3.16) to update beliefs in the wake of a buy order and thus compute:

$$E(d_{t+T} \,|\, \Omega_{t-1}, d_t = 1) - E(d_{t+T} \,|\, \Omega_{t-1}).$$

11. **Empirical analysis of the determinants of spreads and the Amihud illiquidity measure.** The data for this exercise are contained in the Excel file Ch3_ex11_data.xls or in the Stata data file Ch3_ex11_data.dta available on the companion website for this book. These files provide

a record of the average values of the following variables, for a sample of 1,128 stocks traded in U.S. stock markets (based on daily data for April 2009):

- ticker code that identifies each stock (*ticker*);
- bid price (*pb*), ask price (*pa*), and closing price (*p*);
- number of shares (in thousands) traded per day (*vo*);
- trading volume (in millions of dollars) per day (*vp*);
- number of shares (in thousands) outstanding (*ibnosh*);
- sector according to GICS classification (*gics*);
- relative bid-ask spread, in percent (*bas100*);
- Amihud illiquidity measure (*ami100*);
- market capitalization, in millions of dollars (*mktcap*);
- daily return (*ret*);
- realized volatility (twenty-trading-day moving standard deviation of returns, *vola*).

a. Compute the correlation matrix of the closing price, trading volume, market capitalization, bid-ask spread, average return, and return volatility. Which variables are most closely correlated? What does this suggest for the specification of regressions whose dependent variable is the bid-ask spread or the Amihud illiquidity ratio?

b. Estimate regressions where the dependent variable is the bid-ask spread, in six specifications that all include a constant, volatility, and *alternatively* the following other variables: (1) market capitalization, (2) trading volume, (3) log of market capitalization, (4) log of trading volume, (5) turnover rate (defined as *vo/ibnosh*); (6) turnover rate and log of closing price. Compare the explanatory power of these alternative specifications and, based on the models studied in this chapter, interpret the estimates so obtained. In particular, indicate the change in the bid-ask spread associated with a 1% increase in trading volume, according to your estimates.

c. Repeat the empirical analysis under (b) using the Amihud illiquidity measure as dependent variable. How do the results compare with those under (b)?

d. Would the theories studied in this chapter lead one to suppose that financial stocks should have been more illiquid than non-financial, other things being equal, in the estimation period of April 2009? Investigate by generating a financial sector dummy variable (*fin*) that takes the value 1 when the *gics* variable is equal to 40 (the code of the financial sector according to the Global Industry Classification Standard), and then by re-estimating specifications 4 and 6 described under point (b) of this exercise with the addition of this dummy among the regressors. Comment on your results.

e. The specification estimated in answering the previous question allows for the possibility that financial stocks may have been more illiquid than other stocks for given values of all the other explanatory variables. In fact, in the financial sector, the relationships of illiquidity with capitalization, trading volume, and price may not have been the same as in other sectors, in April 2009. Test this hypothesis within specification 6 under point (b) of this exercise (testing the equality of the coefficients of the explanatory variables first separately, and then jointly), and offer an interpretation of your results.

4

Trade Size and Market Depth

Learning Objectives:

- How trade size affects prices
- What market depth is
- How traders choose their trade size
- Why the number of dealers is a determinant of market liquidity

4.1 Introduction

On Friday, January 18, 2008, the top management of Société Générale (the world's leading equity derivative trading house at the time) discovered that one of their traders, Jérôme Kerviel, had accumulated massive unauthorized long positions in European stock index futures (estimated at somewhere between forty and fifty billion euros), which had already accrued losses of about €1.5 billion. On Monday, January 21, the bank began liquidating these positions in a series of small trades and waited until January 24 to go public with the news, giving itself time to unwind the positions and avoid greater losses. Even so, by Friday, January 25, its losses amounted to €4.9 billion, and its stock price slid by 13% relative to the previous Friday's close, while the EuroStoxx price index (which comprises the 50 largest European stocks) dropped by 5%, as shown in Figure 4.1.[1] Yet Société Générale Chairman Daniel Bouton commented: "Had we not acted swiftly, the loss could have been ten times worse." As Société Générale was unwinding its positions, stock markets fell so sharply that Société Générale fire sales probably contributed to the stock market drop, even though the selling was limited to about 10% of daily trading volume.

This episode illustrates three facts. First, the use of a gradual sales strategy demonstrates that when an investor wants to sell a large amount of securities

[1] In the figure, the stock price of Société Générale and the EuroStoxx index are both standardized to 100 on January 11, 2008. Over the same week the S&P 500 was relatively stable, only falling by 0.4%. So the stock market drop was specific to the European stock market, in which Kerviel had taken gigantic exposures.

Market Liquidity: Theory, Evidence, and Policy. Second Edition. Thierry Foucault, Marco Pagano, and Ailsa Röell, Oxford University Press. © Oxford University Press 2023. DOI: 10.1093/oso/9780197542064.003.0005

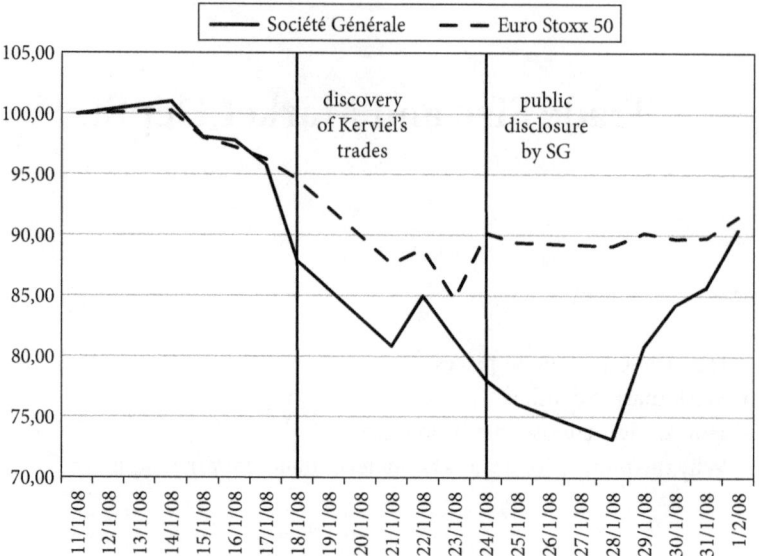

Figure 4.1 Evolution of Société Générale stock price and EuroStoxx 50 Index from January 11, 2008, to February 1, 2008.

he should try to avoid very large orders that are likely to unsettle market prices. Second, the fact that Société Générale kept its exposure secret for a whole week while unwinding it suggests that the news would have had a serious adverse impact on market prices. Finally, the fact that the market turned down illustrates that even this gradual, covert strategy was not entirely successful at insulating the company from loss. In short, even very liquid markets—such as those for equity index futures—have limited depth, so large orders can unsettle prices.

In this chapter we present a framework for analyzing the determinants of market depth (i.e., how and why transaction prices react to order size). Recall that a deep market is one in which large orders do not have a much greater impact on prices than small orders. We shall see that depth depends on three of the factors that affect the bid-spread (see Chapter 3), namely (i) asymmetric information, (ii) risk aversion, and (iii) rents due to imperfect competition among market makers:[2]

---

[2] Order-processing costs do not affect market depth, as long as they are proportional to the number of shares traded. However, if they are more than proportional to trade size, they contribute to widen the bid-ask spread as trade size increases; conversely, if they are less than proportional, they tend to reduce the bid-ask spread as trades grow larger.

(i) Insofar as larger orders reflect more private information than small orders, they induce larger price movements. The sensitivity of prices to trade size is then determined by the degree of asymmetric information between liquidity providers and informed traders: the greater the asymmetry, the shallower the market—that is, the more sensitive prices are to an order of a given size.

(ii) Another factor affecting market depth is the risk aversion of liquidity providers. Filling a large order exposes providers to greater inventory risk; consequently the more risk-averse they are, the larger the price concession that they require to execute trades. To the extent that the order is absorbed by multiple liquidity providers rather than a single one, market depth will depend on their aggregate risk-bearing capacity, hence also on their number.

(iii) Finally, strategic market makers have market power. As liquidity providers' market power is inversely related to their number, this is another reason why market depth increases with the number of liquidity providers.

We present these ideas in Section 4.2, building upon one of the most popular models of price formation under asymmetric information: the static version of the Kyle (1985) model of informed trading and market liquidity. The price impact of orders is increasing in order size, to an extent that depends on the informational advantage of the informed investor and the volume of liquidity or "noise" trading (trades that are not information driven). Section 4.2.4 extends the model to imperfectly competitive market-making, in the context of a call market (also known as a batch auction), where all traders submit supply or demand schedules and a Walrasian auctioneer crosses them at a common market-clearing price (see Chapter 1). Then, in Section 4.3, we analyze a call market where market makers have inventory concerns, being risk averse. We show that also in this setting the price impact of orders is increasing in order size, and depends on the underlying volatility of the stock and the risk aversion and market power of the market makers.

4.2 Market Depth under Asymmetric Information

To understand the determinants of market depth, we start with a model in which some traders have superior information. The logic is similar to that of the Glosten-Milgrom model described in Chapter 3. Here too, the price is set by risk-neutral market makers, but with two differences. First, orders can be of any size. Second, market makers may vary their prices depending on the quantities traded. This extension enables the model to portray the role of trade size in conveying information and driving price movements.

The vehicle for our analysis is the model developed by Kyle (1985), now a standard for studying trading in the presence of asymmetric information. As in Glosten-Milgrom, the demand for liquidity comes from two types of traders, informed and uninformed. But whereas in that model, market makers faced either an informed or an uninformed order, here orders from the two types of traders are batched together. Uninformed investors submit a random aggregate order u, which is normally distributed, with zero mean and variance σ_u^2. The informed trader has advance knowledge of the security's value $v = \mu + \varepsilon$, which other market participants see as a variable drawn from a normal distribution with mean μ and variance σ_v^2, following Kyle's notation (note that σ_v^2 is simply the variance denoted by σ_ε^2 in Chapter 3). Variables u and v are independent, and the informed trader does not know the uninformed order u. He can choose the size of his order and make it contingent on v by placing an order of size $x = X(v)$. Only market orders are allowed, not limit orders. The net batched order (the "order flow") $q = x + u$ is submitted to the market. The market makers do not observe v, but infer it—imperfectly—from the order flow, q, or from the clearing price (depending on the way trading is organized).

In all the models considered below, the relationship between the equilibrium price and the order flow is linear and given by:

$$p = \mu + \lambda q. \tag{4.1}$$

From the standpoint of a trader who wants to buy or sell, the slope λ in this expression measures the price pressure exerted per unit of order size. More formally, this slope measures the price impact dp/dq. A market is deep when even a large order does not shift the price by much, that is, when λ is small. Formally, the depth of the market can be measured by $1/\lambda$, the inverse of the price pressure parameter, in other words, the amount of order flow that drives the price up by one unit.

The value of λ in equilibrium depends on how informative the order flow is (as it drives dealers' inferences about the payoff): in Section 4.2.1, we explain how market makers update their estimate of the security's value on observing the order flow. Section 4.2.2 considers a setting in which competition eliminates all market makers' rents, so that their price is equal to their estimate of the security's value on observing the order flow. In Section 4.2.3, we close the model by deriving both the optimal strategy of a monopolistic informed trader and the equilibrium order flow. This gives us a full description of market participants' strategies in equilibrium, as derived by Kyle (1985). Finally, in Section 4.2.4 we allow for market power in a call auction framework, where the strategic interaction between market makers affects price determination, and market makers earn oligopoly rents.

4.2.1 Learning from Order Size

Market makers know that the order flow for a stock reflects information about the fundamental value v, because one of the orders comes from the informed investor, who knows v in advance. But there are two obstacles to extracting even part of this information from the order flow: (i) the informed order x is overlaid by the noise of the order u of uninformed investors and (ii) market makers must guess how the informed investor's trade is related to his information. This guess must be right; if not, it would lead to systematic losses for market makers, so eventually we shall have to check whether informed investors really do follow the type of strategy that market makers expect. In other words, we have to solve for a rational expectations equilibrium. where market participants' conjectures are verified in equilibrium.[3]

Market makers will obviously expect the informed trader to buy when he knows that the true value v of the security is higher than other market participants' estimate μ, and sell if it is lower. Specifically, suppose that they conjecture the informed investor to trade an amount x that is proportional to the discrepancy $v - \mu$:

$$x = X(v) = \beta(v - \mu) \tag{4.2}$$

for some parameter $\beta > 0$.[4] What the market makers actually observe, however, is not the informed trader's order alone, but the total net order flow, including the noise traders' orders:

$$q = x + u. \tag{4.3}$$

That is, the net order flow is a noisy signal of the asset value v, so market makers can use the noisy signal q to form their expectation of v. The resulting

---

[3] The concept of rational expectations equilibrium is an important tool to model situations of trading with asymmetric information; its application to competitive securities markets was developed by Grossman (1976), Hellwig (1980), Diamond and Verrecchia (1981), and Admati (1985), among others.

[4] In Section 4.2.3, we show that this conjecture is verified: there is a rational expectations equilibrium in which the optimal strategy of the informed investor is linear in $v - \mu$.

conditional expectation $E(v|q)$ will generally differ from their unconditional expectation μ.

As the aggregate order size from noise traders u is normally distributed and independent of v, the expected value of v conditional on q is provided by the ordinary least squares regression rule:[5]

$$E(v|q) = \mu + \frac{\text{cov}(v,q)}{\text{var}(q)} \cdot q$$

$$= \mu + \frac{\beta \sigma_v^2}{\beta^2 \sigma_v^2 + \sigma_u^2} \cdot q$$

$$= \mu + \alpha q, \tag{4.4}$$

where $\alpha = \frac{\beta \sigma_v^2}{\beta^2 \sigma_v^2 + \sigma_u^2}$ measures the sensitivity of expectations to the order flow. That is, α measures how informative the order flow is.

The informativeness of the order flow, α, depends on σ_u^2, σ_v^2, and β. For a fixed value of β, a decrease in the variance of noise trading σ_u^2 makes the order flow a more precise signal of the asset's value, and thereby enhances its informativeness. By the same token, informativeness increases with the variance of the security's value σ_v^2, since this increases the fraction of order flow volatility that can be attributed to the informed trader, and makes the total order flow more informative. The impact of β—the aggressiveness of the informed trader—is non-monotonic. Specifically, it is increasing for small values of β and then decreasing, because an increase in β has two opposite effects: greater aggressiveness by informed traders tends to make the order flow more informative, but at the same time inflates trades for any given value of v, so that the dealer must correspondingly scale down the extent to which he adjusts his estimate of v upon observing any given order flow. The first effect dominates for small values of β; the second dominates for sufficiently large β.

---

[5] Consider two joint normally distributed random variables, and:

$$X \sim N(\mu_x, \sigma_x^2) \text{ and } Y \sim N(\mu_y, \sigma_y^2),$$

and denote their covariance σ_{xy}. A property of the bivariate normal distribution is that the conditional density of Y given $X = x$ is itself normal with conditional mean:

$$E(Y|x) = \mu_y + \frac{\sigma_{xy}}{\sigma_x^2}(x - \mu_x) = \left(\mu_y - \frac{\sigma_{xy}}{\sigma_x^2}\mu_x\right) + \frac{\sigma_{xy}}{\sigma_x^2}x,$$

which is the predicted value of Y from an ordinary least squares (OLS) regression of the equation $Y = a + bX$, upon setting the explanatory variable $X = x$. The slope coefficient σ_{xy}/σ_x^2 is precisely the OLS estimate of b. In our case, the dependent variable is v and the explanatory variable is q.

4.2.2 Perfectly Competitive Dealers

We now consider the case in which dealers are risk-neutral and trading is organized in three steps. In the first step, market orders from the two types of trader are batched into a single net order $q = x + u$. Second, each market maker responds with the price at which he is willing to execute this order in full. Third, the entire batched order is routed to the market maker who posts the best price.[6] Effectively, this means that dealers engage in Bertrand competition.

The expected profit of the dealer who wins the order at price p is:

$$E[q(p-v)|q] = q[p - E(v|q)].$$

Competition between dealers drives this expected profit down to zero. For instance, suppose that $q > 0$ and that $p > E(v|q)$. If a dealer just matches the best offer, p, he is not sure he will execute the order, which will be allocated among all the bidders at price p. So he is strictly better off by slightly undercutting his competitors to win the order. This continues until the best offer is driven down to the dealers' conditional estimate of the security's value (4.4). At this point, it is no longer profitable for anyone to undercut the best offer and an equilibrium is reached. Hence, in this case, the equilibrium price is:

$$p = E(v|q) = \mu + \alpha q, \tag{4.5}$$

and therefore:

$$\lambda = \alpha = \frac{\beta \sigma_v^2}{\beta^2 \sigma_v^2 + \sigma_u^2}. \tag{4.6}$$

Thus, market depth is entirely determined by the informativeness of the order flow. The less informative the order flow, the deeper the market. The intuition is straightfoward. In this model, dealers use the order flow as a signal of the asset's value and adjust their prices accordingly. If the order flow is not very informative, it does not greatly affect dealers' value estimate, which means that it has little impact on prices since quotes are competitive.

Consider now a trader placing an order of size u: what price can he expect to get? He obviously knows his own order size u; he knows nothing about the size of other orders, but expects that, on average, they net out to zero. Therefore, based on equation (4.5), he expects his own order to be executed at price

---

[6] If several post the same price, the order is allocated to one of them.

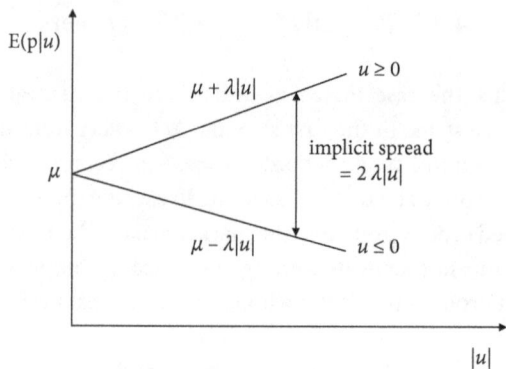

Figure 4.2 Depth and effective bid-ask spread.

$E(p) = \mu + \lambda E(q|u) = \mu + \lambda u$. Figure 4.2 plots the relationship between this price and the investor's average order size, $|u|$.

Relative to traders' prior estimate of the asset payoff (μ), buy market orders execute at a premium and sell market orders at a discount equal to $\lambda|u|$. Thus, $\lambda|u|$ is the effective half bid-ask spread paid by investors on a transaction of size $|u|$. As Chapter 2 explains, the notion of effective bid-ask spread and market depth are closely related: the effective spread increases with the size of the order at a rate of λ.

What does this model tell us about the volatility of stock returns? We can think of the total return as $v - \mu$, the difference between the security's final value v and investors' pre-trading valuation μ (its initial market price). This total return can be split into two components: an initial return up to the time of trading, $p - \mu$, and a subsequent return from the time of trading to the moment when the final value v is revealed, $v - p$.

The volatility of the initial return is:

$$\text{var}(p - \mu) = \lambda^2(\beta^2 \sigma_v^2 + \sigma_u^2) = \frac{\beta^2 \sigma_v^2}{\beta^2 \sigma_v^2 + \sigma_u^2}\sigma_v^2, \tag{4.7}$$

which is increasing in the aggressiveness of informed trading, β. An increase in β means larger trade sizes for the informed trader (the "trade size effect"); thus, for any fixed value of λ, prices deviate more from traders' prior value estimate. This effect is partially offset by the fact that λ decreases with β, for large enough β. But this latter effect is always outweighed by the trade size effect. In short, trading is a source of volatility, because the order flow contains information that moves the price.

The volatility of the return after trading, $v - p$, is:

$$\text{var}(v - p) = \frac{\sigma_u^2}{\beta^2 \sigma_v^2 + \sigma_u^2} \sigma_v^2, \tag{4.8}$$

which is decreasing in the informed trader's aggressiveness, β. Intuitively, this is because if the informed investor trades more aggressively, more of his information is reflected in the market price, so the price is closer to the fundamental v. Price discovery is faster. In this model $\text{var}(v - p)$ equals the "average pricing error," which Chapter 3 defines as $E[(v - p)^2]$, and presents as an inverse measure of price discovery.[7] This finding parallels our result in Chapter 3 that an increase in the fraction of informed traders accelerates price discovery.

The variance of the total return on the security over both periods (before and after trading) is:

$$\text{var}(v - \mu) = \text{var}(v - p) + \text{var}(p - \mu) = \sigma_v^2, \tag{4.9}$$

since $\text{cov}(v - p, p - \mu) = 0$.[8] It is important to note that even though informed trading affects the variance of the pre- and post-trade returns ($p - \mu$ and $v - p$), it leaves the volatility of the total return ($v - \mu$) unchanged. Informed trading does not change the fundamental risk of the security: it simply brings forward the resolution of part of the uncertainty from the final date when v is revealed to the date when trading occurs.

4.2.3 The Informed Trader's Order Placement Strategy

So far, we have taken the trading strategy of the informed trader as given. Now we endogenize his behavior. As in Kyle (1985), we posit that dealers are competitive (so that they obtain no rents), and that the informed trader is risk neutral.

Intuitively, the informed trader's strategy depends on the dealers' pricing policy: the informed investor should trade less aggressively on his information when he expects dealers' prices to be very sensitive to the order flow. In turn, as we have seen, dealers' strategies themselves depend on the informed trader's aggressiveness. Thus, the strategies of dealers and of the informed trader are interdependent. In a Nash equilibrium, each agent behaves optimally given the other agents' behavior. We show that the following strategies constitute a Nash equilibrium:

---

[7] Here the average pricing error is equal to $\text{var}(v - p)$, since $E(v - p) = 0$.

[8] This covariance is zero because the price is the best estimate of the fundamental v at the time of trading, so that $v - p$ is the unanticipated component of the fundamental (the portion not yet reflected in the price), and thus uncorrelated with the price p itself.

$$\text{dealers' quote: } p(q) = \mu + \lambda q, \text{with } \lambda = \frac{\sigma_v}{2\sigma_u}, \qquad (4.10)$$

$$\text{informed investor's trading: } X(v) = \beta(v - \mu), \text{with } \beta = \frac{\sigma_u}{\sigma_v}. \qquad (4.11)$$

Informed investor. Given dealers' pricing strategy (equation (4.10)), the informed investor's expected profit if he trades x shares is:

$$E[(v-p)x] = E[(v - \{\mu + \lambda(x+u)\}x] = (v - \mu - \lambda x)x.$$

Thus, the order size that maximizes his expected profit is:

$$X(v) = \beta(v - \mu), \qquad (4.12)$$

with:

$$\beta = \frac{1}{2\lambda}. \qquad (4.13)$$

The trade size of the informed investor ($|X(v)|$) is inversely related to λ. Intuitively, the informed investor will place larger orders in deeper markets because they have less adverse impact on prices.

Dealers. From Section 4.2.1, we know that if dealers expect the informed investor to follow a linear strategy $X(v) = \beta(v - \mu)$ (equation (4.2)), then their competitive price, for each value of q, is given by:

$$p(q) = \mu + \frac{\beta \sigma_v^2}{\beta^2 \sigma_v^2 + \sigma_u^2} q. \qquad (4.14)$$

Thus, we have:

$$\lambda = \frac{\beta \sigma_v^2}{\beta^2 \sigma_v^2 + \sigma_u^2} \Rightarrow \frac{1}{\lambda} = \beta + \frac{\sigma_u^2}{\beta \sigma_v^2}. \qquad (4.15)$$

Combining (4.13) and (4.15) yields the equilibrium values of λ and β:

$$\lambda = \frac{\sigma_v}{2\sigma_u}, \beta = \frac{\sigma_u}{\sigma_v}.$$

The larger the variance of noise trading σ_u^2 or the lower the variance of the fundamental value σ_v^2, the deeper is the market in equilibrium. Intuitively, the greater σ_u^2, the greater the average order flow in the market, and the less likely that an order of any fixed size will be interpreted as information driven. The smaller

σ_v^2, the smaller the informed investor's average informational advantage, and the less dealers need to protect themselves against it.

In equilibrium, dealers absorb the aggregate market order. Thus, their net supply is q, and their expected profits can be written as:

$$E\big[(p-v)q|q=x+u\big] = E\big[(p-v)x|q=x+u\big] + E\big[(p-v)u|q=x+u\big].$$

The first term in this decomposition is the expected profit on trades with the informed trader; the second is the expected profit on trades with uninformed investors. As the informed investor has an informational advantage, dealers lose on these trades, so that $E\big[(p-v)x|q=x+u\big] < 0$. As in equilibrium, dealers just break even, they must recover this loss by the expected profits on trades with the uninformed investors:

$$E\big[(p-v)x|q=x+u\big] = -E\big[(p-v)u|q=x+u\big].$$

Since this equality must hold for all possible realizations of q, it must also hold unconditionally (by the law of iterated expectations):

$$E\big[(v-p)x\big] = E\big[-(v-p)u\big].$$

Hence, the expected profit of the informed investor is just equal to the expected losses of the uninformed, who ultimately bear the adverse selection costs (as explained in Chapter 3).

In equilibrium, the informed investor's expected profit, conditional on a realized value of v, is:

$$E\big[(v-p)\cdot X(v)|v\big] = \big[v-\mu-\lambda E(q|x)\big]\cdot x$$
$$= \big[v-\mu-\lambda x\big]\cdot x = \frac{1}{2}\frac{\sigma_u}{\sigma_v}(v-\mu)^2,$$

since $x = \frac{\sigma_u}{\sigma_v}(v-\mu)$. Therefore, his unconditional expected profit is:

$$E\big[(v-p)\cdot x\big] = \frac{1}{2}\sigma_u\sigma_v.$$

Thus the informed investor has greater expected profit when there is more uninformed trading (σ_u) or when he has a larger informational advantage (σ_v). A greater volume of uninformed trading, in fact, provides more camouflage, since the aggregate order flow is a noisier signal than the informed investor's actual trade.

Recall that in this model, we can measure price discovery by the average pricing error, $\mathrm{var}(v-p) = \mathrm{E}\left[(v-p)^2\right]$ (see Section 4.2.2). Given the equilibrium actions of the informed investors and the dealers, price discovery is:[9]

$$\mathrm{E}\left[(v-p)^2\right] = \frac{1}{2}\sigma_v^2. \qquad (4.16)$$

Thus, in equilibrium, half the uncertainty about the security's value is resolved at the time of trading.

An instructive way to represent the model graphically is to draw the two relationships that relate β and λ: equation (4.13), which gives the informed investor's choice of trading intensity β as an increasing function of the depth of the market $1/\lambda$; and equation (4.15), which shows the market maker's choice of liquidity $1/\lambda$ as a convex function of the informed investor's trading intensity. This second relationship is non-monotonic because the market maker can afford to provide a deep market both when the informed investor's trading activity is very low *and* when the informed investor trades so aggressively as to give away his presence on the market. These two functions are plotted in Figure 4.3. The intersection indicates the Nash equilibrium point, which happens to coincide with the point where market depth is minimized ($1/\lambda$ is at its lowest point when β equals σ_u/σ_v).

Depth improves whenever the informed investor's trading intensity differs from the level portrayed in Figure 4.3: the line representing the informed investor's response function will then swivel away from the position shown in the figure. This occurs, for instance, if the informed investor is exposed to competition from other informed investors or is risk averse. (We leave the analysis of these two cases to the reader in exercises 3 and 6.) This means that, unlike the simple situation shown in Figure 4.3, the equilibrium may actually be to the left or to the right of the minimum-liquidity point. This suggests to an important caveat for anti-insider-trading regulation and enforcement. In practice, one may not know whether the market equilibrium is to the left or to the right of the minimum-depth equilibrium point, so it is hard to say whether cracking down on insider trading, which steepens the insiders' response function in Figure 4.3, would increase or decrease market liquidity.

---

[9] We obtain equation (4.16) as follows. We have:

$$v - p = v - \mu - \frac{\sigma_v}{2\sigma_u}(x+u) = \frac{v-\mu}{2} - \frac{\sigma_v}{2\sigma_u}u,$$

since in equilibrium, $x = (\sigma_u/\sigma_v)(v-\mu)$. Computing the variance and observing that v and u are independent, we obtain the result in the text.

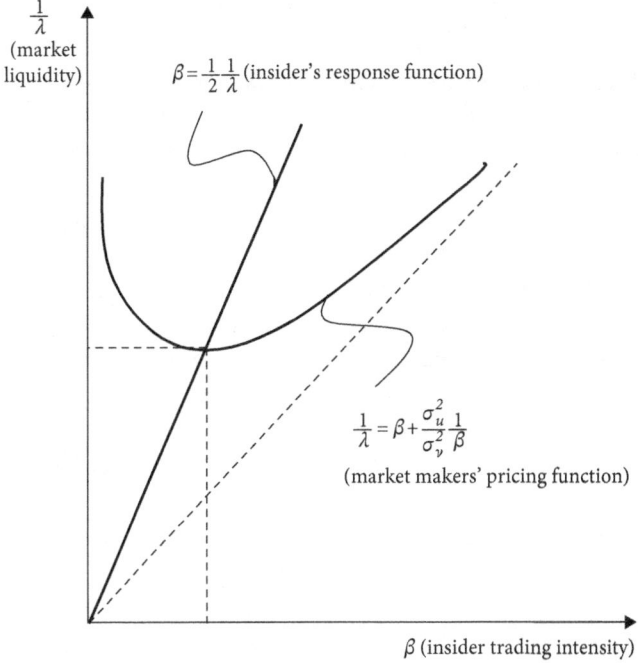

$\frac{1}{\lambda}$ (market liquidity)

$\beta = \frac{1}{2}\frac{1}{\lambda}$ (insider's response function)

$\frac{1}{\lambda} = \beta + \frac{\sigma_u^2}{\sigma_v^2}\frac{1}{\beta}$

(market makers' pricing function)

β (insider trading intensity)

Figure 4.3 Insider's behavior and pricing function in Kyle's model.

To conclude this section, let us discuss some possible extensions. First, we have assumed that the informed investor can trade only once, after which his information becomes publicly known, hence obsolete. This means that he does not worry that by trading aggressively today he alerts the market to his presence and so lowers his potential future gains. Kyle (1985) analyzes the trade-offs involved in a multiperiod version of the model. In keeping with intuition, he shows that the informed investor trades less aggressively than in the one-shot case, in order to avoid dissipating his information advantage too quickly. In this case, information is incorporated into market prices only gradually, as the result of the repeated trading by the informed investor. In the limiting case of trading in continuous time, the rate at which information gets embedded in market prices is constant, and so is the volatility of price changes per unit of time.

Second, we have assumed that there is only one informed investor. The static model can easily be extended to consider multiple informed investors (see exercise 3). In this case, the depth of the market increases with the number of informed investors. Holden and Subrahmanyam (1992) consider the multi-period case and show that competition among informed investors results in a race that dissipates their informational advantage very quickly by comparison with the case of a single informed investor.

4.2.4 Imperfectly Competitive Dealers

The trading mechanism considered in Sections 4.2.2 and 4.2.3 is such that competition among dealers results in zero expected profits for the dealers. This is because risk-neutral dealers submit price bids for the *total* quantity demanded, and the auctioneer selects the best bid to fill the entire net order flow q. We now consider a different trading mechanism, namely a call auction (as described in Chapter 1), in which each dealer submits a schedule of offers that specifies the number of shares he is willing to buy or sell at each possible price, without knowing other dealers' offers. An auctioneer then parcels out investors' aggregate demand, q, among the dealers according to their demand or supply at the price that clears the market. Specifically, let $Y^k(p)$ be the total number of shares that dealer k is willing to supply at price p: if $Y^k(p) > 0$, the dealer is willing to sell shares; if $Y^k(p) < 0$, he is willing to buy $|Y^k(p)|$ shares. If there are K dealers, their aggregate supply at price p is $\sum_{k=1}^{K} Y^k(p)$. Hence, when the aggregate investor demand for the security is $q = x + u$, the clearing price p^* set by the auctioneer is given by the market-clearing condition:

$$\sum_k Y^k(p^*) = q. \tag{4.17}$$

We shall see that with this trading mechanism, competition among dealers does not drive their expected profits to zero unless their number is very large. Moreover, in this setting market depth depends not only on the informativeness of the order flow (as in Section 4.2.2), but also on the number of dealers (which determines their market power). Hence, even fine details of trading arrangements can affect market makers' profits, and market liquidity.

Recall that in Section 4.2.2, the starting point was the market makers' conjecture about the trading strategy of the informed trader. Here, each market maker has to form a conjecture not only about the informed trader's strategy, but also about the behavior of the other market makers. This is because now, in contrast with the model of Section 4.2.2, he cannot take the price as given: he knows he can affect it by changing his own supply of the security, and the response of the equilibrium price depends on how his competitors react to his own action.

Thus, in order to determine the optimal behavior of any dealer, we must specify his beliefs about (i) informed investor trading (x) and how that affects his estimate of the security's value based on total customer demand (q), and (ii) the strategic behavior of his competitors, and what that means for the response of the equilibrium price to his own supply of the security. Suppose that because of informed trading, the best estimate of the security's value, given the total order flow q, is $E(v|q) = \mu + \alpha q$, as in Section 4.2.2. Suppose further that each dealer k will supply shares according to the linear supply function $Y^k(p) = \phi(p - \mu)$. These two conjectures, together with market-clearing condition (4.17), enable each dealer k to identify a "residual demand function" (i.e., net customer demand q minus the supply from his $K-1$ competitors for any price p). He can then compute how the equilibrium price $p^*(q)$ will respond to any possible supply of shares y^k he may decide on, and therefore identify his profit-maximizing supply function (his own best response) $Y^k(p)$.

Note that each dealer's best response $Y^k(p)$ depends also on his estimate of the security's fundamental value $E(v|\Omega^k)$ conditional on his Ω^k. One would think that this information does not contain the aggregate market order q, since dealers do not directly observe q in the call auction and hence they cannot use it to estimate the fundamental value. However, they can infer q from the clearing price, since the clearing price depends on it, by condition (4.17). As dealers submit price-contingent orders, they can take into account the information contained in the clearing price when they bid. Thus, for each possible price p, their estimate of the value of the security is $E(v|p^*(q) = p)$, and they optimally choose the quantity $Y^k(p)$ to buy or sell at this price given this estimate and other dealers' offers.[10] Then, noticing that by symmetry all dealers must choose the same supply function and imposing the equilibrium condition (4.17), one finds the value of the supply parameter ϕ and the relationship $p^*(q)$ consistent with the beliefs assumed. In other words, as in Section 4.2.2, here we also seek a rational expectations equilibrium.

In the context of this model, a rational expectations equilibrium is a set of schedules, $\{Y^k(p)\}_{k=1}^{K}$, for the dealers and a price mapping $p^*(q)$ such that: (i) the schedule of offers posted by each dealer maximizes his expected profit, given his belief about the security's value and the price schedules chosen by his competitors; (ii) dealers correctly anticipate that the clearing price is given by $p^*(q)$ and form their beliefs accordingly; and (iii) for each value of q, the market clears for $p^*(q)$. In this equilibrium, dealers' expectations are rational in the sense that their beliefs are based on the correct relationship between the clearing price and order flow q (the only informative variable about v).

In Appendix A, we show that, if $K \geq 3$, there is a rational expectations equilibrium in which:

$$Y^k(p) = \frac{1}{\alpha} \frac{K-2}{K(K-1)}(p - \mu) \ \forall k \in \{1, \dots, K\}, \qquad (4.18)$$

---

[10] The idea that the clearing price conveys information and that traders should take this information into account in formulating their price-contingent orders is a key insight of rational expectations models such as Grossman (1976).

and the equilibrium price function is:

$$p^*(q) = \mu + \lambda q, \tag{4.19}$$

with $\lambda = \alpha \frac{K-1}{K-2}$ and α defined as in equation (4.4). The equilibrium is linear since both dealers' bidding strategies and the clearing price are linear functions.[11] Note that for equilibrium to exist, there must be at least three market makers. As expected, the market-clearing price reveals information on the payoff v, since it is a linear function of the aggregate order size. In equilibrium, the dealers' estimate of the value of the security when they trade at price p is $E(v|p^*(q) = p) = E(v|q) = \mu + \alpha q$ (the first equality here reflects the fact that there is a one-to-one mapping between the price p and the aggregate market order size q).

When K goes to infinity, we have $\lambda = \alpha$: if the number of dealers is very large, the depth of the market is entirely determined by the informativeness of the order flow, exactly as in Section 4.2.2. As dealers trade at the expected value conditional on their information, they obtain zero expected profits. We refer to this polar case as the competitive case.

In contrast, when the number of dealers is finite, λ is strictly larger than α. Thus, dealers obtain strictly positive expected profits. In fact, we can write equation (4.19) as:

$$p = E(v|q) + \underbrace{\frac{1}{K-2}\alpha q}_{\text{markup}} = \mu + \alpha q + \frac{1}{K-2}\alpha q.$$

Under imperfect competition the dealers' price is higher than their valuation of the security, as illustrated in Figure 4.4 below: when the total order size is q, dealers earn an expected profit per share $p - E(v|q) = \frac{1}{K-2}\alpha q > 0$.

In other words, the trading rules in the call auction enable dealers to compete less aggressively than when they must post a single offer for the entire order, as was assumed in the previous section. The reason is as follows. The risk of trading against an informed investor leads dealers to limit the number of shares that they offer to buy or sell at any given price. As a result, each dealer has pricing power. To see this, suppose that in the aggregate investors want to be net buyers ($q > 0$). For a given market order size, a dealer can raise the clearing price by reducing his supply, very much as a monopolist would do, since the other dealers supply only a limited number of shares at each price. But this possibility is limited by

---

[11] There might be other equilibria in which dealers' bidding strategies or the mapping $p^*(q)$ are non-linear.

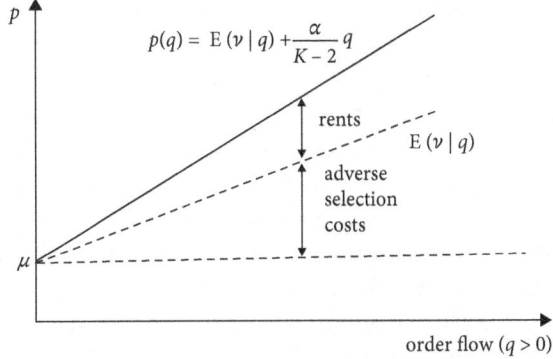

$$p(q) = \mathrm{E}\,(v\mid q) + \frac{\alpha}{K-2}\,q$$

rents

$\mathrm{E}\,(v\mid q)$

adverse
selection
costs

μ

order flow ($q > 0$)

Figure 4.4 Market depth with imperfect competition.

the extent to which his competitors react by increasing their supply. Intuitively, if a small increase in price generates a large increase in other dealers' aggregate supply,[12] then a dealer must shave his own supply by a large amount in order to have a substantial price effect. In this case, the dealer benefits less from the increase in price by reducing his own sale volume. This happens when K is large and the equilibrium price is therefore close to the dealers' valuation $\mathrm{E}(v|q)$. In contrast, when K is small, each dealer has significant market power because the others' aggregate supply response at each price is small. As a result, the wedge between the equilibrium price and dealers' valuation becomes large in markets with few dealers.[13]

For this reason, the depth of the market $1/\lambda$ depends not only on the informational content of the order flow α but also on the number of competing market makers K, as Figure 4.4. shows. More dealers tend to mean lower rents and a deeper market. Thus, liquidity providers' market power is a source of market illiquidity.

In this section, we have taken the informed investor's trade size as given. It is straightforward to endogenize this trade size as we did in Section 4.2.3 (see exercise 8). The behavior of the informed trader is unchanged, except that his trade size now increases with the number of dealers.

---

[12] That is, if the price elasticity of other dealers' aggregate supply is high.
[13] No linear equilibrium exists when $K = 2$ because in this case, by reducing his supply by a small amount, the dealer obtains an infinitely large increase in price. When $K = 1$, the dealer can charge an infinite price to sell q shares, since the investors' aggregate demand is price insensitive.

4.3 Market Depth with Inventory Risk

As we saw in Chapter 3, the need to compensate market makers for holding risky positions is another determinant, in addition to adverse selection, of the bid-ask spread. Here we extend the analysis of price formation with inventory risk to a situation where investors interact via a call auction mechanism where they can place orders of any size. For simplicity, we suppose that there is no informed trading ($x = 0$ so that $q = u$). First, in Section 4.3.1, we posit that risk averse dealers are price-takers (that is, they behave competitively) in the call auction market. In this case, we obtain the same relationship between the equilibrium price and dealers' aggregate inventory as in Section 3.5.1. Then, in Section 4.3.2, we consider risk averse dealers who act strategically in the auction; that is, they realize that the clearing price depends on the way in which they themselves bid. As in the model with asymmetric information, we find that market depth is lower in this case than when dealers behave competitively.

4.3.1 Perfectly Competitive Dealers

Consider again the inventory model of Section 3.5. The main differences between that model and the model analyzed in this section are that now orders may be of any size and trading is assumed to occur via a call auction, as in Section 4.2.4. In the auction, each dealer submits a price schedule $Y^k(p)$ that specifies the number of shares he is willing to buy ($Y^k(p) < 0$) or sell ($Y^k(p) > 0$) if the clearing price is p. For simplicity, we further assume that there is a single trading round (at time $t = 0$) and the asset payoff, v, is realized at its termination (time $t = 1$). In this section, we assume that dealers behave competitively. That is, they neglect the impact of their orders on the equilibrium price (they are "price-takers").

There are K dealers, each with mean-variance preferences. Dealer k has risk-aversion coefficient $\rho^k > 0$ and his expected utility is:

$$U^k = E(w_1^k) - \frac{\rho^k}{2}\text{var}(w_1^k),$$

where w_1^k is the mark-to-market value of the dealer's portfolio at date 1, that is,

$$w_1^k = v \cdot z_1^k + c_1^k = v(z_0^k - y^k) + c_0^k + py^k,$$

where z_t^k is dealer k's inventory in the risky security and c_t^k is his cash position at time t. If at time $t = 0$ the dealer sells y^k shares, this decreases his risky inventory by y^k, and increases his cash position by py^k. Hence, $z_1^k = z_0^k - y^k$ and $c_1^k = c_0^k + py^k$, as shown in the previous equation. As in Chapter 3, the first-order condition for the maximization of dealer k's expected utility is $dU^k/dy^k = 0$, which in the current setting implies:[14]

$$p - \mu + \rho^k \sigma_v^2 (z_0^k - y^k) = 0. \tag{4.20}$$

Thus, the optimal price schedule for dealer k is:

$$Y^k(p) = \frac{p - \mu}{\rho^k \sigma_v^2} + z_0^k. \tag{4.21}$$

Each market maker k's price schedule is related inversely to his risk aversion ρ^k and directly to his initial inventory z_0^k.

As in Section 4.2.4, market-clearing requires that aggregate net sales by dealers equal the net market orders placed by customers:

$$\sum_{k=1}^{K} Y^k(p) = q. \tag{4.22}$$

In this setting, market orders will typically be filled by several dealers, each taking a portion, with some or all customer orders being directly crossed.

Inserting the supply functions (4.21) into the market clearing condition (4.22) yields:

$$\sum_{k=1}^{K} \left(\frac{p - \mu}{\rho^k \sigma_v^2} + z_0^k \right) = q,$$

so that:

$$p = \mu - \rho \sigma_v^2 Z + \rho \sigma_v^2 q, \tag{4.23}$$

where Z denotes the aggregate initial inventory of the market makers $Z = \sum_{k=1}^{K} z_0^k$ and the constant ρ denotes the "collective" risk aversion of all the market makers, defined as:

---

[14] Equation (4.20) corresponds to equation (3.44) in Chapter 3. Beside some slight difference in notation (in particular the use of σ_v^2 instead of σ_ϵ^2 to denote the variance of v), the two equations differ because here the initial inventory position and the risk-aversion coefficients can differ between dealers (as indicated by their subscript k), while in Chapter 3 they do not.

$$\rho \equiv \left(\frac{1}{\rho^1} + \dots + \frac{1}{\rho^K} \right)^{-1}. \tag{4.24}$$

For instance, if all market makers have the same absolute risk aversion $\overline{\rho} = \rho^1 = \dots = \rho^K$ then $\rho = \overline{\rho}/K$. The "collective" risk aversion ρ of the market makers declines as their number K increases, because risk is more widely spread when more dealers are drawn into market-making. So the equilibrium price is:

$$p = \underbrace{\mu - \rho\sigma_v^2 Z}_{\text{midquote } m} + \underbrace{\rho\sigma_v^2}_{\lambda} q. \tag{4.25}$$

As in Chapter 3, the midquote m is inversely related to dealers' aggregate inventory at time $t = 0$. Intuitively, a dealer's marginal valuation for the security is low if his exposure to the risk of the security is already large. Moreover, the previous equation shows that the depth of the market $(1/\lambda)$ is inversely related to dealers' aggregate risk aversion, ρ, and the riskiness of the asset payoff, σ_v^2. So even though dealers are competitive, more dealers means a deeper market when dealers are risk averse, because the higher the number of dealers, the smaller the position that each individual dealer must take to absorb a given market order. Thus, each dealer requires less compensation for bearing inventory risk, and the market is more liquid.

As in Section 4.2.4, we can compute the effective bid-ask spread for an order of size $|q|$. Using equation (4.25), we obtain:

$$s = 2\rho\sigma_v^2 |q|, \tag{4.26}$$

which is proportional to the size of the order imbalance as in the Kyle model (Figure 4.5).

Note that the actual price paid in the call market by any particular investor i depends not just on his own order q^i but on the total order flow from other traders, $q - q^i$. From the standpoint of trader i, the aggregate order flow q may be random, and the variance of the price that he will pay is $\rho^2\sigma_v^4\text{var}(q|q^i)$, where $\text{var}(q|q^i)$ is his estimate of the variance of the total order flow from other investors. So in the call market, as the execution price is not certain ex-ante, investors face an execution risk whose size increases with trading costs: there is a positive relationship between illiquidity and execution price volatility.

4.3.2 Imperfectly Competitive Dealers

The previous section posits that dealers behave competitively: they ignore the effect of their own orders on the clearing price. When the number of dealers

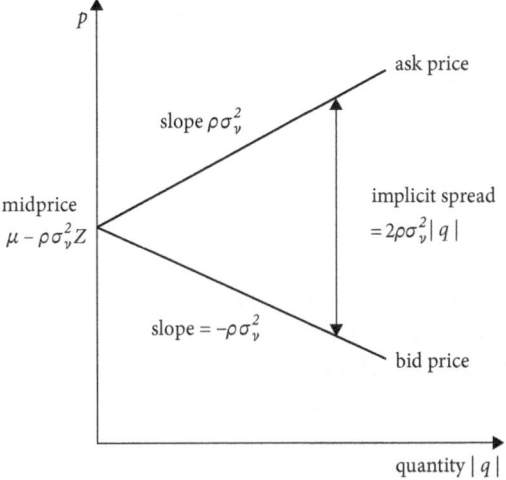

Figure 4.5 Competitive call market price with risk averse market makers.

is small, however, this assumption is unrealistic. Suppose for instance that a buy market order arrives. By reducing the number of shares that he offers for sale in the auction, a dealer drives the clearing price up and obtains a better execution price. Of course, the cost of this strategy is that he receives fewer shares at the equilibrium price. Hence, each dealer faces a trade-off between price and quantity, as in models of imperfect competition between firms (and very much as in the model of imperfect competition considered in Section 4.2.4). To understand this trade-off and its effect on market depth more clearly, we now relax the assumption that dealers are price takers. For simplicity, we assume that all the K market makers have the same coefficient of risk aversion $\overline{\rho}$ and thus, combined risk aversion $\rho = \overline{\rho}/K$.[15]

To analyze the call market equilibrium in this case, we need to account for the interdependence of dealers' bidding strategies. For instance, if a dealer offers a large number of shares at a given price, other dealers will be more inclined to reduce their own orders to obtain a better execution price. We again adopt the concept of Nash equilibrium, which in this case is a set of price schedules $\{Y^k(p)\}_{k=1}^{k=K}$ for the dealers such that the schedule of each one maximizes his expected utility given the price schedule chosen by his competitors.

In Appendix B, we show that, if $K \geq 3$, the following price schedules form a Nash equilibrium:

---

[15] The case where market makers are not all equally risk averse ($\rho^1 \neq \rho^2 \neq \dots \neq \rho^K$) is analyzed by Röell (1998), who shows that for any given aggregate risk tolerance ($1/\rho$), more equal distribution of risk tolerance among them improves market liquidity.

$$Y^k(p) = \frac{K-2}{K-1}\left(\frac{p-\mu}{\rho\sigma_v^2} + z_0^k\right). \tag{4.27}$$

As a consequence, the equilibrium price is a linear function of the market order size q:

$$p = \mu - \rho\sigma_v^2 Z + \left(\frac{K-2}{K-1}\rho\sigma_v^2\right)q. \tag{4.28}$$

The technique used to derive this equilibrium is very similar to that employed in Appendix A. Indeed, the nature of the competition between dealers in the models with asymmetric information and inventory risk is identical. The only difference is that in the former case dealers need to infer information from the clearing price, an effect that is absent here.

Thus, in equilibrium, at each price dealers offer to sell or buy only a fraction $\frac{K-2}{K-1}$ of the number of shares that they would be willing to trade when they behave competitively (compare equations (4.21) and (4.27)). Intuitively, by restricting the size of his order at each price, the dealer shifts the execution price to his advantage, as explained in the introduction of this section.

As a consequence, the aggregate supply schedule is less elastic, so that the price impact of a market order of a given size is larger, that is, λ is greater than in the competitive case. Imperfect competition among dealers reduces the depth of the market, regardless of whether the illiquidity arises from adverse selection or from inventory risk. Now, if the number of dealers increases the market becomes deeper (λ decreases) for *two* reasons: (i) the risk-bearing capacity of the market increases, as in the case of perfectly competitive dealers; and (ii) competition intensifies with the number of dealers, whose scope for affecting the equilibrium price by shading their offers is reduced–an effect captured by the fact that the ratio $(K-1)/(K-2)$ is declining in K. This implies that measures of market illiquidity should be inversely related to the number of dealers in a stock, since a larger number of dealers fosters competition and increases overall risk-bearing capacity.

When the number of dealers becomes infinite, the equilibrium converges to that of the benchmark case, considered in Section 4.3.1. Thus, in presence of either asymmetric information or inventory risk, dealers' rents vanish when the number of dealers is very large (strictly speaking, infinite). This observation has important implications. First, it suggests that in many real-world situations liquidity suppliers' rents should be an important determinant of market illiquidity.[16] As Section 3.4.2 explains, this determinant is often bundled with

---

[16] Biais, Bisière, and Spatt (2010) show empirically that competition among liquidity suppliers is imperfect and provide estimates of their rents on one U.S. electronic market.

order-processing costs in empirical analyses. Yet for policy intervention, it is important to distinguish the two causes of illiquidity. Second, trading rules should foster competition among liquidity providers. For instance, rules that restrict the number of market makers in a security are likely to result in excessive rents and illiquidity.

Finally, in the model with imperfect competition, the expression for the midprice is the same as in the benchmark case. This means that imperfect competition does not affect the conclusions set out in Section 3.5.3 of Chapter 3 regarding the dynamics of quotes and inventories. In fact, those conclusions derive from the relationship between the mid-price and dealers' aggregate inventory, which, as noted, is unaltered by the level of dealers' market power.

4.4 Further Reading

Our analysis in Section 4.2 is based on Kyle (1985). The model of imperfect competition among dealers developed in Section 4.2.4 is based on Kyle (1989), but that work considers a more general case in which bidders are both risk averse and informed. Pagano (1989a) also considers the case of imperfect competition among risk-averse dealers but in a model without asymmetric information, as in Section 4.3.2. Madhavan (1992) compares the properties of dealer markets and call markets under assumptions similar to those used in Sections 4.2.2 and 4.2.4 above. Rostek and Weretka (2015) consider a model of imperfect competition between risk averse dealers similar to that in Section 4.3.2 but use a different method to solve for the equilibrium and, more importantly, consider the case in which dealers can trade over multiple periods (see Vayanos (1999), Du and Zhu (2017), and Duffie and Zhu (2017) for related models). At a more general level, the analysis of imperfect competition among dealers is related to papers on competition in price schedules (e.g., Klemperer and Meyer 1989) and auctions of shares (Wilson 1979).

Many works have used the framework proposed by Kyle (1985) to study a variety of issues. For instance, Chowdhry and Nanda (1991) analyze multi-market trading (see Chapter 7), and Subrahmanyam (1991a) studies the effects of basket trading. Subrahmanyam (1991b) also analyzes the case of risk averse informed investors and market makers in this framework.

The analysis of Sections 4.3 and 4.2.4 emphasizes the importance of modeling imperfect competition among liquidity providers, in that dealers' rents are one cause of market illiquidity. Ho and Stoll (1983) study a model of price competition among dealers in the presence of inventory risk, observing that the best ask price should be set by the dealer with the largest position and the best bid price by the dealer with the smallest position, since there is an inverse relationship between a dealer's bid-ask quotes and his inventory (see Chapter 3). They solve for equilibrium quotes assuming that dealers know each other's inventory (see exercise 9). Biais (1993) relaxes this assumption and, applying the revenue equivalence theorem of auction theory, finds that the average bid-ask spread should be the same whether dealers can observe the inventories of their competitors or not. Yin (2005) considers the effect of search costs in the model of Biais (1993). Biais, Foucault, and Salanié (1997) compare the outcome of competition between dealers with inventory risk in three different trading mechanisms: a floor market, a limit order market, and a dealer market. They find that the limit order market can produce the competitive equilibrium even when the number of dealers is finite, provided that market orders are allocated among dealers tied at the same price on a pro-rata basis (see also Viswanathan and Wang 2002). Biais, Martimort, and Rochet (2000) present a model of imperfect competition between liquidity suppliers in presence of asymmetric information in a discriminatory auction (a market structure that we analyze in Chapter 6).

4.5 Appendix A. Adverse Selection with Imperfect Competition: Derivations

We show that if $K > 3$, under the assumptions of the model in Section 4.2.4, there is a rational expectations equilibrium in which:

$$Y^k(p) = \phi(p - \mu), \ \forall k \in \{1, \ldots, K\}, \tag{4.29}$$

and the equilibrium price mapping is:

$$p^*(q) = \mu + \lambda q, \tag{4.30}$$

with $\phi = \frac{1}{\alpha} \frac{K-2}{K(K-1)}$, $\lambda = \alpha \frac{K-1}{K-2}$ and $\alpha = \frac{\beta \sigma_v^2}{\beta^2 \sigma_v^2 + \sigma_u^2}$.

We first consider the residual demand that a dealer faces for any given total market demand q, when his competitors use the equilibrium supply strategies of equation (4.29). Let y^k be the number of shares offered by dealer k. Market clearing implies that:

$$q = y^k + (K-1)\phi(p - \mu). \tag{4.31}$$

That is,

$$P(y^k) = \mu + \frac{q - y^k}{(K-1)\phi}, \tag{4.32}$$

is the "residual demand function" faced by dealer k.

We next make an educated guess about what the dealer knows. Even though he does not observe q directly, we can see that he can infer it from the market price because for any given value of his supply y^k, there is a one-to-one relationship between q and the market price given by (4.32). Accordingly, we imagine that he knows q and assume that for each given value of q, with its corresponding residual demand function and the corresponding valuation $E(v|q) = \mu + \alpha q$, he picks a price-quantity pair to maximize his expected profit:

$$\max_{y^k} y^k [p - (\mu + \alpha q)],$$

where:

$$p = P(y^k) = \mu + \frac{q - y^k}{(K-1)\phi}.$$

The dealer is assumed to act strategically, and thus to be aware that the clearing price decreases by $\frac{\partial P}{\partial y^k} = -\frac{1}{(K-1)\phi}$ if he increases his supply y^k by one unit. Hence, taking the first-order condition, we obtain:

$$\frac{q - 2y^k}{(K-1)\phi} - \alpha q = 0.$$

Thus dealer k's price-quantity pair for any given q is:

$$y^k = \frac{1}{2}q(1 - \alpha(K-1)\phi),$$

$$p = \mu + \frac{1}{2}\left[\frac{1}{(K-1)\phi} + \alpha\right]q.$$

Eliminating q from these two equations, we find that, as the underlying q varies, dealer k's supply function is traced out:

$$Y^k(p) = \frac{(K-1)\phi[1 - \alpha(K-1)\phi]}{1 + \alpha(K-1)\phi}(p - \mu). \tag{4.33}$$

If the equilibrium is symmetric and all market makers use supply function (4.29), the slope of the supply functions (4.29) and (4.33) must be the same:

$$\phi = \frac{(K-1)\phi[1-\alpha(K-1)\phi]}{1+\alpha(K-1)\phi},$$

which yields:

$$\phi = \frac{1}{\alpha}\frac{K-2}{K(K-1)}.$$

Then market clearing implies:

$$\sum_k \frac{1}{\alpha K}\frac{K-2}{K-1}(p^* - \mu) = q,$$

so that in equilibrium the market price function is:

$$p^* = \mu + \alpha\frac{K-1}{K-2}q.$$

Hence, as claimed,

$$\lambda = \alpha\frac{K-1}{K-2},$$

where $\alpha = \frac{\beta\sigma_v^2}{\beta^2\sigma_v^2+\sigma_u^2}$ as defined in equation (4.4).

4.6 Appendix B. Inventory Risk with Imperfect Competition: Derivations

We show that if $K > 3$, under the assumptions of the model in Section 4.3.2, there is a Nash equilibrium in which:

$$Y^k(p) = \phi(p-\mu) + \varphi z_0^k, \forall k \in \{1, \ldots, K\}, \tag{4.34}$$

with $\phi = \frac{K-2}{K-1}\frac{1}{\overline{\rho}\sigma_v^2}$ and $\varphi = \frac{K-2}{K-1}$.

The reasoning is very similar to that in Appendix A. In particular, we can write the residual demand function facing market maker k: to clear the market, for any given value of total demand q, his supply y^k must equal total demand less the supply from his $K-1$ peers, that is,

$$y^k = q - (K-1)\phi(p-\mu) - \varphi \sum_{j \neq k} z_0^j, \tag{4.35}$$

or equivalently,

$$P(y^k) = \mu + \frac{1}{(K-1)\phi}\left[q - y^k - \varphi \sum_{j \neq k} z_0^j\right], \tag{4.36}$$

so that the sensitivity of the residual demand function faced by a dealer to his supply is again: $\frac{\partial P}{\partial y^k} = -\frac{1}{(K-1)\phi}$. Dealer k chooses his supply y^k to maximize his mean-variance utility:

$$\max_{y^k} \mu z^k + y^k(p-\mu) - \frac{\bar{\rho}\sigma_v^2}{2}(z_0^k - y^k)^2, \tag{4.37}$$

where p is given by (4.36). The first-order condition for this maximization problem is:

$$\frac{1}{\phi(K-1)}\left[q - 2y^k - \varphi \sum_{j \neq k} z_0^j\right] + \bar{\rho}\sigma_v^2(z_0^k - y^k) = 0.$$

Using the market clearing condition (4.35) to substitute for q, we obtain:

$$\frac{\left[y^k + (K-1)\phi(p-\mu) + \varphi \sum_{j \neq k} z_0^j - 2y^k - \varphi \sum_{j \neq k} z_0^j\right] + \bar{\rho}\sigma_v^2(z_0^k - y^k)}{\phi(K-1)} = 0,$$

which yields dealer k's supply schedule:

$$Y^k(p) = \frac{1}{\frac{1}{\phi(K-1)} + \bar{\rho}\sigma_v^2}(p-\mu) + \frac{\bar{\rho}\sigma_v^2}{\frac{1}{\phi(K-1)} + \bar{\rho}\sigma_v^2}z_0^k. \tag{4.38}$$

By equating the coefficients of equation (4.38) with the initially conjectured supply schedule (4.34), it follows that there is a symmetric equilibrium of the form:

$$Y^k(p) = \frac{K-2}{K-1}\left[\frac{1}{\bar{\rho}\sigma_v^2}(p-\mu) + z_0^k\right]. \tag{4.39}$$

To see how the market price varies with demand q, notice that market clearing requires:

$$\sum_{k=1}^{K} Y^k(p) = \sum_{k=1}^{K} \frac{K-2}{K-1}\left[\frac{1}{\rho\sigma_v^2}(p-\mu) + z_0^k\right] = q,$$

which yields:

$$p = \mu - \rho\sigma_v^2 Z + \frac{K-1}{K-2}\rho\sigma_v^2 q,$$

as claimed in equation (4.28) in the text.

4.7 Exercises

1. **Kyle's model with an imperfectly informed investor.** Suppose that in the model presented in Section 4.2 (Kyle 1985), the informed investor observes a noisy signal $s = v + \eta$ about the final value v of the security, where the noise component $\eta \sim N(0, \sigma_\eta^2)$ has no correlation either with the security's value v or with the noise traders' order u ($\mathrm{cov}(\eta, v) = \mathrm{cov}(\eta, u) = 0$).

   a. Assume that competitive market makers post the following price schedule:

   $$p(q) = \mu + \lambda q, \tag{4.40}$$

   where q is the net order flow. Find the optimal value of λ that they will choose if they conjecture that the informed trader's strategy is the following function of his noisy signal s:

   $$X(s) = \beta(s - \mu). \tag{4.41}$$

   How does the market depth $1/\lambda$ chosen by market makers respond to changes in the variance σ_η^2 of the informed investor's error? What is the intuitive explanation for this result? If we plot the depth $1/\lambda$ as a function of the aggressiveness β of informed investors (the former on the vertical axis and the latter on the horizontal axis), how do changes in the variance σ_η^2 affect the position and shape of this curve?

   b. In this case, the informed trader too must solve an inference problem in forming his expectation of the security's value. Show that his expectation of v conditional on the signal s is:

   $$E(v|s) = \mu + \frac{\sigma_v^2}{\sigma_v^2 + \sigma_\eta^2}(s - \mu),$$

and find the value of β as a function of market depth $1/\lambda$. How does the trading aggressiveness β that informed investors choose respond to changes in the variance σ_η^2 of the error term η? What is the intuitive explanation for this result? If we plot β as informed investors' best response to the depth $1/\lambda$ chosen by market makers in the same graph described under point **a**, how do changes in the variance σ_η^2 affect the position and shape of this line?

c. Compute the equilibrium values of λ and β. How do they respond to changes in the variance σ_η^2 of the error made by the informed investor? Graphically, does the equilibrium still correspond to the point of minimum depth as in the baseline version of Kyle's model?

d. Compute the ex ante expected profit of the informed investor. What is the effect of an increase in σ_η^2 on this profit? What is the intuitive explanation for this result?

2. **Noise trading in Kyle's model.** Consider the model presented in Section 4.2 (Kyle 1985), changing only the assumption about noise trading: assume that there are two groups (1 and 2) of noise traders, whose orders are respectively $u_1 \sim N(0, \sigma_{u_1}^2)$ and $u_2 \sim N(0, \sigma_{u_2}^2)$, both uncorrelated with the asset's future value (i.e. $\mathrm{cov}(v, u_1) = \mathrm{cov}(v, u_2) = 0$). All the other assumptions of the model are unchanged: (i) market makers are risk neutral and perfectly competitive, (ii) the asset value is $v \sim N(\mu, \sigma_v^2)$, (iii) the informed investor's order is $x = \beta(v - \mu)$, and (iv) market makers only observe the total net order $q = x + u_1 + u_2$. [Hint: think whether your answers require computing the results of the Kyle model again.]

a. Derive (i) the price schedule $p = \mu + \lambda q$ chosen by competitive market makers, under the assumption that the informed trader's order is $x = \beta(v - \mu)$; (ii) the optimal informed trader's order, given the price schedule chosen by market makers; and (iii) the equilibrium values of λ and β.

b. Now suppose that market makers can observe the actual realization of the order placed by group 1 (for instance, because these are local investors, while those of group 2 are foreign investors) before trading occurs. Under this further assumption, derive again (i) the price schedule $p = \mu + \lambda q$ chosen by competitive market makers, under the assumption that the informed trader's order is $x = \beta(v - \mu)$; (ii) the optimal informed trader's order, given the price schedule chosen by market makers; and (iii) the equilibrium values of λ and β.

c. Compare the results obtained under **a** and under **b**: does the assumption made under **b** change the equilibrium market depth and informed traders' aggressiveness and, if so, what is the intuitive reason for this difference?

3. **Kyle's model with multiple informed traders.** Consider the model presented in Section 4.2 (Kyle 1985), but assume that there are $N > 1$ informed traders, who all perfectly observe the final value of the security v but not the equilibrium price at the time that they determine their quantity demanded q_i.

   a. Suppose that market makers post the price schedule described by equation (4.40), where q is the net order flow $\sum_{i=1}^{N} x_i + \mu$ and $\mu = E(v)$. Assuming that each informed trader uses the following order submission strategy:

   $$x_i = X_i(v) = \beta(v - \mu) \text{ for } i \in \{1, \dots, N\},$$

   find the value of β for which a Nash equilibrium exists, determine how β is affected by N, and explain intuitively why.

   b. Suppose now that investors follow the order submission strategy derived in step a. Show that in this case the market makers' pricing strategy is given by equation (4.40), and find the value of λ that they optimally choose.

   c. What is the market depth in equilibrium, and how is it affected by an increase in the number of informed traders, N? What is the economic intuition for this result? Do you think that this result is robust; that is, does it still hold if the assumptions of the model are relaxed? (For instance, discuss informally whether you would still expect this result to hold if informed traders were risk averse.)

   d. Compute the ex ante expected profit of each informed investor. What is the effect of an increase in N on the aggregate profit of informed investors?

4. **Variance of price change and average pricing error in Kyle's model.** Consider the static model by Kyle (1985), where (i) market makers are risk neutral and perfectly competitive, (ii) the asset value is $v \sim N(\mu, \sigma_v^2)$, (iii) the informed investor's order is $x = \beta(v - \mu)$, and the noise traders' order is $u \sim N(0, \sigma_u^2)$; and (iv) market makers only observe the total net order $q = x + u$.

   a. Based on the price schedule $p = \mu + \lambda q$ chosen by competitive market makers in this model, show that the variance of price changes is:

   $$\text{var}(v - p) = \frac{\sigma_u^2}{\beta^2 \sigma_v^2 + \sigma_u^2} \sigma_v^2,$$

   and explain intuitively why it is decreasing in the informed traders' aggressiveness β.

b. Show that the average pricing error is:

$$\mathrm{var}(p - \mu) = \frac{\beta^2 \sigma_v^2}{\beta^2 \sigma_v^2 + \sigma_u^2}\, \sigma_v^2.$$

Is this expression increasing or decreasing in informed traders' aggressiveness β? Explain intuitively why.

5. **Informed investor with price-contingent orders.** Suppose that in the Kyle (1985) model the informed investor is allowed to set a demand schedule conditioned on price rather than a market order.

  a. Show that the equilibrium is essentially the same as when the informed investor must place a market order, in the sense that average noise trader transaction costs and informed investor profits are the same. The only difference is that liquidity is provided in part by the informed investor as well as by the competitive market makers. [Hint: imagine that the informed investor submits a demand x after observing the uninformed trader demand u.]

  b. What happens under this new assumption if there is more than one informed investor?

6. **Risk-averse informed investor.** Suppose that the informed investor is risk averse (with constant coefficient of absolute risk aversion b) and that he liquidates any amount of the security that he buys at a liquidation value $v + \varepsilon$, where ε is a normally distributed random variable with mean zero and variance σ_ε^2. At the time of trading the informed investor knows the realization of v but not that of ε. This noise in his signal implies that in taking long or short positions based on his privileged information, he bears some risk. Show that in this case his trading intensity is reduced relative to the model with risk neutrality, so that the β function swivels to the left (in Figure 4.3 of the text), increasing the equilibrium liquidity.

7. **Extension of the Glosten-Milgrom model to multiple trade sizes.** Consider the following simple extension of the high-low-value adverse selection model of bid-ask spreads to two trade sizes, as in Easley and O'Hara (1987). A security's true value is v, which may be high (v^H) or low (v^L) with probability $\frac{1}{2}$ each. Market makers do not know the true value. In a trading period one trader comes to the market. Market makers cannot tell who the trader is:

  • With probability $1 - \pi$, he is a "noise trader": either a "retail" customer, who wants to trade one unit, or a "wholesale" customer, who always trades two units. Half the noise traders are retail customers, and half are wholesale customers. Both types of noise trader want to buy or sell the security with probability $\frac{1}{2}$ each.

- With probability π, the trader is an "insider" who knows the security's true value v. He will buy one or two units if the true value is v^H and sell one or two units if the true value is v^L.

Ask and bid prices are set by competitive, risk-neutral market makers.

a. Suppose that the insider always chooses to trade two units. What will be the ask and bid prices quoted by market makers for one unit, that is, $a(1)$ and $b(1)$? In this case, will there be a non-zero bid-ask spread for this trade size? What bid and ask prices correspond to the two-unit trade size, that is $a(2)$ and $b(2)$, under the same assumption?

b. Would the insider always want to trade two units rather than one? Consider this question under two assumptions regarding π: $\pi = \frac{1}{2}$ and $\pi = \frac{1}{4}$. In both cases, compute the insider's profit if he trades two units and compare it with his profit when he trades one unit.

c. Do you have any ideas on what would happen in situations where your answer to point **b** is "No"? In particular, could it be an equilibrium for the insider to always trade one unit? [Hard question: characterize the equilibrium in which the insider always chooses his trade size to maximize his profit!]

8. **Informed traders' optimal trade size with imperfectly competitive dealers.** Consider the model of imperfect competition among dealers in Section 4.2.4. Show that informed investors' trade size in this model is: $x(v) = \beta(v - \mu)$ with $\beta = \sqrt{\frac{K-2}{K}} \cdot \frac{\sigma_u}{\sigma_v}$. Why does the informed investor's trade size increase with the number of dealers, K?

9. **Competition between dealers with different initial inventories.** This exercise analyzes (along the lines of the model by Ho and Stoll 1983) how quotes are determined in a competitive dealer market where dealers have different inventories. Consider the model with inventory risk considered in Section 3.5.1. Instead of a representative dealer, assume that there are two dealers, 1 and 2, with respective initial inventories z_1 and z_2, where $z_1 \geq z_2$. These dealers have mean-variance preferences with the same risk aversion, ρ. An investor contacts the dealers to execute a buy or a sell order of size q. The investor requests a quote simultaneously from both dealers and directs his order to that posting the best offer. If dealers make the same offer, the investor routes his order to either one with probability $\frac{1}{2}$.

a. Suppose that the investor contacts the dealers to execute a buy order. Compute the reservation ask prices, denoted $a^r(z_1)$ and $a^r(z_2)$, that make dealer 1 and 2 indifferent between selling q shares or not. Explain why $a^r(z_1) \leq a^r(z_2)$.

b. Suppose that the investor contacts the dealers to execute a sell order. Compute the reservation bid prices, $b^r(z_1)$ and $b^r(z_2)$, that make dealers 1 and 2 indifferent between buying q shares or not. Explain why $b^r(z_2) \geq b^r(z_1)$.

c. What are the quotes (denoted by $a_1^*, a_2^*, b_1^*, b_2^*$) that will be posted by the dealers in a Nash equilibrium where each dealer knows the inventory of his competitor? [Hint: in such an equilibrium, no dealer can be better off by undercutting the quote of his competitor.]

d. Are dealers' rents increasing or decreasing in the difference between their initial inventories?

e. How would your answer to point **c** change if there is a third dealer with inventory z_3 such that $z_1 > z_2 > z_3$?

10. **Risk-averse market makers active in two correlated markets.** Consider a two-period model with K competitive and identically risk-averse market makers, who in the first period operate in the markets for two assets, 1 and 2. The objective function of market maker $k = (1, 2, \ldots, K)$ is:

$$E(w^k) - \frac{\bar{\rho}}{2}\text{var}(w^k),$$

where $\bar{\rho}$ the individual risk aversion of market makers and w^k denotes the final wealth of market maker k, which is:

$$w^k = v_1 \underbrace{(z_1^k - y_1^k)}_{\substack{\text{final} \\ \text{inventory} \\ \text{of asset 1}}} + v_2 \underbrace{(z_2^k - y_2^k)}_{\substack{\text{final} \\ \text{inventory} \\ \text{of asset 2}}} + \underbrace{p_1 y_1^k + p_2 y_2^k + c^k}_{\substack{\text{final} \\ \text{cash} \\ \text{position}}},$$

where p_j denotes the price of asset j, z_j^k the initial inventory of asset j held by market maker k, and y_j^k is the supply of asset j by market maker k. The final values of assets 1 and 2, v_1 and v_2, have identical mean and variance, and correlation r:

$$E(v_1) = E(v_2) = \mu, \text{var}(v_1) = \text{var}(v_2) = \sigma_v^2, \text{cov}(v_1, v_2) = r\sigma_v^2.$$

a. Derive the optimal supply of the two assets by market maker k.

b. Denoting the total inventories and net demand for asset 1 by Z_1 and q_1 respectively, and those for asset 2 by Z_2 and q_2, derive the equilibrium price of the two assets. (Recall that, since market makers are all identically risk averse, the "collective" risk aversion in the market can be written as $\rho = \bar{\rho}/K$.)

c. How does the equilibrium price of each asset respond to the net order flow of the other? How does that depend on the correlation between the two asset values, r? Would this hold if two separate sets of market makers were active in each of the two markets? Why, intuitively?

11. **Equilibrium number of risk-averse market-makers in a competitive call auction market.** Consider the two-period call auction model with K competitive and identically risk-averse market makers. In that setting, each market maker $k = (1, 2, \ldots, K)$ maximizes the mean-variance objective:

$$U^k = E(w^k) - \frac{\bar{\rho}}{2} \text{var}(w^k),$$

where $\bar{\rho}$ is the risk aversion coefficient and w^k is the final wealth of market maker k. For simplicity, all market makers are assumed to have an identical initial inventory ($z^k = z$) of the risky asset and a zero initial cash position ($c^k = 0$), so that their final wealth is:

$$w^k = v(z - y^k) + py^k,$$

where p denotes the price of the risky asset and y^k the supply of the asset by market maker k, so that $z - y^k$ is his final inventory.

Now suppose that, in order to participate to trading, each market maker must pay a fixed cost $C > 0$, which can be taken to reflect the resource cost of engaging in trading (computer equipment, employees' pay, etc.) and/or that arising from financial frictions (e.g., borrowing costs). Hence, we must consider a *participation constraint*: market maker k participates to the market only if in equilibrium the resulting value of his objective function is at least as large as a threshold level of utility $\bar{U}$, which denotes his utility if he does not supply the asset ($y^k = 0$), thus retaining his whole initial inventory z, and saves the cost C:

$$U^k \geq \bar{U} = E(v \cdot z) - \frac{\bar{\rho}}{2} \text{var}(v \cdot z) + C = \left(\mu - \frac{\bar{\rho}}{2} \sigma_v^2 z \right) \cdot z + C.$$

Denote by K^* the number of market makers who *in equilibrium participate* to the market by supplying a non-zero amount y^k of the risky asset. To help answering the subsequent questions, recall that, *if* market maker k participates to the market, his optimal supply of the risky asset is:

$$y^k = \frac{p-\mu}{\bar{\rho}\sigma_v^2} + z,$$

where μ and σ_v^2 are the mean and the variance of the asset's value, and that the equilibrium price results from equating total supply with net demand q:

$$\sum_{k=1}^{K^*} y^k = q \;\; \Rightarrow \;\; p^* = \mu - \rho\sigma_v^2 Z + \rho\sigma_v^2 q = \mu - \bar{\rho}\sigma_v^2 z + \bar{\rho}\sigma_v^2 \frac{q}{K^*},$$

where Z denotes the total inventory of the K^* market makers who participate to the market and ρ their "collective" risk aversion: $Z = K^* z$ and $\rho = \bar{\rho}/K^*$.

a. Find the equilibrium value of the objective function U^k for a market maker $k \in S^*$ who participates to the market.

b. Determine the marginal market maker, i.e. the market maker for which the participation constraint $U^k \geq \bar{U}$ just binds (in the sense that the constraint would be violated by adding another market maker to the set of participants), and the number K^* of market makers for which the participation constraint $U^k \geq \bar{U}$ is satisfied in equilibrium (neglecting integer constraints, for simplicity).

c. How does K^* vary with σ_v^2, z and q? Why, intuitively?

12. **Inventory effects around treasury auctions.** The data for this exercise are contained in the Excel file Ch4_ex12_data.xlsx, available on the companion website for the book.[17] The file provides data on 105 auctions of French long-term government bonds from 2010 to 2021. The auctions are run by the national debt management office (Agence France Trésor) and the participants are mainly banks, who are active as dealers in the secondary markets for government bonds.

Each row in the Excel file contains the notional amount of bonds issued and the benchmark 30-year yield 5 days before the auction, on the day of the auction, and 5 days after the auction (i.e., $i_{t-5}, i_t,$ and i_{t+5}, where i_t is the bond yield at the auction date). The bond yield is equal to the return from holding the bond to maturity. Since bonds' cash flows are fixed, the yield is inversely related to the bond price: the yield falls when the price of the bond rises,

---

[17] Sources: www.aft.gouv.fr and Bloomberg.

a. As dealers buy bonds at auction, the auction will cause their inventory to increase. Based on the inventory risk model (see equation (4.25)), what effect should we then expect the auction to have on the benchmark yield (recalling that yields and prices move inversely)? Compute the average yield change relative to 5 days before the auction. Is the evidence in line with the model's prediction?

b. Dealers usually decrease their bond holdings in the days following the auction by selling bonds from their inventory to their customers. Which effect should this have on the yield? Is this visible in the data?

c. Based on your replies to questions **a** and **b**, could you devise a trading strategy to exploit the observed pattern in prices? These patterns have actually been observed in many different government bond markets (see Lou, Yan, and Zhang 2013). Auctions are also announced in advance, so the auction itself does not bring any new information. Using the dynamic model presented in Section 3.5.2 (Chapter 3), can you explain why such predictable patterns can persist?

5

Estimating the Determinants
of Market Illiquidity

Learning Objectives:

- What a price impact regression is and how it can be used to measure the various sources of market illiquidity
- How to measure the permanent impact of trades
- How to estimate the level of informed trading in a security

5.1 Introduction

Liquidity varies dramatically from security to security and over time. As Chapters 3 and 4 explain, these variations should reflect changes in the cost of providing liquidity caused by adverse selection, order processing, and risky inventory holding.

The financial crisis of 2008–9 provides a case in point: during the crisis, most stocks became significantly more illiquid. As an illustration, Figure 5.1 plots the average closing bid-ask spread for NYSE stocks in the financial and consumer staples sectors from April 2006 to April 2009. The spreads start rising in all sectors as the first signs of trouble appear in the summer of 2007, and keep increasing as the crisis deepens, especially after the AIG bailout and the Lehman Brothers bankruptcy in the early fall of 2008.

The crisis also generated a huge increase in the volatility of returns by amplifying uncertainty about public policies and companies' prospects. Moreover, it made it harder for liquidity suppliers to get credit to fund their market-making activity. For these reasons, their inventory holding costs increased, which provides a first explanation for the increase in spreads in the sectors of financials and consumer staples.

In addition, the crisis increased asymmetric information for stocks in the financial sector. By their very position, participants from the financial industry were probably better informed about the soundness of the balance sheets of banks and security firms and the likelihood of government bailouts. Thus, the

Market Liquidity: Theory, Evidence, and Policy. Second Edition. Thierry Foucault, Marco Pagano, and Ailsa Röell,
Oxford University Press. © Oxford University Press 2023. DOI: 10.1093/oso/9780197542064.003.0006

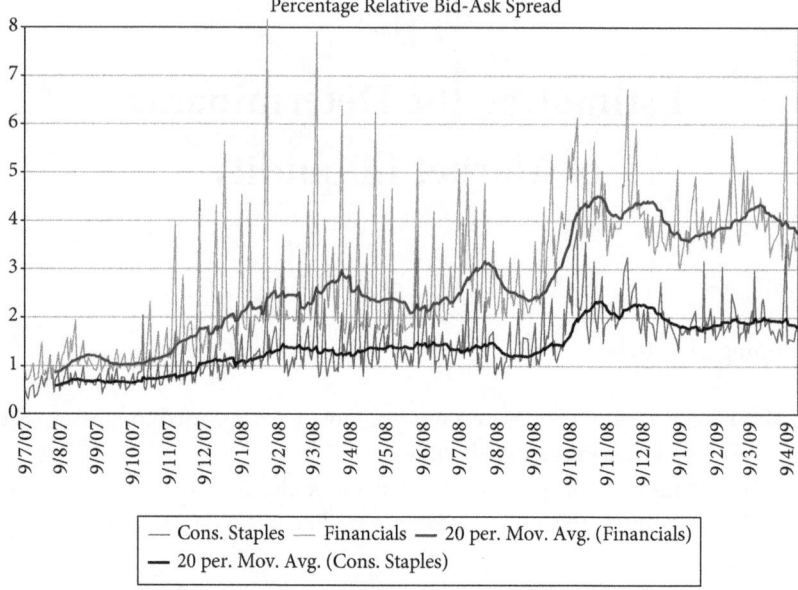

Figure 5.1 Average NYSE closing bid-ask spread, financials, and consumer staples, July 2007–September 2009.

likelihood of informed trading in financials was now greater than before, which may explain why the crisis widened the bid-ask spread on financials more than on consumer staples stocks.

The role of asymmetric information in explaining variations in market liquidity is also illustrated by Figure 5.2, which compares the bid-ask spread for firms that lose analyst coverage (the black line) and firms that do not (the gray line). Financial analysts collect, produce, and disseminate information about the fundamental value of securities. This should level the informational playing field between market participants and thus reduce the opportunities for company insiders. So when analysts' coverage of a company ceases, we expect the bid-ask spread to widen due to adverse selection, and this is precisely what Figure 5.2 shows: when a stock loses its last analyst, its bid-ask spread increases dramatically compared to those of comparable stocks that do not.

The theories set forth in previous chapters, then, have given us a *qualitative* interpretation of cross-sectional and time variations in market liquidity. As we shall see in this chapter, they also serve to *quantify* the contribution of each source of market illiquidity to these variations, using econometric techniques. In Sections 5.2 and 5.3, we explain how one can use time series of transaction prices and signed trade sizes to estimate the contributions of adverse selection

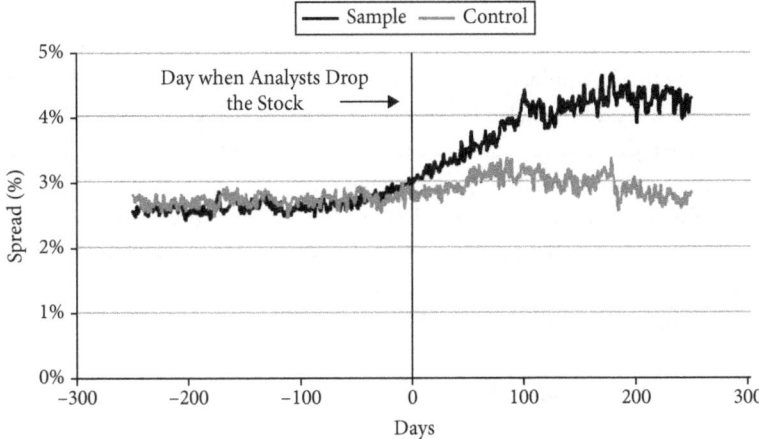

Figure 5.2 Average effective bid-ask spreads for stocks for which analysts coverage is terminated and a control group for which it is continued.
Source: Ellul and Panayides, 2018.

costs, inventory costs, and order processing costs to market illiquidity and price movements. The techniques described exploit the fact that market orders have different effects on the dynamics of securities prices depending on the relative prevalence of adverse selection, order processing, and inventory holding costs (see Chapter 3). Finally, in Section 5.4, we show how one can use order flow data to build a measure of the frequency of informed trading in a security. Armed with this gauge, one can test predictions about the effect of informed trading on liquidity and the sources of informed trading (e.g., whether some trading mechanisms are more prone to informed trading).

5.2 Price Impact Regressions

In this section, we show how to estimate the relative importance of the various costs of providing liquidity by running "price impact regressions," regressions of changes in prices on contemporaneous and lagged measures of order flow. The exact specification of these regressions depends on assumptions about the sources of market illiquidity and the properties of the order arrival process. In Section 5.2.1, we consider the case in which dealers are risk neutral (so as to ignore inventory holding costs) and market orders are serially uncorrelated. Then, Section 5.2.2 explains how to account for inventory holding costs and serial correlation in specifying price impact regressions.

5.2.1 Without Inventory Costs

Consider again the model of trading developed in Section 3.4: liquidity suppliers are risk neutral and they risk trading with better informed investors. They also bear an order-processing cost for each trade. In Chapter 3's scenario, the price of the tth transaction is $p_t = \mu_t + \gamma d_t$, as in equation (3.33), where (i) μ_t is liquidity suppliers' estimate of the asset payoff, (ii) γ is the order-processing cost per share (or a measure of dealers' rent), and (iii) d_t indicates whether the market order triggering the tth transaction is a buy ($d_t = 1$) or a sell ($d_t = -1$).

Accordingly, consecutive price changes are:

$$\Delta p_t = p_t - p_{t-1} = \mu_t - \mu_{t-1} + \gamma \Delta d_t. \tag{5.1}$$

As orders contain information, they affect liquidity suppliers' estimate of the asset's true value (see equation (3.24) in Chapter 3). Specifically:

$$\mu_t = \mu_{t-1} + \lambda d_t + \varepsilon_t, \tag{5.2}$$

where λ measures the informativeness of the order flow,[1] and the error term ε_t is a white noise error that captures the effects of public information (e.g., macroeconomic and corporate announcements) on market participants' value estimates: hence, $E(\varepsilon_t) = 0, \forall t$, and $E(\varepsilon_t \varepsilon_s) = 0, \forall t \neq s$.

Thus, the transaction price can be written as $p_t = \mu_{t-1} + (\lambda + \gamma)d_t + \varepsilon_t$. Recalling that $p_t = a_t$ if $d_t = 1$ and $p_t = b_t$ if $d_t = -1$, the bid-ask spread at the time of the tth transaction is equal to:

$$a_t - b_t = 2(\gamma + \lambda), \tag{5.3}$$

where λ and γ are respectively the adverse selection cost component and the order processing cost component of the bid-ask spread.

Combining equations (5.1) and (5.2) yields:

$$\Delta p_t = \gamma \Delta d_t + \lambda d_t + \varepsilon_t. \tag{5.4}$$

This equation shows that price movements over a short time interval can arise from three sources: the bid-ask bounce due to order-processing costs, the information content of the order flow, and public news. For example, suppose a buy order arrives at time $t-1$ and then a sell order at time t. The buy order

---

[1] The parameter λ corresponds to $s(d_t)$ in equation (3.24), which is time varying, but for simplicity is assumed to be constant, at least over the estimation period.

executes at the best ask price, the sell order executes at the best bid. This "bid-ask bounce" generates a price decrease equal to 2γ, which is captured by the first term $(\gamma \Delta d_t)$ in equation (5.4). Moreover, dealers set the bid price for the tth transaction at a discount from their value estimate after the $(t-1)^{th}$ transaction, reflecting the possibility that the tth order is from an informed investor. This discount also contributes to the change in price between the two transactions, and is captured by the second term (λd_t) in equation (5.4). In this case, it amplifies the price decrease due to the bid-ask bounce by an amount equal to λ. Thus, in this example the total change in price from the $(t-1)^{th}$ to the tth transaction is $\Delta p_t = -\lambda - 2\gamma < 0$, as implied by equation (5.4). By the same token, in the presence of informed trading, Roll's measure underestimates the bid-ask spread, being solely based on the bid-ask bounce (see Box 5.1).

Box 5.1 Revisiting Roll's Measure with Adverse Selection

As Chapter 2 demonstrates, we can use the covariance of consecutive changes in prices to estimate the bid-ask spread. For instance, Roll's estimator of the bid-ask spread $S_{Roll} = 2\sqrt{-\text{cov}\left(\Delta p_t, \Delta p_{t-1}\right)}$ is. As was first noted by Glosten (1987), when the bid-ask spread is in part due to adverse selection costs, this estimator is biased.

To see why, consider again equation (5.4), where only the direction and not the size of trades matters. As d_t and ε_t are independent of each other and over time, equation (5.4) implies that:

$$\text{cov}\left(\Delta p_t, \Delta p_{t-1}\right) = -\gamma(\gamma + \lambda).$$

Thus, Roll's estimate of the bid-ask spread is:

$$\hat{S}_{Roll} = 2\sqrt{\gamma(\gamma + \lambda)},$$

whereas the true spread is $S = 2(\lambda + \gamma)$. The Roll estimator underestimates it by a factor of $\sqrt{(\lambda + \gamma)/\gamma}$. But if S is observed directly by looking at quoted prices in addition to transaction prices, then Roll's measure can be used to estimate the fraction of it that is due to order-processing costs, since $\hat{S}_{Roll}/S = \frac{2\sqrt{\gamma(\lambda+\gamma)}}{2(\lambda+\gamma)} = \sqrt{\frac{\gamma}{\lambda+\gamma}}$. Thus, the order-processing cost component accounts for a fraction $(\hat{S}_{Roll}/S)^2$ of the spread.

More generally, price reversals are a symptom of market illiquidity. For this reason, $-\text{cov}\left(\Delta p_t, \Delta p_{t-1}\right)$ (a measure of the magnitude of price reversals) is sometimes used as a gauge of market illiquidity. However, if illiquidity is mainly due to asymmetric information, this measure of illiquidity will be small even if the spread is large (since in this case $\text{cov}(\Delta p_t, \Delta p_{t-1})$ goes to zero when γ goes to zero). The reason is that the price impact of informed trades is permanent, unlike that of trades due to order-processing costs or inventory holding costs.

Equation (5.4) is the cornerstone of what empiricists call a "price impact regression." Indeed, with trade and quote data like those presented in Table 3.1, the parameters in this equation can be estimated by running a regression of the trade-to-trade changes in price on the contemporaneous order flow (d_t) and the first difference of this variable (Δd_t). The term "price impact" reflects the fact that the estimates of λ and γ provide a way to evaluate the short-term impact ($\lambda + \gamma$) and the long-term impact (λ) of market orders on transaction prices (see Chapter 3). Hence, this methodology enables to assess the relative importance of the various factors affecting price changes over a short period of time.

In general, researchers have used more complex specifications for price impact regressions than that suggested by equation (5.4). First, the order-processing cost may vary with the size of trades. For instance, if this cost has a fixed component, dealers may be willing to execute large orders at smaller markups or discounts. Alternatively, they may offer better quotes to clients making large trades, as those clients have more bargaining power (see exercise 5 in Chapter 10).[2] These effects work to create a negative relationship between the effective spread and trade size. To account for these "quantity discounts," equation (5.1) can be rewritten as follows:

$$\Delta p_t = \mu_t - \mu_{t-1} + \gamma_0 \Delta d_t + \gamma_1 \Delta q_t, \tag{5.5}$$

where γ_1 should be negative in presence of quantity discounts.

Moreover, Chapter 4 shows that not only the direction of orders d_t but also their signed size $q_t = d_t |q_t|$ is informative, since the size of an informed trader's order will increase in the extent of the deviation between his estimate of the asset's value and the prior estimate made by liquidity suppliers (see Section 4.2.3). In this case, it is natural to generalize equation (5.2) in this way:

---

[2] For instance, institutional investors trade larger volumes than retail investors. As they trade more frequently, they have more bargaining power (see Bernhardt et al. 2005). This effect implies that the bid-ask spread may decrease with trade size, a conclusion at odds with the prediction of asymmetric information models but consistent with empirical observations in bond markets (see Green, Hollifield, and Schürhoff 2007) and some equity markets (e.g., Bernhardt et al. 2005).

$$\mu_t = \mu_{t-1} + \lambda_0 d_t + \lambda_1 q_t + \varepsilon_t. \tag{5.6}$$

The coefficient λ_0 should be zero if very small trades have no informational content. Combining equations (5.5) and (5.6), we obtain a more general version of equation (5.4):

$$\Delta p_t = \lambda_0 d_t + \lambda_1 q_t + \gamma_0 \Delta d_t + \gamma_1 \Delta q_t + \varepsilon_t. \tag{5.7}$$

In estimating such a price impact regression, several econometric problems arise.[3] First, data do not always tell whether the trades are triggered by buy or by sell orders (that is, the trade direction d_t, hence the sign of q_t is not always observed). In this case, one must infer market order direction from recorded trades (by using the Lee-Ready algorithm described in Chapter 2), which can induce measurement error in d_t.[4] Second, real-world quotes must be positioned on a discrete grid, so the observed transaction price necessarily differs from the theoretical price by a rounding error. This is a source of error in the regression's dependent variable, which tends to induce negative autocorrelation in residuals. Last, the error term in this regression is likely to be heteroskedastic if, for instance, public information does not arrive at a constant rate during the day: this biases the estimated standard errors of the coefficients.

There are several ways of coping with these econometric problems. One way is to estimate equation (5.7) and an order direction equation jointly, using a maximum likelihood approach, as described in Glosten and Harris (1988), even though this approach retains the assumption that the error term is homoskedastic. In some cases, data sets are richer, so that order direction is observed directly—as in de Jong, Nijman, and Röell (1996). These authors deal with heteroskedasticity and autocorrelation of residuals using Newey-West estimates of the standard errors of the coefficients. Another method is that adopted by Huang and Stoll (1997) and Madhavan, Richardson, and Roomans (1997), who estimate an equation similar to (5.7) using the generalized method of moments (GMM), which can accommodate conditional heteroskedasticity of unknown form and serial correlation of residuals.

Glosten and Harris (1988) estimate equation (5.7) using a sample of eight hundred transaction-by-transaction observations for NYSE stocks between

---

[3] The specification of the regression is a problem in itself as the omission of a single relevant explanatory variable can bias the estimates. This underscores the need for theoretical models of market microstructure, such as those developed in Chapter 3. They provide a starting point to think about economically meaningful specifications of the relationships between returns and order flow.

[4] Errors in measurement of the explanatory variables can lead to biased and inconsistent estimates of the coefficients in the classical linear regression model.

December 1, 1981, and January 31, 1983.[5] They first test the parameter restrictions $\lambda_0 = \gamma_1 = 0$, namely, that small orders carry no information and that order-processing costs are unrelated to trade size. Upon finding that this restriction is not rejected on a subsample, they estimate the following restricted specification of equation (5.7) for each of 250 stocks:

$$\Delta p_t = \lambda_1 q_t + \gamma_0 \Delta d_t + \varepsilon_t. \tag{5.8}$$

They find that λ_1 is significantly positive for 170 stocks and γ_0 is significantly positive for 210 stocks. On average, for the stocks in their sample, they find that for a one–thousand share lot, $\lambda_1 = 0.0102$ and $\gamma_0 = 0.0465$.[6] To interpret these figures, consider a typical stock and suppose that a buy market order for one thousand shares arrives. According to the model, on average, this order executes at a markup (relative to the midquote) equal to: $\gamma_0 + \lambda_1 = 5.67$ cents per share. Thus, the total implicit trading cost on this order is $1,000 \times 0.0567 = \$56.70$. However, after such a trade, the price increases permanently by an average amount equal to 1.02 cents (λ_1). So the liquidity suppliers' expected profit on the transaction (the "realized spread") is only 4.65 cents per share. This example shows how one can use price impact regressions to obtain estimates of effective and realized spreads (see Chapter 2 for their definitions).

Using different data, de Jong, Nijman, and Röell (1996) find that on average the adverse selection component of the spread is weakly increasing in order size, as in Glosten and Harris (1988), but unlike the latter they find that the order-processing cost component is strongly decreasing in trade size (i.e., $\gamma_1 < 0$).

5.2.2 With Inventory Costs

If liquidity suppliers require compensation for inventory risk, as explained in Section 3.5, the price impact regressions (5.4) and (5.7) are misspecified. They will accordingly produce biased estimates of order-processing and adverse selection costs. Indeed, as shown graphically in Figure 3.11 of Chapter 3, part of the change in liquidity suppliers' quotes after a trade reflects the change in inventory. This will dissipate over time as their aggregate inventory reverts to its long-term average. But in the medium term, this impact persists and moves quotes in the same direction as the trade. So the coefficient of the contemporaneous order

---

[5] Our notation differs from that used by Glosten and Harris (1988). They denote by z_0 and z_1 the coefficients that we denote by λ_0 and λ_1, and by c_0 and c_1 the coefficients that we denote by γ_0 and γ_1.
[6] See table 2, panel B on p. 136 of their study.

flow in equation (5.4) will pick up both the impact of asymmetric information and that of inventory risk, and will therefore overestimate the informativeness of order flow.

To see this point, let us expand the model to include not only asymmetric information but also inventory holding costs. For simplicity, we assume that the informational content of the order flow is entirely contained in the signed trade size q_t (so that $\lambda_0 = 0$ in equation (5.6)):

$$\mu_t = \mu_{t-1} + \lambda q_t + \varepsilon_t. \tag{5.9}$$

This means that just before observing the order flow q_t, dealers estimate the security's value as $\mu_{t-1} + \varepsilon_t$, assuming that they expect the order flow to be zero on average. Factoring in inventory holding costs, their valuation before executing the order at time t is:

$$m_t = \mu_{t-1} - \beta z_t + \varepsilon_t, \tag{5.10}$$

where z_t is dealers' aggregate inventory just before the tth transaction and β reflects inventory holding costs, that is, it equals the risk premium parameter $\rho \sigma_\varepsilon^2$ in equation (3.45) of Chapter 3.

Taking the first differences of the midquote in equation (5.10), we obtain:

$$\Delta m_t = \Delta \mu_{t-1} - \beta \Delta z_t + \Delta \varepsilon_t = \lambda q_{t-1} - \beta \Delta z_t + \varepsilon_t, \tag{5.11}$$

where in the second step we have substituted $\Delta \mu_{t-1} = \lambda q_{t-1} + \varepsilon_{t-1}$ from equation (5.9). Using the market-clearing condition $\Delta z_t = -q_{t-1}$ (in equilibrium, the change in inventories mirrors the order flow), we can rewrite equation (5.11) as:

$$\Delta m_t = (\lambda + \beta) q_{t-1} + \varepsilon_t. \tag{5.12}$$

Now the transaction price at time t is the midquote plus or minus half the bid-ask spread, depending on whether the incoming order is a buy or a sell, that is,

$$p_t = m_t + (\lambda + \beta) q_t + \gamma d_t, \tag{5.13}$$

where we assume that the order-processing cost is γ per share. Taking the first difference of this equation and using equation (5.12), the change in consecutive prices can be written as:

$$\Delta p_t = (\lambda + \beta) q_t + \gamma \Delta d_t + \varepsilon_t. \tag{5.14}$$

Thus even if the regression (5.8) estimated by Glosten and Harris (1988) is correctly specified, the estimate of the coefficient of q_t will overestimate the informativeness, λ, of the order flow in the presence of inventory effects. The problem is that this specification is not rich enough to distinguish the adverse selection and the inventory cost components, because in the short run they have the same effect on prices.

To overcome this identification problem, one can enrich the model to account for the fact that market orders are serially correlated, as suggested by Huang and Stoll (1997). As explained below, taking this into account allows a decomposition of the bid-ask spread in its three components: adverse selection, order-processing costs and inventory-holdings costs. Serial correlation in the flow of market orders may arise for at least three reasons. First, informed investors often react to the same signal, which generates a flurry of orders on the same side of the market. This generates positive serial correlation in order flow (see exercise 1). Second, an investor who wants to make a large trade may elect to trickle it into the market as a series of smaller orders to lessen its price impact. This also tends to generate positive serial correlation in the order flow. Third, as Chapter 3 explains, dealers react to an unbalanced order flow by changing their quotes to induce more orders from the opposite side of the market and so rebalance their inventories. This induces negative autocorrelation in the order flow.

Regardless of its sign, the autocorrelation implies that there is a predictable component of the order flow. Let $\eta_t \equiv q_t - \mathrm{E}(q_t|\Omega_{t-1})$ be the unexpected component (i.e., the "innovation") in the tth transaction (Ω_{t-1} being all the relevant information available before the tth transaction relevant for predicting its size). As Hasbrouck (1988) observes, only this unexpected component contains new information and therefore affects dealers' value estimate. Thus equation (5.9) becomes (see exercise 1 for a derivation in the framework analyzed in Chapter 3):

$$\mu_t = \mu_{t-1} + \lambda\left[q_t - \mathrm{E}\left(q_t|\Omega_{t-1}\right)\right] + \varepsilon_t. \tag{5.15}$$

Recalling that the transaction price is the midquote plus or minus half the bid-ask spread, we can rewrite the transaction price at time t as follows:

$$p_t = m_t + \lambda\left[q_t - \mathrm{E}\left(q_t|\Omega_{t-1}\right)\right] + \beta q_t + \gamma d_t, \tag{5.16}$$

where m_t is given by equation (5.10). The adverse selection cost component of the spread (that is, $\lambda[q_t - \mathrm{E}(q_t|\Omega_{t-1})]$) depends only on the trade innovation for the reasons that we just explained. But the inventory cost component (βq_t) is determined by the actual trade size, since the change in dealers' inventory (and thereby their inventory risk exposure) depends on the entire (not just the unexpected) trade size. This provides a way to measure separately the contribution of asymmetric information (λ) and inventory risk (β) to market illiquidity.

As an example, let us assume, as in Huang and Stoll (1997), that market orders are generated by a first-order autoregressive process:

$$q_t = \phi q_{t-1} + \eta_t, \tag{5.17}$$

where the innovation η_t in the order flow is assumed to be independent of current information Ω_{t-1}. Hence, the expected value of the order flow is $E(q_t|\Omega_{t-1}) = \phi q_{t-1}$. In this case the order flow innovation $q_t - E(q_t|\Omega_{t-1})$ is $q_t - \phi q_{t-1}$. Inserting this innovation in expression (5.16) and taking first differences yields the change in transaction prices:

$$\Delta p_t = \Delta m_t + \lambda \left[\Delta q_t - \phi \Delta q_{t-1} \right] + \beta \Delta q_t + \gamma \Delta d_t. \tag{5.18}$$

As in the first step of equation (5.11), the change in the midquote is $\Delta m_t = \Delta \mu_{t-1} - \beta \Delta z_t + \Delta \varepsilon_t$. Again using the market-clearing condition $\Delta z_t = -q_{t-1}$ and the fact that the change in dealers' value estimate is:

$$\Delta \mu_t = \lambda (q_t - \phi q_{t-1}) + \varepsilon_t, \tag{5.19}$$

we obtain:

$$\Delta m_t = (\lambda + \beta) q_{t-1} - \lambda \phi q_{t-2} + \varepsilon_t. \tag{5.20}$$

Substituting this expression for Δm_t in equation (5.18), we finally obtain the following specification for the price impact regression:

$$\Delta p_t = (\lambda + \beta) q_t - \lambda \phi q_{t-1} + \gamma \Delta d_t + \varepsilon_t. \tag{5.21}$$

When estimated jointly with the autoregressive process for the order flow (5.17), this specification of the price impact regression allows us to identify the three determinants of the bid-ask spread: λ, β, γ, and the coefficient of the order flow process, ϕ. Hence, this approach is called a *three-way decomposition* of the bid-ask spread. Identification comes from the additional assumptions that dealers' estimate of the fundamental value is affected only by surprises in order flow and that inventory holding costs are affected by the actual order flow.

Madhavan, Richardson, and Roomans (1997) estimate a special case of equation (5.21), assuming that $q_t = d_t$ (i.e., all trades are posited as being for one share) and $\beta = 0$ (no inventory effect). So, while their approach distinguishes only between the adverse selection and order-processing cost components of the bid-ask spread, as already done by Glosten and Harris (1988), it takes into account that only the unforeseen component of the order flow conveys information. In their case, equation (5.21) becomes:

$$\Delta p_t = (\lambda + \gamma)d_t - (\lambda\phi + \gamma)d_{t-1} + \varepsilon_t. \tag{5.22}$$

Using GMM they estimate this equation jointly with (5.17) (to estimate ϕ) for various intervals during the trading day for NYSE stocks. They show that the adverse selection cost component is relatively high at the opening (about 4 cents in the first half hour of trading: see their table 2) and then declines (to about 2.8 cents in the last half hour). In contrast, the order-processing cost component is lower at the opening (about 3.4 cents) than at the end of the day (about 4.6 cents). This pattern may reflect the fact that dealers' bargaining power increases towards the end of the trading day, since liquidity demanders are more and more impatient to trade. Hence the daily evolution of the adverse selection cost and order-processing cost implies a U-shaped curve of bid-ask spreads in equity markets: high at the beginning and the end of the trading day, low in the middle.

When data on dealers' inventories are available, there is another way to estimate the various components of the bid-ask spread and to relate price changes to order flow. To see this, add and subtract βq_{t-1} from the right hand side of equation (5.21) to obtain:

$$
\begin{aligned}
\Delta p_t &= (\lambda + \beta)q_t - \beta q_{t-1} + \beta q_{t-1} - \lambda\phi q_{t-1} + \gamma\Delta d_t + \varepsilon_t \\
&= \lambda q_t + \beta(q_t - q_{t-1}) - (\lambda\phi - \beta)q_{t-1} + \gamma\Delta d_t + \varepsilon_t \\
&= \theta_0 q_t + \theta_1(q_t - q_{t-1}) + \theta_2(z_t - z_{t-1}) + \gamma\Delta d_t + \varepsilon_t,
\end{aligned}
\tag{5.23}
$$

with $\theta_0 = \lambda, \theta_1 = \beta$, and $\theta_2 = \lambda\phi - \beta$, after using the market clearing condition $z_t - z_{t-1} = -q_{t-1}$ in the last step of (5.23). Thus, with data on dealers' inventories, we can evaluate the strength of inventory effects by estimating a regression of price changes on inventories and order flow. In practice, the coefficient of $\Delta q = q_t - q_{t-1}$ may also reflect the effect of order-processing costs if these have a fixed component, as explained in the previous section. Thus, the coefficient of the price impact regression on the change in inventories, $z_t - z_{t-1}$, is likely to be more informative about the effect of inventory risk on prices. It should be negative if $\beta > \lambda\phi$ (i.e., if inventory effects are strong enough).

Lyons (1995) tests a specification similar to equation (5.23) with data on trades of one dealer in the Deutsche Mark/Dollar market in 1992 (over one week, August 3–August 7, 1992). For each transaction in which the dealer acts as a liquidity supplier, Lyons observes its size and the dealer's inventory. He finds very strong inventory effects. One possible reason is that in foreign exchange markets, inventory risk is large, as trades are typically larger there than in equity markets. Moreover, dealers tend to avoid carrying large inventories overnight, so they must adjust their quotes more substantially after trades in order to get faster mean reversion in their positions. Exercise 4 invites the reader to use the data in Lyons (1995) to estimate various specifications of the price impact regressions described in this section.

5.3 Measuring the Permanent Impact of Trades

The previous section models order arrival as an AR(1) process. That is, traders' expectations regarding the next trade depend only on the last trade. Accordingly, the order flow process is assumed to have a very "short memory." This assumption is problematic: with inventory effects, an order's impact is likely to ripple far in the future, suggesting that we should consider autoregressive process with lags greater than one. Consider, say, the arrival of a large sell order at time t. This order leads to a decrease in price, due in part to the increase in liquidity suppliers' risk exposure rather than a true decline in the asset value. Thus, the new order at time $t+1$ is more likely to be a buy than a sell, which corresponds to the case where $\delta < 0$ in the model of Section 3.5.2. But unless dealers' inventories revert very quickly to their long-run level, prices—even after the next trade— will continue to look relatively low to investors. Thus, at time $t+2$, a buy order is again more likely than a sell. In fact, this will continue to be the case until dealers' aggregate inventory reverts to its long-run level. This suggests that the trade size at time t should affect expectations about trades at time $t+1$ but also at $t+2, t+3$, and so on. Moreover, as dealers' inventories revert to their long-run level, a reversal in prices will temper the initial negative impact of the sell order. Hence, in the presence of inventory effects, the permanent impact of a trade is smaller than its immediate impact, and the short-run impact takes time to dissipate (see Figure 3.11).

To account for these observations, Hasbrouck (1991) proposes to measure the permanent impact of trades (a measure of their informativeness) by jointly modelling the dynamics of price changes and orders by a vector autoregressive model (VAR). More specifically, changes in midquotes and trades are assumed to behave according to the following processes:

$$m_t - m_{t-1} = \sum_{i=1}^{\infty} a_j \Delta m_{t-j} + \sum_{i=1}^{\infty} b_j q_{t-j} + \varepsilon_t, \qquad (5.24)$$

$$q_t = \sum_{i=1}^{\infty} c_j \Delta m_{t-j} + \sum_{i=1}^{\infty} h_j q_{t-j} + \eta_t,$$

with the assumptions that the innovations ε_t and η_t have zero means and are jointly and serially uncorrelated.[7] If one sets $b_1 = \lambda + \beta$, $b_2 = -\lambda\phi$, $h_1 = \phi$, and all other coefficients to zero, this specification encompasses as a special case the midquote changes given by equation (5.20).

Besides this particular specification, the VAR approach can encompass richer interactions between returns and order flow: per se, this approach does not place any restrictions on these interactions. Typically, these restrictions will follow from an economic model. For instance, in the presence of inventory effects, one would expect the coefficients h_j to be negative, since inventory and quote management induce mean reversion of the order flow. If, instead, investors tend to execute large orders piecemeal, then one would expect a positive autocorrelation in the order flow and positive values for some of the coefficients h_j. Moreover, the order flow could respond to past price movements: for instance, investors may tend to place buy market orders in response to low quotes and sell market orders in response to high quotes. Such contrarian strategies should result in negative coefficients c_j.

As an illustration, consider the following example inspired by Hasbrouck (1991). Suppose that trades and changes in midquotes for a stock behave according to the following model:

$$m_t - m_{t-1} = 1.998q_{t-1} + 0.096q_{t-2} + 0.053q_{t-3} + 0.025q_{t-4} + \varepsilon_t, \quad (5.25)$$
$$q_t = -0.486q_{t-1} - 0.269q_{t-2} - 0.124q_{t-3} + \eta_t.$$

Using this specification, we can compute the dynamics of midquote returns and trades after a purchase of size 1 ($q_0 = 1$) when the innovations in the system are set at their average value, namely, zero. Table 5.1 below shows the dynamics of the midquotes and trades from the first transaction to the tenth transaction. For the purpose of this discussion, we normalize the initial estimate of the asset value to $m_0 = 100$.

On receiving the buy order at time $t = 0$, the dealers adjusts his midquote at time $t = 1$ up by 1.998, from 100 to 101.998. Models of trading with adverse selection and inventory holding costs typically attribute this increase to the informational content of the buy order *and* to the decrease in dealers' aggregate inventory. In fact, in the aggregate, dealers have sold one unit of the security and now have a short position, so they mark up the price at which they are willing to sell another unit. Hence, the informational content of the trade can be anywhere from 0 to 1.998 depending on the relative magnitude of adverse selection costs and inventory costs.

---

[7] Our notation and timing conventions are different from Hasbrouck (1991).

Table 5.1 Dynamic Responses of Prices and Trades in the Illustrative Model of Hasbrouck (1991)

t	m_t	$m_t - m_{t-1}$	q_t	$\alpha_t(1) = \sum_{\tau=0}^{t} \Delta m_t$
0	100	−.−	1.000	−.−
1	101.998	1.998	−0.486	1.998
2	101.124	−0.875	−0.033	1.123
3	101.064	−0.060	0.023	1.064
4	101.105	0.041	0.058	1.105
5	101.210	0.105	−0.030	1.210
...	...	...	...	...
10	101.1566	-6×10^{-4}	-3×10^{-4}	1.156

Source: Joel Hasbrouck (1991), "Measuring the information content of stock trades," *Journal of Finance* 46, 179–207.

Hasbrouck (1991) proposes to identify the information content of the trade with its long-run average price effect (see exercise 2 for an application). The idea is simple: as Chapter 3 explains, a change in the midquote due to inventory holding costs will dissipate over time as dealers reduce their exposure to the desired level by unwinding positions. Hence, the change in price that persists after a trade must correspond to the value estimation of the asset induced by the trade. Accordingly, the average cumulative price change over T periods after a trade of size q_0 (denoted $\alpha_T(q_0)$) can be used as a proxy for the informational content of a trade of this size. In the analysis of VAR models, $\alpha_T(q_0)$ is called an *impulse response function*, in this case to an innovation in order flow. Impulse response functions are routinely computed by standard software for statistical analysis.

As an application of this idea, let us look again at Table 5.1. The cumulative price change from the first to the tenth transaction, $\alpha_{10}(1)$, is 1.156.[8] This cumulative change in price is less than the initial change ($\alpha_0(1)$), and it can be used as a measure for the informational content of the trade at time $t = 0$. Of course, one can look at an even longer horizon to get a more accurate estimate of the permanent impact of trade (its true informativeness). The choice of horizon should depend on how fast the price impact of a trade that is not due to its information content dissipates.[9]

---

[8] To see how $\alpha_t(1)$ is computed, consider the calculation of $\alpha_2(1)$. First we compute q_1 using the equation for the dynamics of q_t: we obtain $q_1 = -0.486 \times q_0 = -0.486$. Substituting this in the equation for the dynamics of Δm_t, we obtain $\Delta m_2 = 1.998 \times q_1 + 0.096 \times q_0 = -1.998 \times 0.486 + 0.096 = -0.875$. Hence, $\alpha_2(1) = \Delta m_1 + \Delta m_2 = 1.998 - 0.875 = 1.123$.

[9] The econometric model in equation (5.24) assumes that only market orders convey information. However, limit orders may also do so. By extending the methodology of Hasbrouck (1991) to a model

Hasbrouck (1991) implements this methodology using a continuous sequence of trade and quote data from NYSE, AMEX, and consolidated regional U.S. exchanges, over the sixty-two trading days in the first quarter of 1989. He estimates a specification similar to the previous system of equations, truncated at five lags for each variable. The impact of trades on quote revisions is generally positive, and convergence of α_T to its limit value is quite rapid (most being completed within five steps) but not instantaneous. Like other researchers (e.g., Huang and Stoll 1997), Hasbrouck finds that trades are positively autocorrelated (the h_j's are positive) rather than negatively as expected in the presence of inventory effects. But there is a strong negative correlation with midquote changes (the c_j's are negative), which is more consistent with the inventory control hypothesis.

The measure of private information features interesting cross-sectional relationships with company size. After scaling the persistent price impact α_T by the corresponding average share price, Hasbrouck finds that the overall price impact of a trade innovation is greater for stocks with lower rather than higher market capitalization, implying that information asymmetry is more severe for the former. This may reflect the lesser availability of public information about smaller firms, which generally have little or no analyst coverage. So this finding is consistent with the evidence of Ellul and Panayides (2011), quoted at the beginning of this chapter, that stocks that lose analyst coverage have lower liquidity.

5.4 Probability of Informed Trading (PIN)

A completely different approach to evaluating the importance of adverse selection in trading is found in the works of David Easley, Maureen O'Hara, and various coauthors. The method that they propose aims at estimating the probability of informed trading (PIN). Their idea is to infer this probability from the volume and the imbalance of buy and sell orders throughout the trading day: for example, if buy market orders prevail, it seems likely that good news has arrived at the start of trading day, prompting informed buying.

Here we present their approach. The starting point is a specification of the order arrival process over a specific period of time which, in most applications, is put at one trading day. Figure 5.3 gives a graphical summary.

On each trading day, there is a probability α that an information event occurs. An information event is a change in the value of the security, which can be either

---

that includes both market and limit orders, Brogaard et al. (2019) show that limit orders also have permanent impact and therefore contribute to price discovery.

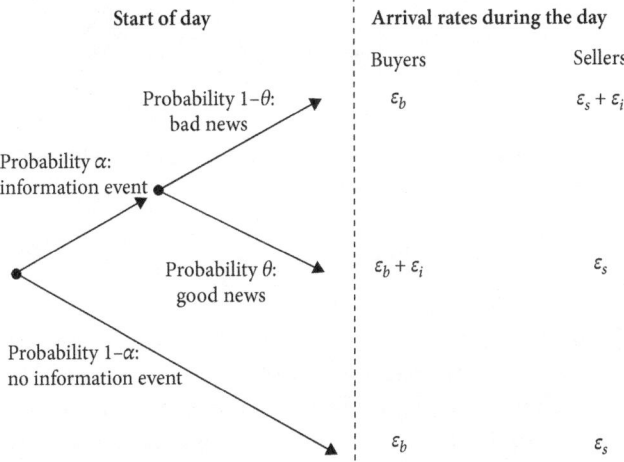

Figure 5.3 Information and order arrival process in the PIN model.

positive with probability θ or negative with probability $1 - \theta$. With probability $1 - \alpha$, there is no information event. A day without an information event is defined as a day without a change in the value of the security.

Dealers do not know whether or not an information event has occurred. If it does, some investors are informed. They know whether the information event is positive (the value of the security rises) or negative. As in Glosten and Milgrom (1985), informed investors will buy on days with good news and sell on those with bad. By definition, there is no informed trading on days without an information event.

More specifically, on days with an information event, orders from informed traders arrive according to a Poisson process with intensity ϵ_i per day. This means that the likelihood of observing k orders from informed traders in a day with an information event is:

$$\frac{\epsilon_i^k e^{-\epsilon_i}}{k!},$$

where $e = 2.71828$ and $k!$ is the factorial of k. Thus, the daily average number of orders from informed traders is ϵ_i. And, whether or not an information event has occurred, buy and sell orders from uninformed investors arrive according to Poisson processes with intensities ϵ_b and ϵ_s, respectively. The order processes for uninformed sellers, uninformed buyers, and informed investors are independent.

The order arrival process differs from the model in Glosten and Milgrom (1985) studied in Chapter 3 in two ways. First, time is continuous and traders arrive at stochastic points in time (in Glosten and Milgrom (1985), time is discrete). Second, there is uncertainty whether an information event has occurred.[10]

As orders from informed and uninformed traders are generated by independent Poisson processes, the likelihood of any given trade being initiated by an informed trader can be shown to be:

$$\text{PIN} = \frac{\alpha \epsilon_i}{\epsilon_b + \epsilon_s + \alpha \epsilon_i}, \tag{5.26}$$

where PIN stands for "probability of informed trading." As one would expect, PIN is the ratio between the rate of arrival of informed traders and the total rate of order arrival. In the limiting case in which uninformed investors do not trade ($\epsilon_b = \epsilon_s = 0$), then PIN=1. This variable plays the same role as the probability π in Chapter 3.

Using this observation, quotes can be computed as in Chapter 3 (see exercise 7). For instance, consider the bid-ask spread for the opening trade and assume that $\theta = \frac{1}{2}$ and $\epsilon_b = \epsilon_s$, so that uninformed investors are equally likely to buy or sell. In this case, using equation (3.12) in Chapter 3 and replacing π with PIN, we obtain:

$$a_1 - b_1 = 2 \times \text{PIN} \cdot (v_H - v_L), \tag{5.27}$$

where v_H is the realization of the asset's value on days with good news and v_L on days with bad news.

Thus market illiquidity is positively related with PIN, which measures dealers' exposure to informed traders. We now explain how to estimate PIN with order flow data. Suppose there are B_n buy and S_n sell market orders on day n. As the order processes of informed and uninformed investors are independent, the likelihood of these realizations conditional on day n being a bad-news day is:

$$\frac{(\epsilon_b)^{B_n} e^{-\epsilon_b}}{B_n!} \cdot \frac{(\epsilon_i + \epsilon_s)^{S_n} e^{-(\epsilon_i + \epsilon_s)}}{S_n!}. \tag{5.28}$$

Conditional on a good-news day, the likelihood of observing B_n buy orders and S_n sell orders is:

$$\frac{(\epsilon_s)^{S_n} e^{-\epsilon_s}}{S_n!} \cdot \frac{(\epsilon_i + \epsilon_b)^{B_n} e^{-(\epsilon_i + \epsilon_b)}}{B_n!}. \tag{5.29}$$

---

[10] This uncertainty implies that the end value of the security has three possible realizations instead of two as in the model of Chapter 3.

Finally, on a no-news day, the likelihood of observing B_n buy orders and S_n sell orders is:

$$\frac{(\epsilon_s)^{S_n} e^{-\epsilon_s}}{S_n!} \cdot \frac{(\epsilon_b)^{B_n} e^{-\epsilon_b}}{B_n!}. \tag{5.30}$$

Now, recall that the probabilities of the three possible configurations of information are:

$$\text{information} = \begin{cases} \text{no news,} & \text{with probability } 1 - \alpha, \\ \text{bad news,} & \text{with probability } \alpha(1 - \theta), \\ \text{good news,} & \text{with probability } \alpha\theta. \end{cases}$$

Hence, using equations (5.28), (5.29), and (5.30), the unconditional probability of B_n buy orders and S_n sell orders on day n is:

$$\begin{aligned} \Pr(B_n, S_n) = {} & (1 - \alpha) \frac{(\epsilon_s)^{S_n} e^{-\epsilon_s}}{S_n!} \cdot \frac{(\epsilon_b)^{B_n} e^{-\epsilon_b}}{B_n!} \\ & + \alpha(1 - \theta) \frac{(\epsilon_b)^{B_n} e^{-\epsilon_b}}{B_n!} \cdot \frac{(\epsilon_i + \epsilon_s)^{S_n} e^{-(\epsilon_i + \epsilon_s)}}{S_n!} \\ & + \alpha\theta \frac{(\epsilon_b + \epsilon_i)^{B_n} e^{-\epsilon_b}}{B_n!} \cdot \frac{(\epsilon_s)^{S_n} e^{-(\epsilon_i + \epsilon_s)}}{S_n!}. \end{aligned}$$

Assuming that the occurrence and direction of information events are independent across days, the likelihood of observing a series of daily number of orders B_n and S_n over N days is therefore:

$$\Pr((B_1, S_1), \ldots, (B_N, S_N)) = \prod_{n=1}^{N} \Pr(B_n, S_n). \tag{5.31}$$

This probability is a function of the five structural parameters: $\alpha, \theta, \epsilon_i, \epsilon_b$, and ϵ_s. Thus we can estimate these parameters, and the PIN, by using the maximum likelihood approach.[11]

Easley, Hvidkjaer, and O'Hara (2002) estimate the PIN of all NYSE common stocks from 1983 to 1998 and obtain a median PIN of about 19%. Their estimate does not vary greatly across stocks (Figure 5.4) and is negatively correlated

---

[11] In order to estimate the PIN, one must know the daily number of buy and sell market orders over the relevant time period. As explained above, some data sets do not identify the direction of market orders, and in these cases, the number of buy and sell orders must be inferred from other variables. This leads to measurement errors that can bias the PIN measure (see Boehmer, Grammig, and Theissen 2006).

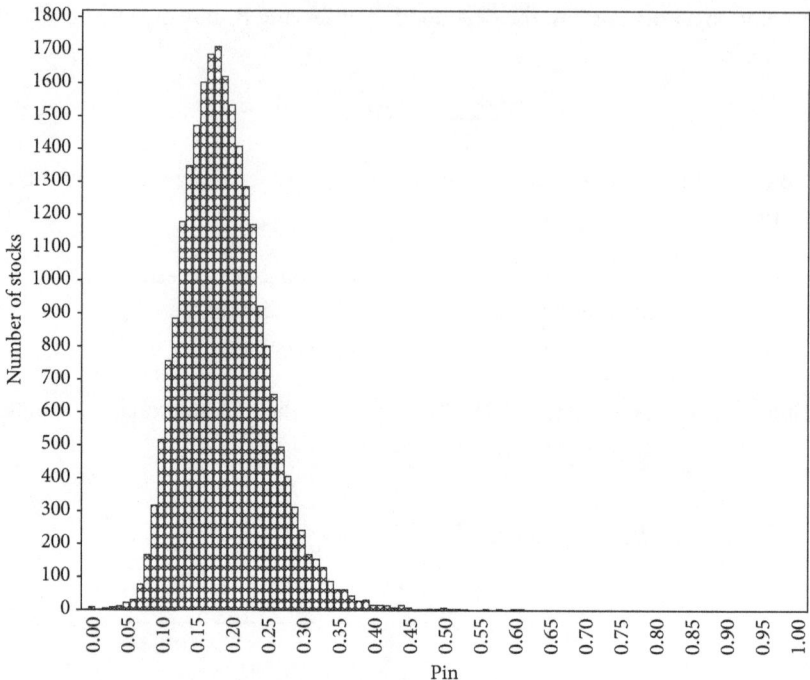

Figure 5.4 Distribution of PIN across NYSE stocks.
Source: panel C of fig. 4 in Easley et al. 2002, p. 2207.

with firm size (with a correlation coefficient of about −0.58): larger firms are characterized by relatively less informed trading, as in Hasbrouck (1991) and many other studies. Meanwhile, the PIN is positively correlated in the cross-section with volatility (0.239) and the bid-ask spread (0.353). The correlation with volatility may reflect the fact that information events are more likely for volatile stocks (α is higher), which also present greater profit opportunities for informed traders (so that ϵ_i is higher for more volatile stocks).

Easley, Hvidkjaer, and O'Hara (2002) also find that the PIN is very stable over time: Figure 5.5 shows the fifth, twenty-fifth, fiftieth, seventy-fifth, and ninety-fifth percentiles of the PIN in each year covered by their study. The PIN does not appear to be correlated with trading volume, perhaps because informed investors adjust their strategies to the trading intensity of noise traders so as to maintain the PIN invariant to volume. Last, as explained in Chapter 10, Easley, Hvidkjaer, and O'Hara (2002) shows that stock returns are positively related to the PIN measure.

This methodology has been applied to many different questions. For instance, Grammig, Schiereck, and Theissen (2001) use it to test the hypothesis that there is less informed trading in non-anonymous trading venues. Intuitively, non-anonymous trading can mitigate informational asymmetries by helping

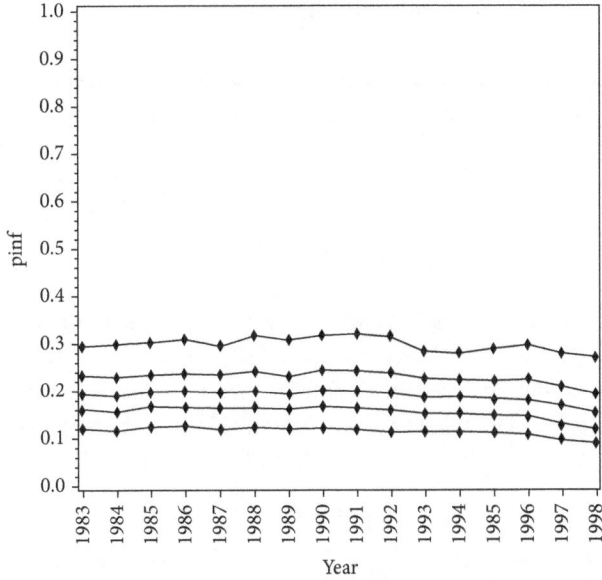

Percentiles shown are 5, 25, 50, 75, and 95.

Figure 5.5 Estimated median PIN for selected trading volume deciles.
Source: panel A of fig. 3 in Easley et al. 2002, p. 2204.

dealers to tell apart informed and uninformed traders (see Chapter 8 for further discussion). Accordingly, when an anonymous and a non-anonymous trading venue coexist, informed traders should choose the anonymous one. The German Stock Exchange offers an ideal laboratory for testing this hypothesis, because its stocks are traded in both an electronic market and a floor market. Using data on trades in both markets, Grammig, Schiereck, and Theissen (2001) estimate the PIN for thirty stocks. As predicted, they find that the PIN is higher in the electronic market for almost all the stocks. Exercise 5 in this chapter is based on their study. Easley, O'Hara, and Paperman (1998) gives another application, showing that the PIN is higher for stocks with less analyst coverage, which may be the reason why the spread widens when analysts stop following a stock (as found by Ellul and Panayides 2011).

PIN measures have become so widely used that some researchers make their estimates of the PIN for different stocks publicly available on their websites (see, for instance, the website maintained by Stephen Brown at the University of Maryland: https://terpconnect.umd.edu/ stephenb/).[12]

---

[12] Other applications of this methodology include Easley et al. (1996a, b); Easley, O'Hara, and Paperman (1998); Easley et al. (2001); Easley et al. (2002); and Heidle and Huang (2002). There is an ongoing debate on the extent to which PIN models match the variability of noise trade in the data and thus provides an accurate measure of informed trading: see Duarte, Hu, and Young (2020) for a discussion of alternative PIN measures and their relative merits.

5.5 Further Reading

This chapter is actually only an introduction to some empirical techniques in the field of market microstructure. For a systematic treatment, see Hasbrouck (2007).

5.6 Exercises

1. **Price impact regressions with order flow predictability.** The goal of this exercise is to derive equation (5.15) using the Glosten and Milgrom model analyzed in Chapter 3. We use the same notations as in Chapter 3. Remember that in Chapter 3, we have shown (see equation (3.24)) that:

$$\mu_t = \mu_{t-1} + s(d_t)d_t,$$

with $s(+1) = s_t^a$ and $s(-1) = s_t^b$ given in equation (3.13) and equation (3.14). Moreover, in exercise 11 of Chapter 3, it is shown that:

$$E(d_t|\Omega_{t-1}) = \pi(2\theta_{t-1} - 1).$$

Define:

$$\lambda_t = \frac{2\pi\theta_{t-1}(1 - \theta_{t-1})(v^H - v^L)}{(1 - \pi(1 - 2\theta_{t-1}))(1 + \pi(1 - 2\theta_{t-1}))}.$$

   a. Using the definition of s_t^a, show that:

$$\mu_t = \mu_{t-1} + \lambda_t(1 - E(d_t|\Omega_{t-1})).$$

   b. Using the definition of s_t^b, show that:

$$\mu_t = \mu_{t-1} + \lambda_t(-1 - E(d_t|\Omega_{t-1})).$$

   c. Deduce that:

$$\mu_t = \mu_{t-1} + \lambda_t(d_t - E(d_t|\Omega_{t-1})).$$

   That is, in line with intuition, dealers' revision of the fair value of the asset are proportional to the innovation in the order flow.

2. **The information effect of orders.** You have a record of transaction prices for all trades on March 26, 2001, for AGF—a French stock listed on

Euronext. There were 519 transactions (trading in Euronext is continuous from 9:00 a.m. to 5:25 p.m.). The index t denotes the tth transaction. The data set contains the following time series (the data are available in two different formats Ch5_AGF_data.xls or Ch5_AGF_data.dta in the companion website of the book.): (i) transaction prices ("traprice"), (ii) the best ask price posted just before the transaction ("ask"), (iii) the best bid price posted just before the transaction ("bid"), (iv) the size of transactions ("tradesize"), and (v) the direction of each trade ("tradedir").

a. Estimate equation (5.22) and interpret the findings.

b. Estimate a VAR model such as equation (5.24) (accounting only for trade direction, not size, for comparability with the findings in **a**). **Note:** Be careful with the timing convention: m_t is the midquote before the tth transaction in the model.

c. Describe the average dynamics of the midquote for AGF after a sell order and infer the estimate of $\alpha_{10}(1)$.

d. How do you explain the difference between the measure of adverse selection obtained in (a) and in (b)?

3. **Empirical specification of price impact regressions.** Suppose that the midprice at time t, m_t, is determined by the best estimate of the stock's fundamental value based on the public information available, namely $\mu_{t-1} + \varepsilon_t$, minus a term reflecting the net inventory position z_t of market makers at time t:

$$m_t = \mu_{t-1} + \varepsilon_t - \beta z_t,$$

where the inventory at time t is related to the order flow at time $t-1$ by the identity:

$$z_t = z_{t-1} - q_{t-1}.$$

When market makers receive an order q_t at time t, they update their estimate of the fundamental value $\mu_{t-1} + \varepsilon_t$ to also reflect the innovation in order flow, $q_t - E[q_t|\Omega_{t-1}]$:

$$\mu_t = \mu_{t-1} + \lambda\{q_t - E[q_t|\Omega_{t-1}]\} + \varepsilon_t.$$

Finally, the order flow is generated by the following AR(2) process:

$$q_t = \varphi_1 q_{t-1} + \varphi_2 q_{t-2} + \eta_t,$$

where η_t is a zero-mean error term uncorrelated with all information at time t (i.e., all variables in the information set Ω_{t-1}).

    a. Define the unexpected component of the order flow, $q_t - E[q_t | \Omega_{t-1}]$ as a function of the current and past values of the order flow.

    b. Determine the change in the best estimate of the fundamental value, $\Delta \mu_t$.

    c. Determine the change in the midprice, Δm_t, as a function only of past values of the order flow.

    d. If you estimate the equation for Δm_t obtained at point (c) jointly with the order flow process assumed in equation $q_t = \varphi_1 q_{t-1} + \varphi_2 q_{t-2} + \eta_t$, can you identify the parameters of the model, namely, β, λ, φ_1, and φ_2? If so, explain how you would infer their values, denoting the coefficients of first three lags of the order flow in the equation obtained at point (c) by b_0, b_1, and b_2.

    e. Do we actually have over-identifying restrictions that can be tested? Specifically, does the above model imply a testable restriction on b_1 / b_2?

4. Price impact estimation. This exercise is based on data collected by Richard Lyons, who used these data to estimate a model of trading with inventory effects (see Lyons 1995). The data are stored in the Excel file Ch5_ex4_data.xls and in the Stata data file Ch5_ex4_data.dta available in the companion website for the book. The data set covers one week of trading (August 3–7, 1992) of one dealer, in the Deutsche Mark/Dollar market, at a major New York investment bank. The data set has two components:

1. A time series of all prices and quantities for all **direct**, **incoming** transactions in which the dealer was involved. **"Direct"** means that the transactions result from direct bilateral negotiations between the dealer and another dealer (in contrast to brokered transactions). **"Incoming"** means that the dealer does not initiate the transaction (that is, he acts as liquidity supplier).

2. A time series of the dealer's inventory. This inventory is observed at the time of each incoming transaction.

    There are 843 observations for the week. Quotes in the Deutsche Mark/-dollar market were firm up to $10 million. The minimal price increment in this market is .0001DM and is referred to as "one pip." Lyons (1995) reports that the median spread quoted by the dealer is three pips. The dataset includes four time series:

1. **price:** transaction prices (p_t).

2. **inventories:** the dealer's inventory (I_t) in million U.S. dollars. I_t is the dealer's inventory just before the tth transaction.

3. **tradesize:** the trade sizes (Q_t) in million U.S. dollars. Trades are signed according to the position taken by the liquidity demander. Purchases (i.e., dealer's sales) are positive, and sales (i.e., dealer's purchases) are negative.

4. **signedtr:** an indicator variable (d_t) that is equal to $+1$ for buy orders (sales by the dealer) and -1 for sell orders (purchases for the dealer).

Overnight observations are suppressed since microstructure effects explain only intraday price dynamics, not overnight changes.

    a. Plot the time series of dealer's inventory at the time of each incoming order in the sample. How do you interpret the graph? Is there evidence of mean reversion in inventories?

    b. Use the data to estimate equation (5.23). How do you interpret the findings?

    c. Propose an estimate of the cost of trading $50 million with the dealer.

5. **PIN estimation.** This exercise uses data from the German Stock Exchange (a subset of the data set used in Grammig, Schiereck, and Theissen 2001).[13] The data set gives, for one stock (BVM) traded on the German Stock Exchange, the number of buy orders and sell orders from June 2 to July 31, 1997 (forty-two days). As usual, the orders are signed according to the position taken by liquidity demanders (i.e., an order is signed positively when the trade initiator is a buyer and conversely). The stock trades on two markets that operate in parallel: a floor market and an electronic trading system. The main difference between the two systems is relative anonymity: a floor market is less anonymous as traders on the floor negotiate prices one-on-one. The data are stored in the Excel file Ch5_ex5_data.xls and the Stata file Ch5_ex5_data.dta available on the companion website for the book. This dataset contains four time series:

    1. **buy_f:** The number of buy orders executed in the floor market on each day t, $t \in \{1, \ldots, 42\}$.

    2. **sell_f:** The number of sell orders executed in the floor market on each day t, $t \in \{1, \ldots, 42\}$.

    3. **buy_e:** The number of buy orders executed in the electronic market on each day t, $t \in \{1, \ldots, 42\}$.

    4. **sell_e:** The number of sell orders executed in the electronic market on each day t, $t \in \{1, \ldots, 42\}$.

    a. Consider the tree describing the order arrival process in Figure 5.3. We modify it to account for the possibility that traders can choose to trade in either the floor market or the electronic market. Specifically, we suppose that informed investors trade at rate μ_F in the floor market and at rate μ_E in the electronic market, while uninformed investors buy and sell at rates ε_{bj} and ε_{sj} in market $j \in \{E, F\}$. On these assumptions, what is the likelihood that this trade is informed, conditional on a trade taking place in the floor market? Conditional on a trade taking place in the electronic market? Call these likelihoods PIN_F and PIN_E.

[13] We thank Erik Theissen for providing the data used here.

b. Using the series of buy and sell orders executed in each system, propose and implement a methodology to estimate PIN_F and PIN_E.

(Note: Estimation by maximum likelihood may not converge if the initial values for the parameters are not well chosen. For this you must calibrate the initial values of the parameters to estimate, so that at least the average number of buy and sell orders per day on each market implied by the Poisson distributions match the actual averages in the data.)

c. Are informed traders more likely to trade in the anonymous market? Is adverse selection greater in the anonymous market?

6. **Decomposition of the bid-ask spread.** Using the data for exercise 1 (Ch5_AGF_data.xls or the Stata file Ch5_AGF_data.dta available in the companion website for the book) and following Glosten and Harris (1988), regress Δp_t on d_t, q_t, Δd_t, and Δq_t.

a. For a transaction of very small size, what is the bid-ask spread and what proportion is attributable to adverse selection versus order-processing cost?

b. Use an F-test to check whether the data support the restriction (imposed by Glosten and Harris 1988) that the coefficients of Δq_t and d_t must both be zero.

c. Use an F-test to check whether the trade size effects (as measured by the coefficients of q_t and Δq_t) are jointly significant over and above the impact of the buy/sell indicators d_t and Δd_t.

d. Relate your answers to the spread measures calculated in the exercises of Chapter 2.

7. **Bid-ask spread and PIN.** Consider the order arrival process described in Figure 5.3. Using equation (3.8) in Chapter 3, derive the ask and bid prices for the first transaction of the day.

8. **Method-of-moments estimator for PIN.** For the PIN model as described in Section 5.4:

a. Derive the first and second moments of the daily buy and sell transactions, that is the expectations $E[B]$ and $E[S]$, the variances $var[B]$ and $var[S]$ and the covariance $cov[B,S]$, as a function of the five underlying parameters of the model (α, θ, ϵ_i, ϵ_b, ϵ_s).

b. Use these five equations to express PIN as well as the underlying parameters of the model in terms of these moments.

PART II

MARKET DESIGN AND REGULATION

6

Limit Order Book Markets

Learning Objectives:

- Why limit order markets require separate analysis
- Adverse selection and market depth in limit order markets
- Effects of trading rules on market liquidity in limit order markets
- Determinants of the choice between market and limit orders

6.1 Introduction

In many markets, trading occurs in continuous time, via an electronic limit order book (LOB), as Chapter 2 describes. For instance, nearly all the major equity markets (the NYSE, Nasdaq, Euronext, the London Stock Exchange, Deutsche Börse, etc.) are continuous limit order markets, sometimes in combination with other trading mechanisms such as a dealer market. Many other instruments (bonds, currencies, derivatives) are also traded in continuous limit order markets. For instance, LIFFE (London International Financial Futures and options Exchange) and the CME (Chicago Mercantile Exchange) use this mechanism to trade derivatives. Likewise, MTS (a trading platform for European sovereign bonds) and BrokerTec (an interdealer trading platform for US Treasuries) are organized as continuous limit order markets.

Limit order markets deserve specific analysis for a number of reasons. First, their trading rules differ from those in call markets or dealership markets, analyzed in Chapter 4. The limit order market is a *discriminatory auction*: all limit orders filled in a given transaction are executed at their own posted price. In contrast, the call market is a *uniform auction*: all traders involved in a given transaction receive or pay the same price.

The following example (Figure 6.1) illustrates the difference. One hundred shares are offered for sale at $A_1 = \$100.50$, two hundred additional shares are offered at $A_2 = \$101$, and an unlimited number of shares is offered for sale at $A_3 = \$101.50$. A buy market order for three hundred shares arrives. It triggers the execution of the sell limit orders placed at $100.50 and $101. In the call

Market Liquidity: Theory, Evidence, and Policy. Second Edition. Thierry Foucault, Marco Pagano, and Ailsa Röell, Oxford University Press. © Oxford University Press 2023. DOI: 10.1093/oso/9780197542064.003.0007

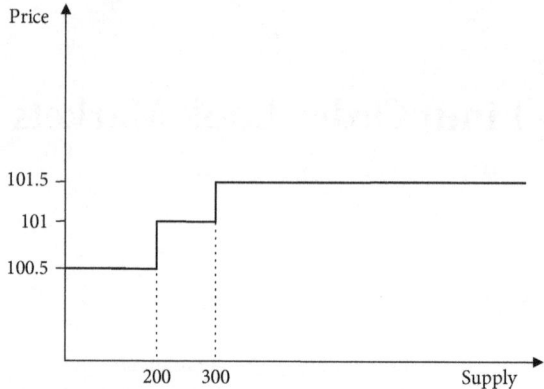

Figure 6.1 A limit order book.

market, all sell limit orders eligible for execution execute at $101, the marginal execution price for the market order. The buyer's payment is therefore $30,300. But in the continuous limit order market, the buy market order "walks up" the book and each limit order executes at its own price. That is, one hundred shares are bought at $100.5 and two hundred shares at $101. The buyer then pays $30,250.

Clearly, for a given LOB, traders submitting market orders get a better deal in the discriminatory auction. However, participants will typically use different order placement strategies in the two types of market since execution prices are determined differently. Chapter 4 analyzes the behavior of investors in a call market. Here, we examine their behavior in a continuous limit order market. To this end, Section 6.2 analyzes a static model of the optimal bidding strategies for limit order traders, maintaining the assumption that traders submitting market and limit orders are different. Thus, this model extends the canonical models considered in Chapters 3 and 4, accounting for the fact that limit order markets operate differently from call auctions. Section 6.3 applies the model to the design of limit order markets: it analyzes the impact of tick size, the role of priority rules and that of designated liquidity suppliers. This model will also be used in Chapter 7 to study how competition between trading platforms affects liquidity (Section 7.4.2).

Another reason why limit order markets deserve a specific analysis is that they feature no strict dichotomy between the traders who "make" the market by posting quotes and those who "take" these quotes by hitting them: any participant can carry out the desired trades by submitting limit orders, market orders, or a combination. Thus, the provision of liquidity does not rest exclusively with a designated group of market makers (as assumed in the models described in Chapters 3 and 4): in these markets, liquidity depends on how agents trade off the costs and benefits of limit orders and market orders.

The benefit of limit orders is straightforward: they enable investors to earn revenues from liquidity provision rather than pay a cost for liquidity consumption. However, limit orders are costly for two reasons. First, limit orders' users are exposed to the risk of losing money to better informed agents, very much like market makers (see Chapter 3). This happens in particular when news arrives to the market. In this case, if limit order traders do not update (or cancel) their limit orders fast enough, they face the risk of trading at a stale price with investors who react to the news faster. This risk, which is called the risk of being picked off, has become particularly acute with the emergence of high-frequency trading (see Chapter 9). Second, limit order users face the risk of non-execution. For instance, a sell limit order is less likely to be filled if its price is not low enough. Non-execution is costly because order management takes time (sometimes it even requires the payment of fees to enter and modify orders), and because it can have opportunity costs (see the discussion about the implementation shortfall in Chapter 2). In Section 6.4 we analyze how these costs affect the pricing of limit orders (hence, the liquidity available to traders who place them) and the choice between market and limit orders. Understanding this choice is important, because the viability of limit order markets depends critically on traders placing both types of order. In making this choice, investors trade off price improvement against the risks of non-execution and being picked off. Thus the determinants of these risks—such as the volatility of asset fundamentals—ultimately shape investors' choice between market and limit orders.

The models presented in this chapter are useful in analyzing data on trades and quotes. The data are basically of two types: snapshots of LOBs at various points in time and flows of market and limit orders over a period of time. Snapshots of the LOB enable measuring the bid-ask spread and the cumulative number of shares offered up to a given ask or bid price. That is, they describe the state of the LOB at a given point in time. The framework presented in Section 6.2 helps to explain why this state may vary from security to security or over time. Order flow data provide information on the terms of completed trades and give insights into the drivers of trading aggressiveness, market orders being more aggressive than limit orders, and limit orders' aggressiveness depending on their price. An important driver, of course, is the state of the book, which is itself is influenced by the order flow. Dynamic models in which traders choose between market and limit orders offer insight into the interactions between the flow of limit and market orders and the state of the LOB (Section 6.4).

6.2 A Model of the Limit Order Book (LOB)

6.2.1 The Market Environment

We consider a limit order market for a risky security with final value $v = \mu + \varepsilon$, where $E(\varepsilon) = 0$. In period 0, traders submit limit orders. Then, in period 1, a market order arrives and executes against the limit orders in the book. In period 2, the value of the security and traders' payoffs are realized. The time line is given in Figure 6.2.

The limit orders are positioned on a price grid. The distance between two consecutive prices on the grid, the tick size, is denoted by Δ. In Figure 6.3, we denote by A_k the kth price on this grid above the expected value μ of the security, and by B_k the kth price on this grid below μ.

In this model, traders never submit sell limit orders at a price lower or buy limit orders at a price higher than μ, as such orders would entail expected losses if executed. For this reason, we refer to $\{B_k\}_{k=1}^{k=\infty}$ as the set of bid prices and to $\{A_k\}_{k=1}^{k=\infty}$ as the set of ask prices. Let y_k be the number of shares offered at price A_k and Y_k be the cumulative depth at price A_k (i.e., the total number of shares offered at price A_k or less). Figure 6.4 represents the ask side of the LOB.

In period 1, a trader submits a market order of size q. A buy market order executes against sell limit orders until it is fully served. Symmetrically, a sell market order executes against buy limit orders. As usual, the size of the market order is signed according to its direction: $q < 0$ for sell and $q > 0$ for buy. Market

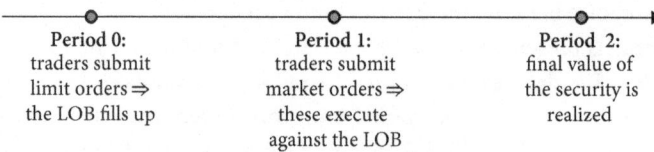

Period 0:
traders submit
limit orders ⇒
the LOB fills up

Period 1:
traders submit
market orders ⇒
these execute
against the LOB

Period 2:
final value of
the security is
realized

Figure 6.2 Timing.

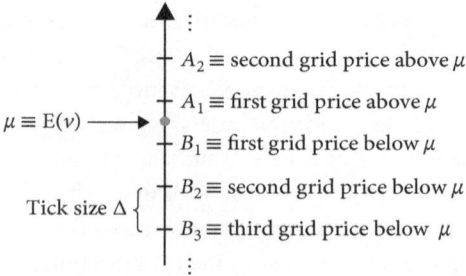

$\mu \equiv E(v)$

$A_2 \equiv$ second grid price above μ

$A_1 \equiv$ first grid price above μ

$B_1 \equiv$ first grid price below μ

$B_2 \equiv$ second grid price below μ

Tick size Δ

$B_3 \equiv$ third grid price below μ

Figure 6.3 The grid of possible quotes in the limit order book.

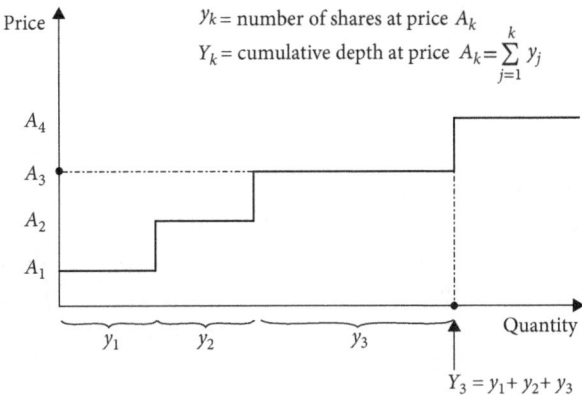

Figure 6.4 The ask side of the limit order book.

orders execute against the book at the limit order prices. Suppose a trader submits a buy market order for q shares such that: $Y_1 < q < Y_2$. His total payment is $Y_1 \cdot A_1 + (q - Y_1) \cdot A_2$.

The market order submitted in period 1 can be a buy or a sell with equal probability. Its size is unknown to the limit order traders when they submit their orders in period 0. The cumulative probability distribution of the order size is denoted by $F(\cdot)$ and its density by $f(\cdot)$. In some of the examples below, the size of market orders is assumed to be exponentially distributed, that is,

$$f(q) = \frac{1}{2}\theta e^{-\theta |q|}. \qquad (6.1)$$

In this case, buy and sell market orders arrive with equal probability, since $\Pr(q > 0) = \Pr(q < 0) = \frac{1}{2}$ and the expected size of a market order, $E(|q|)$, is $\frac{1}{\theta}$.

At time 0, limit orders are submitted by a continuum of risk-neutral traders who arrive sequentially. They fill the book up to the point where there are no expected profit opportunities: a competitive equilibrium is reached when (i) there is no price at which adding a limit order is profitable (the "no entry" condition) and (ii) there is no price at which cancelling a limit order is profitable (the "no exit" condition).

Last, we assume a time-priority rule for tie-breaking.[1] This means that two limit orders at the same price are executed in the order in which they have been submitted. For instance, the last share offered at price A_k (the marginal share at this price) executes if and only if the next market order is a buy order that

---

[1] Other tie-breaking rules are considered in Section 6.3.2.

exceeds the number of shares offered up to price A_k, that is $q > Y_k$. Hence, the execution probability of the marginal share offered at price A_k is:

$$P(Y_k) \equiv \Pr(q \geq Y_k) = 1 - F(Y_k). \tag{6.2}$$

This execution probability declines with cumulative depth at price A_k. As the total number of shares offered up to a given price increases, it becomes less and less likely that the next market order will be large enough to trigger execution of the marginal share. This is akin to a queuing situation in which, as the queue lengthens, the last person has a smaller chance of being served because the object for sale is in unknown but limited supply. The execution probability for the marginal buy limit order at price B_k is obtained in a similar way and is equal to $F(Y_k)$, where $|Y_k|$ is the cumulative quantity demanded at bid price B_k.

This provides a simple framework for analyzing many interesting issues relating to limit order markets. However, two inherent limitations should be noted at the outset.

First, the model says nothing about how the competitive equilibrium is reached. The underlying idea is that the market is sufficiently competitive so that there are no strictly profitable opportunities for adding limit orders to the book. This is an interesting benchmark, but in the real world competition among limit order traders is likely to be imperfect. The competitive equilibrium should therefore be viewed as the limit of the equilibrium obtained when the number of market participants is infinite.

Second, in this model, traders are classed in either one of two groups: (i) those who submit limit orders (supply liquidity) and (ii) those who submit market orders (demand liquidity). They cannot switch from one group to the other. We defer the analysis of how traders choose between a market order or a limit order to Section 6.4.

6.2.2 Execution Probability and Order Submission Cost

To illustrate the notion of competitive equilibrium, we first consider a simple case in which no trader has private information about the final value of the security. Market orders are exogenous, and competing traders place limit orders at a display cost of C per share. This cost represents the time required to submit and monitor the order ("order management cost"), and any entry fee charged to traders submitting limit orders, whether or not they are filled.

This specification of the model illustrates the importance of execution probabilities for limit orders and shows how order submission costs affect cumulative depth. The mechanics here also prepare the ground for the more complex case in which market order traders can be informed (Section 6.2.3). We consider the determination of cumulative depth on the ask side only, leaving the symmetric case of the bid side to the reader.

The zero-profit condition. We write the expected profit on the "marginal" unit offered at price A_k when cumulative depth at this price is Y_k. The trader offering this unit is called the marginal trader at price A_k.

In case of execution, the realized profit on the marginal unit is $A_k - v - C$. In case of non-execution, it is $-C$: the submission cost is paid but the order does not execute. Consequently, the expected profit, $\Pi_k(Y_k)$, on the marginal unit is:

$$\Pi_k(Y_k) = P(Y_k)\left[A_k - E\left(v|q \geq Y_k\right)\right] - C. \tag{6.3}$$

Since we assume that market order traders have no private information, the order flow at time 1 is independent of the value of the security. This means that $E\left(v|q \geq Y_k\right) = E(v) = \mu$. Hence,

$$\Pi_k(Y_k) = P(Y_k)(A_k - \mu) - C. \tag{6.4}$$

The probability of execution for a sell limit order cannot be greater than one-half, as a buy market order is submitted with probability $\frac{1}{2}$. Hence, the expected profit on a marginal limit order at an ask price below $2C + \mu$ is negative, so that no sell limit orders are submitted below $2C + \mu$. The best price on the sell side of the limit order book (the first price at which some shares are offered) is therefore the lowest price on the grid above $2C + \mu$. We denote this price by A^*.

What is the cumulative depth Y_k of the order book at price $A_k \geq A^*$? Consider a trader who contemplates placing a limit order at price A_k. Given the time-priority rule, this order goes to the back of queue Y_k and its execution probability is therefore at most $P(Y_k)$. The trader faces a trade-off between the revenue in case of execution of the limit order, which is $A_k - \mu$ per share, and the order submission cost C. The optimal point along this trade-off depends on the order's execution probability. If the queue Y_k at price A_k is short enough, then the execution probability is high enough so that the trader can expect a positive profit, that is, $\Pi_k(Y_k) \geq 0$. Otherwise, it is unprofitable for the trader to add a limit order to the queue at price A_k, that is, $\Pi_k(Y_k) < 0$.

Thus, the no-entry/no-exit condition for a competitive equilibrium holds when the cumulative depth at price $A_k \geq A^*$ solves:

$$\Pi_k(Y_k) = 0, \tag{6.5}$$

so that the probability of execution of the marginal limit order at price A_k is:

$$P(Y_k) = \frac{C}{A_k - \mu},$$ (6.6)

$$\text{or } A_k = \mu + \frac{C}{P(Y_k)}.$$ (6.7)

Example 1. Consider the case in which the distribution of market order size is exponential, as in equation (6.1). In this case:

$$P(Y_k) = \frac{1}{2}e^{-\theta Y_k}.$$

Thus, solving equation (6.6) for Y_k, we obtain the cumulative depth at price $A_k \geq A^*$:

$$Y_k = \frac{1}{\theta}\ln\left(\frac{A_k - \mu}{2C}\right).$$

The determinants of cumulative depth. In the model, the cumulative depth at price A_k depends on the order submission cost and the probability distribution of market order size. This is clearly shown in example 1. The cumulative depth increases with $1/\theta$, the average order size, because people anticipate "the queue to go faster." Further, cumulative depth at each price is decreasing in the order display cost C. Intuitively, the queue at or below price A_k is shorter when the cost of joining the line is higher. This means that an order entry fee for limit orders impairs the depth of the LOB at every price.

Empirically, the level of trading activity varies across stocks. For instance, firms with a large market value of equity, known as large caps (*LC*), are typically more active, in the sense that trades are more frequent and larger than for small caps (*SC*). This means that the likelihood of a market order larger than any given size is greater for large caps, i.e., $P_{LC}(Y) > P_{SC}(Y)$ for all $Y > 0$. Thus, by equation (6.6), the cumulative depth in the large-cap market in equilibrium will be greater at all prices. In this sense, liquidity demand (active trading) begets liquidity supply, as it improves the chance of execution for limit order traders and so induces them to submit more orders.

6.2.3 Limit Order Trading with Informed Investors

We now explore how adverse selection affects the LOB. We assume that market orders are submitted either by uninformed traders or by informed traders (those who know the true value of the security, $v = \mu + \varepsilon$). Limit order traders do not observe ε but they are aware that market orders may come from informed traders. This model is originally due to Glosten (1994).

Exposure to informed trading has two distinct sources. First, informed traders may have private information not yet available to the market, as Chapters 3 and 4 suggest. Second, as noted in the introduction to this chapter, the arrival of public information exposes limit order traders to the risk of being "picked off" if they are slow in updating their prices to reflect news. In each case, the actions of the informed traders create a positive correlation between the order flow and the change in the estimate of the true value, which is the essence of the adverse selection problem.

The very fact that a limit order is executed contains information. It reveals the direction of the market order and it shows that it was large enough to trigger execution of the limit order. This information is value-relevant, since the size and direction of the market order are correlated with the true value. So when placing a limit order and choosing one's bid, one must take this information into account. Recall that, by equation (6.3), the expected profit on the marginal unit offered at price A_k is:

$$\Pi_k(Y_k) = P(Y_k)\big(A_k - E\big(v|q \geq Y_k\big)\big) - C, \tag{6.8}$$

where the upper tail conditional expectation, $E(v|q \geq Y_k)$, is the estimate of the value of the security conditional on execution of the marginal unit at price A_k.

Intuitively, with informed trading this upper tail expectation increases with Y_k, the cumulative quantity at each price. Consider an informed trader's optimal strategy when he knows that the value of the security is $v > A_k$. If he is not wealth-constrained, his demand is unlimited at any price below v and zero at any price above. Thus, he will definitely sweep up all sell limit orders in the book at prices at or below A_k. In contrast, an uninformed trader only hits the limit orders needed to fill his desired order. Thus, as the queue of limit orders at price A_k lengthens, it becomes more and more likely that the market order triggering execution of the marginal order is from an informed investor who knows that the limit order is "stale," i.e., that $v > A_k$. As a consequence, the marginal trader's valuation conditional on execution gets larger as Y_k increases. The next example illustrates this point.

Example 2. The final value of the security can be either low ($v^L = \mu - \sigma$) or high ($v^H = \mu + \sigma$), with equal probability. The market order trader is either informed with probability π or uninformed with probability $1 - \pi$. The uninformed trader is a buyer or a seller with equal probability, with a desired trade size that is either small (q_S) or large (q_L) with probabilities ϕ and $1 - \phi$, respectively. Let $A(q_S)$ and $A(q_L)$ be the ask prices at which cumulative depth on the ask side is equal to q_S and q_L shares, respectively. Moreover, assume that

$A(q_L) < v^H$.[2] Thus, if the informed investor knows that the value of the security is v^H, he sweeps all limit orders up to price $A(q_L)$, at least.

Let I and U denote the event that the market order is submitted by the informed and the uninformed traders, respectively. Given the order submission strategy of liquidity demanders, we have:

$$\Pr(I|q \geq Y) = \frac{\Pr(q \geq Y|I)\Pr(I)}{\Pr(q \geq Y)} = \frac{\frac{\pi}{2}}{\frac{\pi}{2} + \frac{1-\pi}{2}} = \pi \text{ for } Y \leq q_S.$$

Indeed, an investor is informed with probability $\Pr(I) = \pi$ and, as explained previously, an informed investor buys at least $q_L > q_S$ shares when she learns that the final value is high, that is, $\Pr(q \geq Y|I) = \frac{1}{2}$ for $Y \leq q_S$. As an uninformed investor buys at least q_S shares with probability $\frac{1}{2}$, it follows that $\Pr(q \geq Y) = \frac{1}{2}$ for $Y \leq q_S$ as well. Following the same reasoning, we obtain:

$$\Pr(I|q \geq Y) = \frac{\Pr(q \geq Y|I)\Pr(I)}{\Pr(q \geq Y)} = \frac{\frac{\pi}{2}}{\frac{\pi}{2} + \frac{(1-\pi)(1-\phi)}{2}} = \frac{\pi}{\pi + (1-\pi)(1-\phi)}$$

for $q_S < Y \leq q_L$, because an uninformed investor only buys a large number of shares with probability $\frac{1-\phi}{2}$. It follows that the second expression is greater than the first. Intuitively, a trade smaller than q_S conveys no information about the identity of the person placing the market order, but a trade larger than q_S is more likely to come from an informed trader. It follows that:

$$E(v|q \geq Y) = \Pr(U|q \geq Y)\mu + \Pr(I|q \geq Y)(\mu + \sigma)$$
$$= \mu + \Pr(I|q \geq Y)\sigma. \tag{6.9}$$

Hence $E(v|q \geq Y)$ is weakly increasing in Y because a limit order far back in the queue is more likely to be hit by an informed investor ($\Pr(I|q \geq Y)$ increases in Y). In particular,

$$E(v|q \geq q_S) = \mu + \pi\sigma, \tag{6.10}$$

and:

$$E(v|q \geq q_L) = \mu + \frac{\pi\sigma}{\pi + (1-\pi)(1-\phi)} > E(v|q \geq q_S). \tag{6.11}$$

---

[2] This will in fact be the case in equilibrium.

Let us now go back to deriving the equilibrium LOB. Since $E(v|q \geq Y_k)$ increases with Y_k, the expected profit on the marginal order at a given price decreases along with cumulative depth at this price. As in the previous section, a competitive equilibrium is obtained when cumulative depth Y_k at each price A_k is such that the following zero profit condition is satisfied:

$$\Pi_k(Y_k) = 0 \text{ if } \Pi_k(Y_{k-1}) > 0, \text{ and } Y_k = Y_{k-1} \text{ if } \Pi_k(Y_{k-1}) \leq 0, \tag{6.12}$$

meaning that the marginal unit must yield no profit if offering less were to yield positive profits; otherwise, that unit must not be offered. From equation (6.8), the zero profit condition is equivalent to:

$$A_k = E\left(v|q \geq Y_k\right) + \frac{C}{P(Y_k)} \text{ if } Y_k > Y_{k-1}, \tag{6.13}$$

$$A_k < E\left(v|q \geq Y_{k-1}\right) + \frac{C}{P(Y_{k-1})} \text{ if } Y_k = Y_{k-1}. \tag{6.14}$$

In the remainder of this section, in order to isolate the impact of asymmetric information on the equilibrium price schedule, we assume that the order submission cost C is zero. The example below illustrates, in a simple way, some important and general properties of the limit order market with informed trading.

Example 1, continued. Assume again, as in example 1, that the market order size has an exponential distribution $f(q) = \frac{1}{2}\theta e^{-\theta|q|}$ and that the expected value of the security conditional on the market order size is linear:

$$E\left(v|q = x\right) = \mu + \lambda x. \tag{6.15}$$

Equation (6.15) is the "updating rule" that specifies how liquidity suppliers (limit orders traders) would update their estimate of the asset value if they knew the total size of the market order. The parameter λ is therefore a measure of the informativeness of the order flow. In this example, we take the updating rule and the order size distribution as primitives. This parametric specification of the model is a shortcut for analyzing the properties of the LOB with asymmetric information and has proved useful empirically. Later on, we consider a richer setting in which the updating rule and the distribution of order size are endogenous.

Using the law of iterated expectations and the updating rule, we obtain:

$$E(v|q \geq x) = E(E(v|q = x)|q \geq x)$$
$$= \mu + \lambda E\left(q|q \geq x\right)$$

$$= \mu + \lambda \frac{\int_x^\infty q\theta e^{-\theta q} dq}{\int_x^\infty \theta e^{-\theta q} dq}$$

$$= \mu + \frac{\lambda}{\theta} + \lambda x, \text{ for } x \geq 0.$$

Consider first the case of zero tick size (i.e., prices are not required to take discrete values on a grid). In this case, from equation (6.13) the equilibrium price schedule on the ask side of the book is:

$$A(Y) = E(v|q \geq Y) = \mu + \frac{\lambda}{\theta} + \lambda Y.$$

This price schedule is shown as the upward-sloping line in Figure 6.5. Note that the relationship between bid prices and cumulative depth at each price is the mirror image of the ask side, since the probability distribution for market order sizes is symmetric around zero.

When the tick is not zero, so that prices must be at discrete intervals (no less than ten cents, say), the cumulative depth at each price on the ask side can be derived using equations (6.13) and (6.14). This yields:

$$Y_k = 0 \text{ for } A_k \leq \mu + \frac{\lambda}{\theta} \tag{6.16}$$

$$Y_k = \frac{A_k - (\mu + \frac{\lambda}{\theta})}{\lambda} \text{ for } A_k > \mu + \frac{\lambda}{\theta}. \tag{6.17}$$

Recall that we denote by A^* the lowest price in the limit order book at which some shares are supplied (the best offer). By definition, this price is the first price on the grid at which $Y_k > 0$ and therefore below this price the cumulative

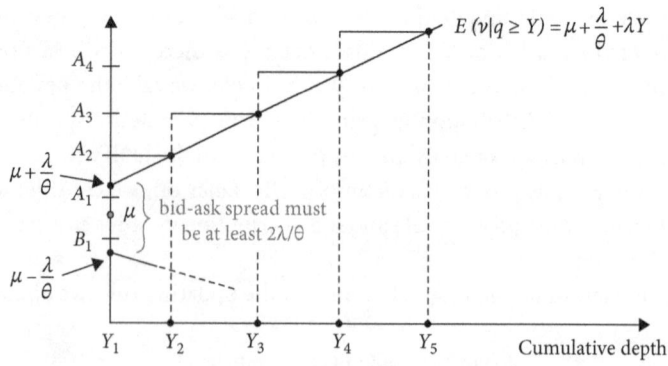

Figure 6.5 Equilibrium limit order book in example 1.

depth is zero. Thus, A^* is the first price on the grid above $E\left(v|q \geq 0\right)$, which in this case is $\mu + \frac{\lambda}{\theta}$. The number of shares offered at this price (the quoted depth) is $\frac{A^* - \mu}{\lambda} + \frac{1}{\theta}$. Graphically, the ask side of the book in this case is represented by the step function in Figure 6.5. The equilibrium has two interesting properties:

- **The limit order market features a non-zero bid-ask spread even for very small orders.** That is, even market orders for an infinitesimal quantity get executed at a premium or discount relative to the expected value of the security. This feature is not an effect of the tick size, since it persists even when the tick is zero, in which case the spread for a very small order is $\frac{2\lambda}{\theta} > 0$. This property does not obtain in the models presented in Chapter 4, such as that of Kyle (1985), in which the spread on an order of size q is given by $2\lambda q$ and goes to zero as the order size goes to zero. The reason is that in the limit order market, liquidity suppliers cannot make their quotes contingent on the total size of market orders. As a result, the limit orders at the top of the book are more exposed to adverse selection. To see this, let us take the sell limit order with the most competitive ask price. It will execute against market buy orders of every size, as it takes precedence over all the other limit orders. So in choosing his offer, the trader at the top of the book must take account of the possibility that his offer can be hit both by very small market orders (which convey very little information) and by very large ones (which are strongly informative). For this reason, his valuation conditional on execution is strictly larger than his prior estimate of the asset value μ.[3]
- **The depth of the LOB is decreasing in the informativeness of order flow.** As λ increases, the LOB thins out (i.e., the cumulative depth at each price diminishes). The intuition should by now be familiar to the reader: the more informative the order flow, the more exposed liquidity suppliers are to adverse selection, so they bid less aggressively (see Chapter 4).

In this example, we have taken the distribution of market order sizes and the updating rule as given. This approach simplifies the analysis but is not entirely satisfactory, as these functions ultimately depend on the informed trader's order placement strategy, which itself depends on the offers available in the book. Thus, in equilibrium the informed investor's order placement strategy and the LOB are

---

[3] The trader's estimate of the value of the security conditional on execution is $E(v|q \geq 0) = \mu + \frac{\lambda}{\theta} > \mu$.

determined *jointly*. We now provide a new example in which this is the case, to show the robustness of the conclusions obtained so far (see also exercise 1).

Example 2, continued. Consider example 2 again and assume that the tick size is zero. In this case, the equilibrium is as follows. If the investor arriving at time 1 is informed, he submits an order of q_L shares, and the LOB displays the following offers:

$$A(Y) = E(v|q \geq Y) = \begin{cases} \mu + \pi\sigma & \text{for } Y \leq q_S, \\ \mu + \dfrac{\pi}{\pi + (1-\pi)(1-\phi)}\sigma & \text{for } q_S < Y \leq q_L, \\ \mu + \sigma & \text{for } Y > q_L. \end{cases} \qquad (6.18)$$

$$B(Y) = E(v|q \leq -Y) = \begin{cases} \mu - \pi\sigma & \text{for } Y \leq q_S, \\ \mu - \dfrac{\pi}{\pi + (1-\pi)(1-\phi)}\sigma & \text{for } q_S < Y \leq q_L, \\ \mu - \sigma & \text{for } Y > q_L. \end{cases} \qquad (6.19)$$

To verify that this is an equilibrium, we must show that the informed investor's behavior is optimal, given the offers in the book, and that the LOB is in a competitive equilibrium, given the behavior of the informed investor.

The first step is straightforward. Suppose that the investor arriving at time 1 is informed and learns that the value of the security is high. He can buy up to q_L shares at a price strictly below the value $v^H = \mu + \sigma$. Thus, buying at least q_L shares is optimal for this informed investor. Additional shares are purchased exactly at v^H. Hence, buying q_L shares is optimal for the informed trader.

Given this behavior, we can follow exactly the same reasoning as in example 2 to show that $E(v|q \geq Y)$ is given by equation (6.9) for $Y \leq q_L$. Moreover, only the informed trader submits a buy market order larger than q_L and he does so upon learning that the true value is v^H. That is,

$$E(v|q \geq Y) = v^H = \mu + \sigma \text{ for } Y > q_L.$$

Thus, in a competitive equilibrium, ask prices in the book are as given by equation (6.18). The analysis for the bid side is symmetric.

This example confirms the robustness of the conclusions drawn from the previous example. First, the book becomes thinner as the exposure to informed trading (π) heightens. And even though the informed investor never submits a small market order, these orders execute at a markup relative to μ. Again, this reflects the fact that limit orders at the top of the book may execute against small orders (with no information content) or large orders (which are informative), leading to a non-zero bid-ask spread for small trades:

$$A(q) - B(q) = 2\pi\sigma, \quad \text{for} \quad 0 \leq q \leq q_S.$$

6.3 The Design of LOB Markets

The model developed in the previous section can be used to address market design issues: how liquidity and the distribution of trading gains among traders are affected by tick size (Section 6.3.1), secondary priority rules (Section 6.3.2), and designated market makers like the NYSE specialist (Section 6.3.3).

6.3.1 Tick Size

Market organizers or regulators usually set a tick size that varies across exchanges and across stocks, as it often is a function of prices. On the NYSE, it was $\$\frac{1}{8}$ for stocks with prices over one dollar until June 1997, when, under regulatory pressure, it was reduced to $\$\frac{1}{16}$ and finally to one cent in 2000. Decimalization was imposed on Nasdaq and AMEX as well. This change was very controversial and the appropriate size of the tick is still debated both in the U.S. and in Europe. For instance, the JOBS Act (2012) required the SEC to conduct a study on "how decimalization affected the number of initial public offerings (IPOs) and the liquidity and trading of smaller capitalization company securities." Following this request, the SEC implemented a pilot program in 2016 to study the effect of raising the tick size to 5 cents for some small-cap stocks.

It may seem surprising that investors, exchanges, intermediaries, and policy makers care so much about tick size. After all, it is often very small compared to stock prices. Yet as the model shows, the tick determines liquidity suppliers' total expected profits. In the model, the number of shares offered at each price is such that the expected profit on the last share (the marginal limit order) is just zero. However, inframarginal limit orders (those ahead of the marginal order in the queue at a given price) obtain strictly positive expected profits *if* the tick size is strictly positive. Consider for instance the trader at the head of the queue of limit orders at price $A_k > A^*$ (i.e., a price strictly above the best offer in the limit order book). His expected profit on the first share offered is:

$$\Pi_k(Y_{k-1}) = (1 - F(Y_{k-1}))(A_k - E(v|q \geq Y_{k-1})) - C, \qquad (6.20)$$

because this order is filled if and only if the size of the market order exceeds the cumulative depth offered at price A_{k-1}. In a competitive equilibrium, the zero profit condition on the marginal share at price A_{k-1} requires:

$$A_{k-1} = E(v|q \geq Y_{k-1}) + \frac{C}{(1 - F(Y_{k-1}))}. \qquad (6.21)$$

Equations (6.20) and (6.21) imply:

$$\Pi_k(Y_{k-1}) = (1 - F(Y_{k-1}))(A_k - A_{k-1}) = (1 - F(Y_{k-1}))\Delta > 0.$$

Thus, the expected profit on the "first" share sold at A_k is proportional to the tick size. The expected profit on additional shares offered at A_k is lower because their probability of execution is lower. Thus, the aggregate expected profit of all limit orders submitted at A_k decreases when the tick size declines. This is also the case for limit orders submitted at the best offer price.[4] In the extreme case of a zero tick size, limit order traders get zero expected profits. Otherwise, their aggregate expected profit is strictly positive and bounded by the tick size.

Consistent with this mechanism, Yao and Ye (2018) empirically find that liquidity providers' rents are higher for stocks with larger relative tick sizes and that they fiercely compete to be at the head of the queue of limit orders at a given price. Indeed, time priority implies that these traders obtain larger expected profits than those at the back of the queue.

The tick size is a source of profit for liquidity providers because it hinders competition: it stops them from bidding the security price up or down to their marginal valuation. As we have just seen, the marginal valuation for the first share offered at price $A_k > A^*$ is A_{k-1}, which is less than A_k if the tick size is positive. Traders could thus earn a strictly positive expected profit by undercutting this offer by an infinitesimal amount, but given the tick, they cannot. If they undercut a quote, they must do so by at least Δ. In equilibrium, the depth at each price is just enough to make undercutting unprofitable.

Figure 6.6 shows the effects of cutting the tick in half from Δ to $\frac{\Delta}{2}$ in the context of example 1. This cut creates new eligible prices on the grid, which are referred to as "new" in Figure 6.6 (other prices are eligible in both grids). The graph shows that the reduction in the tick size can reduce the best offer and therefore the quoted bid-ask spread. When this happens, a reduction in the tick size can reduce the number of shares offered at the best quotes (the quoted depth), as in Figure 6.6. Moreover, the number of shares posted at any given price on the old grid is reduced as well. Intuitively, some of the shares formerly offered at any price A_k are now offered at price $A_k - \frac{\Delta}{2}$. However, the

---

[4] Indeed, the best offer is the first price on the grid above $E(v|q \geq 0) + 2C$. Therefore the expected profit on the first share offered in the LOB is the difference between this price and $(E(v|q \geq 0) + 2C)$. Therefore, as the tick size declines, the aggregate expected profit of limit orders submitted at the best offer declines.

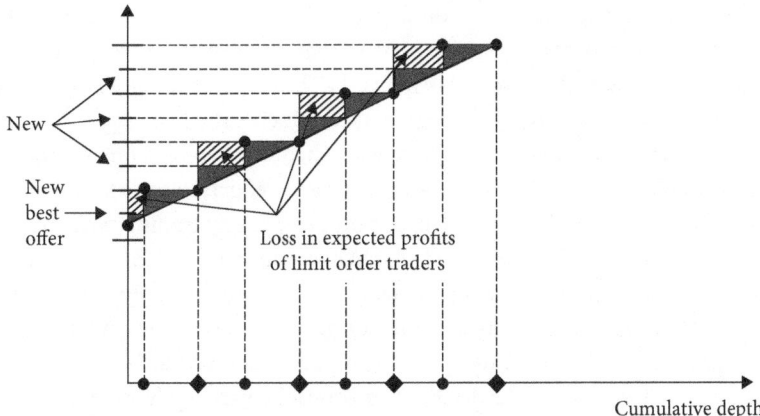

Figure 6.6 Effect of a reduction in the tick size. The dots (diamonds) on the x axis represents the cumulative depth at each new (old) offer price (y axis) on the grid. The dashed areas represent the loss in expected profits for liquidity suppliers following the reduction in the tick size.

smaller tick does not affect the cumulative depth at a given price on the old grid, because cumulative depth at each price must adjust so that the valuation of the marginal seller just equals the price. If this valuation is unaffected by the change in the tick size (as assumed here), then the cumulative depth *at a given price* is independent of the tick size. Thus, reducing the tick size unambiguously lowers the total trading cost for market orders in the framework considered here.

For instance, consider a buy market order of size q. Its total purchase cost is given by the area under the step function $A(q)$, mapping cumulative depth and quotes in equilibrium. Clearly this area becomes smaller when the tick size is reduced. The decrease in trading costs for liquidity demanders reflects the fact that the smaller tick intensifies competition among liquidity suppliers. For instance, the offers posted at price $A_k - \frac{\Delta}{2}$ compete away some of the profits at price A_k on the old grid and so reduce total trading costs.

To sum up, the model predicts that a decrease in tick size:

(i) increases price competition (undercutting) between liquidity suppliers;

(ii) reduces expected profits of liquidity suppliers and therefore trading costs for liquidity demanders;

(iii) reduces the number of shares offered at each price, leaving cumulative depth at a given price unchanged;

(iv) reduces the bid-ask spread;

These points explain why reducing the tick size is such a controversial measure. It clearly hurts the "sell-side" firms that supply liquidity (e.g., firms with market-making activities), and it benefits the "buy side" that demands liquidity. Not surprisingly, the two sides disagree over reducing the tick.

There is evidence that a finer price grid encourages price competition. For instance, Foley et al. (2023) study a (temporary) reduction in tick size in 2009 by Chi-X, BATS, and Turquoise (three European equity trading platforms) for stocks listed on the London Stock Exchange and various Nordic Exchanges (Denmark, Norway, and Sweden). They find that liquidity providers used the finer grids on these platforms to undercut quotes posted on the main markets for these stocks (which were using a coarser grid). They also show that as a result trading costs for these stocks declined and consolidated depth increased.

Other empirical studies find that changes in tick size have different effects on the liquidity available to small and large traders. For instance, Chung et al. (2020) study the effect of an increase in the tick size for small cap stocks that are part of the SEC (2016) pilot program ("pilot stocks"), and find that this increase raises trading costs for small orders, but decreases trading costs for large orders (between five hundred and five thousand shares) due to an increase in cumulative depth throughout the consolidated limit order book of pilot stocks. Interestingly, these findings mirror those reported by Goldstein and Kavajecz (2000) who studied the effect of the reduction in the tick size from $\frac{1}{8}$ to $\frac{1}{16}$ on the NYSE in 1997.[5]

Overall, these empirical findings paint a more complex picture than is suggested by the simple model analyzed in this section. They confirm the prediction that a decrease in the tick size should reduce bid-ask spreads and trading costs for small orders. However, they also suggest that such a decrease can increase trading costs for large orders, in contrast to what the model predicts. This may be due to the fact that the model ignores several possible side-effects. First, as a non-zero tick size guarantees minimal profits for liquidity providers, reducing it may prompt them to exit the market and so reduce total liquidity provision. Moreover, limit order traders may pay less attention to the LOB as the reduction in the tick size diminishes the gain from being at the head of the queue. Or they may choose to improve non-competitive offers in the book by a smaller amount rather than directly posting a competitive offer (since the expected profit obtained at the competitive offer is smaller). In both cases, it will take longer for

---

[5] Bacidore (1997), Porter and Weaver (1997), and Ahn, Bae, and Kalok (1998) studied the impact of a *reduction* in the tick size on the Toronto Stock Exchange in April 1996. They found a reduction of 17.27% in the quoted spread and of 27.52% in the quoted depth at the best price (depending on study and sample).

the LOB to be replenished after a trade, and market orders will execute more frequently against non-competitive offers.[6] Lastly, if the return to limit order trading is lower, traders might use market orders more frequently. Again, this effect could decrease liquidity when the tick size is reduced.

6.3.2 Priority Rules

The LOB can be seen as a queue. Priority rules determine the sequence in which the orders in the queue are "served." Price priority comes first. That is, limit orders at a given price are executed before those at worse prices. Secondary priority rules determine the sequence of execution of multiple limit orders at any given price. The most common is time priority. That is, limit orders at the same limit price are eligible for execution in the sequence in which they were submitted. But there are also other rules. For instance, the electronic futures markets for the leading short-term interest rate in the United States (Eurodollar), Europe (Euribor), and the United Kingdom (Short Sterling) and for the two-year U.S. Treasury Note future have a pro-rata allocation rule.

To see how this rule operates, consider two sell limit orders tied at the best ask price, the first offering one thousand shares, and the second four thousand shares. Suppose a buy market order for four thousand shares arrives. Under the pro-rata rule, the first limit order serves 20% of the incoming order (800 shares) and the second serves the remaining 80% (3,200 shares). Other tie-breaking rules can also be considered. For instance, the market order could be assigned randomly to all the limit orders at the same price.

Priority rules affect traders' bidding behavior and thereby market liquidity. To see this, we compare the LOB with time priority and that with pro-rata allocation. Let Y_k^r be the cumulative depth at price A_k under the pro-rata allocation rule. Using equation (6.8), the aggregate expected profit of all the limit orders posted at price A_k is:

$$\int_{Y_{k-1}^r}^{Y_k^r} \Pi_k(y)\, dy = \int_{Y_{k-1}^r}^{Y_k^r} \{P(y)\left[A_k - \mathrm{E}\left(v|q \geq y\right)\right] - C\} dy. \tag{6.22}$$

Under the pro-rata rule, this expected profit is shared among all the investors with a limit order at price A_k in proportion to the size of each one's order. Thus,

---

[6] This effect is analyzed in Cordella and Foucault (1999) and Foucault, Kadan, and Kandel (2005). Both studies conclude that the tick size that minimizes trading costs for liquidity demanders is strictly positive.

a competitive equilibrium is reached when the cumulative depth at each price in the LOB satisfies:

$$\int_{Y_{k-1}^r}^{Y_k^r} \Pi_k(y)\, dy = 0 \ \forall k. \tag{6.23}$$

Otherwise, it would be profitable either to add limit orders to the book (to get a fraction of the aggregate expected profit at price A_k) or to withdraw limit orders from the book (if the aggregate expected profit is negative).

As $\Pi_k(\cdot)$ is a decreasing function, the zero profit condition (6.23) implies that $\Pi_k(Y_k^r) < 0$. But recall that under time priority, the cumulative depth at price A_k, which we denote here by Y_k^t, satisfies $\Pi_k(Y_k^t) = 0$. Hence,

$$Y_k^r > Y_k^t. \tag{6.24}$$

Thus, the market is always deeper under pro-rata allocation, holding the distribution of market order flow constant (see exercise 3).

This result assumes that the probability distribution of the market order size does not change when the priority rule is changed. Actually, liquidity demanders are likely to submit larger orders when the book is deeper. In Section 6.2.2 such a shift in the distribution of uninformed market orders results in larger cumulative depth. Thus, with an endogenous distribution for market order size, the positive effect of the pro-rata allocation rule on market depth would be even stronger. However, the effect is less clear-cut with informed trading, since informed traders' strategies and the depth of the LOB are jointly determined (see Section 6.2.3). Thus, the net liquidity effect of a change in the priority rule (or, more generally, any change in market design) ultimately requires an analysis of the reaction of both limit order traders and informed traders. Exercise 2 provides an example.

Last, one may wonder why time priority is used in real markets if the pro-rata allocation rule results in a more liquid LOB. As with tick size, a broader perspective is required. In a dynamic setting, time priority rewards liquidity suppliers who are quick to replenish the book when it is depleted. This effect is not considered in the model. Also, exchanges may want to guarantee some minimal profit for limit order traders to encourage liquidity provision. For instance, some exchanges give rebates to limit order traders in case of execution, which shows that they see the profitability of limit orders as critical to their success. Indeed, if the profitability of a limit order is too low compared to its cost or the potential gain from alternative strategies (e.g., placing market orders), the liquidity of the LOB could dry up, endangering the viability of the limit order market.

6.3.3 Hybrid LOB Markets

In limit order markets, trading platforms sometimes assign one or several market makers to a stock. In this case, liquidity is provided both by the LOB and by the designated market makers' offers. In some exchanges (like Euronext), the designated market makers simply post additional limit orders in the LOB, under the constraint that their spread not exceed a threshold set by contract with the exchange or the issuer.[7] In other exchanges, like the NYSE or the Frankfurt Stock Exchange, designated market makers were allowed to make offers contingent on the size of incoming market orders ("last mover advantage"). That is, instead of providing liquidity ex ante (before observing the size of the incoming market orders) like regular limit order traders, they could also do so ex post, i.e., after observing the size of the orders). The NYSE suppressed this arrangement in 2008. However, as explained at the end of this section, this possibility is often implicitly or explicitly allowed by some trading platforms (see Box 6.1).

Is granting such a last mover advantage a good idea? To study this, we extend the model developed in Section 6.2.3 as described in Figure 6.7. After the arrival of a market order, one market maker—the "specialist"—chooses a "stop-out price" $p^s(q)$ at which he is willing to execute all or part of the market order.[8] This price depends on the direction and size of the market order, since unlike limit order traders the specialist sets his stop-out price *after* the market order arrives.

We assume that the specialist must yield both price and time priority to the book (as was the case on the NYSE until 2008). Say the LOB displays one thousand shares at $A_1 = 100$ and six hundred shares at $A_2 = 100.1$. A buy market

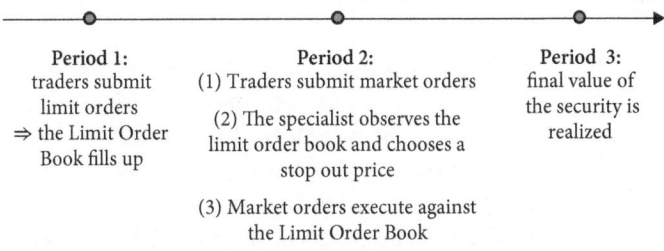

| Period 1:
traders submit
limit orders
⇒ the Limit Order
Book fills up | Period 2:
(1) Traders submit market orders

(2) The specialist observes the
limit order book and chooses a
stop out price

(3) Market orders execute against
the Limit Order Book | Period 3:
final value of
the security is
realized |

Figure 6.7 Timing with a specialist granted a last mover advantage.

---

[7] In compensation, the designated market makers receive a payment from the issuer or are exempted from the exchange's trading fees. We discuss further the role of designated market makers in Section 1.2.3 and in Section 10.5.2.

[8] We refer to the market maker as the "specialist" because this used to be the term used to refer to the market maker assigned to one stock on the NYSE. The NYSE specialist for a stock had the last mover advantage that we analyze in this section. See, for instance, Seppi (1997).

order for two thousand shares arrives and the specialist decides to "stop" the order out at $p^s(2000) = 100.1$. In this case, the buy order executes first against the limit orders at $A_1 = 100$ and $A_2 = 100.1$, after which the specialist fills the order for the remaining four hundred shares at $p^s = 100.1$.

At first glance, it seems that the specialist's intervention could only enhance market liquidity since he expands that offered by the LOB. But this thesis neglects the impact of the specialist on the bids of limit order traders. In the presence of asymmetric information, the specialist's ability to condition his intervention on the exact size of the market order allows him to cream-skim orders with little information content (small orders). This last-mover advantage reinforces the exposure of limit orders to informed trading and so impairs liquidity.

To see this, let us revisit example 2 in Section 6.2.3. As noted, in the equilibrium described in this example, small market orders (of size q_S) are submitted only by uninformed investors. The specialist can exploit this in the following way. When a small order arrives, he stops it out by slightly undercutting the prices offered by limit order traders for an order of this size, that is, at $A(q_S)$ or $B(q_S)$ (respectively given by equations (6.18) and (6.19)) depending on the direction of the order; when a large order arrives, he refrains from trading. This strategy yields a positive expected profit amounting to:

$$\frac{(1-\pi)\phi}{2}\left(A\left(q_S\right)-\mu\right)+\frac{(1-\pi)\phi}{2}\left(\mu-B\left(q_S\right)\right)=(1-\pi)\pi\phi\sigma>0.$$

Intuitively, by cherry-picking the small orders, the specialist captures the compensation required by limit order traders for their exposure to informed trading without being exposed himself. The specialist can do this because, unlike limit order traders, he can condition his intervention on the exact size of the market order.

But then the equilibrium described in example 2 unravels. Indeed, in this case, limit orders at the top of the book execute if and only if a market order for at least q_L shares arrives. Hence, they no longer break even at price $A(q_S)$. Instead, the equilibrium of the hybrid market with a last mover advantage can be readily determined as follows. If the investor arriving at time 1 is informed, he submits an order of at least q_L shares and the LOB displays the following prices (where the superscript h stands for "hybrid"):

$$A^h(Y)=\begin{cases} \mu+\dfrac{\pi}{\pi+(1-\pi)(1-\phi)}\sigma & \text{for } Y\leq q_L, \\ \mu+\sigma & \text{for } Y> q_L, \end{cases} \qquad (6.25)$$

$$B^h(Y)=\begin{cases} \mu-\dfrac{\pi}{\pi+(1-\pi)(1-\phi)}\sigma & \text{for } Y\leq q_L, \\ \mu-\sigma & \text{for } Y> q_L. \end{cases} \qquad (6.26)$$

Moreover, at time $t = 1$, the specialist stops small market orders out by slightly improving on the best quotes in the book ($A(q_L)$ or $B(q_L)$ depending on whether the market order is a buy or a sell). If a large market order arrives, the specialist stays put.

Thus in equilibrium the difference between the quotes at the top of the book now is:

$$A^h(0) - B^h(0) = \frac{2\pi\sigma}{\pi + (1-\pi)(1-\phi)} > A(q_S) - B(q_S) = 2\pi\sigma, \qquad (6.27)$$

so that the quoted spread for small orders in the hybrid market is strictly larger than in the pure limit order market, i.e., $A(q_S) - B(q_S)$. Indeed, the specialist's intervention has a perverse effect. It increases limit order traders' exposure to informed trading. As the spread on large orders is identical in the two market structures, all liquidity demanders are worse off in the hybrid limit order market: in the pure limit order market, small and large market buy orders execute wholly or at least partially against the limit orders at $A(q_S)$, while in the hybrid, all market orders execute at a higher price, namely $A(q_L)$.

To sum up, the hybrid market with a last mover advantage aggravates the adverse selection problem for those without this advantage, and so reduces the liquidity of the LOB. In our analysis, only one liquidity provider (the specialist) benefits from the last mover advantage, which dramatically increases trading costs. Exercise 4 shows that competition among multiple liquidity providers alleviates the problem raised here, but does not eliminate it.

This problem is just an illustration of a more general principle. The possibility for some liquidity providers to post quotes contingent on the observation of some trader or order characteristic (here the size of the trade) enables them to cream-skim uninformed trades. Cream-skimming raises the exposure of other liquidity providers to adverse selection and ultimately impairs liquidity. This issue resurfaces regularly in debates about market design (see Box 6.1 for an example or the discussion on payment for order flow in Section 7.2.4 and in Section 8.3).

Box 6.1 Flash Orders

With the development of algorithmic trading and the intensification of competition for order flow, some electronic trading platforms (e.g., Nasdaq and BATS) introduced flash orders in 2009. In the United States, market orders must be executed at the national best bid and offer price (NBBO), i.e., the best of all competing trading venues for a stock. So a platform that receives a buy market order and does not have the best ask price, must reroute the buy order to the platform that posts the best ask (see Section 7.5.1). If it is a flash order, though, before doing so the platform shows ("flashes") the order to its participants at the national best offer for flash orders to buy, and the national best bid for flash orders to sell. Market participants that receive the flashed order information then have a very brief period (generally less than a second) to respond with their own order to execute against the flashed order at a price that matches the nationwide best quote. Flashed orders are a way for a platform to avoid losing order flow (and therefore revenues) to competing platforms.

As the permitted response time to flash orders is fleeting, only liquidity providers using algorithms have a chance to execute the flashed order. Thus, flash orders give a first look advantage to the traders who can actually respond to flashed orders. As a result, as the model developed in this section shows, such orders can increase the exposure of slow limit order traders (who do not react fast enough to respond to flashed orders) or those active in competing platforms to adverse selection and ultimately raise trading costs. In fact, this problem was pointed out by a number of market participants. For instance, after Nasdaq and BATS requested authorization from the SEC for flash orders, Morgan Stanley said the proposed rule changes "will provide a material disincentive to publicly display limit orders on exchanges, thereby impairing price discovery."[9] Given the controversies raised by flash orders and political pressure, both NASDAQ and BATS voluntarily discontinued their flash orders functionality on September 1, 2009.[10]

6.4 The Make or Take Decision in LOB Markets

A key feature of limit order markets is that traders can choose whether to act as makers or takers (either post or hit a limit order). These markets operate well when some investors are makers and others are takers. As we shall see here, the make or take decision hinges on the trade-off between the benefit of trading at a better price and the cost of being exposed to non-execution and pick-off risk. Section 6.4.1 formalizes this trade-off. Sections 6.4.2 and 6.4.3 investigate

---

[9] SEC release no. 34 - 60684: "Elimination of Flash Order Exception from Rule 602 of Regulation NMS."

[10] Skjeltorp, Sojli, and Tham (2016) study empirically the impact of Nasdaq decision to introduce and then remove the flash order functionality. In contrast with the argument developed here, their findings suggest that flash orders improve market quality. They argue that this may be due to the fact that flash orders increased competition for order flow between limit order traders.

how the risk of non-execution and the risk of being picked off affect the bid-ask spread and its relationship with volatility. Section 6.4.5 analyzes how the state of the LOB (the number of shares offered on the bid and ask sides) affects traders' choices between market and limit orders.

6.4.1 Risk of Being Picked Off and Risk of Non-Execution

Consider the market for a security. Its final payoff v_T is realized at time T and is equal to:

$$v_T = \mu_0 + \sum_{t=1}^{t=T} \varepsilon_t, \qquad (6.28)$$

where ε_t is a zero-mean innovation of which market participants are informed at the beginning of period t; ε_t is equal to $+\sigma$ ("good news") or $-\sigma$ ("bad news") with equal probability. The final payoff time, T, is random. Specifically, in each period, there is a probability $1 - \tau$ that this payoff is realized, so that the market for the asset is closed. The parameter τ is an inverse measure of the participants' eagerness to clinch the trade: the closer τ is to zero, the more impatient they are.

At time t, if the asset has not yet paid off, its expected value—its "fair value"—is:

$$v_t = E_t(v_T) = \mu_0 + \sum_{k=1}^{k=t} \varepsilon_k = v_{t-1} + \varepsilon_t. \qquad (6.29)$$

Thus, σ is the per-period volatility of the security's fair value.

After the realization of each ε_t, a new trader comes to the market. Traders have different valuations of the stock. The utility of trader i if he trades $q \in \{+1, 0, -1\}$ shares at price p is:

$$U(q, y_i, p) = q(v_T + y_i - p).$$

Parameter y_i is specific to each trader; it represents his "private value" from trading. It takes one of two values, $+L$ or $-L$, with equal probability. Intuitively, traders with a large gain from holding the security ($y_i = +L$) should buy from those with a low valuation ($y_i = -L$).[11]

---

[11] Several stories come to mind for why traders have different valuations y_i. One is that traders have a long or short position in the security or in another asset whose payoff is correlated with v_T. In this case, traders with a long position value a purchase of the security less than traders with a short

The trader arriving at time t observes v_t and the state of the LOB. Given this information and his private valuation, the trader must choose whether to buy or sell, and whether to place a limit order or a market order. The market order executes immediately at the best quotes available.

In this setting, traders submitting limit orders are exposed to both the risk of being picked off (see Box 6.2) and the risk of non-execution. To see this, consider a trader who submits, at time t, a buy limit order at bid price B valid for only one period. If the trader is of type y_i, his expected utility with this order is:

$$E_t\left[U\left(q_{t+1},y_i,B\right)\right] = E_t\left[\left(v_T+y_i-B\right)\cdot q_{t+1}\right], \qquad (6.30)$$

where $q_{t+1} = 1$ if the order executes and $q_{t+1} = 0$ otherwise. Let $P_t(B)$ be the execution probability of this order. Then we can rewrite (6.30) as:

$$E_t\left[U\left(q_{t+1},y_i,B\right)\right] = E_t\left[\left(v_T-v_t+v_t+y_i-B\right)\cdot q_{t+1}\right]$$

$$= \left[\left(v_t+y_i-B\right)+E\left(\sum_{k=t+1}^{k=T}\varepsilon_k|q_{t+1}=1\right)\right]P_t(B)$$

$$= \left[\left(v_t+y_i-B\right)+E\left(\varepsilon_{t+1}|q_{t+1}=1\right)\right]P_t(B), \qquad (6.31)$$

where we have used the fact that $E\left(\sum_{k=t+2}^{k=T}\varepsilon_k|q_{t+1}=1\right) = E\left(\sum_{k=t+2}^{k=T}\varepsilon_k\right) = 0$. Indeed, the decision of the trader arriving at date $t+1$ (i.e., q_{t+1}) cannot depend on the innovations in the asset value subsequent to date $t+1$ (ε_{t+2} etc....) because these are unknown to this trader. The first component (v_t+y_i-B) is what the trader would gain with certain execution of his limit order if execution were uncorrelated with changes in the expected value of the security, so that $E(\varepsilon_{t+1}|q_{t+1}=1) = E(\varepsilon_{t+1}) = 0$. His expected utility is less than this, however, because there is both a risk of non-execution ($P_t(B) < 1$) and of being picked off (the trader's buy limit order is more likely to be filled when $\varepsilon_{t+1} < 0$ than when $\varepsilon_{t+1} > 0$, so that $E(\varepsilon_{t+1}|q_{t+1}=1) \leq 0$).

To illustrate these effects, consider a numerical example with $\sigma = 0.7$ and $L = 1$. A trader arrives at time t when $v_t = 100$. The LOB at time t has a single sell limit order at $A_t = 100.1$. If the trader submits a buy market order, his expected utility is:

position and conversely, as explained in Chapter 3. Or traders may have different discount factors or face different tax treatment and hence have different valuations for identical payoffs. For instance, for individual investors in the United States, interest on municipal bonds is tax-exempt while payouts of other securities are not; in contrast, pension funds are income tax-exempt irrespective of the securities they hold. Thus, other things being equal, individuals value munis more than tax-exempt institutions. Last, one could interpret y_i as reflecting differences of opinion among traders about the final payoff.

$$E_t[U(1,1,100.1)] = 101 - 100.1 = 0.9.$$

Now, suppose that instead he submits a buy limit order at $B = 99.9$. The expected utility from this order depends on whether it executes and on the evolution of the fair value of the security. There are four possible events at time $t+1$:

1. Public information is good ($\varepsilon_{t+1} = +0.7$) and the trader arriving at time $t+1$ submits a sell market order. The expected utility of the trader who arrived at time t is:

$$E_{t+1}[U(1,1,99.9)] = 100.7 + 1 - 99.9 = 1.8.$$

2. Public information is good ($\varepsilon_{t+1} = +0.7$) and the trader arriving at time $t+1$ submits a limit order. In this case the trader who arrived at time t does not trade, obtaining expected utility of $E_{t+1}[U(0,1,99.9)] = 0$.
3. Public information is bad ($\varepsilon_{t+1} = -0.7$) and the trader arriving at time $t+1$ submits a sell market order. The expected utility of the trader who arrived at time t is then:

$$E_{t+1}[U(1,1,99.9)] = 99.3 + 1 - 99.9 = 0.4.$$

4. Public information is bad ($\varepsilon_{t+1} = -0.7$) and the trader arriving at time $t+1$ submits a limit order. The trader who arrived at time t does not trade and gets zero.

Let φ be the probability of an increase in the value conditional on execution, that is, the probability of event 1 relative to the total probability of execution (events 1 and 3). Then, at time t, the expected utility from the limit order is:

$$\begin{aligned}
E_t[U(q_{t+1},1,99.9)] &= \{(v_t + y_i - B) + E_t(\varepsilon_{t+1}|q_{t+1} = 1)\}P_t(B)\\
&= \{1.1 + [0.7\varphi - 0.7(1-\varphi)]\}P_t(B)\\
&= [1.1 + 0.7(2\varphi - 1)]P_t(B) = (0.4 + 1.4\varphi)P_t(B),
\end{aligned}$$

If $\varphi < 0.5$, we have $E(\varepsilon_{t+1}|q_{t+1} = 1) < 0$ because execution is more likely if the fair value goes down than if it goes up. This effect clearly reduces the expected gain from the limit order. Thus, the lower is φ, the higher is the investor's risk of being picked off.

The limit order at 99.9 dominates a market order if:

$$E_t[U(q_{t+1},1,99.9)] \geq 0.9.$$

Thus, the decision on order type depends on φ and $P_t(B)$. For instance, if $P_t(B)$ is large and φ is close to $\frac{1}{2}$, then a limit order at 99.9 dominates the market order. But suppose instead that the limit order is only executed when the news is bad at time $t+1$ and that the next trader has a low private valuation: $P_t(B) = 0.25$ and $\varphi = 0$. In this case, the trader's expected utility with a limit order at 99.9 is:

$$E_t[U(q_{t+1}, y_i, B)] = (1.1 - 0.7) \cdot 0.25 = 0.1,$$

implying that he would be better off with a market order.

Of course, there may be another limit order at a different price that yields a larger expected utility, so that eventually the trader will submit a limit order. Finding the optimal limit order requires knowledge of the execution probability and the probability φ of good news conditional on execution associated with each possible limit order. These probabilities cannot be arbitrarily specified, since they depend on future traders' order choices in each possible future state of the market (defined at any given time by the type of trader arriving, the fair value of the security, and the offers present in the LOB). In a rational expectations equilibrium, the probabilities must be consistent with the order submission strategies that are used in equilibrium.

For this reason, it is difficult to solve for the equilibrium when traders can choose between market and limit orders.[12] In particular, the number of possible future states is very large if limit orders can stay on the LOB for many periods. To simplify the analysis, let's assume that all limit orders expire after one period, as in the last example. In Sections 6.4.2 and 6.4.3, we show how traders' optimal order submission strategies can be derived in this case. As we shall see, this analysis affords insights into the impact of execution risk and volatility on liquidity in limit order markets.

Box 6.2 SOES Bandits

The risk of being picked off stems from the fact that traders do not monitor their limit orders continuously and/or react too slowly to the arrival of value-relevant news. Hence, they may be too slow in updating their quotes when new information emerges. Market makers too are exposed to this risk. The controversy in the 1990s over Nasdaq's small order execution system (SOES) provides a good illustration. SOES was introduced by Nasdaq to provide automatic execution of small orders (say, less than five hundred shares)

---

[12] Another reason why the problem is difficult is that investors submitting limit orders may also want to revise them as market conditions change.

against dealers' quotes. Hence SOES also allowed traders who were quick in reacting to news to pick off Nasdaq dealers who were slow to adjust their quotes. By contrast, for larger orders, dealers had to first confirm that they were willing to execute, which gave them time to first check that their quotes were in line with current available information (e.g., other dealers' quotes). Thus, although initially intended for retail investors, SOES quickly became a trading tool for professional traders. As they were inflicting losses on market makers by picking off their quotes, the latter used to call them "SOES bandits," and maintained that the practice forced them to quote larger spreads.

6.4.2 Bid-Ask Spreads and Execution Risk

We first solve for the equilibrium of the limit order market in the simplest case, when the security is riskless ($\sigma = 0$), so that traders are only exposed to non-execution risk. If a trader of type y_i trades q shares at price p, he obtains:

$$U(q, y_i, p) = q(\mu_0 + y_i - p).$$

For instance, suppose the trader sells one share (i.e., $q = -1$). This gives a payoff equal to $p - (\mu_0 + y_i)$, which is positive if and only if $p > \mu_0 + y_i$, i.e., if the sale price is higher than the trader's valuation of the asset. As this valuation is never lower than $\mu_0 - L$, no trader will submit a sell order if the transaction price is below $\mu_0 - L$. By symmetry, no trader submits a buy order at a price above $\mu_0 + L$. Therefore, when $\sigma = 0$, we can restrict our attention to the case in which quotes are in the range $[\mu_0 - L, \mu_0 + L]$. For prices in this range, traders of type $+L$ submit only buy orders and those of type $-L$ submit only sell orders. Hence, in what follows, we study only the optimal buy orders for traders of type $+L$ and sell orders for traders of type $-L$.

Let $\widehat{A}$ be the maximum ask price that a trader of type $+L$ arriving at time t is willing to take using a buy market order. The trader's strategy is:

submit a buy market order if $A_t \leq \widehat{A}_t$,

submit a buy limit order at price B_t^* if $A_t > \widehat{A}_t$.

Similarly, let $\widehat{B}$ be the minimal bid price that a trader of type $-L$ arriving at time t is willing to take with a sell market order. The strategy is:

submit a sell market order if $B_t \geq \widehat{B}_t$,

submit a sell limit order at price A_t^* if $B_t < \widehat{B}_t$.

Suppose that a (high-valuation) investor submits a limit order to buy at bid price B at time t and recall that the successor trader is a low-valuation type with probability $\tau/2$. Given the above strategies for the successor at time $t+1$, the execution probability P_t of the limit order is:

$$P_t(B) = 0 \text{ if } B < \widehat{B}_{t+1},$$
$$P_t(B) = \frac{\tau}{2} \text{ if } B \geq \widehat{B}_{t+1},$$

Hence, if the trader opts for a buy limit order, the optimal bid price is $B_t^* = \widehat{B}_{t+1}$, because a lower bid will not execute, and a higher bid yields no improvement in execution probability. Thus, the highest expected utility from a buy limit order is:

$$E_t\left[U\left(q_{t+1}, +L, \widehat{B}_{t+1}\right)\right] = \frac{\tau}{2}\left(\mu_0 + L - \widehat{B}_{t+1}\right).$$

Therefore, the cut-off ask price $\widehat{A}_t$ that makes the buyer indifferent between a buy market order and a buy limit order solves:

$$\mu_0 + L - \widehat{A}_t = \frac{\tau}{2}\left(\mu_0 + L - \widehat{B}_{t+1}\right) \tag{6.32}$$

The argument for a low-valuation seller is analogous. The seller's optimal ask price is $A_t^* = \widehat{A}_{t+1}$, and the cut-off bid price $\widehat{B}_t$ that makes the seller indifferent between a sell market order and a sell limit order solves:

$$\widehat{B}_t - (\mu_0 - L) = \frac{\tau}{2}\left(\widehat{A}_{t+1} - (\mu_0 - L)\right). \tag{6.33}$$

As the parameters (τ, μ_0, L) are time-invariant, traders face exactly the same problem in each period. Hence, it is natural to focus on steady-state equilibria in which traders choose strategies that do not depend on time, that is:

$$\widehat{B}_t = \widehat{B} \text{ and } \widehat{A}_t = \widehat{A} \ \forall t. \tag{6.34}$$

We can now easily compute traders' equilibrium bids, offers and cut-off prices by solving equations (6.32), (6.33), and (6.34). We obtain:

$$A^* = \widehat{A} = \mu_0 - L + \frac{4L}{2+\tau}, \tag{6.35}$$

$$B^* = \widehat{B} = \mu_0 + L - \frac{4L}{2+\tau}. \tag{6.36}$$

As τ increases, execution risk decreases. There are two possible reasons why a limit order may not be taken: either trading is terminated (probability $1-\tau$), or the next period's trader's private valuation is the same as the current trader's (probability $\tau/2$), so there is a non-execution probability $1-\tau/2$. Thus, in this model parameter τ measures execution risk, which is a key determinant of the bid-ask spread since:[13]

$$A^* - B^* = 2\left(\frac{2-\tau}{2+\tau}\right)L.$$

The bid-ask spread is decreasing in the parameter τ, and thus increasing in execution risk. Indeed, as τ rises, the cost of not trading immediately upon arrival with a market order becomes smaller because the likelihood of a limit order being filled increases. Thus, in equilibrium, limit orders must be more aggressive if they are to attract counterparties; accordingly ask and bid prices become more aggressive as τ gets larger $\left(\frac{\partial A_t^*}{\partial \tau} \leq 0 \text{ and } \frac{\partial B_t^*}{\partial \tau} \geq 0\right)$.

This effect of execution risk on traders' order placement strategies can explain the fact that, in real-world markets, bid-ask spreads widen at the end of the trading day. Indeed, as the end of the day nears, the likelihood that limit orders will remain unfilled gets higher. This prospect increases market makers' power, as traders are willing to pay greater price concessions to avoid losing a trading opportunity.

6.4.3 Bid-Ask Spreads and Volatility

Now we turn to the more complex case in which the security is risky, so that $\sigma > 0$. Let $\widehat{B}_{t+1}(y_{t+1}, v_{t+1})$ be traders' sell cut-off price at time $t+1$. Intuitively, $\widehat{B}_{t+1}(\cdot)$ increases with v_{t+1} and y_{t+1}, other things equal, since traders should demand a higher price to sell when (i) the asset expected payoff is higher or (ii) their valuation for the asset is higher. But it is not clear a priori whether $\widehat{B}_{t+1}(-L, v_t + \sigma)$ is higher or lower than $\widehat{B}_{t+1}(+L, v_t - \sigma)$. To fix things, suppose that:

$$\widehat{B}_{t+1}(-L, v_t - \sigma) < \widehat{B}_{t+1}(-L, v_t + \sigma) < \widehat{B}_{t+1}(+L, v_t - \sigma) < \widehat{B}_{t+1}(+L, v_t + \sigma).$$
$$(6.37)$$

Under this conjecture, which will be verified in equilibrium, Figure 6.8 shows the execution probability of a buy limit order at price B submitted at

---

[13] The structure of the model is such that the limit order book features either a buy limit order at price B^* or a sell limit order at price A^* but not both orders at once. However, as all buy market orders execute at A^* and all sell orders at B^*, it is natural to define the bid-ask spread as $A^* - B^*$.

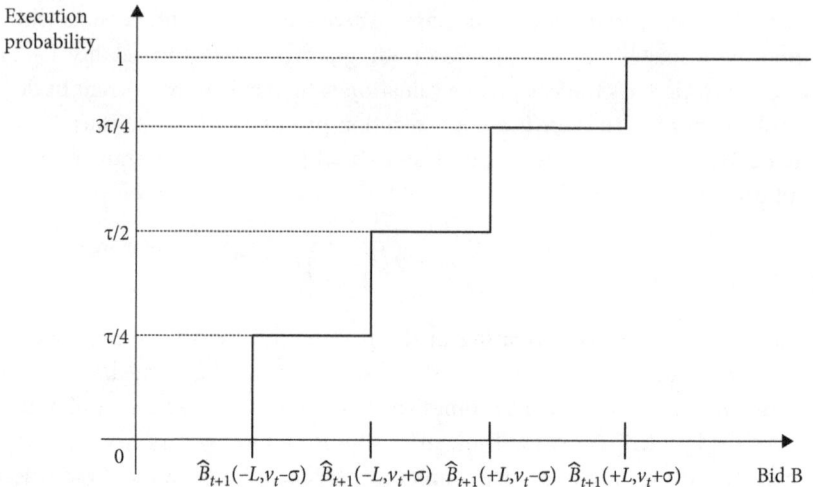

Figure 6.8 Bid price and execution probability.

time t. For example, a buy limit order with a low bid price in the interval $[\widehat{B}_{t+1}(-L, v_t - \sigma), \widehat{B}_{t+1}(-L, v_t + \sigma)]$ executes if and only if (a) the next trader's private valuation is $-L$ and (b) bad news arises about the asset ($\varepsilon_{t+1} = -\sigma$). This event happens with probability $\frac{\tau}{4}$.

A trader who places a buy limit order loses money if her limit order is hit by traders with a high private valuation ($y = +L$). Indeed, the latter is willing to sell only when her valuation for the asset is below the price of the buy limit order. As this valuation is the highest, this means that the limit order submitter necessarily buys at a price above her own valuation for the asset. Thus, she bears a loss when trading with a trader with a high valuation. This argument rules out any buy limit orders at prices of $\widehat{B}_{t+1}(+L, v_t - \sigma)$ or higher, because the resulting increased execution probability is achieved solely by attracting high-private-valuation counterparties in addition to those who would be willing to take a lower bid.

Thus a trader of type $+L$ who places a buy limit order must choose one of only two prices: a conservative low price B_l with a low execution probability of $\frac{\tau}{4}$,

$$B_l \equiv \widehat{B}_{t+1}(-L, v_t - \sigma),$$

and a more aggressive price B_h with a greater execution probability $\frac{\tau}{2}$,

$$B_h \equiv \widehat{B}_{t+1}(-L, v_t + \sigma).$$

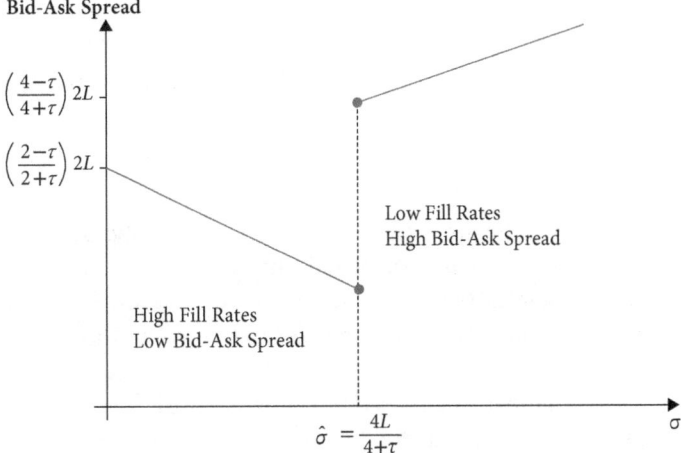

Figure 6.9 Impact of volatility on the bid-ask spread.

Intuitively, the trader faces a trade-off between paying less and having a higher probability of execution. The optimal choice depends on volatility. In equilibrium, traders choose the low-execution-risk strategy if volatility is sufficiently low, so that the utility loss when the asset value drops remains small. Specifically, in equilibrium, traders of type $+L$ adopt the following bidding strategies:

$$\text{post a buy limit order at } B_h = v_t + L - \frac{2(2L-\sigma)}{2+\tau} \text{ if } \sigma \leq \hat{\sigma},$$

$$\text{post a buy limit order at } B_l = v_t + L - \sigma - \frac{8L}{4+\tau} \text{ if } \sigma > \hat{\sigma},$$

where the threshold volatility $\hat{\sigma}$ is defined by:

$$\hat{\sigma} = \frac{4L}{4+\tau}.$$

Similarly, traders of type $-L$ post the following quotes in equilibrium:

$$\text{post a sell limit order at } A_h = v_t - L + \frac{2(2L-\sigma)}{2+\tau} \text{ if } \sigma \leq \hat{\sigma},$$

$$\text{post a sell limit order at } A_l = v_t - L + \sigma + \frac{8L}{4+\tau} \text{ if } \sigma > \hat{\sigma}.$$

The method of proof to obtain this result is the same as that used for the case $\sigma = 0$, as explained in the Appendix to this chapter. Of course, if $\sigma = 0$, the expressions for bid and ask prices are identical to those obtained in Section 6.4.2.

The bid-ask spread in equilibrium is:

$$A_h - B_h = 2\frac{2-\tau}{2+\tau}L - \frac{4}{2+\tau}\sigma \text{ if } \sigma \le \hat{\sigma},$$

$$A_l - B_l = 2\frac{4-\tau}{4+\tau}L + 2\sigma \quad \text{ if } \sigma > \hat{\sigma}.$$

Figure 6.9 shows the spread as a function of volatility, σ. Interestingly, in contrast to most other models of bid-ask spreads, the effect of volatility here is non-monotonic. The reason is that an increase in σ raises the cost of being picked off, but also reduces the market power of those who submit limit orders.

To see this, recall that when $\sigma \le \hat{\sigma}$, investors optimally choose limit orders with a high execution probability, i.e. that execute whether the asset value goes down or up. Now an increase in volatility raises the lowest price (e.g., $\hat{B}_{t+1}(-L, v_t + \sigma)$) required by investors to sell when the value goes up. As a result, if a buyer wants to retain a high execution probability, he must submit limit orders at increasingly high prices as volatility increases. By symmetry, a seller must submit limit orders at increasingly low prices. In other words, an increase in σ reduces the market power of those submitting limit orders. Thus, when $\sigma \le \hat{\sigma}$ the bid-ask spread declines as volatility increases, and as a result, limit order investors obtain less and less surplus.

At $\sigma = \hat{\sigma}$, this surplus is so small that it becomes more profitable for limit order traders to submit less aggressive quotes at the cost of a lower execution probability. As noted earlier, such quotes only execute when there is bad news. Hence, they are shaded by the amount of the adverse movement that triggers their execution, so when $\sigma > \hat{\sigma}$ the spread is increasing in σ.

When $\sigma \le \hat{\sigma}$, limit orders have a higher execution probability than when $\sigma > \hat{\sigma}$. There are more market orders relative to limit orders, and the volume of trading is higher. This means that markets where limit orders are relatively more prevalent ($\sigma > \hat{\sigma}$) are not necessarily more liquid. Indeed, such intensive use of limit orders may simply reflect the fact that traders find it too costly to submit a market order, as in the model for $\sigma > \hat{\sigma}$.

6.4.4 Indexed Limit Orders, Monitoring, and Algorithmic Trading

Pegged limit orders. The risk of being picked off makes the market more illiquid. One solution to this problem is to peg limit orders to changes in the fair value of the security. That is, traders' limit orders can be automatically "repriced" when there is a change in the fair value of the security, and so protected against pick-off risk. The equilibrium is therefore identical to the case in which $\sigma = 0$.[14]

In practice, some trading platforms allow indexed limit orders. Since market organizers do not know the fair value of the security, they peg the prices of indexed limit orders to the price of some other, related security (e.g., an index) or to the quotes posted for the same security on other platforms.[15] But the protection offered by this form of indexing is imperfect and does not fully eliminate the risk of limit orders being picked off.

Monitoring limit orders. Traders can also mitigate pick-off risk by monitoring. For instance, if bad news arrives a buyer can quickly cancel his limit order and resubmit it at a lower price, and similarly in case of good news he can resubmit it at a higher price to keep a high execution probability. If this monitoring is costless, then we are back to the case where $\sigma = 0$. In practice, however, monitoring is not costless (it takes work) and trading platforms sometimes charge a fee for order cancellations.

The cost of monitoring limit orders has declined considerably in recent years, as traders increasingly automate their routing decisions to get better protection against pick-off and non-execution risk. Traders also invest to reduce trading latency, the time it takes for their messages (e.g., a request to cancel an order) to be processed by the exchange. For instance, they pay fees to have their servers close to trading platforms (a practice known as colocation). However, automation can also be used to pick off stale limit orders more quickly. Thus, its net effect on liquidity depends on whether it is a greater help to those who seek protection against the risk of being picked off or to those who want to pick off stale quotes. We analyze this evolution in details in Chapter 9.

Box 6.3 Limit Orders as Free Options

There is an interesting analogy between options and limit orders. For instance, submitting a sell limit order is similar to writing an American call option: it enables investors to buy a security at a "strike" price equal to the ask price of the limit order.[16] Market participants want to exercise these options

---

[14] As Figure 6.9 shows, authorizing pegged limit orders does not necessarily minimize the spread. Indeed, in the model, suppressing limit order traders' exposure to changes in the asset value can increase their market power, as explained at the end of the previous section.

[15] For instance, limit orders in a given stock traded on the NYSE can be pegged to the best bid and ask prices for this stock on the NYSE via the use of Primary Pegged Orders. Pegged limit orders are then automatically repriced every time there is a change in the best bid or ask price, so that their limit price remains at a fixed distance from the best price.

[16] A buy limit order, by symmetry, is similar to an American put option.

when they are "in the money," that is, when the price attached to a sell limit order is below the fair value of the security.

The options implicit in limit orders are "free," since the investors who submit them receive no payment for "writing" (selling) them. Yet, these options can be profitable because, unlike actual options, limit orders sometimes execute even when they are "out the money," simply because some investors (liquidity traders) need to buy the security (say, to hedge), even in the absence of solid information about its value. Limit order traders must therefore price their orders to balance the expected loss when the implied option goes into the money and is exercised against the expected gain when it is exercised out of the money.

This balancing act is very similar to that of market makers who compensate for the cost of trading with better informed investors with the revenue from dealing with liquidity traders, as seen in Chapter 3 (see also Copeland and Galai 1983). There are some significant differences, though: the exposure to pick-off risk also depends on how fast the trader can access the market and how intensively he monitors his quotes. Thus, the liquidity effect of pick-off risk is linked to investment decisions in routing and monitoring technologies. Moreover, competition between traders seeking to pick off limit orders forces them to race to do so as soon as the option is even slightly in the money, thus endogenously forcing accelerated exercise of the option and limiting its potential value.

6.4.5 Order Flow and the State of the LOB

In the previous sections we have analyzed how execution risk and pick-off risk affect the bid-ask spread, the composition of the order flow, and order aggressiveness. However, the model remains too simple to illuminate the relationship between the depth of the LOB and order flow. In particular, it does not allow us to study how variations in depth affect the aggressiveness of traders' orders. Yet intuitively, the depth of the book on both sides should affect order placement strategies.

Consider a buyer. If a large number of shares are offered at the best bid, then the likelihood of quick execution with a limit order is low. In this case, the buyer is more likely to submit a limit order that improves upon the best bid price, or even a market order. That is, an increase in depth on the buy side of the book makes aggressive buy orders more likely.

Similarly, sellers are more likely to submit a market order when the LOB is deep at the best ask price. Hence, when the number of shares offered at the best ask price increases, the execution probability of buy limit orders improves, other things equal. That is, an increase in the depth on the sell side of the LOB makes aggressive buy orders less likely.

In this section, we modify the model developed above to formalize these intuitions. Suppose there is no uncertainty about the time at which the asset pays off, and that we count time backward. That is, $t = 1$ denotes the last period of the trading day, $t = 2$ the penultimate period, and so on. For simplicity, consider only the last three periods. The results generalize to an arbitrary number of periods.

To simplify the analysis further, we assume that traders must position their limit orders on a grid with tick size Δ. The first quote on the grid below the fair value is $b = \mu_0 - \frac{\Delta}{2}$, the first above it is $a = \mu_0 + \frac{\Delta}{2}$. The tick size is such that:

$$\frac{\Delta}{2} < L < \Delta. \tag{6.38}$$

Thus, investors of type $+L$ never trade at a price above a and investors of type $-L$ never trade below b. Submitting a limit order with a price outside the range $[b, a]$ is never optimal, since it has zero execution probability. As we shall see, several buy limit orders will queue at price b, several sell limit orders at a. Time priority is used to determine the sequence in which they are filled.

In addition, a market maker stands constantly ready to sell shares at a and buy shares at b. This market maker does not have priority of execution over limit orders placed at the same price. Thus, arriving traders face a simple choice. Consider a trader of type $+L$ for instance. Since he can always trade immediately at price a using a market order, his choice boils down to a market order filled at price a or a limit order to buy at b.

If a trader of type $+L$ submits a buy market order at time t, he obtains:

$$U(1, L, a) = L - \frac{\Delta}{2}.$$

If he submits a buy limit order instead, he obtains:

$$U(1, L, b) = P_{bt}(n_{bt}, n_{at})\left(L + \frac{\Delta}{2}\right),$$

where $P_{bt}(n_{bt}, n_{at})$ is the execution probability of a buy limit order submitted at time t when the book has n_{bt} buy limit orders (each for one share) at price b and n_{at} sell limit orders (each for one share) at price a (not counting the shares offered by the market maker).

Thus, submitting a buy limit order is optimal if and only if:

$$P_{bt}(n_{bt}, n_{at}) > \frac{2L - \Delta}{2L + \Delta}. \tag{6.39}$$

We obtain the same decision rule for a seller. That is, a trader of type $-L$ optimally submits a sell limit order at price a if and only if:

$$P_{st}(n_{bt}, n_{at}) > \frac{2L - \Delta}{2L + \Delta}, \tag{6.40}$$

where $P_{st}(n_{bt}, n_{at})$ denotes the execution of a sell limit order at price a at time t when the state of the book is $\{n_{bt}, n_{at}\}$.

Hence, the decision for a limit order depends on execution probability, which varies over time, insofar as non-execution gets more likely as the end of the trading day approaches, and the state of the book varies.

Equilibrium. In equilibrium, the execution probability of a limit order at a given time in each state of the LOB depends on future traders' order placement decisions. In turn, these decisions depend on execution probabilities. At time $t = 1$, however, execution probabilities are zero for limit orders, since the trader arriving at this time is the last. Thus, we can solve for traders' optimal actions at each time by "backward induction": first, we derive traders' optimal decision at time $t = 1$; we obtain limit order execution probabilities at time $t = 2$, and using conditions (6.39) and (6.40), we infer traders' optimal orders in each state of the book. We can then proceed to time $t = 3$.

Time t = 1. If the trader arriving at time $t = 1$ were to place a limit order, it would certainly not execute, since he is the last trader of the day. Thus, the trader submits a buy market order if he is type $+L$ and a sell market order if he is type $-L$.

Time t = 2. Suppose that the trader arriving at $t = 2$ is a buyer ($y_i = +L$). Given the equilibrium actions of the trader arriving at time $t = 1$, the execution probabilities are:

$$P_{b2}(0, n_{a2}) = \frac{1}{2},$$

$$P_{b2}(n_{b2}, n_{a2}) = 0 \text{ if } n_{b2} \geq 1.$$

Notice that $\frac{2L-\Delta}{2L+\Delta} < \frac{1}{2}$ since $L < \Delta$. Thus, if $n_{b2} = 0$, condition (6.39) is satisfied and the investor optimally submits a buy limit order; otherwise, a buy market order. The optimal strategy of a seller is symmetric: a sell market order if $n_{a2} \geq 1$ and a sell limit order if $n_{a2} = 0$.

Time t = 3. Finally, we derive the optimal strategy of the trader arriving at time $t = 3$. Again, suppose that this trader is a buyer. Given traders' optimal actions at times $t = 1$ and $t = 2$, we have:

$$P_{b3}(0, n_{a3}) = \frac{3}{4} \text{ if } n_{a3} \geq 1,$$

$$P_{b3}(0, n_{a3}) = \frac{1}{2} \text{ if } n_{a3} = 0,$$

$$P_{b3}(1, n_{a3}) = \frac{1}{4} \text{ if } n_{a3} \geq 1,$$

$$P_{b3}(1, n_{a3}) = 0 \text{ if } n_{a3} = 0,$$

$$P_{b3}(n_{b3}, n_{a3}) = 0 \text{ if } n_{b3} \geq 2.$$

Thus, the buyer arriving at time $t = 3$ submits a buy limit order at b if $n_{b3} = 0$. If $n_{b3} = 1$ and $n_{a3} \geq 1$, the optimal order placement strategy depends on L/Δ. If $\frac{L}{\Delta} \leq \frac{5}{8}$, then a buy limit order is optimal since its execution probability $(1/4)$ is such that condition (6.39) is satisfied. Otherwise, a buy market order is optimal. In other states of the LOB, a trader of type $+L$ submits a buy market order, since a limit order has zero execution probability. The strategy of a seller is symmetric. Table 6.1 summarizes the optimal action for a buyer arriving at time $t = 3$ for each possible state of the book and the execution probability of a buy limit order in each state, when $\frac{L}{\Delta} \leq \frac{5}{8}$. The table shows the optimal order for a buyer arriving at time $t = 3$ ("lo" denoting limit order and "mo" market order) and the execution probabilities of a buy limit order at this time for each possible state of the LOB.

Order flow and state of the book. The equilibrium obtained in this example has several interesting properties (see Table 6.1). First, at each time the execution probability of a new limit order decreases as the number of shares offered on that side increases $\left(\text{e.g., at time 3, } P_{b3}(0,1) = \frac{3}{4} > P_{b3}(1,1) = \frac{1}{4}\right)$, and it increases

Table 6.1 Optimal Order Submission Strategy and Execution Probabilities for a Buyer at $t = 3$

n_a3:	n_b3:	0	1	≥ 2
0		$\left(\text{lo}, \frac{1}{2}\right)$	$(\text{mo}, 0)$	$(\text{mo}, 0)$
1		$\left(\text{lo}, \frac{3}{4}\right)$	$\left(\text{lo}, \frac{1}{4}\right)$	$(\text{mo}, 0)$
2		$\left(\text{lo}, \frac{3}{4}\right)$	$\left(\text{lo}, \frac{1}{4}\right)$	$(\text{mo}, 0)$
3		$\left(\text{lo}, \frac{3}{4}\right)$	$\left(\text{lo}, \frac{1}{4}\right)$	$(\text{mo}, 0)$
≥ 4		$\left(\text{lo}, \frac{3}{4}\right)$	$\left(\text{lo}, \frac{1}{4}\right)$	$(\text{mo}, 0)$

along with the number of shares on the opposite side (e.g., $P_{b3}(0,1) = \frac{3}{4} >$ $P_{b3}(0,0) = \frac{1}{2}$). These properties extend to any time. For instance, at all times, $P_{bt}(n_{bt}, n_{at})$ decreases in n_{bt} and increases in n_{at}.

The first property follows from the fact that limit orders queuing at the same price execute in the sequence in which they were submitted (time priority). Hence traders are more likely to submit market orders when the LOB on their side is deeper. But this means that a limit order has a better chance of execution when the book on the other side is deeper, which is the second property. Thus, at any given time, a buy limit order is more likely when the book on the sell side is deep and less likely when the buy side is deep. Several empirical studies (e.g., Biais, Hillion, and Spatt 1995; Griffiths et al. 2000; Ranaldo 2004) confirm this prediction. Using data from the Swiss Stock Exchange, Ranaldo (2004) finds that traders submit more aggressive orders (higher-priced limit orders or market orders) when the LOB is deeper on their side and less aggressive orders when it is deeper on the opposite side. In the same vein, in a pioneering study of the Paris Bourse, an electronic limit order market, Biais, Hillion, and Spatt (1995) observe that: "Improvements in the best quote are especially frequent when the depth at the quotes is already large. This reflects the trade-off between the execution probability and price" (p. 1657).

These properties of execution probability imply that successive orders submitted to the market are not independent, even though traders' types (buyer/seller) are not serially correlated. To see this, let $I_{bt} = 1$ if a buy limit order is submitted at time t, and $I_{bt} = 0$ otherwise. Similarly $I_{st} = 1$ if a sell limit order is submitted at time t, and $I_{st} = 0$ otherwise. In equilibrium, we have:

$$\Pr(I_{k2} = 1 \mid I_{k3} = 1) \leq \Pr(I_{k2} = 1 \mid I_{k3} = 0) \text{ for } k \in \{b, s\}.$$

That is, the likelihood of two consecutive limit orders in the same direction (e.g., buy-buy) is smaller than that of two limit orders in opposite directions (e.g., buy-sell).[17] In other words, the model predicts that the direction of limit orders should be negatively serially correlated.[18] Suppose that a buy limit order arrives at time t. This order increases the depth at the best bid price, making it less attractive for the next trader to also submit a buy limit order and more attractive to submit a sell limit order.

The model also implies a positive serial correlation in the direction of trades (remember that this is defined as the direction of the market order side). The

---

[17] Here, we just consider dates $t = 3$ and $t = 2$ since the model has only three dates. But this property of the model is more general.

[18] For instance, suppose that $n_{b3} = 0$ and $n_{a3} = 0$. If a sell limit order is submitted at time 3, the likelihood of observing a buy limit order at time $t = 2$ is $\frac{1}{2}$. In contrast, if a buy limit order is submitted at time 3, the likelihood of observing a buy limit order at time 2 is zero.

intuition is as follows. Suppose that a buy market order arrives at time t. The depth of the book on the ask side decreases by one share. As a consequence, the execution probability for an investor submitting a sell limit order improves. Sell limit orders become more attractive and the likelihood that the next investor will submit a sell market order consequently declines. Hence, the likelihood of observing a buy market order at time $t-1$ is greater given a buy market order at time t than given a sell market order. For instance, suppose that one share is offered on each side of the book at time 3 ($n_{b3} = n_{a3} = 1$) and a sell market order now arrives. Then the likelihood of another sell market order at time 2 is $\frac{1}{2}$ in equilibrium. If instead a buy market order hits the market at time 3 then the likelihood of a sell market order at time 2 is nil. Thus, the likelihood of two consecutive transactions in the same direction is greater than that of two transactions in opposite directions.

These properties imply that variations in the state of the LOB can generate time-series dependence in the order flow endogenously, even though traders' types (buyer/seller) are not correlated over time. In fact, in limit order markets orders are serially correlated. For instance, the likelihood of an order of a given type at a given time (say, a buy market order) is greater following the arrival of an order of the same type—which is partly consistent with the model presented here, where two consecutive transactions are more likely to be in the same direction than in opposite directions. But the model presented here does not explain why, empirically, a buy (sell) limit order is more likely after another buy (sell) limit order. This effect may stem from the fact that traders often split large orders into small consecutive trades, a strategy that is outside the model considered in this section.

6.5 Further Reading

Garman (1976) and Cohen et al. (1981) provide early formal analyses of dynamic limit order markets. But they specify traders' beliefs on the execution probabilities of their limit orders exogenously.

Glosten (1994) develops the first equilibrium model of trading in a limit order market. His model is similar to that developed in Section 6.2.3 but he assumes that a pro-rata allocation rule is used to determine how limit orders tied at the same price are executed (as in Section 6.3.2). He also assumes that the number of traders submitting limit orders is infinite. Biais, Martimort, and Rochet (2000) relax this assumption and characterize the equilibrium of the limit order market when there is imperfect competition among limit order traders (see also Baruch and Glosten (2019)).

Using data from the Stockholm Stock Exchange, Sandas (2001) tests the specification of the model considered in example 1 (in its more elaborate version with asymmetric information). He tests whether snapshots of LOBs collected at the time of each transaction satisfy the restrictions imposed on cumulative depth and quotes by equations (6.16) and (6.17). He rejects the model, principally because the LOB predicted by the model appears too deep relative to the actual LOBs that he observes. One possible explanation is that competition among limit order traders is imperfect, so that the zero profit conditions that characterize the competitive equilibrium are not satisfied in reality.

In the model considered in Section 6.2.3, informed investors are assumed to submit market orders. Bloomfield, O'Hara, and Saar (2005) run laboratory experiments in which informed and uninformed participants trade in a limit order market. They find that informed traders sometimes use limit orders. Brogaard et al. (2019) find that limit orders significantly contributes to price discovery, which also suggests that informed investors sometimes use limit orders. Kaniel and Liu (2006) and Rosu (2020) develop theoretical models in which informed traders submit limit orders.

Seppi (1997) introduces the model of limit order trading without asymmetric information considered in Section 6.2. He extends this model to account for adverse selection and analyzes the last-mover advantage of the NYSE specialist (see Section 6.3.3). Parlour and Seppi (2003) use this model to study competition between a hybrid and a pure limit order market. In this framework, Foucault and Menkveld (2008) analyze competition between two pure limit order markets (see Section 7.4.2).

Seppi (1997), Viswanathan and Wang (2002), and Back and Baruch (2007) compare limit order markets and uniform price auctions. Back and Baruch (2007) show that a dynamic uniform auction in which informed investors can split their market orders over time always has an equilibrium that is identical to that obtained in Glosten (1994).

Dynamic models of limit order trading have been developed by Foucault (1995); Parlour (1998); Foucault (1999); Goettler, Parlour, and Rajan (2005); Foucault, Kadan, and Kandel (2005); Van Achter (2006); Rosu (2009); Large (2009); Hoffmann (2014); and Dugast (2018). The model presented in Section 6.4.1 is based on Foucault (1999). Foucault, Kadan, and Kandel (2005) and Rosu (2009) study the role of impatience and time to execution. Parlour (1998) offers a systematic equilibrium treatment of the relationships between the depth of the LOB and the aggressiveness of order submission, as discussed in Section 6.4.5. Buti and Rindi (2013) and Buti, Rindi and Werner (2017) build on this model to study theoretically the role of hidden orders and dark pools in limit order book markets. Goettler, Parlour, and Rajan (2005) develop a more general version of the framework considered in Section 6.4.1, allowing traders to submit multiple limit orders when they arrive, and to stay for more than one period, and drawing traders' private valuations from a continuous distribution. They develop an algorithm to find a stationary Markov-perfect equilibrium of the limit order market numerically and run it to derive various comparative statics. In particular, they consider the effect of reducing tick size. They show that a smaller tick reduces limit order traders' surpluses but increases investors' total surplus. Goettler et al. (2009) apply the same methodology to analyze the decision to acquire information in a limit order market.

A natural question is whether order choices that are observed in reality can be explained by the trade-offs described in Section 6.4.1. Hollifield, Miller, and San-das (2004) test this, using a more general version of that framework. Their test consists in estimating execution probabilities and pick-off risks for limit orders. Then they check whether observed limit orders maximize expected payoffs.[19] They do not reject the model when they test it for buy and sell orders separately.

Hollifield et al. (2006) use this framework to measure the efficiency of a limit order market empirically (the Vancouver Stock Exchange). They find that the limit order market is quite efficient, in that about 90% of the maximum gain from trades is realized, according to their estimates. Interestingly, unexecuted limit orders constitute the main source of inefficiency.

There is also a rich empirical literature on the determinants of order submission choices (see, for instance, Griffiths et al. 2000; Ellul et al. 2007; Ranaldo 2004) and the references therein) and the cost and benefits of using market and limit orders (see Handa and Schwartz 1996; Harris and Hasbrouck 1996). Parlour and Seppi (2008) provide a survey of the literature on limit order markets.

6.6 Appendix. Volatility and Make or Take Decisions: Derivations

Here we briefly sketch the derivation of the equilibrium of the model of Section 6.4.3, which extends the model presented in Section 6.4.2 when $\sigma > 0$. As for $\sigma = 0$, we consider steady state equilibria in which investors' strategies do not depend on time. Assume first that $\sigma \leq \hat{\sigma}$. In this case, in equilibrium, buyers and sellers post only limit orders with high execution probability, that is: $B^* = B_h = \widehat{B}(-L, v_t + \sigma)$ and $A^* = A_h = \widehat{A}(+L, v_t - \sigma)$. Thus, traders' cutoff prices are:

$$\mu_0 + L - \widehat{A}(+L, v_t) = \frac{\tau}{2}\left(\mu_0 + L - \widehat{B}(-L, v_t + \sigma)\right), \quad (6.41)$$

$$\widehat{B}(-L, v_t) - (\mu_0 - L) = \frac{\tau}{2}\left(\widehat{A}(+L, v_t - \sigma) - (\mu_0 - L)\right). \quad (6.42)$$

[19] They show that this can be checked by testing a simple monotonicity condition, using the estimates obtained for execution probabilities and pick-off risk.

Further, it must be that the expected payoff with aggressive (high-execution-probability) orders is greater than that obtained with conservative (low execution probability) limit orders. Thus the following inequalities must hold:

$$\frac{\tau}{2}\left(\mu_0 + L - \widehat{B}(-L, v_t + \sigma)\right) \geq \frac{\tau}{4}\left(\mu_0 + L - \widehat{B}(-L, v_t - \sigma)\right) \qquad (6.43)$$

$$\frac{\tau}{2}\left(\widehat{A}(+L, v_t - \sigma) - (\mu_0 - L)\right) \geq \frac{\tau}{4}\left(\widehat{A}(+L, v_t + \sigma) - (\mu_0 - L)\right) \qquad (6.44)$$

Investors' equilibrium cutoff prices are obtained by solving the system of equations (6.41) and (6.42). This yields closed-form solutions for B_h and A_h. Armed with these solutions for the cut-off prices, we can verify that conditions (6.37), (6.43), (6.44) are satisfied if and only if $\sigma \leq \widehat{\sigma}$. The derivation of the equilibrium when $\sigma > \widehat{\sigma}$ follows similar steps; see Foucault (1999) for a full analysis.

6.7 Exercises

1. **Deriving a competitive LOB.** Consider the model developed in section 6.2.3. We make the following parametric assumptions:
   1. The trader who arrives in period 1 knows the final value of the security v with probability π. Otherwise, he is uninformed.
   2. If the trader who arrives in period 1 is uninformed, he buys or sells (with equal probability) a number of shares x that has an exponential distribution with parameter θ. That is, the size distribution of the market order submitted by an uninformed trader arriving in period 2 is $f(x) = \frac{1}{2}\theta e^{-\theta|x|}$.
   3. The final value of the security in period 2 has the following probability distribution: $g(v) = \frac{1}{2\sigma}\exp\left(-\frac{|v-\mu|}{\sigma}\right)$. This implies that σ is the mean absolute deviation of v and $E(v|v \geq z) = z + \sigma$.
   4. The tick size is nil ($\Delta = 0$).
   Let $Y(A)$ be the cumulative depth up to ask price A in the book and A^* be the lowest ask price in the LOB.
   a. Show that when $v \geq A^*$, the optimal strategy of the informed trader is to buy $Y(v)$ shares.
   b. Using this observation and the zero profit condition (6.13), show that in equilibrium:

   $$Y(A) = \frac{1}{\theta}\left[\ln\left(\frac{1-\pi}{\pi}\right) + \ln\left(\frac{A-\mu}{\sigma}\right) + \frac{A-\mu}{\sigma}\right] \text{if } A > A^*.$$

   c. Show that the book becomes thinner on the ask side when (i) π increases or (ii) σ increases. What is the economic intuition for this result?

2. **Time priority vs. random tie-breaking rule.** Consider example 2 in Section 6.2.3 but assume that the tick size Δ is strictly positive, such that:

$$A_1 = \mu + \Delta < \mu + \sigma < \mu + 2\Delta.$$

Time priority is enforced as in the baseline model of Section 6.2.3.

a. Explain why the LOB will feature at least q_L shares offered at price A_2.

b. Let Y_1 be the number of shares offered at price A_1. Define $r = \sigma/\Delta$. Observe that $r \in [1,2]$. Using the assumptions regarding the order flow at time 1, show that:

$$(a)\ Y_1 = 0 \text{ iff } \frac{(r-1)\pi}{1-\pi} \geq 1.$$

$$(b)\ Y_1 = q_s \text{ iff } \frac{(r-1)\pi}{1-\pi} \in [1-\phi, 1).$$

$$(c)\ Y_1 = q_L \text{ iff } \frac{(r-1)\pi}{1-\pi} \in [0, 1-\phi).$$

c. Why does Y_1 decrease with π?

d. Now assume that $\frac{(r-1)\pi}{1-\pi} \in [1-\phi, 1)$ and suppose that time priority is not enforced any more. Instead, if two traders post a limit order at price A_1, then the offer that is executed first is determined randomly. Specifically, the limit order posted by trader $j \in \{1,2\}$ is executed first with probability 0.5. Let Y_1^j be the number of shares offered by trader $j \in \{1,2\}$ at price A_1. Explain why, in equilibrium, Y_1^1 and Y_1^2 must satisfy the following conditions for $j = 1$ and $j = 2$:

$$\left(A_1 - E\left(v | q \geq Y_1^j\right)\right) \Pr\left(q \geq Y_1^j\right)$$
$$+ \left(A_1 - E(v | q \geq Y_1^1 + Y_1^2)\right) \Pr\left(q \geq (Y_1^1 + Y_1^2)\right) \leq 0,$$

with a strict inequality if $Y_1^1 = Y_1^2 = 0$.

e. Suppose that $q_L = 2q_S$. Deduce that $Y_1^1 + Y_1^2 = q_S$ form an equilibrium if:

$$\frac{(r-1)\pi}{1-\pi} \in \left[(1-\phi), \frac{1+(1-\phi)}{2}\right],$$

when the "random" tie-breaking rule is used.

f. Why is cumulative depth greater when the random tie-breaking rule is used for $\frac{(r-1)\pi}{1-\pi} \in \left[(1-\phi), \frac{1+(1-\phi)}{2}\right]$?

3. **Time priority vs. pro-rata allocation.** Consider the model developed in Section 6.2.2 and suppose $C < A_1 - v_0$. The size of the incoming market order (in absolute value) has a uniform distribution on $[0,Q]$, that is,

$$F(q) = \frac{q}{Q}.$$

a. Show that in this case the cumulative depth at price A_k is:

$$Y_k = Q\left(1 - \frac{C}{A_k - \mu}\right), \forall k.$$

b. Now suppose that instead of time priority, a pro-rata allocation rule is used, as described in Section 6.3.2. Further assume that $A_1 - \mu > 2C$. Then show that the cumulative depth at price A_1 is $Y_1^r = \frac{(A_1-\mu)Q}{2C}$.

c. Why does the pro-rata allocation rule yield greater cumulative depth at all ask prices?

4. **Competition among specialists and liquidity.** Consider the model of Section 6.3.3 and assume that two specialists can stop out a market order. When a market order arrives, they post a stop-out price at which they are ready to fill. The specialist with the more competitive price executes the order. If there is a tie, the order is split equally between the two specialists.

   a. Show that if:

   $$\frac{q_L}{q_S} > 1 + \frac{\pi}{(1-\pi)(1-\phi)},$$

   then, in equilibrium, the offers in the LOB are as described by equations (6.25) and (6.26), and the specialists stop out the small orders at a price (bid or ask) equal to μ.

   b. In this case, do the specialists improve liquidity?

5. **Make/take fees and bid-ask spreads.** Consider the model of section 6.4.1 with $\sigma = 0$ and $\tau = 1$. As Chapter 7 explains, trading platforms often charge different fees for market and limit orders. Let f_{mo} be the fee per share paid by a market order placer and f_{lo} the fee per share paid by a limit order placer when the limit order executes (there is no entry fee for limit orders). Finally let f be the total fee earned by the platform on each trade, that is, $f = f_{mo} + f_{lo}$.

   a. Compute bid and ask quotes in equilibrium.

   b. Show that the bid-ask spread decreases in f_{mo} and increases in f_{lo}. Explain.

   c. Trading platforms often subsidize traders who submit limit orders. That is, they set $f_{lo} < 0$ and $f_{mo} > 0$, maintaining that this practice ultimately helps to narrow the spread and benefits traders submitting market orders. Holding the total trading fee f fixed, is this argument correct?

6. **Cryptocurrency limit order books.** The data for this exercise are contained in the Excel file Ch6_ex6_data.xlsx, available on the companion website for the book. The Excel file has three worksheets: *BTCUSD_Quotes* contains a snapshots of the limit order books for Bitcoin-USD (BTCUSD) on July 1, 2019, *ETHUSD_Quotes* contains a snapshot of the limit order book for Ethereum-USD (ETHUSD) on March 1, 2020 on the Coinbase exchange, and *BTCUSD_Trades* provides the first 10,000 trades in BTCUSD on July 1, 2019. To facilitate comparisons of the limit order books for Bitcoin and Ethereum, all amounts of cryptocurrencies in *BTCUSD_Quotes* and *ETHUSD_Quotes* are expressed in dollars, that is, number of units of the relevant currency multiplied by the price in each case (in the original data, these amounts were in units of each cryptocurrency). In contrast, in *BTCUSD_Trades*, amounts are in units of Bitcoin.

   a. Produce a table with summary statistics (the mean, median, standard deviation, and number of observations) for the trade amount and price (using data in the sheet *BTCUSD_Trades*) and the bid and ask price for BTCUSD (using data in the sheet *BTCUSD_Quotes*).

   b. For both BTCUSD and ETHUSD, calculate the cumulative dollar amounts that can be purchased or sold at the various bid and ask prices posted in the limit order book of each currency and represent them graphically in a single figure, placing prices on the vertical axis and quantities (measured in dollars) on the horizontal axis, as in Figure 6.5. The one-period LOB model with asymmetric information covered in example 1 of Section 6.2.3 predicts that there should be a strictly positive bid-ask spread even for very small order sizes. Is this true in both markets?

   c. The model in Section 6.2.3 predicts that the bid-ask spread should be equal to $\frac{2\lambda}{\theta}$. If we assume that θ is the same in both markets, based on the relative bid-ask spread found in your answer to question **b**, which of the two markets has more informed trading?

   d. Another prediction of Section 6.2.3 is that market depth should be inversely related to the orders' informativeness. According to your answer to question **c**, which market should have the deeper order book? Estimate the bid and ask market depth for both markets by calculating the total amount of liquidity available 5% away from the midprice. For example, to calculate the depth on the bid side of BTCUSD, find the total dollar amount of Bitcoin that could be sold up to price $10222 ($= 0.95 \times 10760.7$). Are the estimates of market depth in line with the theoretical prediction?

e. At different points in Chapter 6, we assumed that the bid and ask side are symmetric. Using your answer to question **d**, does this assumption seem to hold in the data? What could be an explanation for why it might not hold?

f. We have often assumed that the market order is exponentially distributed. Using the trade data in BTCUSD, plot the empirical distribution together with an exponential distribution with parameter of $\lambda = 6.13$.[20] Is this specification of the exponential distribution a good fit for the empirical distribution? (Note that outliers have been removed from the trade data so that no trade amounts are higher than 2.)

---

[20] This parameter is chosen so that the mean of the exponential distribution, $1/\lambda$, matches the mean of the sample distribution.

7

Market Fragmentation

Learning Objectives:

- Market fragmentation
- Costs and benefits of market fragmentation
- How these costs and benefits relate to liquidity externalities
- Implications for regulation of competition among trading platforms

7.1 Introduction

It is common for a security to trade in several venues. For instance, large companies often have their primary listing in their home country and a secondary listing abroad (the Italian energy company ENI, for instance, is listed not only on the Italian Stock Exchange but also on the NYSE). Moreover, several trading platforms permit trading of securities listed elsewhere. For instance, in the United States, stocks listed on Nasdaq or the NYSE can be traded on a myriad of other trading platforms: Cboe's four exchanges, IEX, NYSE Arca, and more. These platforms compete fiercely to attract order flow, and the market share of incumbent exchanges has declined steadily in the United States.

Table 7.1 shows the market shares of the main trading venues for U.S. equities in 2019: NYSE and Nasdaq have market shares of less than 20% each, and electronic communication networks (such as the four exchanges run by Cboe), which operate electronic limit order markets, capture about 16%. Trading is also conducted on regional exchanges and venues known as "dark pools" (crossing networks with minimal transparency requirements), while a relatively large fraction of U.S. trading (27%) is "internalized," executed directly in house by broker-dealer firms (see Chapter 1 for a description of these trading methods).

The same phenomenon has been observed in the EU since 2007 with the implementation of the Market in Financial Instruments Directive (MiFID), the regulatory framework for European Union securities markets. Prior to MiFID, each member state could require all trading in domestically listed stocks to be executed on the national market. MiFID abolished this "concentration rule," triggering the entry of new trading platforms (Chi-X, BATS Europe, Turquoise, etc.). Further, the market share of "dark trading"—"dark pools",

Market Liquidity: Theory, Evidence, and Policy. Second Edition. Thierry Foucault, Marco Pagano, and Ailsa Röell,
Oxford University Press. © Oxford University Press 2023. DOI: 10.1093/oso/9780197542064.003.0008

Table 7.1 Market fragmentation in the United States, 2019

Trading Venue	Market share
Nasdaq	17.2%
Nasdaq BX	1.8%
NYSE	13.5%
NYSE Arca	8.4%
Cboe BYX	3.8%
Cboe BZX	5.5%
Cboe EDGA	2.2%
Cboe EDGX	4.8%
IEX	2.7%
Other registered exchanges	2.9%
Broker-Dealer Internalization	27%
Dark Pools (about 33)	10.2%

Source: Securities and Exchange Commission (2020), Staff Report on Algorithmic Trading in U.S. Capital Markets.

over the counter (OTC) trading and systematic internalizers' (SI) trading—has increased. As a consequence, the market shares of incumbent exchanges (Euronext, LSE, Deutsche Börse, etc.) have declined. The 2021 annual report on EU Securities Markets published by the European Securities Markets Authority (ESMA) estimates that 45% of equity trading occurs outside regulated markets (via OTC trading or SIs), up from 22% in January 2018 and 38% in December 2019. Table 7.2 shows that, as of August 2020, Euronext retained only 66.4% of the trading activity in the CAC40 stocks, and the LSE retained only 61.5% of trading in the FTSE100 stocks.

When a security trades in multiple venues, orders submitted to the different venues do not necessarily contribute jointly to price formation. In this case, the market for the security is said to be "fragmented." For instance, an aggressively priced sell limit order for AXA on Euronext does not have priority of execution over a simultaneous, higher one in Cboe, a competitor to Euronext for European stock trading. Hence, the Euronext and Cboe markets for AXA operate independently. OTC markets like bond and foreign exchange markets, are generally highly fragmented since they have no mechanisms for consolidating quotes.

Market fragmentation raises several concerns that have been at the forefront of recent regulatory debates, in the United States and in Europe. Market fragmentation may lead to excessive "price dispersion," meaning that the same security may trade at different prices at the same instant. Worse, outright arbitrage opportunities—the sign of a dysfunctional market—can arise: for instance, the best offer price in one platform may be below the best bid price in another. Such situations of "locked" or "crossed" markets are not at all

Table 7.2 Market fragmentation in Europe, August 2020

Trading Platforms	Market share	
	CAC40 Stocks	FTSE100 Stocks
Euronext	66.4%	n.a.
LSE	n.a.	61.5%
Cboe CXE	16.1%	18.2%
Cboe BXE	4.4%	4.8%
Aquis	6.0%	7.5%
Turquoise	5.0%	7.6%

Source: Cboe Global Markets.

uncommon.[1] In principle, arbitrageurs should exploit these inefficiencies, which should make them both rare and fleeting. If a security trades at two different prices, arbitrageurs can theoretically make a certain profit by buying in one market and reselling in the other. However, there are many reasons why they may decide not to intervene if price differences are small. For instance, for a cross-listed stock, investment or short-sales restrictions may raise the cost of building an arbitrage portfolio. Moreover, arbitrageurs may not monitor all markets continuously and so may react late to transient price divergences. They may even choose to purposefully neglect some arbitrage opportunities, to avoid the risk of being forced to close their arbitrage position prematurely at a loss due to withdrawal of funding or margin calls, as explained in Chapter 11.

Another concern is that market fragmentation could raise trading costs for investors compared to centralized trading for at least three reasons:

(i) Fragmentation heightens informed investors' ability to exploit their information, allowing them to trade on various platforms and thereby making them harder to detect by other traders (Section 7.2.1). Moreover, by hindering interactions among investors located in different trading venues, fragmentation reduces the scope for risk sharing among investors (Section 7.2.2). Fragmentation also gives local market power to liquidity suppliers in each trading platform, since they do not have to compete with counterparts operating on other platforms (Section 7.2.3).

(ii) In a fragmented market, investors have to conduct a search for the best price, since quotes are not centralized. This search is costly for several reasons. For instance, it takes time to find the intermediary that posts

[1] For instance, Shkilko, Van Ness, and Van Ness (2008) find that ask and bid prices for NYSE- and Nasdaq-listed stocks that are traded on multiple markets are locked or crossed 10% and 3.5% of the time, respectively. For more recent evidence on this phenomenon, see Wah (2016) and Chapter 9.

the best price. In electronic trading platforms (as in European and U.S. equities markets), the search can be automated by using "smart order routing systems" that scan the platforms for the best price. But these technologies are costly. Search costs also exacerbate agency problems between investors and brokers, as the brokers bear the cost of search while the benefit accrues to their client: fragmentation increases the risk that brokers will not shop around systematically for the best possible price (Section 7.2.4), which may in turn reduce the incentives for liquidity providers to post good quotes (Section 7.4.3).

(iii) Fragmentation prevents investors from taking full advantage of the "thick market externalities" (also called "liquidity externalities") that arise from the fact that each additional market participant reduces trading fees or increases liquidity for all other traders. Economies of scale are one source of thick market externalities: in the past, the fixed cost of running a market was high,[2] so that platforms with large volumes could spread this cost over many traders and so charge lower fees. Thus, concentrating trading in a single market place produced efficiency gains. In today's securities markets, this argument for concentration is less compelling since automation has considerably shrunk the fixed-cost component of running a market. Another positive externality of market participation is that it makes it more likely to find a trading partner quickly enough: this is easier if the market attracts many traders. Hence, by joining a platform, an investor indirectly increases other market participants' likelihood of trading and so makes them better off. In Section 7.3, we explore other mechanisms for these externalities, such as reduced adverse selection and improved risk-sharing.

Fragmentation does not only have drawbacks, however. It can benefit investors in various ways. First, competition among platforms tends to reduce fees and foster innovation in trading technology. The recent evolution of US and European equities markets shows the relevance of this argument very well. The entry of new trading platforms (such as BATS in the United States or Chi-X in Europe) drove trading fees sharply down. In the United States, competition has also prompted the NYSE and Nasdaq to overhaul their trading systems. At the turn of the millennium, the NYSE was still predominantly a floor market and Nasdaq was a dealer market; both now have electronic limit order books (LOBs) at their core. Moreover, to serve the trading needs of some clients (in particular, algorithmic traders), trading platforms strive to reduce their "latency" period,

---

[2] For instance, traders had to meet in a physical location, which could involve substantial real estate costs.

which is the time it takes to receive and send messages (such as orders or information on standing quotes). For instance, in 2009 the NYSE introduced a new trading system (Super Display Book) that reduced latency from 105 to 5 milliseconds.

Another benefit of intermarket competition is that different trading needs of investors can be best served by different trading mechanisms. For instance, unlike retail investors, institutional investors often execute very large trades, which can have a significant price impact in transparent electronic limit order markets. They accordingly seek to arrange their trades OTC or in dark pools. Section 7.4 explores these benefits of market fragmentation in greater detail.

In the light of these costs and benefits, ideally one would want to organize securities markets so as to promote intermarket competition while allowing interactions between orders placed in different markets. One approach is to let market forces decide on the level of fragmentation. But, it is unlikely that the socially optimal amount of market fragmentation will arise spontaneously. For instance, liquidity externalities act as a barrier to entry, conferring market power on the incumbent markets. Conversely, strategic considerations by trading platforms may lead to excessive fragmentation. For instance, one trading platform might not allow a competitor to access its quotes.[3]

For this reason, market fragmentation is high on the regulatory agenda. Section 7.5 describes the regulatory framework that rules competition among trading platforms in the United States (RegNMS) and in Europe (MiFID). For instance, the SEC describes the main objectives of Regulation National Market System (NMS), that is, the set of rules under which the U.S. equities market has operated since 2005) as follows:

> The NMS is premised on promoting fair competition among individual markets, while at the same time assuring that all of these markets are linked together, through facilities and rules, in a unified system that promotes interaction among the orders of buyers and sellers in a particular NMS stock [....] Accordingly, the Commission [...] has sought to avoid the extremes of: (1) isolated markets that trade an NMS stock without regard to trading in other markets and thereby fragment the competition among buyers and sellers in that stock; and (2) a totally centralized system that loses the benefits of vigorous competition and innovation among individual markets. Achieving this objective and striking the proper balance clearly can be a difficult task. (Regulation NMS, SEC Release No. 34-51808)

---

[3] This situation is similar to that of a firm choosing to make its product compatible or not with its competitors' product. For instance, surcharges can be used to deter depositors who are not clients of a bank from using its ATMs.

One way to reduce fragmentation is to link markets together so that trades for a given security always occur at the best possible price. And this is the approach taken in Regulation NMS. The so-called order protection rule (or trade-through rule) obliges a market center such as an electronic communication network to reroute marketable limit orders to the trading platform that posts the best price when the order is submitted. But this approach has proven very controversial. In particular, it prioritizes execution price over speed of execution, whereas, for some investors, the latter might actually be more important. In Section 7.4.3, we discuss the effects of a trade-through rule on market liquidity.

7.2 The Costs of Fragmentation

In this section, we analyze three channels through which market fragmentation can reduce liquidity compared to centralized trading:

1. asymmetric information (Section 7.2.1),
2. risk bearing capacity (Section 7.2.2),
3. market power (Section 7.2.3).

In all three cases, fragmentation is a source of illiquidity because investors cannot (or do not) access all the possible trading venues for a security: if they could, each platform would simply be a different portal to the same single market. But in practice, multimarket trading is marred by technical hurdles (e.g., differences in time zones or in clearing and settlement systems) and institutional barriers (e.g., divergent tax treatments of groups of investors). Investors may also be unable to split their orders optimally across markets, because this requires costly investment in technology or because their brokers lack the incentive to do so (see Section 7.2.4).

7.2.1   Information Effects

We first analyze the effect of fragmentation in a multimarket version of the model presented in Chapter 4 (Kyle 1985). We assume that the security is traded in two markets, A and B, and that liquidity traders are captive customers of one of the two markets. Let u_A and u_B denote their liquidity demand in markets A and B, and assume that these variables are independently and normally distributed with zero mean and variances σ_A^2 and σ_B^2. As in Chapter 4, the informed trader knows the final value of the security, v, which is normally distributed with mean μ and variance σ_v^2. Unlike the liquidity traders, he can trade in both markets, placing an order x_A in market A and x_B in market B. This structure captures the idea that traders with superior information tend to coincide with sophisticated market professionals (for instance, hedge funds), whose greater trading activity gives them an economic interest in securing access to several markets.

In each market, order imbalances are absorbed by risk-neutral market makers. In market A, market makers set the price p_A conditional on the order flow $u_A + x_A$. The same process occurs in market B. As in Chapter 4, we seek an equilibrium in which market makers post linear price schedules in each market:

$$p_A = \mu + \lambda_A(u_A + x_A), \; p_B = \mu + \lambda_B(u_B + x_B). \tag{7.1}$$

The optimal order placement strategy for the informed trader (his choice of x_A and x_B) maximizes his expected profits from trading in the two markets:

$$E\big[x_A(v - p_A) + x_B(v - p_B) \mid v\big]. \tag{7.2}$$

Substituting into this expression the prices p_A and p_B from equations (7.1), the first-order conditions of the informed trader with respect to x_A and x_B yield the following order placement strategy:

$$x_A = \frac{v - \mu}{2\lambda_A}, \; x_B = \frac{v - \mu}{2\lambda_B}.$$

Hence, the expression for the informed trader's strategy in each market is the same as in Chapter 4 for a single market. In particular, note that the optimal order size in one market does not depend on the depth of the other. This is because in this setting, an order placed in one market has no impact on the price in the other. Indeed, the informed trader submits orders *simultaneously* in the two markets, so that in market A the price cannot be immediately adjusted in response to concomitant orders in market B, or vice versa.[4]

Proceeding as in Chapter 4, we can then compute the equilibrium values of λ_A and λ_B:

$$\lambda_A = \frac{\sigma_v}{2\sigma_A}, \; \lambda_B = \frac{\sigma_v}{2\sigma_B}. \tag{7.3}$$

The corresponding equilibrium prices in the two markets are:

$$p_A = \mu + \frac{1}{2}(v - \mu) + \frac{\sigma_v}{2\sigma_A} u_A, \; p_B = \mu + \frac{1}{2}(v - \mu) + \frac{\sigma_v}{2\sigma_B} u_B. \tag{7.4}$$

[4] A crucial assumption here is that market makers in one market cannot make their quotes contingent on the order flow in the other, and vice versa. If they could, then the equilibrium would simply be that obtaining in a single market. Hence, the speed of information flows between markets is one determinant of the extent of fragmentation.

Thus, equilibrium prices differ and the two markets are not perfectly integrated. At least in the very short run, such pricing differences are in fact often observed for securities that trade in different markets, even when their trading hours overlap. For instance, Biais and Martinez (2004) document significant price discrepancies between the home and foreign prices for French stocks cross-listed in Frankfurt and for German stocks cross-listed in Paris. Similar evidence is reported for Dutch stocks cross-listed on the NYSE by Hupperts and Menkveld (2002), for Canadian stocks cross-listed in the U.S. by Eun and Sabherwal (2003) and for American Depository Receipts (ADRs)—claims on non-U.S. stocks traded on U.S. exchanges—by Rösch (2021). Such transient discrepancies suggest that continuous arbitrage is impossible due to the limitations of the trading mechanisms available to market professionals, which prevent them from stepping in to cross offsetting orders in the two markets.

Now consider the depth λ and the price that would prevail in equilibrium if the two markets were consolidated (see Chapter 4):

$$\lambda = \frac{\sigma_v}{2\sqrt{\sigma_A^2 + \sigma_B^2}}, \quad p = \mu + \frac{1}{2}(v - \mu) + \frac{\sigma_v}{2\sqrt{\sigma_A^2 + \sigma_B^2}}(u_A + u_B). \quad (7.5)$$

Thus, the market is deeper when it is not fragmented since $\lambda < \min\{\lambda_A, \lambda_B\}$. The reason is that consolidation increases overall liquidity demand, as measured by $\operatorname{var}(u_A + u_B)$. This effect reduces the informativeness of order flow, and market orders' price impacts are smaller when trading is consolidated in a single market. (This may not hold when liquidity demands in each market are negatively correlated: see exercise 1.)

Thus, fragmentation redistributes the trading gains from liquidity traders to informed traders. In the fragmented environment, the informed trader's profits are on average:

$$E[x_A(v - p_A) + x_B(v - p_B)] = \frac{\sigma_v \sigma_A}{2} + \frac{\sigma_v \sigma_B}{2} = \frac{\sigma_v\sqrt{\sigma_A^2 + \sigma_B^2 + 2\sigma_A\sigma_B}}{2}, \quad (7.6)$$

whereas in a consolidated market they are:

$$E[x(v - p)] = \frac{\sigma_v\sqrt{\sigma_A^2 + \sigma_B^2}}{2}, \quad (7.7)$$

where x is the order placed by the insider and p is the equilibrium price in the consolidated market (see Chapter 4). Comparing these two expressions, it is clear that the informed trader's expected profits are larger in the fragmented market. Since market makers have zero expected profits, the profits of informed traders are equal to the losses of the liquidity traders. Hence, the increased profits of the informed trader in the fragmented market come at the expense of liquidity traders.

Dealers in one market can better forecast the asset payoff by observing the price set by dealers in the other market. Hence, the price in one market will adjust after a transaction in the other. This process can explain the lead-lag relations that exist between returns of related or identical securities. To see how this works, suppose that after transactions in their respective markets, market makers in one observe the transaction price in the other. Market makers in both markets then adjust their estimate of the value of the security and set their new (long-run) midprice p_l equal to:

$$p_l = E(v|p_A, p_B).$$

Using equation (7.1) and the fact that v, p_A, and p_B are normally distributed, we obtain the long-run price:

$$p_l = \mu + \alpha_A(p_A - \mu) + \alpha_B(p_B - \mu), \tag{7.8}$$

with $\alpha_A = \alpha_B = 2/3$.[5] This equation shows that market makers' estimate of the fundamental value of the security depends on the informational content of the price changes, $p_j - \mu$, in the two markets. Here the coefficients on these price changes are identical because the informational content of both innovations is identical. In a more general model, the coefficients would differ, with the ratio $\frac{\alpha_j}{\alpha_A + \alpha_B}$ being a natural measure of the "share" of market j in price discovery.

For instance, if α_B is lower than α_A, this means that dealers consider trades (and therefore prices) in market B less informative than those in market A. Hence, market B's response to a price change in market A is stronger than the reverse. In this sense, market A "leads" market B, or contributes more to price discovery: its "share" of price discovery is higher. Using this intuition, researchers have developed methodologies to estimate the price discovery

---

[5] To do this, we must compute the expectation of the security's value v conditional on the two prices, p_A and p_B. Recall that the unconditional expectation is $E(v) = \mu$. Denote by Θ the row vector of covariances $(\text{cov}(v, p_A), \text{cov}(v, p_B))$ and by Ω the variance-covariance matrix of p_A and p_B. From the expressions for the equilibrium prices, we have:

$$\Theta = \frac{\sigma_v^2}{2}(1,1) \text{ and } \Omega = \sigma_v^2 \begin{bmatrix} 1/2 & 1/4 \\ 1/4 & 1/2 \end{bmatrix}.$$

As v, p_A, and p_B are normally distributed, $E(v|p_A, p_B) = \mu + \Theta\Omega^{-1}(p_A - \mu, p_B - \mu)'$, where the notation $'$ indicates the transpose of a vector. Equation (7.8) follows.

share of a given market for securities that trade on several markets (see Has-brouck 1995).[6]

One concern about market fragmentation is that it may harm price discovery. This is not the case in the situation posited here. Indeed, consider the variance of the asset payoff conditional on the realization of prices in market A and market B, that is, $\mathrm{var}(v|p_A,p_B)$. This variance measures the uncertainty that still remains for market participants after trading in markets A and B. The lower this variance, the more accurate the price discovery. Calculations show that:[7]

$$\mathrm{var}(v|p_A,p_B) = \frac{\sigma_v^2}{3}. \tag{7.9}$$

Instead, when trading is concentrated in a single market, we have:

$$\mathrm{var}(v|p) = \frac{\sigma_v^2}{2}.$$

Hence, price discovery is better with two markets. The intuition behind this finding is simple: prices in the two markets provide different signals about the value of the security; as these signals are not perfectly correlated (because liquidity trades in each market are not perfectly correlated), they combine to produce a more accurate forecast than the single price signal in a single marketplace.

7.2.2 Risk-Sharing Effects

The previous section examines the cost of market fragmentation consisting in trading costs due to breaking up total liquidity into separate pools. In that model, this effect damages liquidity traders but benefits informed traders to the same extent, since trading is modeled as a zero-sum game. Here, instead, we shall see that the reduction in liquidity caused by fragmentation can generate a net social

---

[6] The parameters α_A and α_B can be estimated by a regression of the returns in market A on their own lagged value and the lagged returns in the other market, because equation (7.8) can be rewritten as follows:

$$p_l - p_A = -(1-\alpha_A)(p_A - \mu) + \alpha_B(p_B - \mu),$$

where the differences $p_l - p_A$ and $p_A - \mu$ are returns in market A over two consecutive periods. Hence, returns in market A are negatively auto-correlated, *conditional* on returns in market B. In contrast, the return $p_l - p_A$ in market A is positively correlated with the return $p_B - \mu$ in market B, because a high return in market B is more likely when the informed investor is buying in this market.

[7] Let Θ and Ω be as defined in Footnote 5. Then $\mathrm{var}(v|p_A,p_B) = \mathrm{var}(v) - \Theta\Omega^{-1}\Theta'$, which yields equation (7.9).

loss (in the sense that gains may not fully offset losses), because it reduces the extent to which traders can share risks.[8]

As an illustration, consider the model of a competitive call market developed in Chapter 4 (Section 4.3.1), where market makers are assumed to be risk averse, and suppose that the security is traded on two separate call markets. Let the number of market makers be K_A in market A and K_B in market B. For simplicity, we assume that they have no initial inventory ($Z = 0$) and are all equally risk averse, with coefficient $\bar{\rho}$.

Now consider an investor who wants to place a market order of size q on either of the two markets. Using equation (4.25) in Chapter 4 (Section 4.3.1), the equilibrium price at which he will trade in market A is:

$$p_A = \mu + \frac{\bar{\rho}}{K_A}\sigma_v^2 q.$$

Hence, the expected price impact of his order is:

$$\frac{\bar{\rho}}{K_A}\sigma_v^2 |q|,$$

which shows that the liquidity of the market is inversely related to the number of dealers, K_A. Similarly, his expected price impact if he were to trade in market B would be:

$$\frac{\bar{\rho}}{K_B}\sigma_v^2 |q|.$$

If instead the two markets were to merge, the expected price impact on this consolidated trading platform would be:

$$\frac{\bar{\rho}}{K_A + K_B}\sigma_v^2 |q|.$$

Hence, the liquidity of the consolidated market is greater: by increasing the number of market makers, consolidation improves the risk-bearing capacity of the market, and thereby reduces the compensation required by market makers to absorb risky inventories. As in the model of the previous section, consolidation again improves liquidity, but for a different reason.

Market fragmentation not only impairs liquidity but also diminishes the opportunities for risk sharing among market participants. To see this point,

[8] In Chapter 12, we see that it also increases the cost of capital to firms, and thereby lowers the level of investment in the economy.

consider a situation where the market makers' inventories are unbalanced, so that a reallocation among market makers is Pareto improving. If this reallocation could occur only by trading at competitive prices separately on each of the two markets, then trading would equalize market makers' inventories *within* each market. However, since the participants in the two markets will generally have different per-capita inventory endowments, their holdings after trading would not be equalized *across* the two markets. In that case, there will be further gains from trading if the two markets are merged or fully connected, because there are further opportunities for risk sharing.

The costs of market fragmentation described so far hinge crucially on the assumption that customers cannot access both markets simultaneously, and thus split their orders across them. To illustrate, let us go back to the customer who wants to trade q shares with a market order. Assume now that he can split the order across the two markets by placing an order q_A in market A and an order q_B in market B so that $q_A + q_B = q$. In this case, he splits the order so as to minimize his total trading cost. As the reader can verify by solving exercise 2, the optimal order placement strategy is:

$$q_A^* = \frac{K_A}{K_A + K_B} q, \ q_B^* = \frac{K_B}{K_A + K_B} q. \tag{7.10}$$

The trader submits a relatively larger order in the deeper market. This strategy equalizes the execution price the two markets since:

$$p_A(q_A^*) = p_B(q_B^*) = \mu + \frac{\bar{\rho}\sigma_v^2}{K_A + K_B} q.$$

Interestingly, the execution price is identical to the price that the customer would obtain if there were a single market. Hence, fragmentation is innocuous if traders can split their orders seamlessly between markets.

These findings suggest two ways of overcoming the costs of fragmentation. The first approach is to merge markets or require concentration of trading in a single market. The second approach consists in facilitating traders' access to all the markets in which a security is traded. Technological advances, such as data aggregators (which consolidate quotes in different markets) and smart order routing technologies (which optimally split orders between trading platforms), lower the cost of multimarket trading. Yet, obstacles remain such as differences in clearing and settlement systems across markets (see Box 7.5), differences in transparency, different trading hours, and agency problems.

Box 7.1 Stock Exchange Mergers and Liquidity

The analysis developed in this section implies that concentration of trading in a single market generates liquidity gains. Some empirical evidence on this point can be garnered from results on the mergers between stock exchanges. Arnold et al. (1999) study the effects of three successive mergers of regional U.S. stock exchanges in the 1940s and 1950s, which transformed them from venues for listing local securities to competitors for the order flow of NYSE-listed companies. The merged exchanges attracted a larger market share and their bid-ask spreads narrowed. A more recent example is the Euronext merger between September 2000 and November 2003: the French, Belgian, Dutch, and Portuguese stock exchanges merged into a single exchange called Euronext, with a single trading platform and a single clearing and settlement system. This consolidation was associated with a significant increase of liquidity, as measured both by trading volume and bid-ask spreads. Following the consolidation, the average spreads on the securities included in the main indices of the Paris, Brussels, Amsterdam, and Lisbon exchanges fell by an estimated 16% to 21%, controlling for other determinants (Padilla and Pagano 2006).

7.2.3 Competition among Liquidity Suppliers

Another cost of market fragmentation is that it hinders competition among liquidity providers, by weakening interactions between market makers active in different liquidity pools and thereby decreasing their incentives to offer good quotes. We illustrate this point below by extending the model analyzed in the previous section to allow for imperfect competition. Then, we analyze a further instance of fragmentation, when market makers can also internalize order execution, that is, execute them against their own inventory at market prices. This effectively turns each market maker into a "separate market." We show that internalization further reduces competition.

Fragmentation and Market Power

When risk-averse market makers behave as imperfect competitors, the bid-ask spread for investors placing market orders is larger than under perfect competition, as was shown in Section 4.3.2 of Chapter 4. As in the previous section, consider the price impact of a market order of size q on either one of two separate markets A and B, but now assume that each is imperfectly competitive, so that in market A the equilibrium price is:

$$p_A = \mu + \frac{K_A - 1}{K_A - 2} \frac{\bar{\rho}}{K_A} \sigma_v^2 q.$$

Thus, the price impact of an order of size $|q|$ on market A is:

$$\frac{K_A - 1}{K_A - 2} \frac{\bar{\rho}}{K_A} \sigma_v^2 |q|,$$

and similar in market B. If A and B were instead consolidated into a single market with $K_A + K_B$ active market makers, the expected price impact of an order of size $|q|$ would be:

$$\frac{K_A + K_B - 1}{K_A + K_B - 2} \frac{\bar{\rho}}{K_A + K_B} \sigma_v^2 |q|.$$

This expression is lower than its analogue under fragmentation, because the consolidated market has not only greater risk-bearing capacity but also a lower markup. As before, for traders on market A (or market B), the price impact reduction to better risk–sharing is captured by the reduction of the second fraction in the expression from $\bar{\rho}/K_A$ to $\bar{\rho}/(K_A + K_B)$. The further reduction due to more aggressive competition is reflected in the lowering of the first fraction from $(K_A - 1)/(K_A - 2)$ to $(K_A + K_B - 1)/(K_A + K_B - 2)$.

Again, the negative effect of fragmentation on market liquidity would vanish if traders could split their orders between the two markets, or if all market makers were active on both markets simultaneously. In this case, order splitting effectively forces the two pools of market makers to compete against one another.

Internalization and Market Power

Even when trading is centralized, an intermediary can sometimes respond to a client's order in a dual capacity as both broker and dealer. He can choose to channel only a fraction of the order to the market (in his capacity as broker) and take the rest himself (in his capacity as dealer)—a practice known as internalization. In this case, so-called best execution rules require that the broker-dealer executes the internalized order at the current market price or better. This practice is common in the U.S., and has also become increasingly common in Europe, since the MiFID regulation in 2007 allowed it (see Section 1.2.3 and Section 7.5.2). The impact of internalization on market liquidity is controversial.

To analyze this effect, consider the following variant of the previous model. Assume that there is a single centralized market with K imperfectly competitive broker-dealers. One receives a buy market order of size q, and decides what portion (if any) to internalize and what to execute on the main market.[9] If he does internalize, he will refrain from selling shares in the main market; otherwise, he would be competing against himself on the internalized portion.[10] Denote by q_I the number of shares internalized and by $q_M = q - q_I$ the remaining shares routed to the market. In this case, the portion of the order routed to the market executes at the following equilibrium price:

$$p(q_M) = \mu + \frac{K-2}{K-3}\frac{\bar{\rho}\sigma_v^2}{K-1}q_M,$$

which is the same expression as in the previous subsection under the assumption that only $K-1$ markets are active.

Now, consider the broker-dealer's optimal strategy, assuming for simplicity that his initial inventory is zero (the case where it is not zero is left as an exercise). The expected utility from routing a buy order for q_M shares to the market is:

$$E\left[U(q_M)\right] = E\left[p(q_M) - \mu\right]q_I - \frac{\bar{\rho}\sigma_v^2}{2}q_I^2$$

$$= \left[E(p(q_M)) - \mu\right](q - q_M) - \frac{\bar{\rho}\sigma_v^2}{2}(q - q_M)^2.$$

In increasing q_M, the market maker faces a trade-off, three effects being at play. First, by routing additional shares to the market, he loses the excess return $E(p(q_M)) - \mu$ on each internalized share. Second, by doing so, he increases the price impact for each of the remaining shares and thereby increases the price at which he eventually executes the internalized order (since he will match the market price). Thirdly, by routing more shares to the market, he internalizes less of them and thus decreases his inventory risk. So the first effect of lower internalization reduces his expected utility, while the other two increase it. The best point along this trade-off is found by maximizing the previous expression. The solution to this maximization problem is to route a fraction τ of the order to the market:

---

[9] In other words, the internalizer behaves as a Stackelberg leader vis-à-vis all the other broker-dealers, as he chooses the amount executed on the market anticipating the price response by the other broker-dealers.

[10] Selling shares on the main market can never be optimal for him: to see why, suppose that he were to participate to the market alongside with other broker-dealers in filling a portion of the order that he routed to the market. Then, he would put downward pressure on the price and therefore he would lose on the internalized portion of the order. He would, of course, get to sell additional shares in the main market, but he could have sold such shares by internalizing them as well, without affecting the market price adversely.

$$q_M^* = \frac{(K-2)+(K-3)(K-1)}{2(K-2)+(K-3)(K-1)}q \equiv \tau q,$$

and to optimally internalize the remaining fraction $1-\tau$.

Substituting q_M^* into the expression for $p(q_M)$, we find that, with internalization, the execution price for a market order of size q is:

$$p(q_M^*) = \mu + \frac{K-2}{K-3}\frac{\bar{\rho}\sigma_v^2}{K-1}\tau q.$$

If instead internalization were prohibited, the market maker would have to route the entire order to the market and compete with the other dealers if he wished to be a counterparty to the order. As the previous section shows, the expected execution price for the order in this case would be:

$$p_A = \mu + \frac{K-1}{K-2}\frac{\bar{\rho}\sigma_v^2}{K}q.$$

It is readily confirmed that under internalization the price impact of the order, i.e., $\frac{K-2}{K-3}\frac{\bar{\rho}\sigma_v^2}{K-1}\tau$, is greater than when internalization is banned, in which case the price impact is $\frac{K-1}{K-2}\frac{\bar{\rho}\sigma_v^2}{K}$. For instance, if $K=4$ and $\bar{\rho}\sigma_v^2 = 10$, the price impact of an order is 4.76 per share when internalization is authorized compared to 3.75 when it is banned.

There are two reasons for this result. First, the dealer who internalizes the order does not take part in filling the portion of the order that he routes to the market. This effectively reduces competition for this order and works to increase the rents earned by all dealers, including himself (on the internalized portion of the order). Second, the dealer strategically executes a significant fraction of the order on the market in order to amplify its market impact, thereby increasing his rent. However, the dealer takes a larger position than he would in the absence of internalization. Indeed, in that case, the dealer would on average absorb a fraction $1/K$ of the order in equilibrium. Under internalization, instead, he absorbs a fraction $1-\tau$ of the order, which can be shown to be larger than $1/K$. The dealer is willing to take more risk in equilibrium (that is, take a larger position) because internalization allows him to trade at a less competitive price and therefore to obtain a larger expected return per share than without internalization.

Notice that the illiquidity of the main market increases a broker-dealer's ability to extract rents through internalization. Conversely, his scope for rent extraction is minimal if the main market is very liquid: when the number of market makers (K) is very large, τ tends to 1, so that the fraction of the order internalized tends to zero. In short, internalization impairs market quality, and the damage is greater when the main market is more illiquid. Besides reinforcing dealers' market power, internalization can also impact on liquidity in a context of asymmetric information, if internalizers skim off uninformed order flow (because of a similar mechanism, see exercise 3). For a detailed discussion of this point, see Section 8.4.

7.2.4 Fragmentation and the Broker-Client Relationship

When the market is fragmented, it is harder for investors to locate good prices. The proliferation of "dark pools," hidden orders on traditional exchanges and crossing networks of unknown depth have compounded the problem.

Thus, in fragmented markets, finding the best trade is more costly and time consuming, a task investors often delegate to their brokers. This delegation creates an agency problem. That is, brokers incur the costs of searching for and implementing the best execution strategy for their clients (which requires technological investment, expertise, and time) without necessarily being able to entirely charge this cost to these clients. As usual in any agency relationship, one should expect brokers to expend less effort in finding the most desirable execution strategy than would be optimal for clients.

Performance-based contracts cannot fully solve this incentive problem for two reasons. First, clients often lack the data and expertise to verify whether their broker did indeed use the best possible strategy to execute their order, especially when the market is fragmented. Second, a trading strategy that is optimal ex ante may prove disastrous ex post, just because of bad luck. Say, a broker decides to split a client's buy orders into multiple lots to reduce the immediate impact of the order. For large orders, this strategy is often optimal *on average*, but the realized cost in any particular instance is random, as it depends on the evolution of prices over the period during which the order is executed. If prices have risen, the actual average execution price for the client's buy order might prove to be considerably higher than the client could have gotten by executing his order more aggressively. Yet, this poor performance does not indicate a lack of effort or expertise. This example simply shows that it is hard for clients to disentangle what depends on the broker's effort and what is due to bad luck. In this situation, writing incentive contracts is difficult, as one wants to penalize brokers for shirking but not for events beyond their control. To alleviate these agency problems, regulators often require brokers to comply with "best execution rules," which codify how clients' orders must be handled (see Section 7.5).

Brokers' interests may also conflict with those of their clients because they sometimes receive monetary inducements for routing orders to specific markets or dealers. In particular, in the United States, dealers or exchanges can make payments to brokers who route specific orders to them (e.g., small orders or orders from retail investors).[11] A study by the SEC (2000) investigated whether this practice, known as "payment for order flow" (PFOF), affects order-routing decisions in U.S. options markets. Until 1999, there was not much competition among U.S. options exchanges, stock options often being traded only on the exchange where they were listed. For instance, Dell options were listed on the Philadelphia Stock Exchange (PSX) and traded exclusively there. This situation changed in August 1999 when the Chicago Board Options Exchange (CBOE) and the American Stock Exchange (AMEX) announced that they would start trading these options as well. The decision triggered a very fierce battle for market share. As a result, option exchanges started making payments for order flow. The SEC (2000) study shows that by August 2000, 78% of retail customers' orders were routed pursuant to PFOF arrangements. This study further found that PFOF has an impact on routing decisions: the brokerage firms accepting the payments rerouted their customers' orders to the exchanges that paid for order flow (and away from those that did not) much more often than did other brokers (who were much more likely to direct their orders simply to the exchange with the largest market share in the option).

Battalio and Holden (2001) suggest that competition between brokers will force them to pass payments for order flow to their clients, via either lower commissions or improved services. Consistently with this hypothesis, Battalio, Jennings, and Selway (2001) find that the net cost of trading via brokers who sell the order flow to a major Nasdaq dealer is lower than the net cost of trading using brokers who do not sell order flow. This suggests that brokers may pass at least part of their payments along to their clients. But the evidence is mixed: the SEC (2000) reports that in the options markets "few firms are passing along the benefits of payment for options order flow onto their customers in the form of either reduced commissions or rebates." Ernst and Spatt (2022) find that the conflicts of interest associated with PFOF are particularly strong in option markets—indeed stronger than in equity markets.

In any case, payment for order flow could also result in transfers among the different categories of investors. Indeed, several studies suggest that payments for order flow are used to cream-skim orders from uninformed traders (in particular, those from retail investors). Executing these orders at best quotes is

[11] This practice is controversial, both in the U.S. and in the E.U. See "EU lawmaker calls for ban on 'payment for order flow'", *Financial Times*, July 27, 2022, and "SEC aims to stem trading practice of payment for order flow," *Financial Times*, June 8, 2022.

profitable since the bid-ask spread contains a compensation for adverse selection costs (see Chapter 3). However, if a dealer or an exchange attracts these orders by paying for them, it increases the likelihood that other dealers or exchanges will receive a larger fraction of informed orders and so will be more exposed to adverse selection. As a result, the bid-ask spreads offered by these other dealers or exchanges will be wider with payment for order flow than without (see Röell 1990, and exercise 3 in this chapter; for empirical evidence, see Bessembinder and Kaufman 1997). If this is the case, the investors whose brokers do not receive payments for order flow will ultimately be worse off, and even those whose brokers do receive payments might be worse off if the practice widens the spread enough. Again, there is conflicting evidence on this issue. For instance, Easley, Kiefer, and O'Hara (1996) find that orders routed pursuant to payments do show larger effective bid-ask spreads. In contrast, Battalio (1997); Battalio, Greene, and Jennings (1997); and Battalio, Greene, and Jennings (1998) find that the introduction of market makers who pay for order flow in equity markets is associated with a narrowing of bid-ask spreads.

7.3 Liquidity Externalities

As the previous sections observe, order splitting between different market segments can neutralize the potential damage done by market fragmentation. Alternatively, trading naturally gravitates to a single marketplace because each trader benefits from the presence of others. Intuitively, as traders expect a market to be more active, they are more inclined to participate, and by patronizing a market, they reinforce other traders' incentive to join. This liquidity-begets-liquidity effect is a force that works naturally to consolidate trading. Here (Section 7.3.1) we illustrate this point using the asymmetric information model set out earlier. Liquidity externalities carry two important implications. First, they imply that securities markets are subject to market tipping, situations in which order flow migrates swiftly from one platform to another (See Box 7.2). Second, they isolate incumbent markets from competition with strong entry barriers. We discuss these implications and illustrate them with empirical evidence in Section 7.3.2.

7.3.1 Liquidity Begets Liquidity

The model developed in Section 7.2.1 can be easily adjusted to capture the idea that liquidity begets liquidity, by assuming that some liquidity traders have discretion in choice of trading venue. Specifically, suppose that M liquidity traders may choose to participate either in market A or in market B. The liquidity demand of discretionary trader $k \in \{1, \ldots, M\}$, denoted by u_k, is normally distributed with mean zero and variance σ_d^2. The other liquidity traders are locked into one of the two markets. The total liquidity demand of the "captive" liquidity traders in market A, denoted by u_{Ac}, is normally distributed with mean zero and variance σ_{Ac}^2. We use a similar notation for the total liquidity demand of those based in market B. Last, we assume that all liquidity demands are independently distributed and that $\sigma_{Ac}^2 > \sigma_{Bc}^2$, that is, the mass of captive investors is larger in market A than in market B.

Suppose that M_A liquidity traders with discretion in their trading location choose market A and $M_B = M - M_A$ discretionary liquidity traders choose market B. Then equation (7.3) in Section 7.2.1 yields the depth of market A, and of market B:

$$\lambda_A = \frac{\sigma_v}{2\sqrt{M_A \sigma_d^2 + \sigma_{Ac}^2}}, \quad \lambda_B = \frac{\sigma_v}{2\sqrt{M_B \sigma_d^2 + \sigma_{Bc}^2}}.$$

Suppose that $M_A \sigma_d^2 + \sigma_{Ac}^2 > M_B \sigma_d^2 + \sigma_{Bc}^2$. In this case, $\lambda_A < \lambda_B$: market A is deeper than market B. A discretionary liquidity trader in market B can get lower trading costs by switching to the deeper market A. This relocation makes market A deeper still and so reinforces the incentive for liquidity traders to gravitate to it. Eventually, this "gravitational pull" or liquidity-begets-liquidity effect leads all the discretionary traders to cluster in market A. This situation is an equilibrium, since no trader now has an incentive to move his liquidity demand to market B.

If $M_A \sigma_d^2 + \sigma_{Ac}^2 < M_B \sigma_d^2 + \sigma_{Bc}^2$, the same reasoning implies that trading will concentrate in market B. Such an equilibrium can only arise if $\sigma_{Ac}^2 - \sigma_{Bc}^2 < M\sigma_d^2$.

Last, if $M_A \sigma_d^2 + \sigma_{Ac}^2 = M_B \sigma_d^2 + \sigma_{Bc}^2$, the two markets have exactly the same depth and discretionary liquidity traders are indifferent between them. Again, the condition for obtaining this third equilibrium can be satisfied only if $\sigma_{Ac}^2 - \sigma_{Bc}^2 \leq M\sigma_d^2$.

Thus, when $\sigma_{Ac}^2 - \sigma_{Bc}^2 \leq M\sigma_d^2$, there are three equilibria.[12] In two of them, discretionary liquidity traders cluster in one market, which is therefore the most liquid. In the third equilibrium, they split equally and the two markets have exactly the same liquidity. This equilibrium is fragile, however: defection by even a single trader from one market to the other tips the balance and leads to concentration of trading there—a phenomenon known as market tipping.

The evolution of trading volume for cross-listed securities is a good illustration of the gravitational pull effect. Halling et al. (2008) study the distribution of trading volume between the domestic and the foreign market for cross-listed

---

[12] When $\sigma_{Ac}^2 > M\sigma_d^2 + \sigma_{Bc}^2$, the sole equilibrium is such that all trading concentrates in market A.

stocks. They observe that foreign trading is active just after the cross-listing date but decreases dramatically over the subsequent six months. In other words, trading activity "flows back" to the home market in the months after the cross-listing, which is consistent with the presence of liquidity externalities that induce the concentration of trading in a single marketplace.

The analysis in this section also shows that one must be careful in interpreting measures of price impacts as measures of the level of informed trading in a market. For instance, when discretionary liquidity traders concentrate in market A, trades have smaller impacts in market A ($\lambda_A < \lambda_B$). Yet, the informed trader trades more aggressively in this market. Thus, in equilibrium, one can simultaneously observe high liquidity (low price impact) and a high level of informed trading activity. This simply reflects the fact that liquidity and informed traders' aggressiveness are endogenous variables that are jointly determined. Consistent with this logic, Collin-Dufresne and Fos (2015) find empirically that informed traders' (activist investors) accumulate shares on days in which liquidity is high. Thus, paradoxically, measures of adverse selection may appear low when the level of informed trading is high.

Box 7.2 Tipping: the Case of MATIF in 1998

The evolution of trading on the Matif, a French bond futures market, is a good illustration of how trading volume can shift quickly from one venue to another. Matif was an open outcry market since 1986. In 1998, the market organizers decided to switch to an electronic market. Floor brokers went on strike to oppose the switch; during the strike, trading migrated to a competing electronic trading system (Eurex) in Germany. After the strike, this trading never migrated back to Matif, despite several coordinated attempts by French banks to reactivate it. This episode can be seen as an instance of multiple equilibria in the model described above, where the closure of Matif—say, market B—induced discretionary liquidity traders to opt for Eurex—market A—independently of their expectations regarding other traders. In other words, the mere suspension of trading on market B permanently coordinated traders' choices on a different equilibrium with all trading concentrated in market A.

7.3.2 Low-Liquidity Traps

The gravitational pull effect is a force that naturally consolidates trading in securities markets. It implies that it is hard for a new trading platform to cut into the market of an incumbent, even if the platform has the potential to be more liquid.

For instance, in the previous model, trading can concentrate in market B even though liquidity traders with discretion would trade more cheaply if they all reconvened in market A. Indeed, if one liquidity trader expects the others to remain in market B, then he is better off staying there. This expectation is self-fulfilling and inefficiently locks traders into market B. All discretionary liquidity traders would benefit from switching to market A if they could do so collectively, but they individually have no incentive to do so. This coordination problem traps them in a low-liquidity equilibrium.

From the point of view of an exchange that wants to compete for the order flow, this translates into a powerful barrier to entry. To overcome it, entrant venues may disseminate information on their trading volumes to show that they attract some trading and make other potential participants more optimistic about their success. This is one reason why the new electronic platforms often publicize their volume statistics so aggressively. Another strategy is to organize meetings among prospective intermediaries ("users") to facilitate coordination. For instance, in the previous model, suppose that market A manages to attract at least $M_A > (M\sigma_d^2 + \sigma_{Ac}^2 - \sigma_{Bc}^2)/2\sigma_d^2$ discretionary liquidity traders. In this case, the condition $M_A\sigma_d^2 + \sigma_{Ac}^2 > M_B\sigma_d^2 + \sigma_{Bc}^2$ is satisfied and the balance tips in favor of market A. There is a sharp decline of activity in market B, since all the remaining discretionary traders will also switch to market A. The decline thus becomes permanent, as trading is now concentrated in market A in equilibrium.

7.4 The Benefits of Fragmentation

Section 7.2 portrays the dark side of market fragmentation, and Section 7.3 explains how liquidity externalities may lead to the concentration of trading in a single venue. Yet market fragmentation also has a benefit: it enhances "competition for order flow," by which markets try to attract buy and sell orders. This competition operates at two levels: between platforms and between liquidity providers operating within different platforms.

7.4.1 Curbing the Pricing Power of Exchanges

The concentration of trading on a single trading platform gives this venue monopoly power. Hence, in the absence of competition, a profit-maximizing exchange will set its fees at the monopolistic level, constrained only by the elasticity of traders' demand for liquidity services.[13] The evolution of trading fees in the United States and Europe suggest that this concern is realistic. In fact, the entry of new trading platforms in the United States (BATS) and in Europe (Chi-X or BATS Europe) triggered a cut in the fees charged by incumbent markets. As an example, Box 7.3 chronicles the evolution of fees on Euronext in 2003 and 2004 when Deutsche Börse and then the LSE launched trading platforms that allowed brokers to trade Dutch blue chips listed on Euronext Amsterdam.

The escalation of intermarket competition has also led some trading platforms to offer "liquidity rebates" to brokers who submit limit orders (or the reverse). Table 7.3 indicates that in 2020 most U.S. trading platforms paid brokers who submitted limit orders, but charged them a fee for market orders. The table shows that the revenue per share traded for the platforms is a fraction of a cent. For instance, NYSE charges 27.5 cents per round lot (one hundred shares) to "takers" (investors submitting market orders) and rebates 12 cents to "makers" (those submitting limit orders). Thus, it earns 0.155 cents per share traded. On December 18, 2020, 953,501,858 shares of Tape A stocks were traded on NYSE (about 43% of the day's total trading volume in these stocks). Thus, limit order traders collectively received about $1.14 million in rebates from NYSE, while market order traders paid about $2.62 million in fees to NYSE.

Table 7.3 Fees per share in cents per round lot for limit orders (make fee) and market orders (take fee)

	Tape A stocks		Tape B stocks		Tape C stocks	
	Make Fee	Take Fee	Make Fee	Take Fee	Make Fee	Take Fee
NYSE	−12	27.5	−12	27.5	−12	27.5
NASDAQ	−20	30	−20	30	−15	30
Cboe EDGX	−17	27	−17	27	−17	27
Cboe EDGA	30	−18	30	−18	30	−18
Cboe BZX	−20	30	−20	30	−20	30
Cboe BYX	19	−5	19	−5	19	−5

Note: Tape A consists of stocks originally listed on the NYSE, while Tape C are stocks listed on NASDAQ. Tape B includes stocks listed on all other exchanges (so-called regional exchanges). *Source*: NYSE, NASDAQ, and Cboe company websites, August 2020.

[13] Fees will be low only if the elasticity of the demand for trading services is high. The evidence on the elasticity of trading volume with respect to transaction costs is mixed: summarizing the available evidence, Schwert and Seguin (1993) report estimates ranging from as little as −0.25 to as much as −1.35.

Liquidity rebates are similar to the payments for order flow discussed in Section 7.2.4. They differ in two important ways, however. First, they go to liquidity suppliers, not demanders. Second, payments for order flow are usually contingent on some characteristics of the clients (e.g., retail orders), while liquidity rebates are not. Hence, their economic role is likely to be different. In both cases, their effect might depend on whether brokers pass their rebates along to their clients, or charge clients for the fees they pay to platforms. Exercise 5 in Chapter 6 considers the effects of make and take fees on the bid-ask spread.

Competition among trading platforms also forces them to install cutting-edge trading technologies. For instance, competition from electronic communication networks in the United States prompted Nasdaq and the NYSE to revamp their trading mechanisms. Another example is the "latency" war among platforms. Some high-frequency traders (e.g., Virtu Financial, Citadel, Optiver, etc.) specialize in automated market making and therefore play a critical role in the provision of liquidity to other market participants (see Chapter 9). To attract them, platforms have updated their trading systems to reduce latency, that is, the lag between an event on the platform (e.g., submission of an order) and the sending of a message about this event to market participants (e.g., "Your order has been executed"). As a consequence, the time interval between orders and trades is now around one millisecond.

Box 7.3 Rivalry among Stock Exchanges

In May 2003, the Deutsche Börse and the LSE separately announced their intention to launch new trading platforms in the Dutch equity markets. At that time, trading in Dutch stocks was mainly concentrated on NSC, a platform operated by Euronext. Euronext reacted to this competitive threat by repeatedly reducing its fees in 2003 and 2004. For instance, in January 2004, Euronext set at €0.3 its order entry fee (in addition to execution fees). Then it halved this fee for limit orders on April 4, 2004, less than two months before the LSE launched its own trading platform for Dutch stocks, EuroSETS, on May 24, 2004. On that day, Euronext suspended the order entry fee on market orders until the end of July and even offered a rebate on total execution costs for these orders. Eventually, on January 31, 2005, Euronext announced that it would stop charging order entry fees on both market and limit orders and also cut its execution fees. EuroSETS's market share remained a modest at 3.5%, but the mere presence of this platform was sufficient to trigger a significant decrease in trading fees for Dutch stocks.

7.4.2 Sharper Competition among Liquidity Providers

Beside encouraging competition between platforms, market fragmentation can also intensify competition among liquidity providers, and thereby increase consolidated liquidity in comparison to trading concentrated in a single platform. At first glance, this possibility seems to contradict the analysis set out in Section 7.2.2. There, however, it was assumed that liquidity demanders could not split their orders between markets and that liquidity providers could not operate simultaneously on several markets. These assumptions may not adequately describe today's electronic equities markets, where traders often have the technology to provide liquidity where it is most profitable or to demand liquidity where it is cheapest at any instant in time.

In this section we study the effects of market fragmentation when traders can split their orders freely in the context of platforms that use limit order markets, not call markets as in previous sections of this chapter. At the end of Section 7.2.2, we showed that when platforms operate as call markets, fragmentation has no effect in the presence of order splitting. With limit order markets, this is not the case: here, the coexistence of multiple LOBs results in greater consolidated depth, that is, a greater number of shares posted at each price in the market.

To see this point, consider Figure 7.1, which describes an extension of the model of limit order trading considered in Section 6.2. At time 1, investors can submit their limit orders for a security in two limit order markets, the "incumbent" I and the "entrant" E. The payoff v of the security is realized at time 3 and $E(v) = \mu$. The tick size, Δ, is identical in the two markets, and $A_1 = \mu + \Delta$ is the first ask price on the grid above the expected value of the security. For brevity, we focus on the determination of the number of shares, denoted by Y_I and Y_E, offered at price A_1 in each market. Considering other possible prices for limit orders delivers the same insights (see Foucault and Menkveld 2008).

At time 2, a liquidity trader comes to buy or sell shares with equal probabilities. The cumulative probability distribution of the trade size q is denoted by

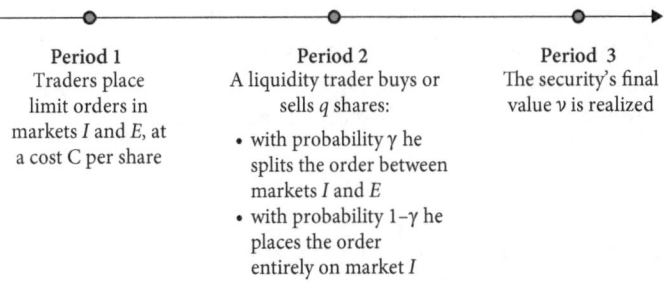

Figure 7.1 Competition between limit order markets: time line.

$F(q)$. For simplicity, we assume that there is no informed trading, but investors submitting limit orders pay an order submission cost C (equal in the two platforms, for simplicity). As in Section 6.2, this cost is the friction that limits the supply of shares at price A_1.

With probability $1 - \gamma$, the liquidity trader can access market I only. This possibility captures the fact that some brokers may ignore offers posted in some platforms (especially new ones) in order to achieve faster execution or to economize on search costs. Moreover, without an adequate routing technology, monitoring prices in both platforms and splitting orders is cumbersome and time-consuming. With probability γ, the liquidity trader can access both platforms. He then splits his order between the two platforms to minimize the total price impact.

To see how this splitting strategy works, suppose that the liquidity trader wishes to buy q shares of the security. If $q \geq Y_I + Y_E$, he optimally fills all limit orders posted at price A_1 in both trading platforms. The remainder of the order executes against limit order at higher prices. If $q < Y_I + Y_E$, the liquidity trader has several ways to execute the order against the limit orders standing at price A_1 in each market. He may give priority to market I, that is, first buy shares in market I and then consider market E if needed, or else may tap market E first and then buy more shares in market I if necessary. The liquidity trader is indifferent between these routing strategies since they result in the same total payment, $A_1 \times q$. Hence, we assume that the liquidity trader gives priority to market I with probability $\frac{1}{2}$.

As in Section 6.2, the depth at price A_1 in market j (for $j \in I, E$) is determined by a zero-profit condition for the marginal limit order posted at this price in that market. To derive this zero-profit condition, we must first compute the probabilities of execution of the marginal limit order placed at price A_1 in the two markets.

Consider the marginal limit order placed at price A_1 in market I. If the liquidity trader at time 1 only has access to I or gives priority to market I, the marginal limit order at the best ask price in market I executes if and only if $q > Y_I$. Thus, in this case, its execution probability is $1 - F(Y_I)$. If the investor arriving at time 1 can trade in both markets and gives priority to market E, the marginal sell limit order at price A_1 in market I executes if and only if $q > Y_I + Y_E$. In this case, therefore, its execution probability is equal to $1 - F(Y_I + Y_E)$. Hence the unconditional execution probability of the marginal limit order posted at price A_1 in market I is:

$$P_I(Y_I, Y_E; \gamma) = \frac{1}{2}\left[(1 - \gamma + \frac{\gamma}{2})(1 - F(Y_I)) + \frac{\gamma}{2}(1 - F(Y_I + Y_E))\right]. \quad (7.11)$$

Now consider the marginal limit order posted at price A_1 in market E. If the liquidity trader trades in both markets and gives priority to market E, this marginal limit order executes if and only if $q > Y_E$. If priority is instead given to market I, it executes if and only if $q > Y_I + Y_E$. In all other cases, this marginal limit order does not execute. Hence its unconditional execution probability is:

$$P_E(Y_I, Y_E; \gamma) = \frac{\gamma}{4}[(1 - F(Y_E)) + (1 - F(Y_I + Y_E))]. \tag{7.12}$$

In a competitive equilibrium, the number of shares supplied in each market at price A_1 must be such that no limit order trader finds it profitable to expand the queue of limit orders at this price, in either market. Let $Y_{1j}^*(\gamma)$ be the number of shares offered in equilibrium at price A_1 in market j. Obviously, if $\gamma = 0$, market E attracts no order since there are no investors routing market orders to it. Thus, $Y_I^*(0)$ is the number of shares offered at price A_1 when all trades take place in market I. As in Section 6.2, if $Y_I^*(0) > 0$, it solves:

$$P_I(Y_I^*(0), 0; 0)(A_1 - \mu) = C,$$

that is, using equation (7.11) for $\gamma = 0$,

$$\frac{1}{2}[1 - F(Y_I^*(0))] = \frac{C}{\Delta}. \tag{7.13}$$

As $1 - F(Y_I^*(0)) < 1$, a necessary condition for the existence of an equilibrium with $Y_I^*(0) > 0$ is $2C < \Delta$. In the rest of this section, we assume that this condition is satisfied, i.e., competitive dealers in market I are willing to sell a positive number of shares at price A_1 if market E is inactive.

Now suppose that $\gamma > 0$. If both markets attract limit orders at price A_1, then $Y_I^*(\gamma) > 0$ and $Y_E^*(\gamma) > 0$. In this case, the zero-profit conditions on the marginal limit order in the two markets require (again from Section 6.2):

$$P_I(Y_I^*, Y_E^*; \gamma) = \frac{C}{A_1 - \mu} = \frac{C}{\Delta}, \tag{7.14}$$

$$P_E(Y_I^*, Y_E^*; \gamma) = \frac{C}{A_1 - \mu} = \frac{C}{\Delta}, \tag{7.15}$$

For a specific parameterization of the probability $F(\cdot)$, the equilibrium number of shares offered in each market at price A_1 can be computed explicitly by solving the system of equations (7.14) and (7.15) (see exercise 4).

In any case, if the two markets coexist (i.e., both attract limit orders at price A_1), in equilibrium the number of shares offered in each at the best price must be such that their execution probabilities of the marginal limit orders are equal:

$$P_I(Y_I^*, Y_E^*; \gamma) = P_E(Y_I^*, Y_E^*; \gamma).$$

This condition is intuitive; otherwise, the investor who placed the marginal limit order in the market with the smaller execution probability would have an incentive to cancel and resubmit it in the other market at the same price. This would increase his expected profit, since the submission cost is the same.

Figure 7.2 illustrates how the equilibrium is determined, by plotting the number of shares Y_I and Y_E offered in the two markets at price A_1. The two solid lines in the figure are drawn for $\gamma = 1$, the case in which liquidity traders always access both platforms: the black curve P_I is the set of pairs (Y_I, Y_E) such that the execution probability of the marginal limit order in market I is equal to $\frac{C}{\Delta}$. Similarly, the grey curve P_E is the set of pairs (Y_I, Y_E) such that the execution probability of the marginal limit order in market E is equal to $\frac{C}{\Delta}$. The equilibrium numbers of shares offered at price A_1 in each market are found at the intersection of the two curves. (The two dashed curves instead show how the equilibrium changes when γ decreases below 1, i.e., the case in which liquidity traders cannot always access both platforms, discussed in the next section.)

When $\gamma = 1$, the expressions for the execution probabilities in the two markets are symmetric. Hence, $Y_I^* = Y_E^*$, as shown in Figure 7.2: the number of shares offered at price A_1 is the same in both platforms, so that the total number of shares offered at price A_1 (the consolidated depth at this price) is $2Y_I^*(1)$. Why is there no concentration of trading in a single platform in this case? To answer

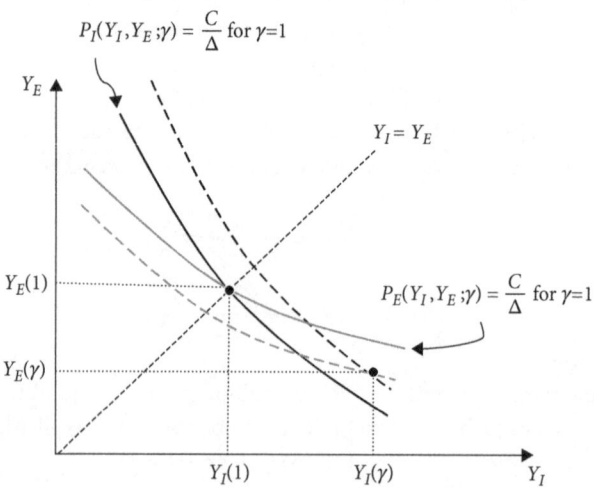

Figure 7.2 Zero-profit depth at the best quote in market I (black) and market E (gray).

this question, suppose that some shares were offered at price A_1 in market I but not yet in market E, and consider an investor who wants to place a limit order at price A_1. If it is placed in market I, the investor's execution probability is $P_I(Y_I, 0; 1) = \frac{1}{4}(1 - F(Y_I))$. If instead it is placed in market E, the execution probability is $P_E(Y_I, 0; 1) = \frac{1}{4}(2 - F(Y_I)) > \frac{1}{4}(1 - F(Y_I))$. Thus, the investor is better off submitting the limit order at price A_1 in market E, as it yields a higher execution probability: by doing this, the investor jumps the queue of limit orders already posted in market I at the same price, because time priority is not enforced across markets.

Intuitively, this "queue-jumping" possibility intensifies competition among limit order traders, as it allows latecomers to reduce the rents of those who submitted their limit orders first.[14] As a result, the cumulative depth at price A_1 is greater when the two markets coexist, that is, $Y_I^*(1) + Y_E^*(1) > Y_I^*(0)$. To see this, notice that the zero-profit conditions (7.14) and (7.15) imply:

$$\frac{1}{4}[(1 - F(Y^*(1))) + (1 - F(2Y^*(1)))] = \frac{C}{\Delta}, \qquad (7.16)$$

where $Y^*(1) \overset{def}{=} Y_I^*(1) = Y_E^*(1)$. Equations (7.16) and (7.13) in turn imply that:

$$F(Y_I^*(0)) = \frac{F(Y^*(1)) + F(2Y^*(1))}{2}. \qquad (7.17)$$

As $F(x)$ increases with x, equation (7.17) implies:

$$2Y^*(1) > Y_I^*(0) > Y^*(1).$$

That is, when both markets are active the total number of shares offered at price A_1 (the consolidated depth) is greater, even though the number of shares offered at price A_1 in each market is smaller than when only market I is active. Hence, for traders who can submit market orders in both markets, the coexistence of two limit order markets improves liquidity at the best quotes.

This analysis shows that it can be misleading to consider the effect of market fragmentation on one platform only. For instance, suppose that initially market I operates alone. In this case, the depth of market I at price A_1 is $Y_I^*(0)$. Now suppose that platform E enters and that $\gamma = 1$. We should observe a drop in the liquidity of market I since $Y_I^*(0) > Y^*(1)$. Yet investors submitting market orders smaller than $2Y^*(1)$ and larger than $Y_I^*(0)$ are better off, since they can

---

[14] The logic is similar to that of the pro-rata allocation rule in a single limit order market: see Section 6.3.2.

execute at a better price. Investors who submit market orders smaller than $Y_I^*(0)$ are indifferent, and those whose market orders are larger than $2Y^*(1)$ can be shown to be better off. Indeed, the improvement in liquidity at the best quote is propagated throughout the LOB via the channel just described for the depth at price A_1. Hence, despite the decrease in liquidity of market I, liquidity demanders are better off because consolidated depth increases at all prices.

The lack of time priority across markets is crucial to this result. The argument also relies on the fact that traders placing limit orders at the head of the queue in each market earn positive expected profits. As explained in Section 6.3.1, this is because the tick size is strictly positive; if it were nil, the number of competing platforms would have no effect on consolidated depth in the framework considered here.

Box 7.4 Competition for Orders and Liquidity: Some Evidence

In 2004, the LSE launched a new limit order market (EuroSETS) to enable Dutch brokers to trade stocks listed on Euronext Amsterdam. Until then, these stocks were traded almost exclusively on NSC, a limit order market operated by Euronext. The launch of EuroSETS accordingly constitutes a good experiment to test whether intermarket competition enhances liquidity in an environment that resembles the one in this section (as NSC and EuroSETS are both limit order markets and their tick size is the same). Foucault and Menkveld (2008) analyze the effects of EuroSETS entry on consolidated depth, using snapshots of the LOBs in each market, and find that consolidated depth increased dramatically, as implied by the model presented in this section.

More evidence on the impact of fragmentation on the liquidity of limit order markets comes from Degryse, de Jong, and Van Kervel (2015), a study of a sample of 52 Dutch stocks (large and mid-cap) in 2006–9. This is an interesting period, since after 2007 the European market became significantly more fragmented owing to the implementation of MiFID (see Section 7.5.2). The sample stocks are listed on Euronext Amsterdam and trade on Chi-X, Deutsche Börse, Turquoise, BATS trading, Nasdaq OMX, and SIX Swiss Exchange. Degryse, de Jong, and Van Kervel (2015) measure market fragmentation using the Herfindahl index, a measure of the dispersion of the trading volume in a stock across the available trading platforms. Their data are very rich, covering limit order books of each trading platform for each stock, so they can study the relationship between their index of market fragmentation and measures of cumulative depth at each price point in all these limit order books. They find a positive relationship between the market fragmentation and the consolidated liquidity of a stock, as predicted.

7.4.3 Trade-Throughs

Let us compare the case in which liquidity traders do not always have access to both the incumbent and the entrant market ($\gamma < 1$) with the previously analyzed case in which they do ($\gamma = 1$). A decrease in γ reduces the execution probability of the marginal limit order in market E, other things being equal. As a consequence, it becomes less profitable to submit a limit order in market E. But the execution probability of the marginal limit order in market I increases, so it becomes more profitable to submit a limit order there. Thus, in Figure 7.2, the curve that shows the pairs (Y_I, Y_E) such that the execution probability of the marginal limit order in market I is equal to C/Δ shifts upward, while the other curve shifts downward, as shown by the dashed curves. The new equilibrium point is at the intersection of these two curves—clearly, in equilibrium,

$$Y_I^*(\gamma) > Y^*(1) > Y_E^*(\gamma) \text{ when } \gamma < 1.$$

Hence, when $\gamma < 1$ the cumulative depth in market I is greater than when $\gamma = 1$, while that in market E is lower. More generally, the cumulative depth in market E diminishes as γ decreases, and there is a value γ^c such that $Y^{E*}(\gamma^c) = 0$. Below this threshold γ^c, no limit order can be profitably posted at price A_1 in market E. Solving for the value of γ such that the solution to the system of equations (7.14) and (7.15) is $Y_E^*(\gamma^c) = 0$ yields $\gamma^c = \frac{4\Delta}{\Delta+2C}$.[15] It can also be shown that if $\gamma < \min(\gamma^c, 2/3)$, then no limit order will be submitted in this market at any price. Intuitively, in this case the expected revenue from a limit order in market E is too low to cover the cost, because this order is unlikely to execute, due the paucity of investors who track limit orders in market E. Thus, to be active, a trading platform needs some *critical mass* of traders who pay attention to its quotes.

This feature is a barrier to entry for a new platform. To see this, suppose that market E is a new trading platform. It will attract some trades if and only if γ is large enough. Actually, in reality, the value of γ is partly determined by investors' beliefs about the chances of success of the new market. Traders will indeed develop technologies to trade in both markets ("smart routers") if and only if they expect the new market to be liquid enough, so that the reduction in trading costs achieved by accessing both markets exceeds the additional cost

---

[15] Note that $\gamma^c < 1$, since $2C < \Delta$ by assumption.

of multimarket trading. But, as we have just seen, the liquidity of the entrant market depends critically on the fraction of traders who monitor quotes in both markets. This can lead to a self-fulfilling prophecy, in which traders expect the entrant market to be unsuccessful and so do not consider the offers on it, and—precisely for this reason—market E fails to attract liquidity, thus confirming traders' expectations.

In other words, the entry of the new trading platform is blocked by a chicken-and-egg problem: to take off it needs a critical mass of traders following its quotes, but traders will pay attention only if they expect the platform's liquidity to be great enough. For example, this was the key hurdle for Tradepoint, a limit order platform that tried to draw order flow away from the LSE in the late 1990s, as described by Tradepoint's CEO at the time, Nic Stuchfield:

> When I was CEO of Tradepoint [...], my team and I spent a considerable amount of effort "selling" the exchange to traders. However, although they all signed up as members, they did not use the market. One major reason was that access to the market was not connected to their trading systems. Even when better bids and offers appeared on our order book, the (momentarily) inferior prices available on the LSE were hit and lifted. Potential users simply could not see, nor easily access the market. If the Tradepoint terminal was at the end of the desk, it was not accessible. The solution [...] was to get Tradepoint integrated into the main order management systems [....] This proved to be easier negotiated than implemented [....] The traders had many other priorities and we could not demonstrate the required liquidity. Think chicken and egg again!   (Stuchfield 2003)

This problem can be alleviated if regulation bans violations of price priority between trading platforms—so-called "trade-throughs," in which a security trades at a worse price in one platform than in another at the same moment. For instance, suppose one hundred shares are offered for sale at $A_1 = \$50$ in markets I and E. The second best ask price is $51, at which two hundred shares are offered in each market. Now consider a broker who wants to purchase two hundred shares and plans to execute this trade with a market order. Ignoring the offer in market E, the broker buys one hundred shares at $50 and one hundred shares at $51 in market I only. This routing decision is a "trade-through," because a buy order executes at $51 while a sell limit order at $50 is posted in market E.

Trade-throughs do occur in practice. In their study of competition between EuroSETS and NSC (see Box 7.4), Foucault and Menkveld (2008) find that a significant fraction of market orders were executed on NSC (the incumbent) even when EuroSETS (the entrant) offered a better price. Similarly, trade-throughs occur on U.S. equities markets, albeit much less commonly as they are forbidden (see Hendershott and Jones (2005b)). Indeed, in the United States, the order protection rule (or trade-through rule) require venues to reroute incoming market orders to the market posting the best quote (provided that automatic execution at this quote is possible). This is the order protection rule or trade-through rule, designed specifically to prevent trade-throughs. The rationale is that trade-throughs discourage liquidity provision, as the SEC noted in its June 2005 release of Regulation NMS (Federal Register Vol. 70, No. 124, pp. 37496–644):

> Price protection encourages the display of limit orders by increasing the likelihood that they will receive an execution in a timely manner and helping preserve investors' expectations that their orders will be executed when they represent the best displayed quotation.   (p. 37505)

This reasoning is consistent with the model developed in this section whereby trade-throughs will occur when $\gamma^c < \gamma < 1$. Consider an investor who wishes to place a market order size equal to $q > Y_I^*(\gamma)$. He should optimally buy part or all of the shares posted at price A_1 in market E. However he will do so only with probability γ. With probability $1 - \gamma$, he will instead buy $q - Y_I^*(\gamma)$ shares at higher prices in market I, a trade-through whose likelihood is therefore $(1 - \gamma)(1 - F(Y_I^*(\gamma)))$. Trade-throughs never happen only if $\gamma = 1$ because in this case all investors optimally execute their market orders against limit orders available in both markets.

Thus, comparing a situation in which $\gamma = 1$ with one in which $\gamma < 1$ is like comparing market structures with and without a trade-through rule. As noted, the number of shares offered in market E is smaller when $\gamma < 1$, because a small γ implies a low likelihood of execution for limit orders placed in market E, and therefore low profitability of limit orders in this market. Hence, a no-trade-through rule effectively encourages investors to submit limit orders in market E by improving their chance of execution.[16]

In this model we have analyzed competition between two platforms, taking their design (both being limit order markets) as given. This is of course incomplete. A full-fledged analysis of intermarket competition would have to allow the design of competing trading platforms to be itself endogenous: the venues choose their fees (which could affect C in the previous model) and design their trading mechanisms. In particular, platforms may want to differentiate their mechanisms to relax competition in fees, in the same way that firms differentiate

---

[16] The model readily generalizes to account for fee differences between trading venues (say, in order submission costs). These fees create asymmetries between the platforms (much like parameter γ does), but do not change the overall logic of the model (see exercise 4).

their products. Such an analysis is needed to see why there is heterogeneity in trading mechanisms and to grasp the logic behind pricing policies such as liquidity rebates.

7.5 Regulation

This chapter begins by setting out the risks and costs of fragmentation: violations of price priority across markets, price dispersion, and diminished liquidity externalities. The second part of the chapter, however, shows that fragmentation also benefits investors by fostering competition among trading platforms. Hence, regulators have the problem of capturing the benefits while lowering the costs of market fragmentation. In this section we explain how the U.S. regulator tried to achieve this difficult balance in designing Regulation NMS and the very different way in which the European Union approached the matter with its MiFID legislation (see also Chapter 1).

7.5.1 Regulation NMS

Regulation NMS went into force in 2006 and 2007.[17] It consists of a series of rules to promote intermarket competition in U.S. equities markets while curtailing the harmful effects of fragmentation.

To understand RegNMS, the historical perspective is helpful. In the 1970s, NYSE-listed stocks traded mainly on the NYSE and not elsewhere. But regional U.S. exchanges and the OTC market gradually captured a larger part of this trading. The U.S. Congress was concerned that this evolution could lead to inefficiencies; in 1975, it mandated the SEC to create a National Market System (NMS). Congress envisioned five purposes for the NMS: (i) economically efficient execution of securities transactions; (ii) fair competition among brokers and dealers and between markets; (iii) availability to brokers, dealers, and investors of information about quotes and transaction; (iv) best execution for investors' orders; and (v) the opportunity to execute orders without the participation of a dealer.

The SEC initially proposed to consolidate all limit orders for each stock in a single file where orders would be executed according to price and time priority. However, this proposal met with strong opposition from exchanges and market makers (see Colby and Sirri 2010). In the end, the SEC opted

---

[17] It was first released on June 9, 2005. See Securities Exchange Act Release No. 51808, Federal Register Vol. 70, No. 124, pp. 37496–644.

for a more decentralized approach: the NMS would be composed of multiple trading venues, linked together by technology. The resulting market structure that emerged to achieve this goal was based on two pillars: the intermarket trading system (ITS) and the Consolidated Tape Association (CTA). The ITS was intended to make sure that price priority would be enforced across all markets. Hence, an order routed first to one exchange (say the NYSE) would then be rerouted to another (a regional exchange perhaps) if the latter posted a better price, unless brokers or market makers on the first exchange decided to improve the price. Implementation of this no-trade-through rule required real-time information on best bids and offers in every trading venue for a security.[18] The CTA was designed to collect and disseminate this information. Importantly, the no-trade-through rule did not apply to stocks traded on the OTC market, in particular stocks listed on Nasdaq.

However, the developments of technology called for revision of this system. The possibility of computerized trading venues to match buy and sell orders with no need for market makers or floor brokers led to the development of electronic communication networks (ECNs), such as POSIT (a crossing network) and Island (a limit order book) in the 1990s. Speed of execution was a strong selling point of theirs against the more traditional markets, such as Nasdaq and NYSE. The no-trade-through rule, however, required orders to be routed to the NYSE when it was quoting a better price, even though it had slower execution (handled manually by the specialist assigned to each stock). For this reason, several ECNs elected to stay out of the NMS. This became problematic as the ECNs' market share grew, in sync with traders' intensifying demand for rapid execution.

The so-called order protection rule (or trade-through rule) of RegNMS is intended to resolve this problem. The rule extends the protection against trade-through to all NMS stocks, but a quote is protected only if it is immediately and automatically accessible. An implication is that manual quotes sourced by floor-based trading systems (such as the NYSE) were no longer protected against trade-throughs. This new regulatory regime lent further impetus to electronic trading and led to an erosion of the NYSE's market share in its listed stocks. As a result, the NYSE had to overhaul its trading system to ensure its quotes were electronic, so that trade execution would be sufficiently immediate to qualify for order protection.

The rise of the ECNs also prompted platforms to devise new pricing strategies. In particular, ECNs now use the so-called maker-taker pricing model. On a limit order market, each transaction involves a match between a limit order (the "maker") and a market order (the "taker"). Market orders are viewed as

---

[18] The effects of the no-trade-through rule on market liquidity are analyzed in Section 7.4.3.

consuming ("taking") the liquidity supplied ("made") by limit orders. For a platform, the maker-taker model consists in charging a fee for market orders that fill against limit orders on the platform and rebating a fraction of this fee to the filled limit orders (see Table 7.3).

This business model can produce price distortions when combined with the trade-through rule. Liquidity rebates do narrow bid-ask spreads in that they decrease the cost of providing liquidity.[19] Thus, liquidity rebates are a way for a platform to display the best prices in the market more frequently. It does not follow, however, that routing market orders to this platform is optimal because the total trading cost for takers includes the take fee. Yet the trade-through rule applies to quotes, not quotes cum fees. Thus, by granting very generous liquidity rebates, a platform can capture a large share of the order flow (thanks to the trade-through rule) while still earning significant profits by charging a high take fee.

The access rule of RegNMS addresses this problem by capping the take fee (or access fee) at $0.003 per share. The access rule also prevents platforms from giving preferential treatment (in terms of priority, speed of execution, or fees) to members/subscribers over non-members/subscribers.

Over the years, the CTA's revenues from the sale of trade and price information became a significant source of income for NMS-members. The allocation of this revenue between members was based on the *number* of trades reported to the consolidated tape, a sharing rule that was creating perverse incentives for platforms. To obtain a larger share, they had an incentive to induce traders to shred their trades into multiple small trades or even engage in wash sales to artificially inflate trading volume.

The market data rules of RegNMS address this issue by changing the revenue-sharing mechanism. The new mechanism is based more on each platform's contribution to finding the right price. In particular, the new formula rewards the trading venues that frequently set the best bid and ask prices for a given stock.

The last ingredient of RegNMS is the "sub-penny rule," which imposes a minimum price variation (tick size) of $0.01 for all NMS securities over $1.[20] The intent was to prevent platforms from competing in the coarseness of their grid size. By setting a very fine grid (with a tick smaller than a penny), a platform could attract limit orders that just barely undercut the best bid or offer price in another market. These orders can generate trades for the platform (due to the trade-through rule), but they gain priority by improving prices for insignificant amounts while undermining the incentives of other traders to quickly post good prices.

---

[19] They can be viewed as a negative order-processing cost (see Chapter 3).

[20] The sub-penny rule does not prevent trading in increments of less than a penny. For instance, traders can agree to match a trade at a price within the best bid and offer price.

RegNMS is designed to secure the benefits of competition without incurring the costs of fragmentation, but it stops short of emulating a nationwide consolidated LOB with multiple points of entry. Indeed, while the regulation ensures that small market orders are executed at the best possible price available on any trading platform, price protection is not given to displayed limit orders that provide market depth at prices outside the best bid and offer. This means that traders who need to fill a large order that cannot be fully executed at the NBBO (after first executing against the protected orders) must hunt around for further market depth, which is often not publicly posted but available in hidden orders on the exchanges or in "dark pools" of liquidity. In this sense, RegNMS does not eliminate all the adverse price disparity and uncertainty effects of fragmentation.

7.5.2   MiFID

Until 2007, E.U. security market regulations allowed member countries to impose "concentration rules": under the 1993 Investment Services Directive (ISD), member states could require transactions in equity securities to be carried out on a "regulated market." Therefore some member states—France, Italy, and Spain, among others—maintained rules requiring execution of share trades on their national stock exchange. Others, such as the United Kingdom, left intermediaries free to execute trades off-exchange and also to internalize them, provided they complied with general best execution requirements.

In 2004 the European Union introduced MiFID, whose regulatory regime went into effect on November 1, 2007. The main change relating to fragmentation was a ban on the concentration rules, ushering in free competition between trading platforms. Specifically, MiFID allows three types of trading systems: (i) regulated markets (RMs), (ii) systematic internalizers (SIs), and (iii) multilateral trading facilities (MTFs). Regulated markets are the incumbent exchanges (e.g., NYSE-Euronext and Deutsche Börse). Multilateral Trading Facilities are functionally similar but operate under different regulatory requirements (Cboe or Turquoise are examples of MTFs). Systematic internalizers are "investment firms" (i.e., brokers or banks) that opt to match ("internalize") buy and sell orders from their clients in-house (either by acting as market makers or by crossing buy and sell orders from different clients).

The abolition of the concentration rules triggered the entry of a series of MTFs.[21] Meanwhile, anticipating entry by other trading platforms, the existing

---

[21] Chi-X (March 2007), Turquoise (March 2007), BATS Europe (April 2008), NasdaqOMX (September 2008), NYSEArca (March 2009), and Burgundy (May 2009).

exchanges pushed for consolidation: the Paris, Amsterdam, Brussels, and Lisbon stock exchanges merged into Euronext; Stockholm's OMX AB acquired stock exchanges in Sweden, Finland, Denmark, Iceland, Estonia, Lithuania, and Latvia; the LSE acquired Borsa Italiana and Turquoise. Many of the new trading platforms and regulated markets also launched "dark pools," which are simply crossing networks that match buy and sell orders at pre-determined points in time at the midquote set in some other market (see Chapter 1). As of April 2010, the stock and bond trading venues registered in thirty different European countries comprised 127 RMs, 142 MTFs, and 172 SIs.

Thus, with the advent of MiFID, Europe moved closer to the U.S. regulatory framework which encourages competition among platforms. However, there are important differences. With the Order Protection Rule, the U.S. approach interconnects platforms to enforce best execution at the best price nationwide. In Europe, there is no formal order protection rule requiring the routing of market orders to the platform posting the best price. In fact, the notion of cross-market best bid and offer is not yet defined in Europe. Rather, MiFID mitigates the harmful effects of market fragmentation by best execution rules and order handling rules.

More specifically, Article 21 requires that "investment firms take all reasonable steps to obtain, when executing orders, the best possible result for their clients taking into account price, costs, speed, likelihood of execution and settlement, size, nature or any other consideration relevant to the execution of the order," unless the firm receives a specific instruction from the client. Thus, MiFID does not define best execution only with reference to the price, as RegNMS effectively does with the order protection rule. Consequently, as empirical studies show, trade-throughs happen relatively frequently in European markets.[22]

In handling orders, investment firms must abide by transparency rules that mimic the U.S. display rule (Rule 11Ac1-1) and quote rule (11Ac1-4). First, when dealing in shares listed on a regulated market, market makers must immediately disclose any unfilled limit orders so as to make them easily accessible to other market participants, unless instructed otherwise by the customers (MiFID, Article 22). This in effect exposes market markers to competition from public limit orders as in the United States. Second, if they deal in shares traded on regulated and liquid markets, investment firms qualifying as "systematic internalizers" must publish firm quotes on a regular and continuous basis during

---

[22] For instance, Ende and Lutat (2011) estimate the frequency of trade-throughs in the constituent stocks of the Euro Stoxx 50 index traded in eight European markets over twenty trading days in 2007 and 2008 at 12% of the trades in their sample.

normal trading hours (Article 27).[23] These must be firm quotes, in the sense that the intermediary must execute at the quoted prices the orders received from their retail clients: the directive prohibits them from offering price improvements to retail customers and limits the scope of price improvements on large orders from professional clients. This measure is designed to encourage firms to display the liquidity that they offer.

After the implementation of MiFID, European policy makers realized that, in spite these transparency rules, the new regulatory framework had reduced the overall transparency of equity trading in Europe, as the increased competition between platforms induced by MiFID had resulted in "lit markets" (RMs and MTFs) losing market share to more opaque ones (SIs and dark pools). This was a reason for concern, as most of the price discovery process still occurs on lit platforms, with more opaque venues relying on the guidance of prices determined on lit platforms. That opaque platforms free-ride on price formation in lit platforms is witnessed by the fact that their activity typically grinds to a halt when trading stops on their reference lit platforms: for instance, on October 29, 2018, following an unintentional halt of Euronext trading, trading in the French CAC40 stocks almost stopped in most alternative European trading venues, to resume as soon as Euronext trading started again (see Comerton-Forde and Zhong 2021, for systematic evidence regarding the spillover effects of outages across European equity trading platforms).

To address these concerns, in January 2018 the EU enacted the MiFID 2 directive, an updated version of MiFID, and the associated regulation (MiFIR), aimed at moving trading activity back to regulated markets. The updated rules included a mandatory requirement for equity to be traded on RMs, MTFs, or SIs, effectively prohibiting OTC trading of equities. MIFID 2 also mandated a cap on equity trading in dark pools, extended pre-trade and post-trade transparency rules to SIs and investment firms, and broadened their scope to non-equity markets. However, the enactment of MiFID 2 in January 2018 did not result in an increase in the share of trading on lit platforms, as the significant drop in OTC trading triggered by the new rules was largely offset by an expansion of SI.

7.5.3 Comparing the U.S. and E.U. Approaches

To sum up, RegNMS and MiFID are two different regulatory approaches, aimed at the same objective: securing the benefits of intermarket competition for

---

[23] Transaction reporting to the competent authority can be made by the investment firm itself, a third party representing the investment firm, a reporting system approved by the competent authority, or the MTF through which the investment firm completes the transaction.

investors without the adverse effects of market fragmentation. With its trade-through rule, RegNMS enforces strict price priority. That is, "best execution" is essentially defined with respect to prices. MiFID defines best execution more flexibly since there is no rule against trade-throughs in Europe. In making their routing decisions, brokers must consider price, of course, but can also weigh other dimensions, such as speed and likelihood of execution.

Another important difference between MiFID and RegNMS lies in the consolidation of market data. In the United States, trading platforms are free to disseminate their trade and quote data, but they must also transmit them to an agency that consolidates them across platforms and provides information in real time on the best bids and offers. At the time of writing, such consolidation of market data does not yet exist in Europe, which makes multimarket trading more complicated and costly. A consolidated tape, bundling together data from Europe's patchwork of trading venues, would in fact require the ability to enforce common technical and operational standards of trade reporting on all trading platforms and punish transgressors—a role that in the U.S. is played by the Financial Industry Regulatory Authority (FINRA).[24] So far, in the EU equity market platforms and bond dealers have resisted the introduction of consolidated record collection and provision of standardized data on order flows, transaction sizes, and prices: equity platforms see a consolidated tape as a threat to their revenues from data sales, and bond dealers see it as a threat to the informational rents that they obtain from opacity (see Chapter 8, especially Section 8.5.1). As a result, many fund managers complain that even MiFID 2 rules failed to improve market transparency as intended. This demonstrates that, when security trading occurs simultaneously on various platforms—which by now is typically the case—a sufficient level of transparency is required to overcome market fragmentation.

Yet another difference between the European and U.S. equities markets is that clearing and settlement systems are much less unified in Europe. As a consequence, cross-border trading is more costly for investors than domestic trading (see Box 7.5). This friction hinders multimarket trading (which in Europe is often cross-border trading) and therefore works against the integration of the various trading platforms. For instance, a French institutional investor may find it optimal to trade on Euronext even if a better price is available on Cboe, because the extra clearing and settlement costs of the latter exceed the price gain.

---

[24] FINRA is a U.S. government-authorized, not-for-profit organization that oversees U.S. broker-dealers to provide investor protection, by testing and licensing anyone who sells securities to the public and by ensuring truthfulness of advertising of securities and complete disclosure about the investment product before purchase.

Box 7.5 Clearing Houses and Custodians

Trading platforms enable buyers and sellers to find one another and agree on the terms of a trade. After a transaction, however, each party needs post-trading services.

First, the trade has to be cleared. That is, for each match on the platform, the account of the buyer to which the security needs to be delivered and that of the seller to which the payment is due must be identified. This task is performed by a clearing house or central counterparty (CCP). The CCP also serves to minimize counterparty risk (the risk that one party to the transaction fails to honor its obligation). If one party defaults, the CPP completes the trade, so the other party gets the security or the payment due. For these services, the CCP collects a fee on each trade from the buyer and the seller.

Second, the trade needs to be settled. Settlement—the actual delivery of the security to the seller and its payment by the buyer—usually takes place through a central securities depository (CSD). CSDs also act as custodians for securities, as they keep track of ownership and enable the holders to receive the benefits (dividends, issue rights, etc.).

In the United States, there is a single CCP and CSD for all equity trades. In Europe, there are more than twenty CCPs and CSDs for equities alone, and different platforms use the services of different CCPs or CSDs. Moreover, MTFs have often chosen to connect to incumbent CSDs via new CCPs and agent banks. For instance, Cboe Europe use EuroCCP as its CCP while Euronext uses Euronext clearing. As a consequence, cross-border transactions are more complex and costlier than domestic transactions since they involve more layers of intermediation.

7.6 Further Reading

Several authors have analyzed thick market externalities in securities markets. Mendelson (1982, 1985, 1987) and Hendershott and Mendelson (2000) show how an increase in the number of participants on a platform (a call market in Mendelson (1982, 1985), a crossing network in Hendershott and Mendelson (2000)) raises the likelihood of finding a match for all traders. Pagano (1989b) considers a different source of thick market externality. In his model, risk-averse traders perceive their demand for the stock as adversely affecting the market price. A greater number of market participants implies a lower price sensitivity to each trader's net demand, thus increasing the market's liquidity. The analysis of risk-sharing effects and market fragmentation in Section 7.2.2 is based on Pagano (1989b).

The tengle market also emerges in models with asymmetric information, such as Admati and Pfleiderer (1988) and Chowdhry and Nanda (1991). Admati and Pfleiderer were the first to consider "discretionary liquidity traders," in a setting in which trading is fragmented across different times of day. Chowdhry and Nanda use a similar model to analyze the fragmentation of trading across different venues; the setting analyzed in Sections 7.2.1 and 7.3.1 is a simplified version of their model.

Parlour and Seppi (2003) develop a model of competition between a dealer market and a LOB. Foucault and Menkveld (2008) extend this model to analyze competition between two limit order markets. The model developed in Section 7.4.2 is based on Foucault and Menkveld (2008). Foucault and Parlour (2004), Colliard and Foucault (2012), Pagnotta and Phillipon (2018), Chao, Chen, and Ye (2019), and Baldauf and Mollner (2021) analyze competition between trading platforms and endogenize their fees.

There is also a rich empirical literature on the effects of market fragmentation and intermarket competition on market liquidity and price discovery. Among others see Foerster and Karolyi (1998), Mayhew (2002); Barclay, Hendershott, and McCormick (2003); Bessembinder (2003); Boehmer and Boehmer (2003); De Fontnouvelle et al. (2003); Battalio, Hatch, and Jennings (2004); Jennings, Boehmer, and Wei (2007); Foucault and Menkveld (2008); Biais, Bisière, and Spatt (2010); O'Hara and Ye (2011); Degryse, de Jong, and Van Kervel (2015); Gresse (2017); Haslag and Ringgenberg (2021).

7.7 Exercises

1. **Market consolidation with correlated noise trading.** Consider the model developed in Section 7.2.1, but assume that u_A and u_B are correlated. Denote by ρ the correlation between these two variables.

   a. How does market depth depend on ρ when order flow is consolidated in a single market?

   b. Does order flow consolidation increase or decrease market depth?

   c. How does the informed investor's expected profit differ from those obtained in the model of Section 7.2.1?

2. **Optimal order splitting.** Consider an order of total size q that can be split into two orders q_A and q_B to be executed in markets A and B. The security traded in these two markets has expected value μ and variance σ_v^2. Markets A and B are populated by K_A and K_B competitive dealers with no initial inventories and identical risk aversion $\bar{\rho}$ as in Section 7.2.2. Show that equation (7.10) is the optimal split of the total order q between the two markets.

3. **Payments for order flow.** Consider the market for a risky security. Its payoff at time 1 is either $v^H = \mu + \sigma$, or, $v^L = \mu - \sigma$ with equal probabilities. At time 0, an investor gives to his broker an order to buy or sell one share of the security to a broker. With probability ϕ, the investor is a retail investor and has no information on the payoff. In this case he buys or sells the security with equal probability. With probability $1 - \phi$, the investor is an institutional investor. In this case, he is perfectly informed about the payoff with probability α, or uninformed with probability $1 - \alpha$. In the latter case, the investor is a buyer or seller with equal probability. Bid and ask quotes for the broker's order are posted by three risk-neutral dealers 1, 2, and 3 before the broker contacts them. The broker cannot split his order among dealers. Dealers have no private information on the payoff of the security. For this exercise, you need also to refer to the material in Section 3.3.2.

   a. Assume that there is no payment for order flow between the broker and the three dealers. In this case, the broker randomly selects one dealer among those posting the best price for his order. Compute the bid and ask quotes posted by the dealers.

   b. Assume now that dealer 1 has a payment for order flow arrangement under which the broker gives dealer 1 all orders from retail investors and the dealer commits to execute all these orders at the best quotes (i.e., the ask and bid price set by the remaining dealers, 2 and 3). Other orders are sent to dealer 2 or 3 (as in question **a**). What are the quotes posted by dealers 2 and 3? Deduce that the bid-ask spread is higher in this case than where there is no payment for the order flow.

   c. Let P be the payment of dealer 1 to the broker. What is the largest possible value of P?

   d. Is payment for order flow beneficial or detrimental to investors?

4. **Competition between limit order markets with uniformly distributed market orders.** Consider the model of Section 7.4.2 and assume that the size of the market order $\tilde{X}$ has a uniform distribution on $\left[0, \bar{X}\right]$ That is, $F(x) = x/\overline{X}$. We denote by $Y^*_{jk}(\gamma)$ the cumulative depth posted at the ask price $A_k = \mu + k\Delta$ in market $j \in \{I, E\}$ when the fraction of investors submitting market orders in both markets I and E is γ, and by c_j be the submission cost in market j.

   a. Assume that $2c_I \leq \Delta$ and that $\gamma = 0$. Show that the equilibrium cumulative depth at price A_k is:

   $$Y^*_{I1}(0) = \overline{X}(1 - \frac{2c_I}{\Delta}). \qquad (7.18)$$

b. Now suppose that $\frac{4c_E}{\Delta+2c_I} < \gamma$ and that the other parameters are such that $Y_{I1}^*(\gamma) > 0, Y_{E1}^*(\gamma) > 0$, but $Y_{I1}^*(\gamma) + Y_{E1}^*(\gamma) < \bar{X}$. Compute $Y_{I1}^*(\gamma)$ and $Y_{I1}^*(\gamma)$ as a function of γ. Deduce further from the result that the conditions $Y_{I1}^*(\gamma) > 0$ and $Y_{E1}^*(\gamma) > 0$ are satisfied if and only if $\frac{4c_I}{\Delta(2-\gamma)+2c_E} < 1$. Moreover deduce that the condition $Y_{I1}^*(\gamma) + Y_{E1}^*(\gamma) < \bar{X}$ is satisfied if $4(\gamma c_I + (2-\gamma)c_E) > (2-\gamma)\gamma\Delta$.

c. Deduce from question **b** that the two markets can coexist even if their order submission costs differ and $\gamma = 1$.

d. Why does the cumulative depth at price A_1 in one market decrease with the order submission cost in this market but increase with the cost in the competing market?

e. Consider the case $\gamma = 1$ and suppose that $4(c_I + c_E) < \Delta$ and $4c_I < \Delta$. Compute $Y_{I1}^*(1)$ and $Y_{E1}^*(1)$.

f. Under the assumptions in question (e), what is the number of shares offered at price $A_k > A_1$? Is the result different when $\gamma = 0$?

8

Market Transparency

Learning Objectives:

- What market transparency is
- Its different dimensions
- How it differs across markets
- How it affects liquidity and price discovery
- The implications for regulation

8.1 Introduction

Securities markets are often taken to be the archetype of transparency, whereby all participants are perfectly informed of the terms of past trades and those at which they could trade at every point in time. In practice, of course, this is rarely the case. Consider a retail investor trying to buy a share of IBM. He could check the latest prices available on the internet, but these are delayed, so that he would still be uncertain about the exact current price. For more accurate information, he could subscribe to a real-time data feed such as Bloomberg or Reuters. But these services are costly, and they indicate the price of the most recent past transaction, not the quotes available for the next trade. To get such quotes, our investor must hire a broker or subscribe to Openbook Ultra, a service that displays all posted limit orders for NYSE stocks.

And the market for IBM is a relatively transparent one. Consider instead an investor who wants to buy or sell a U.S. corporate bond. This is an OTC market, for which data on past trades are available only with a delay of 15 minutes (via a system called TRACE) and no information on dealers' quotes is published: the only way to learn about the price you might get in this market is—again—to contact a broker or your bank's brokerage office, who will in turn inquire about the prices quoted by the various dealers.

This lack of transparency pervades securities markets worldwide. And by no means does it affect only retail investors: even mutual fund managers or brokers often do not have a full picture of the trading process, especially if the relevant market is highly fragmented. For instance, a broker or dealer in an OTC market,

Market Liquidity: Theory, Evidence, and Policy. Second Edition. Thierry Foucault, Marco Pagano, and Ailsa Röell, Oxford University Press. © Oxford University Press 2023. DOI: 10.1093/oso/9780197542064.003.0009

such as the foreign exchange market, cannot possibly know all the opportunities that are available simultaneously. Yet it is important for market professionals to have access to as much information as possible about market conditions, since these professionals quote prices on the market and are crucial to the price discovery process.

The foregoing implies that transparency may refer to different kinds of information, such as the quotes on future trades—pre-trade transparency—or past trades and prices—post-trade transparency. These types of information play different roles. Information on quotes enables market participants to limit execution cost and risk, and fosters competition between liquidity providers, as explained in Section 8.2. Meanwhile, post-trade data help market participants hone their estimates of a security's value and of other participants' strategies, as shown in Section 8.3. Transparency can also extend to the identities of market participants—those involved in past transactions or those currently posting a quote. That is, transparency also encompasses the issue of "anonymity" of trading, an issue raised in Section 8.4.

Transparency is one of the most hotly debated issues in securities market regulation. As explained in Section 8.5, different degrees of transparency mean different distributions of rents across market participants and can even shut some of them out of the market altogether. Moreover, fine-tuning transparency is a crucial choice variable for competing exchanges, as it affects their relative attractiveness to traders. Each market must disclose some data to attract trading, but in doing so it may enable competitors to piggy-back on price discovery.

8.2 Pre-Trade Transparency

Different market structures impose different constraints on pre-trade transparency. The least transparent are OTC markets, such as those for small company stocks, municipal bonds, corporate bonds, or bespoke derivatives like credit default swaps (CDSs). Typically, these are thinly traded securities; no firm quotes are publicly posted, and prices are only available from a dealer upon request. Such markets, where trading interest is at best sporadic, do not repay the time and effort that dealers would have to expend to monitor price-relevant information continuously. At the other extreme, there are the electronic LOB markets for blue chips, where any potential trader can purchase real time information on prices and quantities before placing an order. In between, there is a range of intermediate cases. An example is a dealer market with firm quotes publicly displayed on screen for limited trade sizes, where customers can obtain price improvements by contacting individual dealers.

There are three forms of pre-trade transparency: (i) visibility of quotes, (ii) visibility of incoming orders, and (iii) visibility of traders' identities. These three forms of pre-trade transparency have different effects:

(i) Visibility of quotes reduces dealers' rents and so enhances liquidity (Section 8.2.1); moreover, it enables customers to fine-tune their orders to the liquidity supply and so reduce execution risk (Section 8.2.2).

(ii) Visibility of incoming orders helps dealers to detect informed investors, leading to narrower bid-ask spreads and better price discovery (Section 8.2.3).

(iii) Visibility of order submitters' identities has an ambiguous effect on liquidity: it reduces trading costs for investors who are identified as uninformed, but it may impair liquidity for the others (Section 8.4).

8.2.1 Quote Transparency and Competition between Dealers

This section shows how the lack of pre-trade information on quotes can lessen competition among dealers and thus reduce market liquidity. To see this, consider again the model developed in Chapter 3. There we assumed that dealers' quotes are freely and perfectly observable, so customers costlessly compare quotes and choose the best price. Dealers are accordingly driven to offer zero-profit quotes, and liquidity is maximal. For instance, if there is no asymmetric information, risk aversion, or order-processing cost, the competitive bid and ask quotes are both equal to the expected value of the security, and the spread is zero.

Now suppose instead that dealers' quotes are not visible and clients must contact dealers sequentially to get quotes. On receiving a quote, the investor can either accept it and trade or reject it and contact another dealer. Getting a new quote is costly: investors pay a search cost c for each request of a quote. Each client can be a buyer or a seller with equal probabilities. Buyers are willing to pay up to $\mu + \tau$ (where μ is the expected value of the security) to buy the security, while sellers want to receive at least $\mu - \tau$ for it. Dealers value the security at μ. These differences in valuation might reflect, for instance, different hedging needs (an investor with a long position in a bond, say, is willing to buy a CDS at a markup to its fair value). These differences generate a motivation for trading.

In this setup, the presence of a search cost, however small, enables dealers to charge monopoly prices in equilibrium, that is, bid and ask quotes that are respectively equal to buyers' and sellers' reservation values. To see that this is an equilibrium, suppose that dealers quote these prices. Consider a buyer who is matched with one dealer. The dealer offers to sell at $\mu + \tau$. Since the investor expects other dealers to quote the same price, he has no incentive to use resources to shop around. Now consider the dealers. The dealer that the investor contacted has no incentive to offer a better price than $\mu + \tau$, since he expects the investor to accept it. Nor do other dealers have any reason to quote a better price: they cannot advertise their quotes, because the market is opaque. Replicating this argument symmetrically on the bid side, the bid price will be $\mu - \tau$, so the bid-ask spread is 2τ instead of zero.

Interestingly, there is no equilibrium except for the monopoly pricing equilibrium. To see this, suppose that this is not so—that is, that there is an equilibrium in which at least one dealer quotes an ask price less than $\mu + \tau$. Denote him as dealer 1 and suppose the investor is matched with this dealer. Dealer 1 can raise his offer by a small amount (up to c) without losing this customer since the client cannot get a better offer (dealer 1 being the cheapest) and would have to pay the search cost c. As dealer 1 has a profitable deviation, this cannot be an equilibrium. This argument has been standard in the literature on industrial organization since Diamond (1971), and extends beyond our specific assumptions regarding the shape of customers' demand and supply curves.

Thus pre-trade opaqueness is conducive to market power for dealers, and hence to less liquidity. Dispersion in dealers' prices could be a symptom of such market power: if investors have different private value estimates (that is, different τ), the above model suggests that the prices they receive will be highly dispersed, as dealers' market power enables them to price discriminate (assuming that they know investors' private valuations). Moreover, different types of investors have different search costs: sophisticated ones such as hedge funds or mutual fund managers have smaller search costs than retail investors thanks to their continuous market presence. One therefore expects sophisticated investors to get better prices, which should result in a less-dispersed distribution of the prices they get. For instance, in the previous model, if there are investors for whom $c = 0$, they all receive a price of μ, regardless of their private valuations.

Evidence from the municipal bond market (SEC 2004; Harris and Piwowar 2006; Green, Hollifield, and Schuerhoff 2007) is consistent with these implications. The trading costs for municipal bonds are substantially higher than for equities, and particularly high for retail-sized rather than institutional trades. This is presumably because retail investors are less sophisticated. Furthermore, the SEC report (2004) shows that prices for retail transactions (below \$10,000) are dispersed: intraday price differences exceeding 3% across dealers are quite common (over 9% of transactions), even though intraday fluctuations in the fundamental value of municipal bonds are minimal. By contrast, there is less price dispersion for large, institutional transactions: for trades of size around \$1 million, a difference exceeding 1% is rare (0.4% of transactions) in the sample. In 2004, the National Association of Securities Dealers (NASD) sanctioned major dealers that had failed to meet their obligation to buy and sell at fair prices, after finding major discrepancies in pricing: one bond was sold on behalf of a customer for less than half the price that it traded for later in the day; another client received seventy cents on the dollar for a bundle of bonds with a fair value of 97 cents.

8.2.2 Quote Transparency and Execution Risk

Investors do not always observe all the limit orders posted in the market in real time. This is problematic, since there is considerable time variation in the liquidity available in LOBs. This situation creates uncertainty for investors about the prices they may get: they may end up trading at the wrong time (when price impacts are large) or the wrong amount (too much when the LOB is thin). In other words, if the market is opaque, it will be harder for investors to adjust to market conditions, so that on average they will gain less from trading.

A simple example can illustrate these points. Assume that quotes are given by the following schedule, as in Chapter 4:

$$p(q) = \mu + \lambda q, \tag{8.1}$$

where $p(q)$ is the price obtained by a customer who places an order of size q. Unlike the previous chapters, now suppose that the price impact parameter, λ, is random. For instance, it could be high ($\lambda = \lambda^H$) or low ($\lambda = \lambda^L$) with equal probability. We denote the expected value of λ by $E(\lambda)$.

As in the previous section, consider again a buyer who values the security at $\mu + \tau$ and wishes to place a market order. If the market is opaque, when the investor chooses the size q of this order, he does not know the realization of λ, though he correctly anticipates that his order will affect the market price according to price impact function (8.1) and accordingly sets his order size to maximize:

$$\max_q E\left[(\mu + \tau)q - pq\right] = \tau q - E(\lambda)q^2.$$

The first order condition of this problem yields the optimal order size, q^O, when the market is opaque:

$$q^O = \frac{\tau}{2E(\lambda)}. \tag{8.2}$$

Thus, the investor optimally trades more when the wedge τ between his valuation of the security and that of liquidity suppliers increases, and less if he expects his price impact to be greater.

In contrast, in a transparent market where the investor knows his price impact, λ, he sets his order size, q^T, to maximize:

$$\max_q \tau q - \lambda q^2.$$

The first order condition to this problem yields the optimal order size:

$$q^T(\lambda) = \frac{\tau}{2\lambda}. \qquad (8.3)$$

Hence, when the market is transparent, the investor fine-tunes his strategy to the exact amount of liquidity present in the market, λ. Thus, in contrast to q^O, his order size, $q^T(\lambda)$, depends on the realized value of λ and therefore is itself random. By Jensen's inequality,[1]

$$E\left(\frac{1}{\lambda}\right) > \frac{1}{E(\lambda)}. \qquad (8.4)$$

Thus, comparing equations (8.2) and (8.3), the average optimal order size is greater in the transparent than in the opaque market:

$$E(q^T(\lambda)) > q^O.$$

The intuitive reason is as follows. The investor trades more in the transparent market when the price impact of his own trade is small (when $\lambda = \lambda^L$) and less when the price impact is large (when $\lambda = \lambda^H$). The increase in size in the first case more than offsets the restraint in the second. Hence, on average he ends up trading more.

Interestingly, the investor's expected gain from the trade is also greater in the transparent market. To see this, observe that on average his profit in the transparent market is:

$$E(\tau q^T - \lambda (q^T)^2) = \frac{\tau^2}{4} E\left(\frac{1}{\lambda}\right),$$

whereas in the opaque market, it is:

$$\tau q^O - E(\lambda)(q^O)^2 = \frac{\tau^2}{4} \frac{1}{E(\lambda)}.$$

---

[1] This inequality states that, for any random variable x, $E[f(x)] > f[E(x)]$ if $f(\cdot)$ is a convex function. Here we apply this principle to the function $1/x$, which is convex.

Again using inequality (8.4), we see that the investor fares better in the transparent market—once again, transparency enables him to make better trading decisions.

These findings carry three implications. First, pre-trade transparency is valuable, so people are willing to pay for real-time quote information or to employ intermediaries who have access to it. Second, pre-trade transparency increases the volume of trade, that is, it encourages participation in the market. Third, if there is some persistence in the illiquidity parameter λ over time, investors have an incentive to make their trades conditional on past measures of market liquidity, since these are informative about current liquidity—a point formalized by Hong and Rady (2002).

8.2.3 Order Flow Transparency

In some markets—foreign exchange or bond markets, to name two—different orders get filled almost simultaneously by different liquidity providers, who may know very little about trades made simultaneously by their competitors. In this situation, the order flow is not transparent. What effects does this have?

To address this issue, we compare two market structures, using a slightly modified version of the framework developed in Chapter 3: (i) a completely opaque dealer market in which each dealer observes only his own order flow and (ii) a transparent market where liquidity providers see all the orders submitted before setting their prices. The latter situation captures the wealth of information available to speculators on the floor of an open-outcry auction market (such as the London Metal Exchange).

As in Chapter 3, we consider the market for a risky security with payoff v that can be high (v^H) or low (v^L) with equal probability, so that the expected payoff is $\mu = (v^H + v^L)/2$. Quotes are set by risk-neutral dealers and are valid for one share. Dealers can be contacted either by informed or uninformed investors. Specifically, with probability π two risk-neutral informed traders are present on the market: they both place a market order to buy one share if they know $v = v^H$ or to sell if $v = v^L$. With probability $1 - \pi$, there are two liquidity traders, one buyer and one seller. These assumptions represent the simplest possible way to capture the idea that informed trading tends to generate positively correlated orders, while uninformed trading does not (the case in which noise trades are not perfectly negatively correlated yields similar conclusions—see exercise 1). Figure 8.1 describes the order arrival process.

Traders randomly contact one of the dealers quoting the best price and can trade with only one dealer at a time. The crucial difference from the model considered in Chapter 3 is that now two trades (not one) may happen simultaneously

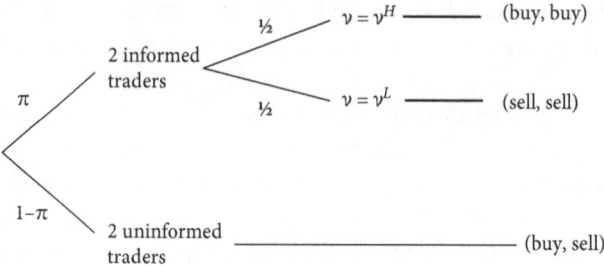

Figure 8.1 Order arrival process in the order flow transparency.

in the market. As noted, in the opaque market dealers only observe the order that comes to them, while in the transparent market they see all orders, whether they receive them or not.

At the time he accepts an order in an opaque market, a dealer does not know the direction of the other order that has come to the market. Hence, his ask price, a^O (where the superscript O stands for "opaque") is the expected value of the security, conditional only on the fact that he has received a buy order. As π is the probability that the order comes from an informed trader, equation (3.10) in Chapter 3 yields the dealer's ask price:

$$a^O = \mu + \pi(v^H - \mu). \tag{8.5}$$

The bid price symmetrically is:

$$b^O = \mu - \pi(\mu - v^L), \tag{8.6}$$

so that the bid-ask spread is:

$$s^O = \pi(v^H - v^L). \tag{8.7}$$

In the transparent market, dealers have more information when they set their quotes, because they observe the orders that go to their competitors as well. Hence, their quote is the estimate of the security's value, *given all the orders submitted*. Under our assumptions, this information reveals whether the traders are informed and tells the direction of their signal. For instance, if two buy orders are submitted, then dealers infer that informed traders know that $v = v^H$ and therefore quote an ask price equal to v^H. The dealers' valuation and price for each possible configuration is given below, where the superscript T stands for "transparent":

(i) two buy orders: $E(v\,|B,B) = v^H$, so that $a^T = v^H$,

(ii) one buy and one sell order: $E(v\,|B,S) = \mu$, so that $a^T = b^T = \mu$,

(iii) two sell orders: $E(v\,|S,S) = v^L$, so that $b^T = v^L$,

The average price paid or received by liquidity traders is μ, which means that the bid-ask spread for them is zero. In this example, transparency eliminates their trading cost. Hence, again in this case, opaqueness increases the trading costs for liquidity traders. The reason is that with transparency dealers detect informed traders more easily, so they can charge a lower spread to the uninformed. This inverse relationship between transparency and uninformed investors' trading costs holds more generally, as Pagano and Röell (1996) show. In the transparent market, by contrast, informed investors obtain no profit since they must always pay the maximum bid-ask spread, $v^H - v^L$. As a result, the average spread in the transparent market is $\pi(v^H - v^L)$, as in the opaque market. In the transparent market, the allocation of trading costs differs between uninformed and informed investors as transparency—unlike opacity—allows dealers to discriminate between the two groups.

In this model, the lower trading costs for liquidity traders mirror a decrease in trading profits for the informed trader, since trading is a zero-sum game and dealers make zero expected profits. Thus a change in market transparency can redistribute gains between different types of participants. This explains why transparency is such a controversial issue.

Order flow transparency also has implications for price discovery. To see this, let us use the average squared pricing error as an inverse measure of price discovery. Let p^O denote the price paid to or by a dealer in the opaque market. This will be a^O if a dealer executes a buy market order and b^O if he executes a sell market order. In the opaque market, the average squared pricing error is:

$$E\left[(p^O - v)^2\right] = \frac{\pi}{2}(a^O - v^H)^2 + \frac{\pi}{2}(b^O - v^L)^2$$
$$+ \frac{1-\pi}{2}\left[\frac{1}{2}(a^O - v^H)^2 + \frac{1}{2}(b^O - v^H)^2\right]$$
$$+ \frac{1-\pi}{2}\left[\frac{1}{2}(a^O - v^L)^2 + \frac{1}{2}(b^O - v^L)^2\right].$$

The first two terms correspond to the cases in which the dealer trades with an informed investor (receiving good news in the first case and bad news in the second). The third term corresponds to the case in which the dealer receives an order from an uninformed investor and the true value of the security is high. The last term corresponds to the symmetric situation of an order from an uninformed investor when the true value is low. Substituting out for the ask price a^O from (8.5) and the bid price b^O from (8.6), this expression simplifies to:

$$E[(p^O - v)^2] = (1 - \pi^2)(v^H - \mu)^2,$$

which is decreasing in π: as the frequency of informed trading increases, the price discovery process improves.

In the case of the transparent market, the transaction price p^T is either equal to the true value if there are informed investors (with probability π), or equal to μ if there are uninformed traders (with probability $1 - \pi$). Hence, the average squared pricing error is:

$$E[(p^T - v)^2] = (1 - \pi)\left[\frac{1}{2}(v^H - \mu)^2 + \frac{1}{2}(v^L - \mu)^2\right] = (1 - \pi)(v^H - \mu)^2.$$

This pricing error is clearly smaller than the corresponding expression in the opaque market, the difference between the squared pricing errors being:

$$E[(p^O - v)^2] - E[(p^T - v)^2] = \pi(1 - \pi)(v^H - \mu)^2 > 0.$$

Thus, transparency also improves price discovery because it helps market participants to learn about the presence of informed traders.

8.3 Post-Trade Transparency

Another issue regarding transparency is the timeliness of disclosure of past trades. In some markets, information is released in real time to all market participants (for a fee); in others, past trades are disclosed with a significant delay, if ever. The speed of publication of information on past trades is one of the most controversial issues in the organization of securities markets. Dealers often oppose prompt disclosure on the ground that it makes it more difficult for them to manage their inventory (and therefore raises inventory holding costs). In this section, we use a variant of the previous section's model to show how the lack of post-trade transparency may enable dealers to capture rents at the expense of other traders. That is, we have another instance of transparency redistributing profits and costs.

Assume that the orders are filled in sequence over two periods, $t = 1$ and $t = 2$, as in Figure 8.2. With probability π, two successive identical orders are placed by informed investors and executed at their arrival times, $t = 1$ and $t = 2$. With probability $1 - \pi$, two orders of opposite signs are placed by uninformed traders in random sequence.

Consider first a market with post-trade transparency: dealers have to report their trades as they take place, and the exchange publishes the information

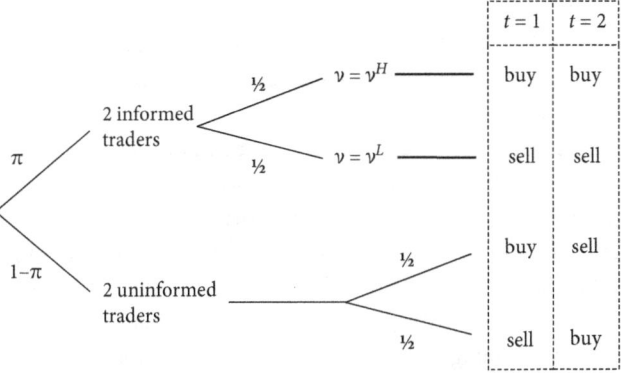

Figure 8.2 Order arrival process in the post-trade transparency model.

immediately. In this case, the quotes posted by dealers at time $t = 1$ are the same as those prevailing in the opaque market analyzed in the previous section, since in the first period dealers have no information on forthcoming orders. Hence, in the first period, the bid-ask spread is:

$$s_1^T = \pi(v^H - v^L). \tag{8.8}$$

In contrast, at time $t = 2$, the dealer who receives the second order is in the same position as in the transparent market analyzed before: he and all his peers observe his new order, and they have all learned about the previous trade. Consider first the case in which the first-period order was a buy. If another buy order arrives at time $t = 2$, dealers infer that the investor is informed and $v = v^H$. Hence, their ask price is equal to v^H. If instead, a sell order arrives, they infer that the investor is uninformed, so $v = \mu$ and their bid price is μ. Hence, following a buy order in the first period, the bid-ask spread in the second period is $v^H - \mu = (v^H - v^L)/2$. If the first-period order is a sell, the analysis is symmetric. Thus, the bid-ask spread posted in the second period is:

$$s_2^T = \frac{1}{2}(v^H - v^L).$$

To summarize, with post-trade transparency, the spread will vary over time, and trading costs for uninformed and informed investors will differ. For instance, liquidity traders pay a spread of s_1^T in the first period, and zero in the second. Summed over the two periods, the average trading cost of uninformed investors in the post-trade transparent market is:

$$TC^T = \frac{1}{2} \times s_1^T + \frac{1}{2} \times 0 = \frac{\pi}{2}(v^H - v^L). \tag{8.9}$$

This shows that post-trade transparency is an imperfect substitute for pre-trade transparency: on average, over the two periods, the trading cost for uninformed traders is intermediate between what they would pay with pre-trade transparency and pre-trade opacity.

Let us now compare the outcome with and without post-trade transparency. Where it is absent, first-period transactions are not disclosed before second-period trading. In this case, in the second period the dealer who has already received an order in the first period has an informational advantage: if it was a buy order, he knows that the value of the security is high with a greater probability than other dealers; with a sell order, he knows that it is low. In general, he will exploit this advantage by adjusting his quotes to capture profitable trading opportunities that his peers are not aware of.

To see this as simply as possible, assume that in the second period dealers set their quotes sequentially and that the dealer who received the first-period order goes last.[2] This dealer can always undercut any competitor's quote that could yield a positive expected profit and refrain from undercutting those that are loss-making. This is an extreme instance of the well-known "winner's curse" problem in auction theory: if you win the trade, it can only be because better informed bidders know that the price you are paying is already too high! In response to this problem, the best quotes that competing dealers can offer without losing money are the highest and lowest possible values that the informed dealer may place on the security, i.e., $a = v^H$ and $b = v^L$.

Now consider the best response of the dealer who executed the order arriving at date $t = 1$. Assume first that it was a sell order. If another sell order comes in, the dealer knows that the security has a low value so that his bid price is v^L. like that of the other dealers. In this case, if he executes, he makes no profit. But if a buy order comes in next, he knows that there is no informed trading and so he estimates the security to be worth μ. He will then slightly undercut the ask price of v^H set by his competitors. Thus, he will get to execute the buy order (as he offers the best price) and will make a profit almost equal to $v^H - \mu$. Therefore, the only scenario in which a dealer makes money in the second period is a sequence of two orders in opposite directions. This only happens with probability $1 - \pi$, since it occurs if and only if the two orders are placed by liquidity traders. That

---

[2] This dealer behaves as a "Stackelberg follower." Though unrealistic, this assumption ensures the existence of a pure-strategy equilibrium in the price-setting game between asymmetrically informed dealers. If instead dealers were assumed to set their quotes simultaneously, the equilibrium is necessarily a mixed-strategy one. This has been shown for first-price common value auctions with differentially informed bidders, to which our game is equivalent (see Engelbrecht-Wiggans, Milgrom, and Weber 1983). For a treatment of the problem in our setting, see Röell (1988). See exercise 3 as well.

is, the dealer who manages to capture the first-period trade earns an expected informational rent in the second period of $(1-\pi)(v^H - \mu)$.

This expected second-period gain comes at the expense of investors, since other dealers are careful to set their quotes so as to make zero profits. Hence, the second-period trading costs are as high as they can possibly be in our setup: the second-period spread is always:

$$s_2^O = v^H - v^L.$$

This result shows that lack of post-trade transparency, which increases informational asymmetries among dealers, is a source of informational rents and thereby impairs market liquidity.

At the same time, however, the prospect of such informational rents can sharpen first-period competition between dealers to capture order flow and the attendant information.[3] In our setting, first-period quotes will be driven down to levels such that the total expected profit of each dealer over both periods is nil. The implied first-period ask price is obtained by subtracting the second-period informational rent $(1-\pi)(v^H - \mu)$ from expression (8.5):

$$a_1^O = \mu + \pi(v^H - \mu) - (1 - \pi)(v^H - \mu) = \mu + (2\pi - 1)(v^H - \mu). \qquad (8.10)$$

The bid price is symmetric, so that the first-period spread is:

$$s_1^O = (2\pi - 1)(v^H - v^L), \qquad (8.11)$$

which is clearly smaller than the second-period spread computed above: $s_1^O < s_2^O$. Therefore, in a market with post-trade opacity, the time profile of the bid-ask spread is rising: initially dealers accept low spreads and incur losses, which they subsequently recoup by higher spreads. This pattern for the bid-ask spread has been found experimentally by Bloomfield and O'Hara (1999, 2000).[4] Interestingly, dealers often argue that post-trade opacity enables them to offer better quotes to their clients. This is in fact the case in the first period of the model, but the practice is really just a way to prepare the ground for much less competitive quotes in subsequent periods.

Note that if π is low enough $\left(\text{less than } \frac{1}{2}\right)$, the model predicts that with post-trade opacity, the first-period spread can be negative! This may seem

---

[3] In this respect, dealers have been compared to the bookmaker who declared that he was happy to lose money to a particularly successful bettor: "He is my most valuable client. I always shorten the odds when he bets and he saves me a fortune" (*Financial Times*, December 6, 1987).

[4] Most experimental work regarding pre-trade transparency has found that markets with greater pre-trade transparency feature lower bid-ask spreads. See for instance Flood et al. 1999.

paradoxical, although such "crossed quotes" (or "locked quotes") do sometimes arise briefly in some markets. However, it is a situation that cannot last, since it is a clear opportunity for arbitrage profit—you can buy a security and resell it at the same time for a higher price! If arbitrage prevents a negative bid-ask spread, then dealers will retain strictly positive expected profits over the two periods, which could explain why they generally oppose post-trade transparency. And their hostility to transparency will be further reinforced if first-period competition is too weak to fully dissipate their overall profit.

Who gains and who loses from post-trade opacity? If price competition among dealers in the first period drives their overall expected profits to zero, all we need to do to find out is compute the total trading costs of the liquidity traders in the opaque market. We get:

$$TC^O = \frac{1}{2}s_1^O + \frac{1}{2}s_2^O = \pi(v^H - v^L), \qquad (8.12)$$

which is double the trading cost under post-trade transparency (see equation (8.9)). Thus, post-trade opacity ultimately raises informed traders' expected profits at the expense of liquidity traders.[5] The reason is that in the opaque market the problem of adverse selection persists into the second period, whereas in the transparent market it is eliminated by last-trade publication at the end of the first period. More precisely, in the opaque market adverse selection persists because a dealer gleans from the first-period order flow information that enables him to gain a competitive edge, so as to both outbid other dealers and exploit this edge at the expense of liquidity traders.

This model highlights the fact that dealers may wish to acquire order flow information, either with smaller spreads or through direct monetary inducements such as payment for order flow (i.e., compensation offered to brokers by a dealer in return for channeling orders to him). In the model, these rebates dissipate the informational rents created by opaqueness. In reality, dealers may be able to set them so as to keep some rents. Thus, both dealers and informed traders could benefit from post-trade opacity at the expense of noise traders. This again illustrates how changes in transparency redistribute trading profits and costs among market participants.

As for price discovery, it can be shown that it is less efficient in the opaque market (see exercise 2). Intuitively, in the opaque market, quotes underadjust relative to the information contained in the order flow. In the first period, dealers

---

[5] At first glance, this is surprising since competition among dealers in the first period dissipates their rents. Hence one would expect uninformed investors to entirely recoup their second period losses with lower trading costs in the first period. But this is not the case, because informed investors capture part of the benefits of the lower spread in the first period.

are willing to execute a buy order at a price below their current value estimate, conditional on receiving a buy order. But in the second period, dealers set quotes that are independent of the first-period order and that are therefore totally uninformative, generating a discrepancy between transaction prices and fair value. In contrast, in the transparent market, second-period quotes are perfectly informative.

8.4 Revealing Trading Motives

Transparency need not be limited to prices and quantities but may extend to the identity of potential counterparties. This information can be price relevant insofar as it offers insight into the reasons why people want to trade, and specifically whether they have superior information about the value of the security. For example, consider a broker who receives a large sell order from a mutual fund facing substantial customer redemptions. He may get a better price for his client if he can reassure market makers that, given its source, the order is most unlikely to be driven by superior information.

Market designs differ in the scope for conveying such detailed information about trading motives. For example, floor markets allow participants to see one another and interpret subtle cues like impatience and nervousness, as well as to voluntarily share information about their clients. Similarly, dealer markets enable brokers to interact with dealers by phone and explain their clients' reason for trading. This exchange of pre-trade information can be seen as a way of increasing pre-trade transparency for the parties involved.[6] Whether it improves the overall transparency of the market depends on how many people are included in the exchange of information. Knowing their motivations enables liquidity suppliers to offer different prices to different traders, opening up the possibility of price discrimination.

Transmission of information about trading motives—and the attendant price discrimination—is less easy in electronic LOB exchanges, where liquidity providers must post quotes without observing the identities of the brokers who are placing market orders. Of course, there are still ways of getting around the problem. If the exchange reveals the codes of the limit order submitters, which not all exchanges do, then a broker could reveal his identity by placing a marketable limit order at the best existing quotes. But the broker's identity provides at best imperfect guidance about the motives for the order.

---

[6] In principle, the exchange of information need not be only from traders to liquidity suppliers, as is assumed in this section. For instance, market makers may also reveal their identities to traders who place orders with them, or they may not—an issue touched on in the next section.

Alternatively, the broker may call up counterparties to arrange a transaction before clearing it in the main market—but this takes time and effort.

In some cases, the need to disclose the trading motives and the identities of the liquidity demanders is so great that non-anonymous trading mechanisms emerge, not necessarily at the exchange authorities' initiative. For instance, an investor could publicly announce a trade and its planned execution date some days in advance, a practice is called "sunshine trading." To this purpose, in 1997, the Swiss stock exchange (SIX Swiss Exchange) created a "second trading line," where firms can buy their own shares back openly on a separate market segment, to avoid exacerbating adverse selection in the main market—firms being generally considered well informed about their own prospects (Chung, Išakov, and Pérignon 2007).

How does the exchange of information about trading motives affect liquidity? To answer, we resort once more to the one-period model presented in Chapter 3, where π and $1-\pi$ are the probabilities of an order coming from an informed and a liquidity trader, respectively. But we now assume that before trading, a fraction κ_U of the uninformed traders is recognized as such, perhaps because they manage to reveal their lack of information via a sunshine trading announcement.[7] Symmetrically, a fraction κ_I of the informed traders is also found out, possibly because they have developed a reputation of trading in advance of news. An important assumption, for the moment, is that a trader's identity, if revealed, is observed by all market makers. This assumption will later be relaxed. The order arrival process is summarized in Figure 8.3.

Now, a trader who places a buy order will face a different ask price, depending on whether he is recognized or not; if he is recognized, he will pay a different

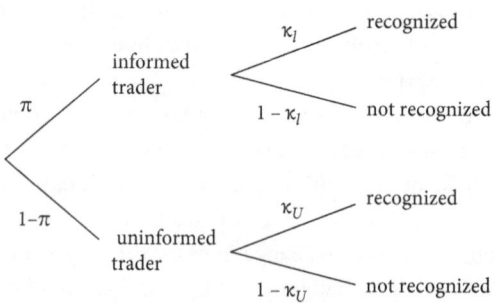

Figure 8.3 Order arrival and recognition of trading motives.

---

[7] For models that study how investors can signal their trading motives, see Seppi (1990) or Admati and Pfleiderer (1991) for instance.

price depending on his type. The easiest cases are those in which traders' motives are recognized. If the buyer is known to be informed, the market makers' best value estimate is v_H, while if he is known to be uninformed, it remains at its unconditional value μ. Now consider the case in which the trader's type is unknown. We need to compute the probability that this trader is informed, conditional on not having been identified. This probability is:

$$\pi' = \frac{\pi(1-\kappa_I)}{\pi(1-\kappa_I)+(1-\pi)(1-\kappa_U)},$$

that is, the fraction of informed traders within the population of unidentified traders. As this probability plays the same role as π in the model of Chapter 3, we deduce that the ask and bid prices posted for an order of unknown origin are:

$$a = \mu + \frac{\pi(1-\kappa_I)}{\pi(1-\kappa_I)+(1-\pi)(1-\kappa_U)}(v^H - \mu), \tag{8.13}$$

$$b = \mu - \frac{\pi(1-\kappa_I)}{\pi(1-\kappa_I)+(1-\pi)(1-\kappa_U)}(v^H - \mu).$$

As expected, the revelation of information on trading motives results in price discrimination. Recognized uninformed traders trade at a zero spread, since they can buy or sell the security at price μ, while informed traders identified as such trade at the fair price and therefore see their trading profits eliminated. Last, all unrecognized traders, regardless of type, trade at the pooled, partially informative prices given in equations (8.13).

The model is open to different interpretations for different values of κ_I and κ_U. The case of $\kappa_U > 0$ and $\kappa_I = 0$ can be interpreted as the coexistence of two populations of uninformed traders: some are identified as such and obtain a zero spread, because they can access the upstairs market or practice sunshine trading; others are pooled with informed traders. Clearly, uninformed traders in the former group benefit from being recognized, while the others are disadvantaged because they face a larger bid-ask spread than they would under anonymous trading. The bid-ask spread faced by unidentified traders is:

$$s = \frac{\pi}{\pi + (1-\pi)(1-\kappa_U)}(v^H - v^L),$$

which increases in κ_U and is therefore minimal for $\kappa_U = 0$. The reason is that the pool of unidentified traders now has a smaller proportion of uninformed traders than in an anonymous market. However, the average uninformed trader is better off, since only a proportion $1-\kappa_U$ pay this spread s, and the average spread $(1-\kappa_U)s$ decreases with κ_U. Intuitively, since there are fewer uninformed traders in the main market, the expected profits of the informed traders will decrease. So reducing anonymity increases the posted bid-ask spread, even though it reduces average trading costs for uninformed traders.

Consider now the opposite case in which some informed traders—but no uninformed traders—can be recognized, that is $\kappa_U = 0$ but $\kappa_I > 0$. This can be thought of as a situation in which regulation obliges some potentially informed traders to disclose their intentions. For example, a potential takeover raider may be forced to disclose that the fraction of the target company's equity (his "toehold") has breached some regulatory threshold (often 5% of the company's voting equity): if subsequent large buy orders are attributed by market participants to such an investor, they should have a larger price impact.

In this case, the bid-ask spread for unidentified traders is:

$$ s' = \frac{\pi(1-\kappa_I)}{\pi(1-\kappa_I)+(1-\pi)}(v^H - v^L), $$

which is decreasing in κ_I: identifying informed traders improves market liquidity.

This analysis suggests that disclosing trading motives benefits uninformed traders, at least on average, but the conclusion rests on a crucial assumption: namely, that information on trading motives is disclosed to *all* market participants. If it were revealed only to a subset of price setters, the conclusion might be different. To see this, in the context of the model with $\kappa_U > 0$ and $\kappa_I = 0$, suppose that the customer's type is observed only by the dealer he contacts, possibly owing to a long-standing relationship that confers credibility on the information revealed by the customer—a situation that cannot be replicated with other dealers.

This situation gives the dealer market power, as he can appropriate some or all of the informational rent involved in the transaction. To see this, suppose that a buyer is identified by his dealer as uninformed. The best price that this buyer can then expect from the dealer is μ, which corresponds to zero spread and zero profit for the dealer. At the opposite extreme, the worst possible price that he will accept from the dealer is his outside option $\mu + s/2$, the ask price that he would get in the main market. In this situation of bilateral monopoly, the relative bargaining power of the buyer and the dealer determines which price within the interval $[\mu, \mu + s/2]$ the traders actually settle upon. If the client has some bargaining power, he negotiates a discount from $\mu + s/2$, his main market price. Such price improvements were in fact quite common in dealer markets, such as Nasdaq and the LSE (Reiss and Werner 2004).

In the extreme case in which the dealer has all the bargaining power, the client gets the same price as unrecognized traders who buy on the main market, that is $\mu + s/2$. As a result, all traders will be strictly worse off than under completely anonymous trading, since s is smallest when $\kappa_U = 0$. In fact, it is easy to verify that this remains true whenever the dealer's bargaining power is great enough that the discount is low. This shows that revealing trading motives may not lower the trading costs of uninformed traders (even those whose motives are revealed) if the information remains confidential (disclosed to just one dealer).

Channeling the orders of uninformed clients to specific dealers or markets is known as cream-skimming, the practice for which brokers often obtain a payment for order flow. If brokers also have a market-making capability (i.e., they are broker-dealers), they may skim off the uninformed orders for in-house execution, a practice known as internalization, modelled by Röell (1990) and Battalioc and Holden (2001).

There is evidence that cream skimming does take place: Easley, Kiefer, O'Hara, and Paperman (1996b) find that orders diverted from the NYSE are less informative than those that remain on the NYSE. Grammig and Theissen (2012) obtain the same result for orders internalized on Deutsche Börse's Xetra trading system. They also find that investors whose orders are internalized do not capture the entire benefit of lower adverse selection costs. Since skimming deprives the main market of a proportion κ_U of the uninformed order flow, it should reduce market liquidity according to this model. However, the evidence is mixed (Battalio 1997; and Battalio, Greene, and Jennings 1998).

We deal with internalization, payment for order flow, and cream-skimming when discussing market fragmentation in Chapter 7. Questions about these practices resurface here, because opacity and fragmentation are intertwined. For instance, order flow transparency (discussed in Section 8.2.3) is harder to achieve when traders can split market orders among multiple trading platforms, unless there are extremely efficient linkages among them.

8.5 Why Are Markets So Opaque?

The previous sections lead to the conclusion that transparency about quotes, orders, and traders' identities generally enhances market liquidity, at least as far as uninformed traders are concerned. The natural question, then, is why we see so little of it: why are so many real-world securities markets so opaque along one or more of the dimensions we have analyzed. A simple explanation may be that these market structures are not designed to benefit uninformed traders but market-making intermediaries or informed traders (see Section 8.5.1). Indeed there is good reason to think that these market professionals have far greater influence in the design of trading rules than uninformed and occasional traders.

Even if market making is competitive, so that it yields no rents to intermediaries, the incentive to offer opacity to large trades still exists, even though this may decrease the liquidity available to retail traders. This issue is examined in Section 8.5.2.

But the opacity of securities markets may also reflect concerns about economic efficiency, at least in some cases. For instance, transparency may be problematic—it may even reduce liquidity—if it exposes limit-order placers to a high risk of being picked off by more informed traders. Moreover, if markets are opaque, market makers may find it more difficult to sustain collusive agreements because it will be harder to detect and punish violations of the cartel's rules. In this sense, opacity may foster competition between market makers. Section 8.5.3 discusses these brighter sides of market opacity.

8.5.1   Rent Extraction and Lobbying

As Section 8.2.1 shows, market makers can extract rents in a market with little pre-trade transparency on quotes, and informed traders can do so in one with little post-trade transparency. In some cases these two categories actually coincide: intermediaries may have superior information (partly due to their advance knowledge of the order flow), and so they may resist making their quotes visible, in part to retain informational rents.[8]

This is consistent with the empirical evidence that transaction costs fall when markets become more transparent. For example, the bid-ask spread on the NYSE declined when the exchange started releasing information about the LOB of its listed stocks (Boehmer, Saar, and Yu 2005); similarly, investors' trading costs in the corporate bond market dropped substantially after the TRACE trade reporting system was implemented in 2002 (Bessembinder and Maxwell 2008). And even in such inherently opaque markets as real estate or travel services, the introduction of web-based search engines has reduced the profits of incumbent firms.

Trading platforms themselves can also extract rents from opacity by restricting access to data on prices and trades, thus increasing the value of the data they sell, even to the point of provoking complaints from some participants. For instance, the NYSE's decision to charge a fee for real time information on quotes and trades in Archipelago (a trading platform acquired in 2006) stirred up strong opposition from investors. More generally, the pricing of market data has become very controversial, as investors need information about quotes

---

[8] In Bolton, Santos, and Scheinkman (2016), opaque asset markets ("OTC markets") enable informed intermediaries to sustain abnormal profits. Moreover, informed intermediaries cream-skim high quality assets, worsening the quality of the pool of assets that trade on exchanges (transparent markets). This generates a negative externality, which leads to excessive intermediation in equilibrium.

and trades to make optimal routing decisions in fragmented markets.[9] Buy side investors complain that trading platforms charge too high prices for their data, while exchanges respond that they incur costs that they need to cover to disseminate those data. Revenues from sales of market data account for an increasing share of exchange revenues. For instance, revenues from data sales for Nasdaq increased from $413 million in 2014 to $779 million in 2019 (including co-location revenues).

A way in which trading platforms can squeeze even more profits from the data that they generate is by selling "low-latency" (super-fast) access to data feeds, even granting to some traders the opportunity to co-locate their computers in physical proximity to the platform's own computer. Such preferential high-speed access is keenly sought by algorithmic traders, who can make money by beating their competitors even by nanoseconds. This again creates tiered access to market data, and enables high-frequency traders to reap large informational rents at the expense of other market participants, as explained in Chapter 9.

Besides enabling intermediaries to retain rents from market power and informed traders to extract profits from superior information, opacity may allow brokers to cheat their customers by misreporting trade prices, or to simply conceal the fact that they exerted little effort or care to make sure their customer got the best price available on the market at the time of execution. This may occur even where best-execution rules are in place, because enforcing such rules is harder in opaque markets: investors are less likely to discern that they are poorly served by their brokers, and to assemble the evidence necessary to demonstrate dishonesty or negligence.

Therefore, in general market professionals should be expected to favor limiting the transparency of the markets where they operate. And it is no surprise that their interests influence market regulation more than those of other market users. Not only do the professionals have a more regular market presence, but nowadays they largely own, control, and manage stock exchanges and multilateral trading facilities, as a result of the trend towards demutualization (described in Chapter 2).

The resistance of market professionals (the "sell side" of the market) to raising transparency standards in security trading can explain why regulatory reforms with this aim often have disappointing outcomes. This was the case, for instance, for the MiFID 2 directive in 2018, which was explicitly aimed at raising the transparency of security markets in the EU (see Section 7.5.2). A survey of data prices in Europe, carried out by the European Securities and Markets

---

[9] This is an enduring issue: Mulherin, Netter, and Overdhal (1991) provide a fascinating historical account of how the NYSE asserted its property rights over prices set on the NYSE in the nineteenth century.

Authority (ESMA) in 2019, found that the 2018 implementation of MiFID 2 had not resulted in market data being supplied to the market on a "reasonable commercial basis," as the regulation had stipulated. Moreover, a consultation conducted in 2020 by the ESMA found that all market participants shared the view that the reform failed to achieve its objective to create meaningful transparency for non-equity markets. However, interestingly, respondents had split views on whether transparency standards should be raised further to overcome this failure: a handful of sell-side firms and trade associations objected to it, emphasizing the role played by banks and other intermediaries in putting their capital at risk, while a much larger group of respondents, including trading venues and proprietary traders, broadly supported it—consistent with the idea that raising transparency standards tends to hurt liquidity suppliers and benefit liquidity demanders.

8.5.2   Opacity Can Withstand Competition

The previous section may suggest that there is an intrinsic connection between opacity and rent extraction (or collusion) by trading intermediaries. If so, one might expect that competition from new entrants, unaffiliated with incumbents, would spark a race towards transparency. But in fact opaque markets are resilient to competition.

To see why, consider again the model of post-trade transparency presented in Section 8.3. Suppose that dealers are allowed to choose whether to publicize their trades. In this case the only equilibrium is such that none chooses to publicize trades. The reason is that the market maker who does not publicize trades can undercut those who do, because he can use the information gleaned from the first-period trades to make a profit in the second period. To see this, recall that the competitive bid-ask spread at time $t = 1$ in the opaque market (equation (8.11)) is lower than the spread that a transparent market maker could charge (equation (8.8)). Thus, in that model all first-period trading will be captured by opaque market makers. Note that the choice about the degree of opacity can be made not only by individual dealers but also at the level of trading platforms on which they operate. Under this interpretation, what the model predicts is that competing platforms will inevitably opt for opacity in the design of their trading system, and such platforms will capture all trading.

In reality, opaque market makers or platforms will compete aggressively only for large orders: small trades, which are unlikely to be informative, will be of little or no interest, since they can be filled just as well by transparent market makers.

This leads to a two-tier market, where large trades execute opaquely and small ones transparently.

The foregoing implies that market forces alone are unlikely to produce post-trade transparency, at least for large trades. Regulation is required to mandate a minimum level of transparency. For instance, the U.S. corporate bond market was opaque until 2002, when the SEC mandated the TRACE system to disseminate price and trade information, albeit with a lag.

Even mandatory disclosure, however, encounters considerable problems of enforcement. First, there may be regulatory arbitrage: if trading can migrate to venues that do not impose less post-trade transparency, it will. Many observers of the migration of the wholesale markets in European blue-chip equities to SEAQ International in London in the early 1990s argued that a primary determinant was the lack of trade publication there. Europe-wide negotiations on market regulation and transparency typically pitted the looser, more free-wheeling regime of the London wholesale markets against the more centralized, transparent regime prevailing in the home markets. Nowadays, the increasing role of dark pools and of the OTC market in the United States and post-MiFID Europe can be explained using the same logic.

Second, it may be possible to evade post-trade transparency requirements. Franks and Schaefer (1995) point out that trade reporting deadlines can be circumvented by using "protected trades": market makers informally offer a price to a customer for a large deal (with the understanding that they will, in practice, honor the commitment), but the deal is not officially finalized and confirmed until they have had time to unwind the resulting inventory. This delays the trade report—and its publication—beyond the regulators' intention. Moreover, it reduces immediacy and imposes some execution risk on large traders.

8.5.3   The Bright Side of Opacity

Is the self-interest of market professionals the only explanation for the prevalence of opaque trading systems? The fact that even the most transparent marketplaces allow for some opaque forms of order placement suggests otherwise. For instance, most electronic order book systems—otherwise known for their high degree of pre-trade transparency—allow traders to enter hidden limit orders or iceberg orders. In this case, only a small portion of the order is visible to other traders, and the rest gradually becomes visible as the order executes against incoming orders. Of course, other investors will eventually realize when a hidden order is present on the LOB, and adapt their trading strategies accordingly (De Winne and D'Hondt 2004). This takes time, however, and even then the total size of the order remains unknown.

One reason why an investor may want to place such an order is to avoid giving away his private information to the market by placing a visible large order.[10] This motivation would be in line with the idea that opacity benefits informed traders. A trader may also consider placing a hidden order to protect himself against the risk of being picked off by better informed traders, if he is afraid, say, that his information may be (or may become) stale and his order accordingly mispriced. Indeed, placing a buy limit order is tantamount to offering a free put option to other market participants (Copeland and Galai 1983); likewise, a sell limit order is a free call option. Investors who receive new information can exploit such an option by hitting existing limit orders before they can be cancelled (see Chapter 9). Therefore, traders who submit limit orders bear an adverse selection cost similar to that facing market makers: the difference is that with limit orders, the possible losses to informed trading are more limited, as limit orders vanish once hit (and they are typically hit as soon as they go into the money), while dealer quotes remain available for trading until the dealer manages to update them.[11]

Therefore, if uninformed investors could not place hidden orders, they would most likely place market orders, possibly trickling them into the market to minimize price impact. As a result, the LOB would be less deep than with hidden orders, which in practice do provide a considerable amount of liquidity. For example, in an active LOB such as that for the CAC 40 blue-chip French stocks on average, the displayed depth at the best five quotes accounts for less than 55% of the total depth at these prices, that is, more than 45% is provided by hidden orders (De Winne and D'Hondt 2004). Here, then, we have an instance in which imposing a greater degree of transparency (banning hidden orders) would be likely to reduce liquidity, by discouraging the use of limit orders.

A similar argument holds for anonymity, again insofar as it applies to limit-order traders, who provide liquidity, rather than to market-order traders, who consume it. Recall again the analogy between limit orders and options: as the value of an option depends on the volatility of the underlying security, the value of a limit order to the market—and hence the cost to its placer—increases with volatility. Hence in anticipation of increased volatility, traders should be less willing to place limit orders, or at least bid less aggressively to reduce the

---

[10] A cost however is that hidden orders have a lower execution probability and longer time to completion: see Bessembinder, Panayides, and Venkataraman (2009).

[11] Equivalently, they can be seen as auction participants exposed to the winner's curse problem, because their buy limit orders are more likely to be filled when they overestimate the true value, and their sell orders are more likely to be filled when they underestimate it (see Chapter 6).

risk of being picked off. As a result, the bid-ask spread should widen. So a wide bid-ask spread signals that limit-order traders expect high volatility. Now suppose that some traders know future volatility and others do not: the latter can infer volatility from the limit order book, which also contains offers posted by the informed traders. But if trading is anonymous, uninformed traders can no longer pick out the limit orders from informed participants. So, when they see a wide spread, they don't know precisely whether or not it reflects high future volatility.

In this setting, Foucault, Moinas, and Theissen (2007) show that if the fraction of informed traders is high, the uninformed will tend to see a large spread as a hint that future volatility is high. They will cave in, thus contributing to a large bid-ask spread. But if their fraction is low, the uninformed traders will consider a large spread as relatively uninformative, and so will trade aggressively, thereby tending to narrow the spread. So in the first scenario anonymity increases the spread, while in the second it reduces it. They show empirically that the latter result is consistent with the data from Euronext (the French Stock Exchange), where identifiers for the brokers placing limit orders ceased to be disclosed after April 23, 2001. After this date, the average quoted spread became significantly smaller; in this case, anonymity increased liquidity. Notice that this result does not contradict those of Section 8.4, which refer to the anonymity of market-order placers, not to that of limit-order placers.

The anonymity of quotes may also deter collusion between quote setters, or at least make it more complicated. When identities of quote setters are unknown, it may be difficult or impossible to "punish" quote setters who violate previous accords, so quote setting is likely to become more competitive. This is another channel through which pre-trade opacity may increase liquidity: Simaan, Weaver, and Whitcomb (2003) find that market makers are more likely to quote on odd ticks and actively narrow the spread when they can do so anonymously by posting limit orders on ECNs. Thus, from a public policy perspective, decreasing the level of pre-trade transparency by allowing anonymous quotes could improve price competition and narrow spreads.

8.6 Further Reading

In this chapter, we have mainly analyzed transparency in models of trading with asymmetric information. However, the literature on pre-trade quote transparency also covers situations where market-maker pricing is determined by inventory holding costs. Biais (1993) posits that market makers differ in inventories (and thus in their inventory holding costs) but are otherwise approximately risk neutral and in agreement on the fundamental value. He compares two market structures: a transparent market in which dealer inventories (or equivalently quotes) are observed by all market participants and an opaque market in which dealers have no information on the inventories (quotes) of their competitors. Effectively, the former is an English auction and the latter is a sealed-bid auction, and the two produce different market maker bidding strategies. The revenue equivalence theorem of auction theory applies to this setting (risk neutral bidders with independent, identically distributed private values) so that, as Biais concludes, the expected spread will be the same in the two markets.

Beyond this stylized setting, auction theory states that revenue equivalence breaks down if the bidders (the market makers) are risk averse, if their private valuations are correlated or asymmetrically distributed, or if there is an imperfectly known common value generating a winner's curse problem (see, e.g., Bolton and Dewatripont 2004). Within Biais's framework, de Frutos and Manzano (2002) relax the assumption of low market-maker risk aversion and conclude that the opaque market is more liquid. Yin (2005) extends the analysis by Biais by incorporating the idea that quote transparency exerts competitive pressure by eliminating customers' search costs. He considers the case in which customers must pay a search cost in the opaque market and finds that the average spread is smaller in the transparent market.

A few empirical studies have examined how a change in pre-trade transparency affects market quality. Hendershott and Jones (2005) consider the impact of a SEC regulatory action that prompted the Island ECN to stop displaying limit orders in three of the most actively traded ETFs for about a year. They find that this was associated with a drop in liquidity for these ETFs. Boehmer, Saar, and Yu (2005) find that liquidity increased when the NYSE started releasing information on the LOBs of its listed stocks in 2002, as predicted by Baruch (2005). However, Madhavan, Porter, and Weaver (2005) consider a similar change on the Toronto Stock Exchange and obtain the opposite conclusion.

The empirical evidence on post trade transparency is also mixed. Gemmill (1996) considers three different reporting regimes (no publication, 90 minutes delay, and 24 hours delay) for dealers on the LSE, and finds no significant impact on liquidity. In contrast, more recent empirical work (Bessembinder, Maxwell, and Venkataraman 2006; Edwards, Harris, and Piwowar 2007; and Goldstein, Hotchkiss, and Sirri 2007) suggests that the implementation of post-trade transparency in the U.S. corporate bond market led to a significant fall in trading costs. Röell (1988, 1995) models post-trade transparency and finds that post-trade transparency benefits retail uninformed traders in particular.

Foucault, Pagano, and Röell (2010) offer a brief survey of the theoretical and empirical literature on transparency.

8.7 Exercises

1. **Uncorrelated noise traders' orders.** Modify the setting of Section 8.2.3 by assuming that if noise traders are present, each independently chooses to place either a buy or a sell order. In other words, we can have the following orders by noise traders: (buy, buy), (buy, sell), (sell, buy), (sell, sell), each occurring with probability $(1-\pi)/4$. Compute the bid and ask prices under pre-trade transparency and opaqueness. How do the predictions of the model change?

2. **Price discovery and transparency.** Consider the model of post-trade transparency described in Section 8.3. Consider the time-averaged expected squared deviation between the transaction price and the true value of the security, that is:

$$\frac{\mathrm{E}\left[(p_1^k - v)^2\right]}{2} + \frac{\mathrm{E}\left[(p_2^k - v)^2\right]}{2},$$

where p_t^k is the transaction price in period $t = 1, 2$ in regime $k = T, O$ (transparent, opaque). Show that price discovery is more efficient in the transparent market. You may limit your analysis to the case $\pi > \frac{1}{2}$ in which the equilibrium first-period spread is positive.

3. **Asymmetric information and dealers.** (Hard question!) Analyze the opaque regime of the model described in Section 8.3 under the assumption that in the second period the market maker who has inherited order flow information from the first period posts his quotes simultaneously with the other market makers—that is, that there is no Stackelberg leader in the second period. First, provide an intuitive argument that there is no pure-strategy equilibrium of the quote-setting game among market makers in the second period. Then, characterize the ensuing mixed-strategy equilibrium.

9

Algorithmic and High-Frequency Trading

Learning Objectives:

- Algorithmic trading and high-frequency trading
- Types of algorithmic trading strategies
- Effects of algorithmic trading on liquidity and price discovery
- Is there too much investment in trading speed?
- Algorithmic trading and financial markets stability
- Market design and trading speed

9.1 Introduction

As described in Section 1.4.3, trading in financial markets has become increasingly automated and often occurs at phenomenal speed, as a result of progress in information and computing technologies. This evolution raises questions. Many have voiced concerns about possible negative effects of high-frequency trading on market liquidity, price efficiency and informativeness, as well as financial market stability. For instance, the best-selling writer Michael Lewis argues that U.S. equity markets are "rigged" in favor of high-frequency traders (HFTs) at the expense of slower investors in his popular book titled *Flash Boys: A Wall Street Revolt*. Others debate the role that automation and HFTs may have played in several market disruptions such as the flash crash in U.S. stock markets of May 6, 2010, in U.S. treasuries on October 15, 2014, and in the British pound market on October 7, 2016.

These concerns have led to proposals to slow down markets. For instance, some trading platforms (e.g., IEX in the U.S. or Alpha in Canada) now use "speed bumps" that delay the time elapsed between the arrival of an order at a trading platform and its entry into the trading platform's matching engine. Alternatively, Budish, Cramton, and Shim (2015) propose a switch from continuous trading (the current norm for electronic markets) to frequent batch auctions, in which market clearing would take place at discrete points in time (say, every few seconds). Yet another proposal is to introduce a tax on security transactions (known as a Tobin tax), falling disproportionately on HFTs, due to

Market Liquidity: Theory, Evidence, and Policy. Second Edition. Thierry Foucault, Marco Pagano, and Ailsa Röell, Oxford University Press. © Oxford University Press 2023. DOI: 10.1093/oso/9780197542064.003.0010

their extremely high trading frequency. Such a tax has already been implemented in France in 2012 and in Italy in 2013.

To understand these debates, we start in Section 9.2 by describing the main trading strategies used by high-frequency traders. Then, in Section 9.3, we use the concepts presented in previous chapters to analyze the channels through which high-frequency trading could affect liquidity and price informativeness, and present the main empirical findings about the effects of algorithmic and high-frequency trading. In Section 9.4, we study speculators' decision to invest in speed-enhancing technologies and the effects of such investment on liquidity. Section 9.5 inquires whether computerized trading is destabilizing, in the sense that it amplifies price movements, increases market vulnerability to manipulation and/or transmits mispricing more rapidly across markets. In light of these models, Section 9.6 discusses the main policy interventions that have been proposed to alleviate the potentially harmful effects of HFTs.

9.2 Trading Strategies

Algorithmic trading relies on sophisticated computer programs to generate, route, and execute orders so as to implement a variety of trading strategies.[1] Importantly, not all algorithmic trading occurs at high frequencies. Only a subset of algorithmic traders use strategies that require very fast reaction (in the order of a few milliseconds) to market events (such as quote updates or public news arrivals) and are called high-frequency traders for this reason.[2] Algorithmic traders' strategies can be classified into four broad types (SEC 2010), the first three of which are widely used by HFTs:

1. *Passive market making*: the submission of non-marketable buy and sell limit orders, providing liquidity to market participants, very much like traditional dealers do. However, high-frequency market makers use highly automated routines for the submission and revision of their quotes (based on inventory exposure, price signals from other markets, etc.), and limit their activity to electronic trading platforms.

---

[1] This definition encompasses very different types of activities, such as quantitative asset management, agency trading (the placement of orders on behalf of other traders) or high-frequency trading.
[2] There is no statutory or regulatory definition of high-frequency trading. Well-known high-frequency trading firms include Virtue Financial, Citadel Securities, Two Sigma Securities, Jump Trading, FlowTraders, or Optiver. Some are standalone for-profit companies (like Virtue Financials) while others (like Citadel Securities or Two Sigma Securities) are part of broader financial institutions with asset management activities.

2. *Arbitrage*: exploiting price discrepancies between related securities. Algorithmic trading can enable one to detect and benefit from discrepancies between the prices of related securities (e.g., derivatives and their underlying securities or exchange rates that should be tied by triangular arbitrage) before other market participants. An obvious example of arbitrage opportunities is the case of a stock traded on two platforms, say the French stock Sanofi, which trades on both Cboe Europe and Euronext. If the bid price for Sanofi on Cboe Europe exceeds the ask price on Euronext, it is profitable to buy it on Euronext and sell it on Cboe Europe.[3] Speed is of the essence, though, as the profit will be locked in only if the two transactions are virtually simultaneous. Such straightforward arbitrage opportunities are rare and fleeting, precisely because participants take advantage of them in a split second: for instance, Chaboud, Chiquoine, Hjalmarsson, and Vega (2014) find that most arbitrage opportunities on the foreign exchange market last for less than a second.

3. *Directional trading*: aiming to exploit information not yet reflected in prices. The informational advantage of investors can be very fleeting. For instance, consider a news release that leads investors to mark up the value of a firm. Investors who can place buy market orders almost instantaneously can profit by picking off "stale" sell limit orders whose prices do not yet reflect the new value. Again, speed is of the essence because investors who trade on such information can make a profit only by moving before traders on the other side cancel their limit orders or a competing buyer materializes. This "rat race" between directional HFTs is a salient issue in the public debate about HFTs and is analyzed in detail in Section 9.4. Nowadays directional algorithms can exploit an array of techniques to search, extract, and process information: for instance, they can scan the Internet for relevant keywords, and use machine learning techniques to analyze big data or apply textual analysis to the statements of top managers or firms' regulatory filings (e.g., 10-K or 8-K forms in the U.S.).[4]

4. *Execution algorithms*: implementing trading strategies that reduce the execution cost for large orders. Buy-side institutional trading desks use in-house algorithms or suites of algorithmic execution services provided

---

[3] Wah (2016) shows that arbitrage opportunities of this type are frequent for a large sample (495) U.S. stocks. For these stocks, she finds an average of 69 arbitrage opportunities per day. These opportunities are very short-lived (their median duration is 870 milliseconds). The average potential profit per opportunity is small ($81) but as arbitrage opportunities are frequent, they generate a large aggregate profit of $3 billion.

[4] For instance, Barbopoulos et al. (2021) find that a large number of downloads of new regulatory filings on the SEC Edgar website just after they appear on this site stem from machines. This number has increased over time from less than 1 million in 2008 to more than 8 million in 2016.

by brokerage firms when they rebalance their portfolios. This rebalancing often involves the submission of large orders ("parent orders") that algorithms optimally split in smaller orders ("child orders") both over time and across trading platforms in order to minimize portfolio managers' trading costs. Brokers often provide off-the-shelf algorithms such as "Volume-weighted average price" (VWAP) (which split orders to target the VWAP over a certain period of time; see Chapter 2), "Minimum Implementation Shortfall" (which split orders to minimize the implementation shortfall on a given parent order; see Chapter 2), or "Percent of Volume" (which split orders to target a certain fraction of participation to total trading volume per unit of time).[5] These algorithms often use limit orders (see Beason and Wahal 2019) and continuously adjust the order placement strategy given changing market conditions (as formalized by Bertsimas and Lo 1998 or Huberman and Stanzl 2007). They also use Smart Order Routing Systems to optimally navigate in fragmented markets, by identifying quickly where are the best possible prices for executing their orders.

This evolution has led to important structural changes in the provision of trading services and financial information. Firstly, algorithmic trading is possible only to the extent that trading platforms are electronic. Thus, algorithmic trading has been enabled by the gradual electronification of trading (that started in the 1960s in equities markets) and in turn has accelerated this evolution in instruments that used to trade over the counter (e.g., currencies and more recently Treasury and corporate bonds).

Moreover, algorithmic trading has triggered a considerable increase in the volume of orders relative to trading volume on trading platforms, forcing the latter to improve the capacity of their matching engines to process very high traffic. In particular, algorithmic trading is often associated with the placement of a large number of limit orders that are subsequently cancelled and repriced. As a result the cancel-to-trade ratio (the number of cancellation divided by the number of trades) has considerably increased over time. This ratio can vary enormously. For instance, between 2013 and 2020 the average daily value of this ratio ranged from 9 (in 2020) to more than 33 (in 2015) for U.S. stocks.[6]

Lastly, the profitability of high-frequency traders' trading strategies critically depends on their speed of access to information about market events (a quote

---

[5] Institutional investors often allocate trades to brokers using an "algo wheel," which enables them to track the performance of the algorithms provided by different brokers and pick these algorithms optimally depending on the characteristics of their trades and specific constraints. See Johnson (2019), "Trends in global equity execution," Greenwich Associates.

[6] See https://www.sec.gov/marketstructure/ to view various statistics of interest for U.S. stocks and trading platforms.

update, a new trade, a corporate announcement about a stock, etc.) and their ability to minimize communication times ("latencies") with trading platforms. To do this, they rely on in-house algorithms and computing power but also on external technology providers. First, they buy co-location services from trading platforms, that is, the ability to locate their computers right next to trading platforms' matching engines and connect these computers by subscribing to high-speed communication services. These services are provided by specialized companies that build infrastructure catering specifically to high-frequency traders. This has led to massive investments. For instance, the Spread Networks fiber-optic cable between the Chicago area (where many U.S. futures markets are located) and New Jersey (where stock and ETF markets are located in the U.S.) alone required a $300 million investment, and setting up 15 different microwave networks linking the same areas costed about $120 million. There are also plans to use low earth orbit satellites to transmit information faster between Wall Street and the City of London, requiring investments of at least $3 billion (see Shkilko and Sokolov 2020). This raises questions about the social benefits of these investments and whether they are not excessive—a point analyzed in detail in Section 9.4.

9.3 Algorithmic Trading and Market Quality

9.3.1 Liquidity

Does algorithmic trading, and more specifically high-frequency trading, affect market liquidity and, if so, why? Addressing this question requires understanding how algorithmic trading affects each of the components of the bid-ask spread analyzed in Chapter 3, namely: (i) order processing costs or liquidity providers' rents, (ii) inventory holding costs, and (iii) adverse selection costs.

Order processing costs. Automation of the order submission process should naturally reduce order processing costs for liquidity providers. For instance, replacing human traders with machines reduces the variable labor cost of liquidity provision. Indeed, the development of new trading algorithms involves a fixed cost (required to design and code algorithms), which can be amortized over a large number of trades at negligible variable costs.

Also, recall from Chapter 3 (Box 3.1) that order processing costs may also include liquidity providers' rents from market power. Algorithmic trading can be expected to intensify competition between liquidity providers and therefore reduce such rents. For instance, consider the arrival of a market order that depletes the limit order book for a stock and thereby increases the bid-ask spread.

By receiving quicker feedback on the state of the limit order book, processing this information faster and automating order submission, liquidity providers can react more quickly to this situation by undercutting posted quotes and thus accelerate the reversal of the bid-ask spread to its competitive level (Cordella and Foucault 1999; Bongaerts and Van Achter 2021). Moreover, as explained in Chapter 6, traders whose limit order has time priority at a given price obtain larger rents. By reacting fast to changes in the state of the limit order book, high-frequency liquidity suppliers can capture these rents.

Inventory holding costs. As explained in Chapter 3, inventory holding costs are smaller for securities in which liquidity providers can unwind their positions more quickly (see, for instance, the discussion of Figure 3.7). High-frequency market makers do so by using very fast access to information on quotes posted in different markets. For instance, consider a high-frequency market market in Unilever, a stock that trades on various electronic trading platforms in Europe, including Euronext and Cboe. A market maker who fills a sell market order for Unilever on Euronext can immediately place a sell limit order on Cboe and thus turn around his position quickly, possibly faster than if he had traded only on Euronext, especially if Euronext and Cboe attract different types of buy side investors.

Figure 9.1, drawn from Menkveld (2013), presents evidence consistent with this idea. It shows the change in the cumulative positions of a high-frequency market maker in Unilever stock on Euronext and Chi-X (now Cboe) and the sum of these two cumulative positions (i.e., the net change in the market maker's aggregate inventory position), over 200 days. The figure shows that as the market maker buys shares of Unilever on Euronext, he sells shares on Cboe. As a result, his aggregate position fluctuates around zero and his inventory risk exposure never lasts long. More generally, computerized trading enables high-frequency market makers to manage the risk of their positions more efficiently and thus reduce their inventory holding costs (Ait-Sahalia and Sağlam 2017).

Adverse selection costs. Automation of the order submission process also enables traders, in particular high-frequency traders, to react very fast to new information. This possibility has an ambiguous effect on adverse selection costs. To see why, suppose that good news about a stock arrives. It will take some time (from a few milliseconds to minutes) for liquidity providers in this stock to impound the news in their quotes by repricing their limit orders. In the meantime, some traders can submit buy market orders to trade at advantageous prices, that is, against sell limit orders whose prices have not been updated yet. These trades are profitable for the buyers but are costly for sellers. Thus, news arrivals exposes liquidity suppliers to the risk of being adversely selected: they are more likely to sell than buy when news is good (as in our example) and vice versa when news is bad.

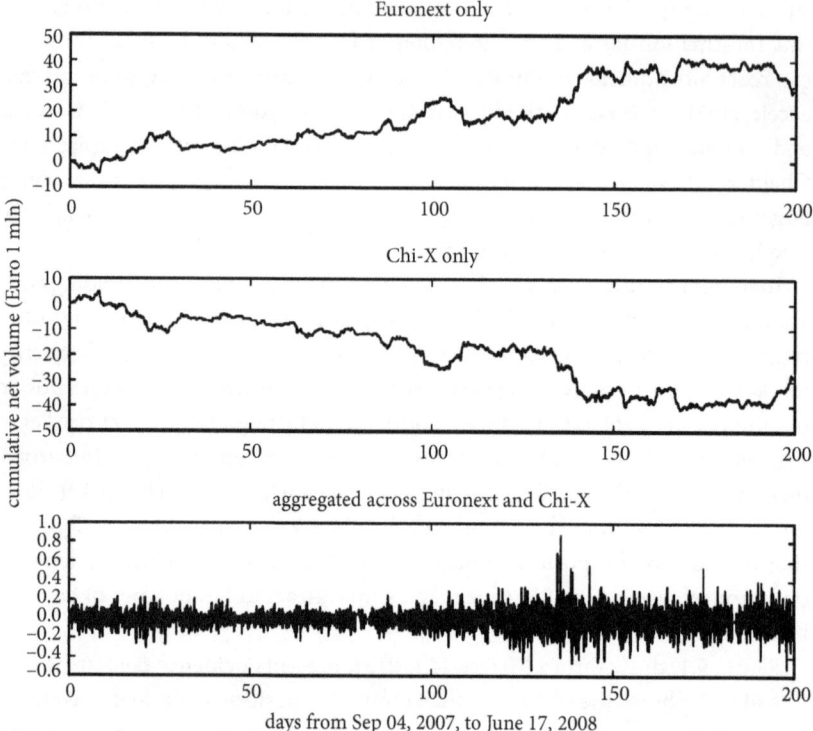

Figure 9.1 Net change in the aggregate inventory (in euros) of a high-frequency dealer in Unilever from September to June 2008.

Source: Menkveld (2014).

This source of adverse selection (referred to as "picking off," "sniping," or "free option" risk) is due to differences in traders' effective reaction time to news (possibly due to differences in technological investments or "jitters," i.e., randomness in communication times) rather than to differences in their ability to obtain superior information or data processing skills.[7] This is not specific to modern markets. For instance, around 1835 the reporter Daniel Craig started selling advance access to news from Europe arriving in the U.S. by steamships. Steamships stopped in Halifax, allowing Craig's agents to read and deliver the news in Boston through carrier pigeons before the steamships arrived there. Craig charged $500 for each hour of advance access to the news. More recently,

---

[7] It is also due to liquidity providers' obligation to post firm quotes. In some markets, dealers have the possibility to adjust their quotes after receiving an order. This option, called "last look" in currency markets, considerably reduce the risk of trading at stale quotes. It may however create room for opportunistic pricing by dealers, as recent controversies in currency markets show. See, for instance, "The role of last look in foreign exchange markets," Norges Bank Investment Management, 2015 for further discussion.

day traders in the 1990s took advantage of the automated execution of small market orders on Nasdaq to pick off dealers who were slow to update their quotes after news arrival (see Foucault, Röell, and Sandas 2003). What is novel is the time scale at which this game is played: high-frequency traders react to news in a few milliseconds, rather than in a matter of hours or minutes.

As an illustration, Figure 9.2 (from Brogaard, Hendershott, and Riordan 2014) describes the evolution of stock returns for a sample of Nasdaq stocks over the ten seconds following the arrival of positive macro-economic announcements in the U.S. (left-axis; solid curve) and the net order flow from high-frequency traders, measured by the difference between the dollar volume of buy and sell market orders over the same period (right axis; dashed dotted curve). The figure shows that it takes about 10 seconds on average for stock prices to adjust to their new level after positive announcements. Immediately after the arrival of positive news, HFTs submitting market orders are net buyers of Nasdaq stocks: in about 2 seconds, their net buy is worth on average 2 million dollars. These trades are filled against stale sell limit orders, oftentimes posted by other high-frequency trading firms, who have been slow in cancelling their quotes. This fact is shown by the dotted line, which plots the net dollar difference between buys and sales of high-frequency traders whose limit orders are executed over the 10 seconds following news arrivals. This difference is negative, reflecting the fact that these traders sell more shares than they buy after positive news announcements. As these announcements are followed by an increase in prices on average, these traders are adversely selected.

Interestingly, Figure 9.2 also suggests that the speed game is largely played among high-frequency traders at the expense of each other (the gains of fast traders picking off stale quotes are obtained at the expense of fast liquidity suppliers).[8] It may however negatively affect all market participants because it leads fast dealers to charge larger bid-ask spreads than they would in the absence of the risk of being picked off, as shown below in Section 9.4.

The exposure to the risk of being picked off decreases if liquidity suppliers become faster in updating their quotes in case of news arrivals *relative* to traders submitting market orders when news arrives (and increases in the opposite case). The effect of high-frequency trading on this risk and its effect of adverse selection costs is therefore ambiguous. If high-frequency trading enables liquidity suppliers to be relatively faster, it should reduce their exposure to the risk of being picked off and through this channel reduces adverse selection. If instead automation makes high-frequency traders faster in picking off stale limit

---

[8] In Figure 9.2, the aggregate losses of fast liquidity suppliers exceed the aggregate gains of fast liquidity demanders. This suggests that fast liquidity suppliers' quotes are also picked of by traders who are not classified as high-frequency traders.

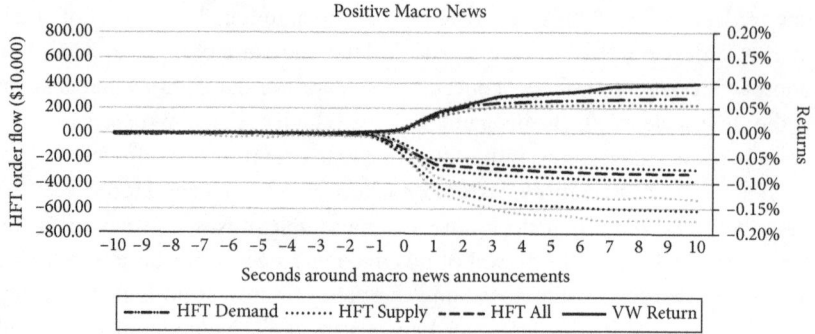

Figure 9.2 Stock prices and trades in Nasdaq stocks following macro-economic announcements.

Source: Brogaard, Hendershott, and Riordan (2014).

orders, it increases liquidity suppliers' exposure to the risk of being picked off and raises adverse selection costs.

Our previous example considered the case of news arrival. It is worth stressing that high-frequency traders do not even need to observe news to pick off stale quotes. Consider, for instance, the case of the E.mini Nasdaq-100 futures and the QQQ Exchange Traded Fund (ETF), which tracks the same index. These two securities are indexed on the same asset. However, liquidity suppliers in each market are distinct (the Nasdaq-100 futures trade on the Chicago Mercantile Exchange in Chicago and the QQQ ETF trade on the Nasdaq data center in Carteret, NJ). When news arrives regarding Nasdaq-100 stocks, these liquidity suppliers will therefore not update their quotes at exactly the same moment, except by chance. Such asynchronous updates of prices in related markets can create very short-lived arbitrage opportunities.

In exploiting these opportunities, high-frequency arbitrageurs create adverse selection for liquidity suppliers in the market whose quotes lag behind (see Budish, Cramton, and Shim 2015). For instance, if liquidity suppliers in the E.mini futures raise their quotes first after good news, fast arbitrageurs can pick off stale sell limit orders in the ETF market while submitting sell market orders in the E.mini futures to hedge their position. Even though these arbitrage trades do not exploit information about subsequent price changes (arbitrageurs do not even need to anticipate them to lock in a profit), they raise adverse selection costs for liquidity providers. Importantly, not all arbitrage opportunities are due to asynchronous reactions of quotes to news arrival and therefore a source of adverse selection. As explained in Chapter 11, even at high-frequency, some are also due to transient demand shocks arising from noise traders: in exploiting these opportunities, arbitrageurs implicitly act as liquidity suppliers and therefore improve liquidity rather than impair it (see Foucault, Kozhan, and Wah 2017).

In sum, the net effect of algorithmic and high-frequency trading on adverse selection costs is theoretically ambiguous. Hence, unsurprisingly, empirical findings regarding this effect are equally ambiguous. For instance, Chakrabarty et al. (2020) consider the SEC ban on unfiltered market access (so-called "naked access"), requiring brokers to verify that their clients' orders are compliant with credit and capital thresholds. This verification takes time and therefore reduces the speed with which traders can react to market events. As this ban did not affect traders registered as broker-dealers, it most likely affected high-frequency traders that do not specialize in market making. Consistent with the view that fast trading by HFT can raise adverse selection costs, Chakrabarty et al. (2020) find that the unfiltered access ban is associated with a significant reduction in adverse selection costs and accordingly a drop in trading costs. Similarly, Shkilko and Sokolov (2020) show that rainfalls, which slow down the microwaves transmission of information between Chicago and New York, reduces adverse selection costs in ETFs traded in New York (see Box 9.1 for a description of their methodology). Consistently with these results, Foucault, Kozhan, and Wah (2017) find that a technological innovation that raises arbitrageurs' relative speed in the foreign exchange market results in an increase in adverse selection costs. All these findings suggest that slowing down arbitrageurs or directional traders exploiting lags in price adjustment across markets reduces adverse selection.

In contrast, Hendershott et al. (2011) find that the introduction of Autoquote on the NYSE (which allows liquidity suppliers to become more quickly informed about changes in the limit order book) is associated with an improvement in liquidity. Similarly, Brogaard et al. (2015) show that market makers become significantly better at avoiding adverse selection after upgrading their co-location with Nasdaq OMX.

In reality, algorithmic and high-frequency trading affect all costs of liquidity provision. Thus, one might find empirically that high-frequency trading improves liquidity because its benefits more than offsets its costs. Thus to better understand how algorithmic and high-frequency trading affects liquidity, it is important to separately analyze its effects on the various components of illiquidity for instance using techniques for decomposing bid-ask spreads described in Chapter 5.

Box 9.1 Rainfall and Liquidity

Various methods are used to transmit information between the Chicago Mercantile Exchange (CME, based in the Chicago area), where investors can trade futures on equity indexes and the NYSE and Nasdaq trading platforms, in New Jersey, where investors can trade Exchange Traded Funds (ETFs). The fastest consists in using microwave networks, which transmit information 30% faster than fiber cable networks (cutting transmission times from 6.5 milliseconds to 4.5 milliseconds). Users of these networks have therefore a speed advantage in accessing information on quote updates and trades relative to non-users. However, this advantage is reduced when it rains or snows on the transmission path between Chicago and New-York because bad weather conditions slow down information transmission via microwave networks.

Shkilko and Sokolov (2020) shows that during precipitation episodes, effective bid-ask spreads on ETFs drop by about 2.5% and price impacts by about 3.8%. In other words, events that reduce the speed differentials between fast and slow traders mitigate adverse selection costs for liquidity suppliers and thereby improve liquidity.

Last, it is worth stressing that algorithmic trading reduces search costs. As explained in Chapters 2 and 7, equity markets in North America and in Europe are very fragmented. FX and bond markets are even more so given that OTC markets are inherently fragmented (e.g., there are more than 75 trading venues in FX markets; see BIS (2019)). In such an environment, investors or their brokers must decide how to split their orders across trading venues in a way that minimizes their total trading costs. In this sense, they must "search" for liquidity and using algorithms (e.g., smart order routing systems) minimize the time and cognitive costs of this search.

9.3.2 Price efficiency and Informativeness

As explained in previous chapters, another dimension of market quality is the speed at which asset prices impound information about fundamentals. The activity of high-frequency traders can be expected to raise this speed, as these traders are very quick in (i) taking advantage of arbitrage opportunities (thus eliminating them) and (ii) reacting to the arrival of new public information, either by updating quotes to reflect it or by picking off stale quotes (thereby pushing prices in the direction of new information). Intuitively, this behavior should contribute to make prices more efficient, namely, closer to a random walk (see Chapter 3). Empirical findings support this conjecture. Chaboud et al. (2014) find that the introduction of algorithmic trading on foreign exchange trading platforms significantly reduced the duration of arbitrage opportunities in foreign exchange markets. Moreover, Brogaard et al. (2014) find that high-frequency traders' orders reduce the noise in prices, making them closer to a random walk. Similarly, Conrad et al. (2015) find a positive cross-sectional relationship between the number of quote updates and price efficiency for U.S. stocks.

In addition, algorithmic and high-frequency traders can exploit information about future price movements or future trades contained in market data. For instance, as explained in Chapter 3, market orders can be seen as noisy signals about investors' private information. Combining computing power with access to vast amounts of market data (e.g., trades in different trading venues involving assets with correlated fundamentals), algorithmic and high-frequency traders can filter out the noise in such data more efficiently than other market participants. In this way, they can "piggyback" on private signals about fundamentals produced by other traders (e.g., hedge funds). This is especially the case when the latter split their orders over time. Doing so, they leave footprints in transactions data, which act as signals for other algorithmic traders.

Korajczyk and Murphy (2018) and Menkveld and van Kervel (2019) provide empirical findings supporting this scenario. Their data allow them to identify episodes of different durations (ranging from a few hours to multiple days) during which institutional investors executed large orders. They observe that high-frequency traders in their samples initially provide liquidity to institutional investors (e.g., place sell orders when institutional investors buy) but eventually trade in the same direction as institutional investors. This behavior is consistent with the existence of a learning phase during which high-frequency traders detect the presence of an institutional investor executing a large order, followed by an exploitation phase in which they trade in the same direction. Interestingly, this behavior is detectable only for trades that appear to be information-based, in line with the idea that high-frequency traders extract information about institutional investors' private signals from their orders.

This behavior has two effects. First, it raises trading costs for institutional investors. Second, it accelerates the speed at which institutional investors' informational advantage decays. Both effects reduce institutional investors' profits from trading on private information and therefore their incentive to produce fundamental information (e.g., through careful analysis of firms' financial reports and prospects). Thus, even though algorithmic or high-frequency trading make prices more efficient, it might reduce the overall production of information and thereby asset price informativeness (see Dugast and Foucault 2018). Consistent with this possibility, Weller (2017) finds that earnings announcements have a stronger impact on the price of stocks with more algorithmic trading, suggesting that the information in these announcements is less frequently anticipated by the market, that is, there is less information production about future earnings in these stocks.

9.3.3 Market Manipulation

Market manipulation is defined by regulators as an activity that artificially changes the supply or demand for a security to affect its price. Actions of this type are not new. For instance, "pump and dump" schemes (spreading false positive rumors about a stock), "wash trades" (the simultaneous entry of buy and sell orders offsetting each other by the same trader or his/her affiliates) or "banging the close" (moving the price of a derivative asset to make profit on a position in the underlying asset) are manipulative practices that existed before the advent of algorithmic trading. However, the use of machines to place orders has raised concerns about new forms of market manipulation, based on quick entry and cancellations of orders. We discuss two examples below.

Spoofing and layering. Spoofing and layering consists in placing and quickly cancelling limit orders on one side of the limit order book for an asset to convey the false impression that the demand or supply for a stock is stronger than it really is. Some algorithmic and high-frequency traders have been accused of market manipulation via such schemes and the number of market manipulation cases brought to courts by regulators (e.g., the SEC and the CFTC in the U.S.) has steadily increased since 2010. For instance, JPMorgan agreed to pay a $920 million fine in 2020 for spoofing by its traders in metal and Treasury markets from 2008 to 2016 (see "US regulators step up battle with spoofing," *Financial Times*, October 10, 2020).

As an example, consider an algorithm ("the manipulator") quickly submitting a series of sell limit orders in a futures market (say, the E.mini futures on the S&P 500) for 1,000 contracts at prices ranging from the best ask price upward, without real intent to sell the futures. Other algorithms may almost instantaneously interpret this change in the state of the book as reflecting weak demand and therefore offer to sell at lower prices. The manipulator can then quickly cancel his own sell limit orders and buy the stock at a better price than he could have otherwise obtained.

By giving the impression of an artificially weak demand, the manipulator influenced the price at which he can buy the futures. Clearly, if successful, this practice defrauds the manipulator's counterparties and temporarily pushes prices away from fundamental values, thereby impairing price discovery.[9]

Over time, other algorithms may adapt to the risk of spoofing or may find a way to trade at the manipulator's disadvantage. For instance, in the previous example, algorithms seeking liquidity (e.g., to execute a large buy order) might

---

[9] Using Canadian data, Brogaard, Li, and Yang (2022) provide evidence that spoofing harms market liquidity and price discovery. Williams and Skryzpack (2020) presents a model in which spoofing arises in equilibrium, using an extension of Glosten and Milgrom (1985).

take advantage of the attractive sell limit orders submitted by the manipulator by quickly submitting buy market orders before the manipulator cancels them.

Box 9.2 "Make Sure to Always do Your Gravy in Large Size"

In October 2014, in the first market manipulation case involving a high-frequency trading firm in the U.S., the SEC sanctioned a New York City-based high-frequency trading firm for quickly placing large orders, using an algorithm called "Gravy," with the intent of affecting the closing prices of stocks listed on Nasdaq.[10]

On Nasdaq, traders can submit limit and market "on-close orders" that execute at the close of the market. The closing auction price is set at 4:00 p.m. to maximize the number of shares traded at the close under the constraint of not deviating too far from the last price in the continuous session, to reduce volatility.

A few minutes before the closing auction, Nasdaq disseminates information (the "Net Order Imbalance indicator") about the imbalance between the volume of buy and sell on-close orders at the current market price. Based on this information, market participants can react by entering "Imbalance-Only-Orders" on the opposite side of the imbalance. For instance, a positive imbalance for a stock signals that the demand exceeds the supply for that stock at the close. Thus, market participants anticipate an increase in the price, which encourages them to simultaneously place buy orders in the continuous auction and offsetting sell orders in the close auction. Such a strategy enables traders to profit from the difference between the price at which they accumulate their position in the continuous auctions and the price at which they offset it in the call auction (in a way similar to the optimal behavior of dealers in the presence of anticipated shocks, considered in Chapter 3). In principle, this behavior works to make the price in the continuous auction closer to the closing price.

This strategy is risky, however, unless traders can guarantee the execution of their Imbalance-Only-Order with a high degree of confidence. To do so, one can very quickly place an Imbalance-Only-Order as soon as the Imbalance message is released to gain time priority in the closing auction while progressively accumulating an offsetting position in the continuous auction, particularly in the few milliseconds before the close. The "gravy algorithm" was designed to do so, while making sure that the high-frequency

---

[10] See https://www.sec.gov/news/press-release/2014-229 for more information on this case.

trader using it would account for a very large fraction of the trading volume in the milliseconds preceding the auction, as revealed by internal e.mails exchanges between traders such as "make sure we always do our gravy in large size."

This latter feature (a large size trade) was intended to push the price of the auction in a favorable direction for the trader. It is the one that triggered a regulatory sanction because of the high-frequency trading firm's explicit intent to affect closing prices. In addition, the SEC argued that by accumulating very large positions, this firm had become a dominant player with significant market power.

Quote Stuffing. This is a strategy that entails submitting a large number of buy and sell orders and cancelling them almost instantaneously. This practice is viewed as a form of market manipulation because it can create a false impression of trading activity in a stock. Moreover, a sudden burst of order submissions delays order processing and the reporting of trade information to all market participants, which creates arbitrage opportunities for investors aware of these delays.[11] Hence, some market participants may deliberately swamp platforms with messages (quotes and cancellations) solely to manipulate the tape (the quote and trade information reported to other participants). Egginton et al. (2016) find that quote stuffing events (defined as extreme bursts in the number of quotes submitted per minute) are frequent in U.S. equities markets (on average they count 125 such events per day in their sample), short (more than 70% last less than one minute) and pervasive (74% of all U.S. equities are affected). Moreover, they find that these events are associated with increases in measures of illiquidity (e.g., effective bid-ask spreads) and volatility.

9.4 Investment in Speed as an Arms Race

Huge investments in infrastructure have been made to respond to high-frequency traders' demand for trading speed (see Section 9.2). These systems are not built by high-frequency trading firms themselves but by third parties (trading platforms or others) who sell access to their infrastructure to

---

[11] See "SEC probes canceled trades," *Wall Street Journal*, September 1, 2010, regarding the case of Procter & Gamble stock on April 28, 2010. On that day, a burst of limit orders in this stock was transmitted to the NYSE shortly before 11:48 a.m. and cancelled almost immediately, triggering a several-second outage of the NYSE reporting system, sufficient to create an apparent arbitrage opportunity between the prices of Procter & Gamble on the NYSE and the competing BATS platform.

high-frequency traders. However, the cost of these investments is recouped by charging fees to HFTs, which are paid out of their trading revenue.

The demand for trading speed has often been compared to an arms race. In this section, we analyze traders' incentives to become fast (invest in speed) and explain why the race to be fast is indeed, in some respects, comparable to an arms race. To this end, we present a stylized four-period model. This model is similar in many ways to the model of trading with asymmetric information presented in Chapter 3, with two key differences: (i) the asymmetric information stems from differences in the moment at which traders observe public information rather than from private information and (ii) traders can choose the speed at which they react to public information.

Figure 9.3 presents the timeline of the model, which considers the market for a risky asset whose value v can be $v^H = \mu + \sigma$ or $v^L = \mu - \sigma$ with equal probabilities. At the initial date ($t = 0$), traders decide whether to invest in a technology that enables them to react quickly to public information. Then at $t = 1$ a risk neutral dealer posts bid (b) and ask (a) quotes, and at $t = 2$ public information may become available and trade occurs. At the final date ($t = 3$) the asset's value v becomes known, irrespective of whether public information has been revealed at the trading stage.

Denoting the dealer's bid-ask spread by S, the ask and bid quotes posted at $t = 1$ are:

$$a = \mu + \frac{S}{2} \quad \text{and} \quad b = \mu - \frac{S}{2}. \tag{9.1}$$

In choosing these quotes, the dealer anticipates that one of two possible events can occur at the trading date $t = 2$: with probability $1 - \pi$, a liquidity trader submits, with equal probabilities, a buy or a sell order for one share; alternatively, or with probability π, public information (news) is released about the value v of the asset. Such public information might be revealed via announcements by firms, news reports in financial media, discussions in social media, etc.

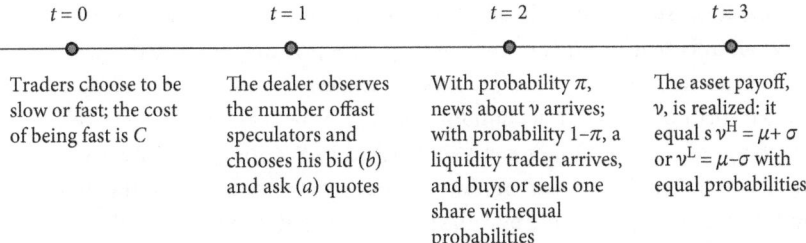

$t = 0$	$t = 1$	$t = 2$	$t = 3$
Traders choose to be slow or fast; the cost of being fast is C	The dealer observes the number offast speculators and chooses his bid (b) and ask (a) quotes	With probability π, news about v arrives; with probability $1-\pi$, a liquidity trader arrives, and buys or sells one share withequal probabilities	The asset payoff, v, is realized: it equal s $v^H = \mu + \sigma$ or $v^L = \mu - \sigma$ with equal probabilities

Figure 9.3 Investment in speed as an arms race: time line.

Indeed, some firms (like Ravenpack and Thomson Reuters) specialize in selling trading signals ("buy" or "sell") to investors based on such announcements. They typically release these signals a few milliseconds after new information arrives (see Keim, Massa, and von Beschwitz 2019), enabling traders subscribing to their services to quickly submit orders based on these signals. For simplicity, we assume that the public signal released at $t = 2$ about the firm is perfect (it reveals v). We first show in Section 9.4.1 how an increase in speculators' speed of reaction to news raises adverse selection costs for the dealer and therefore the equilibrium bid-ask spread. Then, in Section 9.4.2, we study how traders make investments to be fast.

9.4.1 Trading Speed and Adverse Selection

Now suppose that the dealer's bid and ask quotes at date $t = 1$ are such that $v^L < b$ and $a < v^H$ (i.e., $S < 2\sigma$). In this case, if public information is released and the dealer does not cancel his quotes, some speculators can trade profitably at the expense of the dealer. For instance, if public information indicates that the value of the asset is high, a speculator can swiftly place a buy market order. His order executes at price a and the speculator makes a profit equal to $v^H - a = \sigma - S/2$, at the expense of the dealer.

This loss is similar to an adverse selection cost for the dealer (see Chapter 3). When he posts quotes at $t = 1$, the dealer must account for the possibility that he might trade, at a loss, with investors who observe public information about the asset value, v, at $t = 2$ before he can cancel (or refresh) his quotes.

However, there is an important difference with the situation analyzed in Chapter 3, where informed traders were assumed to possess private information unavailable to other participants, including dealers. In this case, instead, speculators exploit public information, that is, information in principle available to all market participants. Yet, in a world where traders can react very fast to public information, the frontier between public and private information becomes blurred. In reality, traders do not get the chance to react to public information simultaneously and therefore those who can do so before others have an information advantage, as if they were privately informed.

This asynchronicity in the reaction of traders to news arrival creates a particular form of adverse selection for liquidity providers, which effectively is the "picking off risk" or "sniping risk" described in Section 9.3.1. The exposure of dealers to this risk depends on how fast they react to public information *relative* to other traders. We denote by l_i the probability that trader i "wins the race," i.e., is the first to react when public information arrives at $t = 2$, where $i = 0$ denotes the dealer and $i = 1, \ldots, N$ denotes a speculator.

The expected profit of the dealer (i.e., trader 0) is:

$$\Pi_0(S) = (1 - \pi)\frac{S}{2} - \pi(1 - l_0)\left(\sigma - \frac{S}{2}\right). \tag{9.2}$$

The first term in expression (9.2) is the dealer's realized profit ($S/2$) from trading with a liquidity trader times the likelihood of this event. In this trade, the dealer earns half the bid-ask spread (because he either buys or sells one share with equal probability). The second term is the expected dealer's loss if (i) public information arrives at $t = 2$ and (ii) the dealer is not fast enough to cancel his quotes so as to avoid being picked off. The likelihood of this event is $\pi \times (1 - l_0)$. The bid-ask spread, S^*, such that the dealer breaks even ($\Pi_0(S^*) = 0$) is:

$$S^* = \frac{2\pi(1 - l_0)}{1 - \pi l_0}\sigma. \tag{9.3}$$

We refer to S^* as the "competitive bid-ask spread," in the sense that it cannot be profitably undercut by another dealer operating at the same speed. It increases with the likelihood of the dealer being picked off, $1 - l_0$, as such an increase raises the adverse selection for the market maker. In the limiting case where the dealer is picked off with certainty ($l_0 = 0$), we obtain the same expression for the bid-ask spread as in the basic adverse selection model presented in Chapter 3: see equation (3.12).

Given the dealers' bid-ask spread S, each speculator's expected profit is:

$$\Pi_i(S) = \pi l_i\left(\sigma - \frac{S}{2}\right), \quad \text{for} \quad i \geq 1, \tag{9.4}$$

that is, the profit earned by the speculator, $(\sigma - S)/2$, times the probability that (i) public information arrives at $t = 2$ and (ii) speculator i is the first to observe it and to place a market order to pick off the dealer, before the latter cancels his quotes: the joint probability of (i) and (ii) is $\pi \cdot l_i$. Hence, when the dealer quotes the competitive bid-ask spread, we obtain the expected profit of speculator i by substituting S^* for S in equation (9.4):

$$\Pi_i(S^*) = \pi l_i\left(\sigma - \frac{S^*}{2}\right) = \frac{\pi(1 - \pi)}{1 - \pi l_0}l_i\sigma, \quad \text{for} \quad i \geq 1. \tag{9.5}$$

Thus, a speculator's expected profit increases with his likelihood of being first to react to the news l_i, because this makes him more likely to trade. It also increases with the volatility of the asset payoff, σ, as this increases the value of the information that the speculator can exploit by trading. Instead, the likelihood of news (π) has an ambiguous effect on the speculators' expected profit. On the one hand, more frequent news arrival increases it by raising the frequency of his trading opportunities; on the other hand, it lowers it by increasing the competitive bid-ask spread.

9.4.2 Is Investment in Trading Speed Excessive?

So far, trader i's probability of winning the race, l_i, has been treated as a parameter. But in fact traders may invest in technology to raise their probability of winning the race. To study this investment, consider a simple specification where trader i chooses his "speed" Y_i, and faster traders have a comparative advantage in winning the race, so that the likelihood l_i that trader i is the first to react to the arrival of public information is:

$$l_i(Y_i; Y_{-i}) = \frac{Y_i}{Y_0 + Y_1 + \ldots Y_N} \quad \forall i, \tag{9.6}$$

where Y_{-i} is the vector of all traders' speeds, except trader i. Thus, trader i can increase his likelihood of being the first to react to public information by becoming faster, i.e., by increasing Y_i, but even so he cannot be sure to win the race.[12] This makes sense because in reality a myriad of events outside the traders' control can affect the transmission of their orders to an exchange, so that by chance orders submitted by a slow trader might be executed before faster traders' orders.

For simplicity, we assume that traders can choose between only two possible speed levels, slow or fast. We denote these levels as Y (slow) or $\delta \cdot Y$ (fast), where $\delta > 1$. That is, a fast trader reacts "δ times faster" to events than a slow trader. We initially assume that the dealer is slow (case 1), and then turn to the case in which the dealer can choose to be fast (case 2).

Case 1. Equilibrium with slow market makers
Suppose that there are $F \le N$ fast speculators and thus $N - F \ge 0$ slow ones. In this case, the dealer's likelihood of being first to update his quotes in response to public information is:

$$l_0 = \frac{1}{1 + N + (\delta - 1)F}. \tag{9.7}$$

---

[12] This functional form would emerge naturally if the time it takes trader i to react to public information arrival has an exponential distribution with intensity Y_i and reaction times are independent across traders. It is used by Foucault, Röell, and Sandas (2003) and Foucault, Kozhan, and Tham (2017) to analyze a similar problem.

Thus, the chance that dealer manages to move first and avoids being picked off is decreasing in the number of speculators N and, for given N, in the number of fast speculators F active in the market.

Substituting l_0 from equation (9.7) into equation (9.5), we obtain each speculator's expected profit as a function of the number of fast speculators:

$$\Pi_i^j(F) = l_i^j \frac{1+N+(\delta-1)F}{1-\pi+N+(\delta-1)F}(1-\pi)\pi\sigma, \text{ for } i \geq 1, \qquad (9.8)$$

where l_i^j is the likelihood that speculator i of type $j \in \{slow, fast\}$ is first to react to news. For a slow speculator this probability is, from expression (9.6),

$$l_i^{slow}(F) = \frac{Y}{(N+1-F)Y+\delta FY} = \frac{1}{1+N+(\delta-1)F}, \qquad (9.9)$$

while for a fast speculator it is:

$$l_i^{fast}(F) = \frac{\delta Y}{(N+1-F)Y+\delta FY} = \frac{\delta}{1+N+(\delta-1)F}. \qquad (9.10)$$

Thus, a fast speculator is δ faster than a slow one and is therefore δ times more likely to win the race among speculators. For this reason, the expected trading profit of a fast speculator is δ times larger than that of a slow speculator:

$$\Pi_i^{fast}(F) = \delta\Pi_i^{slow}(F). \qquad (9.11)$$

The expected profit of all speculators decreases with the total number of speculators, N, and for given N it decreases with the number of fast ones, F, because an increase in the number of fast speculators lowers any trader's chance of winning the race. Indeed, revenues from high-frequency trading have sharply declined over time, from over \$9 billion in 2009 to about \$2 billion in 2016.[13] This drop may reflect entry of new fast trading firms (higher F), as well as a reduction in volatility (lower σ).

At date 0, speculators simultaneously choose whether to invest or not in a fast trading technology (e.g., more powerful computers or access to market data via colocation or microwave transmission), whose cost is C. The outcome of this choice by speculators is observed by all at date 1: hence, the market maker observes F when he sets his quotes.

---

[13] See "How high-frequency trading hit a speed bump," *Financial Times*, January 1, 2018.

The situation in which all speculators are fast (i.e., $F = N$) is a Nash equilibrium if each speculator is better off investing (being fast) than not investing when he expects (i) all $N-1$ other speculators to be fast and (ii) the bid-ask spread to be equal to that charged by the market maker when all other speculators are fast. A necessary and sufficient condition for this equilibrium to exist is that no speculator can be better off by choosing to be slow unilaterally at date 0, when all others are fast. This requires:

$$\Pi_i^{fast}(N) - C \geq \Pi_i^{slow}(N-1). \tag{9.12}$$

As $l_i^{slow}(N-1) = \frac{1}{2+\delta(N-1)}$ and $l_i^{fast}(N) = \frac{\delta}{1+\delta N}$, this condition becomes:

$$(\delta-1)\frac{1-\pi+\delta(N-1)}{(1-\pi+\delta N)(2-\pi+\delta(N-1))}(1-\pi)\pi\sigma \geq C, \quad \text{for} \quad i \geq 1. \tag{9.13}$$

The left-hand side of this inequality is increasing in the relative speed advantage of being fast, δ, and the volatility of the asset, σ, and decreasing in the number of speculators, N. Thus, an equilibrium in which all speculators are fast is more likely to obtain when the speed advantage of the fast trading technology is large, asset volatility is high and there are not too many speculators trying to pick off the dealer, so that speed confers a non-negligible advantage.

Arms Race between Speculators. The previous argument shows that under certain conditions all speculators find it optimal to invest in high-frequency trading technologies when they expect others to do so. Is this a desirable outcome from the viewpoint of speculators? Not necessarily: the availability of such technology can lead to over-investment, i.e., expenses that speculators would prefer to avoid if they could precommit to do so. This is the case when speculators are better off when they are all slow ($F = 0$) than when they are all fast ($F = N$), that is when:

$$\Pi_i^{fast}(N) - C - \Pi_i^{slow}(0) = \frac{(\delta-1)}{(1-\pi+N)(1-\pi+\delta N)}\pi(1-\pi)^2\sigma - C < 0. \tag{9.14}$$

It is easily seen that this condition is always satisfied, even if C is small, when π is sufficiently close to 1. In this case, speculators would be better off if they could commit to being all slow instead of being all fast. The reason is that the fast trading technology has two opposite effects on speculators' expected trading profit. It raises the likelihood that one of them will be able to react to news before the market maker updates his quotes. However, when this happens, a speculator obtains a smaller expected profit because the dealer charges a larger bid-ask spread to protect himself from faster speculators. When π increases, the second effect strengthens and can eventually dominate the first.

Thus, when conditions (9.13) and (9.14) hold, there is an equilibrium in which all speculators are fast and yet, they would all be better off if they could all commit to be slow.[14] In this case, the equilibrium features overinvestment even from speculators' standpoint. This is one reason why one can compare investment in the high-frequency trading technology to an arms race. Such an investment can ultimately make all speculators worse off after accounting for the cost of investing in speed and the adjustment in bid-ask spreads. Yet, individually each speculator has no incentive to remain slow ("unarmed") if he expects all others to be fast ("build up weaponry"). Figure 9.4 shows that the set of values for δ and C for which conditions (9.13) (the solid curve) and (9.14) (the dashed curve) hold is non-empty (other parameters being fixed at $\pi = 0.2$, $N = 10$, and $\sigma = 10$).

The inefficiency comes on top of the inefficiency of high-frequency trading from the standpoint of liquidity traders, because an increase in the number of high-frequency traders reduces the likelihood, l_0, that the dealer can cancel his quotes before being picked off, which raises the bid-ask spread by equation (9.3). Thus, the bid-ask spread is always larger when all speculators are fast than when they are all slow.

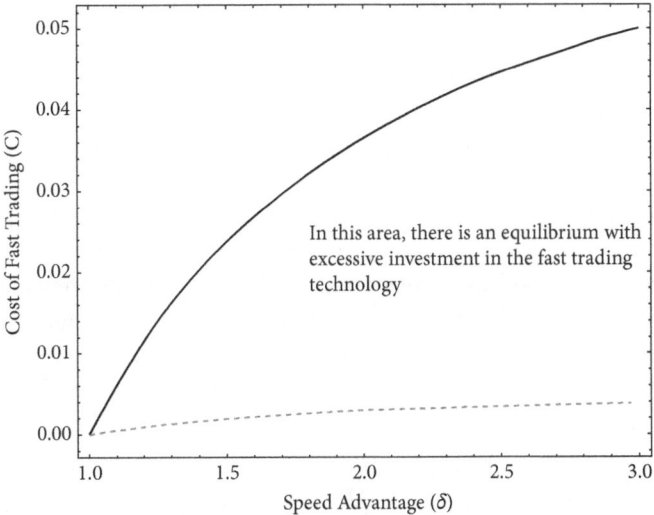

Figure 9.4 Excessive investment in the fast trading technology.

[14] The case in which all speculators are slow is not an equilibrium in this case. Indeed, one can check that if condition (9.13) is satisfied, then a speculator is better off becoming fast if he expects other speculators to be slow, that is $\Pi_i^{fast}(1) - C - \Pi_i^{slow}(0) > 0$.

Not only can there be overinvestment from the viewpoint of speculators and increased trading costs for liquidity traders: there is also always overinvestment from the overall social viewpoint. This is because the "arms race" to pick off stale quotes has no social benefit in the model. The aggregate expected profit of speculators is just equal to the expected trading cost for liquidity traders, because trading is a zero sum game. Thus, for traders as a whole, total expected profit is zero, so that the speculators' investment in trading speed is just a social loss. Nobel prize winner Paul Krugman voiced precisely this concern about high-frequency trading in a 2009 *New York Times* column:

> High-frequency trading probably degrades the stock market's function, because it's a kind of tax on investors who lack access to those superfast computers—which means that the money Goldman spends on those computers has a negative effect on national wealth. As the great Stanford economist Kenneth Arrow put it in 1973, speculation based on private information imposes a "double social loss": it uses up resources and undermines markets.[15]

This is exactly what happens in the case in which only speculators invest in fast trading: (i) high-frequency trading uses up resources and (ii) undermines markets (the bid-ask spread increases in equilibrium). It remains however to be checked whether this conclusion still stands when one considers that market makers may also choose to invest in fast trading: this is what we turn to next.

Case 2: Incentives to be fast for market makers.
Differently from the analysis developed so far, we now allow the dealer to invest in the fast trading technology at date 0. To simplify the analysis, we initially suppose that the dealer ($i = 1$) faces competition from a fringe of slow dealers who stand ready to offer liquidity at their competitive bid-ask spread, given by equation (9.3). That is, if the dealer were to charge a larger spread, one of them would step in and post the competitive spread. Otherwise they remain inactive.

Suppose that condition (9.13) is satisfied. Then, if the active dealer does not invest in the fast trading technology, there is an equilibrium in which all speculators choose to invest (see Case 1). In this case, the dealer charges a bid-ask spread equal to:

$$S^* = \frac{2\pi(1 - l_0)}{1 - \pi l_0}\sigma = \frac{2\pi\delta N}{1 - \pi + \delta N}\sigma, \qquad (9.15)$$

[15] P. Krugman, "Rewarding bad actors," *New York Times*, August 2, 2009.

because $l_0 = \frac{1}{1+\delta N}$ when all speculators are fast and the active dealer is slow. So the active dealer just obtains an expected trading profit of zero

If instead the active dealer chooses to be fast, she still charges the same bid-ask spread S^*. Indeed, a smaller bid-ask spread would reduce her expected profit while a larger expected bid-ask spread would be undercut by slow dealers. However, in contrast to case in which she is slow, her likelihood of being able to cancel her quotes before being picked off, is larger than when she is slow: it is $l_0 = \frac{1}{1+N}$ rather than $l_0 = \frac{1}{1+\delta N}$. Thus, the active market maker's expected trading profit is:

$$\Pi_0(S^*) = (1-\pi)\frac{S^*}{2} - \pi(1-l_0)\left(\sigma - \frac{S^*}{2}\right)$$
$$= \frac{N(\delta - 1)\sigma(1-\pi)\pi}{(N+1)(1-\pi+\delta N)} > 0. \tag{9.16}$$

It is strictly positive because the dealer's adverse selection cost is smaller when she is fast than when she is slow and, as she is assumed to be the only fast dealer, she can afford to charge a non-competitive bid-ask spread from her own standpoint.[16]

However, the active dealer will not want to invest in the fast trading technology if her expected trading profit when she is fast net of the cost of the technology, $\Pi_0(S^*) - C$ is negative, that is, if:

$$\frac{N(\delta - 1)\sigma(1-\pi)\pi}{(N+1)(1-\pi+\delta N)} < C, \tag{9.17}$$

Thus, when conditions (9.13) and (9.17) hold (the set of parameters such that this is the case is non empty), there is an equilibrium in which all speculators are fast and the active dealer optimally choose not to be fast, so that the equilibrium is as in case 1.

This analysis highlights an important difference between the decision to be fast for speculators and the decision to be fast for dealers. The former compares the expected profit they can obtain by picking off stale quotes to the cost of being fast. The latter compares the expected profit from liquidity provision (stemming from trades with liquidity traders) with the cost of being fast. This profit is constrained by the extent of competition from other dealers, even the slow ones. This difference between the speculators and the dealer explains why

---

[16] This situation is akin to a situation in which two firms compete in prices with different unit costs. The firm with the lowest unit cost can charge a price just below the cost of its competitor and earn a profit equal to the difference in cost.

an equilibrium can exist where the former choose to be fast while the latter does not.[17]

Competition between fast dealers reduces even more dealers' incentives to be fast. Indeed, when at least two market makers are fast, price competition at date 1 drives their expected trading profit to zero, preventing them to recoup the cost of investing in the fast trading technology. If dealers correctly anticipate this outcome, not investing in the fast trading technology is optimal for the dealers.[18]

9.4.3 Selling Information to Fast Traders

The previous model can be interpreted as a model of information acquisition. Paying the cost C at date 0 enables traders to obtain information about the asset payoff at date 1. In fact, trading platforms that provide co-location services, companies that provide quick data feed using high-speed fiber or microwave transmissions or sell high-speed access to newswires are indeed selling information. By charging fees for their services, they capture a fraction of the rents earned by traders subscribing to their services.

The risk of overinvestment in information might not be specific to the type of information obtained by these traders. However, it might be more acute. Compare two cases: an asset manager who hires an analyst to assess a firm's prospect and a trading firm that subscribes to a fast data feed to obtain information on quote updates (or public news) a few milliseconds before other participants.

In the former case, the analyst produces information that would not necessarily be available otherwise. By trading on this information the asset manager generates adverse selection for other market participants but this has the benefit of making the firm's stock price more informative. Hence, the investment made by the manager to obtain private information has social value (see Chapter 12), even though it is a source of adverse selection. In contrast, the information obtained by the trading firm would have been released to market participants in any case and therefore the social return on the cost paid by the trading firm to obtain this information is probably negligible. In the words of Hirshleifer (1971), the trading firm just obtains "foreknowledge" (information about events that in due time will anyway become known to all) while the analyst contributes to information discovery (i.e., produce information that otherwise would never be available).

---

[17] This is consistent with evidence in Aquilina et al. (2021) who find that the fastest traders in their data tend to submit market orders rather than limit orders.

[18] However, if all dealers are slow, one may find attractive to become fast if condition (9.17) is not satisfied. This reasoning implies that there is no equilibrium in which dealers decide to invest or not invest in the fast technology with certainty (pure strategy equilibrium). One must then consider equilibria in which the investment decision of a dealer is determined using a mixed strategy.

9.5 Algorithmic Trading and Financial Stability

Another concern about algorithmic trading is its impact on the stability of financial markets. This concern stems from the fact that the automation of trading creates new risks or changes existing ones (in addition to increasing the risk of market manipulation, as discussed in Section 9.3.2).

Operational Risks. First, the scale and speed at which algorithms can deploy trading strategies increase operational risks due to malfunctioning of algorithms. The demise of Knight Capital following the deployment of an ill-designed algorithm in 2012 provides a vivid illustration of this type of risk (see Box 10.3).[19] To reduce operational risks, regulators have begun to require that trading algorithms are appropriately checked and tested before going live. For instance, the SEC's regulation Systems Compliance and Integrity Rule (SEC (2013) requires exchanges and traders using computerized trading systems to:

> establish written policies and procedures reasonably designed to ensure that their systems have levels of capacity, integrity, resiliency, availability and security adequate to maintain their operational capability and promote the maintenance of fair and orderly markets, and that they operate in the manner intended.

MIFID II (Article 48(1)) in Europe has even more explicit requirements regarding risk controls in place for algorithmic traders. For instance, it requires firms to have a "kill switch" function to completely stop transactions in case an algorithm malfunctions.

Box 9.3 The Demise of Knight Capital

Knight Capital (KC) was one of the largest market making firm in the U.S. until the dramatic events of August 1, 2012. On that day, before the market opening, KC updated its smart order routing algorithms, but by mistake it forgot to disable a particular functionality used to test these algorithms in artificial markets. As a result, its algorithms could not recognize whether

---

[19] Another example is the failure of the IPO of BATS Global market on March 23, 2012, because of a mishap in the algorithm used by BATS to run the electronic auction for its own IPO. See "IPO software behind BATS failure," *Financial Times*, March 26, 2012. Ironically, BATS Global Market (now Cboe) is one of the major equity markets, both in the U.S. and in Europe. More generally, exchanges around the world often experience outages due to software malfunctions. Recent examples are discussed in the article "Exchange outages spark demands for action," *Financial Times*, May 18, 2021.

orders sent for execution were executed or not. Thus, they kept sending million of buy or sell orders in various stocks over the first 30 minutes of the trading day. As a result, KC accumulated large long and short positions in about 150 stocks for a total value of about $7 billion.[20]

To avoid bankruptcy due to margin calls on the next day, KC quickly tried to reduce its positions. However, this could be done only at significant discount or markup relative to the purchase price for long or short positions, respectively. Eventually, KC agreed to sell its entire remaining net position to Goldman Sachs at a 5% discount, resulting in a total trading loss of $460 million. The week after it received a rescue package of $400 million from six different trading firms and was eventually acquired by GETCO (another high-frequency market maker) in December 2012.

Interestingly, this event had significant effects on the prices and liquidity of stocks bought or sold by KC, as shown by Bogousslavsky et al. (2020). The price of bought stocks first rose (and those sold dropped) very significantly, as predicted by the models considered Chapters 3 and 4. Then, once the glitch became public information and market participants understood that the massive buys and sells were not due to private information, prices started reverting toward the pre-glitch level. But they did so slowly, consistent with models based on inventory risk (see Chapter 3), and it took about one day for the initial price effects to dissipate. Moreover, trading costs for institutional investors who were seeking to trade in the same direction as KC increased significantly for several days.

Market Liquidity Risks. Another potential risk of algorithmic and high-frequency trading is that it increases the likelihood of sudden liquidity dry-ups, that is situations in which liquidity indicators (bid-ask spreads and depth) for a security (or several securities) deteriorate very quickly.

There might be several reasons for this. First, high-frequency market makers control their inventory holding costs by turning around their positions quickly. However, this is possible only if the order flow is not too large and one-sided for too long. If not, high-frequency market makers switch from supplying to demanding liquidity, which results in a sudden evaporation of liquidity and an amplification of price impacts. Another, related, reason is that high-frequency market making firms are more likely to stop their machines in periods of abnormal market conditions (e.g., large unexplained price changes), because their algorithms are trained to operate in normal times or because large price

---

[20] See Bogousslavsky et al. (2021) for a detailed description of this event and its consequences.

movements lead them to reassess the risk of their positions. Last, algorithms might be more prone to "herding" because they are trained to react in the same way to the same signals or are so good at forming predictions that this leaves little disagreement among them in the interpretation of the same data. In this case, high-frequency market makers might decide to curtail or expand liquidity provision in the same situations, triggering extreme ups and downs in liquidity supply.

The U.S. Treasury market crash on October 15, 2014, offers an interesting example of such sudden liquidity dry ups: the yield on the recently issued ("on-the-run") 10-year Treasury security (an important benchmark for other interest rates) experienced a "Flash rally" (a sudden sharp increase in prices followed by a reversal) between 9:33 and 9:45 a.m., without any apparent cause. Over this period, the 10-year Treasury yield decreased and then increased by about 16 bps. A movement of this size over such a period of time is highly unusual in U.S. Treasury markets, which are among the most liquid in the world.

For this reason, and given the importance of U.S. Treasury markets for the functioning of the world economy, this event was followed by an in-depth investigation by various agencies (including the FED, the SEC, and the CFTC).[21] The inquiry established that the sharp decrease in yields (increase in Treasury prices) coincided with a sudden decrease in the depth of the limit order book for the 10-year Treasury Bill. Interestingly, at the beginning of the event window (9:33–9:45), the bulk of the liquidity supply came from Principal Trading Firms (PTFs) using quantitative trading strategies rather than market making trading desks. However, as the event unfolded, they reacted by reducing the size of their limit orders (depth at the best quotes) while bank dealers reacted by raising their bid-ask spreads. The inquiry concluded that: "Both actions served as risk management strategies by reducing the number and size of orders that could be executed, and also caused a sharp drop in the supply of liquidity to the market."

The inquiry could not find a clear catalyst for the Treasury crash. In particular, in contrast to the 2010 Flash crash (discussed below), it could not attribute the initial trigger of the price movement to the arrival of large buy orders. One possibility is that this type of event reflects technological changes that happened over the last twenty years in Treasury markets. In particular, trading in "on-the-run" Treasuries is now done on electronic trading platforms. This automation has triggered entry of PTFs, which now dominate liquidity provision in on the run Treasury markets.

---

[21] See "Joint Staff Report: The U.S. Treasury Market on October 15, 2014," 2015, available at: https://home.treasury.gov/system/files/276/joint-staff-report-the-us-treasury-market-on-10-15-2014.pdf.

Another contributing factor are new regulations in the wake of the 2007–8 financial crisis that increased inventory holding costs for traditional liquidity providers (market-making trading desks of large banks). It is possible that PTFs compensated the lower ability of traditional liquidity providers to post tight spreads by using trading strategies that are less exposed to inventory risk in normal times. However, as PTFs are more lightly capitalized, they cannot keep positions for long.

Propagation Risks. Many securities are closely related, for instance stocks that are part of a well-diversified index (say, the EuroStoxx 50), futures on this index and Exchange Index Funds tracking this index. As explained in Section 9.2, algorithmic traders will often seek to quickly take advantage of temporary price discrepancies between these assets. One concern is that in doing so they might transmit non-fundamental shocks in one asset to other assets, possibly triggering large non-fundamental price movements that would not have occurred in the absence of fast arbitrageurs.

The Flash Crash of May 6, 2010, is a good example of this propagation risk. On that day, the Dow Jones Industrial Average experienced its second-largest intra-day point swing ever recorded, falling by 9% in a matter of minutes before rebounding by 5% by the end of the day. The stocks making up the index lost about $1 trillion in market value in the half hour between 2:30 p.m. and 3:00 p.m., before bouncing back to a level not too far from the initial one. Some individual stocks underwent even more dramatic swings. For instance, Accenture shares fell by over 99%, from $40 to $0.01, while Sotheby's shares rose three-thousand-fold, from $34 to $99,999.99.

A joint report by the Commodity Futures Trading Commission (CFTC) and the SEC (CFTC-SEC 2010) found that the crash may have been triggered by a single very large sell order in the E-mini S&P 500 index: a large mutual fund sold an unusually large number of futures; first the order exhausted available buy limit orders, and then it precipitated additional sales by high-frequency traders, which spread the crash quickly from the futures market to the stock market.

Figure 9.5 (drawn from the CFTC-SEC report on the flash crash) shows the evolution of the depth of the LOBs of the E-mini futures contract on the S&P 500 index, the SPY Exchange-traded fund and the stocks in the S&P 500 index (averaged across all its individual constituents). Depth is measured as a fraction of the depth available at 1:30 p.m. (the start of the crash). The evaporation of liquidity in all these securities is evident: by 2:45 p.m., the liquidity available in each market was down to just 20% of its level at 1:30. The LOBs for these securities then started replenishing as traders submitted new limit orders. This injection of new limit orders was a factor in the upturn of prices and liquidity observed towards the end of the crash. These dynamics after a large sell order

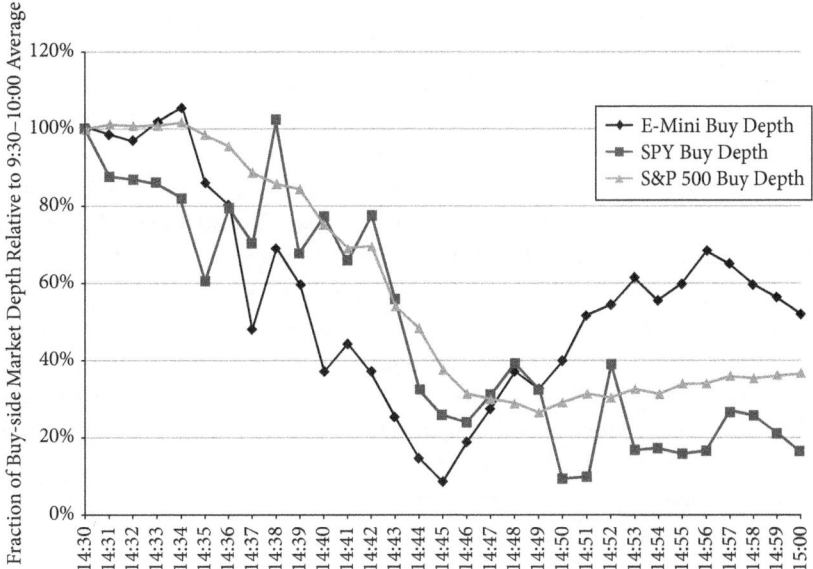

Figure 9.5 Market liquidity of the E-mini futures on the S&P 500, the SPY ETF, and the constituent stocks of the S&P 500 from 2:30 p.m. to 3 p.m. on May 6, 2010. *Source*: CFTC-SEC 2010.

(a drop in price and liquidity followed by an upturn) is an extreme manifestation of a more general phenomenon in illiquid markets: buy and sell market orders trigger transient price movements followed by reversals (see Figure 0.2 in the Introduction). Chapter 3 explores the reason for such reversals.

The pathological nature of the flash crash lies not only in the extraordinary magnitude of the collapse in price and liquidity and the subsequent recovery, but also in the fact that it propagated so widely and so quickly across different markets. The reason for this is not completely clear, but algorithmic trading is likely to have been a factor. Indeed, in the face of a drop in the price of E.mini futures relative to the underlying basket of stocks, high-frequency arbitrageurs probably purchased the E.mini futures (and in this way they dampened the price pressure exerted by the large seller) and simultaneously sold stocks in the underlying basket (and this transmitted the initial price shocks to underlying securities). Moreover, directional algorithms may have mistakenly interpreted the drop in the E.mini futures price as a negative signal about the value of underlying stocks, selling them. These actions could have contributed to propagating the E.mini futures crash to underlying stocks, even those that were not constituents of the S&P 500 index. In this way, even though they were not at the origin of the crash, high-frequency traders are likely to have exacerbated the resulting price decline and spread it across markets.

In sum, the automation of trading makes markets more interconnected. While in principle this should contribute to better and faster price discovery, insofar as prices are noisy signals, it also increases the likelihood that traders in one security may react to price movements in another security that are actually triggered by uninformative trades.

Some market participants also claim that "mini-flash crashes," large and short-lived price movements affecting one or just a few stocks simultaneously, have become more frequent with the advent of algorithmic and high-frequency trading.[22] The academic literature on this topic is still scarce. However, existing findings do not support this view.[23] Brogaard et al. (2018) examine high-frequency traders' behavior for a large sample of Nasdaq stocks during extreme price movements (increases or decreases in returns in the 99.9th percentile of the return distribution in their sample). On average, they find that during these episodes, high-frequency traders' aggregate net trade is in a direction opposite to the price movement. Thus, rather than amplifying extreme price movements, HFTs seem to dampen them by trading against "the wind."

9.6 Slowing Down High-Frequency Traders

As explained in previous sections, high-frequency traders can increase the exposure to adverse selection for liquidity providers. Moreover, we have seen in Section 9.4.2 that the technological race by traders to pick off stale limit orders following news arrival or avoid being picked off can lead to overinvestment. Last, the trading strategies of high-frequency and algorithmic traders generate a very high level of cancellations and order resubmissions, which puts a strain on electronic trading platforms and can make financial markets fragile.

Various changes in the design of continuous limit order markets have been proposed to mitigate these problems. These proposals include:

1. **Minimum resting times for limit orders.** According to this proposal, limit orders must remain in limit order books before cancelled for a minimum amount of time. For instance, in June 2009, ICAP introduced a minimum resting time (of 250 milliseconds) for quotes posted on EBS

---

[22] See "Mini Flash Crashes Worry Traders," *USA today*, May 17, 2011, and "German Bundesbank: High-Frequency Trading Can Worsen 'Flash Crashes,'" *Wall Street Journal*, October 24, 2016.

[23] Some mini-flash crashes seem to be due to erroneous orders. In 2016, Merrill Lynch agreed to pay a $12.6 million fine for submitting erroneous large orders (due to bad internal control procedures) and causing mini-flash crashes. See "Merrill Lynch charged with trading controls failures that led to mini-flash crashes," available at https://www.sec.gov/news/press-release/2016-192.

(Electronic Broking Service), an electronic limit order book used in currency markets.

2. **Caps (or fees) on Messages-to-Trade Ratios.** This intervention sets a cap the number of orders (cancellations and resubmissions) relative to the number of trades for a given trader (or charge a fee for exceeding this cap).

3. **Speed bumps.** They consist in delaying the time at which new orders submitted to a trading platform are processed by its matching engine. IEX ("The Investors Exchange") was the first trading venue to develop this feature using 38 miles of fiber cable coiled in a small box (called the "magic shoe box" by IEX) to delay the arrival of all orders at its matching engine by 350 millionths of a second. Several futures and stock exchanges are now considering to use speed bumps.[24] Many (like for instance the Cboe) have proposed asymmetric speed bumps such that incoming market orders face longer delays than cancellations.

4. **Randomized execution times for market orders.** This is a particular form of speed bump in which the time between the moment a market order arrives at an exchange and its entry in the exchange's matching engine is chosen randomly. For instance, the Toronto Stock Exchange (TSX) introduced such a randomized speed bump on "Alpha" (one of its trading platforms). Alpha delays all incoming market and limit orders by a random time ranging from 1 to 3 milliseconds. However, traders can bypass the delay by paying a fee to the TSX.

5. **Frequent batch auctions.** Budish, Cramton, and Shim (2015) argue that, by design, continuous limit order markets encourage excessive investment in speed because the continuous-time serial processing (i.e., in their sequence of arrivals) of orders creates very frequent arbitrage opportunities (i.e., opportunities to pick off stale limit orders). Therefore, they propose to replace continuous limit order markets with batch auctions taking place at discrete points in time (such auctions would be run at very high-frequency but not continuously). Indriawan et al. (2021) consider a switch from batch auctions to continuous trading by the Taiwan Stock Exchange and find, as proposed by Budish et al. (2015), that this switch triggers an increase in adverse selection for liquidity providers.

Speed bumps, randomized execution times for market orders and batch auctions aim at reducing (in different ways) the speed advantage of fast traders (δ in the model of Section 9.4) to make investment in fast trading less attractive.

---

[24] See "More platforms add speed bumps. Defying high frequency traders," *Wall Street Journal*, July 29, 2019 and "Futures exchanges eye shift to 'flash boys' speed bumps," *Financial Times*, May 30, 2019.

From equation (9.11), one obtains that the difference between the expected profit of fast and slow speculators (when all dealers are slow) is:

$$\Pi_i^{fast}(F) - C - \Pi_i^{slow}(F) =$$
$$(\delta - 1)\Pi_i^{slow}(F) - C =$$
$$(\delta - 1)\frac{(1 - \pi)\pi\sigma}{(1 - \pi + N + (\delta - 1)F)} - C.$$

(9.18)

Thus, when δ decreases, the difference in expected profit between fast and slow speculators declines and the largest possible number of speculators who choose to be fast in equilibrium (the largest value of F such that the previous expression is positive) must decline as well. In this sense, "slowing down" high-frequency traders is a way to mitigate investment in speed.

Others have proposed that a financial transaction tax (FTT), the so-called "Tobin Tax," could be a way to curb high-frequency trading and other forms of speculative activities. For instance, the Inclusive Prosperity Act proposed by the 2020 U.S. presidential candidate Bernie Sanders stated that an FTT would "reduce speculation and high-frequency trading that is destabilizing financial markets." Colliard and Hoffman (2017) study the effects of the introduction of a Financial Transaction Tax on August 1, 2012, on the daily change in net positions (purchases) for stocks traded on Euronext (the French Stock Exchange).[25] They find that stocks affected by the French FTT (stocks with a market capitalization exceed \$1 billion) experience a significant drop in trading volume, no change in volatility and a moderate increase in measures of illiquidity. As intraday transactions were exempt from the tax, the FTT did not directly affect high-frequency traders operating on Euronext.[26] However, the trading activity of HFTs declined by 35% due to (i) the increase in bid-ask spreads (so that submitting market orders is less profitable for HFTs) and (ii) a decrease in intermediation needs, as trading volume drops. Interestingly, Colliard and Hoffman (2017) also show that market orders submitted by high-frequency traders have the strongest price impact among orders submitted by all market participants (in line with the idea that these traders are well informed). Thus, the drop in their activity reduces adverse selection costs but this is insufficient to offset the increase in bid-ask spreads due to other effects of the tax.

---

[25] In October 2012, 11 E.U. countries committed to the introduction of an harmonized tax on financial transactions.

[26] In addition to the Financial Transaction Tax, France imposed a tax of 1 bps on the notional amount of modified and cancelled orders for HFTs with an order-to-trade ratio larger than 5. However, this tax only applied to HFTs based in France and market making activities were exempt. De facto, the most active high-frequency trading firms were therefore exempt from the tax.

9.7 Further Reading

The literature on algorithmic and high-frequency trading is growing fast. Surveys of this literature are provided by Biais and Foucault (2014), Goldstein et al. (2014), O'Hara (2015), Menkveld (2016), Foucault and Moinas (2018), SEC (2020), and Duffie et al. (2022) (Chapter 4).

Theoretical studies. Copeland and Galai (1983) is the first paper to note that limit orders are exposed to the risk of being picked off after news arrival. Foucault et al. (2003), Hoffman (2014), Budish et al. (2015), Foucault et al. (2017), Menkveld and Zoican (2017), and Baldauf and Mollner (2020) analyze theoretically races to pick off stale quotes due to news arrivals. Foucault et al. (2003), and Foucault, Kozhan, and Tham (2017) consider models in which investors can choose the speed to which they react to news or arbitrage opportunities as in the model of Section 10.4. Hoffman (2014) considers the possibility for fast traders to post limit orders in a model of limit order trading (similar to that considered in Section 6.4.1). Budish et al. (2015) analyze how batch auctions can reduce liquidity providers' exposure to the risk of being picked off and reduce incentives to overinvest in speed.

Using a model similar to Budish et al. (2015), Menkveld and Zoican (2017) consider the effect of delays in order processing by trading platforms on bid-ask spreads. Baldauf and Mollner (2020) extend Budish et al. (2015)'s model to a multi-market setting and show that high-frequency traders reduce incentives to produce fundamental information. They then analyze the effects of speed bumps and batch auctions on bid-ask spreads and incentives to produce information.

Other papers assume that high-frequency trades have information about short-term price movements. Biais et al. (2015) study a model in which high-frequency trading enables investors to obtain information about short-term price movements and posted prices in a fragmented market. They show that in equilibrium, the fraction of investors choosing to be fast always exceeds the social optimum. Foucault et al. (2016) extends the Kyle (1985) model when the informed trader has both long-lived private information about the long run payoff of the asset and short-lived private information about public news about the asset payoff. They show that the latter possibility significantly affects the informed investor's optimal trading strategy. Yang and Zhu (2019) consider a two trading periods model similar to Kyle (1985). After the first period, some traders ("back runners") receive a signal about informed investors' trades in the first period and trade on this signal in the second period. They show that the presence of back runners induce the informed investors to play a mixed strategy in period 1 (as in Levine et al. (2001)).

In Cespa and Vives (2022) multiple exchanges control the fraction of speculators who can access a fast trading technology (e.g., pay a co-location fee). In their model, fast speculators have more trading opportunities (can trade at multiple dates) than slow traders. An increase in the number of fast speculators increases market liquidity and welfare (by intensifying competition in the provision of liquidity supply). Competition induces exchanges to reduce the fee charged for accessing the fast technology and improves welfare. However, it leads to excessive entry (market fragmentation) relative to the first best outcome.

In contrast to the previous studies, Aït-Sahalia and Sağlam (2017) derive the optimal pricing behavior of a high-frequency market maker facing inventory holding costs. They show that his bid-ask spread is smaller on average when the dealer is faster because she can then better manage her inventory risk.

Empirical studies. Several authors study the effect of algorithmic and high-frequency trading on various aspects of market quality. Hendershott, Jones, and Menkveld (2011), Hendershott and Riordan (2013), Brogaard, Hendershott, and Riordan (2014), Brogaard, Hagstromer, and Norden (2015), Conrad, Wahal, and Xiang (2015), and Boehmer, Li, and Saar (2018) provide evidence of a positive effect of algorithmic or high-frequency trading on liquidity and price efficiency. Other studies focus more specifically on the effect of trading on adverse selection costs and find a positive effect of fast trading on adverse selection costs (e.g., Foucault, Röell, and Sandas (2003), Foucault, Khozan, and Tham (2017), Chakrabarty et al. (2020), Shkilko and Sokolov (2020), Aquilina, Budish, and O'Brien (2021), Indriawan et al. (2021)).

Baron et al. (2018), Chordia et al. (2018), and Brogaard and Garriott (2018) estimate high-frequency traders' profits in various environments and study the determinants of these profits. Chao, Chen, and Ye (2018) show that high-frequency traders compete for time priority and are therefore more likely to provide liquidity when the tick size is large because the profits of being ahead of the queue of limit orders at a given price is larger in this case (in line with the analysis in Chapter 6).

Kirilenko et al. (2017) study the role played by high-frequency traders in the 2010 U.S. equity Flash crash. They do not find that high-frequency traders significantly changed their behavior during the day of the crash relative to other days. As on other days, high-frequency market orders appear to be informed on very short-term price movements. Brogaard et al. (2018) study the behavior of high-frequency traders during stock-specific extreme price movements. They do not find evidence that these traders amplify these movements. Rather, they trade against the direction of these movements.

9.8 Exercises

1. **Private vs. social benefits.** Consider the model of Section 9.4. Suppose that the parameters of the model are as follows: $\pi = 0.3$, $\delta = 2$, $\sigma = 2$,

and $N=5$. Moreover, suppose that the cost of being fast is $C = 0.02$ (one percent of the largest possible profit per trade, σ).

a. Suppose that all speculators are slow. What is the equilibrium bid-ask spread?

b. Show that if the dealer expects all speculators to be slow, at least one speculator is better off paying C to become fast.

c. Suppose that all speculators are fast. What is the equilibrium bid-ask spread?

d. Show that if the dealer expects all speculators to be fast, all speculators are better off paying C to be fast. Is this situation a Nash equilibrium?

e. Show that speculators' expected profit is larger if they are all slow than if they are all fast. Why is this not an equilibrium? What is the problem?

2. **Risk of being picked off and investors' attention.** In limit order markets, all investors, including retail investors, can submit market or limit orders. Benamar (2019) analyzes the performance of retail investors submitting limit orders at a French on-line broker over the period 2002–10. His dataset contains more than 100,000 retail investors over the whole period, 60% of their orders are market orders and 20% of their orders are limit orders (the remaining 20% include more exotic types of orders such as stop-loss orders). In June 2003, the on-line broker began offering a new technology called "TradeRobot," a computerized system enabling retail investors to better monitor their limit orders (e.g., by obtaining customized alerts conditional on stock movements and sending multiple orders very quickly in reaction to these alerts). Only a subset of retail investors (about 2,000) have used TradeRobot. Let us call "treated group" the group of retail investors using TradeRobot and "control group," a group of retail investors that never used TradeRobot but are otherwise (in terms of education, age, location trading behavior, etc.) very similar to those in the treatment group.

Each time the limit order (sell or buy) of a retail investor executes, Benamar (2019) computes the following measure:

$$R = d \times \frac{P_c - P_{exe}}{P_{exe}},$$

where (i) P_c is the closing price on the day in which the order is executed, (ii) P_{exe} is the execution price and (iii) $d = +1$ if the limit order is a buy limit order and $d = -1$ if this is a sell order. Figure 9.6 shows the evolution of the **average** monthly value of this measure for investors in the treatment group (thick line) and in the control group (dashed line) from 2001 to 2010 (the light gray line is the value of R for investors who are in none of the two

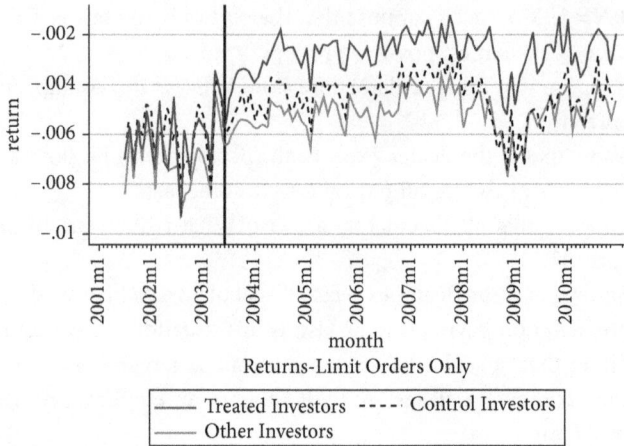

Figure 9.6 Returns to investors from placing limit orders.
Source: Benamar (2019), fig. 4.

previous groups: investors who never used TradeRobot but had different characteristics from investors in the treated group).[27]

a. How do you explain that the average value of R is always negative for both groups? Is this surprising?

b How do you explain that the average value of R becomes more negative for both groups after 2008?

c. How do you explain that after the introduction of TradeRobot in June 2003 (corresponding to the vertical line in Figure 9.6), the average value of R is smaller in absolute value (though still negative) for investors in the treatment group than for investors in the control group? (Note that the difference between the average value of R for the two groups is statistically significant after June 2003 but not before.)

d. If you were a broker, would the evidence in Figure 9.6 lead you to advise your retail customers to use market orders rather than limit orders? What further information would you need to be able to advise your retail customers about this choice?

---

[27] For instance, suppose that in January 2009, there are two investors, A and B, in the treated group and that for investor A, $R = 2\%$ whereas for investor B, $R = -3\%$. Then, the average value of R for investors in the treated group in January 2009 would be $\frac{1}{2} \times 2\% - \frac{1}{2} \times 3\% = -0.5\%$.

PART III

IMPLICATIONS FOR ASSET PRICES, FINANCIAL INSTABILITY, AND CORPORATE POLICIES

10

Liquidity and Asset Prices

Learning Objectives:

- What is the illiquidity premium?
- Role of the holding horizon and liquidity clienteles
- Determinants of the bid-ask spread and illiquidity premia
- Search frictions, execution delay, and illiquidity premia in OTC markets
- Liquidity risk and illiquidity premia

10.1 Introduction

A recurrent theme of this book is that the various costs of liquidity provision (attributable to adverse selection, inventory holding, and order processing) create a wedge between transaction prices and the fundamental values of assets. This wedge is a measure of market illiquidity. But we have not yet considered that illiquidity may affect the asset's value.

The main reason for this is that transaction costs reduce the return to investors, just as a tax on capital gains does. Hence, insofar as they expect to pay transaction costs in the future, investors are willing to pay less for less liquid assets, so asset returns contain an illiquidity premium in addition to a risk premium. As investors care about asset returns net of expected trading costs, the illiquidity premium is determined both by the bid-ask spread and their trading frequency, as the latter determines how often they "pay the bid-ask spread."

Section 10.2 makes this point focusing on the simple case where both the bid-ask spread and investors' trading frequency are taken to be exogenous, and shows that an asset's illiquidity premium depends not only on its bid-ask spread but also on the horizon over which investors wish to hold the asset: the greater the holding period, the lower the impact of the bid-ask spread on investors' valuation of the asset, because they pay the bid-ask spread less frequently. Insofar as investors have different desired holding periods, they will require different illiquidity premia from assets, and this can generate "investor clienteles": investors that tend to trade more frequently will tend to prefer assets with lower bid-ask spreads while those that trade infrequently will specialize in

Market Liquidity: Theory, Evidence, and Policy. Second Edition. Thierry Foucault, Marco Pagano, and Ailsa Röell, Oxford University Press. © Oxford University Press 2023. DOI: 10.1093/oso/9780197542064.003.0011

illiquid assets. As shown in Section 10.2.2, in the presence of such clienteles, the illiquidity premium should increase less than proportionately with the bid-ask spread.

Since the illiquidity premium reflects investors' expected trading costs, it is affected by all the determinants of the bid-ask spread examined in Chapter 3: the higher are adverse selection, inventory holding costs, and order processing costs, the higher the illiquidity premium, hence the lower the market price and the higher the expected return that an asset will command in equilibrium. Section 10.3 illustrates this point with reference to the adverse selection component of the bid-ask spread, and presents empirical evidence indicating that assets with greater probability of informed trading feature a higher illiquidity premium.

In centralized markets investors can execute their trades without delay. In contrast, in decentralized markets, such as OTC ones, order execution takes time because trading requires searching for a counterpart. This search generates delays in execution and, insofar as these delays are costly, they will also contribute to the illiquidity premium, in addition to the bid-ask spread that investors pay when trading. In addition, the delays caused by search frictions confer market power on dealers, and therefore increase the bid-ask spread charged to investors, thereby contributing to the illiquidity premium also via this channel, as explained in Section 10.4.

Risk-averse investors can be expected to care not only about expected trading costs but also about their randomness: as liquidity varies over time in ways that cannot be fully anticipated, its fluctuations may add "liquidity risk" to the fundamental risk of assets, such as default risk and unknown future dividend streams. As usual in asset pricing theory, if investors are sensitive to risk, they will require compensation for liquidity risk as well, unless it can be diversified. Liquidity risk and how it affects illiquidity premia is discussed in Section 10.5.

10.2 The Illiquidity Premium

This section presents a simple framework drawn from Amihud and Mendelson (1986), which illustrates the effect of liquidity on asset prices and required returns and shows how this relationship is affected by the investors' time horizon, with empirical evidence on the relationship.

10.2.1 Illiquidity Premia and Investors' Holding Period

To illustrate how the level of liquidity affects the prices of asset, consider a simple example. U.S. Treasury notes and bills are bonds of different initial maturity. They have exactly the same default risk but are traded on distinct markets. At issue, notes have longer maturities (two to ten years) than bills (twelve months or less). But at any given point in time there will coexist bills and notes with identical residual maturity of less than six months, with a single payout remaining at maturity. As those securities are identical in risk and payout timing, standard arbitrage arguments would imply that in a frictionless world they should have the same price per dollar of payout. However, Amihud, and Mendelson (1991) (and many subsequent papers) find that notes typically trade at a substantial discount relative to identical bills; on average, at the time of their study, the annualized yield on notes exceeded that on bills by 43 basis points, in a sample with an average maturity of about 95 days.

A natural explanation for this significant premium is that the markets for bills and notes are not equally liquid. Amihud and Mendelson (1991) report that the bid-ask spread and brokerage fees on notes are greater than that on bills. Hence notes must offer extra compensation to attract investors.

To see this, consider the following simple model. An investor buys a security that he plans to sell after h periods; during this time the security does not pay dividends or interest. The market is illiquid, and the proportional bid-ask spread at date t is s_t, so that the ask and bid prices at that time are given by:

$$a_t = m_t(1 + \frac{s_t}{2}), \tag{10.1}$$

$$b_t = m_t(1 - \frac{s_t}{2}). \tag{10.2}$$

Henceforth, we assume that the midquote is equal to the fundamental value of the security, that is, $m_t = \mu_t$. For brevity, we call s_t a bid-ask spread, but it should be interpreted more broadly as a measure of trading cost, which includes, for instance, the price impact of large transactions and brokers' commissions. Suppose that investors require a return of r per period on the security, given its risk characteristics. For example, for a riskless security like a Treasury bill, the required return is simply the risk-free rate. If the market were perfectly liquid (i.e., $s_t = 0$ at any time) then μ_t would grow at rate r on average.

Under these assumptions, the maximum price that the investor is willing to pay is given by the standard discounted cash flow model:

$$a_t = \frac{b_{t+h}}{(1 + r)^h}, \tag{10.3}$$

that is, using (10.1) and (10.2):

$$\underbrace{\mu_t\left(1 + \frac{s_t}{2}\right)}_{a_t} = \underbrace{\mu_{t+h}\left(1 - \frac{s_{t+h}}{2}\right)}_{b_{t+h}} \frac{1}{(1 + r)^h}.$$

This equation can be used to express the current value of the asset as its discounted future value adjusted for current and future transaction costs:

$$\mu_t = \mu_{t+h} \times \frac{1}{(1+r)^h} \times \frac{1 - \frac{s_{t+h}}{2}}{1 + \frac{s_t}{2}}. \tag{10.4}$$

The last term is a measure of illiquidity because it decreases in both s_t and s_{t+h}. The fundamental value at date t is determined by illiquidity: the greater the current or future spread, the higher the transaction costs for investors and the lower the value of the asset to them. This is consistent with our example, in which the more liquid Treasury bills traded at a premium over notes, notwithstanding their identical payoffs at maturity.

Empirical researchers often find it easier to test asset pricing models by investigating the properties of returns rather than prices. Therefore, we use equation (10.4) to derive a relationship between gross returns and bid-ask spreads:

$$\frac{\mu_{t+h}}{\mu_t} = (1+r)^h \times \frac{1 + \frac{s_t}{2}}{1 - \frac{s_{t+h}}{2}},$$

and thus R, the gross return per period over the holding horizon h, is defined by the following expression:

$$(1+R)^h = (1+r)^h \times \frac{1 + \frac{s_t}{2}}{1 - \frac{s_{t+h}}{2}}. \tag{10.5}$$

The gross return R is the average per-period percentage change in the security's fundamental value required to induce the investor to hold the security. As the last term on the right-hand side of the equation exceeds 1, R is greater than the net return r: the difference compensates investors for transaction costs. This explains why the yield on notes can be greater than the yield on bills.

The gross return in (10.5) also depends on the investors' holding period h. It is easiest to see the effect of this factor if the percentage spread s_t is assumed constant, so that $s_t = s_{t+h} = s$. Using this assumption in equation (10.5), the gross return R is given by the following approximation (for r and s small):[1]

---

[1] A way to derive this approximation is to take logarithms of both sides in equation (10.5) and recall that $ln(1+x) \simeq x$, for x small.

$$R \simeq r + s/h. \tag{10.6}$$

This expression shows that R is increasing in the spread s at a rate that is inversely proportional to the holding period h. The reason is that an investor who holds the security incurs the transaction cost only once every h periods, and thus the per-period cost is reduced.

The foregoing analysis may seem restrictive, in that it assumes the asset to be safe. But this assumption is not indispensable: if μ_t (the fundamental value) is uncertain, the discount rate should be the rate of return required by investors, given the risk of the security. According to the capital asset pricing model (CAPM), this risk adjustment is determined by adding to the risk-free rate r a premium that is proportional to its "beta," that is, the covariance between the return on the stock and that on the market portfolio, divided by the variance of the latter. Specifically, the required rate of return on asset j should be:

$$E(r_j) = r + \beta_j[E(r_M) - r], \tag{10.7}$$

where $E(\cdot)$ is the expectation operator, r_M is the uncertain return of the market portfolio, and $\beta_j \equiv \text{cov}(r_j, r_M)/\text{var}(r_M)$. This expression indicates that the risk premium is the product of the contribution of asset j to the risk of a well-diversified portfolio (β_j) multiplied by the risk premium on the market portfolio ($E(r_M) - r$). Hence, the β of a security captures its specific risk, which cannot be suppressed by holding it in combination with many others. For this reason, this parameter is often called the security's systematic risk.

For asset j, equation (10.5) becomes:

$$[1 + E(R_j)]^h = [1 + E(r_j)]^h \times \frac{1 + \frac{s_{jt}}{2}}{1 - \frac{s_{jt+h}}{2}}, \tag{10.8}$$

where R_j is the gross return, and s_{jt} the bid-ask spread at date t. Substituting $E(r_j)$ from equation (10.7) into (10.8) and making the same approximation as before, we obtain:

$$E(R_j) = r + s_j/h + \beta_j[E(r_M) - r]. \tag{10.9}$$

This expression shows that the required gross rate of return on asset j is equal to the risk-free rate plus the illiquidity premium s_j/h plus the risk premium $\beta_j[E(r_M) - r]$. Hence, the CAPM relationship (10.7), which applies to net returns (because that is what investors care about), must be suitably modified if it is estimated using gross returns (i.e., in our setting, returns based on mid-quotes

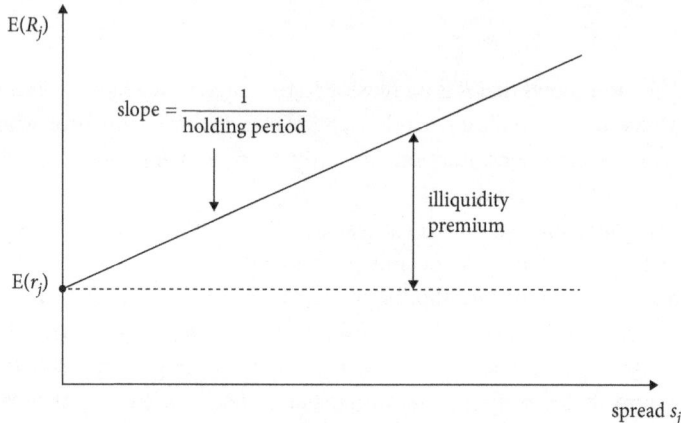

Figure 10.1 Expected return and bid-ask spread.

instead of transaction prices). Figure 10.1 depicts the relationship between the expected gross return on asset j and the spread, where the intercept is the expected net return, $E(r_j) = r + \beta_j[E(r_M) - r]$, and the slope is $\frac{1}{h}$, the inverse of the holding period.

Thus gross expected returns have two determinants: (i) the classical determinants of required asset returns, such as the beta in the CAPM, and (ii) an additional premium that compensates for transaction cost. We refer to this premium s_j/h as the illiquidity premium. If all investors have the same holding period h, then the illiquidity premia are approximately linearly related to spreads, with slope $1/h$, as depicted in Figure 10.1. If equation (10.9) holds in reality, the inverse of the coefficient of the spread in a regression for the gross rate of return should provide an estimate of the holding period of the representative investor.

Another assumption in the foregoing analysis is that the future spread is known with certainty at the initial date. But in reality the spread may change unpredictably, so that the riskiness of the liquidation price will be determined both by fluctuations of the fundamental value μ_{t+h} (due to news about future cash flows, for example) and by fluctuations in the spread s_{t+h}. The latter generate what is known as "liquidity risk." If the liquidity risk of a security is idiosyncratic—that is, uncorrelated with market returns—then the analysis is unchanged, except that the actual spread s_{t+h} must be replaced by its expected value $E(s_{t+h})$. Investors will not require any compensation for liquidity risk, since they can diversify it away.[2]

---

[2] According to the CAPM, an asset risk premium is determined by the co-variation of its net return with the net return of the market portfolio. If trading costs are uncorrelated across securities,

In reality, however, future liquidity tends to worsen precisely at times of low market returns (i.e., when μ_{t+h} is low) and high fundamental volatility. This means that liquidity risk amplifies the systematic fundamental risk of securities—it increases their beta. In equilibrium, this prompts investors to demand an additional compensation for liquidity risk, as analyzed in more detail in Section 10.5.

Finally, the analysis can be extended to the case in which the security pays cash flows (coupons or dividends) before the liquidation date $t + h$. These cash flows do not affect the basic insights developed so far. However they reduce the magnitude of the liquidity premium because investors receive part of the return directly via these cash flows, without having to liquidate the security (see exercise 1).

10.2.2 Clientele Effects

So far, we have implicitly assumed that all investors have the same holding period. But in practice different investors typically have different holding periods. For instance, pension funds tend to hold securities for longer periods than mutual funds. The cost of trading weighs more heavily on investors who trade frequently, so one would expect them to prefer highly liquid stocks, while low-turnover investors should be more willing to invest in illiquid securities. Amihud and Mendelson (1986) show that this "clientele effect" implies that equilibrium gross returns should be a concave rather than a linear function of the spread.

To see this, consider a simple example with just two securities, a liquid zero-coupon bond with spread s_1 and a relatively illiquid one with spread $s_2 > s_1$, and two types of investors, one with short holding period h_1 and another with long holding period $h_2 > h_1$. Consider a situation in which the first group buys only the liquid bond at the gross rate R_1 and the second buys the illiquid bond at the rate R_2.

This situation is an equilibrium if each of the two clienteles has no incentive to switch out of its candidate "preferred habitat" (in the wording of Modigliani and Sutch 1966). This is the case for the first group of investors, if they earn at least as large a net return r_1 by investing in the liquid asset as by investing in the illiquid one:

$$R_1 - s_1/h_1 \geq R_2 - s_2/h_1.$$

---

they do not contribute to the cross-sectional covariations in net returns and therefore do not affect the risk premium required to hold a security.

Conversely, the second group of investors will not want to switch to the liquid security if their net return on the illiquid security, r_2, is at least equal to the return per period on the liquid security:

$$R_2 - s_2/h_2 \geq R_1 - s_1/h_2.$$

These two conditions, taken together, imply the inequality:

$$\frac{1}{h_2} \leq \frac{R_2 - R_1}{s_2 - s_1} \leq \frac{1}{h_1}. \tag{10.10}$$

This condition implies that investor 1 is in his preferred habitat purchasing security 1, while investor 2 prefers security 2. Graphically, the middle expression in inequality (10.10) is the slope of the segment $\overline{BC}$ that connects the equilibrium return-spread pairs for the two assets in Figure 10.2. The condition requires it to lie between the indifference curve of clienteles 1 and 2: the indifference curve of clientele i depicts the gross return-spread combinations that yield a given net return r_i to clientele i. Thus, the indifference curve of clientele i has slope $1/h_i$, for $i = 1, 2$. In the figure, the short-horizon clientele 1 prefers point B to point C (i.e., prefers security 1 to security 2). It also prefers point B to point A, which corresponds to a zero-spread asset. Conversely, clientele 2 is best off at point C, and therefore will hold security 2. Group 2 cares less about liquidity because it has a longer holding period, and so finds the extra return associated with a high spread s_2 sufficiently attractive to prefer C over B, while group 1 cares more about liquidity and therefore prefers B over C.

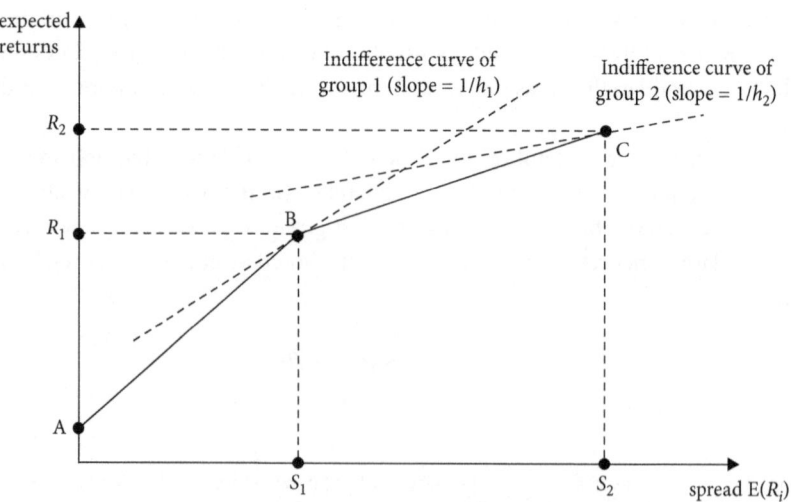

Figure 10.2 Expected return and spread with two clienteles.

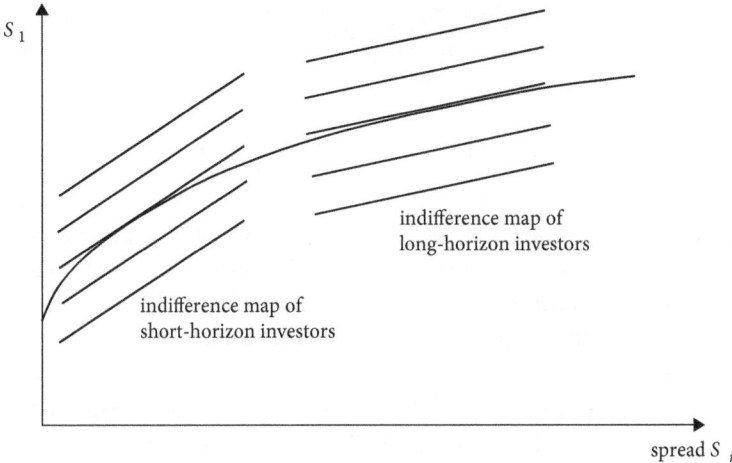

Figure 10.3 Expected return and spread with many clienteles.

Extending the logic to three or more securities ranked by liquidity, we would find that a "preferred habitat" equilibrium requires gross returns to form a (weakly) concave locus such as that drawn in Figure 10.3. Clienteles with different holding periods congregate at different points on the curve. Therefore, the gross return increases with the spread s_h, but at a decreasing rate.

10.2.3 Evidence

Equation (10.9) is that illiquid securities must provide investors with a higher expected return to compensate them for their higher transaction costs, controlling for the determinants of the required net rate of return: the security's market risk, as measured by its beta. Observe that the realized gross return R is the expected return $E(R_j)$ plus an expectation error. If investors have rational expectations, this error will have zero mean and be independent of any other observed variable. Thus, according to equation (10.9), the observed gross return for security j should satisfy:

$$R_i = \gamma_0 + \gamma_1 \beta_i + \gamma_2 s_i + \varepsilon_i, \tag{10.11}$$

where γ_0 is an estimate of the risk-free return, γ_1 is an estimate of the risk premium on the market portfolio and γ_2 is an inverse measure of the average holding period.

Equation (10.11) can be tested and estimated by running a cross-sectional regression of stock returns on betas and relative bid-ask spreads. Such an estimation was first applied to monthly returns by Amihud and Mendelson (1986) using NYSE and AMEX stock data for 1961–80.[3] In their basic specification, which also includes year dummies, they obtain the following estimates for equation (10.11):

$$R_i = 0.0036 + \underset{(6.18)}{0.00672}\,\beta_i + \underset{(6.83)}{0.211}\,s_i,$$

(t-statistics in parenthesis). These estimates imply that a 1-percentage-point increase in the bid-ask spread for a stock is associated with a 0.211% increase in its monthly expected return–that is, more than 2.5% per year. This coefficient also suggests that the marginal investor trades once every five months (holding period $= \dfrac{1}{0.211} \simeq 5$).

If—as is argued in Section 10.2.2—the relationship between expected return and spread is concave, it can be estimated as a piecewise linear regression. Amihud and Mendelson (1986) do this and find that the slope of the relationship does tend to decline as the spread increases. They also estimate other specifications, controlling for additional firm-specific variables that may affect required stock returns, such as firm size, tax treatment, and market-to-book ratio; they find that the effect of the spread is robust to such changes in specification and that it accounts for a good portion of the so-called small firm effect (small firms offering higher returns than larger firms with comparable risk).

Amihud and Mendelson point out that the increases in required returns called for by larger spreads translate into substantial reductions in asset valuations:

> Consider an asset which yields $1 per month and has a bid-ask spread of 3.2% (as in our high-spread portfolio group) and its proper opportunity cost of capital is 2% per month, yielding a value of $50. If the spread is reduced to 0.486% (as in our low-spread portfolio group), our estimates imply that the value of the asset would increase to $75.8. about a 50% increase, suggesting a strong incentive for the firm to invest in increasing the liquidity of the claims it issues.   (p. 246)

This estimate makes it clear that corporate financial policies that enhance liquidity have a considerable payoff in terms of asset valuation. For instance, a company may reduce its cost of capital by listing on a more liquid stock exchange. Foerster and Karolyi (2000) provide evidence of a 44 basis points decline in intraday effective spreads for 52 Canadian companies listing in the United States, and Miller (1999) finds that the market reaction to the issuance of

---

[3] They use 49 portfolios sorted according to the previous-year average bid-ask spread for the stocks in the portfolios and the previously estimated betas of the portfolios. They regress the monthly returns of these portfolios on their average bid-ask spreads and their betas in the previous year.

American Depository Receipt (ADR) is highest for firms that list on more liquid and better-known markets such as the NYSE and Nasdaq. We will return to the impact of liquidity on corporate policies in Chapter 10.

Amihud and Mendelson's study has spawned a vast empirical literature. Many subsequent studies confirmed the significant positive cross-sectional association between various illiquidity measures and asset returns, controlling for risk (e.g., Brennan and Subrahmanyam 1996 and Amihud 2002). Brennan and Subrahmanyam use the coefficient of price impact regressions (see Chapter 5) to develop a measure of illiquidity. If λ_i is the price impact coefficient for stock i, then its illiquidity in a given month is measured by $\lambda_i q_i / P_i$, where q_i is the average trade size in that month for stock i and P_i is its average price. Using NYSE stock returns for 1984–91, they also find a positive cross-sectional relationship between monthly average stock returns and this measure of illiquidity, after controlling for other factors that are known to affect stock returns (e.g., the so-called Fama-French factors).

One problem with this approach is that illiquidity may simply be proxying for some risk factor that has not yet been identified. One way to cope with this problem is to compare returns for securities that have similar risks but different illiquidity. Bonds issued by highly rated sovereign issuers are ideal candidates, since they present no risk of default. They should therefore offer the same yields if they have the same residual maturity. Amihud and Mendelson (1991) were first to use this approach. As the beginning of Section 10.2.1 explains, they show that the yield to maturity of U.S. Treasury notes with six months or less to maturity exceeds that on Treasury bills with similar maturity. This supports the theory since Treasury bills are more liquid. Their findings are also confirmed by subsequent studies (e.g., Kamara 1994 or Longstaff 2004).

Differential liquidity also provides a possible explanation for the "on/off-the-run" yield differential: "off-the-run" issues, like T-bonds and T-notes issued before the last auction for the same instruments, are typically less liquid than "on-the-run" issues for the same maturity. Thus, on-the-run bonds should offer lower yields. And this is indeed the case, as found empirically in various studies (Krishnamurthy 2002 or Goldreich, Hanke, and Nath 2005, among others).[4] Goldreich et al. (2005) show that the yield differential between on-the-run and off-the-run securities narrows as the date at which securities go off-the-run nears. This finding shows that investors are forward looking and care about future rather than current liquidity in pricing on-the-run securities (this is

---

[4] On-the-run bonds are often borrowed by traders making short sales (to play on the yield difference between these bond and the off-the-run bonds). Holders of on-the-run bonds can therefore earn lending fees from short sellers. These fees also help to widen the yield spread between on and off the run bonds (see Duffie et al. 2002 and Krishnamurthy 2002).

consistent with the fact the gross required return on a security depends both on current liquidity, s_t, and future liquidity, s_{t+h}).

Another way to assess the impact of liquidity on asset prices and the cost of capital is to consider changes in trading rules known to affect liquidity (see exercise 2). For instance, Muscarella and Piwowar (2001) study a sample of 134 stocks listed on the Paris Bourse that switched from call trading to continuous trading (86 stocks) or vice versa (48 stocks). Those switching from call to continuous trading improved their liquidity, while those going over to call trading suffered a deterioration. Accordingly, a switch from periodic call auctions to continuous trading should reduce the cost of capital and produce a jump in stock's price between the date at which the switch is announced and the date at which it is implemented. A switch from continuous trading to a call market should have the opposite effect. This is precisely what Muscarella and Piwowar (2001) find: stocks that switch to continuous trading register a price rise of about 5.5% while those switching to call trading undergo a decline of 4.9%.

10.3 Illiquidity Premia and Sources of the Spread

In the previous section, the bid-ask spread was taken to be exogenous. In Chapter 3 we have seen that the bid-ask spread in turn depends on asymmetric information, order-processing costs, inventory holding costs, and the rents arising from imperfect competition among market participants. Hence, ultimately each of these determinants of transaction costs should affect asset prices. And by the same token, they should affect asset returns via the illiquidity premium (Section 10.2.1). In this section we show that therefore the illiquidity premium is increasing in the likelihood of informed trading, order processing costs and inventory holding costs, and report evidence supporting some of these predictions. The next section will show that in the context of OTC markets, where trade is not centralized, the illiquidity premium is also affected by search frictions, both directly and via their effect on the bid-ask spread, and report some relevant evidence from the corporate bond market.

10.3.1 Predictions from Models of the Bid-Ask Spread

To illustrate the impact of determinants of the bid-ask spread on assets' illiquidity premia in the simplest possible way, we consider the expressions for the bid-ask spread derived in the one-period models presented in Chapter 3.

Recall that in the model where informed and liquidity traders place orders with uninformed, risk-neutral dealers, the opening bid-ask spread is

$S = \pi(v^H - v^L)$ (expression 3.12), and the midquote m equals the unconditional estimate μ of the fundamental value. Expressing the final value of the security as $v^H = \mu(1 + \sigma)$ when high and $v^L = \mu(1 - \sigma)$ when low, where σ measures the advantage of informed traders, the relative spread is:

$$s = \frac{S}{m} = \frac{\pi(v^H - v^L)}{\mu} = 2\pi\sigma.$$

Therefore, for small values of π and σ, using the approximation for the gross return in expression (10.6) for $h = 1$, the illiquidity premium becomes:

$$R - r \simeq 2\pi\sigma, \tag{10.12}$$

and therefore it is greater for securities where informed traders are more numerous and have more valuable information. This prediction also holds in a more general model of asymmetric information with multiple securities and risk averse investors. Easley and O'Hara (2004) consider such a model, where investors observe public signals about payoffs and a fraction of them also get private signals. In equilibrium, the expected return on a security is higher when the ratio of private to public signals is larger. In the presence of informed investors, the uninformed end up holding more securities with low payoffs and fewer securities with high payoffs than they would in a market without asymmetric information. Thus, they require a higher return on their holdings.[5] Easley and O'Hara (2004) note that holding several securities does not alleviate this problem, since uninformed investors always end up on the wrong side of the trade.

As shown in Chapter 3, the model of the bid-ask spread based on adverse selection can be easily augmented with order-processing costs and/or imperfect competition rents. Assuming that these amount to γ per dollar traded, the bid-ask spread becomes:

$$s = 2(\pi\sigma + \gamma),$$

so that the illiquidity premium on the asset also reflects the market makers' order processing costs and oligopoly rents:

$$R - r \simeq 2(\pi\sigma + \gamma). \tag{10.13}$$

---

[5] Another reason is that uninformed investors face greater uncertainty when the number of public signals decreases relative to private signals. As they are risk averse, they require a higher premium.

Finally, recall that in the one-period version of the inventory holding cost model presented in Chapter 3, according to expression (3.46), the relative bid-ask spread faced by an investor placing a unit-size order $d = \pm 1$ is $s \equiv S/\mu = 2\rho\sigma_\varepsilon^2/\mu$. Hence, using again expression (10.6) for $h = 1$, in this case the illiquidity premium is approximately:

$$R - r \simeq 2\rho\sigma_\varepsilon^2/\mu = 2\rho\mu\sigma_r^2, \qquad (10.14)$$

where $\sigma_r \equiv \sigma_\varepsilon/\mu$ is the standard deviation of the percentage return on the security. Thus, the illiquidity premium on the asset reflects not only the volatility of fundamentals σ_r^2 but also the dealers' risk aversion ρ and the expected dollar value traded μ.

10.3.2 Evidence

Asymmetric Information. Easley, Hvidkjaer, and O'Hara (2002) test the prediction that stocks more exposed to informed trading command a higher illiquidity premium, using the probability of information-based trading (PIN) in a stock as a proxy for the level of informed trading.[6] In Chapter 5, section 5.4, we explain how to estimate this probability using intraday data on buy and sell orders. Specifically, Easley et al. estimate the following regression in each month over the period between 1984 and 1998 for a large sample of stocks listed on the NYSE:

$$R_{it,l} = \gamma_{0t} + \gamma_{1t}\hat{\beta}_i + \gamma_{2t}PIN_{it-1} + \gamma_{3t}SIZE_{it-1} + \gamma_{4t}BM_{it-1} + \eta_{it}, \qquad (10.15)$$

where $R_{it,l}$ is the excess return of stock i in month l of year t; $\hat{\beta}_i$ is an estimate of the β for stock i over the entire estimation period; PIN_{it-1} is an estimate of the PIN measure using order data for stock i at the end of year $t-1$; $SIZE_{it-1}$ is the logarithm of the stock's market capitalization of stock i at the end of year $t-1$; BM_{it-1} is the logarithm of the stock's book-to-market value at the end of year $t-1$. The authors control for market capitalization and book-to-market ratios because these variables are known to be priced characteristics (i.e., to explain the cross-section of stock returns).

---

[6] Kelly and Ljungqvist (2012) use a different approach. They use a shock (a drop in the number of securities analysts covering a stock because of termination of their research departments by brokerage houses) that increase asymmetric information in a subset of stocks (those covered by closed brokers). They show that the price of stock affected by this shock falls (the cost of capital increases).

Over all the monthly regressions, the average effect of PIN is positive and significant, in various specifications of equation (10.15). Thus, stocks with a higher likelihood of informed trading have higher returns on average, as predicted by equation (10.12). In principle, the PIN measure may capture other characteristics that affect returns. In particular, high-PIN stocks may also be illiquid, but for reasons other than just asymmetric information. However, the effect of PIN on returns does not vanish when the bid-ask spread is included as a control variable in equation (10.15). However, in a more recent study, Duarte and Young (2009) estimate equation (10.15) over a longer sample period (1984–2004) using the Amihud ratio (defined in Chapter 2) to control for illiquidity, and find that, once this variable is controlled for, the estimated coefficient of the PIN measure is no longer statistically significant.

Inventory Holding Costs. Friewald and Nagler (2019) study the effect of inventory holding costs on monthly bond yields (a measure of investors' required gross returns for investing in bonds), based on transaction prices for a large sample of U.S. corporate bonds from 2003 to 2013. Using these data, they estimate time series regressions of monthly changes in bond yields on aggregate factors that should affect these yields according to standard asset pricing models (such as changes in the 10-year Treasury rate, changes in the slope of the yield curve and changes in market volatility), as well as marketwide proxies of trading frictions specific to OTC markets, namely, inventory holding costs and search costs (that we shall analyze in Section 10.4).

They measure dealers' inventory holding costs in four ways: the change in their aggregate inventory in a given month, the change in the amount of bonds outstanding (as greater bond issuance in a given month presumably forces dealers to increase their inventories), and two proxies for dealers' risk aversion (parameter ρ in equation (10.14)), namely, the marketwide fraction of prearranged trades, for which dealers avoid inventory risk, and the TED spread, which in this context is used as a proxy of dealers' funding costs.[7] In line with the prediction from equation (10.14), Friewald and Nagler (2019) find that bond yields are positively correlated with these measures of dealers' inventory holding costs, as well as search costs, while they are not significantly affected by asymmetric information, as the coefficient of the PIN measure is not significantly different from zero (though positive) in their estimates.

---

[7] The TED spread is the difference between the three-month London Interbank Offered Rate (LIBOR) at which banks lend to each other and the three-month Treasury bill rate. As U.S. Treasury bills are seen as risk-free assets, the TED spread is commonly used as a measure of funding costs for dealers (see, for instance, Brunnermeier (2009) or Friewald and Nagler (2019)).

10.4 Illiquidity Premia in OTC Markets

As Chapters 1 and 8 explain, trading in OTC markets (such as swaps, CDSs, corporate bonds, etc.) is decentralized and opaque. As a result, it takes more time for investors in these markets to find a suitable counterparty and execute their trades. Moreover, opacity softens competition between dealers and therefore gives them bargaining power. In this section, we show how delays in execution affect illiquidity premia, both directly and indirectly via their effects on dealers' bid-ask spreads, as highlighted by a recent strand of research on asset pricing in OTC markets, pioneered by Duffie, Gârleanu, and Pedersen (2005, 2007).

10.4.1 Search Frictions and Illiquidity Premia

We consider a simplified version of the model by Duffie, Gârleanu, and Pedersen (2005), where a continuum of risk-neutral investors can invest in two different assets: a riskless security paying one dollar per period forever (a "consol bond") and a bank account offering a rate of interest r. The per-capita supply of the consol bond is denoted by q.

Investors can either hold one share of the security or none, and short-sales are not allowed. Hence, all trades are for a single share. Some investors have a holding cost of c per period: when they hold the asset, their cash flow is only $\$(1-c)$ per period, and thus are "low-valuation" investors; instead, those who bear no holding cost are "high-valuation" investors. The holding cost of low-valuation investors may reflect, for instance, a less favorable tax rate than that faced by high-valuation investors. Thus, in each period t, there are four groups of investors: (i) high-valuation investors who own the security, (ii) high-valuation investors who do not own the security, (iii) low-valuation investors who own the security, and (iv) low-valuation investors who do not own the security.

In each period, after receiving their payoff, investors' valuation may switch (from low to high or high to low) with probability ψ. Intuitively, these shocks explain why investors want to trade in the model. Indeed, investors with a low valuation place a lower value on the asset than investors with a high valuation since they derive smaller cash-flows from holding it. Thus, there are gains from trade between investors with low valuations holding the asset and investors with high valuations not holding the asset. As soon as an investor's valuation switches from high to low, he wishes to sell the asset and starts looking for a potential buyer. For this reason, $1/\psi$ can be seen as investors' holding horizon (h in Section 10.1).

When their valuation switches, investors can trade the security. Investors willing to buy (high valuation non owners) or sell (low valuation owners) can do so by trading with dealers at bid and ask prices b and a. However, finding a dealer takes time. Specifically, in each period, the probability of finding a market maker for an investor who wants to trade is ϕ, so that on average the execution delay for an investor is $1/\phi$ (as we shall see, ask and bid quotes are such that investors immediately trade when they find a counterparty). This delay is costly for investors who need to trade because it postpones the moment at which they obtain their preferred position in the asset. For instance, investors with a low valuation inefficiently bear the holding cost c as long as they hold the asset.

To sum up, in each period, the time line of the model is as follows:

1. Investors holding the asset receive their payoff, \$1 if they have a high valuation or \$$(1-c)$ if they have a low valuation.
2. Each investor changes his valuation for the security with probability ψ.
3. High-valuation non-owners and low-valuation owners search for a dealer and find one with probability ϕ.

The fractions of investors' types and the prices quoted by dealers in each period are endogenous (the appendix of this chapter explains how they are determined). When the per capita supply of the asset is low (i.e., $q < 1/2$ as we assumed), the price paid by investors for the security turns out to be (see the appendix):

$$a = \frac{1}{r} - \underbrace{\frac{2\psi}{r(1+\chi)}\left(1 - \phi\frac{1-\chi}{2}\right)S,}_{\text{illiquidity premium}} \qquad (10.16)$$

where S is dealers' bid-ask spread and χ is an index of dealers' market power when they buy the asset from sellers. This index is the fraction of the gains from trade captured by dealers when they trade with sellers: when $\chi = 1$, dealers' market power is maximal.

As explained in the appendix, a is the maximum price that investors with a high valuation are willing to pay for the asset.[8] Indeed, this is the present (discounted) value of the cash-flows that they expect to receive from the asset, including the resale value when their valuation for the asset will become low. For instance, if $\psi = 0$, investors with a high valuation never need to resell the asset (their holding horizon is infinite). Thus, after buying the asset, they receive a stream of cash flows of \$1 per period forever, whose present value is $1/r$. When

---

[8] Thus dealers extract all the surplus from trades with buyers. The reason is that when $q < 1/2$, there is an excess of buyers relative to sellers at any date (see the appendix). Dealers' ask price is in fact the price that would clear the market if trading were centralized.

$\psi > 0$, this present value is less because (i) at some point (on average in $1/\psi$ periods) investors start bearing holding costs and (ii) bear these costs as long as they do not find a counterparty. Moreover, when they eventually find one dealer, investors bear a bid-ask spread cost S. In anticipation of these costs, buyers require a compensation for holding the asset, captured by the second term in the previous equation. This illiquidity premium compensates investors for (i) holding costs due to delays in finding a counterparty when they resell the asset and (ii) bid-ask spread costs. While the second effect is identical to that highlighted in Section 10.2, the first is novel.

Holding the bid-ask spread constant, the illiquidity premium increases with the probability that trading needs arise, ψ, and decreases with the probability of finding a dealer, ϕ. Thus, it is inversely related to investors' expected horizon, $1/\psi$ (as in Section 10.2) and positively related to their expected delay in execution of their desired trade, $1/\phi$. This shows that delays in execution also affect illiquidity premia.

These parameters also affect the equilibrium bid-ask spread, whose expression is (as shown in the appendix):

$$S = a - b = \frac{(1+\chi)c}{2(r+2\psi) + (1-2\psi)\phi(1-\chi)}. \tag{10.17}$$

Thus, dealers' bid-ask spread increases with their bargaining power, χ. For this reason, the illiquidity premium also increases in dealers' bargaining power, as can be seen more easily upon substituting expression (10.17) for S in expression (10.16) for the illiquidity premium.[9]

The bid-ask spread also increases when investors expect longer delays for the execution of their orders, that is when the probability ϕ of finding a dealer decreases. The reason is that gains from trade between dealers and investors are larger when investors expect larger delays in finding a counterparty. For instance, consider a seller who just found a dealer. If the seller turns down the dealer's offer, he expects to bear holding costs for longer time when ϕ is smaller. Thus, the surplus created by an immediate transaction is larger. As dealers' bid price is set to capture a fraction χ of this surplus, dealers' bid-ask spread increases. In sum, an increase in execution delays affects the illiquidity premium both directly (i.e., holding trading costs constant, as explained previously) and indirectly via the bid-ask spread.

---

[9] The bid-ask spread does not vanish when χ goes to zero because dealers retain market power when they trade with buyers: this is because there is an excess of buyers relative to sellers when $q < \frac{1}{2}$, as explained in n. 6.

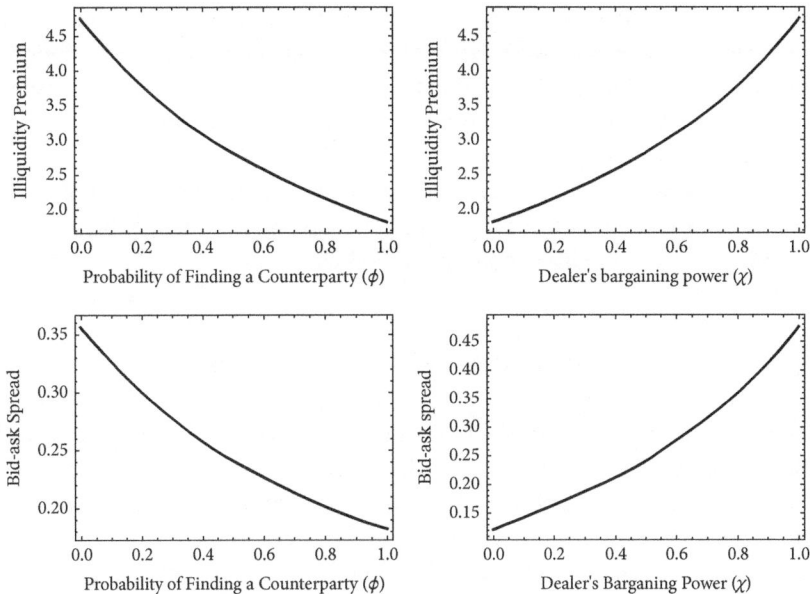

Figure 10.4 Effects of search and bargaining frictions on the illiquidity premium and the bid-ask spread.

Figure 10.4 illustrates the previous results for specific paramater values: $r = 1\%$ (so that the frictionless value of the asset is 100), $c = 0.1$ (i.e., holding costs equal 0.1% of the asset's frictionless value, $\psi = 0.1$ (implying that investors' holding horizon is 10 periods). The figures in the upper panel show the effect of ϕ (fixing dealers' bargaining power at $\chi = 0.5$), while those in the lower panel illustrate the effect of dealers' bargaining power, χ (for $\phi = 0.5$).

Overall, the results in this section provide a rationale for policies that induce a greater centralization of trading in OTC markets. Such policies should reduce illiquidity premia (and ultimately reduce the cost of capital for issuers) by reducing (i) execution delays due to search frictions and (ii) dealers' market power via more intense competition among dealers.

10.4.2 Evidence

As explained in Section 10.3.2, Friewald and Nagler (2019) provide evidence that inventory holding costs affect corporate bond yields, in line with equation (10.14). They also show that dealers' bargaining power (χ) and the time delay in trades due to search frictions ($1/\phi$) increase corporate bond yields. For instance, bond yields tend to rise in months in which trading is concentrated among fewer dealers, so that they have greater bargaining power vis-à-vis their clients, as predicted by model presented above. Moreover, bond yields increase in months in which dealers appear less connected with each other (based on measures drawn from network analysis), so that delays in execution become larger, again in line with the model's predictions.

Overall, Friewald and Nagler (2019) conclude that inventory holding costs, search frictions and dealers' bargaining power jointly account for about 23% of the time-series variations in bond yields in their sample.

10.5 Liquidity Risk and Asset Prices

The previous sections established that future expected liquidity affects required rates of return. Now we turn to the effect of uncertainty about the future level of liquidity on the required rate of return. Intuitively, if liquidity fluctuates over time, it contributes to the volatility of returns: this source of risk is called liquidity risk. To see why and how unexpected changes in future liquidity can contribute to the risk of a security over and above its fundamental risk, we present two seminal approaches: the liquidity-adjusted version of the Capital Asset Pricing Model (LCAPM) developed by Acharya and Pedersen (2005) (Section 10.5.1), and the multifactor model proposed by Pastor and Stambaugh (2003) (Section 10.5.2).

10.5.1 The Liquidity-Adjusted CAPM

Suppose that all investors' holds securities for h periods, and consider again expression (10.5) for security j, denoting by $R_{j,t+h}$ the gross per-period rate of return of the security between date t and date $t+h$, and by $r_{j,t+h}$ its corresponding per-period net rate of return over the same holding horizon:

$$(1 + R_{j,t+h})^h = (1 + r_{j,t+h})^h \times \frac{1 + \frac{s_t}{2}}{1 - \frac{s_{t+h}}{2}}. \tag{10.18}$$

Taking a logarithmic approximation yields:

$$r_{j,t+h} \simeq R_{j,t+h} - \frac{s_{j,t+h} + s_{j,t}}{2h}. \tag{10.19}$$

Analogously the per-period net rate of return of the market portfolio is:

$$r_{M,t+h} \simeq R_{M,t+h} - \frac{s_{M,t+h} + s_{M,t}}{2h}, \tag{10.20}$$

where $s_{M,t}$ and $s_{M,t+h}$ are the average bid-ask spreads of the securities included in the market portfolio at dates t and $t+h$, respectively.

Recall that according to the CAPM, the risk premium for holding a security is proportional to the covariance of its return with the return of the market portfolio. More precisely, the net return required by investors is $E(r_{j,t+h}) = r + \beta_j[E(r_{M,t+h}) - r]$, which, using equations (10.19) and (10.20), can be rewritten as:

$$E(R_{j,t+h} - \frac{s_{j,t+h} + s_{j,t}}{2h}) = r + \beta_j[(E(R_{M,t+h} - \frac{s_{M,t+h} + s_{M,t}}{2h}) - r]. \quad (10.21)$$

where security j's *net* beta is defined as the covariance of security j's *net* return with the *net* return of the market portfolio, divided by the variance of the net return on the market portfolio:

$$\beta_j \equiv \frac{\text{cov}(r_{j,t+h}, r_{M,t+h})}{\text{var}(r_{M,t+h})}. \quad (10.22)$$

Substituting in for the net returns from equations (10.19) and (10.20):

$$\beta_j = \frac{\text{cov}(R_{j,t+h} - \frac{s_{j,t+h}}{2h}, R_{M,t+h} - \frac{s_{M,t+h}}{2h})}{\text{var}(r_{M,t+h})}, \quad (10.23)$$

where we use the fact that at date t investors know the current value of the bid-ask spread of security j, $s_{j,t}$, and of the market portfolio, $s_{M,t}$, so that they do not affect covariances.

Thus the net beta of security j can be expressed as the sum of four betas:

$$\beta_j = \frac{\text{var}(R_{M,t+h})}{\text{var}(r_{M,t+h})} \times \left[\frac{\text{cov}(R_{j,t+h}, R_{M,t+h})}{\text{var}(R_{M,t+h})} + \frac{1}{4h^2}\frac{\text{cov}(s_{j,t+h}, s_{M,t+h})}{\text{var}(R_{M,t+h})} \right.$$
$$\left. - \frac{1}{2h}\frac{\text{cov}(R_{j,t+h}, s_{M,t+h})}{\text{var}(R_{M,t+h})} - \frac{1}{2h}\frac{\text{cov}(s_{j,t+h}, R_{M,t+h})}{\text{var}(R_{M,t+h})} \right] \quad (10.24)$$
$$= \frac{\text{var}(R_{M,t+h})}{\text{var}(r_{M,t+h})} \times \left[\beta_{j1} + \frac{1}{4h^2}\beta_{j2} - \frac{1}{2h}\beta_{j3} - \frac{1}{2h}\beta_{j4} \right].$$

Finally using this expression in equation (10.21), the required risk premium on security j can be written as:

$$E(R_{j,t+h}) - r = \beta_{1j}\lambda_M + \underbrace{\kappa(s_{j,t} + E(s_{j,t+h})) + \beta_{2j}(\kappa^2\lambda_M) - \beta_{3j}(\kappa\lambda_M) - \beta_{4j}(\kappa\lambda_M)}_{\text{illiquidity premium}},$$
$$(10.25)$$

where $\kappa \equiv 1/2h$ and λ_M is the adjusted risk premium on the market portfolio:

$$\lambda_M \equiv \frac{\text{var}(R_{M,t+h})}{\text{var}(r_{M,t+h})} \times \left[E(R_{M,t+h} - s_{M,t+h}) - r \right]. \tag{10.26}$$

The decomposition in equation (10.25) yields a liquidity-adjusted CAPM, which is relevant for any asset pricing test of the CAPM that relies on gross returns—that is, for tests relying on returns measured as percentage changes of midquote prices, rather than net returns. Equation (10.25) shows that the illiquidity premium includes two components: the first is the compensation for the current and expected level of trading costs, $s_{j,t} + E(s_{j,t+h})$, already discussed in Section 10.2.1 and captured in equation (10.9); the second component arises only if there is systematic illiquidity risk, as measured by the three illiquidity betas, β_{2j}, β_{3j}, and β_{4j}.

Each illiquidity beta captures a source of covariance risk arising from innovations in illiquidity: only β_{1j} captures the covariance between the security's fundamentals and those of the market portfolio; the other three are all related to illiquidity risk. Specifically:

1. Parameter $\beta_{2j} = \text{cov}(s_{j,t+h}, s_{M,t+h})/\text{var}(R_{M,t+h})$ measures the commonality in liquidity, namely, the extent to which the illiquidity of stock j ($s_{j,t+h}$) correlates with market-wide illiquidity ($s_{M,t+h}$). Holding stocks that remain liquid when others go illiquid is a way to hedge a drop in asset values due to market-wide illiquidity. Thus, other things being equal, these stocks are attractive and should have a higher price (lower risk premium). Conversely, stocks with a high β_2 must have greater returns on average, because investors require compensation for holding a security that becomes illiquid when the overall market does.

2. Parameter $\beta_{3j} = \text{cov}(R_{j,t+h}, s_{M,t+h})/\text{var}(R_{M,t+h})$ measures the sensitivity of individual security returns to market liquidity, namely, the co-movement between the gross return on stock j ($R_{j,t+h}$) and market-wide illiquidity ($s_{M,t+h}$). A high value of β_{3j} means that the stock does well when market-wide illiquidity increases. Thus, stocks with high β_{3j} offer a hedge against a drop in market-wide liquidity, so investors require a smaller risk premium to hold these stocks.

3. Parameter $\beta_{4j} = \text{cov}(s_{j,t+h}, R_{M,t+h})/\text{var}(R_{M,t+h})$ measures the sensitivity of individual securities' liquidity to market returns, namely, the co-movement between the illiquidity of stock j and the gross return on the market portfolio. Stocks with a high β_{4j} require a lower expected return, because they tend to remain liquid when the market is down: investors value such stocks more highly, as they allow them to sell at low transaction costs in an adverse market phase.

The model implies that, as any other type of risk, liquidity risk will be "priced" by financial markets only if it cannot be eliminated via diversification: if liquidity risk were purely idiosyncratic, security j's future bid-ask spread $s_{j,t+h}$ would by definition not comove either with market-wide illiquidity or with the return of the market portfolio, so that $\beta_{2j} = \beta_{4j} = 0$. Furthermore, a well-diversified portfolio of securities would feature a negligible amount of illiquidity risk, as the unexpected drop in the liquidity of some securities can be expected to be offset by unexpected increases in the liquidity of other securities in the portfolio. Hence, the liquidity risk of the market portfolio would be negligible, implying that $\beta_{3j} = 0$.

However, empirical studies indicate that liquidity risk is not idiosyncratic: Hasbrouck and Seppi (2001); Chordia, Roll, and Subrahmanyam (2000); and Huberman and Halka (2001) show that there is "commonality" in liquidity risk. That is, liquidity measures for various securities (e.g., bid-ask spreads or measures of price impact) are usually positively correlated. This co-movement in liquidity implies that the liquidity risk on a security cannot be easily diversified away and so contributes to its systematic risk. In this situation, the logic of asset pricing models (such as the CAPM) implies that investors will require compensation for liquidity risk, thereby creating a second link between the price and the liquidity of financial assets, beside that highlighted by Amihud and Mendelson (1986).

Acharya and Pedersen (2005) estimate the LCAPM relationship (10.26) on CRSP data for all common stocks listed on NYSE and AMEX from 1962–99 in two stages: first, they estimate the betas as defined above; second, they estimate equation (10.26) on the cross-section of returns and betas. They measure illiquidity by the Amihud ratio, i.e., the ratio between the absolute value of daily returns and the daily volume.[10]

Acharya and Pedersen report three main results. First, illiquid stocks (those with high average transaction costs) tend to be more exposed to illiquidity risk, as the absolute value of their liquidity betas (β_{2j}, β_{3j}, and β_{4j}) are larger. Second, the cross-section of stock returns is explained better by the liquidity-adjusted CAPM than by the traditional CAPM. Last, liquidity risk is priced: overall, the various sources of liquidity risk contribute a 1.1% difference in average annual returns between a portfolio of illiquid stocks and a portfolio of liquid stocks. This yield spread is largely due to the third source of illiquidity risk (captured by β_{4j}): investors seem to value especially highly those securities that remain liquid when the market is down. However, when expected illiquidity and the

---

[10] Since the Amihud ratio is at best proportional to the transaction cost variable s considered by the model, reliance on this empirical measure of illiquidity may affect the estimate of the scaling factor κ in expression (10.25). As a result, the estimate of κ cannot be used to identify the investors' holding period h.

liquidity betas are entered jointly with no restrictions in the specification, their impact on the risk premium is estimated imprecisely because of collinearity.

Both Acharya and Pedersen's (2005) original work and subsequent work, notably by Lee (2011) and Holden and Nam (2019), find similar "first-stage" results: most betas are significantly different from zero, and the first liquidity-related beta, β_{2j}, is positive for most stocks while the remaining two, β_{3j} and β_{4j}, are generally negative (though Holden and Nam find that the betas do not seem to be very stable over time when comparing pre- and post-2000 estimates). Thus for most stocks illiquidity co-moves with market-wide illiquidity, and it worsens when the general market is down, while the stock's return is negatively correlated with market-wide illiquidity.

Regarding the "second stage," which considers the impact of illiquidity on stock returns, the evidence is more mixed. All studies confirm the established finding that the average level of illiquidity, s_j, carries a significant premium. However, Holden and Nam's (2019) replication and extension do not consistently find estimated coefficients on the illiquidity β's that are of the predicted sign and significantly different from zero. Moreover, the implication of the LCAPM, that all four β's should be significant and carry an equal coefficient λ_M, is rejected. However, it should be pointed out that the hypothesis that these coefficients should all be equal is at odds with the predictions from equation (10.25). To see this, observe that in equation (10.25) the liquidity betas have different coefficients whenever the holding period h differs from $\frac{1}{2}$. A further reason to expect this hypothesis to fail is that the measure of illiquidity used is not the bid-ask spread, but at best proportional to it.[11]

10.5.2 The Liquidity-Augmented Factor Model

Pastor and Stambaugh (2003) have proposed an alternative approach to test the pricing of liquidity risk, which rests on a measure of aggregate stock market liquidity as a risk factor (i.e., a source of risk for stock returns for which investors demand a risk premium). More specifically, they estimate the following regression for NYSE and AMEX stocks (over the 1962–2000 period):

$$r_{jt} = \beta_j^0 + \beta_1^{\mathcal{L}}\mathcal{L}_t + \beta_j^M MKT_t + \beta_j^M SMB_t + \beta_j^H HML_t + \epsilon_{jt}, \qquad (10.27)$$

[11] Acharya and Pedersen include the effect of κ in their discussion of the expected illiquidity premium but do not account for its importance in determining the relationship between the coefficients on the betas: their theory predicts that the regression coefficient of liquidity β_{2j} should be κ^2 times that of β_{1j}, while those of liquidity betas β_{3j} and β_{4j} should be $-\kappa$ times that of β_{1j}.

where r_{jt} is security j's excess return (i.e., the difference between its rate of return and the risk-free interest rate), $\mathcal{L}_t$ is the Pastor and Stambaugh liquidity factor (defined below), MKT_t is the excess return on the market portfolio, SMB_t is the size factor (i.e., the difference between the return on a portfolio that is long on small-capitalization stocks and short on large-capitalization stocks), HML_t is the value factor (i.e., the difference between the return on a portfolio that is long on high-book-to-market stocks and short on high-book-to-market stocks). These last three factors were proposed by Fama and French (1993), and are widely used in empirical asset pricing research.[12]

The coefficient of the liquidity factor $\mathcal{L}_t$, $\beta_1^{\mathcal{L}}$, measures the extent to which the return of security j responds to changes in aggregate liquidity. It therefore captures a source of risk similar to the coefficient β_{3j} in equation (10.25) proposed by Acharya and Pedersen (2005). By construction the approach proposed by Pastor and Stambaugh (2003) focuses just on market-wide liquidity risk, but it controls for a larger set of potential risk factors, beside a security's covariance with the return on the market portfolio.

To construct their liquidity factor $\mathcal{L}_t$, Pastor and Stambaugh (2003) estimate monthly regressions of daily security-level stock returns (in excess of the return of the market portfolio) on a lagged measure of signed aggregate trading volume, which is intended to capture past order flow. These individual stocks' regressions produce a monthly estimate of the "reversal coefficient" for each security. These are aggregated across securities into a market-wide illiquidity time series at the monthly frequency, which is the liquidity factor $\mathcal{L}_t$. The idea is that order flow should trigger a price response that is followed by a reversal in the subsequent period, as predicted by the order-processing costs and inventory holding costs models presented in Chapter 3. Therefore, the stronger is this reversal, the more illiquid is a stock. Thus, $\mathcal{L}_t$ is negative (it captures reversals) and a lower value of $\mathcal{L}_t$ means an increase in market wide illiquidity.

The time series $\mathcal{L}_t$ features occasional downward spikes, corresponding to months with particularly low liquidity (large reversals). Most of these correspond to sharp market downturns, the largest of which occurred in the stock market crash of October 1987. In a subsequent extension to more recent data, Pastor and Stambaugh (2019) find that the time series of liquidity sharply drops at the time of the 2008 financial crisis. Moreover, this measure of liquidity tends to be low at times of high market volatility.

---

[12] The Fama-French factors are available on Kenneth French's website at: https://mba.tuck. dartmouth.edu/pages/faculty/ken.french/datalibrary.html. The Pastor and Stambaugh (2003) liquidity factor is available on Lubos Pastor's website here: https://faculty.chicagobooth.edu/lubos-pastor/data.

The estimates of the loading of the liquidity factor $(\beta_1^{\mathcal{L}})$ in equation (10.27) turn out to be positive and statistically significant, indicating that empirically returns tend to be low when illiquidity increases. Moreover, Pastor and Stambaugh (2003) show that there are systematic differences in the average returns of portfolios formed by stocks with different exposures to liquidity risk $(\beta_1^{\mathcal{L}})$, after controlling for the exposure of these portfolios to the other factors included in equation (10.27). In particular, the differential in average returns, adjusted for exposure to other sources of risks in equation (10.27), of a portfolio of stocks with high loadings $(\beta_1^{\mathcal{L}})$ on the liquidity factor and a portfolio of stocks with low loadings is 9.23 %. Thus, investors require a compensation for holding stocks that are more exposed to liquidity risks, after controlling for their exposure to other well known risk factors.

Li, Novi-Marx, and Velikov (2017) have replicated and extended out-of-sample the 2003 study, and have broadly confirmed its results. However, they have raised a debate about the relationship between the liquidity factor $(\beta_1^{\mathcal{L}})$ and the momentum factor, which captures the tendency of stocks to maintain recent price trends in the future. Pastor and Stambaugh (2019) provide a discussion of this issue.

10.6 Further Reading

Amihud, Mendelson, and Pedersen (2005) and Vayanos and Wang (2009) offer in-depth examinations of the effects of illiquidity on asset prices (see also Cochrane 2005). The seminal study by Amihud and Mendelson (1986) was followed by a spate of works confirming the positive cross-sectional relationship between liquidity and returns, controlling for risk: see Brennan and Subrahmanyam (1996); Datar, Naik, and Radcliffe (1998); and Chordia, Roll, and Subrahmanyam (2000); Similarly, the liquidity effects found by Amihud and Mendelson (1991) for fixed-income securities were confirmed by other studies, such as Warga (1992), Daves and Ehrhardt (1993), Kamara (1994), and Krishnamurthy (2002). Some researchers have also considered the effect of exogenous transaction costs on asset prices in dynamic portfolio choices models (e.g., Constantinides 1986 and Vayanos 1998).

It is worth pointing out that asymmetric information poses several important issues for asset pricing beyond those discussed in Section 10.2.4. One issue is which are the effects of asymmetric information in dynamic models of trading. Wang (1993) considers such a model with a single security, and finds that the effect of asymmetric information on expected returns conditional on a liquidity shock is ambiguous. An increase in the fraction of informed traders in his setup has two opposite effects. It increases adverse selection risk for uninformed investors, which works to increase expected returns, but it also increases the amount of information available to investors, which reduces the uncertainty over the final payoff and with it the risk premium required by investors to absorb liquidity shocks.

Another question is whether, in the presence of asymmetric information, a CAPM-like relationship still obtains. Even under the usual CAPM assumptions (i.e., CARA utility functions and normal distributions of securities' payoffs), investors with heterogeneous information have different expectations for returns and their covariance structure. Hence, they do not have the same mean-variance frontier, implying that under asymmetric information the usual two-funds separation theorem of the CAPM does not hold. Biais, Bossaerts, and Spatt (2010) show however that a CAPM-like relationship can be obtained by considering the weighted-average beliefs of informed and uninformed investors (see also Admati 1985).

The model of asset pricing in OTC markets in Section 10.2.5 is based on Duffie, Gârleanu, and Pedersen (2005), from which our presentation differs in two respects. First, their model is cast in continuous time, while we consider a discrete time. Second, in their model investors can trade directly with other investors, as well as with dealers. This model has pioneered the so called search-theoretic approach to OTC markets and gave rise to many subsequent extensions and applications. For instance, Duffie, Gârleanu, and Pedersen (2007) consider the case of a risky security and risk-averse investors, and analyze the dynamics of prices after an aggregate liquidity shock (an exogenous drop in the fraction of investors with a high valuation). Weill (2007) allows market makers to carry inventories over time and thus to counter the negative price effects of liquidity shocks. Vayanos and Wang (2007) posit multiple securities and derive cross-sectional implications for asset returns. See Weill (2020) for a survey of the search-theoretic approach to model trading in OTC markets.

Pastor and Stambaugh (2003) and Acharya and Pedersen (2005) were among the first to study whether liquidity risk is priced. Their approach and findings generated a large following literature and debates about whether liquidity risk is actually priced: see Li et al. (2019), Pastor and Stambaugh (2019), Pontiff and Singla (2019) or Ben-Rephael et al. (2015).

In contrast to the cross-sectional evidence, the longitudinal evidence on the relationship between bid-ask spread and returns is somewhat inconclusive. Using a very long series of monthly data, Jones (2002) finds that at times when spreads are large and so expected to be high in the near future, then expected returns are also high. However, Hasbrouck (2005) gets mixed results using daily data. These conflicting findings may be partly produced by the difficulty of disentangling the impact of time-varying liquidity from that of time-varying volatility, induced perhaps by bouts of noise traders' buy or sell orders.

A few papers highlight the interactions between illiquidity and fundamental risk. For instance, in Vayanos (2004), fund managers are subject to withdrawals when their performance falls below a given threshold. Hence, they are more likely to liquidate when the market is volatile, which increases the illiquidity premium at times of high volatility. In contrast, Favero, Pagano, and von Thadden (2010) predict a negative relationship between the illiquidity premium and volatility, as in their model investors have less use for liquidity when volatility is high since outside investment opportunities also deteriorate.

10.7 Appendix: The Derivation of the Search Model

This appendix shows how to derive the expressions for the ask price and the bid-ask spread in Section 10.4. In each period t, there are four groups of investors in the market: (i) high-valuation investors who own the security, (ii) high-valuation investors who do not own the security, (iii) low-valuation investors who own the security, and (iv) low-valuation investors who do not own the security. Let π_h^o, π_h^{no}, π_l^o, and, π_l^{no} be the fractions of investors in each group, with superscript h and l referring respectively to a high-valuation and a low-valuation individual, and subscripts o and no to an owner and a non-owner.

In each period, the fraction of investors willing to buy the security is $\pi_b = \psi\pi_l^{no} + (1-\psi)\pi_h^{no}$, and the fraction willing to sell is $\pi_s = \psi\pi_h^o + (1-\psi)\pi_l^o$. We first show that when $q < \frac{1}{2}$, we have $\pi_b > \pi_s$. That is, at any date, there are more investors who want to buy the asset than investors willing to sell it.

To see this, let π_h be the steady-state fraction of high-valuation and π_l be the steady-state fraction of low-valuation investors. It must be that $\pi_h + \pi_l = 1$. Next, remember that in each period a fraction ψ of high-valuation investors become low-valuation investors, and vice-versa. Hence:

$$\pi_h = (1-\psi)\pi_h + \psi\pi_l = (1-\psi)\pi_h + \psi(1-\pi_h). \tag{10.28}$$

Solving this equation for π_h yields $\pi_h = \frac{1}{2}$. By definition, $\pi_h = \pi_h^o + \pi_h^{no}$ and $\pi_l = \pi_l^o + \pi_l^{no}$. Moreover, all shares are necessarily owned either by high-valuation investors or by low-valuation ones. Hence $q = \pi_l^o + \pi_h^o$. Thus, we have:

$$\pi_h^o + \pi_h^{no} = \frac{1}{2},$$

$$\pi_l^o + \pi_l^{no} = \frac{1}{2},$$

$$\pi_l^o + \pi_h^o = q.$$

Using these equations, after some straightforward steps one obtains:

$$\pi_b = \pi_s + \left(\frac{1}{2} - q\right),$$

so that $\pi_b > \pi_s$ if and only if $q < \frac{1}{2}$.

Some dealers are contacted by sellers while some are contacted by buyers. Thus, after trading with their clients, dealers are either short one share of the asset or long one share of the asset. Following Duffie et al. (2005), we assume that dealers cannot hold an inventory position at the end of each period. This assumption has two implications. First, dealers must trade together (those with a short position buy the asset from those with a long position). We denote by μ the price at which interdealer trades takes place. Second, dealers' aggregate position after trading with their clients must be zero. As there are more investors seeking to buy the asset than investors seeking to sell it ($\pi_b > \pi_s$), this no aggregate inventory condition implies that some buyers of the asset must eventually decide not buy it. Ultimately, this decision depends on how dealers' ask and bid prices are set, which we explain now.

First, consider the case of a dealer who is contacted by an investor willing to sell the asset and let $\bar{b}$ be the minimum price that this investor is ready to accept. In this case, the potential gains from trade (surplus) between the investor and the dealer are $\mu - \bar{b}$. Following, Duffie et al. (2005), we assume that dealers set their bid price to obtain a fraction χ of this surplus. Thus, dealers' bid price is:

$$b = \chi \bar{b} + (1 - \chi)\mu,$$

with $0 \leq \chi \leq 1$. As dealers' bargaining power χ increases, they extract a larger surplus from sellers. At the limit, for $\chi = 1$, the surplus left to sellers is zero. As $b \geq \bar{b}$, an investor willing to sell the asset trades as soon as he finds a dealer. Thus, there is a mass $\phi \pi^s$ of dealers with a long position after trading with investors in each period.

Now consider the case of a dealer who is contacted by an investor willing to buy the asset and let $\bar{a}$ be the maximum price that this investor is ready to pay. At any ask price a strictly less than a, the investor is strictly better off doing so and at $a = \bar{a}$ he is indifferent between trading or not. Thus, if $a < \bar{a}$, the mass of dealers with a short position after trading with investors is $\phi \pi^b$ and therefore exceeds the mass of dealers with a long position, $\phi \pi^s$ (since $\pi^b > \pi^s$). In this case, the zero aggregate inventory condition cannot be satisfied. In contrast, at $a = \bar{a}$, one can assume that only a fraction $\frac{\pi_s}{\pi_b}$ of investors buy the asset because investors willing to do so are indifferent between buying or not. In this way, the mass of dealers with a short position after trading with investors is $\frac{\pi_s}{\pi_b} \times \phi\pi^b = \phi\pi^s$ and in aggregate dealers' position is zero, as required. In sum, this means that $a = \bar{a}$ and the likelihood that an investor willing to buy the asset trades in a given period is $\rho^b \equiv \phi \cdot \frac{\pi_s}{\pi_b}$.[13]

Finally, following Duffie et al. (2005), assume that these inter-dealer transactions take place at the midpoint between investors' reservations prices:

$$\mu = \frac{\bar{a} + \bar{b}}{2}. \tag{10.29}$$

To obtain the equilibrium ask and bid prices, we must now compute $\bar{a}$ and $\bar{b}$. To this end, we first compute the discounted value of the future stream of cash flows that each type of investor expects to receive just after trading in a given period (i.e., just after stage 3). Let V_j^k be this discounted value for a trader with valuation $j \in \{h, l\}$ and type $k \in \{o, no\}$.

Now, consider a high-valuation non-owner contacting a dealer: he buys the security if and only if:

$$V_h^o - a \geq V_h^{no},$$

since otherwise he is better off staying a non-owner. Similarly, a low-valuation owner will sell the security to a market maker if and only if:

$$V_l^{no} + b \geq V_l^o.$$

Thus, $\bar{a} = V_h^o - V_h^{no} = \Delta V_h$ and $\bar{b} = V_l^o - V_l^{no} = \Delta V_l$. To determine ΔV_h and ΔV_l, we first calculate V_j^k for $j \in \{h, l\}$ and $k \in \{o, no\}$. The value placed by a high-valuation owner on the security is:

$$V_h^o = \frac{1}{1+r} + \frac{(1-\psi)V_h^o}{1+r} + \frac{\psi(1-\phi)V_l^o}{1+r} + \frac{\psi\phi(V_l^{no} + b)}{1+r}. \tag{10.30}$$

To understand this expression, observe that a high-valuation owner always receives \$1 with certainty at the beginning of the next period, which explains the first term here. The last three terms are simply the weighted average of

---

[13] Note that $a = \bar{a}$ means that dealers extract all surplus when they trade with a buyer while they don't when they trade with a seller. This makes sense because there is an excess of buyers relative to sellers. In fact, $\bar{a}$ is the price that would be set to clear the market if trading was centralized as in a Walrassian market.

the discounted cash flow for the investor in each of his possible states at the end of the next period, the weights being the respective probabilities. With probability $1 - \psi$, the investor remains a high-valuation owner and therefore values the discounted cash flow of the asset at V_h^o. This explains the second term in the equation. With probability $\psi(1 - \phi)$, he turns into a low-valuation owner who does not manage to sell to a dealer, and thus the subsequent period ends up valuing it at V_l^o; this explains the third term. Finally, with probability $\psi\phi$, the investor becomes a low-valuation investor who does manage to resell the security at price b in the next period. In this state, the investor receives b but also keeps the option of buying at some point in the future. The value of this option is V_l^{no}. This state is captured by the last term.

Proceeding in the same way, we obtain the discounted value of future cash flows for a high-valuation investor who does not own the asset yet:

$$V_h^{no} = \frac{\psi V_l^{no}}{1+r} + \frac{(1-\psi)(1-\rho^b)V_h^{no}}{1+r} + \frac{(1-\psi)\rho^b(V_h^o - \bar{a})}{1+r}. \tag{10.31}$$

The first term here corresponds to the state in which the investor's valuation drops, so that in the next period he does not want to buy the asset anymore; the second to the state in which his valuation stays high but he does not manage to buy the security from a dealer; and the last term to the situation in which the investor does buy the asset from a dealer (at price $\bar{a}$ with probability ρ^b) and therefore owns the asset at the end of the next period. Following the same reasoning, we get:

$$V_l^o = \frac{1-c}{1+r} + \frac{\psi V_h^o}{1+r} + \frac{(1-\psi)(1-\phi)V_l^o}{1+r} + \frac{(1-\psi)\phi(V_l^{no} + b)}{1+r} \tag{10.32}$$

$$V_l^{no} = \frac{(1-\psi)V_l^{no}}{1+r} + \frac{\psi(1-\rho^b)V_h^{no}}{1+r} + \frac{\psi\rho^b(V_h^o - \bar{a})}{1+r} \tag{10.33}$$

Remember that $\Delta V_h = V_h^o - V_h^{no}$. From equations (10.30), (10.31), (10.32), and (10.33), we obtain:

$$\Delta V_h = \frac{(1-\psi(1-\phi)\Delta V_l + (\psi b + (1-\psi)\bar{a})\phi - (1-\psi)(\phi - \rho^b)(\Delta V_h - \bar{a})}{(1+r) - (1-\psi)(1-\phi)}.$$

Recalling that $\bar{a} = \Delta V_h$, this expression can be rewritten as:

$$\Delta V_h = \frac{1 + \psi(1-\phi)\Delta V_l + (\psi b + (1-\psi)\bar{a})\phi}{(1+r) - (1-\psi)(1-\phi)}. \tag{10.34}$$

Proceeding in the same way and remembering that $\Delta V_l = V_l^{no} - V_l^o$, we obtain:

$$\Delta V_l = \frac{(1-c) + \psi(1-\phi)\Delta V_h + (1-\psi)\phi b + \psi\phi\bar{a}}{(1+r) - (1-\psi)(1-\phi)}. \tag{10.35}$$

Hence:

$$\Delta V_h - \Delta V_l = \frac{c + S(1 - 2\psi)\phi}{(1+r) - (1-2\psi)(1-\phi)}, \tag{10.36}$$

where $S = a - b$ is the bid-ask spread charged by dealers. Now, recalling that:

$$\bar{a} = \Delta V_h, \tag{10.37}$$

$$b = \chi\bar{b} + (1-\chi)\mu. \tag{10.38}$$

and that $\mu = \frac{\bar{a} + \bar{b}}{2} = \frac{\Delta V_h + \Delta V_l}{2}$, we deduce from equations (10.37) and (10.38) that:

$$\Delta V_h - \Delta V_l = \frac{2(\bar{a} - b)}{1 + \chi} = \frac{2S}{1 + \chi}. \tag{10.39}$$

Substituting $\Delta V_h - \Delta V_l$ from this expression into equation (10.36) and solving for S, we get:

$$S = \frac{(1 + \chi)c}{2(r + 2\psi) + (1 - 2\psi)\phi(1 - \chi)}, \tag{10.40}$$

which is expression (10.17) in Section 10.4.1.

Next, using the fact that $\Delta V_l = \Delta V_h - \frac{2S}{1+\chi}$ from equation (10.39) and $\bar{a} = \Delta V_h$, we can solve equation (10.34) for ΔV_h and obtain the ask price:

$$a = \bar{a} = \Delta V_h = \frac{1}{r} - \frac{2\psi}{r(1 + \chi)}\left(1 - \phi\frac{1 - \chi}{2}\right)S,$$

which is expression (10.16) in Section 10.4.1.

10.8 Exercises

1. **Liquidity premium in the presence of dividend income.** Assume that investors hold a stock for one period, and can trade it at a constant percentage bid-ask spread s. The stock's fundamental value at date t, μ_t, equals its midprice at that date. The stock yields a constant dividend yield

d per period, so that the dividend per share at date t is $d\mu_t$. The one-period required rate of return on the stock is given and equal to r.

a. Define the gross-of-transaction-cost return $1 + R$ in terms of μ_t, μ_{t+1}, and d.

b. Determine the equilibrium gross return $1 + R$ as a function of r, s, and d alone.

c. How does the liquidity premium $R - r$ change with the dividend yield d? [Hint: recall that $(1 + x)/(1 + y) \approx x - y$, for x and y small.]

d. Explain the intuitive reason for the result obtained in answering point c.

2. **Transaction costs and clientele effects.** Consider two bonds: bond A yields 2% and has a bid-ask spread of 1.00%, while bond B yields 2.40% and has a bid-ask spread of 2%. Your asset management company caters to two groups of investors: the members of group 1 have a four-year expected holding period, while group 2 has a two-year expected holding period. The company asks you which of the two bonds should be marketed to which group of customers.

a. Does group 1 prefer bond A or B?

b. Does group 2 prefer bond A or B?

c. Denote by $\Delta R = R_B - R_A$ the difference between the gross yields of the two bonds. Given the holding periods of the two groups and the bid-ask spreads of the two bonds assumed above, which are the minimum and maximum yield differentials ΔR that would produce the same clientele equilibrium as in the case considered under **a** and **b**?

d. Suppose that ΔR were higher than the upper bound found under **c**: which bonds would the two groups want to buy?

e. Suppose that ΔR were lower than the lower bound found under **c**: which bonds would the two groups want to buy?

3. **Effect of changes in market structure on expected returns.** Consider an investor who plans to buy stock X at date t and resell it, after one year, at date $t + 1$. The required annual rate of return on this stock is r and each year the stock pays a dividend equal to $\bar{D}$ on *average*. Let b_{t+1} be the expected resale price at $t + 1$. As the market for stock X is illiquid, the resale price is lower than the expected fundamental value μ_{t+1}. Specifically, $b_{t+1} = \mu_{t+1}(1 - s/2)$ where s is the bid-ask spread. Let $a_t = \mu_t(1 + s/2)$ be the ask price that the investor is willing to buy at date t.

a. Show that:

$$\mu_t = \frac{\bar{D}}{\left[(1 + r)\frac{1+s/2}{1-s/2} - 1\right]\left(1 - \frac{s}{2}\right)},$$

where r is the net expected return on the stock.

b. Let $r_t = \frac{D_t + b_{t+1}}{a_t} - 1$ be the actual return of the stock over the period $[t, t+1]$. Note that this differs from the net expected return simply because the actual dividend may differ from the expected dividend in every period. Of course, $E(D_t) = \bar{D}$. Let $r_t - r$ be the "abnormal" return of the stock over the period $[t, t+1]$. What is the average abnormal net return?

c. Now suppose that at some date τ, the stock exchange on which stock X is listed introduces a new trading system. Following this change, the bid-ask spread on stock X becomes s^*. What is the effect of this change in trading organization on the price of the stock at date τ? If this change is unexpected until date τ, what is the effect on the expected abnormal return of the stock from date $\tau - 1$ to date τ.

d. Suppose you measure the average gross and net annual returns of stock X over ten years before the change at date τ, excluding the year preceding date τ; then you perform the same calculation with ten years of data after the change in the trading system, and finally compare the two figures. If the change in the trading system makes the market more liquid (i.e., $s^* < s$), what should be the outcome of this comparison?

4. **Effect on the bid-ask spread of the probability of finding a dealer.** Consider the equilibrium bid-ask S in expression (10.17) in the search model of Section 10.4.

  a. Assuming $\chi < 1$, how does the bid-ask spread respond to changes in the probability ϕ of finding a dealer? How does the answer depend on the value of the probability ψ that the investor's valuation will change in the future?

  b. What is the intuitive explanation for this result?

5. **Bid-ask spreads and trade size in OTC markets.** The Excel file Ch10_ex5_data.xlsx, available on the companion website for the book, contains trades from the over-the-counter market for a Danish residential mortgage bond with a 1% coupon maturing in 2053.[14] The data covers 698 trades from March 2021 to October 2021.

  a. For each trade, compute the quoted bid-ask half spread as a percentage of the midprice. Compare the magnitude of the average spread to the bid-ask spreads from equity markets reported in Table 2.2.

  b. Inspect sell orders with trade ID 15 and 16. Although they were executed almost at the same time, do they have a similar spread? Would such a difference in spreads be possible in a market with a centralized limit order book? What is different about over-the-counter markets?

[14] Source: nasdaqomxnordic.com.

c. Estimate a regression of the spread on the trade size. A priori, based on the Kyle model presented in Section 4.2.2, what sign would you expect the coefficient on trade size to have? What sign does the coefficient actually have?

d. Consider the Duffie, Gârleaneu, Pedersen (DGP) model of an over-the-counter market from Section 10.4. Suppose that there are two (identifiable) types of investors: sophisticated investors (such as hedge funds) and unsophisticated investors (such as retail investors). If sophisticated investors have higher bargaining power than unsophisticated investors and also trade larger amounts, can the DGP model explain the empirical finding from question **b**?

e. Classify all orders as being submitted by sophisticated or unsophisticated investors by using the following crude rule: if the order size is a multiple of 10 million, the investor is sophisticated, if not the investor is unsophisticated. Now estimate a regression of the spread on the order size and a dummy variable indicating whether the investor is sophisticated (without an interaction term). Are the results consistent with the theoretical explanation proposed in question **c**?

11

Financial Stability and Market Liquidity

Learning Objectives:

- The provision of liquidity by market makers and arbitrageurs hinges on their access to funding liquidity
- Funding and market liquidity can feed on each other, generating "liquidity spirals"
- This feedback loop can generate financial instability
- Interconnections between financial intermediaries and markets can propagate instability and generate systemic risk
- Adverse selection due to counterparty risk contributes to instability
- Public provision of funding liquidity can mitigate such instability

11.1 Introduction

Liquidity fluctuates over time, to the point that sometimes it evaporates completely, especially in the context of financial crises. This chapter considers the causes of these sharp drops in liquidity and their effects on asset prices, and the channels by which they can propagate across markets. We shall see that the provision of market liquidity crucially depends on the financial health of the intermediaries who provide liquidity services, and in particular on their access to funding.

These intermediaries not only include the market makers described in Chapter 3, who speedily absorb the orders placed by noise traders into their inventories, but also professional investors such as hedge fund and mutual fund managers, who play the same function at lower frequencies (ranging from hours to weeks). For instance, when a large flow of sell orders placed by uninformed traders tends to push the market price below the fundamental, these professional investors "lean against the wind" by absorbing these sell orders in their portfolios; conversely, in response to large buy orders from noise traders, they tend to sell their holdings or even short-sell the asset.

Market Liquidity: Theory, Evidence, and Policy. Second Edition. Thierry Foucault, Marco Pagano, and Ailsa Röell,
Oxford University Press. © Oxford University Press 2023. DOI: 10.1093/oso/9780197542064.003.0012

Hedge funds that follow "contrarian" strategies for extended periods of time are good examples. They build portfolios with long positions in underperforming stocks and short positions in overperforming stocks, so as to exploit the price reversals that should occur if the price movements are due to transient noise trading shocks. Like traditional market makers, they sustain inventory risks because the extent and the speed of price reversals are uncertain, although the price reversals that they exploit take place at a lower frequency than those on which traditional market makers thrive. And, just as with market makers, their activity tends to mitigate mispricing, that is, the deviation of the market price from fundamentals that noise trading would otherwise generate, or to reduce its persistence. By the same token, their activity helps reassert the "law of one price," which requires assets with the same cash flows to trade at the same price: large orders placed by uninformed traders may otherwise cause prices to violate this non-arbitrage condition. For this reason, these professional speculators are sometimes referred to as "arbitrageurs."

This chapter highlights two novel points regarding the ability of market makers and arbitrageurs to provide market liquidity and prevent persistent mispricing. First, Section 11.2 shows that their ability to provide market liquidity hinges on their access to credit, hence on "funding liquidity." To see why, notice that to absorb large sell orders that exceed the cash in their portfolios, market makers and arbitrageurs must be able to borrow from banks or other financial intermediaries; similarly, to absorb large buy orders that exceed their holdings of the relevant asset, they must be able to short-sell it, and to fund such short sales they may again need to borrow the necessary resources. The need for such funding liquidity is particularly important when the orders generated by noise traders are correlated (Section 11.3).

Second, the availability of "funding liquidity" may itself be affected by dislocations in asset prices, as shown in Section 11.4: the mispricing generated by a bout of noise trading may become so extreme and persistent as to generate a drop in funding liquidity. For instance, if market makers and arbitrageurs have taken long positions in stocks that they consider undervalued, and are booking losses on these positions because stock sales by noise traders persist, the banks that fund these positions may refuse to roll over their loans to them. This is because the drop in stock prices may inflict capital losses on banks, either due to the implied increase in their credit risk exposure to market makers and arbitrageurs or due to banks' own exposure to the mispriced stocks: compliance with regulatory capital ratios requires them to reduce lending in line with their reduced capital. Hence, there can be a feedback effect from market liquidity to funding liquidity.

The mutual interaction between market and funding liquidity just described may generate a perverse feedback loop, as illustrated in Figure 11.1 for the case

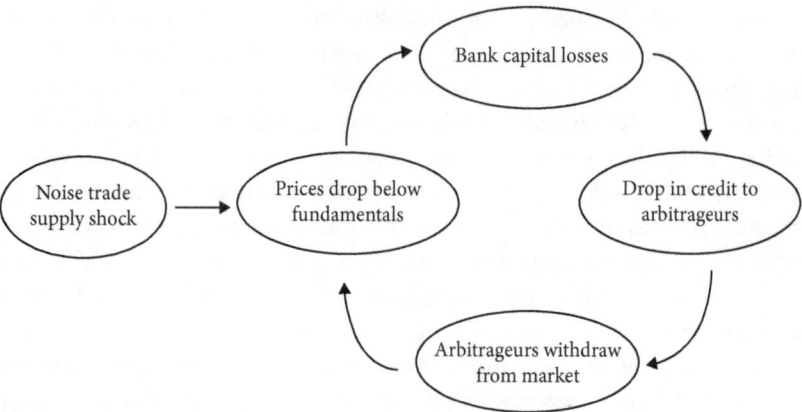

Figure 11.1 Feedback loop between market liquidity and funding liquidity.

where the initial trigger is a large flow of sell orders placed by noise traders. If the market is illiquid, these sales will push asset prices below fundamentals, and if this mispricing is large enough, it may induce a drop in funding liquidity, which in turn impairs the ability of market makers and arbitrageurs' ability to absorb orders, precipitating extreme mispricing and capital losses for banks.

The feedback loop illustrated in this figure can threaten the stability of financial markets, not only because of the magnitude of the asset price changes that they may trigger, but also because these impair simultaneously the balance sheets of market makers, arbitrageurs (e.g., hedge funds) and banks. Insofar as these financial intermediaries are typically interconnected via a network of contractual relationships in different markets, these destabilizing effects can propagate across intermediaries via their interlocking balance sheets, as discussed in Section 11.5: the liabilities of each are the assets of others. In extreme situations, the resulting domino effect can threaten the stability of the whole financial system. Hence, this chapter links market liquidity not only to funding liquidity, but also to the notion of "systemic risk," i.e., the risk that swings in asset prices and in market liquidity may result in a financial crisis.

The chapter closes with Section 11.6, which highlights that the balance sheets of financial intermediaries matter not only for market liquidity because of their role in amplifying and transmitting asset price shocks, but also because they can be a source of adverse selection. Recall that in Chapters 3 and 4 of this book private information about asset fundamentals has been shown to generate adverse selection and thereby market illiquidity. But the same can be said of private information about the balance sheets of financial intermediaries. If there are doubts about the ability of intermediaries to fulfill their obligations, this will generate adverse selection in the markets where they operate. This is relevant for counterparty risk in security markets, as well as in the interbank market, where banks are the issuers of the credit claims being traded, and in structured debt markets where the quality of the asset is affected by the standing of an intermediary. For instance, the value of an asset-backed security (ABS) that is partly guaranteed by a bank depends on the creditworthiness of the bank itself; and the other financial intermediaries typically do not have as accurate and timely a gauge of that as the bank in question.[1] At times of financial stress, creditworthiness typically becomes much more important than in normal times, and therefore the implied adverse selection become a more serious issue for the liquidity of the relevant assets, as witnessed by the dry-up of ABS markets during the financial crisis of 2008. Hence, private information about the state of intermediaries' balance sheets can be an additional threat to systemic stability.

11.2 Funding Liquidity and Limits to Arbitrage

The absence of arbitrage is a central tenet of asset pricing: two assets with identical cash flows should command the same price. Yet there are well-known cases in which this principle appears to be violated, due to frictions that prevent arbitrage between these assets. Transaction costs, for instance, may exceed the profits that can be gained by exploiting a price discrepancy, so that arbitrageurs will have no incentive to eliminate such discrepancy. In this section we focus on a less obvious source of frictions, namely the availability of funding for arbitrage.

One example of persistent deviations from no-arbitrage prices is the failure of the covered interest rate parity (CIP) condition in the foreign exchange market. This condition ensures that investors earn the same return from debt denominated in domestic and foreign currency, if they can rely on forward contracts to eliminate foreign exchange risk. It states that the interest rate differential between the two currencies in the respective cash money markets should equal the differential between the forward and spot exchange rates. The fact that this condition does not always hold opens up potential opportunities to earn riskless profits from covered interest arbitrage. Du, Tepper, and Verdelhan (2018) document that the CIP condition is systematically and persistently violated among G10 currencies, leading to significant arbitrage opportunities in currency and fixed income markets since the 2008 global financial crisis, and

---

[1] ABS are securities backed by a portfolio of income-generating assets such as housing mortgage loans, student or car loans, or credit card receivables. Examples of ABS are mortgage-backed securities (MBS) and collateralized debt obligations (CDO). Investors who purchase these securities receive the cash flow generated by the underlying loan pool. The bank that designs and sells the ABS to investors may provide guarantees to the investors who purchase the ABS to reduce the risk stemming from the possible default of the loans included in its portfolio.

document that these deviations for major currencies are not explained away by credit risk or transaction costs. This is striking, the foreign exchange forward and swap market being among the largest and most liquid derivative markets in the world.

Another instance of persistent arbitrage opportunities is the opening example in Section 10.2.1: in the United States, Treasury notes typically trade at a discount relative to otherwise identical Treasury bills. We argued that this difference in gross rates of return can be accounted for by the greater liquidity of bills. But why don't arbitrageurs eliminate this difference by selling bills, and buying notes, holding them to maturity so as to avoid further trading costs? This looks like a textbook example of a profitable arbitrage opportunity—the kind that according to asset pricing theory cannot last.

But lack of funding can prevent arbitrageurs from taking such an opportunity. In theory, riskless arbitrage should not require arbitrageurs to invest their own wealth or obtain outside funding, because a long position can be funded by an offsetting short position: arbitrage should be self-funding! However, in practice arbitrage does require capital. To understand this point, consider our simple example. It looks as if no capital is required to build the arbitrage portfolio: if the notes are worth 95% of the bills with the same maturity, the arbitrageur can use the proceeds from selling the bills short (say, $100,000) to buy the notes ($95,000), and immediately cash in the difference ($5,000), which is an instantaneous arbitrage profit (a "free lunch"), provided he can hold the position to maturity.

In reality, though, this kind of standard arbitrage portfolio requires capital. For instance, to sell bills short an arbitrageur must borrow them from a broker, who for example may require a margin of 150% of the value of the short sale as collateral (in our example, $150,000); buying the notes will cost another $95,000.[2] Therefore, in this example the total capital, net of the proceeds of the short sale, committed to the arbitrage portfolio would be $145,000, a huge multiple of the arbitrage profits ($5,000).

Hence a reason for the persistence of arbitrage opportunities is that arbitrageurs may not have enough wealth to exploit them. Of course they could borrow so as to carry out the arbitrage. But unless they can secure long-term funding, borrowing exposes them to the risk of having to liquidate their position

---

[2] Under Regulation T, the Federal Reserve Board requires all short sale accounts to have 150% of the value of the short sale at the time the sale is initiated. The sale described in the text is a "covered short sale," where the seller borrows the stock needed to deliver it to the buyer. In principle, even "naked shorting" may be allowed, whereby the seller does not borrow the stock needed and therefore must buy it on the market for delivery, which creates the risk of failure to deliver the stock to the buyer. However, in practice "naked shorting" has been banned in most jurisdictions since the financial crisis of 2008.

before the prices of notes and bills eventually converge at maturity. This risk is particularly great if the mispricing that they try to correct widens: as a result, they may have to meet larger margin requirements or may face a cut in funding due to a loss of confidence in their strategy. So, paradoxically, they may be forced to liquidate their position just when its future profitability is largest.

Limited wealth generally forces arbitrageurs to raise external funds. If these funds come in the form of short-maturity debt or can be withdrawn at will, arbitrageurs risk being unable to refinance their positions before their arbitrage portfolio pays off. For instance, in our example, the lender of the bills may recall them at any point in time, forcing the arbitrageur to either borrow them from another broker or to close out his position, possibly at a loss. Indeed, Du et al. (2018) find that deviations from CIP increase at the end of each quarter, especially for contracts that appear in banks' balance sheets, when banks face tighter capital constraints due to quarterly regulatory filings.[3]

One way out of these problems is to obtain long-term financing, as some arbitrageurs do by imposing lock-up covenants, the condition that investors cannot withdraw their funds for some minimum period. For instance, hedge funds typically raise money in the form of shares that can be redeemed at their market value only after a lock-up period. However, if the claims are short-term, financiers can better control the use of their funds by arbitrageurs: if the latter do not perform well, external investors can simply pull the plug. This threat helps to discipline arbitrageurs and prevent excessive risk taking. Alternatively, short-term financing could be an optimal response to uncertainty: it allows the financier to progressively increase his stake as he becomes more confident about the real ability of arbitrageurs. But, as noted above, it exposes arbitrageurs to the danger of early liquidation. The demise of LTCM, a major U.S. hedge fund, in 1998 (see Box 11.1) offers a vivid illustration.

This reasoning has been used to explain the empirical evidence of persistent arbitrage opportunities. For instance, Rosenthal and Young (1990), Froot and Dabora (1999), and de Jong, Rosenthal, and Van Dijk (2009) show that the prices of dually listed stocks (so-called twin stocks) often differ even though they are claims on the same cash flows.[4] De Jong, Rosenthal, and Van Dijk (2009) show that arbitrageurs who try to exploit these price differences must hold their positions for long periods of time with all the attendant risk. They write: "Since

---

[3] Note that arbitrage can also be performed by a bank's own security trading desk, with funding provided by the bank itself. Even so, its security trading activity is constrained by the bank's capital requirements.

[4] A "dually listed company" is a corporate structure that involves two listed companies with two distinct stocks that are claims on the same assets. A "cross-listed" company is a single firm with a single stock traded in multiple markets; researchers have found that arbitrage opportunities on these stocks are much smaller and less common than for the dually listed.

there is no identifiable date at which dual listed companies prices will converge, arbitrageurs with limited horizons who are unable to close the price gap on their own face considerable uncertainty. In some cases, arbitrageurs would have to wait for almost nine years before prices have converged and the position is closed. In the short run, the mispricing might deepen. In these situations, arbitrageurs receive margin calls, after which they would most likely be forced to liquidate part of the position at a highly unfavorable moment and suffer a loss" (p. 497).

Box 11.1 The LTCM Crisis

Long-Term Capital Management (LTCM) was a hedge fund founded in 1994 with equity of $1.3 billion. Investors had to put up a minimum of $1 million and could not withdraw it for three years. The first four years of its life were extremely profitable. Its main investment was of "market-neutral arbitrage," i.e., arbitrage positions that involve no systematic risk, mainly buying high-yield illiquid bonds (e.g., emerging market bonds and non-investment-grade corporate bonds) and shorting low-yield liquid bonds (e.g., U.S. Treasuries). Many these arbitrage positions were taken indirectly via derivative contracts such as rate swaps. Thus LTCM was betting that the yield spread between low- and high-risk bonds would narrow. Even by the standards of hedge funds, LTCM's leverage was enormous (over $20 of borrowing per $1 of equity), so that even a slight narrowing of yield spreads would translate into huge profits.

In the spring of 1998, however, spreads widened in the wake of the Southeast Asian financial collapse and Russia's troubles. The situation deteriorated further in August, when Russia devalued the ruble and declared a moratorium on public debt payments. By September, the yield spread on the J.P. Morgan index of emerging market bonds had increased to over seventeen percentage points, five times more than in October 1997. Yield spreads on U.S. non-investment-grade bonds also rose fivefold over the period. As a result, LTCM started making huge losses, cutting its equity value to $600 million by September (from $4.8 billion at the start of 1998). At this point, both LTCM and other funds with similar strategies came under pressure to meet margin calls and post additional collateral with creditors and swap counterparties, resulting in pressure to liquidate their positions at a further loss.

However, in fear that a generalized flight to quality might trigger a downward price spiral and a cascade of bankruptcies of financial institutions, the Federal Reserve persuaded a consortium of LTCM's major creditors to inject over $3.6 billion into the fund in return for a 90% equity stake. After the rescue, LTCM was run by these creditors and, helped by the recovery of financial markets, it gained 13% by December 1998. In the following months its portfolio was unwound and LTCM was liquidated.

The sequence of events in the LTCM crisis offers a good illustration of the forces at work in the model of Section 11.2.1: LTCM was arbitraging away yield differences that it considered excessive, but in doing so it was exposed to the risk of early liquidation by its creditors. Its positions were fundamentally sound, in that its portfolio bounced back once its creditors were persuaded to extend long-term financing, but the differences were not eliminated as quickly as LTCM had bet they would be. Other arbitrageurs did not intervene on a sufficient scale, because the Russian and Asian crises had raised volatility and tightened the funding available for arbitrage activity.

11.2.1 Risk of Early Liquidation as a Limit to Arbitrage

To illustrate these points, consider the following simple model, which is inspired by Shleifer and Vishny (1997). There are three dates (0, 1, and 2) and two zero-coupon bonds (A and B) with the same certain payoff V at date 2. The risk-free interest rate is set to zero, so that absent arbitrage opportunities, the price of the two bonds should equal V at both dates 0 and 1.

Suppose that an arbitrage opportunity arises at date 0: the price of bond A falls below that of bond B by an amount $M_0 > 0$ ($P_{0A} = P_{0B} - M_0$), while bond B is priced correctly ($P_{0B} = V$). That is, bond A is undervalued, and the size of this mispricing at date 0 is M_0. At date 1, the mispricing increases to $M_1 > M_0$ with probability κ or disappears with probability $1 - \kappa$. In the first case, the price of bond A is $P_{1A} = P_{1B} - M_1$; in the second case it is simply $P_{1A} = P_{1B} = V$. In the next section, we explain why such mispricing may arise and persist. At date 2, the assets pay off so that any mispricing is eliminated: $P_{2A} = P_{2B} = V$ with certainty.

As the prices of bonds A and B will converge at date $t = 2$, the arbitrage portfolio is a short position in asset B and an offsetting long position in asset A.[5] We assume that arbitrageurs must choose whether to build their arbitrage portfolio at date 0 or at date 1, denoting the decision to intervene at date t by the indicator function $I_t \in \{0,1\}$: if $I_t = 1$, the arbitrageur sells one share of B and buys one share of A at date t. If $I_0 = 1$, the portfolio is built at date 0; if $I_1 = 1$, at date 1. Otherwise the arbitrageur is inactive at both dates ($I_0 = I_1 = 0$). There are two restrictions: the arbitrageur cannot be active in both periods, that

---

[5] This type of arbitrage which bets on the convergence in the prices of two related securities, is known as "convergence trading."

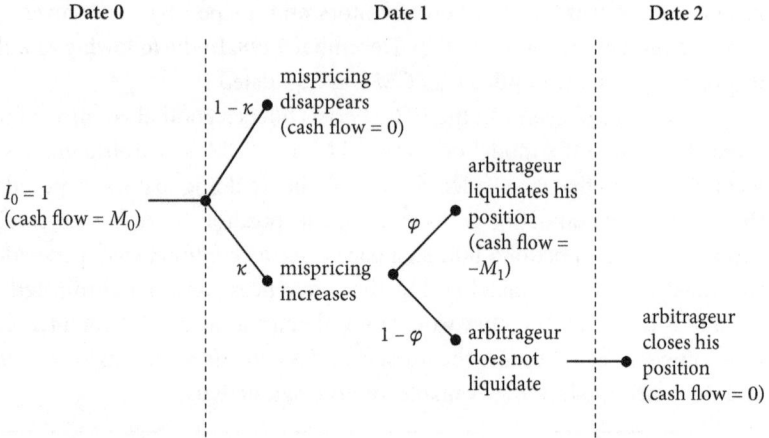

Figure 11.2 Actions and cash flows if the arbitrageur intervenes at date 0.

is, he cannot choose $I_0 = I_1 = 1$, and cannot take a position of more than one unit in the two bonds. These assumptions are intended to capture the funding constraints discussed above.

Suppose that the arbitrageur chooses to intervene at date 0. In this case, Figure 11.2 shows the cash flows of his portfolio at each date and in each contingency. The arbitrageur pockets the mispricing M_0 at date 0. With probability $1 - \kappa$ the mispricing disappears at date 1, so he closes his position. But with probability κ the mispricing increases to M_1.

When the mispricing persists at date 1, outside investors may choose to cut their funding of the arbitrageur's activities because they cannot tell whether it is due to a deepening of the arbitrage opportunity or a miscalculation by the arbitrageur. Then the arbitrageur must close his position at a loss: so the model captures the notion of "performance-based arbitrage," namely, that funds under management are withdrawn from arbitrageurs following trading losses. We assume that such forced liquidation occurs with probability φ. When forced to liquidate, the arbitrageur has a negative cash flow of $-M_1$, because he resells security A at price $V - M_1$ and covers his short position by buying security B at price V. If he is not forced to liquidate at date 1, he has zero cash flow at $t = 1$ and $t = 2$, as at this date the net payoff of his arbitrage portfolio is zero. Hence, intervention at date 0 yields an expected profit equal to $\Pi_0(\varphi) = M_0 - \kappa\varphi M_1$.

If instead the arbitrageur has not intervened at date 0, he will intervene at date 1 if the mispricing persists. The cash flows of his arbitrage portfolio in this case are illustrated in Figure 11.3. By definition he has zero cash flows at date 0. At date 1, he has the opportunity to set up an arbitrage portfolio only if the mispricing of bond A increases: hence he gets a cash flow M_1 with probability κ.

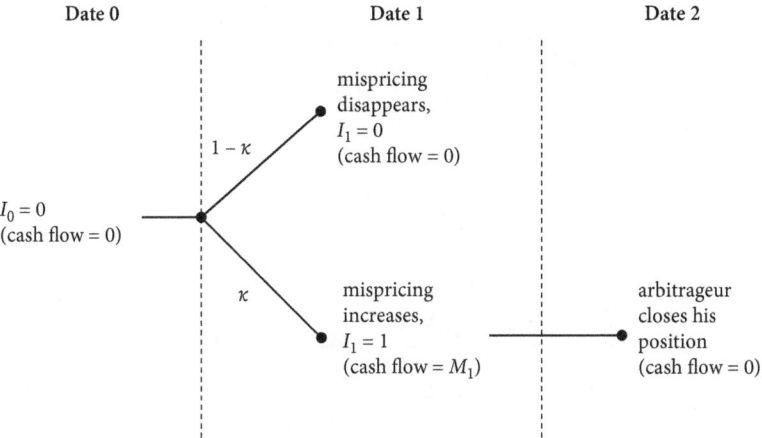

Figure 11.3 Actions and cash flows if the arbitrageur intervenes at date 1.

If instead the mispricing disappears, the arbitrageur can no longer intervene profitably, and will get no cash flow. Thus, the arbitrageur's expected profit is $\Pi_1 = \kappa M_1$.[6]

The choice hinges on the following trade-off. If the arbitrageur chooses to "wait" and intervene at date 1, he expects a gain M_1 if the mispricing persists (which happens with probability κ), and avoids the risk of early liquidation. But he forgoes the gain M_0 from exploiting the mispricing at date 0. Therefore, if $\kappa M_1 \geq M_0$, all arbitrageurs prefer to defer their intervention, as on average the mispricing will be greater at date 1. Hence, from now on, we focus on the more interesting case in which $\kappa M_1 < M_0$, that is, mispricing is expected to decrease. In this case, waiting is optimal if and only if $\Pi_1 > \Pi_0$, that is, if $\kappa M_1 > M_0 - \kappa\varphi M_1$. Hence, waiting is preferable if the future expected future mispricing κM_1 is large enough relative to the current mispricing M_0 and/or if the probability of early liquidation φ is large enough.

The threshold value of mispricing at $t = 1$ that keeps investors just indifferent between intervening early or late is:

$$\hat{M}_1 = \frac{M_0}{\kappa(1 + \varphi)} \tag{11.1}$$

The critical level of future mispricing $\hat{M}_1$ that makes arbitrageurs indifferent between intervening at date 0 or 1, is decreasing in the risk φ of early liquidation,

---

[6] One can imagine a more complex setting in which an arbitrageur is allowed to invest only part of his resources at date 0 and "hoard" the rest to intervene at date 1. This case is more realistic but does not deliver additional insights.

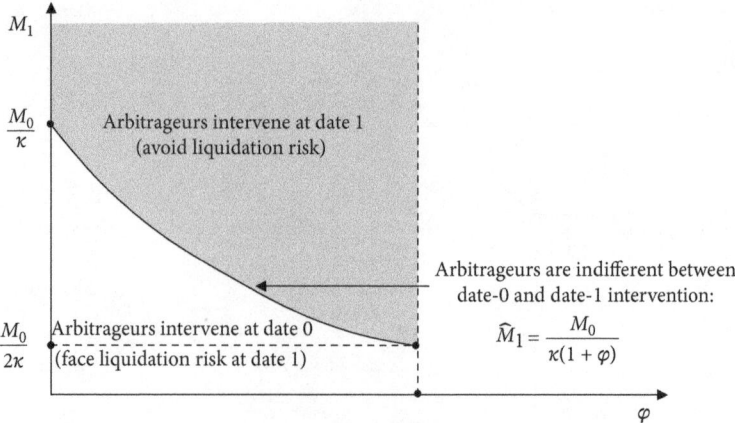

Figure 11.4 Allocation of arbitrage capital between dates 0 and 1.

as shown in Figure 11.4. In the shaded region above the "indifference curve" future mispricing and/or liquidation risk are large, so that arbitrageurs prefer to defer intervention. Below it, future mispricing and/or liquidation risk are low enough that they intervene immediately.

If expected mispricing were to exceed the level in expression (11.1), i.e., $M_1 > \hat{M}_1$, then all investors would choose to keep their powder dry and intervene at date 1.[7] Conversely, if the opposite inequality $M_1 < \hat{M}_1$ were to hold, then all investors would intervene at date 0. Finally, if $M_1 = \hat{M}_1$, then all investors would be indifferent between intervening at date 0 and doing so at date 1. In this case, we assume that a fraction $f \in (0, 1)$ of investors intervenes at date 0 and a complementary fraction $1 - f$ keeps their powder dry for speculation at date 1. The fraction f is determined by market clearing at date 1, as will be seen in the next subsection.

11.2.2 Limited Speculative Capital as a Barrier to Arbitrage

So far, we have considered mispricing (M_0 and M_1) at either date as exogenous. The literature on limits to arbitrage often assumes that mispricing arises from supply or demand shocks that drive prices away from fundamental values, which may occur for various reasons. For instance, some investors ("noise traders") may become irrationally over-pessimistic or over-optimistic (investor

---

[7] Note that, even when mispricing is expected to decline ($\kappa M_1 < M_0$), arbitrageurs will prefer to postpone intervention to date 1 if the risk φ of early liquidation is large enough, that is, it can still be that $M_1 > \hat{M}_1$.

sentiment) about the prospects of a security.[8] Alternatively, some investors (e.g., mutual funds or insurance companies) may suddenly be forced to liquidate positions in financial assets to deal with an unexpected funding need (e.g., to pay back creditors or meet investor withdrawals) or a prudential regulation requiring them to scale back their positions in certain asset classes. Such forced asset liquidations, which typically occur at deeply discounted prices, are known as "fire sales."[9]

To determine in the simplest possible way the mispricing M_1 at date 1, suppose that it arises from a shock to noise traders' supply—a "fire sale"—that occurs with probability κ and pushes the price of bond A further below its fundamental value. Otherwise, the price of bond A reverts to its fundamental value V. When this shock occurs, the aggregate noise traders' supply of bond A at date 1, $y(P_{A1})$, is assumed to be:

$$y(P_{A1}) = 1 + \delta(P_{A1} - V) = 1 - \delta M_1, \tag{11.2}$$

where $\delta > 0$ is the sensitivity of the noise traders' supply to the asset price. Hence, with probability κ, noise traders sell the bond at any price above $V - \frac{1}{\delta}$: they are overly pessimistic, as they value the bond at $V - \frac{1}{\delta}$, even though it will pay V for sure at date 2. Their sell orders exert a downward price pressure as long as the price is higher than $V - \frac{1}{\delta}$, that is, provided its undervaluation M_1 does not exceed $\frac{1}{\delta}$.

Hence, noise traders' orders are a source of mispricing, which can be corrected only if arbitrageurs lean strongly enough against them. However, the arbitrageurs' ability to do this is limited, since they must allocate capital between different strategies (in our model, interventions at date 0 and at date 1). Suppose that mispricing at date 0 is very pronounced. In this case, arbitrage capital will be massively invested to harness the date 0 mispricing, leaving little available to bet against mispricing at date 1. Mispricing will tend to persist and be increasing in its initial value, M_0.

Thus the precise level of mispricing prevailing on the market if noise traders materialize at date 1 depends on the fraction f of arbitrageurs that intervened at date 0: at date 1, these investors are no longer available to speculate against noise traders' sales, and a fraction φ of them will actually exacerbate the depressing effect of noise traders' supply on the price, since these arbitrageurs will have to liquidate their positions prematurely. Note that ex ante φ is the probability that

---

[8] Hence, the literature on limits to arbitrage is also related to that on behavioral finance, which studies how investors' psychological biases affect securities prices and can explain market anomalies (such as the existence of arbitrage opportunities).

[9] Shleifer and Vishny (2011) provides examples of fire sales and a review of the relevant literature.

each arbitrageur attaches to early liquidation, and ex post it is the fraction of arbitrageurs who face early liquidation at date 1.

The mispricing M_1 is determined by market clearing at date $t = 1$ when a noise trader supply shock occurs. The equilibrium price of bond A must be such that its supply is equal to its demand. There are two types of sellers: (i) noise traders who collectively sell an amount $y(P_{A1})$, which is positive for $M_1 < \frac{1}{\delta}$, and (ii) arbitrageurs who are forced to liquidate their position prematurely. As each arbitrageur who intervened at date 0 must liquidate his position with probability φ, the aggregate supply from arbitrageurs who liquidate at date $t = 1$ is $f\varphi$. Sell orders from these two categories of investors must be absorbed by the $1 - f$ arbitrageurs who still have capital to invest at date 1 because they did not intervene at date 0. Hence, the equilibrium price of asset A at date $t = 1$ is given by the condition:

$$\underbrace{y(P_{A1})}_{\text{noise traders' sell orders}} + \underbrace{f\varphi}_{\text{arbitrageurs' sell orders}} = \underbrace{1 - f.}_{\text{arbitrageurs' buy orders.}} \tag{11.3}$$

Replacing $y(P_{A1})$ with its expression in (11.2), this market clearing condition yields the following expression for the equilibrium mispricing of bond A at date $t = 1$ if noise traders materialize (which they do with probability κ):

$$M_1 = \frac{1 + \varphi}{\delta} f. \tag{11.4}$$

Note that, by construction, there is no mispricing at date 1 if all arbitrage capital were deployed at that date, namely, $f = 0$, because the mass of arbitrageurs is just sufficient to offset the noise trading shock. Hence, as announced earlier, the undervaluation of bond A at date $t = 1$ when a noise trading supply shock occurs is increasing in the fraction f of investors who started an arbitrage at date 0, since this will reduce the amount of speculative capital $1 - f$ left in the market at date 1.

In principle, three scenarios can arise: (1) one where $f \in (0, 1)$, i.e., some investors initiate an arbitrage at date 0 and others do so at date 1; (2) an extreme scenario where $f = 1$, i.e., all investors start an arbitrage at date 0; (3) the polar opposite case where $f = 0$, i.e., no investor starts an arbitrage at date 0.

Let us focus first on the more interesting case, namely, the intermediate scenario where $f \in (0, 1)$: this case arises when investors are indifferent between initiating an arbitrage at date 0 and doing so at date 1, i.e. $M_1 = \hat{M}_1$. Combining investors' indifference condition (11.1) with the market clearing condition (11.4) determines the fraction of investors:

$$f^* = \frac{\delta M_0}{\kappa(1+\varphi)^2}. \tag{11.5}$$

If the expression for f^* is smaller than 1, then this is an equilibrium, in the sense that the mispricing expected to clear the market at date 1 is such that investors are indifferent between starting an arbitrage at date 0 and delaying it. This level of mispricing is:

$$M_1^* = \hat{M}_1 = \frac{M_0}{\kappa(1+\varphi)}. \tag{11.6}$$

This equilibrium is illustrated by Figure 11.5, where the fraction f of investors who intervene at date 0 is measured on the horizontal axis and the mispricing occurring at date 1 on the vertical axis. The level of mispricing that satisfies the indifference condition, i.e. expression (11.6), corresponds to the horizontal line where $M_1^* = \hat{M}_1$. The points above this line correspond to levels of future mispricing so high that all investors would rather delay their intervention (implying $f = 0$), while the points below it correspond to levels of future mispricing so low that all of them would prefer intervening at date 0 (implying $f = 1$). Only along this line is f strictly between 0 and 1. The market-clearing condition is instead represented by the upward-sloping line in the figure: the equilibrium mispricing M_1 is increasing in the fraction f of investors who intervene at date 0, because this corresponds to a smaller fraction $1 - f$ of arbitrageurs still available to correct mispricing at date 1.

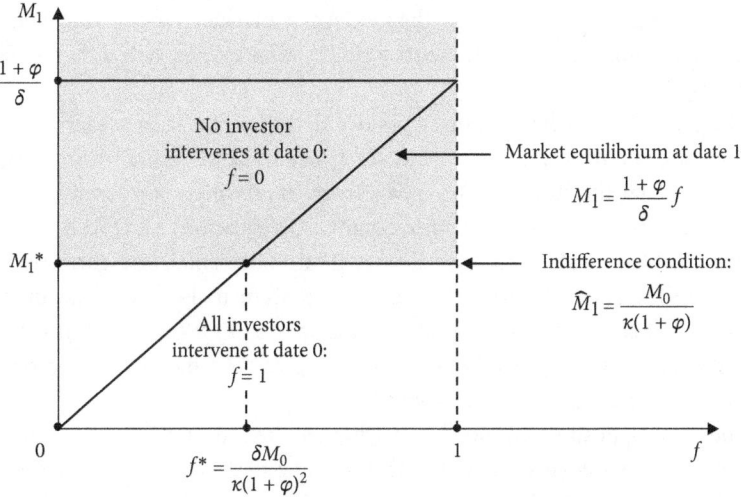

Figure 11.5 Equilibrium mispricing with some arbitrageurs intervening at date 0 and others at date 1.

Figure 11.5 helps understanding the relationship between mispricing at date 0 and at date 1. First of all, it shows that there is persistence in mispricing, as M_1^* is increasing in the initial mispricing M_0. As M_0 increases, the indifference locus shifts upward, so that both M_1^* and f^* increase: intuitively, this is because as initial mispricing increases, it attracts scarce arbitrage capital to early intervention, causing mispricing at date 1 to increase. Hence, when arbitrage capital is limited, mispricing persists and is self-reinforcing. Interestingly, it has been observed that in derivatives markets arbitrage opportunities can be relatively persistent, taking a long time to disappear (see, for instance, Mitchell, Pedersen, and Pulvino 2007 or Gabaix, Krishnamurthy, and Vigneron 2007). This generally is ascribed to the slow entry of arbitrageurs (Duffie 2010), but it could also be due to strategic allocation of arbitrage capital over time (or more generally across various assets), as in the model developed here.

Figure 11.5 can also be used to clarify the role of noise traders and the risk of early liquidation in generating this persistence. As the probability κ of noise traders' presence and/or the risk φ of premature liquidation increase, the horizontal indifference locus shifts downward, so that f^* decreases: intuitively, more noise trading at date 1 and/or greater risk of liquidation raises the attraction of delaying arbitrage to date 1 relative to initiating it at date 0, reducing the fraction of arbitrage capital f^* deployed at date 0, and thus raising the magnitude of future mispricing M_1^*. This is also evident from expression (11.5): the fraction of investors who initiate an arbitrage at time 0 is decreasing in the risk of early liquidation φ and in the probability κ that noise traders materialize at date 1, besides being obviously increasing in the initial mispricing M_0.

Depending on the parameters, the model can alternatively generate scenarios where in equilibrium all arbitrageurs strictly prefer to intervene either at date 0 or at date 1.

The case $f^* = 1$, where all investors decide to initiate an arbitrage at date 0, and no speculative capital is left at date 1, occurs if the initial mispricing M_0 is so large that the threshold level $\hat{M}_1$ from the indifference condition (11.1) exceeds the market-clearing mispricing given by equation (11.4) with $f = 1$, i.e., $(1 + \varphi)/\delta$. Graphically, this case occurs if the horizontal line corresponding to the indifference condition in Figure 11.5 were to lie above the upward-sloping market-clearing line for all possible values of $f \in [0, 1]$. In this case, the equilibrium mispricing would be $M_1^* = (1 + \varphi)/\delta$, obtained by setting $f = 1$ in equation (11.4), since f cannot exceed 1.

The polar opposite scenario $f^* = 0$, where no investor initiates an arbitrage at date 0, and all speculative capital is deployed at date 1, would be an equilibrium only if there is no initial mispricing, that is, $M_0 = 0$. In this case the equilibrium point would shift to the origin, where $f^* = 0$, and by equation (11.4) also the date-1 mispricing would vanish, i.e. $M_1^* = 0$. Intuitively, $M_0 = 0$ implies that nothing can be gained from arbitrage at date 0, so all investors would delay it to date 1; but by doing so they eliminate mispricing also at date 1, because enough arbitrage capital is available to counter the negative effect of noise traders' pessimism on prices. This is because the noise traders' supply function (11.2) is such that the effect of their sales is precisely offset by arbitrageurs if all of them intervene at date 1, i.e., they were to place an aggregate buy order of size 1.

In this section we have taken date-0 mispricing M_0 as given. But this could be generated by exactly the same mechanism illustrated so far for date-1 mispricing M_1: also at date 0 the arrival of pessimistic investors can push the price below fundamental value. The exact level of date-0 mispricing will then depend on how much arbitrage capital is allocated to intervention at date 0 (we leave this analysis as exercise 2). In general, mispricing at date 0 will not disappear because in our model the arbitrage capital available at this date is limited: the prospect that the mispricing of the bond may be greater at date 1 induces some arbitrageurs to wait rather than exploit the opportunity at date 0.

In reality, arbitraging activity may be curtailed not only by the risk of forced liquidation, but by three other frictions as well.

First, arbitrageurs may be risk averse, unlike in our analysis. The cash flows generated by arbitrage portfolios are uncertain when there is a risk of early liquidation, as in our model, and this risk may not be easily diversified if arbitrageurs are specialized (say, because their activity requires expertise).

Second, as noted above, arbitrageurs do not earn the market interest rate on the collateral that they are required to post on their short positions. This point is not captured by our model, which posits a zero market interest rate. When these costs are large relative to the benefit of an arbitrage opportunity, arbitrageurs will simply refrain from taking advantage of it, and the opportunity will persist.

Thirdly, in the model presented above, the number of arbitrageurs that choose to be active either at date 0 or at date 1 is fixed. In reality, the presence of an arbitrage opportunity may attract the attention of outside investors whose intervention will help to close the arbitrage opportunity. However, in some cases it may take time for these further investors to become aware of the mispricing and intervene, so that the mispricing will persist for a long time: Duffie (2010) characterizes this situation as one of "slow-moving capital" and explains that it can reflect institutional impediments, such as search costs for trading counterparties or time to raise capital by intermediaries. Accordinly, Duffie, Gârleanu, and Pedersen (2007) show that the speed with which transaction prices recover after "fire sales" depends to a large extent on search costs and the liquidity of the market: in the case of illiquid environments, price recovery may take considerable time as market participants have to wait for the arrival of counterparties. That is, limits to arbitrage are themselves a function of market liquidity.

11.2.3 Implications for Market Making

As highlighted in the introduction to this chapter, the arbitrageurs modelled in the previous sections can be viewed as providing liquidity to noise traders. For instance, arbitrageurs with capital at date 1 are "leaning against the wind" by absorbing the sell orders for asset A of noise traders and the fire sales of arbitrageurs who liquidate at that date. In doing this and selling asset B short, they act exactly as market makers, who fill sell orders and simultaneously hedge their positions.[10] Thus, one can interpret the magnitude of the mispricing M_1 as the price impact of sell orders due to the lack of liquidity. Indeed, if all arbitrage capital is deployed at date 1, the market at that date is fully liquid, in the sense that it absorbs noise traders' sell orders with no discount.

This interpretation highlights that arbitrageurs' activity closely parallels market-making activity. Market participants such as hedge funds, which take and hold positions for long periods, play a similar role conceptually to that of the market makers described earlier (e.g., NYSE specialists or Nasdaq dealers). The main difference is that they do not operate at the same frequency. They take long positions in underperforming stocks and short ones in overperforming stocks (see Khandani and Lo 2011), seeking to exploit the respective price reversals towards fundamentals. Like the market makers analyzed in Chapter 3, they take inventory risks stemming from uncertainty regarding the extent and the speed of price reversals, the main difference with market makers being that they seek to exploit price reversal at a lower frequency. The analogy between the role of arbitrageurs and market makers is highlighted by Grossman and Miller (1988) and Huang and Wang (2009, 2010).[11]

11.3 Correlated Order Flow and Noise Trader Risk

In the previous section, noise trading was seen to be an important trigger of mispricing, because the price pressure generated may be so great that arbitrageurs are unable to absorb their orders and keep market prices from diverging further from fundamentals. One reason is that noise traders' orders tend to be highly

---

[10] For instance, a market maker taking a long position in a stock can hedge the systematic risk by selling futures on a stock index.

[11] They present a model of market making with inventory risk. If a large number of investors decide to sell a security for liquidity reasons, its price will drop to attract buyers even though its cash flow is unchanged. This temporarily low price makes it attractive for investors to step in and buy, providing liquidity to the sellers—effectively playing the role of market makers. If there are many such investors, large sell orders have little or no impact on price. But if these liquidity suppliers have limited capital, their ability to absorb orders may be impaired, in which case the price will be sensitive to sell orders.

correlated, so that they sell or buy in waves. Dorn, Huberman, and Sengmueller (2008), using data on a sample of retail investors with accounts at a large online broker in Germany, find that their trades are positively correlated.

This can either reflect correlation of their liquidity needs or a tendency to follow the same trading rules (reacting in the same way to the same information). Liquidity needs may be correlated because of macroeconomic shocks to many households at once. During the COVID-19 pandemic, for instance, social distancing rules have reduced many households' spending on leisure activities, such as travel, restaurant meals, and live entertainment; this has led them to accumulate abnormal savings, which they have invested in assets, such as securities and real estate, inflating their prices. Moreover, investors may display "herd" behavior, in the sense that they may imitate one another's trading strategies, stampeding into or out of specific investments. Nowadays, noise traders can also use social media to coordinate their trades in real time, as exemplified by the GameStop saga (see Box 11.2). Alternatively, they may follow common mechanical trading "momentum strategies," which lead them to sell at the same time when securities prices are falling (and buy when they are rising). This type of behavior is modelled by De Long et al. (1990) by assuming that noise traders behave as "positive feedback traders," who buy when prices rise and sell when they fall.

A simple way to grasp this point is to consider the inventory model of Chapter 3, where the dealers' quotes are centered on the price $m_t = \mu_t - \rho\sigma^2 z_t$, which decreases with the dealers' risk aversion ρ, the riskiness of the security σ^2, and the dealers' inventory z_t. In that setting, larger orders (large $|q_t|$) induce greater imbalance in dealers' inventory ($|z_t|$), and thereby in their risk. If the orders of noise traders are correlated, the swings in their trade sizes, and hence in z_t and m_t, are larger. Seen ex ante through the eyes of investors, this phenomenon tends to increase risk: each of them should consider a stock to be riskier if many others can be expected to sell when he wants to sell. Hence, noise traders' behavior is in itself a source of risk, distinct from the fundamental risk due to the arrival of new information regarding the asset payoff (i.e., changes in μ_t).[12]

Interestingly, rational speculators—or arbitrageurs—may not offset the price swings induced by feedback noise traders or by dynamic hedgers, but rather exacerbate them. In De Long et al. (1990), this is because speculators may gain by jumping on the bandwagon and trading ahead of the noise traders; in Gennotte and Leland (1990) it is because they may incorrectly interpret selling by dynamic

---

[12] Building on this observation, several studies attempt to quantify the contribution of noise traders to the volatility of stock returns (see, for instance, Foucault, Thesmar, and Sraer (2011) or Hendershott et al. (2010)).

hedgers as driven by bad news, inducing them to join the latter in a wave of selling.

This risk induced by noise trading is greater in thin markets, which cannot absorb large bulges of buy or sell orders without wide price fluctuations. Pagano (1989a) and Allen and Gale (1994) show that in certain circumstances noise trader risk can trap the market into a self-perpetuating high-volatility, low-volume equilibrium, where noise trader risk deters new investors and low volume makes for acute sensitivity to noise traders' orders.

Box 11.2 The GameStop Short Squeeze of January 2021

The GameStop episode of early 2021 illustrates the dangers of risky arbitrage, namely the prospect of being forced to close the position prematurely before the stock price reaches its predicted long-run level.[13] In 2020 a number of hedge funds, pessimistic about GameStop's prospects, heavily shorted the stock: the short interest reported over the third quarter of 2020 ranged from 66.8 to 70.3 million shares, representing over 100% of the 65.2 million shares issued. Thus conditions were ripe for a classic short squeeze, in which the supply of stock is cornered, forcing short sellers who are obliged to deliver stock to buy it in at an inflated price.[14] Even if the dire forecasts for GameStop's business prospects were to come true eventually, that would be small comfort to short sellers who were forced to liquidate their position before the long awaited stock price correction materializes.

In early January 2021, a series of online posts on Reddit whipped gaming aficionados into action to teach the short sellers a lesson and protect GameStop, a retailer of the gaming merchandise that they valued. As shown by Figure 11.6, the buying frenzy that ensued in the second half of January drove up the GameStop stock price, calibrated on the left-hand axis, to stratospheric heights. It briefly reached $483 on January 28, for a stock that had been trading in the single digits for most of 2020, and many of the short sellers were forced to close out their positions at a crippling loss, and some to exit permanently from short selling altogether. Short interest in GameStop plunged from 62 to 21 million shares in the second half of January, and continued to decline steadily after that, to about 10 million shares in mid-March,

---

[13] GameStop Corp. is a large American bricks-and-mortar video game, consumer electronics, and gaming merchandise retailer.

[14] The SEC's Rule 204 deals with settlement failures by requiring a forced buy-in of stock at any price so as to ensure that it is delivered on time. The rule was instituted in 2005 after a long history of abuses: failures to settle were common, and such failures are tantamount to forcing the short-seller's counterparty to extend a free loan of stock.

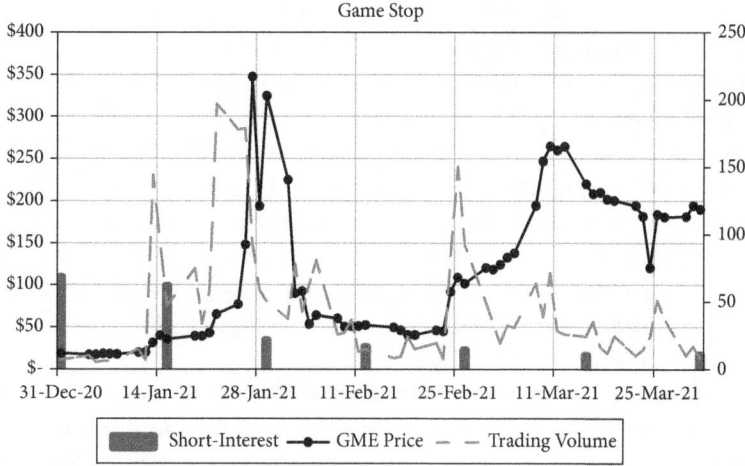

Figure 11.6 GameStop stock price, trading volume and short interest in the first quarter of 2021.

as depicted in Figure 11.6, where short interest and trading volume are measured in millions of shares of the right-hand axis.

One of the novel features of this episode was that the short squeeze involved concerted action by small, unsophisticated traders, fueled by two recent developments. First, the rise of social media such as Reddit enabled direct real-time commentary and coordination, giving rise to ringside excitement far beyond that provided by traditional, less immediate, methods of generating interest in stocks (unsolicited phone calls, newsletters, faxes). Second, commission-free, user-friendly trading apps offered by Robinhood and other brokers made stock trading easy, fast, and ostensibly costless, drawing inexperienced investors into excessive leveraged speculation. These developments have fueled a rash of "meme" stocks caught up in sudden bursts of retail investor excitement, of which GameStop is but one example.

Many of those who bought at the height of the price spike around the end of January lost a large proportion of the money they invested at the behest of their supposed peers—some of whom profited handsomely and may now face class action lawsuits for misrepresenting themselves as amateur investors. And investors were deeply suspicious of the motives of Robinhood in its moves to calm the excesses by raising margins and restricting purchases of GameStop stock. At the height of the frenzy, the GameStop closing price rose by 135% in a single day, Wednesday, January 27. Robinhood imposed trading restrictions on January 28 which contributed to the 44% fall in the closing price between January 27 and 28: by the close, the price had fallen to $193 from its intraday high of $483. Robinhood justified its actions citing dramatic increases in collateral required by its clearinghouse: it was forced to raise money to meet these, drawing down over $500 million in lines of credit, and raising $1 billion from its existing investors late on Thursday, January 28. Several other brokers followed suit. After the Thursday market close, Robinhood announced the restrictions would be loosened, precipitating a 68% price spike on that Friday. A subsequent investor lawsuit against Robinhood accusing it of colluding with Citadel Securities, which paid it to execute orders, to stop investors from buying on January 28 was dismissed by a federal judge in November 2021.

Concerns about market manipulation and the protection of unsophisticated investors from "pump and dump" schemes led to a series of congressional hearings starting on February 18, 2021, which, interestingly, precipitated a renewed wave of buying pressure triggered by the defiant testimony of the protagonists. The relevant investor protection issues are wide ranging, including the use of social media in encouraging small investors to buy, and the role of Robinhood in fueling the price gyrations: its profits from payment-for-order-flow by market makers—in particular, Citadel Securities—are driven by volatility and trading volume.

By late March analyst forecasts for GameStop were up, a boardroom shakeup was announced (the departure of the failed CEO would entail vesting over 1.1 million shares, giving him an outlandish exit payout of over $200 million at reigning stock prices) together with plans to raise equity capital (by the end of June 2021 the company was to sell 8.5 million shares, raising over $1.6 billion) and improve the company's business model. Though prices failed to revisit the stratospheric levels reached at the end of January they remained far above the levels reached before the short squeeze. The cause of this enduring price rise is an open question: have potential short sellers been chastened enough to steer clear of the stock despite their negative views of its fundamental value, or has there been a marked improvement in the company's business model and long-term prospects?

The GameStop frenzy is a perfect example of correlated noise traders' order flow and of its ability to overwhelm arbitrageurs' trading strategies. It illustrates that noise traders may determine not only unwarranted stock market crashes but also booms, which cause short squeezes, i.e., inflict losses on arbitrageurs who short sell when they think a stock is overvalued. It also illustrates that such correlated behavior has been enhanced by noise traders' ability to rely on social media to communicate and coordinate their orders.

11.4 Feedback Loop between Market and Funding Liquidity

A key insight from the limits-to-arbitrage model presented above is that arbitrage requires external funding: a shortage of external funding can force arbitrageurs to scale down their activity or even withdraw completely from some markets, leading to wider mispricing and illiquidity. This explains why a credit crunch affecting market makers often leads to reduced liquidity in security markets: in the words of Brunnermeier and Pedersen (2009), a sudden drying up of "funding liquidity" reduces market liquidity as well.[15]

Market makers can face a drying up of funding liquidity just when it is most needed, precipitating a very sharp fall in asset prices. In turn, a sharp drop in assets prices may jeopardize the ability of banks to provide funding to market makers: for instance, it may reduce the value of banks' assets to the point where they hit a regulatory capital constraint or it may stoke doubts about the solvency of banks among fixed-income investors or depositors. This may generate a feedback loop between market liquidity and funding liquidity, as shown by Figure 11.1: an increase in mispricing triggers a drop in funding by banks, which in turn exacerbates the mispricing in the market. Brunnermeier and Pedersen (2009) refer to this feedback loop as an "illiquidity spiral."

To capture this point in the model of the previous section, suppose that if mispricing at time 1 rises above a critical threshold $\overline{M}_1$, then banks curtail funding to a fraction φ' of arbitrageurs larger than the fraction φ initially anticipated. This can be because the drop in asset prices hits their own balance sheet (possibly to the point of triggering their bankruptcy) and therefore curtails their lending capacity. In other words, from the standpoint of an arbitrageur that opened a position at time 0, there is an unanticipated increase of the risk of facing premature liquidation from φ to φ'. A good example of such an unanticipated collapse in credit is that triggered by the Lehman bankruptcy in September 2008: as Lehman collapsed unexpectedly, it withdrew credit to hedge funds that it was previously funding, and this shock reduced the market liquidity of the assets that those funds were trading (Aragon and Strahan 2012).

We will show that this unexpected drop in funding liquidity may lead mispricing to become so large as to exceed the banks' critical threshold, i.e. to $M_1 > \overline{M}_1$, and thus justify their decision to curtail funding to arbitrageurs more than initially anticipated. In other words, banks' belief of extreme mispricing can be self-fulfilling, i.e. generate a drop in funding to arbitrageurs that determines

---

[15] Here, a market crash is triggered by a reduction of the funding liquidity by banks and of market liquidity by market makers. But in principle, it can also arise from a scramble for liquidity by investors: Huang and Wang (2009) present a theory of market crashes based on the idea that the demand for liquidity may become suddenly too great relative to the supply.

precisely such an extreme mispricing. We refer to this situation as a "crisis equilibrium," and will see that it can coexist with an equilibrium featuring a "normal" level of mispricing such as that shown in Figure 11.5.

We assume that crises are rare events: as of time 0, the probability of a crisis occurring at time 1 is very low. Hence arbitrageurs treat a crisis as a zero-probability event in the choice of their strategy at date 0, neglecting the possibility that φ may increase to φ' at date 1. Hence, f^* is determined by equation (11.5), as before.[16]

If the economy is not in a crisis, the equilibrium mispricing M_1^* is determined by equation (11.6), as in Figure 11.5. If a crisis does occur however, the clearing condition (11.4) is altered since a fraction $\varphi' > \varphi$ of the arbitrageurs who did not intervene at date 0 are forced to liquidate their positions prematurely. Hence, the equilibrium mispricing in a crisis is:

$$M_1^{**} = \frac{1+\varphi'}{\delta}f^* = \frac{1+\varphi'}{1+\varphi}M_1^* > M_1^*. \tag{11.7}$$

Note that, for this to be a "crisis equilibrium," the mispricing in equation (11.7) triggered by the drop in funding must be so large as to jeopardize banks' funding ability, namely, $M_1^{**} > \overline{M}_1$. If this condition were violated, banks would never react to the increase in mispricing by further curtailing funding, so that a crisis could not occur. Compared to its value in the "normal-times equilibrium," given by equation (11.6), asset A is more severely mispriced in the "crisis equilibrium," the percentage increase in mispricing being approximately proportional to the incremental drop in funding: $(M_1^{**} - M_1^*)/M_1^* = (\varphi' - \varphi)/(1+\varphi)$: the sharper the dry-up in bank funding, the more severe the drop in the market price at date 1.

The two equilibria are illustrated in Figure 11.7, where f^* represents the allocation of arbitrage capital between the two dates, which does not change, as it was determined giving a negligible weight to the possibility of crisis; the level of mispricing in a crisis, M_1^{**}, is found on the new market-clearing locus (11.7) in correspondence with the original value of f^*. As Figure 11.7 indicates, the increase in mispricing triggered by the crisis—the market crash—will be more dramatic, the larger the drop in funding liquidity $\varphi' - \varphi$.

The coexistence of a normal-time equilibrium and a crisis equilibrium arises from the feedback loop between market liquidity and funding liquidity present in this model illustrated by Figure 11.1 in the introduction to this chapter: the initial noise trading supply shock moves prices below fundamentals at time 1; if

---

[16] This assumption is made for analytical simplicity: the results obtained in this section would be qualitatively unchanged if arbitrageurs were to consider a crisis as an event with positive probability.

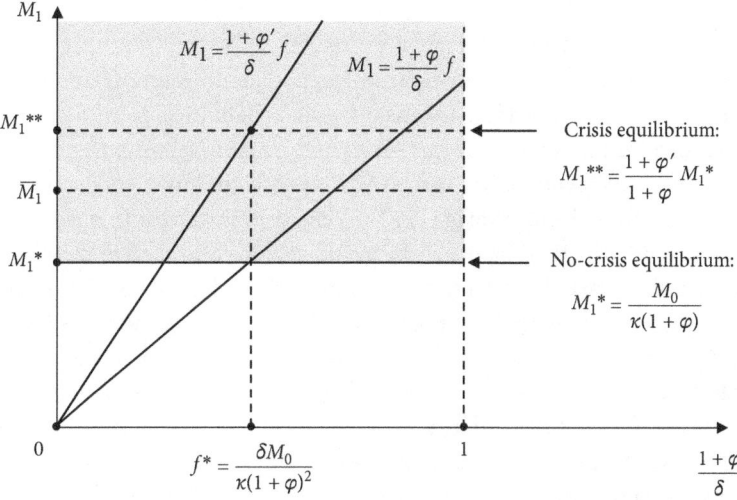

Figure 11.7 Mispricing and allocation of arbitrage capital with and without crisis.

banks are exposed to the asset, they suffer capital losses as a result of the drop in price, and this precipitates a drop in credit to arbitrageurs, who will consequently scale back their trading. This will in turn exacerbate the mispricing, leading to another round of bank losses, credit crunch, and arbitrageurs' withdrawal from the market. This vicious circle lies at the heart of the crisis equilibrium.

This type of feedback loop is modeled more exhaustively by Brunnermeier and Pedersen (2009), who introduce a second feedback channel: insofar as mispricing generates greater expected volatility, it triggers higher margin requirements for speculators, forcing them to reduce their positions, which in turn generates further mispricing. A similar mechanism can arise even in the absence of margin requirements, if speculators are risk averse: high volatility can then trigger a rise in bid-ask spreads, which in turn adds to the volatility of transaction prices (as explained in Chapters 3 and 4), generating a feedback loop akin to that modeled by Brunnermeier and Pedersen (2014).

An important issue is why financial intermediaries respond to increased asset mispricing by curtailing credit to arbitrageurs, and hence precipitate the extreme increase in mispricing that is typical of a financial crisis. In the above notation, why does the expectation of $M_1^{**} > \overline{M}_1$ lead banks to raise the frequency of liquidation from φ to φ'?

One answer is that as mispricing rises, banks will need to mark down their loans to arbitrageurs, in line with the drop in the value of their collateral; moreover, banks may suffer capital losses on their trading book, insofar as their security portfolios are themselves exposed to the mispriced asset. On both accounts, banks will suffer capital losses on the asset side of their balance sheet, and in order to comply with regulatory capital ratios they will have to reduce lending. Prudential regulation imposes such capital requirements on banks precisely on account of their intrinsic fragility, stemming from the maturity transformation that they perform: banks use demand deposits to fund longer term loans, and therefore are themselves exposed to "runs" by depositors, as shown by Diamond and Dybvig (1983). When depositors fear that the payoff of the loans funded by their bank may be insufficient to convert all of their deposits into cash, they have the incentive to withdraw their deposits before the others do. This will in turn force the bank to recall its loans and liquidate its securities at fire-sale prices, thus validating depositors' pessimistic conjecture. In other words, banks themselves are fragile, as their maturity transformation function creates strategic complementarity between depositors, which in turn generates equilibria with runs (beside those with no runs).

Banks are not the only intermediaries exposed to runs: mutual funds are also exposed to runs by their shareholders. In general, insofar as mutual funds invest in diversified bundles of assets featuring different liquidity, they will tend to sell first their most liquid assets (those with the lowest bid-ask spreads and price impact) in response to withdrawals by their shareholders. As a result, when shareholders expect abnormal withdrawals by others, they have the incentive to be first in line in withdrawing their own funds, to avoid being left holding a bundle of less liquid shares, which are going to sell for less upon liquidation. As in the case of banks, these runs arise from strategic complementarities among investors. Consistent with this idea, Chen, Goldstein, and Jiang (2010) find that mutual funds with illiquid assets (where complementarities are stronger) exhibit stronger sensitivity of outflows to bad past performance than funds with liquid assets. Relatedly, Ben-Rephael (2017) documents that at times of extreme market uncertainty, mutual funds reduce their aggregate holdings of illiquid stocks, as a result of larger withdrawals from funds holding such stocks.

11.5 Contagion, Flight to Safety, and Systemic Instability

The mispricing modeled in the previous section with reference to a single asset (bond A in our example) often involves multiple assets at the same time: mispricing can be local, i.e., involve a specific asset, or systemic, i.e. spread across asset classes or intermediaries, which is the key feature of a financial crises. This systemic feature of mispricing may arise either from "commonality" in the liquidity shocks, i.e., their simultaneous effect on many different markets and intermediaries, or from their tendency to propagate across financial intermediaries via chains of lending relationships, or from both mechanisms.

The occurrence of a common liquidity shock can explain why, in the model of the previous section, banks may wish to terminate loans to arbitrageurs precisely at the time when noise traders materialize and generate selling pressure on the security market. The reason may be that banks themselves are hit by a concomitant liquidity shock, such as a run by their depositors. Even if arbitrageurs are not funded by bank loans, but by short-term debt securities such as commercial paper, they may be unable to roll over such funding when they face selling pressure, because the commercial paper market may also dry up (or feature a spike in yields) at the same time due to sales by noise traders occurring also on that market.

Even a liquidity shock that hits a single market can propagate across markets and intermediaries, and generate global, rather than local, mispricing. A clear example of this occurred in the 2008 global financial crisis, which originated in the subprime mortgage lending market, a very specific corner of the credit market, but almost metastasized into a complete financial meltdown. The main reason for such propagation is that financial intermediaries (mutual funds, hedge funds, and market makers, as well as the banks who fund them) are often highly interconnected. For instance, suppose a group of arbitrageurs face premature withdrawals of funding and are forced to liquidate their positions. The drop in security prices that they trigger can inflict losses on other intermediaries: for example, if a bond is used by banks as collateral for their loans, a large drop in its price can make the collateral insufficient to guarantee existing loans and prompt banks to recall them, forcing another round of premature asset liquidations by their borrowers. Hence, withdrawals of funds and fire sales can propagate both across asset classes and across different groups of market participants. In the most extreme instance, this domino effect may precipitate an economy-wide financial collapse, which ultimately requires intervention of the central bank acting as "lender of last resort" to distressed intermediaries in the form of an extraordinary credit expansion and/or massive open market bond purchases.

A specific example of such contagion among financial institutions is the effect of the collapse of the Lehman Brothers investment bank on U.S. money market funds in 2008. Since these funds invest in very safe short-term debt, such as T-Bills, their per-share net asset value (NAV) normally stays constant at $1: this is facilitated by market regulation, which allows these funds to value their assets at cost rather than market value. Hence, U.S. investors treat their shares of money market funds as equivalent to bank deposits. But, following the bankruptcy of Lehman Brothers in September 2008, the NAV of the prominent Reserve Primary Fund fell to 0.97 cents per share (it "broke the buck") because it had invested 1.5% of its assets in Lehman commercial paper, and worried investors started redeeming their holdings, so that the fund's assets declined by nearly two-thirds in 24 hours. Being unable to meet redemption requests, the fund was forced to liquidate. More generally, investors began to doubt the safety of money market funds as a safe, liquid place to invest, and the panic extended to other money market funds that had invested in the commercial paper of banks. This contributed to the dry-up of liquidity in the commercial paper market, which propagated the crisis to yet more financial institutions.

Network analysis is often used to model the interconnections between financial institutions, and thus understand how resilient financial markets are to such forms of contagion. The connections between financial institutions stem from both the asset and the liability sides of their balance sheets, and their connections can be either direct or indirect. For instance, banks are directly connected via mutual exposures on the interbank market; at the same time, they may be indirectly linked if they hold similar security and/or loan portfolios or are funded by the same depositors.

The structure of the network can affect its resilience to financial shocks. Allen and Gale (2000) show that a more densely interconnected network enhances the resilience of the system to the insolvency of any individual bank, as the losses of a distressed bank are divided among more creditors, reducing the impact of its insolvency on the rest of the system, compared to a network where a few institutions play a central role. This underscores the importance of identifying these "systemically important financial institutions" (SIFI), i.e., those whose failure might precipitate a financial crisis, so as to ensure their solvency with higher capital requirements than other banks. Acemoglu, Ozdaglar, and Tahbaz-Salehi (2015) confirm the insight that a more diversified pattern of interbank liabilities leads to a less fragile financial system, provided the magnitude of negative shocks is below a certain threshold, but also show that, faced with sufficiently large shocks, highly diversified financial networks facilitate financial contagion and thus lower systemic stability. The intuition is that, when negative shocks are very large, the excess liquidity of the banking system may no longer be sufficient to absorb the resulting losses. In this case, financial interconnections act as a propagation mechanism, rather than as a stabilizing one. In contrast, a less diversified lending pattern guarantees that the losses are shared with the senior creditors of the distressed banks, rather than transmitting the shocks to other banks in the system.

Contagion helps to account not only for the propagation of mispricing, fund withdrawals, and insolvencies but also for the "commonality" in market liquidity, namely, the tendency of bid-ask spreads to widen simultaneously for many securities, as funding to market makers is curtailed across the board. The commonality in bid-ask spreads is reinforced by the commonality of risk: at times of market turbulence, the risk of assets with correlated returns rises simultaneously, leading risk-averse market-makers to widen their spreads simultaneously for all of them, risk being a key driver of bid-ask spreads, as seen in Chapter 3.

11.6 Adverse Selection and Financial Instability

The feedback loop between funding and market liquidity modeled by Brunnermeier and Pedersen (2008) is not the only explanation for financial crises proposed in the literature. In particular, financial crises have been viewed as situations in which adverse selection problems become so extreme as to generate very high illiquidity or even market collapse.

Adverse selection regarding the quality of an asset may suddenly increase if confidence in the issuer of the asset declines and people start researching the asset's fundamentals. If only a few investors manage to get hold of the information and interpret it correctly, adverse selection will intensify: the asset will become more information-sensitive, and as a result its market will become less liquid. Insofar as this induces unsophisticated traders to withdraw from the market, it may lead to market collapse (Pagano and Volpin 2012 and Dang, Gorton, and Holmstrom 2020). This has been proposed as one possible explanation for the collapse of the U.S. market for securitized mortgage debt in 2008.

Market collapse due to increased adverse selection may also arise from counterparty risk, namely, the probability that the other party in a transaction may default on its contractual obligations. While so far in this book adverse selection has been assumed to concern only the payoffs of assets, in practice it may also concern the solvency of the intermediaries an investor is trading with, hence the counterparty risk the investor is exposed to. When market turbulence increases, the probability that a given financial intermediary may be unable to meet its obligations increases too. This may result in investors losing confidence in the solvency of their potential counterparties and withdrawing from trading. In the extreme, it may lead to market collapse. Heider, Hoerova, and Holthausen (2015) propose a model where an increase in counterparty risk can precipitate a crisis, and use it to interpret developments in interbank markets prior to and during the 2007–9 financial crisis.

Counterparty risk is typically mitigated by central clearing counterparties (CCPs), namely, institutions that take on counterparty credit risk between parties to a transaction and provide clearing and settlement services for trades (see Chapter 7). CCPs share counterparty credit risk among their members in the markets in which they operate. They reduce settlement risks not only by netting offsetting transactions between multiple counterparties,[17] but also by requiring collateral deposits (called "margin deposits") and often by creating a guarantee fund to be used to cover losses in excess of a defaulting member's collateral on deposit.

Multilateral netting reduces the cost of posting collateral, as a given amount of collateral can support a greater number of positions: Duffie and Zhu (2011) argue that this is the key comparative advantage of CCPs over a system where counterparties agree bilaterally on the collateral to be posted as protection against counterparty risk (provided there is "interoperability" across CCPs, that is, links that allow for multilateral netting across them). Hence, CCPs are a cost-efficient way of mitigating adverse selection (as well as moral hazard) issues arising from counterparty risk.[18] A further advantage of CCPs lies in their ability to mitigate fire sales, insofar as they liquidate the securities of members who default on their margin calls via auctions among their surviving members, rather than in the open market. These auctions can be seen as a mechanism to reduce the inefficiencies associated with fire sales due to the scarcity of speculative capital analyzed earlier in this chapter.

The benefits of CCPs are illustrated by Vuillemey (2020) with reference to the creation of the first CCP in Le Havre (France) in 1882, in the coffee futures market. He shows that central clearing changed the geography of trade flows in Europe, to the benefit of Le Havre, and as a result CCPs quickly spread to other exchanges. Of course, the benefits of CCPs are conditional on the CCPs themselves not collapsing. When a large enough fraction of transactions is centrally cleared, as it is now generally the case, the solvency of CCPs becomes crucial to the smooth functioning of security markets. The risk of a CCP failure is not a remote possibility: during the recent COVID-19 crisis, in as many as half a dozen CCPs the clearing members' mark-to-market losses exceeded the collateral they posted by more than 1%, which is the industry standard (Menkveld and Vuillemey 2020).

11.7 Further Reading

The theoretical literature on limits to arbitrage can be traced back to Dow and Gorton (1994) and Shleifer and Vishny (1997). Kondor (2009) develops a continuous-time model of convergence trading in which arbitrageurs do not

---

[17] Netting enables an investor to offset losses in a position with gains in another. For example, an investor who is short 40 shares of a security and long 100 shares of the same security vis-à-vis different counterparties has a net long position of 60 shares.

[18] See Kuong and Maurin (2022) for a theory of the optimal design of CCPs.

immediately allocate all their capital to an opportunity, anticipating that it may become even more profitable in the future. He shows that, in equilibrium, the size of the opportunity must necessarily increase with positive probability over time. Gromb and Vayanos (2002) explicitly model the link between arbitrageurs' past performance and the amount of arbitrage capital available at a given date, in the presence of margin requirements. If performance is bad, arbitrageurs' wealth declines. Thus, margin requirements limit the amount of capital that can be devoted to arbitrage activities more stringently, further depressing prices. Brunnermeier and Pedersen (2008) extend their model to the case of multiple arbitrage opportunities, showing how financial constraints (such as margin requirements) can generate co-movement in liquidity in various securities. Duffie (2010) surveys recent research on these price effects across multiple markets associated with slow-moving capital. Duffie and Strulovici (2009) model the equilibrium movement of capital between asset markets with different levels of invested capital, and show that the greater the difference in capital levels, the greater the intermediaries' effort to re-balance the distribution of capital across markets, and the faster the convergence of the mean rates of return on different assets toward a common level. Xiong (2001) and Kyle and Xiong (2001) consider a dynamic setting in which arbitrageurs have logarithmic utility functions, so that their demand for risky securities increases with their wealth. As a consequence, losses on arbitrageurs' positions induce a decrease in their demand for risky securities and further price decline. Gromb and Vayanos (2010) survey the theoretical literature on the limits to arbitrage.

Many of the empirical studies on limits to arbitrage analyze the temporary underpricing and subsequent price reversal induced by "fire sales." Coval and Stafford (2007) investigate stock market transactions induced by the redemptions of open-end mutual funds, and find that funds undergoing large outflows tend to decrease the size of their positions, which puts pressure on prices of the securities held in common by distressed funds. Mitchell, Pedersen, and Pulvino (2007) study the price reactions of convertible bonds to forced redemptions of hedge funds. Pulvino (1998) shows that financially constrained airlines get lower prices than their unconstrained rivals when they sell used narrow-body aircraft. Campbell, Giglio, and Pathak (2011) show that forced sales of real estate due to foreclosures are associated with substantial price discounts followed by mean-reversion, while unforced sales prices are close to a random walk. Ellul, Jotikasthira, and Lundblad (2011) examine fire sales of speculative-grade corporate bonds by insurance companies arising from regulatory constraints and/or capital requirements. They find that more severely constrained companies are, on average, more likely to sell downgraded bonds, and that bonds whose probability of regulatory-induced selling is higher exhibit significant price declines and subsequent reversals, especially when insurance companies as a group are more distressed and other potential buyers have scarce capital.

A vast literature applies network theory to the analysis of financial contagion and systemic stability. Beside the theoretical studies by Allen and Gale (2000) and Acemoglu et al. (2015) cited in the text, a growing empirical literature applies network-theoretic approaches to the analysis of systemic stability of interbank and securities markets: for instance, Furfine (2003) uses a network-based approach to analyze solvency contagion in the U.S. federal funds market, and Drehmann and Tarashev (2013) use it to measure the systemic importance of interconnected banks.

The commonality in liquidity is well-documented both across stocks (Chordia, Roll, and Subrahmanyam 2000; Hasbrouck and Seppi 2001; and Huberman and Halka 2001), and across stocks and bonds (Chordia, Sarkar, and Subrahmanyam 2005). There is also evidence that connects commonality in liquidity to the availability of credit to market makers (Acharya, Schaefer, and Zhang 2008). Coughenour and Saad (2004) find that the comovements in liquidity for stocks handled by the same specialist on the NYSE are explained both by movements in the liquidity of the relevant specialist's portfolio and by market-wide movements in liquidity. Hence, increases in the cost of capital or increased risk exposure for a specialist leads to a drop in liquidity for the stocks assigned to that specialist.

While this chapter highlights that the mutual feedback between funding and market liquidity may generate financial instability, further mutual feedbacks can develop between financial instability and the real economy. For instance, a financial crisis typically triggers a recession, which results in firm bankruptcies, hence losses by banks and other financial intermediaries, and further retrenchment of credit. These further feedback loops and the resulting non-linearities in the response of the economy to shocks have been the object of a vast macro-finance literature, such as He and Krishnamurthy (2012, 2013), Brunnermeier and Sannikov (2014), and Brunnermeier et al. (2016, 2017). The concern that financial crises may result in real instability and vice versa has led to much recent research regarding macro-prudential policies, i.e., financial policies aimed at reducing the probability of financial crises and/or mitigate their consequences: macroprudential capital buffers for banks, ceilings to loan-to-value (LTV) ratios for real estate lending, minimum liquidity ratios and redemption gates for mutual funds. A key issue in the design of macro-prudential policy is to avoid the pro-cyclicality of micro-prudential policy rules, for instance preventing the capital ratios imposed on banks to ensure their solvency from inducing them to liquidate assets and call back loans in the middle of a severe recession. Freixas, Laeven, and Peydró (2015) provide an early treatment of these topics, while Duffie (2018) examines how capital and failure-resolution rules for systemically important banks adopted after the 2008–9 financial crisis have affected the liquidity of security markets, especially OTC ones.

11.8 Exercises

1. **Maximal mispricing.** Suppose that, in the model of limits to arbitrage presented in Section 11.2.2, the parameters are such that $\delta M_0 > \kappa(1 + \varphi)^2$. What is the resulting equilibrium allocation of arbitrageurs across periods, and the implied equilibrium mispricing at date 1? Provide an intuitive explanation.

2. **Endogenous mispricing at dates 0 and 1.** Consider the model of arbitrage in Section 11.2.2. Assume that, at date 0, the total supply from noise traders is:

$$y(P_{A0}) = 1 + \delta_0(P_{A0} - V), \tag{11.8}$$

where P_{A0} is the price of asset A at date 0. Otherwise the model is unchanged.

   a. Write down the system of equations that determines M_0, M_1, and f in equilibrium.

   b. Compute the equilibrium values of mispricing at dates 0 and 1, M_0^* and M_1^*, and the equilibrium fraction of arbitrageurs intervening at date 0, f^*.

   c. Consider how the parameters κ, δ, δ_0, and φ affect the equilibrium mispricing at each of the two dates and the proportion of arbitrageurs intervening at the two dates, and provide an intuitive explanation for your findings.

3. **Carry-trade arbitrage.** In this exercise we analyze the returns and risks of a currency carry trade. A carry trade involves borrowing money in a low interest-rate currency and investing it in a high interest-rate currency. Based on the theories presented on liquidity risk and limits to arbitrage, we will re-evaluate the attractiveness of investing in such a strategy. The Excel file Ch11_ex5_data.xlsx, available on the companion website for the book, contains data on the monthly risk-free rate in Australian Dollars (AUD) and Swiss Franc (CHF) and the CHFAUD exchange rate (number of Swiss Francs per Australian Dollar), denoted x_{CHFAUD}.[19] It also contains data on the S&P 500 monthly return, the average U.S. stock bid-ask spread and the TED-spread. These variables will be used in the later part of the exercise.

---

[19] Source: Bloomberg.

a. A popular carry trade is to borrow CHF at the risk-free rate, exchange them to AUD and invest at the AUD risk-free rate. The monthly return (in Swiss Francs) from this strategy can be approximated as:

$$R_t \approx r_{AUD,t-1} - r_{CHF,t-1} - \frac{\Delta x_{CHFAUD,t}}{x_{CHFAUD,t-1}},$$

where $r_{y,t}$ indicates the risk-free rate in currency y in month t and $\Delta x_{CHFAUD,t}$ the change in exchange rate from the end of month $t-1$ to month t. Calculate and plot the cumulative returns from investing in this strategy from the start of 2006 to the end of 2014, re-investing the proceeds each period. Does the strategy generate a positive return on average?

b. Based on the liquidity-adjusted CAPM presented in Chapter 10, we know that an asset's expected return should be adjusted for its covariance with the market return and its liquidity risk. Calculate the correlation between the returns of the carry trade strategy and the market portfolio (proxied by the S&P 500). Then calculate the correlation between the carry trade's returns and s_M (proxied by the average bid-ask spread for U.S. stocks). How will these two correlations impact the strategy's required return? Given your findings, does the strategy appear more or less attractive? In answering this question, you may ignore the currency mismatch between the carry trade strategy in CHF and the S&P 500 index, which is in USD.

c. As illustrated by your answer to part a, the carry trade is generally profitable but suffered during the financial crisis in 2008. Based on your knowledge of the limits to arbitrage theory presented in Section 11.2, what could be a reason that more speculative capital did not flow into the carry trade during the 2008 crisis? Now plot the carry trade returns together with the TED spread. The TED-spread is the difference between the rate at which banks can borrow (USD Libor at the time) and the three month Treasury bill rate (a proxy for the USD risk-free rate). It can be used as a measure for the cost of raising speculative capital. Does the figure support your explanation?

d. Imagine that you are raising capital for an investment vehicle targeting carry trades, however you are worried that investors will pull their money out during a crisis and you will not be able to raise new funds. Which of the following fund structures would alleviate such concerns:

1. A structure where investors can withdraw their money at any time.
2. Same as 1, but with a clause allowing the fund to freeze redemptions for up to a year during a market crisis.
3. A fund where investors' money is locked up for a fixed 10-year period.

12

Liquidity, Price Discovery, and Corporate Policies

Learning Objectives:

- Effects of the financial markets' liquidity on firms' investment and corporate governance
- Effects of price discovery on corporate investment and executive compensation
- How corporate policies affect market liquidity

12.1 Introduction

A key function of securities markets is to channel funds from savers to firms, to finance their investment. What role do market liquidity and price discovery play in this process? For instance, is a more liquid market conducive to more investment? Does it lead to a better allocation of funds among alternative investment projects? These are old questions to which the great economists of the past have responded in very different ways.

John Hicks, for instance, argued that the liquidity of securities markets—and not technological progress per se—is what made the industrial revolution possible (Hicks 1969): "According to Hicks, the products manufactured during the first decades of the industrial revolution had been invented much earlier. Thus, technological innovation did not spark sustained growth. Many of the existing innovations, however, required large injections and long-run commitments of capital. The critical new ingredient that ignited growth in eighteenth century England was capital market liquidity" (Levine 1997, p. 692).

Keynes, by contrast, argued that liquidity can lead to inefficient investment decisions, by encouraging short-term speculation at the expense of sound investment decisions based on firms' long-term prospects: "If I am allowed to appropriate the term *speculation* for the activity of forecasting the psychology of the market, and the term *enterprise* for the activity of forecasting the prospective yield of assets over their whole life, it is by no means always the case that

Market Liquidity: Theory, Evidence, and Policy. Second Edition. Thierry Foucault, Marco Pagano, and Ailsa Röell, Oxford University Press. © Oxford University Press 2023. DOI: 10.1093/oso/9780197542064.003.0013

speculation predominates over enterprise. As the organization of investment markets improves, the risk of the predominance of speculation does however increase. These tendencies are a scarcely avoidable outcome of our having successfully organized 'liquid' investment markets. It is usually agreed that casinos should, in the public interest, be inaccessible and expensive. And perhaps the same is true of Stock Exchanges" (Keynes 1936, pp. 158–9).

While these views conflict, they nevertheless both rest on the idea that liquidity is of paramount importance to firms' investment, and therefore ultimately to their performance. In Section 12.2, we go deeper into the mechanisms through which liquidity affects firms' investment decisions and discuss the evidence that has built up. Section 12.3 considers how high liquidity affects the governance of firms, and specifically whether it discourages the formation of large shareholding stakes and therefore the probability that management will be monitored by a large shareholder. But liquidity is not the only aspect of market microstructure that can affect corporate policies: the market's ability to keep prices in line with fundamentals may also be important for firms. So Section 12.4 investigates the link between the accuracy of price discovery, the quality of firms' investment decisions, and their ability to incentivize managers by indexing executives' compensation to stock prices. Finally, Section 12.5 considers the reverse causal link, which is to say, actions that firms themselves can take to fine-tune the liquidity of their securities.

12.2 Market Liquidity and Corporate Investment

Chapter 10 provides an important reason why liquidity should enhance investment: investors will pay a higher price for more liquid securities or else, to the same effect, require a lower expected rate of return to hold them. Hence, a more liquid securities market lowers the cost of capital to firms, which should boost investment, as Hicks argued with reference to the industrial revolution: cheaper capital will increase the number and size of the investment projects with positive net present value, so more liquid markets should be associated with more investment and higher firm valuation.

There is evidence to support these predictions. Levine and Zervos (1998a), with data for 49 countries from 1976 to 1993, find that investment and economic growth are positively correlated with measures of stock market turnover, taken to be a proxy for liquidity. They estimate cross-sectional regressions where the dependent variable for a country is alternatively the investment rate, the growth rate of real per capita GDP, or the growth rate of productivity, averaged over the sample period. The explanatory variables include measures of stock market turnover in 1976, scaled by stock market capitalization or by GDP, plus several control variables capturing other factors associated with capital accumulation and growth (initial income per capita; education; political stability; indicators of exchange rate and trade, fiscal, and monetary policy). The estimated coefficient of stock market turnover is always positive and significant, implying that stock market liquidity is positively and significantly correlated with subsequent investment.

Related evidence is drawn from the analysis of stock market liberalizations via policies relaxing restrictions on foreign investors' share purchases. These policies are associated with an increase in liquidity, a jump in stock prices, and a drop in the cost of equity capital, as well as an increase in private investment. For instance, in a sample of 11 developing countries that liberalized their stock markets, Henry (2000b) finds that the growth rate of private investment rose above the median pre-liberalization investment rate one year later in 9 countries, two years later in 10, and three years later in 8. The average growth rate of private investment in the three years after liberalization exceeds the mean of Henry's sample by 22 percentage points (see Section 12.6 for related studies).

There is also firm-level evidence that liquidity is correlated with company value. Fang, Noe, and Tice (2009) report that firms with more liquid stocks have higher market-to-book value ratios. To identify the causal effect of liquidity on firm performance, they focus on an exogenous shock to liquidity—the decrease of the tick size for U.S. securities in 2000 (see Chapter 6)—and show that the resulting increase in liquidity around that year raises company values. One mechanism that may explain this finding, as explained above, is the decline in firms' cost of capital due to better liquidity. An alternative mechanism is that a more liquid market may induce managers to select better investment opportunities, as the next section explains. Fang, Noe, and Tice (2009) try to discriminate empirically between these alternative mechanisms, and conclude that the cost-of-capital channel plays a minor role compared with the managerial decision channel.

Stock market liquidity is particularly important for the firms that first approach public markets via an IPO: their value is very uncertain, so the stocks of recent IPOs are particularly exposed to problems of asymmetric information. As information about the company progressively emerges in secondary market trading, the problem becomes less severe and market liquidity improves. Ellul and Pagano (2006) show that in a sample of 337 British IPOs between 1998 and 2000, the average bid-ask spread declined from 4.5% in the immediate aftermarket to about 2% several weeks after, as shown by Figure 12.1—a decline that largely reflects the decrease in the adverse-selection component. The figure also shows that the range of variation of the spread is greatest immediately after the IPO and declines steadily thereafter. This observation indicates not only that illiquidity is most severe in conjunction with the IPO, but that illiquidity risk

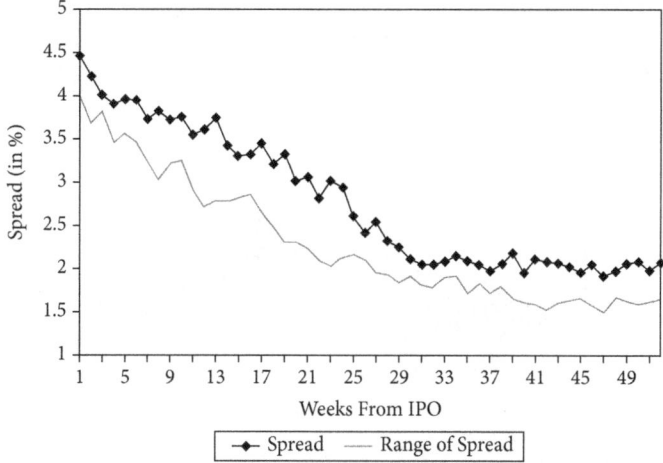

Figure 12.1 Bid-ask spread after an IPO: average value and range of variation (based on data from Ellul and Pagano 2006).

is too. Accordingly, the illiquidity premium that investors require to buy new stocks should be particularly large, especially if these stocks are purchased by "flippers" who want to buy and quickly resell.

Consistent with this argument, IPOs sell at a discount relative to the immediate post-IPO market price, known as "IPO underpricing": relative to the first day of trading in the sample, this underpricing is 47.7%, which implies that firm owners leave a lot of money on the table when their firm goes public. In fact, the underpricing is more pronounced for firms that turn out to be more illiquid, as shown by Figure 12.2. In other words, the more illiquid the secondary market, the higher the cost of equity capital in the primary market for the companies that tap it. Ellul and Pagano (2006) show that this relationship persists even after controlling for other determinants of IPO underpricing, such as the reputation of the underwriter.

Another benefit of a liquid market is that it provides an "exit option" for venture capitalists—a class of intermediaries who invest in startup firms, acting not only as financiers but also as advisors and monitors in the early stages. As these advisory and monitoring services require highly specialized human capital, venture capitalists typically must limit their operations to just a few companies at a time. An increase in market liquidity enables them to exit more rapidly from their investments, because better prices are available to them. Michelacci and Suarez (2004) show that this more quickly frees their scarce human capital for redeployment in a new round of financing, and thereby increases the total number of firms they are able to serve.

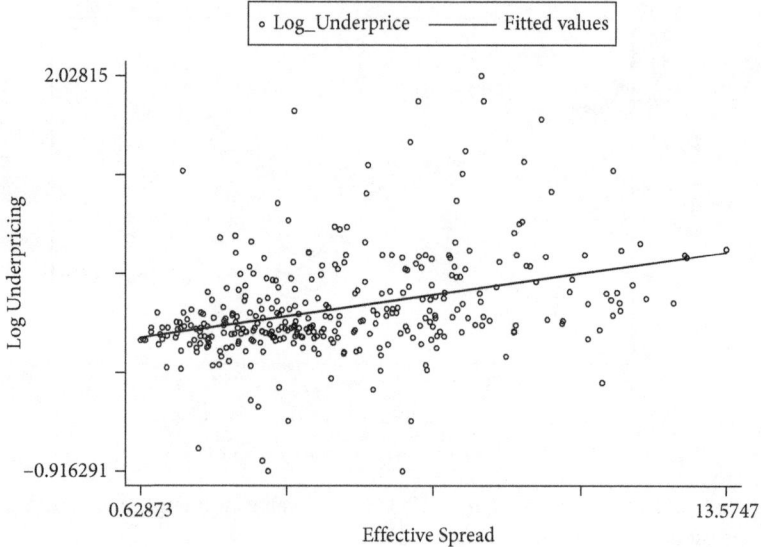

Figure 12.2 IPO underpricing and effective bid-ask spread after an IPO (based on data from Ellul and Pagano 2006).

12.3 Market Liquidity and Corporate Governance

We now turn to a more indirect channel through which liquidity affects firms' investment policies, namely via their corporate governance. In particular, the question is whether greater liquidity encourages investors to monitor companies in order to improve managerial decisions. As Section 10.1 indicates, Keynes would have probably answered in the negative. He viewed liquidity as discouraging investors from emphasizing the long-term prospects of their investments, as they can liquidate their holdings quickly and cheaply if dissatisfied with their performance. In line with this view, some have argued that the U.S. market-friendly regulatory framework, designed to enhance liquidity, ultimately discourages the activism of large shareholders.

Coffee (1991) states this view as follows: "Liquidity and control are antithetical. American law has said clearly and consistently since at least the 1930s that those who exercise control should not enjoy liquidity and vice versa. [...] the separation of liquidity and control is not only a cause of institutional passivity, but to some degree should be. In short, those institutions that most desire liquidity would make poor monitors." He adds that other countries have chosen a different point along the trade-off between liquidity and control: "Advanced industrial economies can be classified along a continuum ranging from those, such as Japan and Germany, that permit financial institutions to control corporate managements, but effectively deny them liquidity, to those that inhibit institutional control, but maximize their liquidity." This is represented by the United States, where disgruntled investors sell their shares rather than challenge management—the well-known "Wall Street Rule." In this vein, Bhide (1993) argues that in the U.S. "public policy has favored stock market liquidity over active investing," at the cost of impaired corporate governance.

The trade-off between liquidity and control described by Coffee (1991) and Bhide (1993) is a special case of A. O. Hirschman's (1970) idea that members of a dysfunctional organization choose between exit and voice. If it is easy and cheap to exit by selling, shareholders will have little interest in exercising a costly voice to intervene actively in the affairs of the company, replacing unsatisfactory managers, and so on. But if exit is blocked because the market is illiquid, then exercising one's "voice" becomes more attractive.

To capture these ideas, consider the time line of events illustrated by Figure 12.3: at date 0, a potentially activist shareholder amasses a block of shares amounting to a fraction φ of the firm's equity, which has current value V; at date 1 the blockholder decides whether to use his control rights to intervene in the company's operation (voice) or to sell his stake (exit). We first analyze the date-1 problem facing the investor after he has already purchased a sizeable block of shares. Then we consider whether, given what he expects to happen at date 1, he wants to buy a block of shares at date 0.

If the blockholder intervenes at date 1, say by replacing lazy or incompetent management, he brings about a gain G in the firm's value. But, to do so he must exert effort at a cost C. His decision whether to intervene or to walk away depends on the liquidity of the stock at date 1. If he stays for the long haul and intervenes, the value of his stake, net of the intervention cost, will be:

$$\varphi(V + G) - C.$$

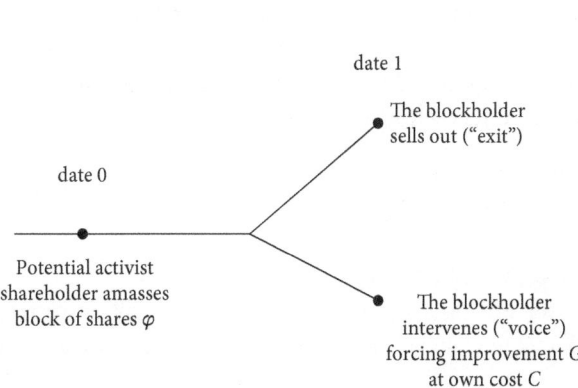

Figure 12.3 Stock market trading and shareholder activism: time line.

To make the problem interesting, we assume that the blockholder's intervention produces an increase in the value of his stake that exceeds the cost of intervention: $\varphi G > C$. Otherwise, there is no chance of activism.

If at date 1 the blockholder sells his stake, he gets:

$$\varphi(\mu_1 - S_1),$$

where μ_1 is the market's perception of the stock's value at date 1, including any downward revision induced by the blockholder's decision to sell, and the half-spread S_1 measures any market illiquidity over and above such price impact. For example, if trading is anonymous and the market believes the blockholder will intervene with probability π, then $\mu_1 = V + \pi G$. If instead regulation forces him to disclose his intention to exit before trading, then $\mu_1 = V$, because the market anticipates no improvement.

Thus, for voice to prevail over exit—i.e., for the shareholder to intervene rather than sell—we must have:

$$\varphi(V + G) - C \geq \varphi(\mu_1 - S_1). \tag{12.1}$$

Let us consider the case most favorable to exit, namely that the blockholder can sell anonymously at a price $\mu_1 = V + \pi G$, where π is a rational estimate of the probability of intervention. Then the previous condition (12.1) becomes:

$$\varphi G - C \geq \varphi(\pi G - S_1). \tag{12.2}$$

Clearly, this condition is always met if it holds for $\pi = 1$, and if so, there will always be intervention by the blockholder. Simple algebra shows that this occurs if $S_1 \geq C/\varphi$, that is, if the market is so illiquid that exit is excessively costly. If $S_1 < C/\varphi$ instead, there is a mixed-strategy equilibrium with the probability of intervention π such that the blockholder is just indifferent between voice and exit. In that case, condition (12.2) holds with equality. Encompassing both cases, the probability of intervention is

$$\pi = \min\left\{1 - \frac{1}{G}\left(\frac{C}{\varphi} - S_1\right), 1\right\}. \tag{12.3}$$

This expression shows that market illiquidity encourages voice by making exit more costly: the probability π of blockholder intervention increases with the illiquidity parameter S_1, rising to 1 when $S_1 \geq C/\varphi$, as shown above.[1] This

---

[1] By assumption, $G - C/\varphi > 0 > -S_1$, so intervention will always occur with strict positive probability ($\pi > 0$), from equation (12.3).

illustrates the "lock-in effect" described by Coffee: the more illiquid the market, the more advantageous it is to monitor actively rather than to exit. Note also that blockholder activism is more likely, the greater the potential gain G, the lower the intervention cost C, and the larger the blockholder's stake, as one would expect.

The lock-in effect just described is heightened if the blockholder is forced to disclose that he is walking away from his stake, so that the market prices the company at non-intervention value $\mu_1 = V$. In this case, exit becomes prohibitively expensive because there is no capital gain from selling, but the trading cost S_1 must still be paid. We leave it to the reader to verify that in this case activism is guaranteed, that is, $\pi = 1$ (see exercise 1).

Up to this point, we have taken the presence of a blockholder for granted. But we must consider whether a potential activist would find it worthwhile to build up a block of shares in the first place. As Bolton and von Thadden (1998) and Maug (1998) point out, the decision to purchase a block is affected by the liquidity of the market at the date of purchase: here liquidity favors activism by reducing the cost of building up the block. Formally, at date 0 the per-share price paid by the potential activist is $\mu_0 + S_0$, where μ_0 denotes the market's valuation of the company and S_0 is the transaction cost. The market valuation μ_0 will range from V when the market does not expect a blockholder to emerge, to $V + \pi G$ when it does expect so (with probability π).

As before, consider the case where a blockholder's presence is not foreseen, so that $\mu_0 = V$. Recall that, from the left-hand side of expression (12.1), the net value of a block after intervention at date 1 is $\varphi(V + G) - C$. Since the cost of amassing the block at date 0 is $\varphi(V + S_0)$, the ex ante net gain from doing so is:

$$\varphi(V + G) - C - \varphi(V + S_0)$$
$$= \varphi(G - S_0) - C,$$

which is decreasing in the market illiquidity parameter S_0. Hence illiquidity is a double-edged sword: it discourages the original formation of a block, but once the block is in place, it locks the blockholder in and encourages activism.

However, if at date 0 the market fully anticipates the presence of a block-holder, then any improvements that he may bring to the company will already be reflected in the date-0 share valuation $\mu_0 = V + \pi G$. In this case, he is certain to lose money if he goes ahead and acquires the block. To see this, note that his net gain is then:

$$\varphi(V + G) - C - \varphi(V + \pi G + S_0)$$
$$= \varphi((1 - \pi)G - S_0) - C,$$

which, inserting the probability of his date-1 intervention from equation (12.3), becomes:

$$-\varphi S_0 - \min(C, \varphi S_1) < 0.$$

Intuitively, the blockholder incurs a transaction cost of S_0 per share when acquiring his stake, and subsequently incurs either the monitoring cost C or the exit transaction cost of S_1 per share, whichever is lower. Any improvements he makes to the company's value are already incorporated into the share price at purchase. Not surprisingly, he loses money on the round-trip transaction and so prefers to avoid it. This idea was first articulated by Grossman and Hart (1980), who argue that other shareholders free-ride on the value improvements they expect the activist investor to make, by refusing to sell at any price that does not fully reflect them. Thus, the potential activist cannot recover his costs, unless he can secretly build up a toehold stake at a lower price. This will largely depend on his ability to camouflage his trades behind noise trading, as Kyle and Vila (1991) note.

The model presented above indicates that the assertion that "liquidity and control are antithetical" by Coffee (1991) is an oversimplification: greater liquidity may actually facilitate block formation, and therefore active intervention in corporate control by blockholders.[2] The relationship between liquidity and activism is further complicated by the fact that, from the standpoint of a large shareholder, liquidity will also depend on the price impact of his trades, in addition to S_0 and S_1, which may discourage the accumulation of a large stake and penalize its decumulation. As noted, the magnitude of this adverse price impact depends on the visibility of the blockholder's trades. If regulators want to promote the formation of activist blockholders, they will have to facilitate accumulation of significant blocks of shares without disclosure to other market participants. But once a blockholder does have a controlling stake, sale of this stake should be highly visible to make his exit as costly as possible. In other words, the formation of a block requires relative opacity, while its retention requires great transparency, a delicate balancing act for regulators.

---

[2] Edmans (2009) points out an additional reason why liquidity and monitoring by large shareholders are complementary, rather than anthitetical. Since in a liquid market a large shareholder has low exit costs after bad investment decisions, his trading decisions can convey more information to the market about the quality of managerial decisions and so reinforce the discipline to which managers are subject. By the same token, liquidity enhances the signal conveyed by the blockholder's retention of his stake when the firm books low earnings: precisely because he could sell at little cost, his decision not to do so signals that the fundamental value of the firm is sound, and keeps the stock price well aligned with fundamentals. Edmans also shows that when the blockholder chooses his stake optimally, greater market liquidity induces the blockholder to choose a larger stake, which makes the stock price more informative about the long-run payoff of the firm and induces management to avoid short-termist investment behavior.

In practice, regulators have addressed this dilemma by allowing the buildup of an initial stake to go undisclosed below some threshold (in the United States, 5% of a firm's equity); beyond it, all further transactions by the blockholder must be disclosed immediately. Thus, once the stake is taken, it becomes hard to decumulate it without a price concession that reflects the lower monitoring incentive by the blockholder.

Empirically, the presence of blockholders varies greatly from country to country. Blocks are commonplace in continental Europe and Asia but much less so in the United States and United Kingdom. Even in the United States, however, the involvement of large institutional shareholders increased dramatically with the advent of public pension fund activism during the mid-1980s and the greater role of mutual funds in equity investing. Davis and Yoo (2003) report that mutual funds manage over 20% of U.S. equity and hold sizeable blocks of 10% or more in many of the largest U.S. companies.

There is evidence that institutional investors do regard corporate governance as important to their investment decisions, but nevertheless tend to exit rather than voice their discontent (see Section 12.6 for details). This aversion to exerting influence may be due partly to the U.S. short-swing profit rule, which obliges investors who actively participate in management decisions (or hold a stake of at least 5%) to hold their stake for at least six months, or else disgorge any capital gains made on the in-and-out transaction. This deters institutions like mutual funds from activism, as they may experience unpredictable outflows that oblige them to liquidate shares.

Another reason for the lack of activism of institutional investors—even a frequent pro-management attitude—is conflict of interest: not opposing or even backing the managers of the companies in which they invest may enable them to get or keep lucrative contracts to run those companies' pension funds. Davis and Kim (2007) analyze proxy voting by U.S. mutual funds in 2004 and find that aggregate pro-management votes at the fund family level are positively correlated with the magnitude of mutual funds' business ties to firms in their portfolio, even though the correlation does not emerge when examining voting behavior at specific firms: in other words, funds with strong business ties with portfolio firms tend to be less activist across the board; they do not necessarily cast their votes specifically in favor of client firm management.

A more fundamental question is whether shareholder activism actually prompts better corporate performance. The evidence is mixed. While some studies document positive short-term market price reactions to announcements of certain kinds of activism, others find that large blockholders fail to improve the long-term operating or stock market performance of the targeted companies (for a survey, see Gillan and Starks 2007). One reason for this mixed evidence may be that often activist shareholders intervene "behind the scenes," so their actions are not picked up by studies that rely on public information. Indeed Becht et al. (2009) document the effectiveness of such behind-the-scenes activity, using data from British Telecom's pension fund manager Hermes on its private engagements with management in companies targeted by its U.K. Focus Fund. They find that the fund intervenes predominantly through such private engagements and, in contrast with most previous studies of activism, they report that the Hermes fund considerably outperforms benchmarks and that its abnormally high returns are correlated with its interventions. McCahery, Sautner, and Starks (2016) provide survey-based evidence that these behind-the-scenes practices by institutional investors are widespread, and are used jointly with governance-motivated exit. These governance mechanisms are viewed as complementary devices, with intervention typically occurring prior to a potential exit. They also find that long-term investors and investors less concerned about stock liquidity intervene more intensively. Becht, Franks, and Wagner (2021) provide further evidence that the monitoring effort of active asset managers may lead to their exit: they show that a large institutional investor that engages in high-level private meetings with executives and board members of portfolio firms gains a sizeable information advantage that it exploits in trading on and around meeting days and votes.

There is more agreement on the evidence regarding shareholder activism by hedge funds. These are more lightly regulated and have fewer conflicts of interests than other institutional investors. Most empirical studies support the view that their activism creates value for shareholders by improving the governance, capital structure decisions, and operating performance of target firms (for a survey, see Brav, Jiang, and Kim 2009). Brav, Jiang, Thomas, and Partnoy (2008), using a large data set from 2001–6, find that activist hedge funds in the United States attain success or partial success in two-thirds of the cases in which they intervene, and that the announcement of their activism is accompanied by an abnormal return of approximately 7%, with no reversal during the subsequent year, and is followed by higher payout, better operating performance, and greater CEO turnover.

Interestingly, Edmans, Fang, and Zur (2013) find that market liquidity increases hedge funds' propensity to acquire large blocks of shares, but that once the stake is acquired, liquidity increases the likelihood of hedge funds opting for "exit" rather than voice, exactly as predicted by the model here: greater liquidity makes it more likely that the blockholder will choose a Schedule 13Gs filing (passive investment) rather than 13Ds (active investment), especially if its manager's wealth is sensitive to the stock price.

12.4 Price Discovery, Corporate Investment, and Executive Compensation

Sections 12.2 and 12.3 examined how market liquidity affects two key aspects of corporate policy, namely investment and governance. But these decisions are also affected by price discovery. An essential function of securities markets is discovering asset values by aggregating investors' private signals about future cash flows. The information conveyed by market prices can then be used by managers to guide their investment decisions; this is the topic of Section 12.4.1. If stock prices provide information about a company's performance, they can also be used by shareholders to index compensation and give executives sharper incentives to maximize the company's value, as will be discussed in Section 12.4.2.

12.4.1 Stock Prices and Investment Allocation

The information conveyed by stock market prices can be useful to firms' managers and stakeholders more generally. For instance, managers may decide to pursue or terminate an investment plan (e.g., a major acquisition, a research and development project, or diversification into new products and markets) after observing the market's reaction to its announcement. In line with this idea, Luo (2005) studies the case of merger announcements empirically and shows that managers use the stock price reaction to these announcements in deciding whether to cancel or consummate the deal. Or a sharp decline in stock prices may suggest to a financier that other investors have adverse information on the firm's prospects and induce him raise the return required for new capital (Goldstein, Ozdenoren, and Yuan 2009).

Box 12.1 Strategy Changes and Stock Price Reactions: HP'S Double U-Turn

On August 19, 2011, the price of the computer company Hewlett Packard's (HP) stock plunged 20.5%, after a decline of 6% the previous day. This followed an announcement by HP's chief executive officer Leo Apotheker that he planned to spin off or sell the personal computer unit for which HP was universally known and refocus the company on software production with the planned $11 billion acquisition of Autonomy, Britain's largest software producer. The new strategy was motivated by considerably larger profit margins in software than in personal computers. Clearly, the stock market did not react well to the announcement. On September 22, the company fired Mr. Apotheker and replaced him with Meg Whitman, former CEO of eBay. On October 27, HP announced that it had dropped the plan to spin off the personal computer unit, largely because it would have lost synergies related to bulk purchasing of components, thus significantly increasing costs. The price of HP shares rose by 22.6% from $22.80 on September 22 to $27.95 on November 30. However, the Autonomy deal was not abandoned, and it later resulted in extensive litigation regarding misleading accounting practices at Autonomy in the runup to the deal; and in 2021, HP wrote down a record $8.8 billion of Autonomy's value.

The possibility that managers' investment decisions may be determined by stock prices creates a complex interdependence between the stock market and the real economy, as first modeled by Dow and Gorton (1997). It is clear that real investment decisions affect stock prices, since the fundamental value of a security is the discounted value of its future cash flows. But if managers gather information from stock prices, causation may also run the other way. That is, stock prices will also affect investment decisions, hence future cash flows.

To capture this feedback from stock price to investment, consider the sequence of actions illustrated in Figure 12.4. At date 0, a firm announces that it is considering a new investment project (e.g., an R&D program for a new chip or a move into a new product line as in the example of Box 12.1), which is equally likely to be of high quality (H) or low quality (L). The project will contribute a net gain $G > 0$ to the company's value (originally equal to V) if it is of high quality or else entail the loss of the investment I:

$$\Delta V = \begin{cases} G & \text{if the company invests and project is high-quality } (H), \\ -I & \text{if the company invests and project is low-quality } (L), \\ 0 & \text{if the company does not invest.} \end{cases}$$

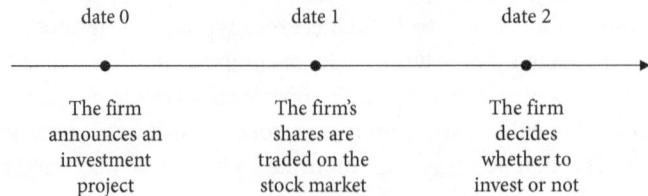

date 0	date 1	date 2
The firm announces an investment project	The firm's shares are traded on the stock market	The firm decides whether to invest or not

Figure 12.4 Stock prices and investment decisions: time line.

It is assumed that, if no information about quality is available, the project is not viable: $G < I$, so that the project's expected net present value, $\frac{1}{2}G - \frac{1}{2}I$, is negative.

At date 1, after the announcement of this investment opportunity, the firm's shares are traded by investors, some of whom have valuable information about the quality of the project. As in Chapter 3, two potential types of traders place orders that are filled by risk-neutral, competitive, and uninformed market makers. With probability π, an informed risk-neutral speculator who knows whether the project's quality is H or L comes to the market, and makes a trade that maximizes his expected profit. With probability $1 - \pi$, a liquidity trader buys or sells one unit of stock with equal probabilities. The market makers price the stock at its expected value, conditional on the arrival of a buy or sell order.

At the same time, with probability γ the firm's manager privately receives a report that enables him to establish the quality of the project; with probability $1 - \gamma$ he does not. Thus, at date 2, when the decision to proceed with the project or not must be taken, the manager considers both his own information (if any) and the reaction of the stock market to the announcement. The issue is whether and how the information conveyed by trades on the stock market can help guide the investment decision.

To solve for the equilibrium, let us conjecture that informed traders buy a unit of the stock if they learn that the project is of high quality and sell a unit otherwise: later we will check that this strategy is indeed optimal in equilibrium.

If the manager has gotten a private report, he needs look no further to decide whether to invest. The interesting case is when he has not received any such report, and so his only guide is the stock market. As in Chapter 3, if a buy order is placed, it executes at the ask a; a sell order executes at the bid b. Hence the transaction price p reveals the direction of trading interest. Depending on whether he observes a transaction at ask or at bid, the manager updates his estimate of the probability of the project being of quality H, using Bayes' Law:[3]

$$\Pr(H|p = a) = \frac{1 + \pi}{2},$$

$$\Pr(H|p = b) = \frac{1 - \pi}{2}.$$

If the manager observes a trade at the ask, then his updated expectation of the project's net present value is:

---

[3] These two probabilities can be obtained from equations (3.16) and (3.17), which describe the updating of the dealer's beliefs in Chapter 3. Setting the prior probability of the stock being high value $\theta_{t-1} = \frac{1}{2}$ yields the updated probabilities $\theta_t^+ = \Pr(H|p = a)$ and $\theta_t^- = \Pr(H|p = b)$.

$$\Pr(H|p = a)G + (1 - \Pr(H|p = a))(-I) \tag{12.4}$$

$$= \frac{1 + \pi}{2}G - \frac{1 - \pi}{2}I.$$

A transaction at the ask will persuade him to invest if this updated expected present value is positive, which requires that:

$$\pi \geq \frac{I - G}{I + G}. \tag{12.5}$$

Recalling that π is the proportion of informed investors, inequality (12.5) states that the executive's decision is guided by the stock market only if the trading is informative enough. This inequality is more easily satisfied if I is very close to G, that is, if the project is borderline in the first place, so that even a little bit of positive news can tip the balance. Naturally, if a transaction is observed at the bid, the manager elects not to invest: his prior estimate of the project's net present value was already negative by assumption, and his posterior estimate will be even lower.

What is the allocative value of the information from the stock market? Let us compare the outcome of the investment decision with and without a stock market. We assume that the informativeness condition (12.5) holds, because otherwise the stock market would clearly play no role.

In the absence of a stock market (that is, if the company is not listed), the manager will only invest with probability $\gamma/2$, namely if he receives private information about the project and if the information is positive. Therefore, ex ante the value of the firm, if privately held, is:

$$V_{private} = V + \frac{\gamma}{2}G. \tag{12.6}$$

If the firm is listed, however, the manager can fine-tune his investment decision and invest even if he does not have private information, as long as he observes a trade at the ask price on the market. As before, he gets positive private information with probability $\gamma/2$, in which case he again invests gaining G. But when he does not receive private information, which occurs with probability $1 - \gamma$, he will observe a transaction at the ask with probability $\frac{1}{2}$ and therefore invest. The net present value of this policy is given by equation (12.4), so that the ex ante value of the firm when publicly listed is:

$$V_{public} = V + \frac{\gamma}{2}G + \frac{1 - \gamma}{2}\left(\frac{1 + \pi}{2}G - \frac{1 - \pi}{2}I\right) \tag{12.7}$$

$$= \underbrace{V + \frac{\gamma}{2}G}_{V_{private}} + \underbrace{(1 - \gamma)\frac{\pi}{2}G}_{\text{informational gain}} - \underbrace{(1 - \gamma)\frac{1 - \pi}{2}\frac{I - G}{2}}_{\text{loss from noise}}.$$

Thus we can think of the total contribution of the stock market to the investment decision as consisting of two components: the gain from investing when the informed trader is present and provides a valuable positive signal by buying the stock, and the loss from overinvesting when the noise trader buys stock (in which case the investment on average is mistaken, given our assumption that $I > G$). Clearly, the net effect is positive whenever the informativeness condition (12.5) is satisfied: the manager will only consider the stock price when it improves the firm's investment decision. And as one would expect, the net gain is increasing in the informativeness of trading, as measured by π.

Under our assumptions, the stock market encourages investment, insofar as it sometimes prompts the manager to invest even in the absence of private information. However, this feature of the model is not robust: if we were to assume that on average the investment is viable (i.e., if we assumed that $G > I$), the stock market would act as a brake on investment, by prompting the manager to forgo investment when traders sell. We leave this case as an exercise to the reader (see exercise 2).

Having obtained the manager's equilibrium investment strategy, we can now compute the bid and ask prices that will prevail on the market in equilibrium. This problem is somewhat more subtle here than in Chapter 3, because market makers must take into account the relationship between market trading, the manager's investment decision, and the probability of the project's being high quality. Recall that market makers have no independent information and simply condition their quotes on whether there is a buy or a sell order. Computing the equilibrium bid and ask prices is also useful to check the validity of our initial conjecture that the informed speculator always finds it profitable to buy when he learns that the company's project is high quality, and to sell if it is low quality.

Since equilibrium bid and ask prices depend on the investment policy, they differ depending on whether the informativeness condition (12.5) holds or not. If it does, market makers know that the manager will invest either when he receives positive private information or when he observes a buy order. So, competitive market makers will set their ask price at:

$$a = V + (1-\pi)\underbrace{\left[\frac{\gamma}{2}G + (1-\gamma)\frac{G-I}{2}\right]}_{\text{NPV if noise trader buys}} + \pi\underbrace{G}_{\substack{\text{NPV if} \\ \text{informed} \\ \text{buys}}} \qquad (12.8)$$

The term in square brackets is the net present value of the investment conditional on the order coming from a noise trader: with probability $\gamma/2$, the manager knows that the project is high quality and invests; with probability $\gamma/2$, he knows that it is low quality and does not invest; and with probability $1-\gamma$, he has no private information and mistakenly takes guidance from the stock market, so that the project's expected value is $(G-I)/2$ (since the noise trade contains no real information). The last term in the expression is the value of the investment conditional on the buy order coming from an informed trader, namely G.

Conversely, a competitive market maker will set his bid price at:

$$b = V + (1 - \pi) \underbrace{\frac{\gamma}{2} G.}_{\substack{\text{NPV if noise} \\ \text{trader sells}}} \tag{12.9}$$

If there is a sell order, the manager will only invest if he has positive private information. In this case, the sell order necessarily comes from a noise trader because the manager's information and the informed trader's signal never conflict. Hence, the market maker anticipates a successful investment (worth G) with probability $(1 - \pi)\gamma/2$ (the joint probability of a noise trade and positive private information).

How will the informed speculator react to the ask and bid prices in (12.8) and (12.9)? If he knows that the project is of high quality, and expects the manager to invest upon observing the speculator's own buy order, he will value the firm at $V + G$. Hence, by placing a buy order at the ask in (12.8) he will book the expected trading profit:

$$(V + G) - a = \frac{1 - \pi}{2} [G + (1 - \gamma)I] > 0. \tag{12.10}$$

Similarly, if he knows that the project is of low quality, the speculator will book a profit from a sell order at the bid price in (12.9). In this case, since the manager will not invest upon observing the speculator's own sell order, the firm will be worth V, so that a sell order implies the expected profit is:

$$b - V = (1 - \pi)\frac{\gamma}{2} G > 0. \tag{12.11}$$

It can also be readily shown that the informed speculator has no incentive to trade against his information (see exercise 3): for instance, he does not short the security when he knows that the investment is intrinsically sound.[4]

Hence, as initially conjectured, in equilibrium the speculator buys upon receiving good news about the project and sells otherwise. We leave it to the reader to show that the same applies if the informativeness condition (12.5)

---

[4] This type of manipulation can happen, however, in more complex models with feedback from the stock market to investment decisions, as shown by Goldstein and Gümbel (2008). In this case, instead of contributing to the efficient allocation of corporate investment, the signals issued by stock market prices would impair it.

does not hold, so that the stock market does not affect the manager's investment decisions (see exercise 4).

To sum up, we have established that there is an equilibrium in which the informed speculator buys if he receives a positive signal about the manager's strategy but sells otherwise, and the manager implements his strategy if he receives good information about the project or if the stock market's reaction to the announcement of his strategy is positive, but not otherwise.

Using equations (12.8) and (12.9), one can compute the equilibrium bid-ask spread:

$$S = \pi G - \frac{(1-\pi)(1-\gamma)}{2}(I-G). \tag{12.12}$$

Clearly, S is increasing in π.[5] So, as in Chapter 3, an increase in the prevalence of informed trading not only increases the informational content of stock prices but also makes the market less liquid. This points to an interesting conclusion: informed trading π increases the stock market's ability to guide investment, as measured by the gain $V_{public} - V_{private}$ in (12.7), at the cost of reducing market liquidity, as measured by the bid-ask spread (12.12). This highlights the danger of considering liquidity as a universally desirable attribute of the stock market, and provides a counterexample to the view that liquidity increases asset values and investment, as suggested by the analysis in Chapter 10. In this model, more frequent informed trading reduces liquidity, but on average raises the stock price, because it improves the allocation of investment, as is attested to by the fact that the average transaction price (the midprice, since buyers and sellers arrive with equal probabilities in this example) is increasing in π:

$$m = \frac{a+b}{2} = V + \frac{1}{2}\left\{[(1-\gamma)\pi + \gamma]G - \frac{(1-\pi)(1-\gamma)}{2}(I-G)\right\}.$$

In this model, the frequency of informed trading also increases the frequency of investment: if π is so low that it does not satisfy condition (12.5), the manager invests only with positive private information, that is, with probability $\gamma/2$; if instead π is above the threshold set by condition (12.5), he invests also when he sees buying in the stock market, that is, with probability $\frac{1}{2}$.[6]

---

[5] The equilibrium spread in (12.12) is positive, since we assume that condition (12.5) holds, that is, $\pi \geq \frac{I-G}{I+G}$ and, by the same token, $1 - \pi \leq \frac{2G}{I+G}$. Using these two conditions for π and $1 - \pi$ and equation (12.5), we find that $S \geq \gamma G(I-G)/(I+G)$, which is non-negative, so that $S \geq 0$ for any π that satisfies condition (12.5).

[6] The argument developed so far has an important limitation: it takes the frequency of informed trading as a given parameter π, whereas in reality it could be endogenous. In markets where there is

We discuss evidence regarding this feedback from stock prices to investment decisions, via managerial learning from prices, in Section 12.6.

12.4.2 Stock Prices and Executive Compensation

A central theme in corporate finance is that, when control is entrusted to professional managers, the interests of shareholders and management may conflict. These conflicts can take many forms. Managers may pursue objectives that are not in the shareholders' best interest: for instance, they may opt for an "easy life" rather than work hard to seek the best profit opportunities for the company; they may pursue unwarranted expansion (empire building) or they may give themselves unduly large salaries or perks, or make nepotistic appointments. Alternatively, they may deviate from shareholder value maximization in the interest of other stakeholders, for example, undertaking loss-making but environmentally friendly projects or retaining unproductive employees. It can be difficult or inconvenient for shareholders to monitor and restrain such opportunism, especially if ownership is dispersed, so that shareholders' stakes are too small to justify the costs of activism.

And even if shareholders could verify managers' behavior, it may be very hard to curtail their opportunism. Consider an executive who is seen to opt for an "easy life," as opposed to hard work: it may be very difficult for the shareholders to take such a manager to court and prove that he did not work as hard as possible. The reason is that "working hard" cannot be accurately described in a contract enforceable in court: it is impossible to foresee all the contingencies that can arise in managing the firm and specify what a "hardworking" manager must do in each. Indeed, in the United States the so-called "business judgment rule" protects managers from legal challenges to their decisions (except in clear cases of negligence or corruption) and thus gives them considerable flexibility to act as they deem appropriate in the company's interest. In more technical jargon, even if shareholders could observe the manager's effort level, such effort may not be verifiable or legally enforceable. This generates a moral hazard (or agency) problem between shareholders and management.

While lawsuits may be ineffective, shareholders can mitigate this moral hazard and thus improve the company's performance by giving management financial

---

more trading by uninformed investors, speculators can obtain higher returns on their information, and so have more incentive to acquire information on the quality of firms' investment projects. Since more uninformed trading also tends to increase liquidity (as in Kyle's model), changes in it may result in a positive correlation between liquidity and the frequency of informed trading, in contrast with the tradeoff between liquidity and the allocative value of prices described in the text.

incentives to work hard.[7] By indexing the manager's compensation to some measure of company performance (based on accounting variables or on stock prices), shareholders can induce the manager to exert effort—a practice known as "pay for performance." Holmstrom and Tirole (1993) contend that linking executive pay to the price of their company's stock may be very effective in sharpening their incentives to exert effort. They argue that if shares are listed and publicly traded, speculators will gather information on the firm's performance and the stock price will thus at least partly reflect this information. The more precise the information conveyed by the firm's stock price, the more effective linking managerial compensation to it will be in eliciting effort, and hence the greater the enhancement of the firm's performance.

In this section, we capture this point in a simple setting where shareholders can choose whether the manager's compensation is to depend on the final value of the company (say, its long-term earnings or its terminal liquidation value) or to the price of the stock at some interim date, when investors observe the effort exerted. Specifically, as illustrated in Figure 12.5, at date 0 shareholders design the compensation contract; at date 1 the manager chooses whether to exert effort at a personal cost c (a choice that is publicly observed, though not verifiable in court); at date 2, the shares are traded on the stock market at price P; finally, at date 3, the final value of the company V—say, its earnings—is either high (V^H) or low (V^L). The manager's effort increases the company's expected value: the

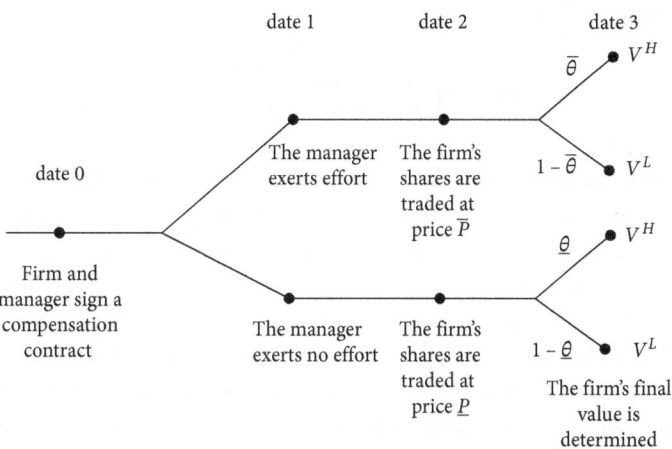

Figure 12.5 Stock prices and managerial compensation: time line.

[7] Other governance mechanisms that can realign the executive's incentives with those of shareholders are the risk of termination (i.e., managerial turnover) or career concerns (performance-based advancement).

probability that $V = V^H$ is $\underline{\theta}$ if the manager exerts no effort, $\bar{\theta} = \underline{\theta} + \Delta\theta$ if he exerts effort.

Thus, if he exerts effort, the manager increases the company's expected value by $\Delta\theta(V^H - V^L) = \Delta\theta\Delta V$. We assume that effort is efficient, i.e., that the effect on the company's expected final value is greater than the cost of the manager's effort: $\Delta V > c/\Delta\theta$. In other words, shareholders would find it worthwhile to just compensate the manager for his effort if they could make sure that the manager does not shirk. For simplicity, we assume that the manager's reservation wage (i.e., what he could get from another employer) is zero, so he will be willing to work for the firm if his expected wage from exceeds his effort cost, that is, his participation constraint is satisfied. Moreover, the manager is assumed to enjoy limited liability: he cannot be made to pay any penalty over and above his compensation. Hence, his wage can never be negative.

Consider first the case in which the manager's pay can only be conditioned on the final value of the company (i.e., incentive pay can only be based on reported earnings: pay $w(v)$ takes one of two values w^H or w^L depending on the firm's final value). It is most economical for the owners to set the salary as low as possible in case of failure: $w^L = 0$. Incentive compatibility requires that the manager be given a high enough compensation w^H in case of success to induce him to exert effort:

$$\bar{\theta}w^H - c \geqslant \underline{\theta}w^H. \tag{12.13}$$

The lowest-cost pay scheme that elicits effort is thus:

$$w(v) = \begin{cases} w^H = c/\Delta\theta & \text{if} \quad V = V^H, \\ w^L = 0 & \text{if} \quad V = V^L. \end{cases} \tag{12.14}$$

The manager's participation constraint is satisfied, since this compensation package gives him a positive expected payoff $\bar{\theta}w^H - c = \underline{\theta}c/\Delta\theta > 0$, which is greater than his zero reservation wage, an example of what is known in the labor economics literature as an "efficiency wage," surveyed by Yellen (1984). So shareholders end up paying the manager a "rent" to stimulate him to exert effort. This is due to the manager's limited liability: if shareholders could inflict a penalty when the company's value is low, they could avoid paying him this rent, since they could incentivize him while just meeting his participation constraint.[8] Hence the company's expected value, at time 0, is:

---

[8] Inflicting a penalty on an underperforming manager is equivalent to paying him a negative salary. If shareholders could pay a negative salary $w^L < 0$ to a manager for poor performance, they could meet his incentive constraint by paying him $w^H = c/\Delta\theta + w^L$ if $V = V^H$ and w^L if $V = V^L$. But now they can also reduce his wages to just barely meet his participation constraint by setting his average wage, net of effort cost, to zero: $\bar{\theta}w^H + (1 - \bar{\theta})w^L = c$, so as to just compensate him for

$$V_0 = \left[\bar{\theta}V^H + (1-\bar{\theta})V^L\right] - \bar{\theta}w^H = V^L + \bar{\theta}\left(\Delta V - \frac{c}{\Delta \theta}\right). \qquad (12.15)$$

So far, it has been assumed that, although the company's shares are publicly traded, shareholders do not take the stock price into account in determining the manager's pay. But, at date 2, the stock price will be higher when the manager exerts effort than when he does not since investors observe the manager's effort.[9] Suppose now that the manager's compensation can be conditioned on the stock price rise associated with his effort: he can be paid a salary $\bar{w}$ if the stock price signals that the manager exerted effort at date 1, and zero otherwise. Hence, at date 2, the company's stock price is:

$$P = \begin{cases} \bar{P} = \underline{\theta}V^H + (1-\underline{\theta})V^L + \Delta\theta\Delta V - \bar{w} & \text{if the manager exerts effort,} \\ \underline{P} = \underline{\theta}V^H + (1-\underline{\theta})V^L & \text{if the manager shirks.} \end{cases}$$
$$(12.16)$$

The incentive constraint now is:

$$\bar{w} - c \geqslant 0. \qquad (12.17)$$

Hence, shareholders optimally offer the following compensation package to the manager:

$$w(P) = \begin{cases} \bar{w} = c & \text{if} \quad P = \bar{P}, \\ \underline{w} = 0 & \text{if} \quad P = \underline{P}. \end{cases} \qquad (12.18)$$

Under this compensation scheme, from expression (12.16), $\bar{P} - \underline{P} = \Delta\theta\Delta V - c$. This difference is positive: as conjectured, the company's stock price is higher when the manager is seen to exert effort $(\bar{P} > \underline{P})$.

The key point is that, by linking the manager's pay to the stock's performance, shareholders can incentivize the manager without leaving any rent to him: they just compensate him for his effort, so his net payoff is zero. The reason is that in this model the stock price is a more precise (in fact, here perfect) signal of the effort than reported earnings. As a result, with stock-based compensation the expected value of the company at date 0 will be greater than under earnings-based compensation:

---

the cost of effort. Hence, the manager's optimal compensation would be $w^H = c(1-\bar{\theta})/\Delta\theta > 0$ if $V = V^H$ and $w^L = -c\bar{\theta}/\Delta\theta < 0$ if $V = V^L$.

[9] The difference is $\Delta\theta\Delta V - c > 0$. The proof is left to the reader as an exercise.

$$V_0' = [\bar{\theta}V^H + (1 - \bar{\theta})V^L] - \overline{w} = V^L + (\bar{\theta}\Delta V - c), \qquad (12.19)$$

which exceeds the value in equation (12.15). The gain in value is $V_0' - V_0 = c\underline{\theta}/\Delta\theta$. Thus the increase in expected value is proportional to $\underline{\theta}$, the likelihood that the company will overperform when the manager shirks, and to c, the private cost of effort to the manager. Intuitively, a higher value of either one of these parameters worsens the problem of moral hazard and so increases the desirability of indexing the manager's compensation to stock prices. In exercise 6, the reader is invited to solve for the optimal compensation scheme when investors do not necessarily observe the manager's effort.

While this model shows that stock-based compensation can benefit share-holders by sharpening managerial incentives, this type of scheme also has some drawbacks. One is pointed out by Holmstrom and Tirole (1993) themselves: stock prices are a reliable device for managerial discipline only if they are infor-mative about the company's future performance, but the greater informativeness of stock prices comes at the cost of lower liquidity, because the informational rents of speculators are gained at the expense of uninformed investors. If these investors are rational, initially, they will be willing to buy the company's shares only at a lower price—they will require an illiquidity discount.

As shown in Section 10.3, more informed trading raises this illiquidity premium and so lowers the initial price that the security will command. This factor works in the opposite direction from that considered so far: while stock price informativeness tends to increase the company's initial value by enabling shareholders to better discipline managers, the related reduction in market liquidity tends to reduce value. The familiar tension between price discovery and market liquidity resurfaces. Holmstrom and Tirole (1993) conclude that companies will have to trade off the beneficial impact of the increase in executive effort against the implied illiquidity discount.

Another disadvantage of stock-based (and option-based) managerial com-pensation is that it may lead managers to divert valuable resources to misrep-resent performance (Goldman and Slezak 2006). This danger has been shown to be empirically relevant by a number of studies, which detect a positive correlation between managerial incentive pay and accounting fraud (see Section 12.6). Moreover, stock- and option-based compensation may induce managers to pursue short-term rather than long-term objectives: for instance, Edmans, Fang, and Lewellen (2017) identify short-termism using the amount of stock and options scheduled to vest in a given quarter, and find that vesting equity is associated with a decline in the growth of research and development and capital expenditure in the same quarter. Last but not least, stock- and option-based compensation has been shown to be associated with excess risk-taking by bank managers, especially in the context of the 2007–9 financial crisis (see Section 12.6).

12.5 Corporate Policies and Market Liquidity

We have seen that a liquid security market can increase corporate investment and that the informational content of stock prices can improve firms' investment decisions and help them to provide incentives to management. This suggests that companies may wish to enhance the liquidity of their stock or the informativeness of its price. And companies can in fact affect these variables by a variety of decisions.

Clearly, the most basic decision in this respect is whether or not to go public. But even after this decision is made, this is not the end of the story: after an IPO on its domestic stock market, a company may decide to cross-list on other exchanges. Alternatively, it can choose from the start to list on multiple exchanges, via a global IPO. The determinants and effects of these choices are discussed briefly in Section 12.5.1.

Public listing, however, is no guarantee that the shares will be actively traded, with narrow bid-ask spreads and informative prices. To achieve this, a company can act on three other fronts. First, it can support the liquidity of its shares directly by paying designated market makers to trade in its stock and maintain a tight bid-ask spread: Section 12.5.2 discusses the effects of these policies on liquidity and company value. Second, the company can affect the liquidity of its securities by disclosing detailed, precise and timely value-relevant accounting data and by encouraging financial analysts to evaluate and convey them to investors, as discussed in Section 12.5.3. Third, it can affect liquidity and informativeness by adjusting its issuance of shares and debt securities, hence its leverage—the key parameter of a firm's capital structure. Alternatively, it can tweak the design of its securities so as to vary the sensitivity of the security's price to performance information. These issues are discussed in Section 12.5.4.

12.5.1 Listing and Cross-Listing

Liquidity is the most obvious benefit from listing a company's shares on a public market: the trading platform for its stock acts as a coordination device, where potential buyers and sellers can meet and trade, instead of searching informally for a counterparty. Per se, this liquidity gain expands the company's shareownership base to investors who would otherwise shun it, for fear of being unable to liquidate the shares at a reasonable price in case of need. In fact, many investors may not even be aware of a company's existence until it lists. As highlighted by Merton (1987), investors' portfolio choices are constrained by their limited awareness of which securities are available for investment.

Hence, going public should enable companies not only to reduce the cost of equity financing—thanks to the lower liquidity premium (see Chapter 10)—but also to access a larger pool of external funds, by expanding their shareholder base. These effects are further amplified by the fact that public companies typically disclose much more information than private ones do (Section 12.5.3). In the United States, young companies tend to use their improved post-IPO access to external equity to increase investment, while more mature companies use it mainly to pay down debt (Mikkelson, Partch, and Shah 1997); in Italy, instead, newly listed companies use the funds mainly to reduce leverage, and negotiate lower interest rates with their banks (Pagano, Panetta, and Zingales 1998).

The benefits of going public extend beyond liquidity and access to finance. An IPO enables the controlling shareholders to divest some of their shares and diversify their portfolios (Pagano 1993b; Chemmanur and Fulghieri 1999). It also allows the company to use the stock price as an input into managerial decisions (Section 12.4.1) and can improve output market performance by enhancing the firm's visibility and reputation.

However going public also entails costs. Some are straightforward: the underwriting fees charged by the investment banks that assist the company in listing and placement, stock exchange listing fees, and the costs of complying with disclosure requirements. Other costs are more subtle, involving the negative fallout of disclosure due to greater visibility to competitors and tax authorities. Since some of these costs have a large fixed cost component, it is not surprising that many small companies refrain from going public: indeed Pagano, Panetta, and Zingales (1998) report that company size is the single most important determinant of the probability of going public. Recently, public liquid markets appear to have lost some of their former appeal for firms, judging from the steep decline in the number of publicly listed U.S. firms since 1997 (Doidge et al. 2017). This may be due both to the phenomenal growth in the availability of private equity funding and to the increased cost of corporate disclosure (see Section 12.5.3).

Most companies that go public do so via domestic IPOs, in the country where they are headquartered. Yet they can still increase their market access further by cross-listing their shares on foreign exchanges. Less frequently, companies undertake their IPO directly in a foreign market or simultaneously at home and abroad—a so-called global IPO. The benefits and costs associated with cross-listing are similar but not identical to those associated with the first listing discussed above.

On the benefit side, cross-listing may increase liquidity and access to new investors; indeed, companies tend to cross-list in more liquid and larger exchanges (Pagano et al. 2001). However, in contrast to an IPO, a cross-listing creates an additional market for the same stock. Hence, in theory, it might reduce the liquidity of the home market, or fail to produce a very active foreign market for the stock. In other words, the fragmentation of trading induced by cross-listing may reduce total liquidity (see Section 7.2)—an issue that has been addressed by a number of empirical studies (see the references in Section 12.6).

The effect of cross-listing on the cost of equity capital appears to vary with company's country of origin: non-U.S. companies from countries with relatively poor shareholder protection tend to get positive stock price reactions when they announce that they will cross-list in the United States, while no such reaction is observed for cross-listings by U.S. companies (Karolyi 1998). Cross-listing also enhances increased visibility and reputation: actually, of 305 cross-listed European companies, 57% reported that the most important benefits of a foreign listing are increased visibility and prestige (Bancel and Mittoo 2001).

This suggests that some benefits of cross-listing stem specifically from the wide range of choices of where to cross-list, while for the original IPO, listing on the domestic exchange is the default option. Hence, cross-listing can be used strategically to "bond" the company to the rules of an investor-friendly foreign jurisdiction or to benefit from the prestige and visibility of an established stock exchange. Indeed, companies tend to cross-list in countries with better investor protection (Pagano et al. 2001)—a choice generally rewarded by the market via a lower cost of capital or equivalently a "cross-listing premium." Consistent with the bonding hypothesis, the premium of companies that cross-list in the United States is positively correlated with measures of improvements in corporate governance (see the survey by Karolyi 2006 and the references in Section 12.6).

Another strategic benefit of cross-listing is to access investors who are best at evaluating its business plans or its technology. Hence, a cross-listing can be used to enhance the informativeness of stock prices to managers and thereby firm value, as is shown by Foucault and Gehrig (2008). For instance, a firm that plans to launch a product in the U.S. market knows that American investors are well placed to judge its potential. One way for the firm to obtain credible feedback from U.S. consumers is to cross-list in the United States, thus encouraging local investors to trade its stock and contribute to price discovery. U.S. investors may also have greater expertise in evaluating the business of high-tech firms, such as software or biotech companies, which have a particularly strong presence in the U.S. economy.

The evidence on cross-listings and foreign IPOs is consistent with the thesis that companies seek to list where investors are better positioned to value their shares. Pagano, Röell, and Zechner (2002) document that the foreign sales of European companies that cross-listed between 1986 and 1997 tended to expand afterwards, and that U.S. exchanges attracted mainly cross-listings of high-tech and export-oriented companies. The same motivations appear to apply to most companies that choose to make their original IPO outside their domestic market. Caglio, Weiss Hanley, and Marietta-Westberg (2011) document that foreign IPOs tend to involve high-tech firms strongly oriented towards foreign markets, and originate from countries with low capital market development and poor disclosure requirements.

12.5.2 Designated Market Makers

As was explained in Section 12.2, companies whose shares are more liquid in secondary market trading fetch a higher price at the IPO stage (Ellul and Pagano 2006): the fact that investors appear to value post-IPO liquidity suggests that firms can benefit from policies that improve the liquidity of their stock. And in fact, IPO underwriting banks sometimes act as market makers to boost the new stock's liquidity in the months following the offering (see Ellis, Michaely, and O'Hara 2000). Firms pay their underwriter an additional fee for this service, which attests the fact that liquidity is particularly valuable at the IPO stage.

But firms can enter into this type of arrangement even after the IPO: they can—and often do—hire a market-maker to maintain a liquid market in their stock, by keeping the spread below some agreed level, for instance. Such designated market makers (DMMs) have been increasingly popular in LOB markets: they have appeared in France, Germany, Italy, the Netherlands, Sweden, and Norway, where they operate with aggressive limit orders on the buy and sell side of the book and thereby increase liquidity to incoming orders. In this sense, their operation is completely different from that of the NYSE specialists, whose last-mover advantage has such potential drawbacks, as the possibility of cream skimming, which might harm liquidity (Section 6.3.3).

Indeed, the evidence shows that DMMs have increased market liquidity— as measured by spreads and other indicators—in all the markets where they have been introduced (see Section 12.6 for the relevant references). The studies by Menkveld and Wang (2011) for the Netherlands and by Skjeltorp and Ødegaard (2015) for Norway also show that the introduction of a DMM is associated with a reduction in liquidity risk, as measured by the "liquidity betas" proposed by Acharya and Pedersen (2005), described in Chapter 10. These studies conclude that the introduction of a DMM corresponds to statistically and economically significant abnormal returns, which vary considerably across markets. The average yearly cumulative abnormal return associated with their announcement ranges from 1% in Oslo to 3.5% in Amsterdam, 5% in Paris, and 7% in Stockholm. In any event, this is concurrent evidence that liquidity is valued by the market, well after the IPO stage.

Since hiring a DMM is a corporate decision, one wonders which companies choose to spend money to enhance market liquidity and what type of benefit is obtained. The study by Skjeltorp and Ødegaard (2015) on DMMs in the Oslo stock market is enlightening. It shows that only relatively illiquid firms choose to hire a DMM (see Figure 12.6). The histogram in panel A shows the frequency distribution of the relative bid-ask spread for the companies that do not have a DMM in a given year; panel B displays that information for firms that do hire a DMM, both the year before and the year after the hire. Comparing the three plots, we see that the most liquid firms do without a DMM—probably because they are confident that their bid-ask spreads are narrow anyway—and for companies that do hire a DMM, the distribution of spreads is distinctly shifted to the left.

This study also sheds light on why companies hire a DMM, showing that the decision is affected by the likelihood that the firm will interact with the capital markets in the future. Firms that choose to hire a DMM have greater growth

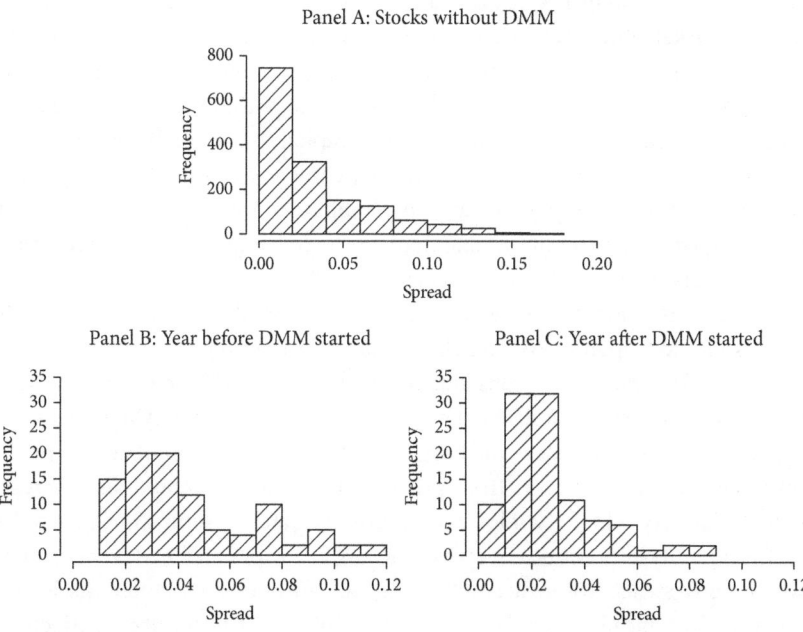

Figure 12.6 Frequency distribution of bid-ask spread for stocks without DMM and with DMM.

Source: Figure 2 in Skjeltorp and Ødergaard 2015.

opportunities (as measured by their Tobin's Q) and are more likely to raise external equity after the appointment of the DMM. Presumably they introduce a DMM precisely because they plan to issue more shares in the future and hope to do so at better prices.

12.5.3 Disclosure Policy

As observed in Section 12.5.1, committing to a high degree of corporate disclosure is part and parcel of the decision to go public. First, at the IPO stage a company must file a prospectus, which provides certified balance sheet data, as well as information about ownership and control, business plans and expected performance, reasons for going public, and so on. Second, from that moment onward, the company commits to periodic disclosure of certified balance-sheet data and regular earnings announcements. Third, blockholders commit to disclose information about trades that imply a substantial change in their stake in the company and on related-party transactions (e.g., deals with important suppliers or customers).

However, if the shareholders want, they can opt for even more disclosure than required by the domestic stock market or regulator. For instance, they can cross-list in a market with more stringent requirements or better enforcement against insider trading, or in a jurisdiction with stronger shareholder protection. All of these policies—see the evidence on the "bonding hypothesis" in Section 12.5.1— enable companies to secure a lower cost of capital. But cross-listing is not the only way to commit to better disclosure: a company can do so by having its accounts certified by reputable auditing companies, by adopting international rather than national accounting standards, or by committing to regular meetings with analysts to set out the company's prospects.

Insofar as they mitigate adverse selection problems, all these disclosure mechanisms should help firms to raise cheaper and more abundant equity capital not only in the IPO but also in subsequent seasoned equity offerings. Indeed, there is empirical evidence that firms that choose greater transparency tend to attract more funding from investors and have a lower cost of capital. Since greater public disclosure reduces the rents from private information, it should also increase market liquidity, which itself lowers the cost of capital, as shown in Chapter 10.

The liquidity-promoting effect of disclosure is documented by several studies: when firms switch to an accounting regime that features better disclosure, their stocks typically become more liquid. This effect is confirmed by cross-country evidence. Lang, Lins, and Maffett (2012) show that firms that choose a higher degree of transparency (as measured by less earnings management, better accounting standards, higher quality auditors, more analyst following, and more accurate analyst forecasts) have narrower bid-ask spreads and fewer non-trading days. They also demonstrate that this increased liquidity is associated with lower cost of capital and higher valuation. Further evidence on the relationship between transparency, liquidity, and access to capital markets comes from what happens to companies when they lose all of their analysts' coverage (Figure 5.2). Their liquidity suffers compared to a control sample of similar companies (Ellul and Panayides 2018), and their investment drops significantly (Derrien and Kecskés 2013), suggesting that their access to capital diminishes or their cost of capital increases. To some extent, firms may compensate for the adverse effects of loss of coverage by analysts by disclosing more information, as found empirically by Balakrishnan et al. (2014). Section 12.6 reports further evidence on these issues.

If disclosure is so beneficial for firms, why is it that not all firms opt for maximum disclosure? The fact is that disclosure also has costs, and the trade-off between costs and benefits differs between companies and countries, depending on a variety of circumstances. The first, and most obvious, cost of transparency is the expense of disseminating the information in a credible way to investors (Section 12.5.1): listing fees, underwriting commissions, auditing fees, regulation compliance costs, and so on. For instance, compliance with the disclosure rules of a foreign jurisdiction sometimes requires switching to a different accounting system. Biddle and Saudagaran (1989) and Saudagaran and Biddle (1992) report that stringent disclosure requirements deter the listing of foreign companies, and the companies surveyed by Bancel and Mittoo (2001) place them among the chief disadvantages of a cross-listing.

A second, and less obvious, cost stems from the non-exclusive nature of information disclosure: once information about a firm's business plans or R&D projects is known to investors, it becomes known to competitors as well, who may exploit it to appropriate the firm's profit opportunities. This should be a particularly acute concern for high-tech, innovative firms—and especially the more successful ones: Campbell (1979) and Yosha (1995) suggest that firms with projects whose value depends on confidentiality may prefer bilateral financing arrangements rather than going public. Regulation may further exacerbate this concern. In the United States, the Regulation Fair Disclosure (known as Reg FD) prevents public companies from disclosing information selectively to certain groups of investors. The value of confidentiality for the increasing number of firms that rely heavily on patents and intangible capital may be one of the reasons why lately more and more firms prefer private equity financing to raising capital via a public listing.

A third, closely related cost arising from the non-exclusive nature of financial disclosure is diminished ability to evade or elude taxes: for instance, if the company provides more detailed accounting information to investors, it also reveals it to the tax authorities, especially if it is incorporated in a country that prescribes "book-tax conformity" (i.e., that bans reporting different earnings to tax authorities and investors). So in choosing accounting transparency, firms must trade off the benefits of access to more abundant and cheaper capital against the cost of a greater tax burden. Ellul et al. (2018) find that cross-country company-level data are consistent with the existence of this trade-off. First, investment and access to finance are correlated positively with accounting transparency and negatively with tax pressure. Second, transparency is nega-tively correlated with tax pressure: firms choose less transparency where the implied tax cost is higher, particularly in sectors where they are less dependent on external finance, so that the implied cost in terms of foregone investment is lower.

Finally, disclosing more information forces investors to work harder to appraise the pricing implications, and these information processing costs—whether in terms of personal effort or of the expense on additional financial advice—must be compensated by higher returns. Worse, if some investors are more sophisticated than others (e.g., better trained at pricing securities), disclosing more detailed information about companies or securities may increase the informational advantage of sophisticated investors over unsophisticated ones. In this case, paradoxically, disclosure may *exacerbate*, rather than mitigate, adverse selection problems. In other terms, the thesis that transparency reduces information asymmetries rests on the important assumption that all investors are equally good at processing the additional information. Failing this assumption, disclosing more information may lead unsophisticated investors to leave the market or to require a larger return on their investment to overcome the expected losses from investing in markets where they are disadvantaged. Thus, issuers may prefer to provide only coarse information for complex securities when information is particularly costly for many investors to process. Pagano and Volpin (2012), who make this point with reference to the asset-backed securities (ABS) created by the securitization process, also observe that while opacity may reduce adverse selection at the issue stage, it creates the danger that adverse selection may reappear in secondary trading, if at that stage sophisticated investors are still able to dig out the undisclosed information.[10]

Some readers may wonder how the notion of "market transparency" exten-sively analyzed in Chapter 8 relates to the transparency that companies achieve

---

[10] Another potentially harmful effect of disclosure is that when it refers to the ownership and control structure of the firm, it may discourage the accumulation of large blocks of shares and so hinder shareholder activism (Section 12.3). Of course, this effect is harmful for companies only insofar as shareholder activism is value-increasing.

via the disclosure policies discussed here. The two notions obviously refer to quite different "objects": Chapter 8 refers to the market trading process—how much is known about past trades, incoming orders, and existing quotes on a company's security. The disclosure policies considered here refer to a company's fundamental value, insofar as this can be gauged from its accounts, business plans, ownership, control, and so on. Bearing this in mind, we may call this "fundamental transparency." In any case, both forms of transparency, though different, can reduce adverse selection and increase liquidity, and both are therefore often rewarded by investors via higher issue prices or more generous funding. These two forms of transparency can be considered as substitutes, in the sense that an issuer who wishes to achieve a certain target level of liquidity and cost of capital may opt for greater corporate disclosure (more "fundamental transparency") to compensate for the opacity of the trading process (less "market transparency").

12.5.4 Capital Structure

Throughout this book the payoff of a stock has been taken to be a random variable v, equal to the fundamental value of the firm that issued the stock (standardizing for simplicity the number of shares to one). Hence, the rate of return offered by the company, $r = v/p - 1$, coincides with the return on its stock. This is appropriate if the firm is entirely equity financed. But if it has also issued some debt securities, the future cash flow v must be split between shareholders and debtholders in proportion to their holdings, and the return on equity will differ from the total return on the company's assets. Denoting the initial value of the company's equity by E and that of its debt by D, the total return on assets is the weighted average of the return to its equity and debt components:

$$r = \frac{E}{E+D} r_E + \frac{D}{E+D} r_D.$$

Hence, the return on the company's stock is:

$$r_E = \frac{E+D}{E} r - \frac{D}{E} r_D.$$

This expression shows that the more highly leveraged the firm, the greater the volatility of a shareholder's rate of return: a 1% change in the firm's total return r will determine a $\frac{E+D}{E}$ percent move in its stock return r_E, if the return on debt r_D stays constant. News about the firm's future cash flow disproportionately affects the payoff to shareholders, because—if debt is and remains risk free—it leaves the rate of return to debtholders unaffected. Hence, the riskiness of stocks is not determined only by the riskiness of fundamentals, but also by the firm's choice of its leverage ratio D/E: more generally, capital structure determines how the final value is split among different securities, such as equity, debt, hybrids, and options, and therefore the stochastic characteristics of the returns to each of these securities.

This has an important implication for liquidity. If some investors have better access to news about fundamentals (or are better at processing it), the asymmetry of information will create illiquidity only for information-sensitive securities, such as stocks, and not for safe ones, such as debt. Gorton and Pennacchi (1990) show that firms can mitigate the trading losses associated with informational asymmetry by designing securities with cash flows that are insensitive to private information and so can be safely bought by uninformed investors who want them only for their liquidity needs. Firms have an incentive to issue such safe securities, because they will be very liquid and, therefore, ex ante their buyers require no liquidity premium to hold them. Informed investors will instead concentrate their trades on information-sensitive securities, because these are the only ones from which they can hope to earn informational rents.

Of course, if the investment needs of uninformed investors are completely satisfied by the issuance of safe corporate debt by companies, then there are no stock market rents to be obtained by informed investors, because such rents arise from the trading losses incurred by the uninformed. If uninformed investors' wealth exceeds the amount of safe debt that companies can issue, in equilibrium they must hold and possibly trade some stocks. And the more leveraged the company, the more information sensitive and therefore the more illiquid these stocks will be. In this case, even the issuance of corporate debt does not completely shelter uninformed investors from the need to hold some illiquid securities and pay some transaction costs. This will restore some rents for informed investors and make stocks attractive for them.

However, as Section 12.4.1 points out, the illiquidity of stocks comes with a potentially countervailing benefit, namely, the improved price discovery implied by informed trading. And, since greater leverage implies that stocks are more information-sensitive, by increasing their leverage firms can increase the attractiveness of their stock to informed traders. If the proportion π of informed traders is not constant, but varies with informational rents, greater leverage will translate into a higher value of π, hence both higher trading costs for uninformed investors (equation (12.12)) and greater overall firm value (equation 12.7).

This suggests that in choosing its degree of leverage, and therefore the extent to which it wants to attract informed trading, a firm may seek to balance the higher trading costs that it thereby inflicts on its uninformed investors—and thus the illiquidity premium that it will have to pay, as argued in Chapter 9—against the benefits of better price discovery. The extent to which a company wishes to leverage and thus attract informed trading will be all the more limited if uninformed traders' participation in the market is sensitive to the bid-ask spread: in response to more informed trading, they may curtail or abandon their trading altogether and thus reduce the profits available to informed traders, which by equations (12.10) and (12.11), are increasing in $1 - \pi$. Thus, information collection will be discouraged and there is a limit to how high π, and with it, stock price informativeness, can be made.

The trade-off between liquidity and the informativeness of stock prices is also affected by the value of information for firms' decisions: Chang and Yu (2010) argue that when information is not very important to improving operating decisions, a firm should limit its debt issuance, thereby reducing the information-sensitivity of its stock price. In this way, the firm discourages acquisition of private information, which reduces the illiquidity premium associated with adverse selection. This may be contribute to explain why many firms issue no or modest amounts of debt, which is one of the main puzzles in corporate finance, given the compelling tax advantages of leveraging up to the hilt.

12.6 Further Reading

Stock market development, investment and growth. There is a vast literature on the relationship between financial market development, investment, and growth, which is surveyed by Pagano (1993a), Demirguc-Kunt and Levine (2001), and Levine (2005), among others. Besides Henry (2000b), other studies of the effects of stock market liberalization are Bekaert, Harvey, and Lundblad (2005), who show that equity market liberalization is associated with a subsequent average annual real economic growth of about 1%, and that this effect is robust to controls for capital account liberalization and other simultaneous reforms, and Gupta and Yuan (2009), who document industries that are more externally dependent and face better growth opportunities grow faster following liberalization. Moreover, Levine and Zervos (1998b) find that such policies are associated with an increase in stock market liquidity, and Henry (2000a) and Bekaert and Harvey (2000) document that they coincide with a jump in stock prices and a drop in the cost of equity capital.

Informational effects of market prices on firms. Bond, Edmans, and Goldstein (2012) offer a good survey of the literature on the real effects that financial markets have on firms' real decisions via the information provided by security prices. Dow and Gorton (1997) and Subrahmanyam and Titman (1999) provide early theoretical analyses of the feedback from asset prices to firms' investment decisions, via managerial learning. Testing for this channel has subsequently attracted a lot of attention by empirical researchers. Using U.S. data, Chen, Goldstein, and Jiang (2007) find that firms' investment decisions respond positively to their stock price, consistent with the thesis that managers gather information from stock prices. Moreover, in accordance with the model presented in Section 12.4.1, the sensitivity of investment to stock prices is greater for firms with more informative stock prices: firms that attract more informed investors (as measured by the PIN variable presented in Chapter 5) feature greater sensitivity of investment to prices. A non-exhaustive list of other empirical studies on this issue includes Durnev, Morck, and Yeung (2004), Luo (2005), Bakke and Whited (2010), Foucault and Frésard (2012), Foucault and Frésard (2014), or Dessaint, Foucault, Frésard, and Matray (2019).

Shareholder activism. Edmans (2014) provides a survey of the literature on blockholders and corporate governance. Several authors have analyzed the positive externality created by a large shareholder's monitoring, and the implied holdout problem. Shleifer and Vishny (1986) show that if a takeover bidder starts with zero initial holdings, he has no incentive to acquire shares and become an activist shareholder. Huddart (1993) and Admati, Pfleiderer, and Zechner (1994) analyze this externality in models where the potentially activist shareholder is risk-averse. Admati and Pfleiderer (2009) show that exit and voice are not always mutually exclusive, since a large shareholder may discipline managers by threatening exit on the basis of private information. Stoughton and Zechner (1997) and Pagano and Röell (1998) analyze models in which the stake of the activist blockholder is determined endogenously at the IPO stage. On the empirical front, Parrino, Sias, and Starks (2003) document the preference for exit over voice by U.S. institutional investors.

Managerial compensation and incentives. The literature on executive compensation is vast. A good number of models have shown that performance-based compensation in the form of stock and options can enhance the incentive to exert effort and take risk (see, for instance, Smith and Stulz 1985; Hall and Murphy 2000; and Dittmann and Maug 2007). But more recent work highlights the possible distortionary effects of such managerial incentives. Theoretical work by Goldman and Slezak (2006) and Peng and Röell (2008b, 2014) focuses on the efficiency costs of manipulation, and empirical work by Bergstresser and Philippon (2006), Burns and Kedia (2006), Kedia and Philippon (2009), and Peng and Röell (2008a) demonstrates that high-powered incentive schemes (especially options) are positively correlated with proxies for accounting fraud, such as discretionary accruals, fraud accusations, accounting restatements, and class action litigation. Another distortionary effect of performance-based compensation is that it may lead to excessive risk taking by financial intermediaries and thus contribute to financial instability: indeed there is evidence of a positive association between performance-based compensation and bank risk taking in the context of the 2008–9 financial crisis (for instance, Boyallian and Ruiz-Verdú 2018 and Kolasinski and Yang 2018).

Cross-listing. Karolyi (1998) surveys the evidence on stock price behavior around cross-listings and finds that the effect differs across companies; even when initially positive, the effect is often dissipated in the subsequent year. On balance, non-U.S. companies listing in the United States have positive cumulative abnormal returns (Foerster and Karolyi 1999) and experience a reduction in the cost of capital (Karolyi 1998). Foerster and Karolyi (1999) show that the stock prices of cross-listed companies rise more significantly when the expansion of the shareholder base is more pronounced. Foerster and Karolyi (1999), Kadlec and McConnell (1994), and Miller (1999) show that the price reaction to a cross-listing is positively correlated with the increase in the shareholder base.

Several studies document that cross-listing is associated with an increase in liquidity, in the form of lower bid-ask spreads and more trading: see Kadlec and McConnell (1994); Noronha, Sarin, and Saudagaran (1996); Foerster and Karolyi (1998, 2000); and Smith and Sofianos (1997). However, cross-listing may not always enhance liquidity, due to the potentially offsetting impact of market fragmentation, as in the models of Pagano (1989), Chowdhry and Nanda (1991), and Madhavan (1995). Indeed the evidence on the emerging markets indicates that cross-listing in the United States tends to depress domestic trading. Domowitz, Glen, and Madhavan (1998) show that the home market liquidity of Mexican companies decreases upon their issuance of American depository receipts; they relate this effect to the poor information linkages between the two markets. This is consistent with Levine and Schmukler (2006), who find that companies in emerging economies experience a drop in domestic trading when they cross-list, and with Halling et al. (2008), who document that a cross-listing has a positive effect on home market liquidity for companies in developed countries, but a negative one in emerging countries.

On the bonding hypothesis, Doidge (2004) ties the premium from cross-listing in the United States to the cross-listing's ability to reduce the voting premium, and therefore produces direct evidence on its effect on the controlling shareholders' ability to extract private benefits and increase the firm's ability to take advantage of growth opportunities. Doidge, Karolyi, and Stulz (2004) document that in 1997 foreign companies listed in the United States had a Tobin's Q ratio 16.5% higher than that of firms from the same country not listed in the United States. This difference is statistically significant and persists even after controlling for several firm and country characteristics. They also find that growth opportunities are valued more highly for firms listed in the United States especially for firms from countries with less investor protection. Doidge, Karolyi, and Stulz (2009) show that in spite of the greater compliance costs associated with the Sarbanes-Oxley Act in the United States, the listing premium associated with a New York listing persists, while no such premium is associated with a London listing.

Designated market makers (DMM). Nimalendran and Petrella (2003) show that the introduction of a specialist-based market-making mechanism for thinly traded Italian Stock Exchange securities was associated with a reduction in execution costs. Venkataraman and Waisburd (2007) find that the introduction of a DMM by relatively illiquid liquid firms listed on the Paris Bourse improves market quality and that its announcement is associated with a 5% cumulative abnormal return. They also show that DMM are mainly hired by younger and smaller firms and by those with less volatile stocks. Hengelbrock (2008) studies the effect of the introduction of DMM for thinly traded stocks on the Xetra platform of the Deutsche Börse, and finds that while quoted and effective spreads narrow when trading with one or two designated sponsors, further increases in the number of specialists do not necessarily result in greater liquidity. Anand, Tanggaard, and Weaver (2009) show that DMM introduction in Sweden increases liquidity, produces a 7% cumulative abnormal price run-up, increases volume, and leads DMMs to trade more in the stocks that they contract for. Menkveld and Wang (2011) study the introduction of DMM in the Amsterdam stock market, when Euronext allowed listed firms to hire DMMs on October 29, 2001, and find that for 74 stocks that hired a DMM, liquidity increased, liquidity risk dropped, and there was an average cumulative abnormal return of 3.5%. Interestingly, DMMs participate in more trades and incur a trading loss on high quoted-spread days (days when their constraint is likely to bind). Finally, Bessembinder, Hao, and Zheng (2015) show that firms can benefit from hiring a DMM as this is a way to make the liquidity for their stock higher than it would be in a competitive market.

Transparency, liquidity, and access to capital. Leuz and Wysocki (2008) survey empirical work on the relationship between transparency and firms' access to capital markets. This literature consistently shows that increased disclosure is associated with greater stock market liquidity and lower cost of capital. Goldstein and Yang (2017) provide a survey of the relevant theoretical literature.

The idea that information disclosure may exacerbate adverse selection problems, discussed in the text with reference to Pagano and Volpin (2012), is also present in the theoretical work by Dang, Gorton, and Holmstrom (2010) and Morris and Shin (2012). In the same line of argument, Kim and Verrecchia (1994) show that earnings announcements decrease market liquidity if they allow sophisticated traders to increase their informational advantage over other traders. The same argument is used by Goel and Thakor (2003) to rationalize earnings smoothing: to maintain a liquid market for their stocks, companies will smooth earnings so as to reduce the informational rents of sophisticated investors. Di Maggio and Pagano (2011) analyze the relationship between financial disclosure ("fundamental transparency") and "market transparency" in a model where investors have different information processing costs and securities are sold via a search market.

Empirically, the practice of selling securities exclusively in bundles, rather than separately, may be considered as one instance in which opacity increases liquidity: Kavajecz and Keim (2005) show that asset managers lower trading costs by 48% via "blind auctions" of stocks, whereby they auction a set of trades as a package to potential liquidity providers, without revealing the identities of the securities in the package to the bidders. Similarly, Vickery and Wright (2010) document that mortgage-backed securities issued by U.S. public agencies (agency MBS) are extremely opaque when placed via the "to-be-announced" market, where MBS sellers specify only a few basic characteristics of the security to be delivered, but are extremely liquid.

Capital structure, liquidity, and stock price informativeness. Gorton and Pennacchi (1990) argue that information-insensitive securities such as debt are more liquid. This thesis is also central to the model of Dang, Gorton, and Holmstrom (2010). The idea that increasing the information sensitivity of the firm's securities can be beneficial because it elicits information collection by sophisticated investors is formalized by Boot and Thakor (1993) and Fulghieri and Lukin (2001).

12.7 Exercises

1. Trading disclosure and shareholder activism. Consider the blockholder's decision whether to intervene or not in the company's management at date 1 in the model in Section 12.3, and suppose that regulation forces him to disclose his intention to exit before trading, so that if he sells the market anticipates that no improvement will occur ($\mu_1 = V$). Show that in this case activism is guaranteed: the probability of intervention is $\pi = 1$.

2. **Stock market as guide to investment.** In the model analyzed in section 12.4.1, we assumed that $G < I$ and found that on average the stock market encourages investment. Consider here the complementary case where $G > I$:

   a. Show that in this case the stock market deters inappropriate investment. Explain the intuition behind this result.

   b. Assume that the market is informative enough for the stock price to affect investment and derive the new expression for the increase in firm's ex ante value resulting from the presence of a stock market.

3. **No price manipulation by speculators.** In the context of the model of Section 12.4.1, verify that in equilibrium the informed speculator does not have an incentive to trade against his information, that is, to sell on good news or buy on bad news. Assume that the informativeness condition (12.5) holds.

4. **Bid and ask prices when investment does not react to stock prices.** In the model analyzed in Section 12.4.1, assume that the informativeness condition (12.5) does not hold.

   a. Compute the equilibrium bid and ask prices, and show that in this case too, in equilibrium the informed speculator will buy upon receiving positive information and sell otherwise.

   b. Compute the bid-ask spread and find out whether in this case it is increasing in the frequency of informed trading π.

   c. Compare this bid-ask spread with that given by equation (12.12) under the informativeness condition (12.5).

   d. Finally, compute the midprice and see whether it depends on the frequency of informed trading π, explaining why.

5. **Bid and ask prices when investment must be chosen before stock trading.** Consider the following change in the model analyzed in Section 12.4.1: assume that, even though the informativeness condition (12.5) holds, the manager cannot react to the stock price because stock trading takes place once the investment decision has already been irrevocably made. (Technically, we are reversing the order of the trading and investment stages of the game along the time line.) Assuming that the manager's investment decision is private and that market participants cannot observe it before trading, derive the ask and bid prices under this new assumption, and establish whether the market is more or less liquid than in the model of Section 12.4.1, by comparing the bid-ask spread that you have computed with that of equation (12.12). Explain the intuition behind your finding.

6. **Incentive pay when stock price is imperfectly informative**. Consider an extension of the model of Section 12.4.2 in which the stock market is informed (i.e., able to observe the manager's effort) only with frequency π, and is uninformed with the complementary probability $1 - \pi$.

   a. Show that if shareholders write an incentive contract conditional on the stock price only, the compensation that they will have to pay is inversely related to π (the proportion of time that the stock market observes effort). [Hint: in your analysis you may assume that the stock market rationally expects the manager to exert effort if his pay contract respects his incentive constraint.]

b. (Harder problem.) Assuming that $\pi < 1$, investigate whether shareholders can obtain a better outcome by conditioning pay $w(P, v)$ on *both* the interim stock price *and* the final value of the firm. What would the pay contract look like?

References

Abdi, Farshid, and Angelo Ranaldo, 2017, A simple estimation of bid-ask spreads from daily close, high, and low prices, *Review of Financial Studies* 30, 4437–80.

Acemoglu, Daron, Ozdaglar Asuman, and Tahbaz-Salehi Alireza, 2015, Systemic risk and stability in financial networks, *American Economic Review* 105, 564–608.

Acharya, Viral V., Stephen Schaefer, and Yili Zhang, 2008, Liquidity risk and correlation risk: a clinical study of the General Motors and Ford downgrade of May 2005, *Quarterly Journal of Finance* 5(2), 1–51.

Acharya, Viral V., and Lasse Heje Pedersen, 2005, Asset pricing with liquidity risk, *Journal of Financial Economics* 77, 375–410.

Admati, Anat, 1985, A noisy rational expectations equilibrium for multiple asset securities markets, *Econometrica* 53, 629–57.

Admati, Anat, and Paul Pfleiderer, 1988, A theory of intraday patterns: volume and price variability, *Review of Financial Studies* 1, 3–40.

Admati, Anat, and Paul Pfleiderer, 1991, Sunshine trading and financial markets equilibrium, *Review of Financial Studies* 3, 443–81.

Admati, Anat R., Paul Pfleiderer, and Josef Zechner, 1994, Large shareholder activism, risk sharing and financial market equilibrium, *Journal of Political Economy* 102, 1097–1130.

Admati, Anat R., and Paul Pfleiderer, 2009, The "Wall Street walk" and shareholder activism: exit as a form of voice, *Review of Financial Studies* 22, 2645–85.

Adrian, Tobias, Michael Fleming, and Erik Vogt, 2017, An Index of Treasury Market Liquidity: 1991–2017, Federal Reserve Bank of New York Staff Report No. 827, https://www.newyorkfed.org/medialibrary/media/research/staff_reports/sr827.pdf.

Ahn, Hee-Joon, Bae Keehong, and Kalok Chan, 2001, Limit orders, depth and volatility: evidence from the Stock Exchange of Hong Kong, *Journal of Finance* 56, 767–88.

Akerlof, George A., 1970, The market for "lemons": quality uncertainty and the market mechanism, *Quarterly Journal of Economics* 84, 488–500.

Allen, Franklin, and Anna Babus, 2009, Networks in finance, in P. Kleindorfer and J. Wind (eds.), *Network-Based Strategies and Competencies*, Philadelphia: Wharton School Publishing.

Allen, Franklin, and Douglas Gale, 1994, Limited market participation and volatility of asset prices, *American Economic Review* 84, 933–55.

Amihud, Yakov, 2002, Illiquidity and stock returns: cross-section and time-series effects, *Journal of Financial Markets* 5, 31–56.

Amihud, Yakov, and Haim Mendelson, 1980, Dealership markets: market-making with inventory, *Journal of Financial Economics* 8, 31–53.

Amihud, Yakov, and Haim Mendelson, 1986, Asset pricing and the bid-ask spread, *Journal of Financial Economics* 17, 223–49.

Amihud, Yakov, and Haim Mendelson, 1991, Liquidity, maturity, and the yields on U.S. treasury securities, *Journal of Finance* 46, 1411–25.

Amihud, Yakov, Haim Mendelson, and Lasse Heje Pedersen, 2005, Liquidity and asset prices, *Foundations and Trends in Finance* 1, 269–364.

Anand, Amber, Carsten Tanggaard, and Daniel G. Weaver, 2009, Paying for market quality, *Journal of Financial and Quantitative Analysis* 44, 1427–57.

Aquilina, Matteo, Eric Budish, and Peter O'Neill, 2022, Quantifying the High-Frequency Trading "Arms Race, *The Quarterly Journal of Economics*, 137, 493–564.

Aragon, George, and Philip Strahan, 2012, Hedge funds as liquidity providers: Evidence from the Lehman bankruptcy, *Journal of Financial Economics* 103, 570–87.

Arnold, Tom, Hersch, Philip, J. Harold Mulherin, and Jeffry Netter, 1999, Merging markets, *Journal of Finance* 49, 1083–1107.

Bacidore, Jeffrey M., 1997, The impact of decimalization on market quality: an empirical investigation of the Toronto Stock Exchange, *Journal of Financial Intermediation* 6, 92–120.

Back, Kerry, and Shmuel Baruch, 2007, Working orders in limit order markets and floor exchanges, *Journal of Finance* 62, 1589–1621.

Bagehot, Walter (Jack Treynor), 1971, The only game in town, *Financial Analysts Journal* 22, 12–14.

Balakhrishnan, Khartik, Mary Brooke Billings, Brian Kelly, and Alexander Ljundqvist, 2014, Shaping liquidity: on the causal effects of voluntary disclosure, *Journal of Finance* 69, 2237–78.

Baldauf, Markus, and Joshua Mollner, 2020, High-frequency trading and market performance, *Journal of Finance* 75, 1495–1526.

Bakke, Tor, and Toni M. Whited, 2010, Which firms follow the market? An analysis of corporate investment decisions, *Review of Financial Studies* 23, 1941–80.

Baldauf, Markus, and Joshua Mollner, 2020, High-frequency trading and market performance, *Journal of Finance*, forthcoming.

Baldauf, Markus, and Joshua Mollner, 2021, Trading in fragmented markets, *Journal of Financial and Quantitative Analysis* 56, 93–121.

Bancel, Franck, and Usha R. Mittoo, 2001, European managerial perceptions of the net benefits of foreign stock listings, *European Financial Management* 7, 213–36.

Barbopoulos, Leonidas G., Rui Dai, Talis J. Putniņš, and Anthony Saunders, 2021, Market efficiency in the age of machine learning Available at SSRN: http://dx.doi.org/10.2139/ssrn.3783221.

Barclay, Michael J., William G. Christie, Jeffrey H. Harris, Eugene Kandel, and Paul H. Schultz, 1999, Effects of market reform on the trading costs and depths of Nasdaq stocks, *Journal of Finance* 54, 1–34.

Barclay, Michael J., Terrence Hendershott, and Timothy D. McCormick, 2003, Competition among trading venues: information and trading on electronic communication networks, *Journal of Finance* 58, 2637–65.

Baron, Matthew, Jonathan Brogaard, Björn Hagströmer, and Andrei Kirilenko, 2019, Risk and Return in High-Frequency Trading, *Journal of Financial and Quantitative Analysis*, 54, 993–1024.

Baruch, Shmuel, 2005, Who benefits from an open limit-order book?, *Journal of Business* 78, 1267–1306.

Baruch, Shmuel and Lawrence R. Glosten, 2019, Tail expectation and imperfect competition in limit order book markets, *Journal of Economic Theory*, 183, 661–697.

Battalio, Robert H., 1997, Third market broker-dealers: cost competitors or cream skimmers?, *Journal of Finance* 52, 341–52.

Battalio, Robert H., Jason Greene, and Robert Jennings, 1997, Do competing specialists and preferencing dealers affect market quality?, *Review of Financial Studies* 10, 969–93.

Battalio, Robert H., Jason Greene, and Robert Jennings, 1998, Order flow distribution, bid-ask spreads, and liquidity costs: Merrill Lynch's decision to cease routinely routing orders to regional stock exchanges, *Journal of Financial Intermediation* 7, 338–58.

Battalio, Robert H., and Craig Holden, 2001, A simple model of payment for order flow, internalization and total trading cost, *Journal of Financial Markets* 4, 33–71.

Battalio, Robert H., Brian Hatch, and Robert Jennings, 2004, Towards a national market system for U.S. exchange-listed equity options, *Journal of Finance* 54, 933–62.

Battalio, Robert H., Robert Jennings, and Jamie Selway, 2001, The potential for clientele pricing when making markets in financial securities, *Journal of Financial Markets* 4, 85–112.

Beason, Tyler, and Sunil Wahal, 2020, The Anatomy of Trading Algorithms, available at SSRN: http://dx.doi.org/10.2139/ssrn.3497001.

Beber, Alessandro, and Marco Pagano, 2013, Short-selling bans around the world: evidence from the 2007–2009 Crisis, *Journal of Finance* 68, 343–82.

Bech, Morten, Anamaria Illes, Ulf Lewrick, and Andreas Schrimpf, 2016, Hanging up the phone: electronic trading in fixed income markets and its implications, *BIS Quarterly Review* March 2016, 79–94.

Becht, Marco, Julian R. Franks, Colin Mayer, and Stefano Rossi, 2009, Returns to shareholder activism: evidence from a clinical study of the Hermes U.K. Focus Fund, *Review of Financial Studies* 22, 3093–129.

Becht, Marco, Julian R. Franks, and Hannes F. Wagner, 2021, The benefits of access: evidence from private meetings with portfolio firms, European Corporate Governance Institute—Finance Working Paper 751/2021, available at SSRN: https://ssrn.com/abstract=3813948 or http://dx.doi.org/10.2139/ssrn.3813948.

Bekaert, Geert, and Campbell Harvey, 2000, Foreign speculators and emerging equity markets, *Journal of Finance* 55, 565–613.

Bekaert, Geert, Campbell Harvey, and Christian Lundblad, 2005, Does financial liberalization spur growth? *Journal of Financial Economics* 77, 3–55.

Bekaert, Geert, Campbell R. Harvey, and Christian Lundblad, 2007, Liquidity and expected returns: lessons from emerging markets, *Review of Financial Studies* 20, 1783–1831.

Benamar, Hedi, 2019, To See Is to Know: Simultaneous Display of Market Data for Retail Investors, *Review of Finance*, 23, 397–437.

Ben-Rephael, Azi, 2017, Flight-to-liquidity, market uncertainty, and the actions of mutual fund investors, *Journal of Financial Intermediation* 31, 30–44.

Ben-Rephael, Azi, Ohad Kadan, and Avi Wohl, 2015, The diminishing liquidity premium, *Journal of Financial and Quantitative Analysis* 50, 197–229.

Benos, Evangelos, Richard Payne, and Michalis Vasios, 2020, Centralized trading, transparency, and interest rate swap market liquidity: evidence from the implementation of the Dodd–Frank Act, *Journal of Financial and Quantitative Analysis* 55, 159–92.

Bergstresser, Daniel B., and Thomas Philippon, 2006, CEO incentives and earnings management, *Journal of Financial Economics* 80, 511–29.

Bernanke, Ben S., and Mark Gertler, 1995, Inside the black box: the credit channel of monetary policy transmission, *Journal of Economic Perspectives* 9, 27–48.

Bernhardt, Dan, Vladimir Dvoracek, Eric Hughson, and Ingrid Werner, 2005, Why do large orders receive discounts on the London Stock Exchange?, *Review of Financial Studies* 18, 1343–68.

Bertsimas, Dimitris, and Andrew W. Lo, 1998, Optimal control of execution costs, *Journal of Financial Markets* 1, 1–50.

von Beschwitz, Bastian, Donald Keim, and Massimo Massa, 2020, First to "read" the news: news analytics and algorithmic trading, *Review of Asset Pricing Studies* 10, 122–78.

Bessembinder, Hendrik, 2003, Quote-based competition and trade execution costs in NYSE-listed stocks, *Journal of Financial Economics* 70, 385–422.

Bessembinder, Hendrik, Allen Carrion, Laura Tuttle, and Kumar Venkataram, 2016, Liquidity, resiliency and market quality around predictable trades: theory and evidence, *Journal of Financial Economics* 121, 142–66.

Bessembinder, Hendrik, Jia Hao, and Kuncheng Zheng, 2015, Market making contracts, firm value, and the IPO decision, *Journal of Finance* 70, 1997–2028.

Bessembinder, Hendrik, and Herbert M. Kaufman 1997, A cross-exchange comparison of execution costs and information flow for NYSE-listed stocks, *Journal of Financial Economics* 46, 296–319.

Bessembinder, Hendrik, William F. Maxwell, and Kumar Venkataraman, 2006, Market transparency, liquidity externalities, and institutional trading costs in corporate bonds, *Journal of Financial Economics* 82, 251–88.

Bessembinder, Hendrik, and William Maxwell, 2008, Transparency and the corporate bond market, *Journal of Economic Perspectives* 22, 217–34.

Bessembinder, Hendrik, Marios Panayides, and Kumar Venkataraman, 2009, Hidden liquidity: An analysis of order exposure strategies in electronic stock markets, *Journal of Financial Economics* 94, 361–83.

Bessembinder, Hendrik, Chester Spatt, and Kumar Venkataraman, 2020, A survey of the market microstructure of fixed income market, *Journal of Financial and Quantitative Analysis* 55, 1–45.

Bhide, Amar, 1993, The hidden costs of stock market liquidity, *Journal of Financial Economics* 34, 31–51.

Biais, Bruno, 1993, Price formation and equilibrium liquidity in fragmented and centralized markets, *Journal of Finance* 48, 157–85.

Biais, Bruno, Christophe Bisière, and Chester Spatt, 2010, Imperfect competition in financial markets: an empirical study of Island and Nasdaq, *Management Science* 5, 2237–50.

Biais, Bruno, Peter Bossaerts, and Chester Spatt, 2010, Equilibrium asset pricing and portfolio choice under asymmetric information, *Review of Financial Studies* 23, 1503–43.

Biais, Bruno, Fany Declerck, James Dow, Richard Portes, and Ernst-Ludwig Von Thadden, 2006, European corporate bond markets: transparency, liquidity, efficiency, City of London and CEPR.

Biais, Bruno, Thierry Foucault, and François Salanié, 1997, Dealer markets and limit order markets, *Journal of Financial Markets* 1, 523–84.

Biais, Bruno, Thierry Foucault, and Sophie Moinas, 2015, Equilibrium fast trading, *Journal of Financial Economics*, 116, 292–313.

Biais, Bruno, and Thierry Foucault, 2014, High-Frequency Trading and market quality, *Bankers, Markets & Investors*, 128, 5–1.

Biais, Bruno, Pierre Hillion, and Chester Spatt, 1995, An empirical analysis of the limit order book and the order flow in the Paris bourse, *Journal of Finance* 50, 1655–89.

Biais, Bruno, David Martimort, and Jean-Charles Rochet, 2000, Competing mechanisms in a common value environment, *Econometrica* 68, 799–837.

Biais, Bruno, and Isabelle Martinez, 2004, Price discovery across the Rhine, *Review of Finance* 8, 49–74.

Biddle, Gary C., and Shahrokh M. Saudagaran, 1989, The effects of financial disclosure levels on firms' choices among alternative foreign stock exchange listings, *Journal of International Financial Management and Accounting* 1, 55–87.

BIS, 2016, Electronic trading in fixed income markets, Markets committee paper 7, 1–50.

BIS, 2020, FX execution algorithms and market functioning, Markets committee paper 13, 1–55.

Bloomfield, Robert, and Maureen O'Hara, 1999, Market transparency: who wins and who loses?, *Review of Financial Studies* 12, 5–35.

Bloomfield, Robert, and Maureen O'Hara, 2000, Can transparent markets survive?, *Journal of Financial Economics* 55, 425–59.

Bloomfield, Robert, Maureen O'Hara, and Gideon Saar, 2005, The "make or take" decision in an electronic market: evidence on the evolution of liquidity, *Journal of Financial Economics* 75, 165–99.

Boehmer, Beatrice, and Ekkehart Boehmer, 2003, Trading your neighbor's ETFs: competition and fragmentation, *Journal of Banking and Finance* 27, 1667–1703.

Boehmer, Ekkehart, Joachim Grammig, and Eric Theissen, 2006, Estimating the probability of informed trading: does missclassification matter?, *Journal of Financial Markets* 10, 26–47.

Boehmer, Ekkehart, Robert Jennings, and Li Wei, 2007, Public disclosures and private decisions: equity market execution quality and order routing, *Review of Financial Studies* 20, 315–58.

Boehmer Ekkehart, Dan Li, and Gideon Saar, 2018, The Competitive Landscape of High-Frequency Trading Firms, *The Review of Financial Studies*, 31, 2227–2276.

Boehmer, Ekkehart, Gideon Saar, and Lei Yu, 2005, Lifting the veil: an analysis of pre-trade transparency at the NYSE, *Journal of Finance* 60, 783–815.

Bogousslavsky, Vincent, and Dimitriy Muravyev, 2021, Who trades at the close? Implications for price discovery and liquidity, http://dx.doi.org/10.2139/ssrn.3485840.

Bogousslavsky, Vincent, Pierre Collin-Dufresne, and Mehmet Sağlam, 2021, Slow-moving capital and execution costs: Evidence from a major trading glitch, *Journal of Financial Economics*, 139, 922–949.

Bolton, Patrick, and Matthias Dewatripont, 2004, *Contract Theory*. Cambridge, MA: MIT Press.

Bolton, Patrick, Tanos Santos, and Jose Scheinkman, 2016, Cream-skimming in financial markets, *Journal of Finance* 71, 709–36.

Bolton, Patrick, and Ernst-Ludwig von Thadden, 1998, Blocks, liquidity, and corporate control, *Journal of Finance* 53, 1–25.

Bond, Philip, Alex Edmans, and Itay Goldstein, 2012, The real effects of financial market, *Annual Review of Financial Economics* 4, 339–60.

Bongaerts, Dion, and Mark van Achter, 2021, Competition among liquidity providers with access to high-frequency trading technology, *Journal of Financial Economics*, 140, 220–249.

Boot, Arnoud, and Anjan Thakor, 1993, Security design, *Journal of Finance* 48, 1349–78.

Boyallian, Patricia and Pablo Ruiz-Verdú, 2018, Leverage, CEO risk-taking incentives, and bank failure during the 2007–10 financial crisis, *Review of Finance* 22, 1763–1805.

Brav, Alon P., Wei Jiang, and Hyunseob Kim, 2009, Hedge fund activism: a review, *Foundations, and Trends in Finance* 4, 185–246.

Brav, Alon P., Wei Jiang, Randall S. Thomas and Frank Partnoy, 2008, Hedge fund activism, corporate governance, and firm performance, *Journal of Finance* 63, 1729–75.

Brennan, Michael J., and Avanidhar Subrahmanyam, 1996, Market microstructure and asset pricing: on the compensation for illiquidity in stock returns, *Journal of Financial Economics* 41, 441–64.

Brogaard, Jonathan, Allen Carrion, Thibaut Moyaert, Ryan Riordan, Andriy Shkilko, and Konstantin Sokolov, 2018, High frequency trading and extreme price movements, Journal of Financial Economics, 128, 253–65.

Brogaard, Jonathan, and Corey Garriott, 2019, High-Frequency Trading Competition, Journal of Financial and Quantitative Analysis, 54, 1469–1497.

Brogaard, Jonathan, Bjorn Hagstromer, Lars Nordén, and Ryan Riordan, 2015, Trading Fast and Slow: Colocation and Liquidity, The Review of Financial Studies, 28, 3407–43.

Brogaard, Jonathan, Terrence Hendershott, and Ryan Riordan, 2014, High-frequency trading and price discovery, *Review of Financial Studies* 27, 2267–306.

Brogaard, Jonathan, Terrence Hendershott, and Ryan Riordan, 2019, Price discovery without trading: evidence from limit orders, *Journal of Finance* 74, 1621–58.

Brogaard, Jonathan, Dan Li, and Jeffrey Yang, 2022, Does High Frequency Market Manipulation Harm Market Quality? Working paper, available at SSRN: http://dx.doi.org/10.2139/ssrn.4280120.

Brunnermeier, Markus K., Sam Langfield, Marco Pagano, Ricardo Reis, Stijn Van Nieuwerburgh, and Dimitri Vayanos, 2017, ESBies: safety in the tranches, *Economic Policy* 32, 175–219.

Brunnermeier, Markus K., and Lasse Heje Pedersen, 2009, Market liquidity and funding liquidity, *Review of Financial Studies* 22, 2201–38.

Brunnermeier, Markus K., and Peter Sannikov, 2014, A macroeconomic model with a financial sector, *American Economic Review*, 104, 379–421.

Budish, Eric B., Peter C. Cramton, and John J. Shim, 2015, The high-frequency trading arms race: frequent batch auctions as a market design response, *Quarterly Journal of Economics*, 130, 1547–1621.

Burns, Natasha, and Simi Kedia, 2006, The impact of performance-based compensation on misreporting, *Journal of Financial Economics* 79, 35–67.

Buti, Sabrina and Barbara Rindi, 2013, Undisclosed orders and optimal submission strategies in a limit order market, *Journal of Financial Economics*, 109, 797–812.

Buti, Sabrina, Barbara Rindi, and Ingrid Werner, 2017, Dark pool trading strategies, market quality and welfare, *Journal of Financial Economics*, 124, Issue 244–265.

Caglio, Cecilia, Kathleen Weiss Hanley, and Jennifer Marietta-Westberg, 2016, Going public abroad, *Journal of Corporate Finance* 41, 103–122.

Cai, Tianwu, and Georges Sofianos, 2006, Multi-day executions, *Journal of Trading* 25–33.

Calcagno, Riccardo, and Stefano Lovo, 2006, Bid ask price competition with asymmetric information between market makers, *Review of Economic Studies*, 73, 329–55.

Campbell, John Y., Stefano Giglio, and Parag Pathak, 2011, Forced sales and house prices, *American Economic Review* 101, 2108–31.

Campbell, Tim, 1979, Optimal investment financing decisions and the value of confidentiality, *Journal of Financial and Quantitative Analysis* 14, 913–24.

Cespa, Giovanni, and Thierry Foucault, 2013, Sale of price information by exchanges: does it promote price discovery, *Management Science* 60, 145–65.

Cespa, Giovanni, and Xavier Vives, 2022, Exchange Competition, Entry, and Welfare, *The Review of Financial Studies*, 35, 2570–2624.

Chaboud, Alain, Benjamin Chiquoine, Erik Hjalmarsson, and Clara Vega, 2014, Rise of the machines: algorithmic trading in the foreign exchange market, *Journal of Finance* 64, 2044–84.

Chaboud, Alain, Dagfinn Rime, and Vladyslav Sushko, 2022, The foreign exchange market, Refet Gürkaynak and Jonathan Wright (eds.), *The Research Handbook of Financial Markets*, Edward Elgar: Northampton, Masschussets 01060, USA. pp: 253–275. Available at SSRN: https://ssrn.com/abstract=4063213.

Chakrabarty, Bidisha, Pankaj Jain, Andriy Shkilko, and Konstantin Solokov, 2020, Unfiltered market access and liquidity: Evidence from SEC Rule 15c3-5 Management Science, 1–16.

Chakrabarty, Bidisha, Roberto Pascual, and Andriy Shkilko, 2015, Evaluating trade classification algorithms: bulk volume classification versus the tick rule and the Lee-Ready algorithm, *Journal of Financial Markets* 25, 52–79.

Chang, Chun, and Xiaoyun Yu, 2010, Informational efficiency and liquidity premium as the determinants of capital structure, *Journal of Financial and Quantitative Analysis* 45, 401–40.

Chao, Yong, Yao Chen, and Mao Ye, 2019, Why discrete price fragments U.S. stock exchanges and disperses their fee structures, *Review of Financial Studies* 32, 1068–1101.

Chemmanur, Thomas J., and Paolo Fulghieri, 1999, A theory of the going-public decision, *Review of Financial Studies* 12, 249–79.

Chen, Qi, Itay Goldstein, and Wei Jiang, 2007, Price informativeness and investment sensitivity to stock price, *Review of Financial Studies* 20, 619–50.

CFTC-SEC, 2010, Findings regarding the market events of May 6, 2010: report of the staffs of the CFTC and SEC to the Joint Advisory Committee on Emerging Regulatory Issues, September.

Choi, Jong Yeon, Dan Salandro, and Kuldeep Shastri, 1988, On the estimation of bid-ask spreads: theory and evidence, *Journal of Financial and Quantitative Analysis* 23, 219–30.

Chordia, Tarun, Richard Roll, and Avanidhar Subrahmanyam, 2000, Commonality in liquidity, *Journal of Financial Economics* 56, 3–28.

Chordia, Tarun, Asani Sarkar, and Avanidhar Subrahmanyam, 2005, An empirical analysis of stock and bond market liquidity, *Review of Financial Studies* 18, 85–129.

Chordia, Tarun, Clifton Green, and Badrinath Kottimukkalur, 2018, Rent Seeking by Low Latency Traders: Evidence from Trading on Macroeconomic Announcements, *Review of Financial Studies* 31, 4650–4687.

Chowdhry, Bhagwan, and Vikram Nanda, 1991, Multimarket trading and market liquidity, *Review of Financial Studies* 4, 483–511.

Christie, William G., and Paul H. Schultz, 1994a, Why do Nasdaq market-makers avoid odd-eight quotes?, *Journal of Finance* 49, 1813–40.

Christie, William G., Jeffrey H. Harris, and Paul H. Schultz, 1994b, Why did NASDAQ market makers stop avoiding odd-eighth quotes?, *Journal of Finance* 49, 1841–60.

Chung, Dennis Y., Dušan Išakov, and Cristhophe Pérignon, 2007, Repurchasing shares on a second trading line, *Review of Finance* 11, 253–85.

Chung, Kee, Albert Lee, and Dominik Rosch, 2020, Tick size, liquidity for small and large orders, and price informativeness: evidence from the Tick Size Pilot Program, *Journal of Financial Economics* 136, 879–99.

Cochrane, John, 2005, Liquidity, trading and asset pricing, *NBER Reporter*, Winter 2004–5.

Coffee, John C., 1991, Liquidity versus control: the institutional investor as corporate monitor, *Columbia Law Review* 91, 1277–1368.

Cohen, Kalman, Steven Maier, Robert Schwartz, and David Whitcomb, 1981, Transaction costs, order placement strategy, and existence of the bid-ask spread, *Journal of Political Economy* 89, 287–305.

Colby, Robert, and Erik Sirri, 2010, Consolidation and competition in the US equity markets, *Capital Markets Law Journal* 5, 169–96.

Colliard, Jean-Edouard, and Thierry Foucault, 2012, Trading fees and efficiency in limit order markets, *Review of Financial Studies* 25, 3389–3421.

Colliard, Jean-Edouard, and Peter Hoffmann, 2017, Financial transaction taxes, market composition, and liquidity, *Journal of Finance* 72, 2685–715.

Collin-Dufresne Pierre and Vyacheslav Fos, 2015, Do prices reveal the presence of informed trading? *Journal of Finance* 70, 1555–82.

Comerton-Forde, Carole, Terrence Hendershott, Charles M. Jones, Pamela C. Moulton, and Mark S. Seasholes, 2010, Time variation in liquidity: the role of market-maker inventories and revenues, *Journal of Finance* 65, 295–331.

Comerton-Forde, Carole, and Zhuo Zhuong, 2021, How do you solve a problem like market outage? Ensuring the resilience of European equities trading, Plato partnership.

Conrad, Jennifer, Sunil Wahal, and Jin Xiang, 2015, High frequency quoting, trading and the efficiency of prices, *Journal of Financial Economics* 116, 271–91.

Conrad, Jennifer, and Sunil Wahal, 2020, The term structure of liquidity provision, *Journal of Financial Economics* 136, 239–59.

Constantinides, Georges, 1986, Capital market equilibrium with transaction costs, *Journal of Political Economy* 94, 842–62.

Copeland, Thomas, and Dan Galai, 1983, Information effects on the bid-ask spread, *Journal of Finance* 38, 1457–69.

Cordella, Tito, and Thierry Foucault, 1999, Minimum price variations, time priority and quote dynamics, *Journal of Financial Intermediation* 8, 141–73.

Coughenour, Jay F., and Mohsen Saad, 2004, Common market makers and commonality in liquidity, *Journal of Financial Economics* 73, 37–69.

Coval, Joshua D., and Shumway, Tyler, 2001, Is sound just noise?, *Journal of Finance* 56, 1887–1910.

Coval, Joshua D., and Erik Stafford, 2007, Asset fire sales (and purchases) in equity markets, *Journal of Financial Economics* 86, 479–512.

Dang, Tri Vi, Gary Gorton, and Bengt Holmström, 2020, The information view of financial crises, *Annual Review of Financial Economics* 12, 39–65.

Datar, Vinay T., Narayan Y. Naik, and Robert Radcliffe, 1998, Liquidity and stock returns: an alternative test, *Journal of Financial Markets* 1, 203–19.

Daves, Philip R., and Michael C. Ehrhardt, 1993, Liquidity, reconstitution, and the value of U.S. treasury strips, *Journal of Finance* 48, 315–29.

Davis, Gerald F, and E. Han Kim, 2007, Business ties and proxy voting by mutual funds, *Journal of Financial Economics* 85, 552–70.

Davis, Gerald F., and Mina Yoo, 2003, The shrinking world of the large American corporation: common ownership and board ties, 1990–2001, *Gérer et Comprendre* 74, 51–62.

de Frutos, Maria Angeles, and Carolina Manzano, 2002, Risk aversion, transparency, and market performance, *Journal of Finance* 57, 959–84.

de Jong, Abe, Leonard Rosenthal, and Mathijs A. Van Dijk, 2009, The risk and return of arbitrage in dual-listed companies, *Review of Finance* 13, 495–520.

de Jong, Frank, Theo Nijman, and Ailsa Röell, 1996, Price effects of trading and components of the bid-ask spread on the Paris Bourse, *Journal of Empirical Finance* 3, 193–213.

De Long, Bradford, Andrei Shleifer, Lawrence Summers, and Robert Waldmann, 1990, Positive feedback investment strategies and destabilizing rational speculation, *Journal of Finance* 45, 379–95.

De Winne, Rudy, and Catherine D'hondt, 2007, Hide-and-seek in the market: placing and detecting hidden orders, *Review of Finance* 11, 663–92.

DeFontnouvelle, Patrick, Raymond P. H. Fishe, and Jeffrey H. Harris, 2003, The behavior of bid-ask spreads and volume in options markets during the competition for listings in 1999, *Journal of Finance* 58, 2437–63.

Degryse, Hans, de Jong, Frank, and Vincent van Kervel, 2015, The impact of dark trading and visible fragmentation on market quality, *Review of Finance* 19, 1587–1622.

Demirguc-Kunt, Asli, and Ross Levine, 2001, *Financial Structure and Economic Growth: A Cross-Country Comparison of Banks, Markets, and Development.* Cambridge, MA: MIT Press.

Derrien, François, and Ambrus Kecskés, 2013, The real effects of financial shocks: evidence from exogenous changes in analyst coverage, *Journal of Finance* 68, 1407–40.

Dessaint, Olivier, Thierry Foucault, Laurent Frésard, and Adrien Matray, 2019, Noisy stock prices and corporate investment, *Review of Financial Studies* 32, 2625–72.

Deville, Laurent, and Fabrice Riva, 2007, Liquidity and arbitrage in options markets: a survival analysis approach, *Review of Finance* 11, 497–525.

Di Maggio, Marco, Amir Kermani, and Zhaogang Song, 2017, The value of trading relations in turbulent times, *Journal of Financial Economics* 124, 266–84.

Di Maggio, Marco, and Marco Pagano, 2011, Financial disclosure with costly information processing, Working Paper, MIT and Università di Napoli Federico II.

Diamond, Douglas W., and Philip H. Dybvig, 1983, Bank runs, deposit insurance, and liquidity, *Journal of Political Economy* 91(3), 401–19.

Diamond, Douglas W., and Robert E. Verrecchia, 1981, Information aggregation in a noisy rational expectations economy, *Journal of Financial Economics* 9, 221–35.

Diamond Douglas W., and Robert E. Verrechia, 1987, Constraints on short-selling and asset price adjustment to private information, *Journal of Financial Economics* 18, 277–311.

Diamond, Peter, 1971, A model of price adjustment, *Journal of Economic Theory* 3, 156–68.

Dittmann, Ingolf, and Ernst Maug, 2007, Lower salaries and no options? On the optimal structure of executive pay, *Journal of Finance* 62, 303–43.

Doidge, Craig, 2004, U.S cross-listings and the private benefits of control: evidence from dual-class firms, *Journal of Financial Economics* 72, 519–53.

Doidge, Craig, G. Andrew Karolyi, and René M. Stulz, 2004, Why are foreign firms listed in the U.S. worth more?, *Journal of Financial Economics* 71, 205–38.

Doidge, Craig, G. Andrew Karolyi, and René M. Stulz, 2009, Has New York become less competitive in global markets? Evaluating foreign listing choices over time, *Journal of Financial Economics* 91, 253–77.

Doidge, Craig, G. Andrew Karolyi, and René M. Stulz, 2017, The U.S. listing gap, *Journal of Financial Economics* 123, 464–87.

Domowitz, Ian, Jack Glen and Ananth Madhavan, 1998, International cross-listing and order flow migration: evidence from an emerging market, *Journal of Finance* 53, 2001–27.

Dorn, Daniel, Gur Huberman, and Paul Sengmueller, 2008, Correlated trading and returns, *Journal of Finance* 63, 885–920.

Dow, James, and Gary Gorton, 1997, Stock market efficiency and economic efficiency: is there a connection? *Journal of Finance* 52, 1087–1129.

Drehmann, Mathias, and Nikola Tarashev, 2013, Measuring the systemic importance of interconnected banks, *Journal of Financial Intermediation* 22(4), 586–607.

Du, Songzi, and Haoxiang Zhu, 2017, What is the optimal trading frequency in financial markets?, *Review of Economic Studies* 84, 1606–51.

Du, Wenxin, Alexander Tepper, and Adrien Verdelhan, 2018, Deviations from covered interest rate parity, *Journal of Finance* 73, 915–57.

Duarte, Jefferson, Edwin Hu, and Lance Young, 2020, A comparison of some structural models of private information arrival, *Journal of Financial Economics* 135, 795–815.

Duarte, Jefferson, and Lance Young, 2009, Why is PIN priced?, *Journal of Financial Economics* 91, 119–38.

Dugast, Jérôme, 2018, Unscheduled News and Market Dynamics, *Journal of Finance*, 73, 2537–2586.

Dugast, Jérôme, and Thierry Foucault, 2018, Data Abundance and Asset Price Informativeness, *Journal of Financial Economics* 130, 367–391.

Duffie, Darrell, 2010, Presidential address: asset price dynamics with slow-moving capital, *Journal of Finance* 65, 1237–67.

Duffie, Darrell, 2012, Market making under the proposed Volker rule, A report to the Securities Industry and Financial Markets Association.

Duffie, Darrell, 2018, Post-Crisis Bank Regulations and Financial Market Liquidity, 13th Paolo Baffi Lecture.

Duffie, Darrell, 2020, "Still the world's safe haven? Redesigning the U.S. Treasury market after the COVID-19 crisis," Hutchins Center Working Paper Number 62, Brookings Institution.

Duffie, Darrell, and Strulovici Bruno, 2012, Capital mobility and asset pricing, *Econometrica* 80, 2469–509.

Duffie, Darrell, Nicolae Gârleanu, and Lasse Heje Pedersen, 2002, Securities lending, shorting, and pricing, *Journal of Financial Economics* 66, 307–39.

Duffie, Darrell, Nicolae Gârleanu, and Lasse Heje Pedersen, 2005, Over-the-counter markets, *Econometrica* 73, 1815–47.

Duffie, Darrell, Nicolae Gârleanu, and Lasse Heje Pedersen, 2007, Valuation in over-the-counter markets, *Review of Financial Studies* 20, 1865–1900.

Duffie, Darrell, Thierry Foucault, Laura Veldkamp, and Xavier Vives, 2022, Technology and finance, in The Future of Banking 4.

Duffie, Darrell, and Haoxiang Zhu, 2011, Does a central clearing counterparty reduce counterparty risk? *Review of Asset Pricing Studies* 1, 74–95.

Duffie, Darrell, and Haoxiang Zhu, 2017, Size discovery *Review of Financial Studies* 30, 1095–1150.

Dunne, Peter, Moore Michael, and Richard Portes, European government bond markets: transparency, liquidity, efficiency, CEPR, 1–83.

Durnev, Art, Randall Morck, and Bernard Yeung, 2004, Value-enhancing capital budgeting and firm-specific return variation, *Journal of Finance* 59, 65–105.

Easley, David, Robert F. Engle, Maureen O'Hara, and Liuren Wu, 2001, Time-varying arrival rates of informed and uninformed trades, Economics Working Paper Archive at WUSTL.

Easley, David, Soeren Hvidkjaer, and Maureen O'Hara, 2002, Is information risk a determinant of asset returns? *Journal of Finance* 57, 2185–221.

Easley, David, Nicholas M. Kiefer, Maureen O'Hara, and Joseph Paperman, 1996a, Cream-skimming or profit-sharing? The curious role of purchased order flow, *Journal of Finance* 51, 811–33.

Easley, David, Nicholas M. Kiefer, Maureen O'Hara, and Joseph Paperman, 1996b, Liquidity, information, and less-frequently traded stocks, *Journal of Finance* 51, 1405–36.

Easley, David, and Maureen O'Hara, 1987, Price, trade size, and information in securities markets, *Journal of Financial Economics* 19, 69–90.

Easley, David, and Maureen O'Hara, 1992, Time and the process of security price adjustment, *Journal of Finance* 47, 576–605.

Easley, David, and Maureen O'Hara, 2004, Information and the cost of capital, *Journal of Finance* 59, 1553–83.

Easley, David, Maureen O'Hara, and Joseph Paperman, 1998, Financial analysts and information-based trade, *Journal of Financial Markets* 1, 175–201.

Easley, David, Maureen O'Hara, and Gideon Saar, 2001b, How stock splits affect trading: a microstructure approach, *Journal of Financial and Quantitative Analysis* 36, 25–51.

Edmans, Alex, 2009, Blockholder trading, market efficiency, and managerial myopia, *Journal of Finance* 22, 4881–917.

Edmans, Alex, 2015, A survey of blokholders and governance, *Annual Review of Financial Economics* 6, 23–50.

Edmans, Alex, Vivian W. Fang, Katharina A. Lewellen, 2017, Equity vesting and investment, *Review of Financial Studies* 30, 2229–71.

Edmans, Alex, Vivian W. Fang, and Emanuel Zur, 2013, The effect of liquidity on governance, *Review of Financial Studies* 26, 1443–82.

Edwards, Amy K., Lawrence E. Harris, and Michael S. Piwowar, 2007, Corporate bond market transaction costs and transparency, *Journal of Finance* 62, 1421–51.

Egginton, Jared, Bonnie Van Ness, Bonnie, Robert Van Ness, 2016, Quote Stuffing. Financial Management, 45, 583–608.

Eisfeldt, Andrea, Bernard Herskovic, Sriram Rajan and Emil Siriwardane, 2023, OTC Intermediaries, *Review of Financial Studies* 36, 615–677.

Ellis, Katrina, Roni Michaeli, and Maureen O'Hara, 2002, The market making of a dealer market: from entry to equilibrium in the trading of Nasdaq stocks, *Journal of Finance* 57, 2289–316.

Ellul, Andrew, Craig W. Holden, Pankaj Jain, and Robert H. Jennings, 2007, Determinants of order choice on the New York Stock Exchange, *Journal of Empirical Finance* 14, 636–61.

Ellul, Andrew, Chotibhak Jotikasthira, and Christian Lundblad, 2011, Regulatory pressure and fire sales in the corporate bond market, *Journal of Financial Economics* 101, 596–620.

Ellul, Andrew, and Marco Pagano, 2006, IPO underpricing and after-market liquidity, *Review of Financial Studies* 19, 381–421.

Ellul, Andrew, and Marios Panayides, 2018, Do financial analysts restrain insiders' informational advantage? *Journal of Financial and Quantitative Analysis* 53, 203–41.

Ende, Bartholomaus, and Marco Lutat, 2011, Trade-throughs in European cross-traded equities after transaction costs: empirical evidence for the EURO STOXX 50, Working Paper, Goethe Universität.

Engelbrecht-Wiggans, Richard, Paul R. Milgrom, and Robert Weber, 1983, Competitive bidding and proprietary information, *Journal of Mathematical Economics* 11, 161–9.

Ernst, Thomas, Jonathan Sokobin, and Chester Spatt, 2021, The value of off exchange data, Working paper, Carnegie Mellon University.

Ernst, Thomas, and Chester Spatt, 2021, Payments for order flow and asset choice, Working paper, Carnegie Mellon University.

ESMA, 2021a, EU Securities Markets, https://www.esma.europa.eu/.

ESMA, 2021b, MiFID II review report on algorithmic trading, https://www.esma.europa.eu/.

Eun Cheol S., and Sanjiv Sabherwal, 2003, Cross-border listings and price discovery: evidence from U.S.-listed Canadian stocks, *Journal of Finance* 58, 549–76.

European Commission, 2017, Drivers of corporate bond market liquidity in the European Union, available at https://ec.europa.eu/info/sites/default/files/171120-corporate-bonds-study_en.pdf.

Fahlenbrach, Rudiger, and René M. Stulz, 2011, Bank CEO incentives and the credit crisis, *Journal of Financial Economics* 99, 11–26.

Fang, Vivian W., Thomas H. Noe, and Sheri Tice, 2009, Stock market liquidity and firm value, *Journal of Financial Economics* 94, 150–69.

Favero, Carlo, Marco Pagano, and Ernst-Ludwig von Thadden, 2010, How does liquidity affect government bond yields?, *Journal of Financial and Quantitative Analysis* 45, 107–34.

Fleming, Michael J., 2003, Measuring treasury market liquidity. Federal Reserve Bank of New York, *Economic Policy Review* 9, 83–108.

Flood, Mark D., Ronald Huisman, Kees G. Koedijk, and Ronald J. Mahieu, 1999, Quote disclosure and price discovery in multiple-dealer financial markets, *Review of Financial Studies* 12, 37–59.

Foerster, Stephen, and G. Andrew Karolyi, 1998, Multimarket trading and liquidity: a transactions data analysis of Canada-U.S. interlistings, *Journal of International Financial Markets* 8, 393–412.

Foerster, Stephen R., and G. Andrew Karolyi, 2000, The long-run performance of global equity offerings, *Journal of Financial and Quantitative Analysis* 35, 499–528.

Foerster, Stephen, and G. Andrew Karolyi, 1999, The effects of market segmentation and investor recognition on asset prices: evidence from foreign stocks listing in the U.S., *Journal of Finance* 54, 981–1013.

Foley, Sean, Tom Meling, and Bernt Arne Odegaard, 2023, Tick size wars: the market quality effects of pricing grid competition, *Review of Finance*, 659–692.

Foucault, Thierry, 1995, Price formation and order placement strategies in a dynamic order driven market, Working Paper, Universitat Pompeu Fabra.

Foucault, Thierry, 1999, Order flow composition and trading costs in a dynamic limit order market, *Journal of Financial Markets* 2, 99–134.

Foucault, Thierry, and Laurent Frésard, 2012, Cross listing, investment sensitivity to stock price, and the learning hypothesis, *Review of Financial Studies* 25, 3305–50.

Foucault, Thierry, and Laurent Frésard, 2014, Learning from peers' stock prices and corporate investment, *Journal of Financial Economics* 111, 554–77.

Foucault, Thierry, and Thomas Gehrig, 2008, Stock price informativeness, cross-listings, and investment decisions, *Journal of Financial Economics* 88, 146–68.

Foucault, Thierry, Johan Hombert, and Ioanid Rosu, 2016, News Trading and Speed. *The Journal of Finance*, 71, 335–382.

Foucault, Thierry, Ohad Kadan, and Eugene Kandel, 2005, Limit order book as a market for liquidity, *Review of Financial Studies* 18, 1171–1217.

Foucault, Thierry, Ohad Kadan, and Eugene Kandel, 2013, Liquidity cycles, and make/take fees in electronic market, *Journal of Finance* 68, 299–341.

Foucault, Thierry, Roman Kozhan, and Wing Wah Tham, 2017, Toxic Arbitrage, *The Review of Financial Studies*, 30, 1053–1094.

Foucault, Thierry, and Albert J. Menkveld, 2008, Competition for order flow and smart order routing systems, *Journal of Finance* 63, 119–58.

Foucault, Thierry, Sophie Moinas, and Erik Theissen, 2007, Does anonymity matter in electronic limit order markets?, *Review of Financial Studies* 20, 1707–47.

Foucault, Thierry, Marco Pagano, and Ailsa Röell, 2010, *Market Transparency* in Encyclopedia of Quantitative Finance, vol. 23, ed. R. Cont. Chichester: John Wiley 7 Sons.

Foucault, Thierry, and Christine Parlour, 2004, Competition for listings, *RAND Journal of Economics* 35, 329–55.

Foucault, Thierry, Ailsa Röell, and Patrik Sandas, 2003, Market making with costly monitoring: an analysis of SOES trading, *Review of Financial Studies* 16, 345–84.

Foucault, Thierry, David Sraer, and David Thesmar, 2011, Individual investors and volatility, *Journal of Finance* 66, 1369–1405.

Franks, Julian, and Steven Schaefer, 1995, Equity market transparency on the London Stock Exchange, *Journal of Applied Corporate Finance* 8, 70–7.

Frazzini, Andrea, Ronen Israel, and Tobias Moskowitz, 2018, Trading costs, working paper, available at https://papers.ssrn.com/sol3/papers.cfm?abstract_id=3229719.

Freixas, Xavier, Luc Laeven, and José-Luis Peydró, 2015, *Systemic Risk, Crises, and Macroprudential Regulation*. Cambridge, MA: MIT Press.

Freixas, Xavier, Bruno M. Parigi, and Jean-Charles Rochet, 2000, Systemic risk, interbank relations, and liquidity provision by the central bank, *Journal of Money, Credit and Banking* 32(3), 611–38.

French, Kenneth, and Richard Roll, 1986, Stock return variances: the arrival of information and the reaction of traders, *Journal of Financial Economics* 17, 5–26.

Froot, Kenneth A., and Emil M. Dabora, 1999, How are stock prices affected by the location of trade?, *Journal of Financial Economics* 53, 189–216.

Fulghieri, Paolo, and Dmitry Lukin, 2001, Information production, dilution costs, and optimal security design, *Journal of Financial Economics* 61, 3–42.

Furfine, C.H., 2003, Interbank exposures: quantifying the risk of contagion. *Journal of Money Credit Banking* 35(1), 111–28.

Gabaix, Xavier, Arvin Krishnamurthy, and Olivier Vigneron, 2007, Limits of arbitrage: theory and evidence from the mortgage-backed securities market, *Journal of Finance* 62, 557–96.

Garman, Mark, 1976, Market microstructure, *Journal of Financial Economics* 3, 257–75.

Gemmill, Gordon, 1996, Transparency and liquidity: a study of block trades on the London Stock Exchange under different publication rules, *Journal of Finance* 51, 1765–90.

Gennotte, Gerard, and Hayne Leland, 1990, Market liquidity, hedging, and crashes, *American Economic Review* 80, 999–1021.

George, Thomas J., Gautam Kaul, and Mahendrarajah Nimalendran, 1991, Estimation of the bid-ask spread and its components: a new approach, *Review of Financial Studies* 4, 623–56.

Gillan, Stuart, and Laura Starks, 2007, The evolution of shareholder activism in the United States, *Journal of Applied Corporate Finance* 19, 55–73.

Glosten, Lawrence R., 1987, Components of the bid/ask spread and statistical properties of transaction prices, *Journal of Finance* 42, 1293–1308.

Glosten, Lawrence R., 1989, Insider trading, liquidity, and the role of the monopolist specialist, *Journal of Business* 62, 211–35.

Glosten, Lawrence R., 1994, Is the electronic open limit order book inevitable?, *Journal of Finance* 49, 1127–61.

Glosten, Lawrence R., and Lawrence Harris, 1988, Estimating the components of the bid/ask spread, *Journal of Financial Economics* 21, 123–42.

Glosten, Lawrence R., and Paul R. Milgrom, 1985, Bid, ask, and transaction prices in a specialist market with heterogeneously informed traders, *Journal of Financial Economics* 13, 71–100.

Goel, Anand, and Anjan Thakor, 2003, Why do firms smooth earnings?, *Journal of Business* 76, 151–92.

Goettler, Ronald L., Christine A. Parlour, and Uday Rajan, 2005, Equilibrium in a dynamic limit order market, *Journal of Finance* 60, 2149–92.

Goettler, Ronald L., Christine A. Parlour, and Uday Rajan, 2009, Informed traders and limit order markets, *Journal of Financial Economics* 93, 67–87.

Goldman, Eitan, and Steve Slezak, 2006, An equilibrium model of incentive contracts in the presence of information manipulation, *Journal of Financial Economics* 80, 603–26.

Goldreich, David, Bernd Hanke, and Purnendu Nath, 2005, The price of future liquidity: time-varying liquidity in the U.S. treasury market, *Review of Finance* 9, 1–32.

Goldstein, Itay, and Alexander Gümbel, 2008, Manipulation and the allocational role of prices, *Review of Economic Studies* 75, 133–64.

Goldstein, Itay, Hao Jiang, and David T. Ng, 2017, Investor flows and fragility in corporate bond funds, *Journal of Financial Economics* 126, 592–613.

Goldstein, Itay, Emre Ozdenoren, and Kathy Yuan, 2013, Trading frenzies and their impact on real investment, *Journal of Financial Economics* 109, 566–82.

Goldstein, Itay, and Liyan Yang, 2017, Information disclosure in financial markets, *Annual Review of Financial Economics* 9, 101–25.

Goldstein, Michael, Kumar, Pavitra, and Graves, Frank, 2014, Computerized and High-Frequency Trading. *Financial Review*, 49, 177–202.

Goldstein, Michael A., Edith S. Hotchkiss, and Erik Sirri, 2007, Transparency and liquidity: a controlled experiment on corporate bonds, *Review of Financial Studies* 20, 235–73.

Goldstein, Michael, and Kenneth Kavajecz, 2000, Eighths, sixteenths, and market depth: changes in tick size and liquidity provision on the NYSE, *Journal of Financial Economics* 56, 125–49.

Goldstein, Michael, and Kenneth Kavajecz, 2004, Trading strategies during circuit breakers and extreme market movements, *Journal of Financial Markets* 7, 301–33.

Gorton, Gary, and George Pennacchi, 1990, Financial intermediaries and liquidity creation, *Journal of Finance* 45, 49–71.

Goyenko, Ruslan, Craig W. Holden, and Charles A. Trzcinka, 2009, Do liquidity measures measure liquidity? *Journal of Financial Economics* 92, 153–81.

Grammig, Joachim, and Erik Theissen, 2012, Is best really better? Internalization in Xetra BEST, *Schmalenbach Business Review* 64, 82–100.

Grammig, Joachim, Dirk Schiereck, and Eric Theissen, 2001, Knowing me, knowing you: trader anonymity and informed trading in parallel markets, *Journal of Financial Markets* 4, 385–412.

Green, Richard C., Burton Hollifield, and Norman Schuerhoff, 2007, Financial intermediation and the costs of trading in an opaque market, *Review of Financial Studies* 20, 275–314.

Green, Richard, Dan Li, and Norman Schuerhoff, 2010, Price discovery in illiquid markets: do financial asset prices rise faster than they fall? *Journal of Finance* 65, 1669–1702.

Gresse, Carole, 2017, Effects of lit and dark market fragmentation on liquidity, *Journal of Financial Markets* 35, 1–20.

Griffiths, Mark D., Brian F. Smith, D. Alasdair S. Turnbull, and Robert W. White, 2000, The costs and determinants of order aggressiveness, *Journal of Financial Economics* 56, 65–88.

Gromb, Denis, and Dimitri Vayanos, 2002, Equilibrium and welfare in markets with financially constrained arbitrageurs, *Journal of Financial Economics* 66, 361–407.

Gromb, Denis, and Dimitri Vayanos, 2010, Limits of arbitrage: the state of the theory, *Annual Review of Financial Economics* 2, 251–75.

Grossman, Sanford, 1976, On the efficiency of competitive stock markets where trades have diverse information, *Journal of Finance* 31, 573–85.

Grossman, Sanford J., and Oliver D. Hart, 1980, Takeover bids, the free-rider problem, and the theory of the corporation, *Bell Journal of Economics* 11, 42–64.

Grossman, Sanford J., and Merton H. Miller, 1988, Liquidity and market structure, *Journal of Finance* 43, 617–37.

Gupta, Nandini, and Kathy Yuan, 2009, On the growth effect of stock market liberalizations, *Review of Financial Studies* 22, 4715–52.

Hagströmer, Björn, 2021, Bias in the effective bid-ask spread, *Journal of Financial Economics* 142, 314–37.

Hall, Brian J., and Kevin J. Murphy, 2000, Optimal exercise prices for executive stock options, *American Economic Review* 90, 209–14.

Halling, Michael, Marco Pagano, Otto Randl, and Josef Zechner, 2008, Where is the market? Evidence from cross-listings in the United States, *Review of Financial Studies* 21, 724–61.

Handa, Puneet, and Robert A. Schwartz, 1996, Limit order trading, *Journal of Finance* 51, 1835–61.

Hansch, Oliver, Narayan Y. Naik, and S. Viswanathan, 1998, Do inventories matter in dealership markets? Evidence from the London Stock Exchange, *Journal of Finance* 53, 1623–56.

Harris, Lawrence E., 1990, Statistical properties of the Roll serial covariance bid/ask spread estimator, *Journal of Finance* 45, 579–90.

Harris, Lawrence E., 2003, *Trading & Exchanges, Market Microstructure for Practitioners.* Oxford: Oxford University Press.

Harris, Lawrence E., and Joel Hasbrouck, 1996, Market vs. limit orders: the superdot evidence on order submission strategy, *Journal of Financial and Quantitative Analysis* 31, 213–31.

Harris, Lawrence E., and Michael S. Piwowar, 2006, Secondary trading costs in the municipal bond market, *Journal of Finance* 61, 1361–97.

Hasbrouck, Joel, 1988, Trades, quotes, inventories, and information, *Journal of Financial Economics* 22, 229–52.

Hasbrouck, Joel, 1991, Measuring the information content of stock trades, *Journal of Finance* 46, 179–207.

Hasbrouck, Joel, 1995, One security, many markets: determining the location of price discovery, *Journal of Finance* 50, 1175–99.

Hasbrouck, Joel, 2002, Stalking the "efficient price" in market microstructure specifications: an overview, *Journal of Financial Markets* 5, 329–39.

Hasbrouck, Joel, 2005, Trading costs and returns for U.S. equities: the evidence from daily data, Unpublished Working Paper, New York University.

Hasbrouck, Joel, 2007, *Empirical Market Microstructure*. Oxford: Oxford University Press.

Hasbrouck, Joel, 2009, Trading costs and returns for U.S. equities: estimating effective costs from daily data, *Journal of Finance* 64, 1445–77.

Hasbrouck, Joel, and Duane J. Seppi, 2001, Common factors in prices, order flows, and liquidity, *Journal of Financial Economics* 59, 383–411.

Hasbrouck, Joel, and George Sofianos, 1993, The trades of market makers: an empirical examination of New York Stock Exchange specialists, *Journal of Finance* 48, 1565–94.

Haslag, Peter, and Matthew Ringgenberg, 2021, The demise of the NYSE and NASDAQ: market quality in the age of market fragmentation, available at SSRN: https://ssrn.com/abstract=2591715 or http://dx.doi.org/10.2139/ssrn.2591715.

He, Zighuo, and Arvin Krishnamurthy, 2012, A model of capital and crises, *Review of Economic Studies*, 79, 735–77.

He, Zighuo, and Arvin Krishnamurthy, 2013, Intermediary asset pricing, *American Economic Review* 103, 732–70.

Heider, Florian, Marie Hoerova, and Cornelia Holthausen, 2015, Liquidity hoarding and interbank market spreads: the role of counterparty risk, *Journal of Financial Economics* 118, 336–54.

Heidle, Hans, and Roger D. Huang, 2002, Information-based trading in dealer and auction markets: an analysis of exchange listings, *Journal of Financial and Quantitative Analysis* 37, 391–424.

Hellwig, Martin, 1980, On the aggregation of information in competitive markets, *Journal of Economic Theory* 22, 477–98.

Hendershott, Terrence, and Charles Jones, 2005a, Island goes dark: transparency, fragmentation, and regulation, *Review of Financial Studies* 18, 743–93.

Hendershott, Terrence, and Charles M. Jones, 2005b, Trade-through prohibitions and market quality, *Journal of Financial Markets* 8, 1–23.

Hendershott, Terrence J., Charles M. Jones, and Albert J. Menkveld, 2011, Does algorithmic trading improve liquidity, *Journal of Finance* 66, 1–33.

Hendershott, Terrence, Sunny X. Li, Albert J. Menkveld, and Mark S. Seasholes, 2010, Risk sharing, costly participation, and monthly returns, Working Paper, Vrije University.

Hendershott, Terrence, and Haim Mendelson, 2000, Crossing networks and dealer markets: competition and performance, *Journal of Finance* 55, 2071–115.

Hendershott, Terrence, and Albert J. Menkveld, 2014, Price pressures, *Journal of Financial Economics* 114, 405–23.

Hendershott, Terrence J., and Ryan Riordan, 2013, Algorithmic trading and the market for liquidity. *Journal of Financial and Quantitative Analysis*, 48, 1001–1024.

Hengelbrock, Jördis, 2008, Designated sponsors and bid-ask spreads on Xetra, Working Paper, Bonn Graduate School of Economics.

Henry, Peter Blair, 2000a, Stock market liberalization, economic reform, and emerging market equity prices, *Journal of Finance* 55, 529–64.

Henry, Peter Blair, 2000b, Do stock market liberalizations cause investment booms?, *Journal of Financial Economics* 58, 301–34.

Hicks, John, 1969, *A Theory of Economic History*, Oxford: Clarendon Press.

Hirschman, Albert O., 1970, *Exit, Voice, and Loyalty: Responses to Decline in Firms, Organizations, and States*, Cambridge, MA. Harvard University Press.

Ho Thomas, and Hans Stoll, 1981, Optimal dealer pricing under transaction and return uncertainty, *Journal of Financial Economics* 9, 47–73.

Ho, Thomas, and Hans Stoll, 1983, The dynamics of dealer markets under competition, *Journal of Finance* 38, 1053–74.

Hoffmann, Peter, 2014, A dynamic limit order market with fast and slow traders, *Journal of Financial Economics* 113, 156–69.

Holden, Craig W., 2009, New low-frequency liquidity measures, *Journal of Financial Markets* 12, 778–813.

Holden, Craig W., and S. Jacobsen, 2014, Liquidity measurement problems in fast, competitive markets: expensive and cheap solutions. *Journal of Finance* 6, 1747–85.

Holden, Craig W., Stacey Jacobsen, and Avanidhar Subrahmanyam, 2014, The empirical analysis of liquidity, *Foundations and Trends in Finance* 8, 263–365.

Holden, Craig W., and Nam Jayoung, 2019, Do the LCAPM predictions hold? Replication and extension evidence, *Critical Finance Review*, 8, 29–71.

Holden, Craig W., and Avanidhar Subrahmanyam, 1992, Long-lived private information and imperfect competition, *Journal of Finance* 47, 247–70.

Hollifield, Burton, Robert Miller, and Patrik Sandas, 2004, Empirical analysis of limit order markets, *Review of Economic Studies* 71, 1027–63.

Hollifield, Burton, Robert Miller, Patrik Sandas, and Joshua Slive, 2006, Estimating the gains from trade in limit order markets, *Journal of Finance* 61, 2753–804.

Holmstrom, Bengt, and Jean Tirole, 1993, Market liquidity and performance monitoring, *Journal of Political Economy* 101, 678–709.

Hong, Harrison, and Sven Rady, 2002, Strategic trading and learning about liquidity, *Journal of Financial Markets* 5, 419–50.

Huang, Jennifer, and Jiang Wang, 2009, Liquidity and market crashes, *Review of Financial Studies* 22, 2607–43.

Huang, Jennifer, and Jiang Wang, 2010, Market liquidity, asset prices, and welfare, *Journal of Financial Economics* 95, 101–27.

Huang, Roger D., and Hans R. Stoll, 1996, Dealer versus auction markets: a paired comparison of execution costs on NASDAQ and the NYSE, *Journal of Financial Economics* 41, 313–57.

Huang, Roger D., and Hans R. Stoll, 1997, The components of the bid-ask spread: a general approach, *Review of Financial Studies* 10, 995–1034.

Huberman, Gur, and Dominika Halka, 2001, Systematic liquidity, *Journal of Financial Research* 24, 161–78.

Huberman Gur, and Werner Stanzl, 2005, Optimal liquidity trading, *Review of Finance* 9, 165–200.

Huddart, Steven, 1993, The effect of a large shareholder on corporate value, *Management Science* 39, 1407–21.

Hupperts, Erik C.J., and Albert J. Menkveld, 2002, Intraday analysis of market integration: Dutch blue chips traded in Amsterdam and New York, *Journal of Financial Markets* 51, 57–82.

IBM, 2008, Tackling latency: the algorithmic arms race, IBM Global Business Services.

Indriawan, Ivan, Pascual, Roberto, and Shkilko, Andriy, On the Effects of Continuous Trading (October 7, 2020). Available at SSRN: https://ssrn.com/abstract=3707154

Jain, Pankaj, 2005, Financial market design and the equity premium: electronic vs. floor trading, *Journal of Finance* 60, 2955–85.

Jones, Charles, 2002, A century of stock market liquidity and trading costs, Unpublished Working Paper.

Jurkatis, Simon, 2022, Inferring trade directions in fast markets, *Journal of Financial Markets* 58, 1006–1035.

Kadlec, Gregory B., and John J. McConnell, 1994, The effect of market segmentation and illiquidity on asset prices: evidence from exchange listings, *Journal of Finance* 49, 611–36.

Kamara, Avraham, 1994, Liquidity, taxes, and short-term treasury yields, *Journal of Financial and Quantitative Analysis* 29, 403–17.

Kaniel, Ron, and Hong Liu, 2006, So what orders do informed traders use?, *Journal of Business* 79, 1867–1913.

Karolyi, Andrew G., 1998, *Why Do Companies List Shares Abroad? A Survey of the Evidence and its Managerial Implications*, New York: New York University Salomon Bros. Center Monograph, Vol. 7, No. 1.

Karolyi, Andrew G., 2004, The role of American depositary receipts in the development of emerging markets, *Review of Economics and Statistics* 86, 670–90.

Karolyi, Andrew G., 2006, The world of cross-listings and cross-listings of the world: challenging conventional wisdom, *Review of Finance* 10, 73–115.

Kavajecz, Kenneth, and Donald Keim, 2005, Packaging liquidity: blind auctions and transaction efficiencies, *Journal of Financial and Quantitative Analysis* 40, 465–92.

Kedia, Simi, and Thomas Philippon, 2009, The economics of fraudulent accounting, *Review of Financial Studies* 22, 2169–99.

van Kervel, Vincent, and Albert J. Menkveld, 2019, High-frequency trading around large institutional orders, *Journal of Finance* 74, 1091–1137.

Keynes, John Maynard, 1936, *The General Theory of Employment, Interest, and Money*, New York: Harcourt, Brace, and Co.

Khandani, Amir E., and Andrew W. Lo, 2011, What happened to the quants in August 2007? Evidence from factors and transactions data, *Journal of Financial Markets* 14, 1–46.

Kim, Oliver, and Robert Verrecchia, 1994, Market liquidity and volume around earnings announcements, *Journal of Accounting and Economics* 17, 41–67.

Kirilenko, Andrei, Albert Kyle, Mehrdad Samadi, and Tugkan Tuzun, 2017, The Flash Crash: High-Frequency Trading in an Electronic Market, *The Journal of Finance* 72, 967–98.

Kissell, Robert, and Morton Glantz, 2003, *Optimal Trading Strategies: Quantitative Approaches For Managing Market Impact and Trading Risk*, New York: Amacom.

Klemperer, Paul, and Margaret Meyer, 1989, Supply function equilibria in oligopoly under uncertainty, *Econometrica* 57, 1243–77.

Kolasinski, Adam and Nan Yang, 2018, Managerial myopia and the mortgage meltdown, *Journal of Financial Economics* 128, 466–85.

Kondor, Peter, 2009, Risk in dynamic arbitrage: the price effects of convergence trading, *Journal of Finance* 64, 631–55.

Korajczyk, Robert A., and Dermot Murphy, 2019, High frequency market making to large institutional trades, *Review of Financial Studies* 32, 1034–67.

Krishnamurthy, Arvind, 2002, The bond/old-bond spread, *Journal of Financial Economics* 66, 463–506.

Kuong, John and Vincent Maurin, 2022, The design of a central counterparty, *Journal of Financial of Quantitative Analysis*, forthcoming.

Kyle, Albert S., 1985, Continuous auctions and insider trading, *Econometrica* 53, 1315–35.

Kyle, Albert S., 1989, Informed speculation with imperfect competition, *Review of Economic Studies* 56, 317–55.

Kyle, Albert S., and Jean-Luc Vila, 1991, Noise trading and takeovers, *RAND Journal of Economics* 22, 54–71.

Kyle, Albert S., and Wei Xiong, 2001, Contagion as a wealth effect, *Journal of Finance* 56, 1401–40.

Lang, Mark H., Karl V. Lins, and Mark G. Maffett, 2012, Transparency, liquidity, and valuation: international evidence on when transparency matters most, *Journal of Accounting Research* 50, 729–74.

Large, Jeremy, 2009, A market clearing role for inefficiency on a limit order book, *Journal of Financial Economics* 91, 102–11.

Lee, Charles M.C., and Mark J. Ready, 1991, Inferring trade direction from intraday data, *Journal of Finance* 46, 733–46.

Lee, Kuan-Hui, 2011, The world price of liquidity risk, *Journal of Financial Economics* 99, 136–61.

Lee, Ruben, 2000, *What Is an Exchange? The Automation, Management, and Regulation of Financial Markets*, Oxford: Oxford University Press.

Leinweber, David J., 1995, Using information from trading in trading and portfolio management, *The Journal of Investing* 4, 40–50.

Lesmond, David A., 2005, Liquidity of emerging markets, *Journal of Financial Economics* 77, 411–52.

Lesmond, David A., Joseph J. Ogden, and Charles Trzcinka, 1999, A new estimate of transaction costs, *Review of Financial Studies* 12, 1113–41.

Leuz, Christian, and Peter D. Wysocki, 2008, Economic consequences of financial reporting and disclosure regulation: a review and suggestions for future research, Working Paper, available online at http://ssrn.com/abstract=1105398.

Levine, Ross, 1997, Financial development and economic growth: views and agenda, *Journal of Economic Literature* 35, 688–726.

Levine, Ross, 2005, Finance and growth: theory and evidence, in Philippe Aghion and Steven Durlauf (eds.), *Handbook of Economic Growth*, Amsterdam: Elsevier Science.

Levine, Ross, and Sergio L. Schmukler, 2006, Internationalization and stock market liquidity, *Review of Finance* 10, 153–87.

Levine, Ross, and Sara Zervos, 1998a, Stock markets, banks, and economic growth, *American Economic Review* 88, 537–58.

Levine, Ross, and Sara Zervos, 1998b, Capital control liberalization and stock market development, *World Development* 26, 1169–83.

Li, Dan, and Norman Schürhoff, 2019, Dealer networks, *Journal of Finance* 74, 91–144.

Li, Hongtao, Robert Novy-Marx, and Mihail Velikov, 2019, Liquidity risk and asset pricing, *Critical Finance Review*, 8, 223–55.

Longstaff, Francis A., 2004, The flight-to-liquidity premium in U.S. treasury bond prices, *Journal of Business* 77, 511–26.

Lou, Dong, Hongjun Yan, and Jinfan Zhang, 2013, Anticipated and repeatd shocks in liquid markets *Review of Financial Studies* 26, 1797–1829.

Luo, Yuanzhi, 2005, Do insiders learn from outsiders? Evidence from mergers and acquisitions, *Journal of Finance* 60, 1951–82.

Lyons, Richard K., 1995, Tests of microstructural hypotheses in the foreign exchange market, *Journal of Financial Economics* 39, 321–51.

Lyons, Richard K., 2001, *The Microstructure Approach to Exchange Rates*, Cambridge, MA: MIT Press.

Madhavan, Ananth, 1992, Trading mechanisms in securities markets, *Journal of Finance* 47, 607–41.

Madhavan, Ananth, 1995, Consolidation, fragmentation, and the disclosure of trading information, *Review of Financial Studies* 8, 579–603.

Madhavan, Ananth, David Porter, and Daniel G. Weaver, 2005, Should securities markets be transparent?, *Journal of Financial Markets* 8, 266–88.

Madhavan, Ananth, Matthew Richardson, and Mark Roomans, 1997, Why do security prices change? A transaction-level analysis, *Review of Financial Studies* 10, 1035.

Madhavan, Ananth, and Seymour Smidt, 1993, An analysis of changes in specialist inventories and quotations, *Journal of Finance* 48, 1595–1628.

Maloney, Michael T., and J. Harold Mulherin, 2003, The complexity of price discovery in an efficient market: the stock market reaction to the challenger crash, *Journal of Corporate Finance* 9, 453–79.

Maug, Ernst, 1998, Large shareholders as monitors: is there a tradeoff between liquidity and control?, *Journal of Finance* 53, 65–98.

Mayhew, Stewart, 2002, Competition, market structure and bid-ask spreads, *Journal of Finance* 57, 931–58.

McCahery, Joseph A., Zacharias Sautner, and Laura T. Starks, 2010, Behind the scenes: the corporate governance preferences of institutional investors, *Journal of Finance* 71, 2905–32.

Mendelson, Haim, 1982, Market behavior in a clearing house, *Econometrica* 50, 1505–24.

Mendelson, Haim, 1985, Random competitive exchange: price distributions and gains from trade, *Journal of Economic Theory* 37, 254–80.

Mendelson, Haim, 1987, Consolidation, fragmentation and market performance, *Journal of Financial and Quantitative Analysis* 22, 187–207.

Menkveld, Albert J., 2013, High-frequency trading and the new-market makers, *Journal of Financial Markets* 16, 712–40.

Menkveld, Albert J., and Guillaume Vuillemey, 2021, The economics of central clearing, *Annual Review of Financial Economics* 13, 153–178.

Menkveld, Albert J., and Ting Wang, 2011, How do designated market makers create value for small-caps?, *Journal of Financial Markets* 16, 571–603.

Menkveld, Albert, and Marius Zoican, 2017, Need for Speed? Exchange Latency and Liquidity, *The Review of Financial Studies*, 30, 1188–1228.

Menkveld, Albert, 2016, The Economics of High-Frequency Trading: Taking Stock, *Annual Review of Financial Economics*, 8, 1–24.

Merton, Robert, 1987, A simple model of capital market equilibrium with incomplete information, *Journal of Finance* 42, 483–510.

Michelacci, Claudio, and Javier Suarez, 2004, Business creation and the stock market, *Review of Economic Studies* 71, 459–81.

Mikkelson, Wayne H., Megan Partch, and Ken Shah, 1997, Ownership and operating performance of companies that go public, *Journal of Financial Economics* 44, 281–308.

Miller, Darius P., 1999, The market reaction to international cross-listings: evidence from depository receipts, *Journal of Financial Economics* 51, 103–23.

Mitchell, Mark, Lasse Heje Pedersen, and Todd C. Pulvino, 2007, Slow moving capital, *American Economic Review* 97, 215–20.

Mitchell, Mark, Todd C. Pulvino, and Erik Stafford, 2004, Price pressure around mergers, *Journal of Finance* 59, 31–63.

Mizrach, Bruce, and Christopher J. Neely, 2007, The microstructure of the U.S. treasury market, Federal Reserve Bank of St. Louis Working Paper 2007-052B.

Modigliani, Franco, and Richard Sutch, 1966, Innovations in interest rate policy, *American Economic Review* 91, 99–127.

Morris, Stephen, and Hyun Song Shin, 2012, Contagious adverse selection, *American Economic Journal: Macroeconomics* 4, 1–21.

Mulherin, J. Harold, Jeffrey M. Netter, and James A. Overdahl, 1992, Prices are property: the organization of financial exchanges from a transaction cost perspective, *Journal of Law and Economics* 34, 591–644.

Muscarella, Chris J., and Michael S. Piwowar, 2001, Market microstructure and securities values: evidence from the Paris bourse, *Journal of Financial Markets* 4, 209–29.

Naik, Narayan Y., Anthony Neuberger, and S. Viswanathan, 1999, Trade disclosure regulation in markets with negotiated trades, *Review of Financial Studies* 12, 873–900.

Nimalendran, Mahendrarajah, and Giovanni Petrella, 2003, Do "thinly-traded" stocks benefit from specialist intervention?, *Journal of Banking and Finance* 27, 1823–54.

Noronha, Gregory M., Atulya Sarin, and Shahrokh M. Saudagaran, 1996, Testing for micro-structure effects of international dual listings using intraday data, *Journal of Banking and Finance* 20, 965–83.

O'Hara, Maureen, and Ye Mao, 2011, Is market fragmentation harming market quality, *Journal of Financial Economics* 100, 459–74.

O'Hara, Maureen, 2015, High frequency market microstructure, *Journal of Financial Economics*, 116, 257–270.

O'Hara, Maureen, and Xing Zhou, 2021, The electronic evolution of corporate bond dealers, *Journal of Financial Economics* 140, 368–90.

Oxera, 2019, The design of equity trading markets in Europe, prepared for the Federation of European Securities Exchanges.

Padilla, Jorge A., and Marco Pagano, 2006, Effects of stock exchange integration: the Euronext evidence, Working Paper, University of Naples, Frederico II.

Pagano, Marco, 1989a, Endogenous market thinness and stock price volatility, *Review of Economic Studies* 56, 269–87.

Pagano, Marco, 1989b, Trading volume and asset liquidity, *Quarterly Journal of Economics* 104, 255–74.

Pagano, Marco, Fabio Panetta, and Luigi Zingales, 1998, Why do companies go public? An empirical analysis, *Journal of Finance* 53, 27–64.

Pagano, Marco, 1993a, Financial markets and growth: an overview, *European Economic Review* 37, 613–22.

Pagano, Marco, 1993b, The flotation of companies on the stock market: a coordination failure model, *European Economic Review* 37, 1101–25.

Pagano, Marco, Otto Randl, Ailsa Röell, and Josef Zechner, 2001, What makes stock exchanges succeed? Evidence from stock listing decisions, *European Economic Review* 45, 770–82.

Pagano, Marco, and Ailsa Röell, 1996, Transparency and liquidity: a comparison of auction and dealer markets with informed trading, *Journal of Finance* 51, 579–611.

Pagano, Marco, and Ailsa Röell, 1990, Trading systems in European stock exchanges: current performance and policy options, *Economic Policy* 10, April, 63–115.

Pagano, Marco, and Ailsa Röell, 1993, *Shifting Gears: An Economic Evaluation of the Reform of the Paris Bourse*, in *Financial Market Liberalization and the Role of Banks*, ed. V. Conti and R. Hamaui, Cambridge: Cambridge University Press.

Pagano, Marco, and Ailsa Röell, 1998, The choice of stock ownership structure: agency costs, monitoring and the decision to go public, *Quarterly Journal of Economics* 113, 187–225.

Pagano, Marco, Ailsa Röell, and Josef Zechner, 2002, The geography of equity listing: why do companies list abroad?, *Journal of Finance* 57, 2651–94.

Pagano, Marco, and Ernst-Ludwig von Thadden, 2004, The European bond markets under EMU, *Oxford Review of Economic Policy* 20, reprinted in Xavier Freixas, Philipp Hartmann, and Colin Mayer (eds.), 2008, *Handbook of European Financial Markets and Institutions*, New York: Oxford University Press.

Pagano, Marco, and Paolo Volpin, 2012, Securitization, transparency and liquidity, *Review of Financial Studies* 25, 2417–53.

Pagnotta, Emiliano, and Thomas Philippon, 2018, Competing on speed, *Econometrica* 86, 1067–1115.

Palomino, Frederic, Luc Renneboog, and Chendi Zhang, 2009, Information salience, investor sentiment, and stock returns: the case of British soccer betting, *Journal of Corporate Finance* 15, 368–87.

Panayides, Marios A., Thomas Shohfi, and Jared D. Smith, 2019. Bulk Volume Classification and Information Detection, Journal of Banking & Finance 103, pp. 113–129.

Parlour, Christine, 1998, Price dynamics in limit order markets, *Review of Financial Studies* 11, 789–816.

Parlour, Christine A., and Duane J. Seppi, 2003, Liquidity-based competition for order flow, *Review of Financial Studies* 16, 301–43.

Parlour, Christine A., and Duane J. Seppi, 2008, Limit order markets: a survey, in *Handbook of Financial Intermediation and Banking*, Elsevier, Amsterdam.

Parrino, Robert, Richard W. Sias, and Laura T. Starks, 2003, Voting with their feet: institutional ownership changes around forced CEO turnover, *Journal of Financial Economics* 68, 3–46.

Pastor, Lubos, and Robert F. Stambaugh, 2003, Liquidity risk and expected stock returns, *Journal of Political Economy* 111, 642–85.

Pastor, Lubos, and Robert F. Stambaugh, 2019, Liquidity risk after 20 years, *Critical Finance Review* 8, 277–99.

Peng, Lin, and Ailsa A. Röell, 2008, Executive pay and shareholder litigation, *Review of Finance* 12, 141–84.

Peng, Lin, and Ailsa A. Röell, 2008b, Manipulation and equity-based compensation, *American Economic Review Papers and Proceedings* 98, 285–290.

Peng, Lin, and Ailsa A. Röell, 2014, Managerial in centives and stock price manipulation, *Journal of Finance* 69, 487–526.

Perold, Andre, 1988, The implementation shortfall: paper versus reality, *Journal of Portfolio Management* 14, 4–9.

Petram, Lodewijk O., 2014, *The World's First Stock Exchange*, New York: Columbia University Press.

Petrescu, Monica, and Michael Wedow, 2017, Dark pools in European equity markets: emergence, competition and implications, ECB Occasional Paper No. 193.

Pontiff, Jeffrey, and Rohit Singla, 2019, Liquidity risk? *Critical Finance Review* 8, 257–76.

Porter David, and Daniel Weaver, 1997, Tick size and market liquidity, *Financial Management* 26, 5–26.

Pulvino, Todd C., 1998, Do asset fire sales exist? An empirical investigation of commercial aircraft transactions, *Journal of Finance* 53, 939–78.

Ranaldo, Angelo, 2004, Order aggressiveness in limit order book markets, *Journal of Financial Markets* 7, 53–74.

Reiss, Peter C., and Ingrid Werner, 1998, Does risk sharing motivate interdealer trading?, *Journal of Finance* 53, 1657–1703.

Reiss, Peter C., and Ingrid Werner, 2004, Anonymity, adverse selection, and the sorting of interdealer trades, *Review of Financial Studies* 18, 599–636.

Roll, Richard, 1984, A simple implicit measure of the bid-ask spread in an efficient market, *Journal of Finance* 39, 1127–39.

Roll, Richard, 1988, R-Squared, *Journal of Finance* 43, 541–66.

Röell, Ailsa, 1988, Regulating information disclosure among stock exchange market makers, LSE Financial Markets Group Discussion Papers 51.

Röell, Ailsa, 1990, Dual-capacity trading and the quality of the market, *Journal of Financial Intermediation* 1, 105–24.

Röell, Ailsa, 1995, Stock market transparency, Working Paper, ECARE (Université Libre de Bruxelles).

Röell, Ailsa, 1998, Liquidity in limit order book markets and Walrasian auctions with imperfect competition, Princeton, NJ: Princeton University.

Rösch, Dominik, 2021, The impact of arbitrage on liquidity, *Journal of Financial Economics*, 142, 195–213.

Rosenthal, Leonard, and Colin Young, 1990, The seemingly anomalous price behavior of Royal Dutch/Shell and Unilever N.V./PLC, *Journal of Financial Economics* 26, 123–41.

Rostek, Marzena, and Marek Weretka, 2015, Dynamic thin markets, *Review of Financial Studies* 28, 2946–92.

Rosu, Ioanid, 2009, A dynamic model of the limit order book, *Review of Financial Studies* 22, 4601–41.

Rosu, Ioanid, 2020, Liquidity and information in limit order markets, *Journal of Financial and Quantitative Analysis* 55, 1792–1839.

Sandas, Patrik, 2001, Adverse selection and competitive market making: empirical evidence from a limit order market, *Review of Financial Studies* 14, 705–34.

Saudagaran, Shahrokh M., and Gary C. Biddle, 1992, Financial disclosure levels and foreign stock exchange listing decisions, *Journal of International Financial Management and Accounting* 4, 106–47.

Schwert, G. William, and Paul J. Seguin, 1993, Securities transaction taxes: an overview of costs, benefits and unresolved questions, *Financial Analysts Journal* 49, 27–35.

SEC, 2000, Special study: payment for order flow and internalization in the options markets. Available at http://www.sec.gov/news/studies/ordpay.htm.

SEC, 2004, Report on transactions in municipal securities, Office of Economic Analysis. Available at https://www.sec.gov/news/studies/munireport2004.pdf.

SEC, 2005, Regulation NMS. Securities Exchange Act Release No. 34-51808; File No. S7-10-04, Federal Register 70(124), 37496–644.

SEC, 2010, Concept release on equity market structure Release No. 34-61358; File No. S7-02-10.

SEC, 2012, Report on the municipal securities market. Available at: https://www.sec.gov/files/munireport073112.pdf.

SEC, 2020, Staff Report on Algorithmic Trading in U.S. Capital Markets, available at: https://www.sec.gov/files/algo_trading_report_2020.pdf.

Seppi, Duane, 1990, Equilibrium block trading and asymmetric information, *Journal of Finance* 45, 73–94.

Seppi, Duane, 1997, Liquidity provision with limit orders and a strategic specialist, *Review of Financial Studies* 10, 103–50.

Schrimpf, Andreas, and Vladyslav Sushko, 2019, FX trade execution: complex and highly fragmented, *BIS Quarterly Review*, 39–50.

Shkilko, Andriy, and Konstantin Sokolov, 2020, Every cloud has a silver lining: fast trading, microwave connectivity and trading costs, *Journal of Finance* 75, 2899–927.

Shkilko, Andryi, Bonnie F. Van Ness, and Robert Van Ness, 2008, Locked and crossed markets on Nasdaq and NYSE, *Journal of Financial Markets* 11, 308–37.

Shleifer, Andrei, 2000, *Inefficient Markets*, Clarendon Lectures, Oxford: Oxford University Press.

Shleifer, Andrei, and Robert Vishny, 1986, Large shareholders and corporate control, *Journal of Political Economy* 94, 461–88.

Shleifer, Andrei, and Robert W. Vishny, 1997, The limits of arbitrage, *Journal of Finance* 52, 35–55.

Shleifer, Andrei, and Robert W., Vishny, 2011, Fire sales in finance and macroeconomics, *Journal of Economic Perspectives* 25, 29–48.

Simaan, Yusif, Daniel G. Weaver, and David Whitcomb, 2003, Market maker quotation behavior and pre-trade transparency, *Journal of Finance* 58, 1247–67.

Skjeltorp, Johannes A., and Bernt Arne Ødegaard, 2015, When do listed firms pay for market making in their own stock?, *Financial Management* 44, 241–66.

Skjeltorp, Johannes A., Elvira Sojli, and Wing Wah Tham, 2016, Flashes of trading intent at Nasdaq, *Journal of Financial and Quantitative Analysis* 51, 165–96.

Smith, Clifford, and René Stulz, 1985, The determinants of firm's hedging policies, *Journal of Financial and Quantitative Analysis* 20, 391–405.

Smith, Katherine, and George Sofianos, 1997, The impact of an NYSE listing on the global trading of non-US stocks, NYSE Working Paper 97-02.

Stoll, Hans R., 1978, The supply of dealer services in securities markets, *Journal of Finance* 33, 1133–51.

Stoll, Hans R., 2000, Friction, *Journal of Finance* 55, 1479–1514.

Stoughton, Neal M., and Josef Zechner, 1997, IPO-mechanisms, monitoring and ownership structure, *Journal of Financial Economics* 49, 45–77.

Stuchfield, Nic, 2003, Is exchange liquidity contestable? *The Handbook of World Stock, Derivative and Commodity Exchanges.*

Subrahmanyam, Avanidhar, 1991a, A theory of trading in stock index futures, *Review of Financial Studies* 4, 17–51.

Subrahmanyam, Avanidhar, 1991b, Risk aversion, market liquidity, and price efficiency, *Review of Financial Studies* 4, 417–41.

Subrahmanyam, Avanidhar, and Sheridan Titman, 1999, The going-public decision and the development of financial markets, *Journal of Finance* 54, 1045–82.

U.S. Department of Treasury, 2017, A financial system that creates economic opportunities, Capital Markets.

Van Achter, Mark, 2006, A dynamic limit order market with diversity in trading horizons, Working Paper, available at http://ssrn.com/abstract=967610.

Vayanos, Dimitri, 1998, Transactions costs and asset prices: a dynamic equilibrium model, *Review of Financial Studies* 11, 1–58.

Vayanos, Dimitri, 1999, Strategic trading and welfare in a dynamic market, *Review of Economic Studies* 66, 219–54.

Vayanos, Dimitri, 2004, Flight to quality, flight to liquidity, and the pricing of risk, NBER Working Paper No. 10327, February.

Vayanos, Dimitri, and Jiang Wang, 2009, Liquidity and asset prices: a unified framework, NBER Working Paper 15215, DOI 10.3386/w15215.

Vayanos, Dimitri, and Tan Wang, 2007, Search and endogenous concentration of liquidity in asset markets, *Journal of Economic Theory* 136, 66–104.

Venkataraman, Kumar, and Andrew C. Waisburd, 2007, The value of the designated market maker, *Journal of Financial and Quantitative Analysis* 42, 735–58.

Vickery, James, and Joshua Wright, 2010, TBA trading and liquidity in the agency MBS market, Federal Reserve Bank of New York, Staff Report 468.

Viswanathan, S., and J. Wang, 2002, Market architecture: limit order books versus dealership markets, *Journal of Financial Markets* 5, 127–68.

Vuillemey, Guillaume, 2020, The value of central clearing, *Journal of Finance* 75, 2021–53.

Vives, Xavier, Thierry Foucault, Laura Veldkamp, and Darrell Duffie (eds), 2022, *Barcelona 4: Technology and Finance*, CEPR Press, London, 1–173.

Wah, Elaine, 2016, How prevalent and profitable are latency arbitrage opportunities on U.S. Stock Exchanges? available at https://dx.doi.org/10.2139/ssrn.2729109.

Walras, Léon, 1874, *Elements d'Economie Politique Pure, ou Théorie de la Richesse Sociale*, Paris: R. Pichon and R. Durand-Ausiaz.

Wang, Jiang, 1993, A model of intertemporal asset prices under asymmetric Information, *Review of Economic Studies* 60, 249–382.

Warga, Arthur, 1992, Bond returns, liquidity, and missing data, *Journal of Financial and Quantitative Analysis* 27, 605–17.

Weill, Pierre-Olivier, 2007, Leaning against the wind, *Review of Economic Studies* 74, 1329–54.

Weill, Pierre-Olivier, 2020, The search theory of OTC markets, *Annual Review of Economics* 12, 747–73.

Williams Basil and Andrzej Skrzypacz, 2020, Spoofing in Equilibrium. Stanford University Graduate School of Business Research Paper, available at SSRN: http://dx.doi.org/10.2139/ssrn.3742327.

Wilson, Robert, 1979, Auctions of shares, *Quarterly Journal of Economics* 94, 675–89.

Xiong, Wei, 2001, Convergence trading with wealth effects: an amplification mechanism in financial markets, *Journal of Financial Economics* 62, 247–92.

Yao, Chen, and Mao, Ye, 2018, Why trading speed matters: a tale of queue rationing under price controls, *Journal of Financial Economics* 31, 2157–83.

Yang, Liyan, Haoxiang Zhu, 2020, Back-Running: Seeking and Hiding Fundamental Information in Order Flows, *The Review of Financial Studies*, 33, 1484–1533.

Yellen, Janet L., 1984, Efficiency wage models of unemployment, *The American Economic Review Papers and Proceedings* 74, 200–205.

Yin, Xiangkang, 2005, A comparison of centralized and fragmented markets with costly search, *Journal of Finance* 60, 1567–90.

Yosha, Oved, 1995, Information disclosure and the choice of the financing source, *Journal of Financial Intermediation* 4, 3–20.

Name Index

Subject Index